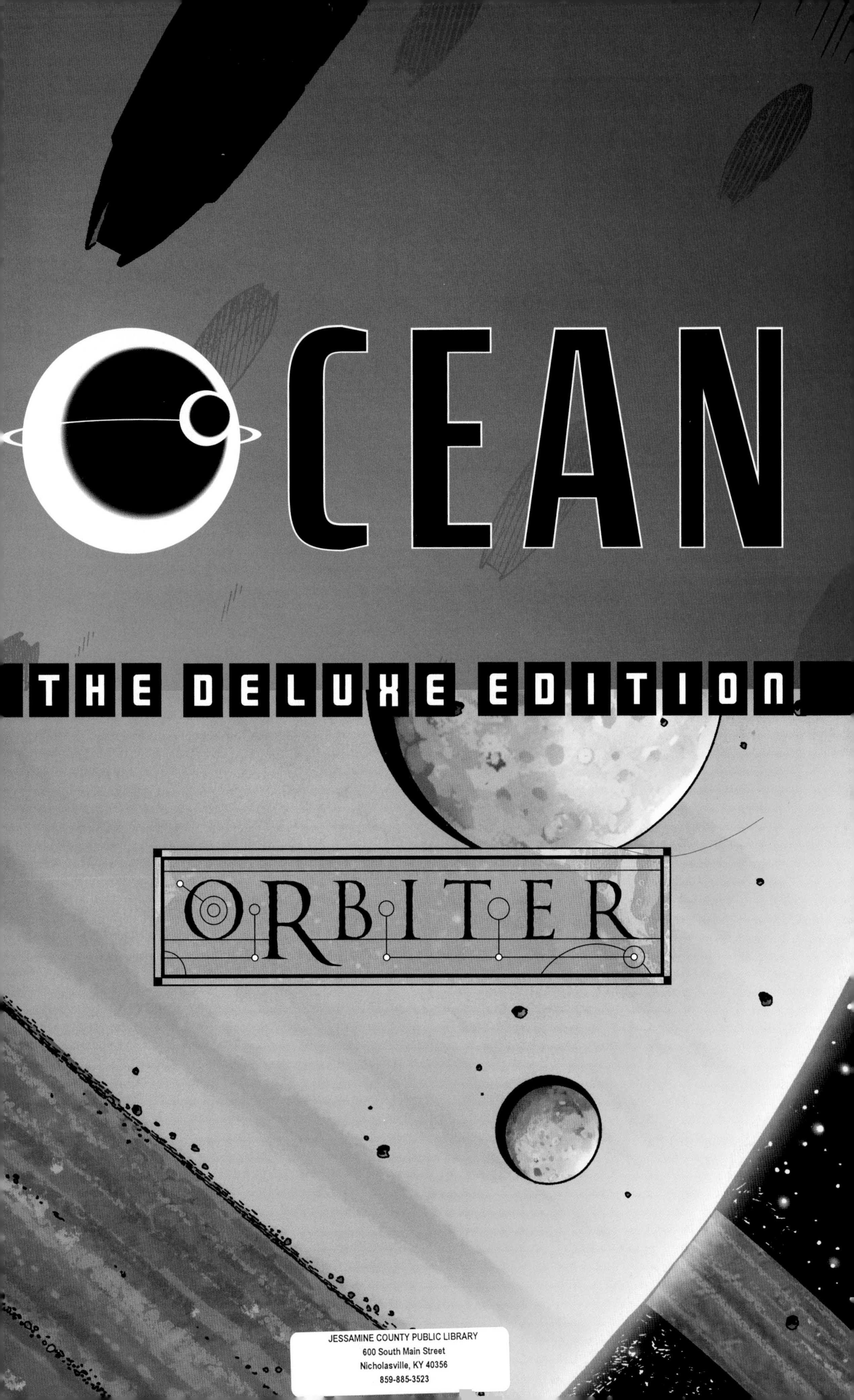

OCEAN

THE DELUXE EDITION

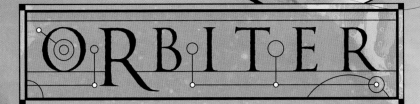

ORBITER

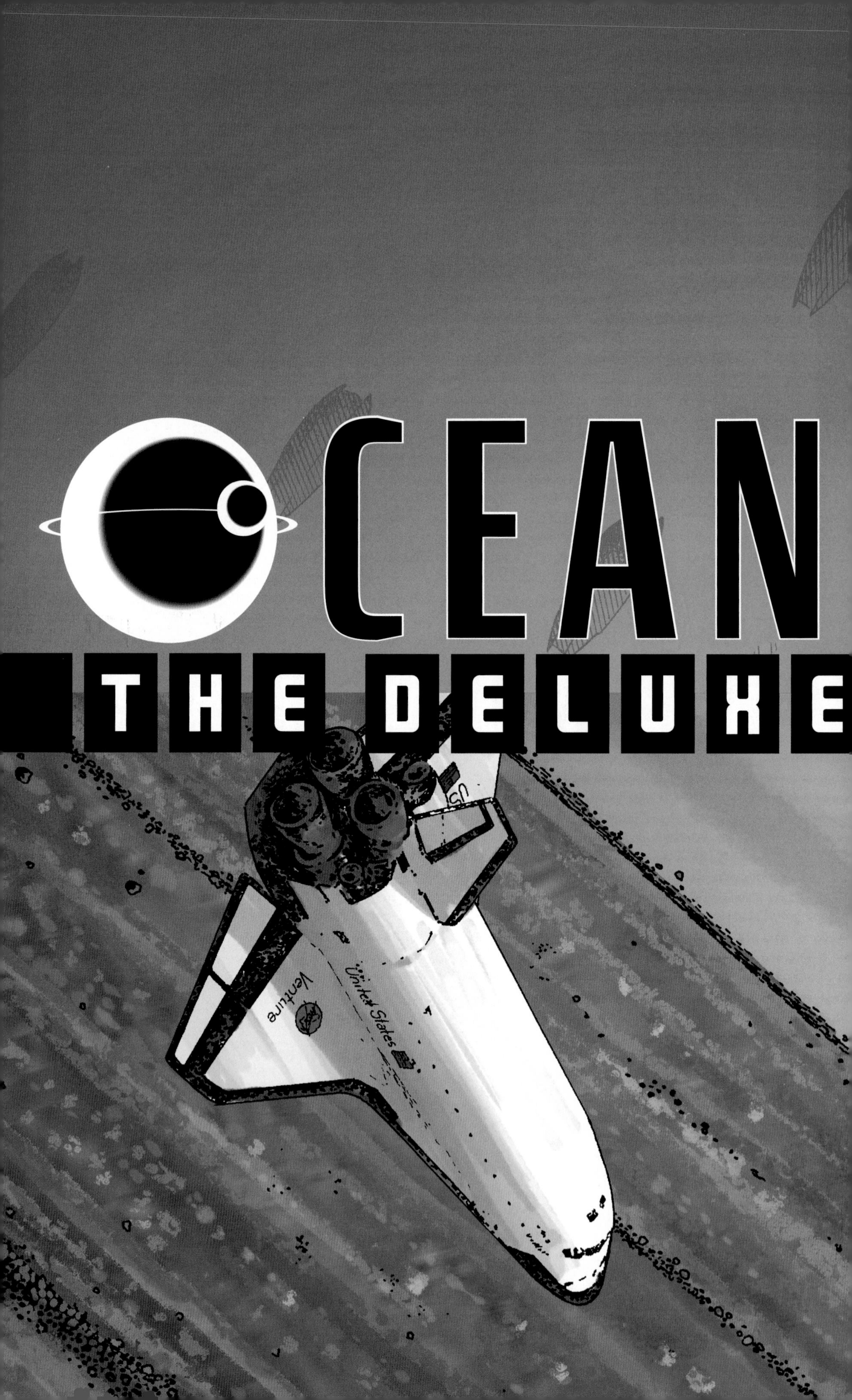
OCEAN
THE DELUXE
Venture
United States

WARREN ELLIS
Writer

CHRIS SPROUSE   KARL STORY   COLLEEN DORAN
Artists

RANDY MAYOR   DAVE STEWART   WENDY BROOME
TONY AVIÑA   WILDSTORM FX
Colorists

JARED K. FLETCHER   CLEM ROBINS
Letterers

MICHAEL GOLDEN   COLLEEN DORAN
Cover Art and Original Series Covers

OCEAN created by **WARREN ELLIS** and **CHRIS SPROUSE**
ORBITER created by **WARREN ELLIS** and **COLLEEN DORAN**

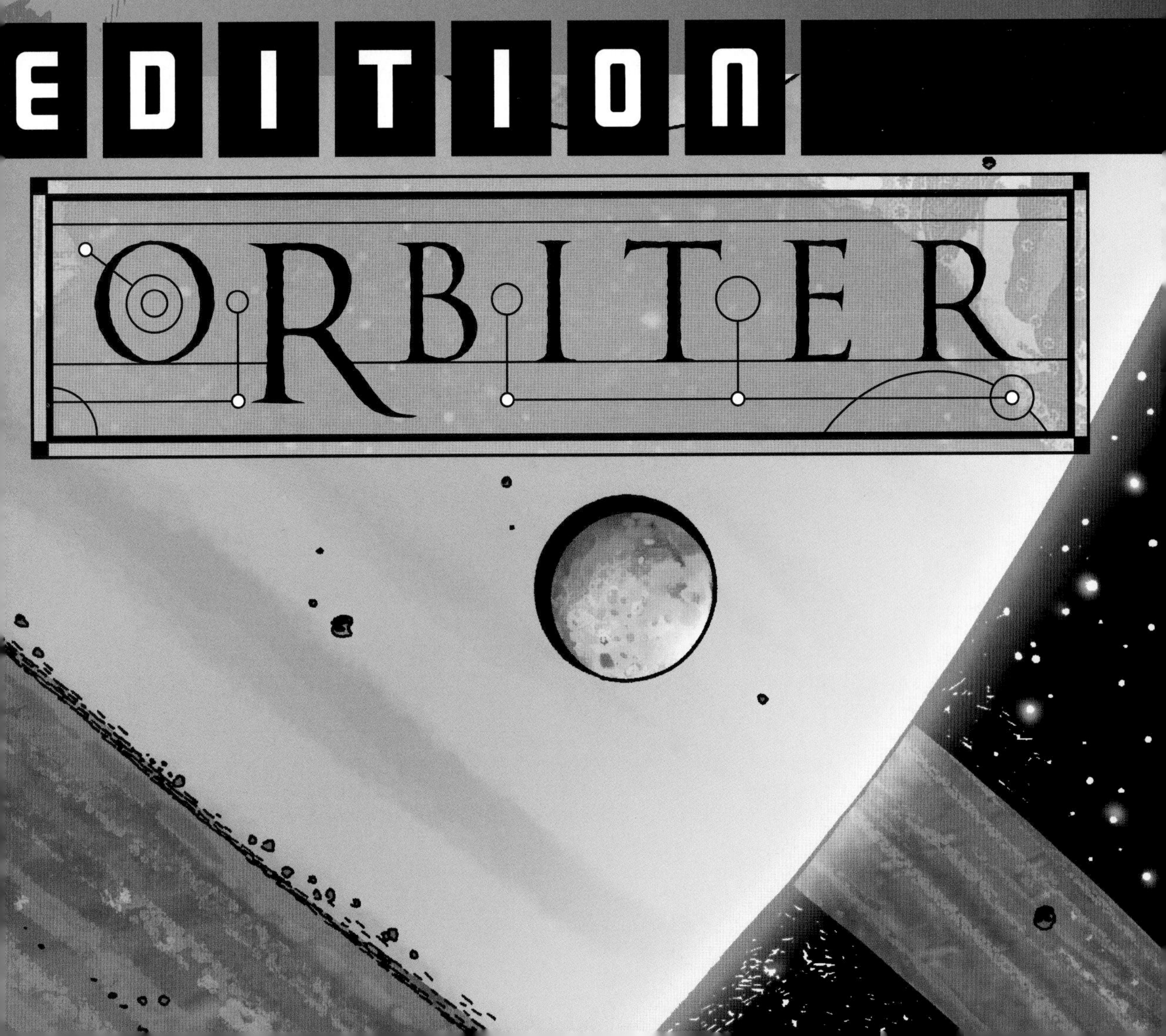

EDITION

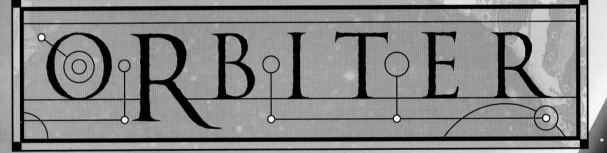

ORBITER

Scott Dunbier Will Dennis Heidi MacDonald
Editors – Original Series

Kristy Quinn Zachary J. Rau
Assistant Editors – Original Series

Scott Nybakken
Editor

Robbin Brosterman
Design Director – Books

Damian Ryland
Publication Design

Shelly Bond
Executive Editor – Vertigo

Hank Kanalz
Senior VP – Vertigo & Integrated Publishing

Diane Nelson
President

Dan DiDio and Jim Lee
Co-Publishers

Geoff Johns
Chief Creative Officer

Amit Desai
Senior VP – Marketing & Franchise Management

Amy Genkins
Senior VP – Business & Legal Affairs

Nairi Gardiner
Senior VP – Finance

Jeff Boison
VP – Publishing Planning

Mark Chiarello
VP – Art Direction & Design

John Cunningham
VP – Marketing

Terri Cunningham
VP – Editorial Administration

Larry Ganem
VP – Talent Relations & Services

Alison Gill
Senior VP – Manufacturing & Operations

Jay Kogan
VP – Business & Legal Affairs, Publishing

Jack Mahan
VP – Business Affairs, Talent

Nick Napolitano
VP – Manufacturing Administration

Sue Pohja
VP – Book Sales

Fred Ruiz
VP – Manufacturing Operations

Courtney Simmons
Senior VP – Publicity

Bob Wayne
Senior VP – Sales

OCEAN/ORBITER: THE DELUXE EDITION

DC Comics 1700 Broadway, New York, NY 10019
A Warner Bros. Entertainment Company.
Printed in Canada. First Printing. ISBN: 978-1-4012-5534-3

Library of Congress Cataloging-in-Publication Data

Ellis, Warren.
Ocean/Orbiter deluxe edition / written by Warren Ellis ; illustrated by Chris Sprouse, Colleen Doran.
pages cm
ISBN 978-1-4012-5534-3 (hardback)
1. Graphic novels. I. Sprouse, Chris. II. Doran, Colleen, 1963- III. Title.
PN6727.E448O28 2015
741.5'973 — dc23
2014049011

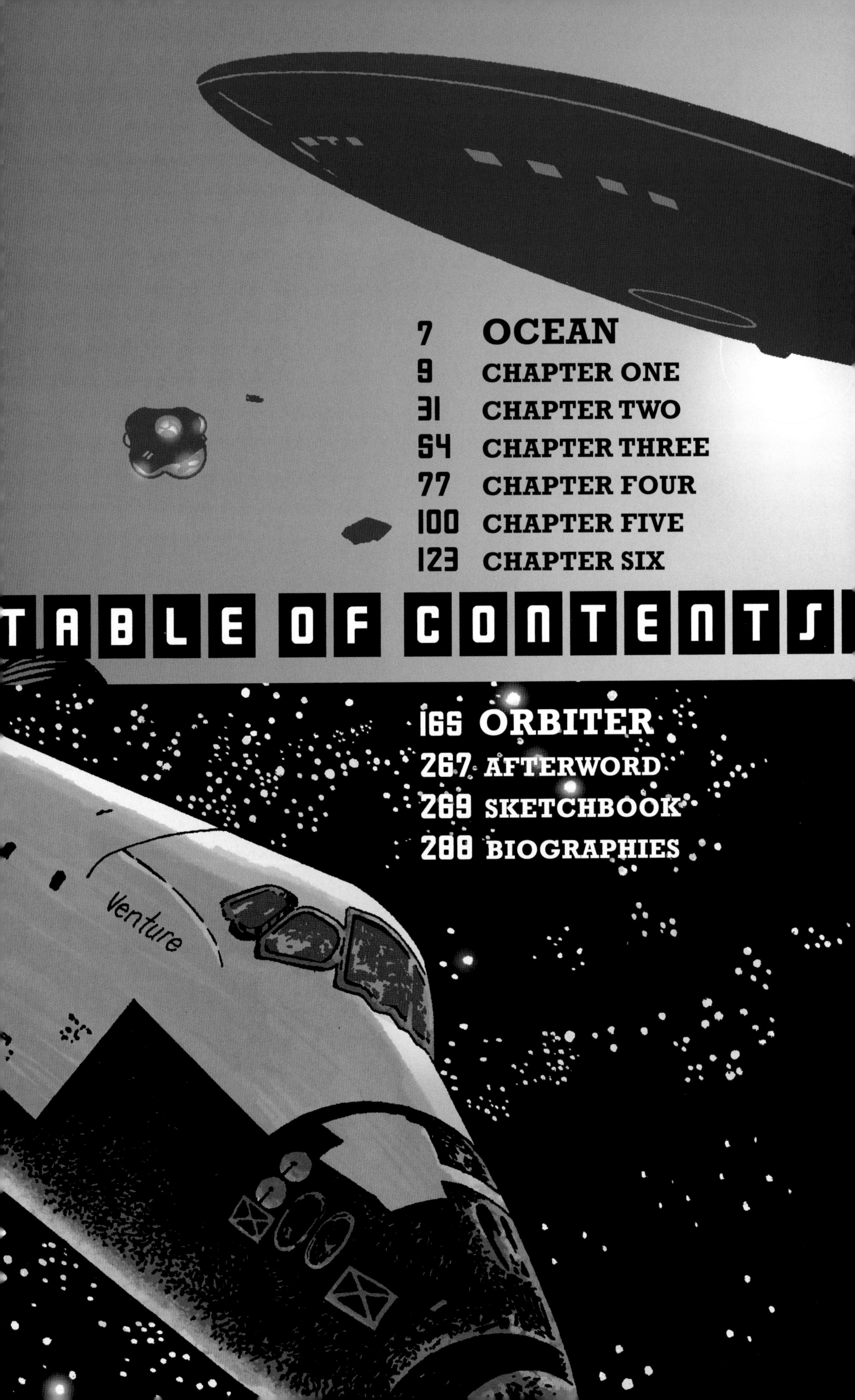
Venture

TABLE OF CONTENTS

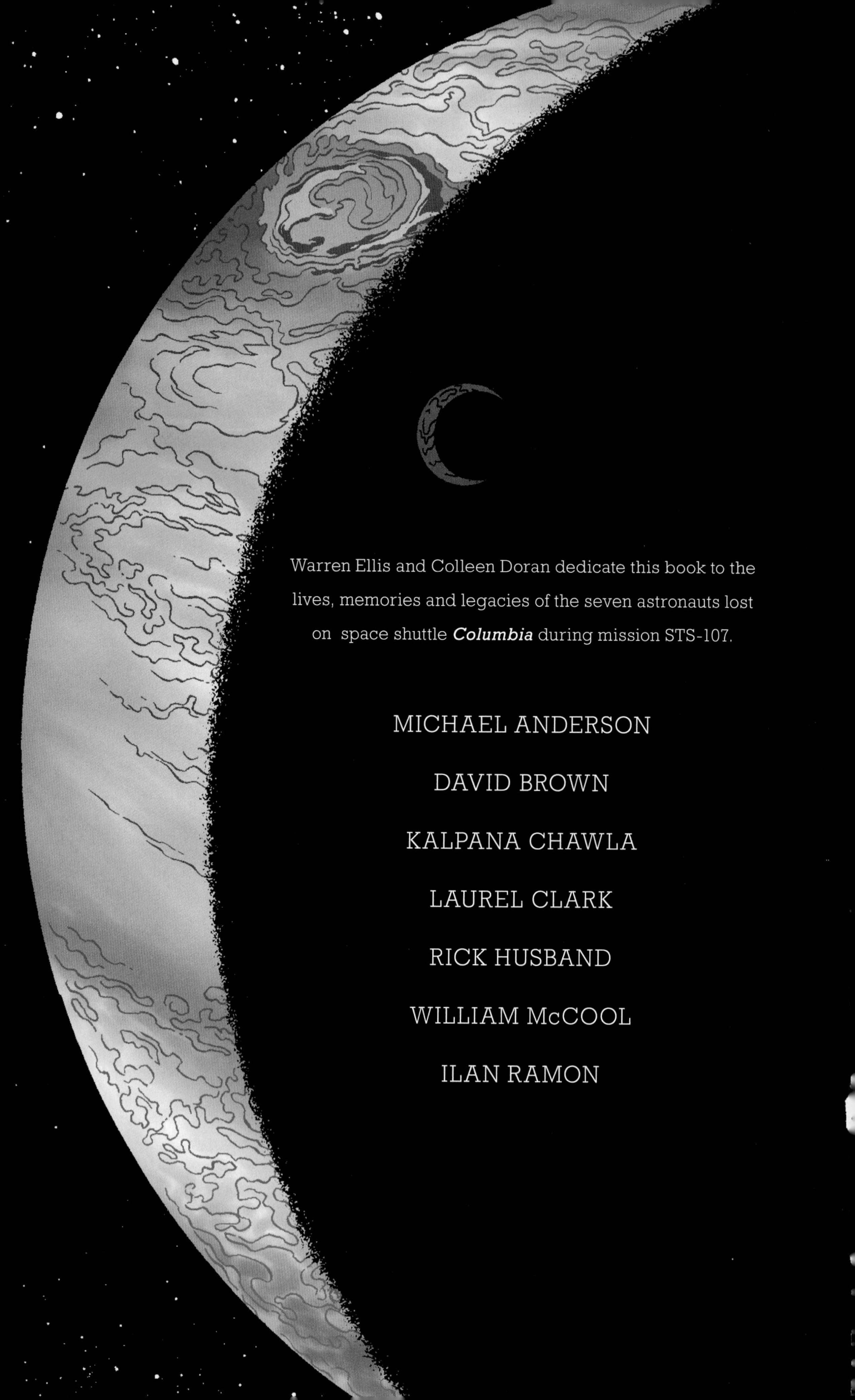

Warren Ellis and Colleen Doran dedicate this book to the lives, memories and legacies of the seven astronauts lost on space shuttle ***Columbia*** during mission STS-107.

MICHAEL ANDERSON

DAVID BROWN

KALPANA CHAWLA

LAUREL CLARK

RICK HUSBAND

WILLIAM McCOOL

ILAN RAMON

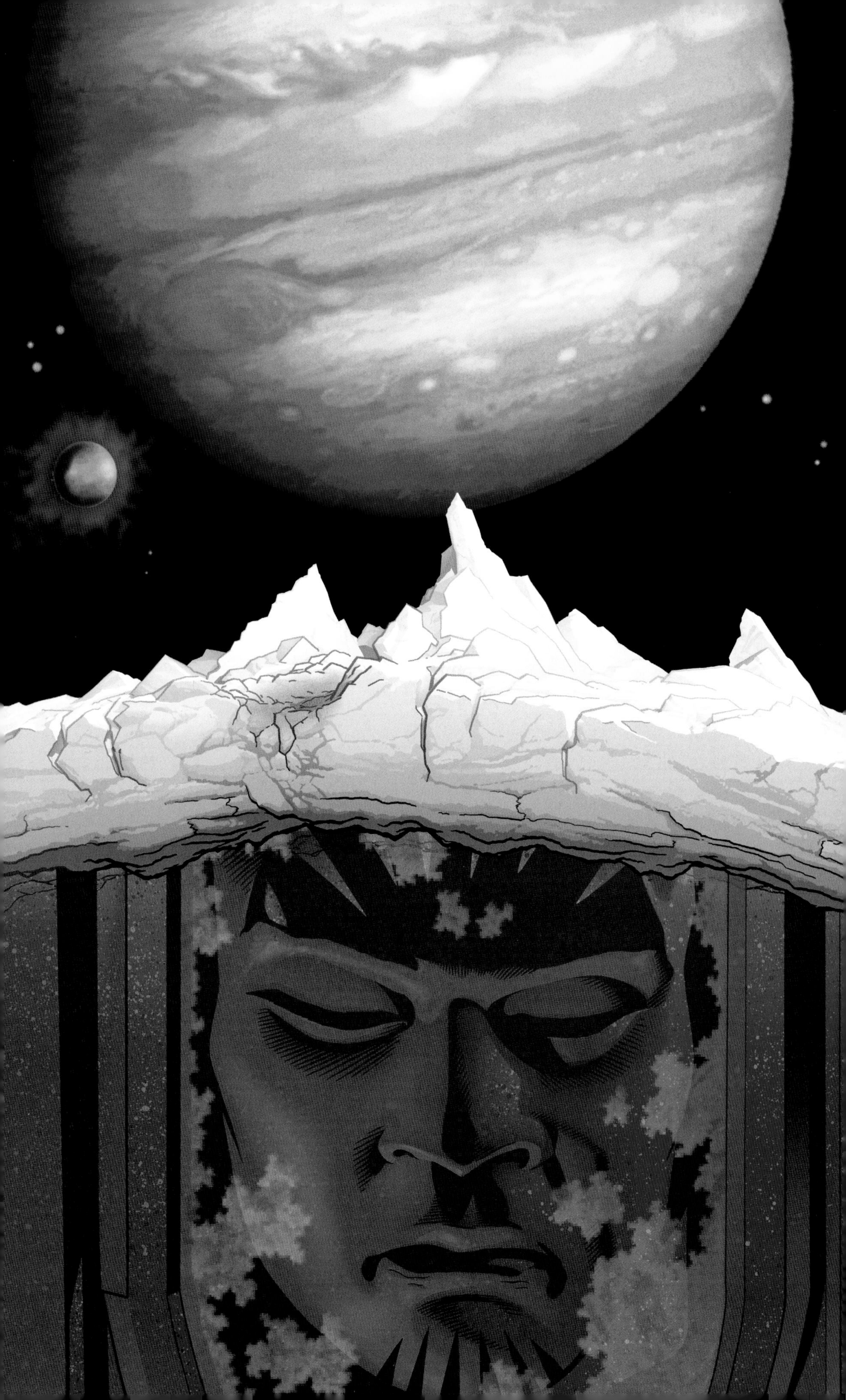

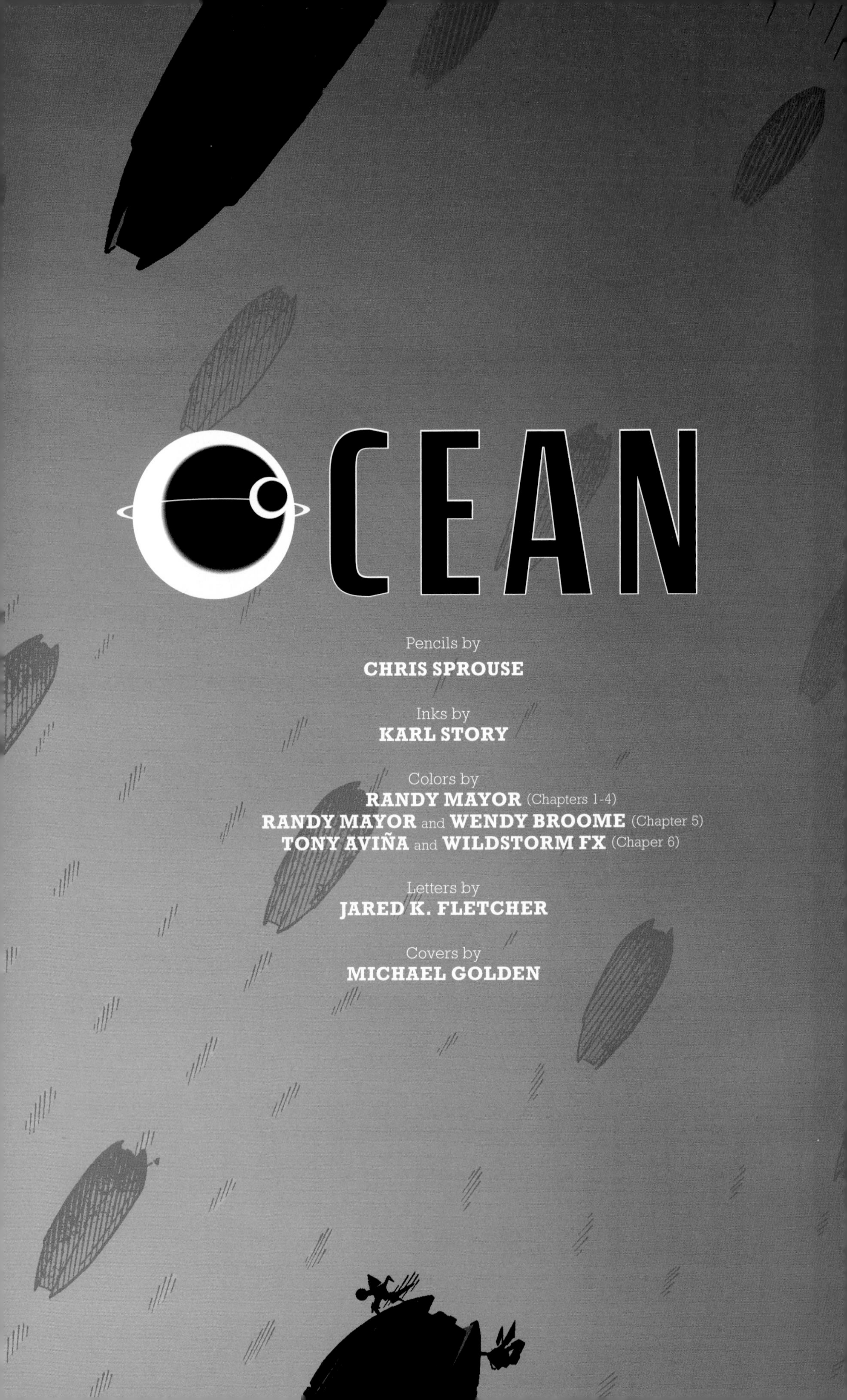

OCEAN

Pencils by
CHRIS SPROUSE

Inks by
KARL STORY

Colors by
RANDY MAYOR (Chapters 1-4)
RANDY MAYOR and **WENDY BROOME** (Chapter 5)
TONY AVIÑA and **WILDSTORM FX** (Chaper 6)

Letters by
JARED K. FLETCHER

Covers by
MICHAEL GOLDEN

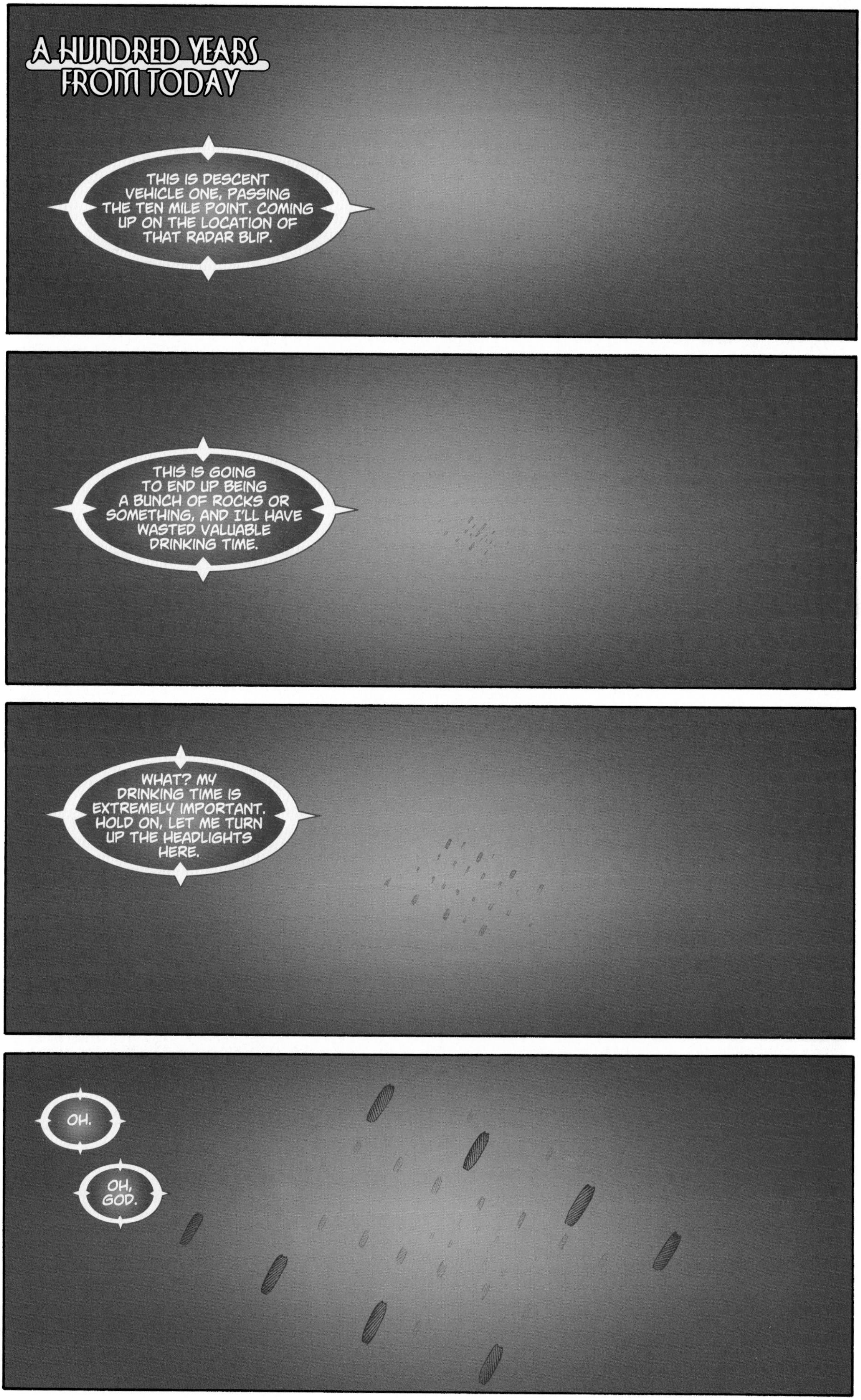

A HUNDRED YEARS FROM TODAY

THIS IS DESCENT VEHICLE ONE, PASSING THE TEN MILE POINT. COMING UP ON THE LOCATION OF THAT RADAR BLIP.

THIS IS GOING TO END UP BEING A BUNCH OF ROCKS OR SOMETHING, AND I'LL HAVE WASTED VALUABLE DRINKING TIME.

WHAT? MY DRINKING TIME IS EXTREMELY IMPORTANT. HOLD ON, LET ME TURN UP THE HEADLIGHTS HERE.

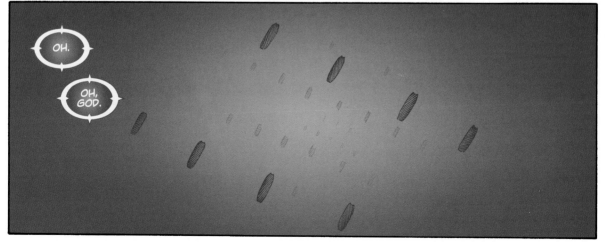

OH.

OH, GOD.

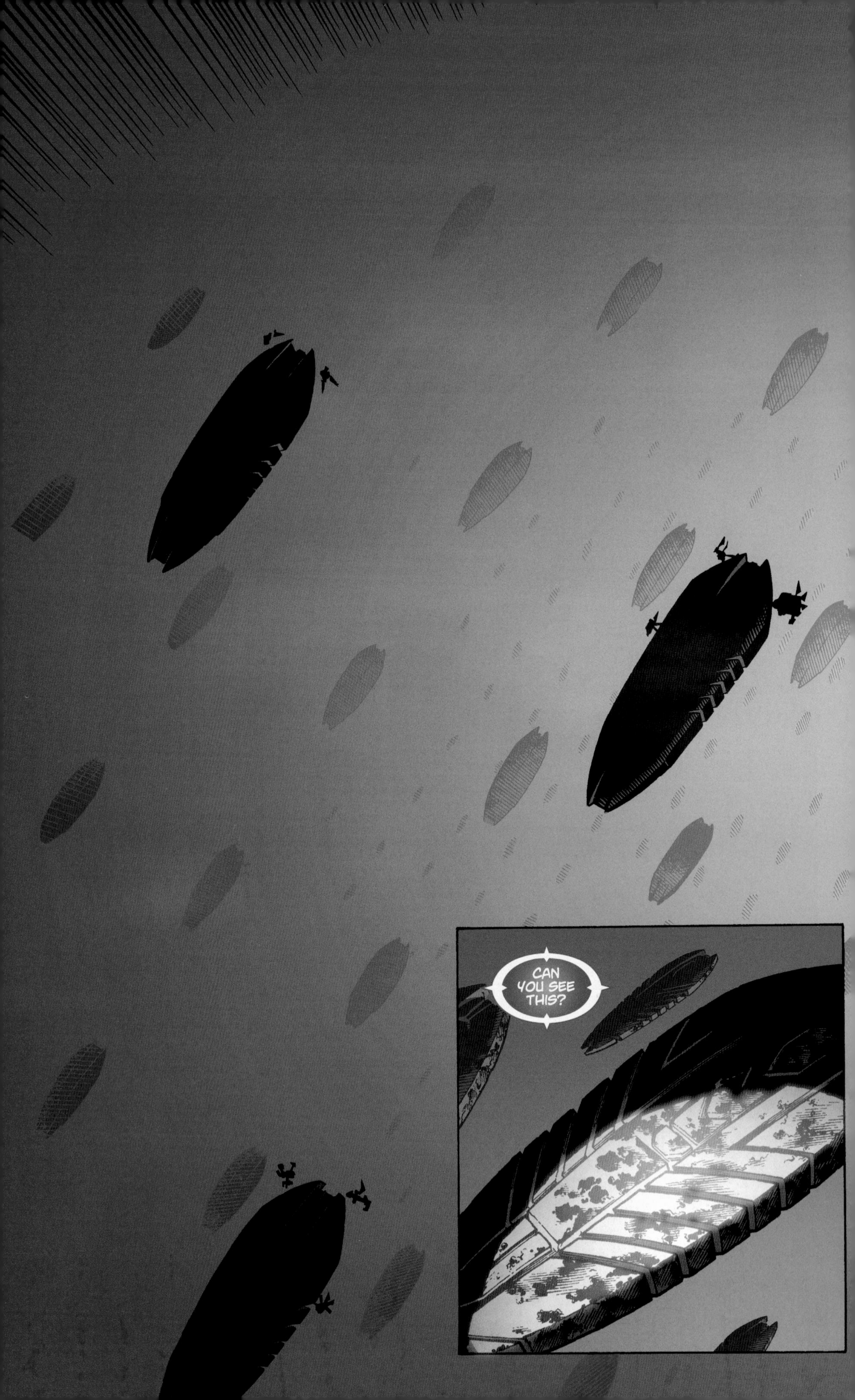
CAN YOU SEE THIS?

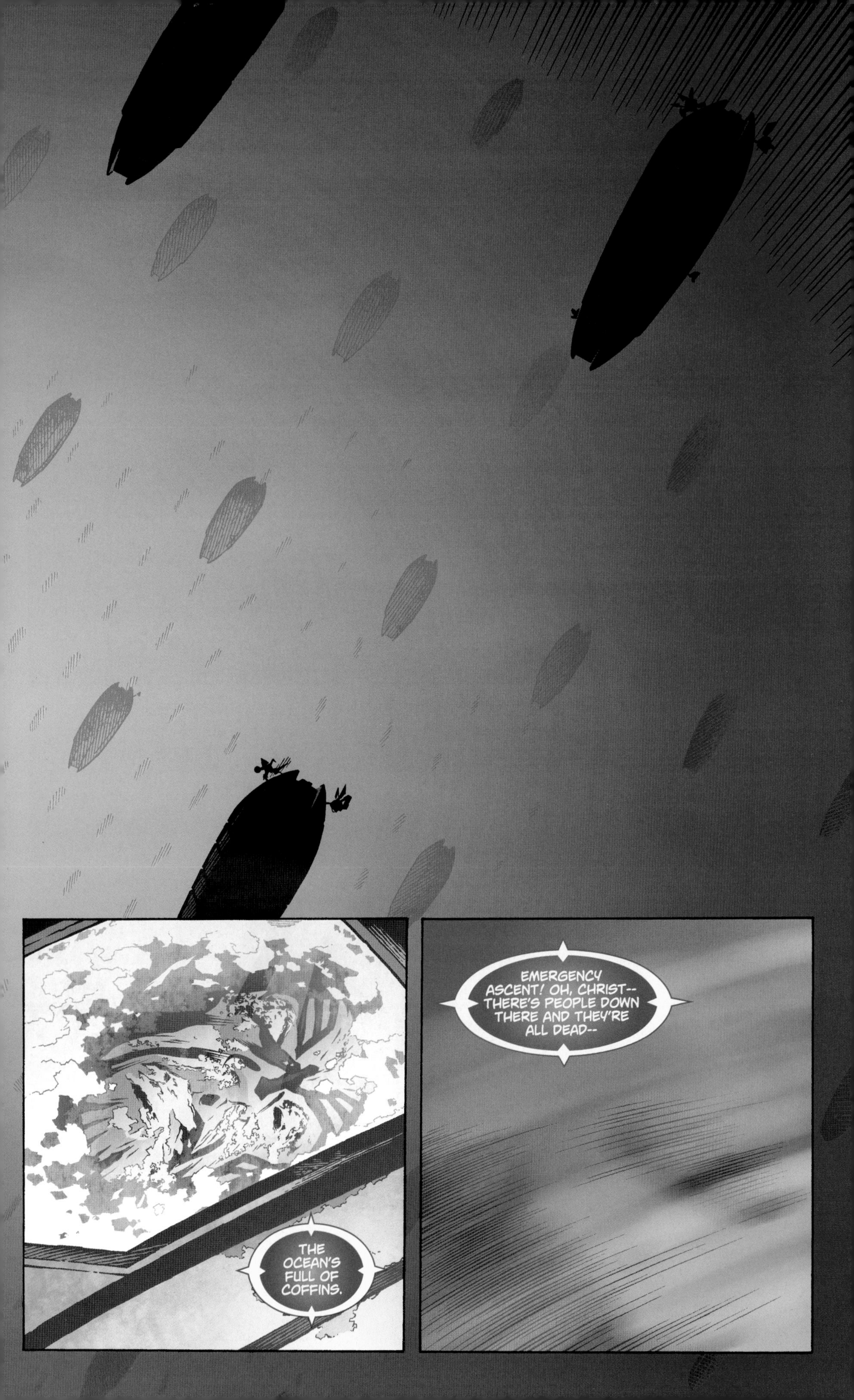
THE OCEAN'S FULL OF COFFINS.
EMERGENCY ASCENT! OH, CHRIST-- THERE'S PEOPLE DOWN THERE AND THEY'RE ALL DEAD--

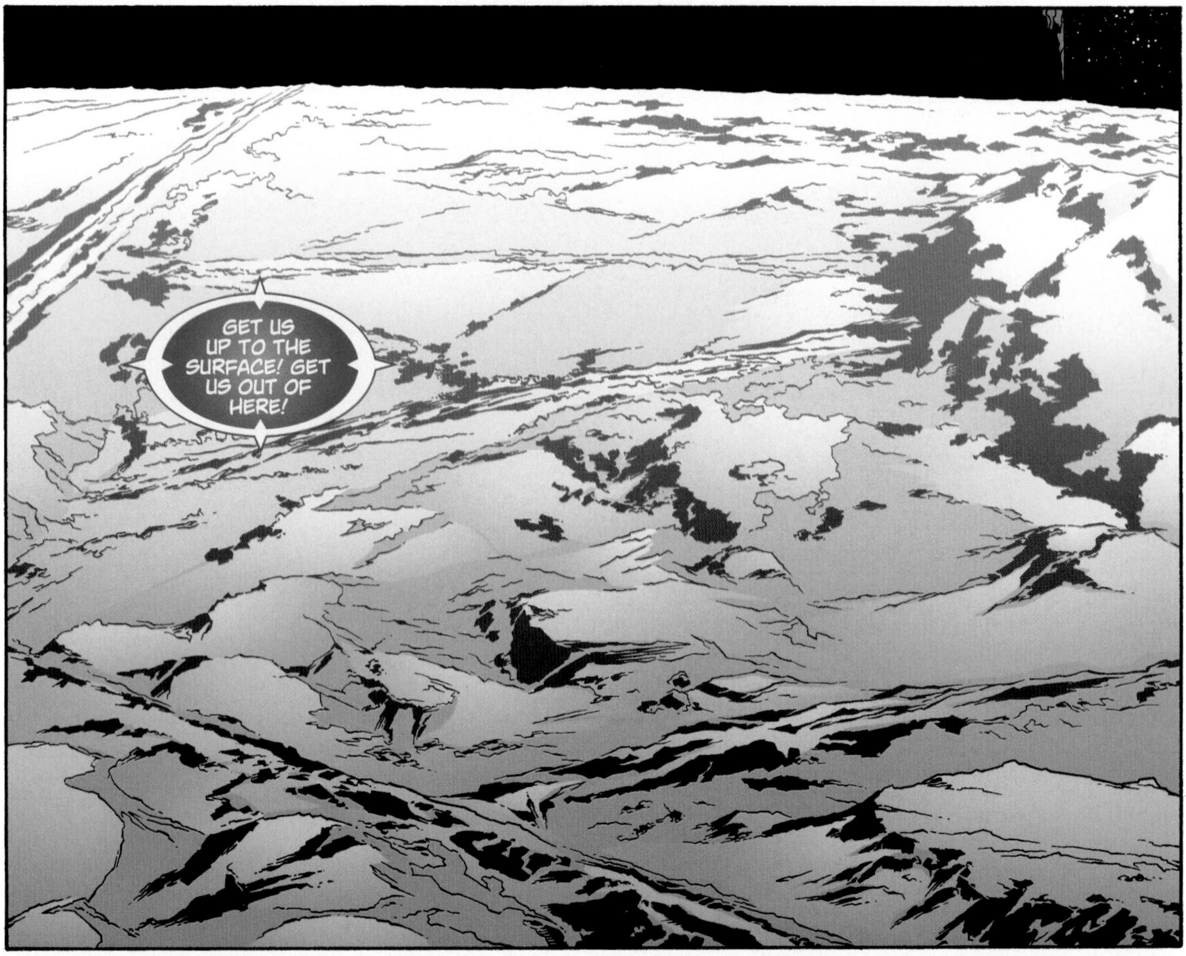
GET US UP TO THE SURFACE! GET US OUT OF HERE!

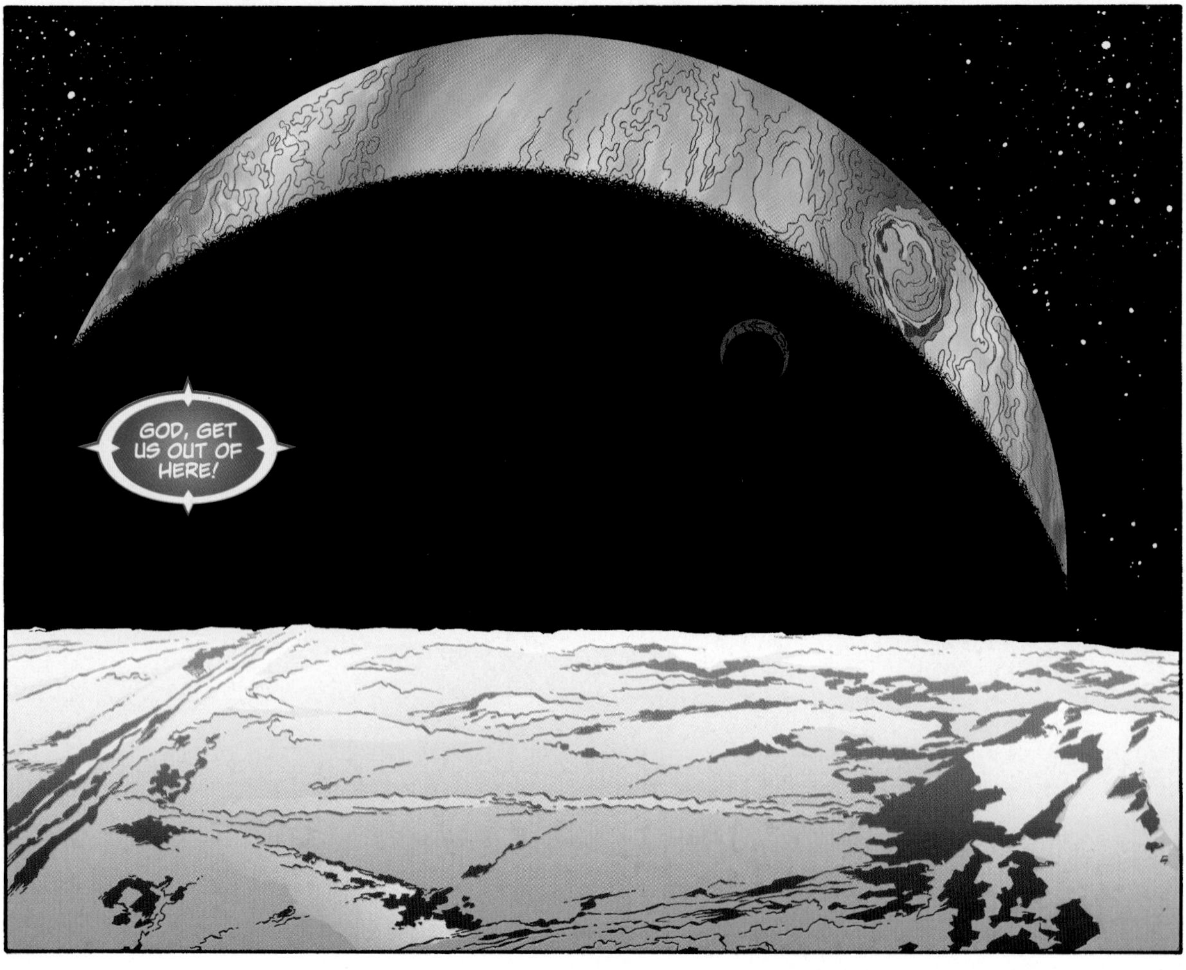
GOD, GET US OUT OF HERE!

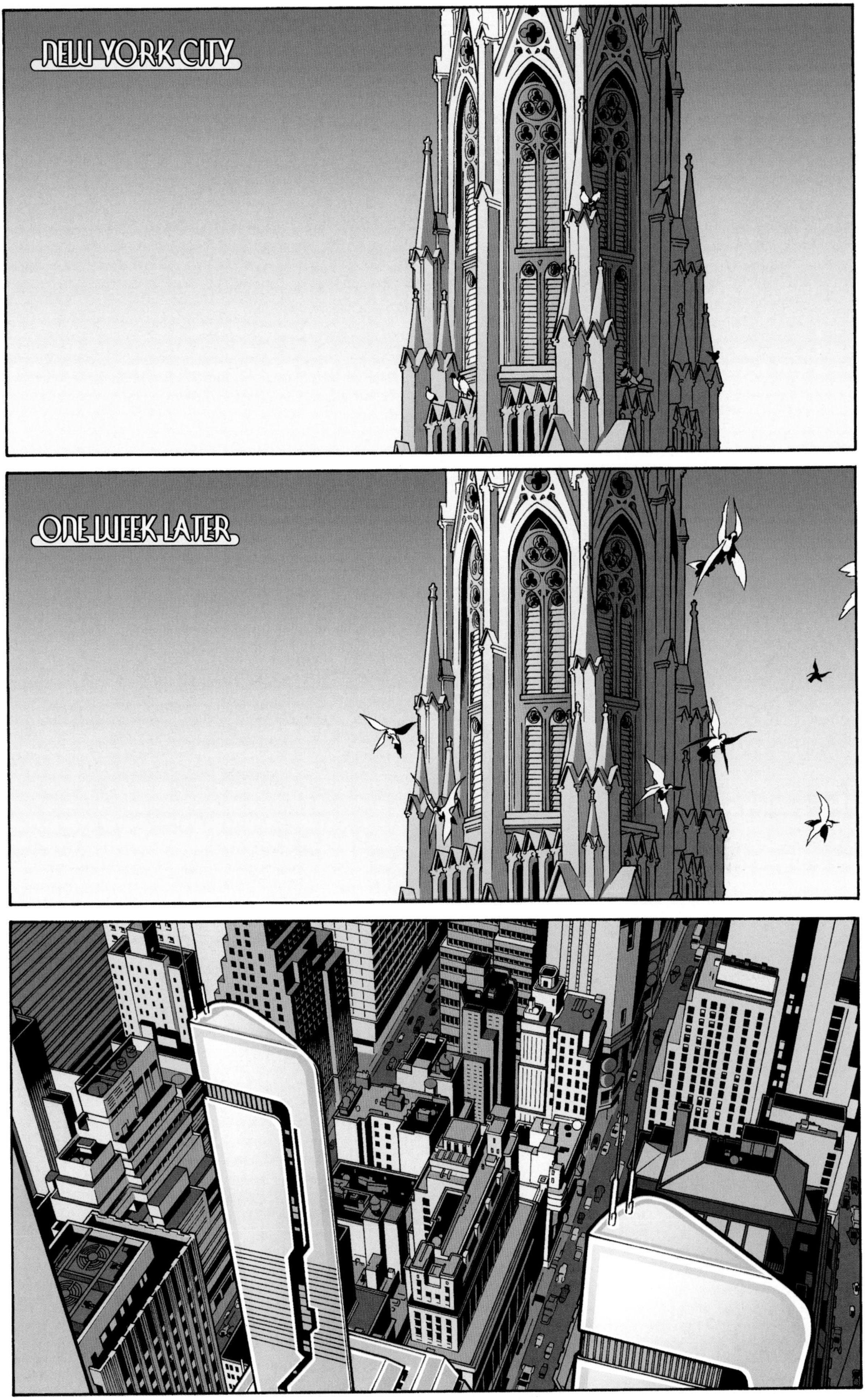
NEW YORK CITY
ONE WEEK LATER

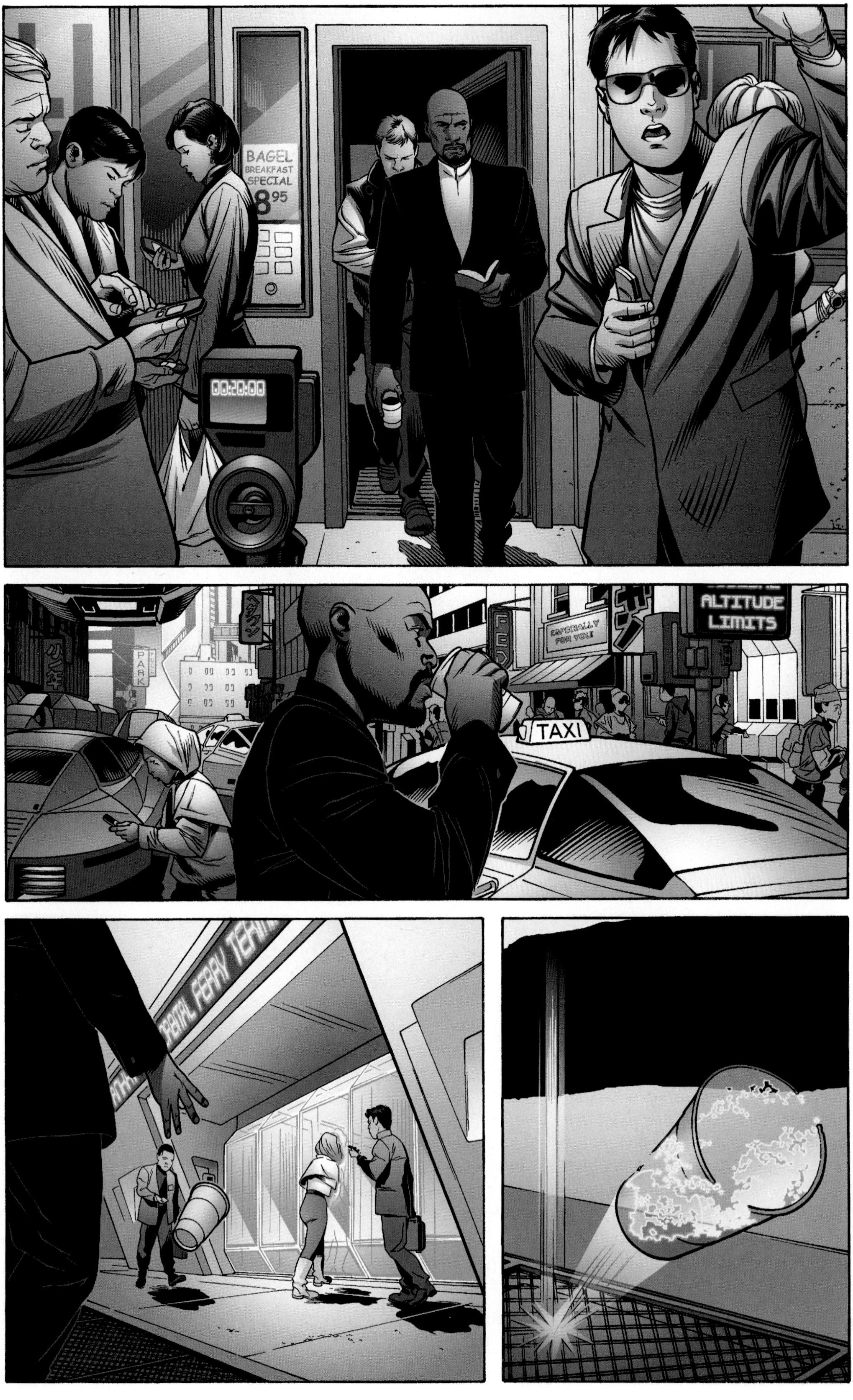
BAGEL
BREAKFAST
SPECIAL
8.95
00:20:00
PARK
ESPECIALLY FOR YOU!
ALTITUDE LIMITS
TAXI
ORBITAL FERRY

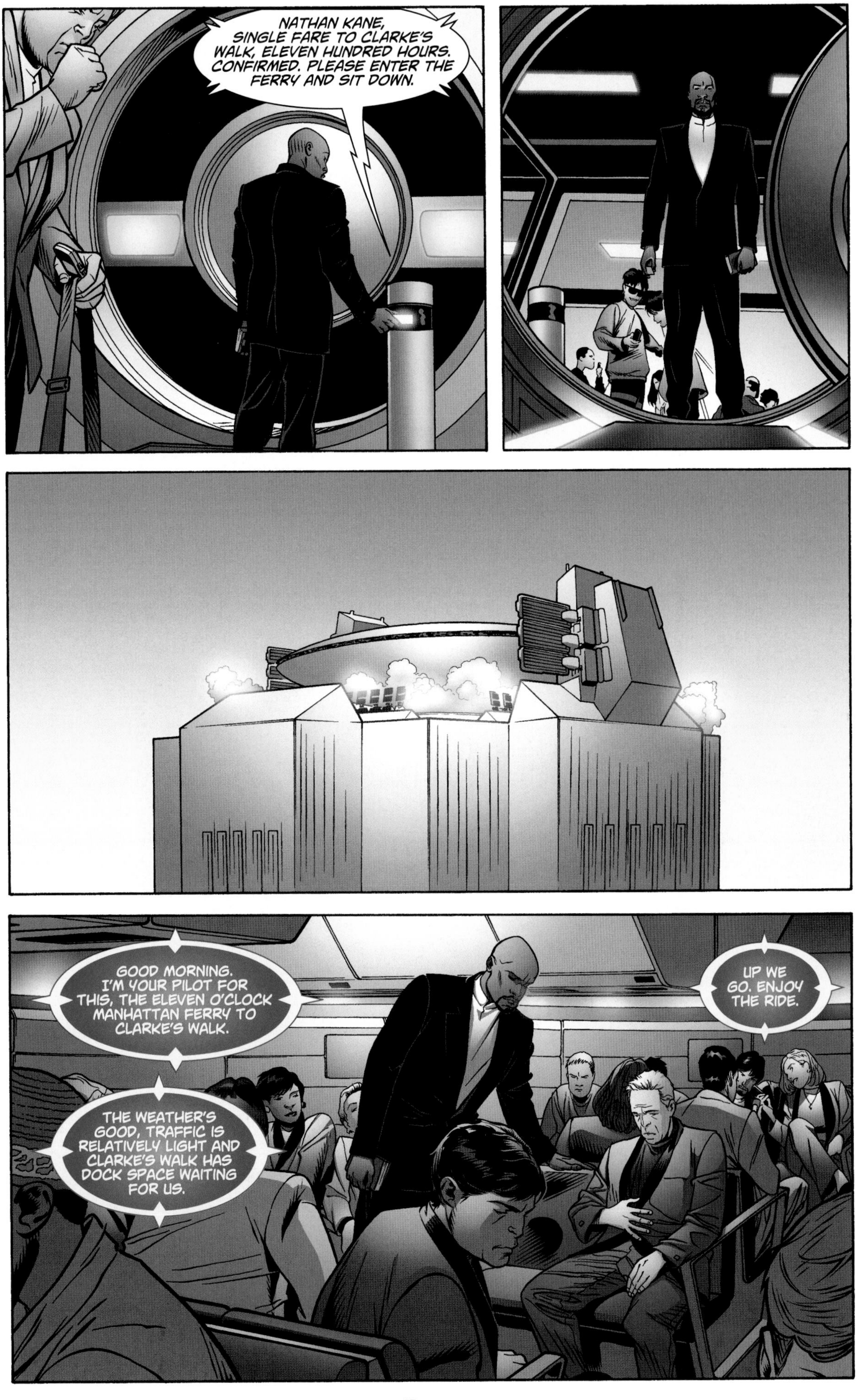
NATHAN KANE, SINGLE FARE TO CLARKE'S WALK, ELEVEN HUNDRED HOURS. CONFIRMED. PLEASE ENTER THE FERRY AND SIT DOWN.
GOOD MORNING. I'M YOUR PILOT FOR THIS, THE ELEVEN O'CLOCK MANHATTAN FERRY TO CLARKE'S WALK.
THE WEATHER'S GOOD, TRAFFIC IS RELATIVELY LIGHT AND CLARKE'S WALK HAS DOCK SPACE WAITING FOR US.
UP WE GO. ENJOY THE RIDE.

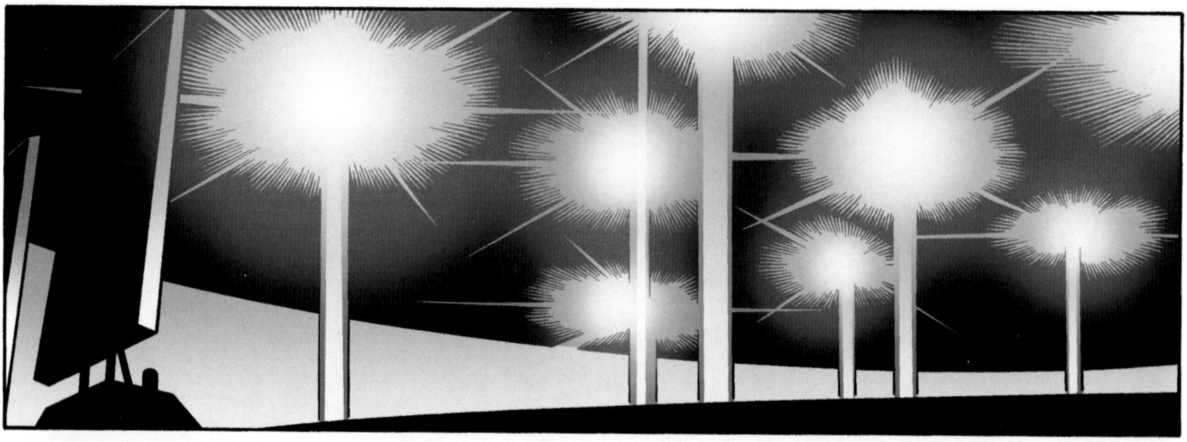

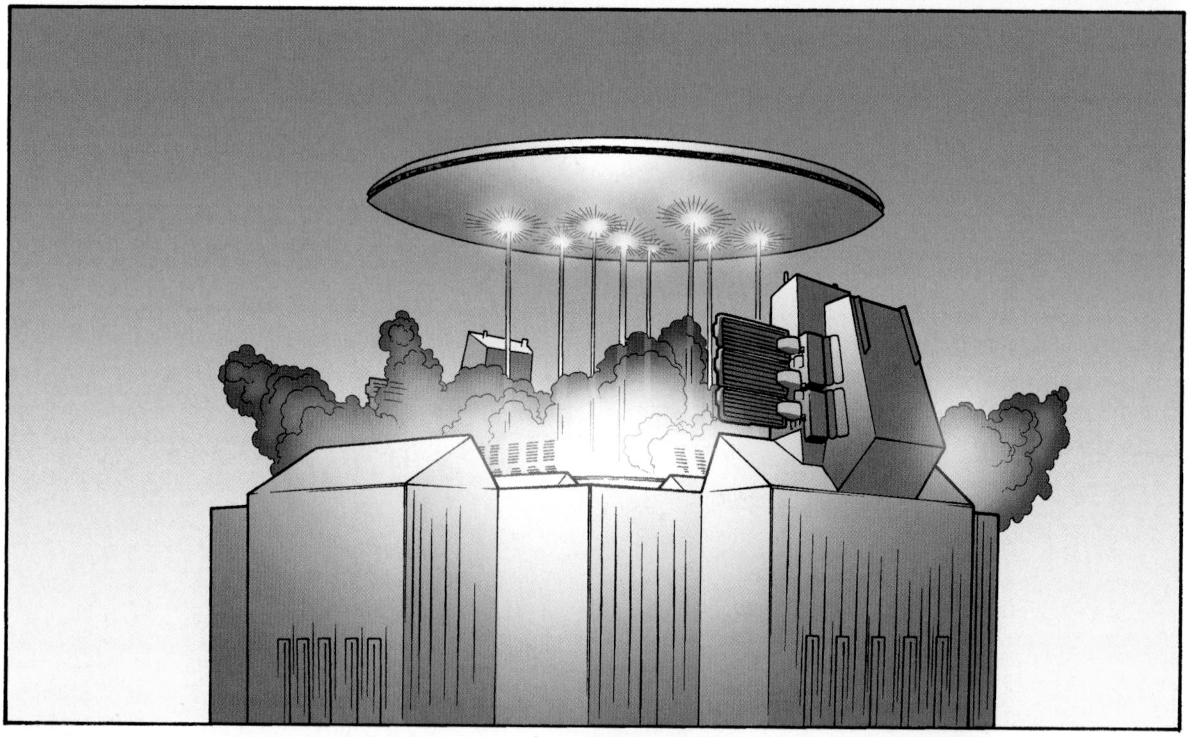

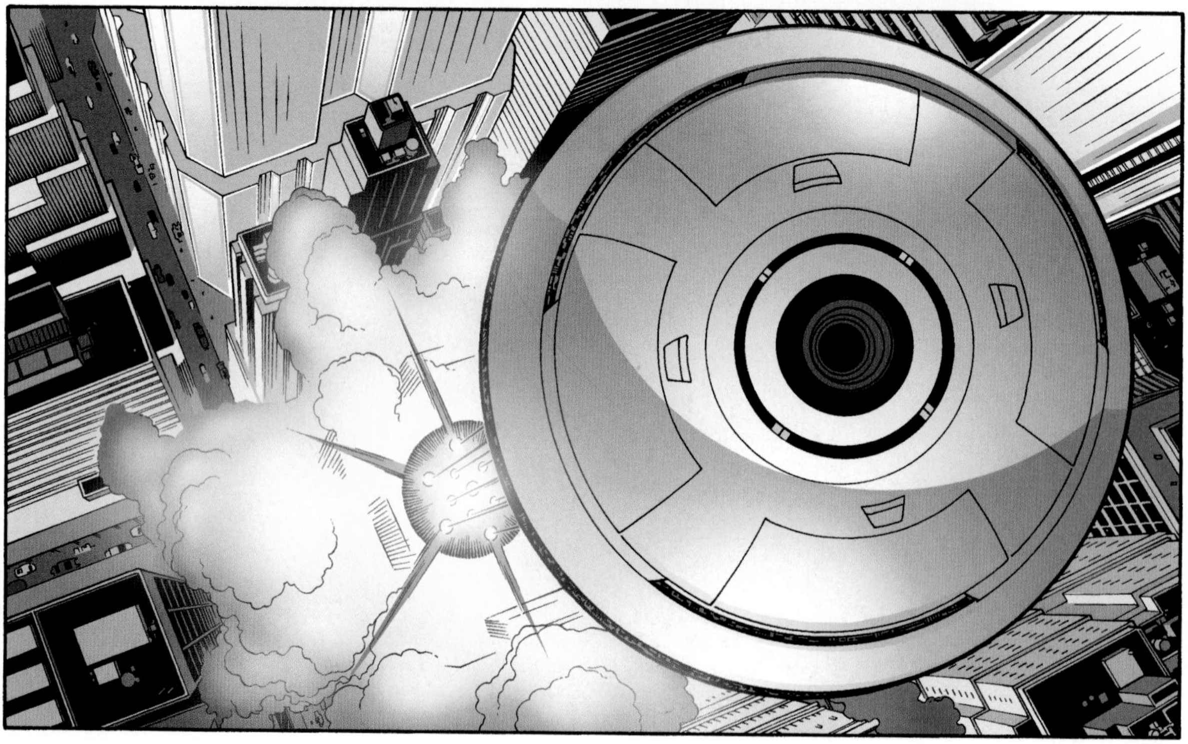

YOU KNOW HOW PEOPLE USED TO GO UP? ON TOP OF SOMETHING THE SIZE OF AN OFFICE BLOCK, FULL OF CHEMICAL EXPLOSIVES.

IS THAT BERSERK OR WHAT? RIDING A BOMB TO ORBIT.

YEAH. LISTEN, I DON'T TRAVEL TOO WELL--

NO, LISTEN, IT GETS WORSE. I MEAN, THIS FERRY HERE? IT'S GOING TO JUST DRIFT BACK SLOWLY ON A REDUCED LASER PULSE.

BACK IN THE OLD DAYS? THEY DID BALLISTIC RE-ENTRY. JUST AIMED AT THE PLANET LIKE A BULLET OUT OF A GUN, IN A LITTLE CAPSULE WITH A FAT BASE.

HEAT SHIELD, YOU SEE? TO STOP 'EM ROASTING ON THE WAY IN.

FIRST STEP TO SPACE: A history of the 20th Century space program

I SWEAR. MERCURY, APOLLO, ISS. FASCINATES MY ASS.

YOU KNOW THERE ARE CLOUDS OF FLASH-FROZEN URINE EJECTED BY APOLLO ASTRONAUTS STILL ORBITING THE EARTH AT HUNDREDS OF MILES AN HOUR?

ANY MINUTE NOW WE COULD BE HOLED AND KILLED BY A HAIL OF ANTIQUE BALLISTIC PISS.

LITTLE SPACESHIPS THE SIZE OF YOUR BATHROOM, JUST DROPPING ON EARTH FROM SPACE, CATCHING FIRE AND DROPPING IN THE OCEAN...

HORK

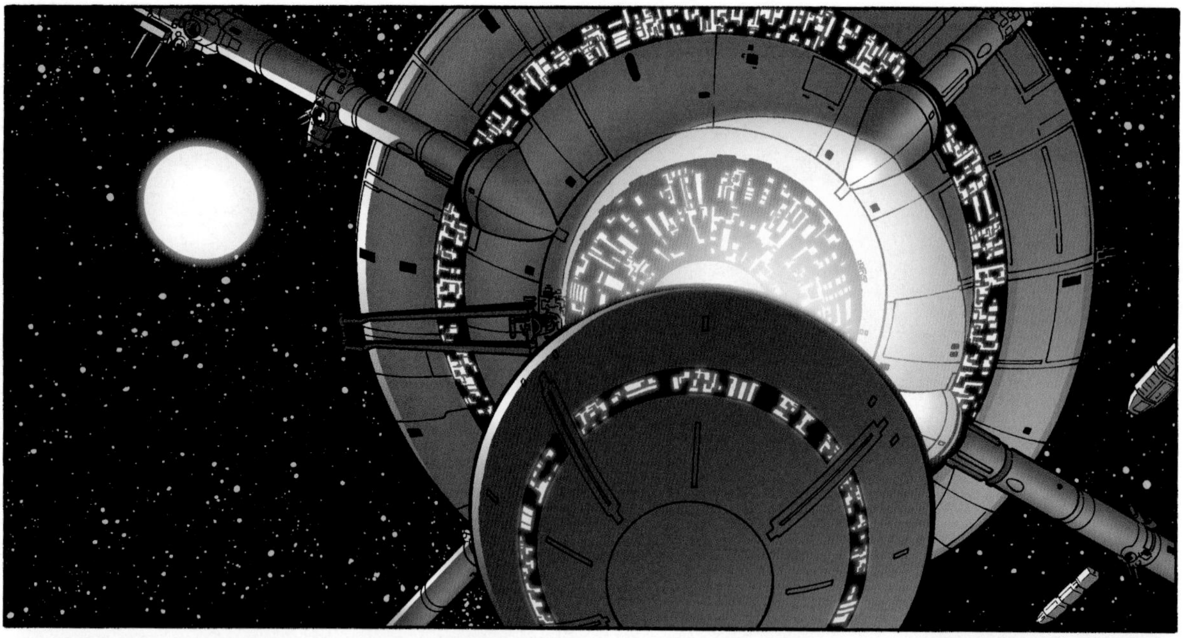

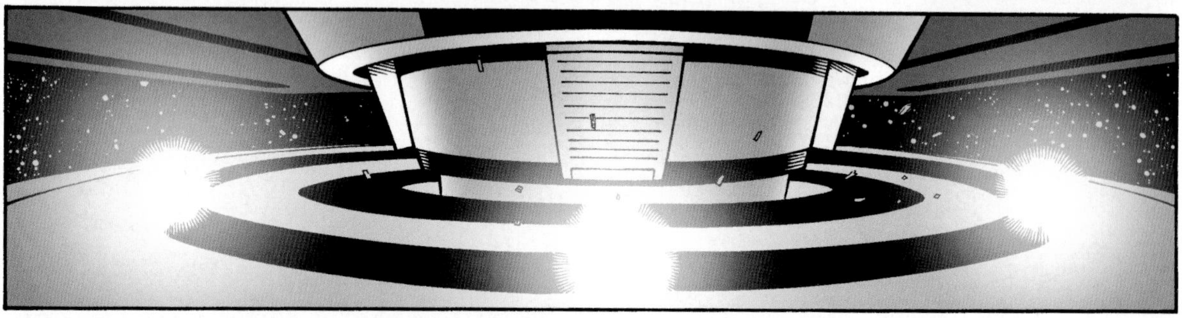

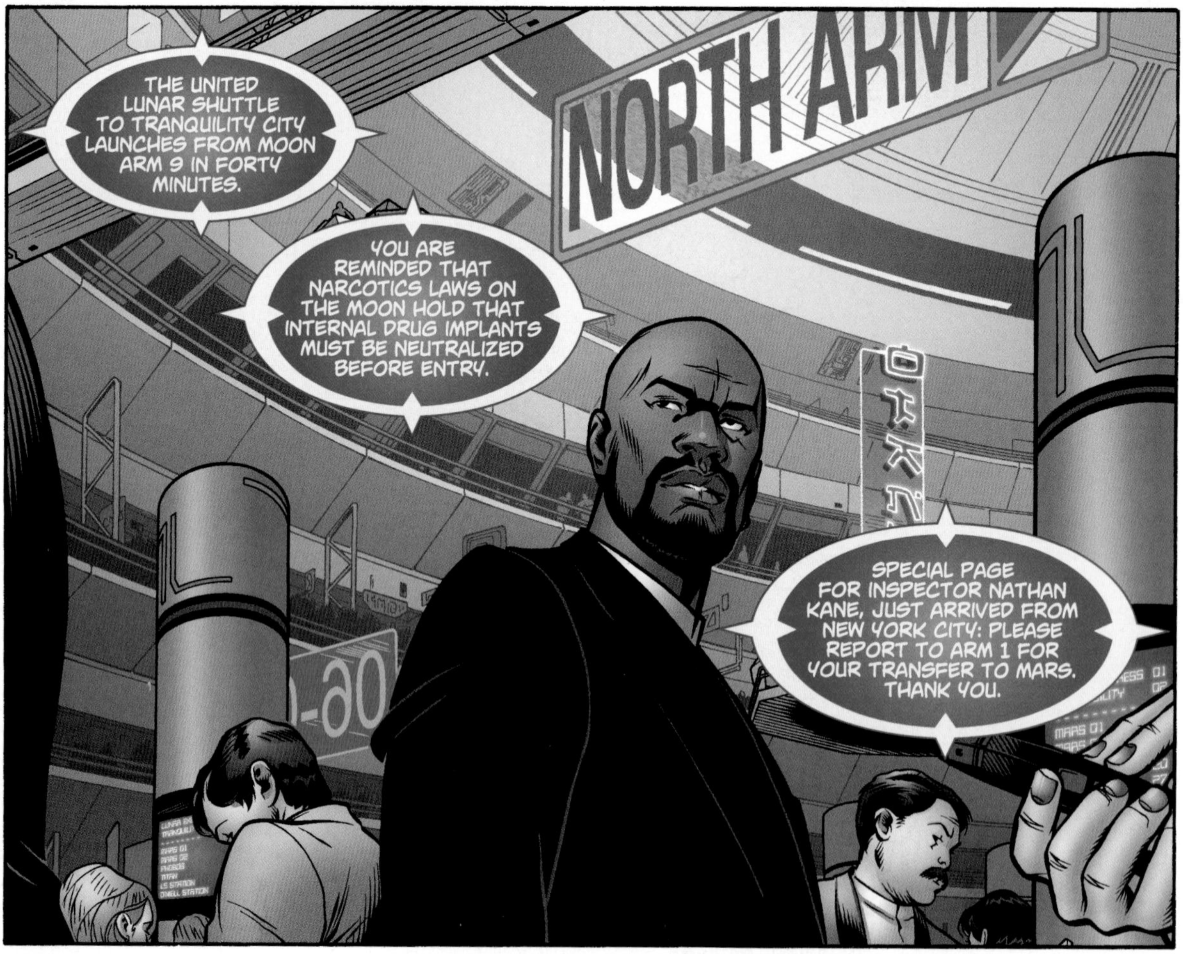
THE UNITED LUNAR SHUTTLE TO TRANQUILITY CITY LAUNCHES FROM MOON ARM 9 IN FORTY MINUTES.
YOU ARE REMINDED THAT NARCOTICS LAWS ON THE MOON HOLD THAT INTERNAL DRUG IMPLANTS MUST BE NEUTRALIZED BEFORE ENTRY.
NORTH ARM
SPECIAL PAGE FOR INSPECTOR NATHAN KANE, JUST ARRIVED FROM NEW YORK CITY: PLEASE REPORT TO ARM 1 FOR YOUR TRANSFER TO MARS. THANK YOU.

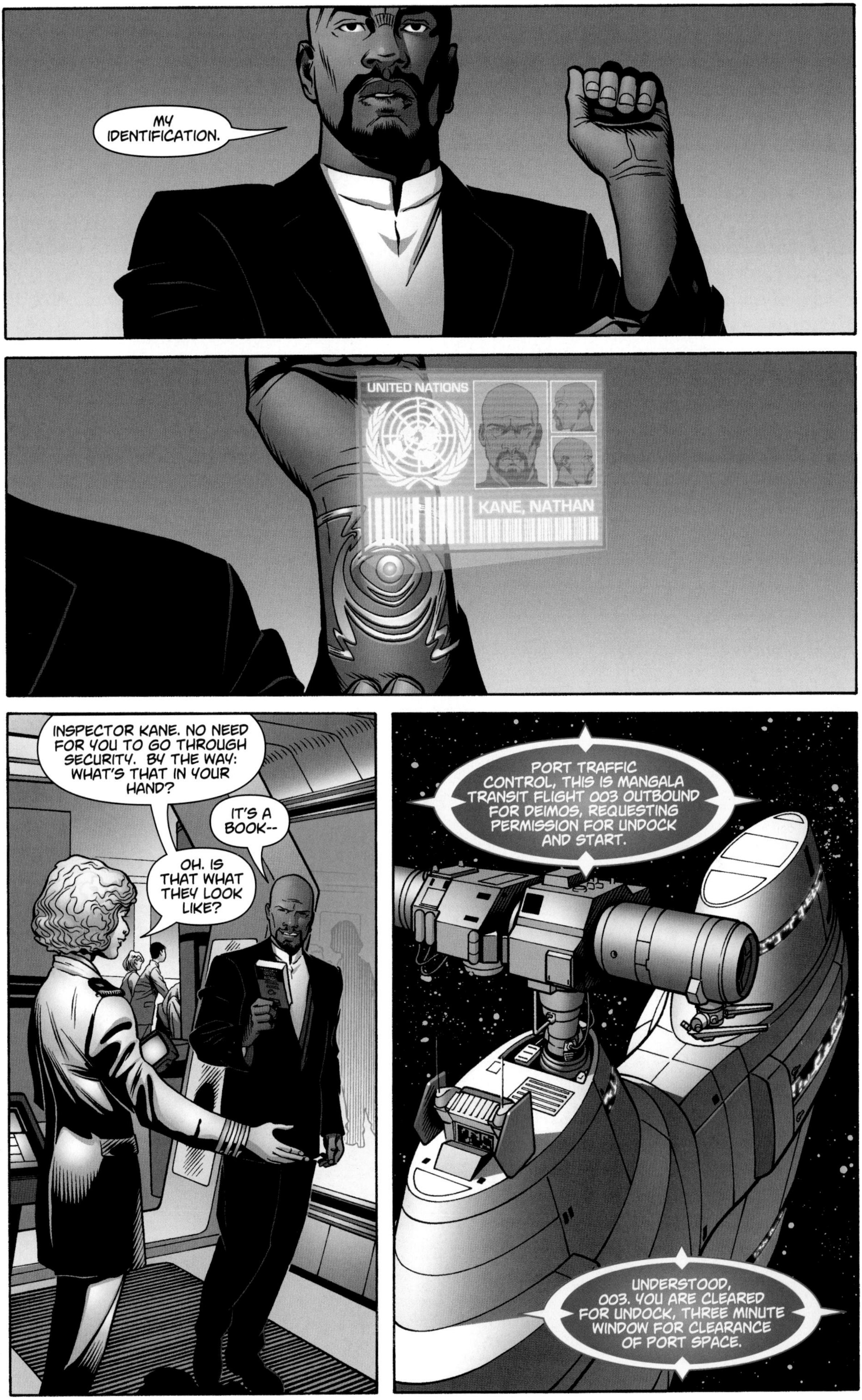
MY IDENTIFICATION.
UNITED NATIONS
KANE, NATHAN
INSPECTOR KANE. NO NEED FOR YOU TO GO THROUGH SECURITY. BY THE WAY: WHAT'S THAT IN YOUR HAND?
IT'S A BOOK--
OH. IS THAT WHAT THEY LOOK LIKE?
PORT TRAFFIC CONTROL, THIS IS MANGALA TRANSIT FLIGHT 003 OUTBOUND FOR DEIMOS, REQUESTING PERMISSION FOR UNDOCK AND START.
UNDERSTOOD, 003. YOU ARE CLEARED FOR UNDOCK, THREE MINUTE WINDOW FOR CLEARANCE OF PORT SPACE.

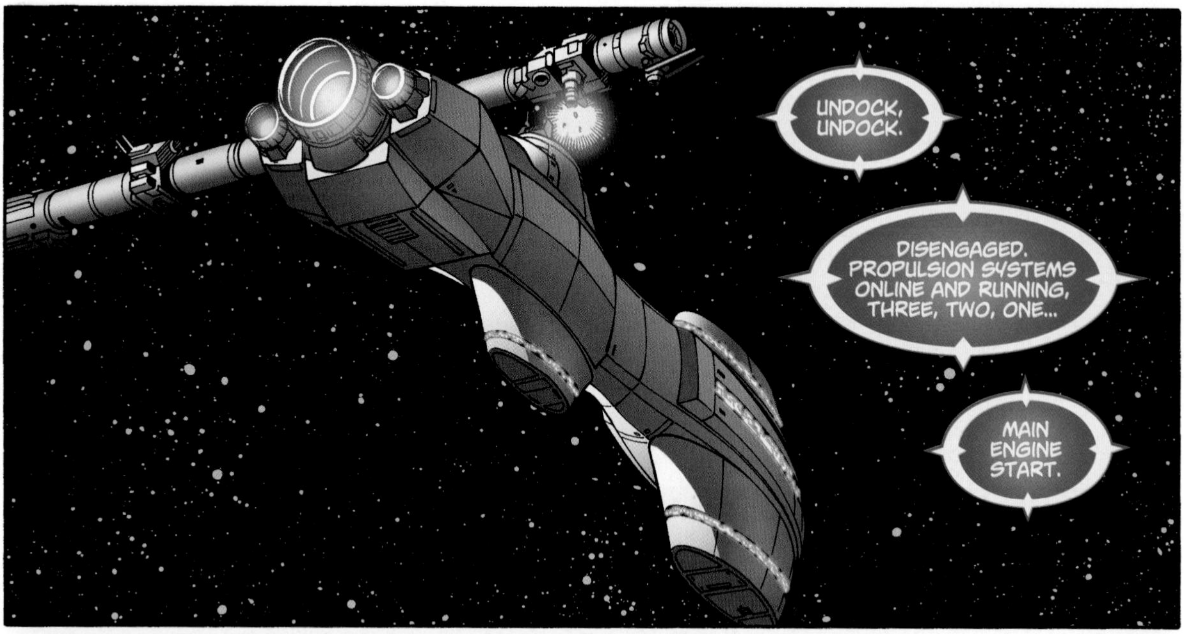
UNDOCK, UNDOCK.
DISENGAGED. PROPULSION SYSTEMS ONLINE AND RUNNING, THREE, TWO, ONE...
MAIN ENGINE START.

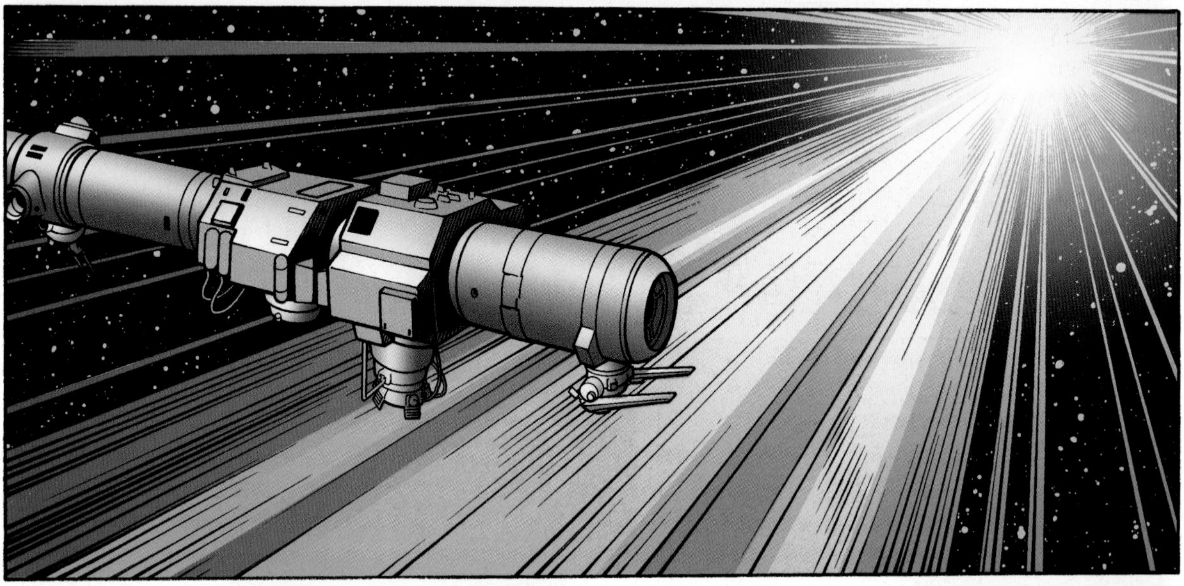

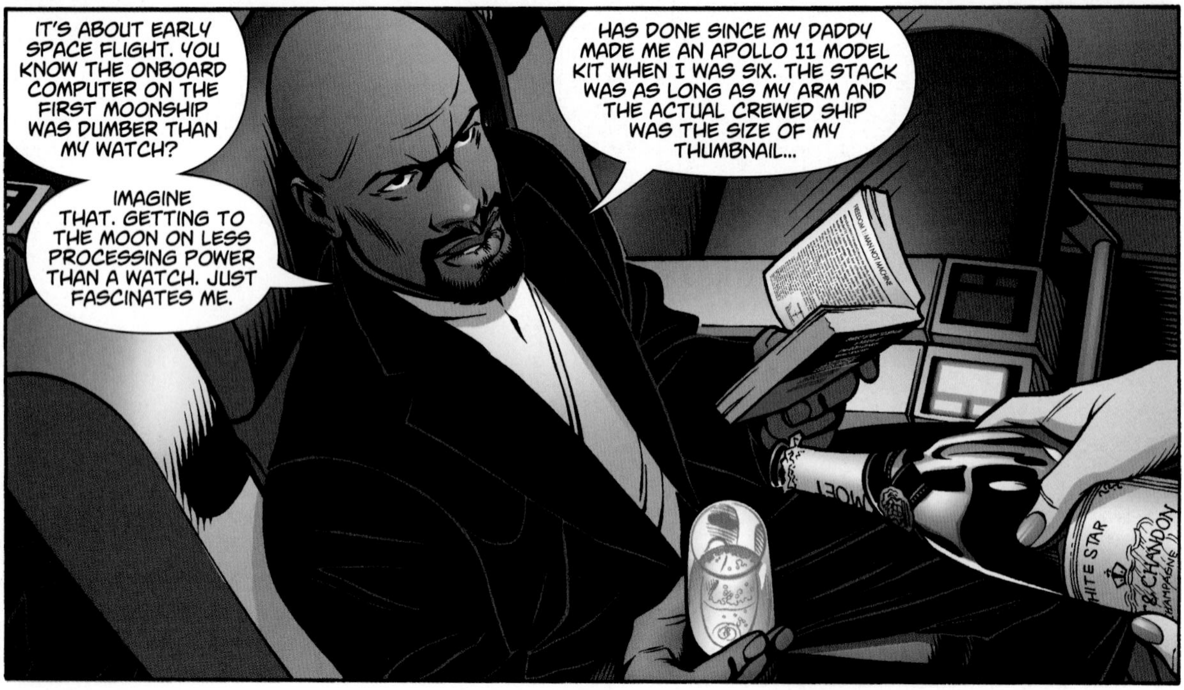
IT'S ABOUT EARLY SPACE FLIGHT. YOU KNOW THE ONBOARD COMPUTER ON THE FIRST MOONSHIP WAS DUMBER THAN MY WATCH?
IMAGINE THAT. GETTING TO THE MOON ON LESS PROCESSING POWER THAN A WATCH. JUST FASCINATES ME.
HAS DONE SINCE MY DADDY MADE ME AN APOLLO 11 MODEL KIT WHEN I WAS SIX. THE STACK WAS AS LONG AS MY ARM AND THE ACTUAL CREWED SHIP WAS THE SIZE OF MY THUMBNAIL...

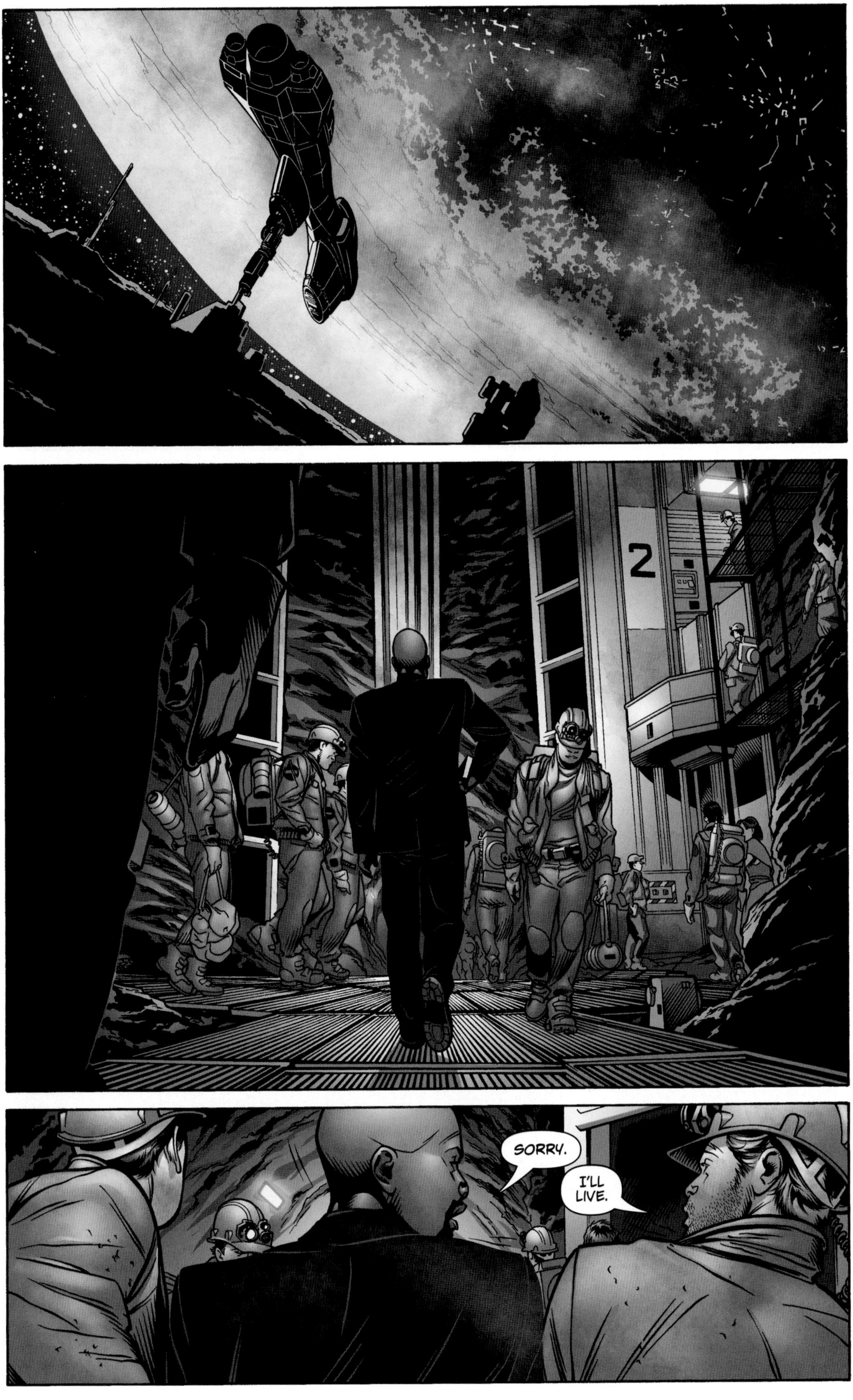
SORRY.
I'LL LIVE.

YOU KNOW WHAT THE WORST THING ABOUT WORKING IN SPACE IS? YOU CAN'T OPEN A GODDAMN WINDOW.

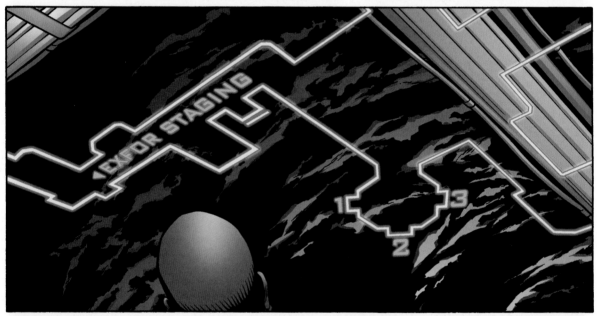

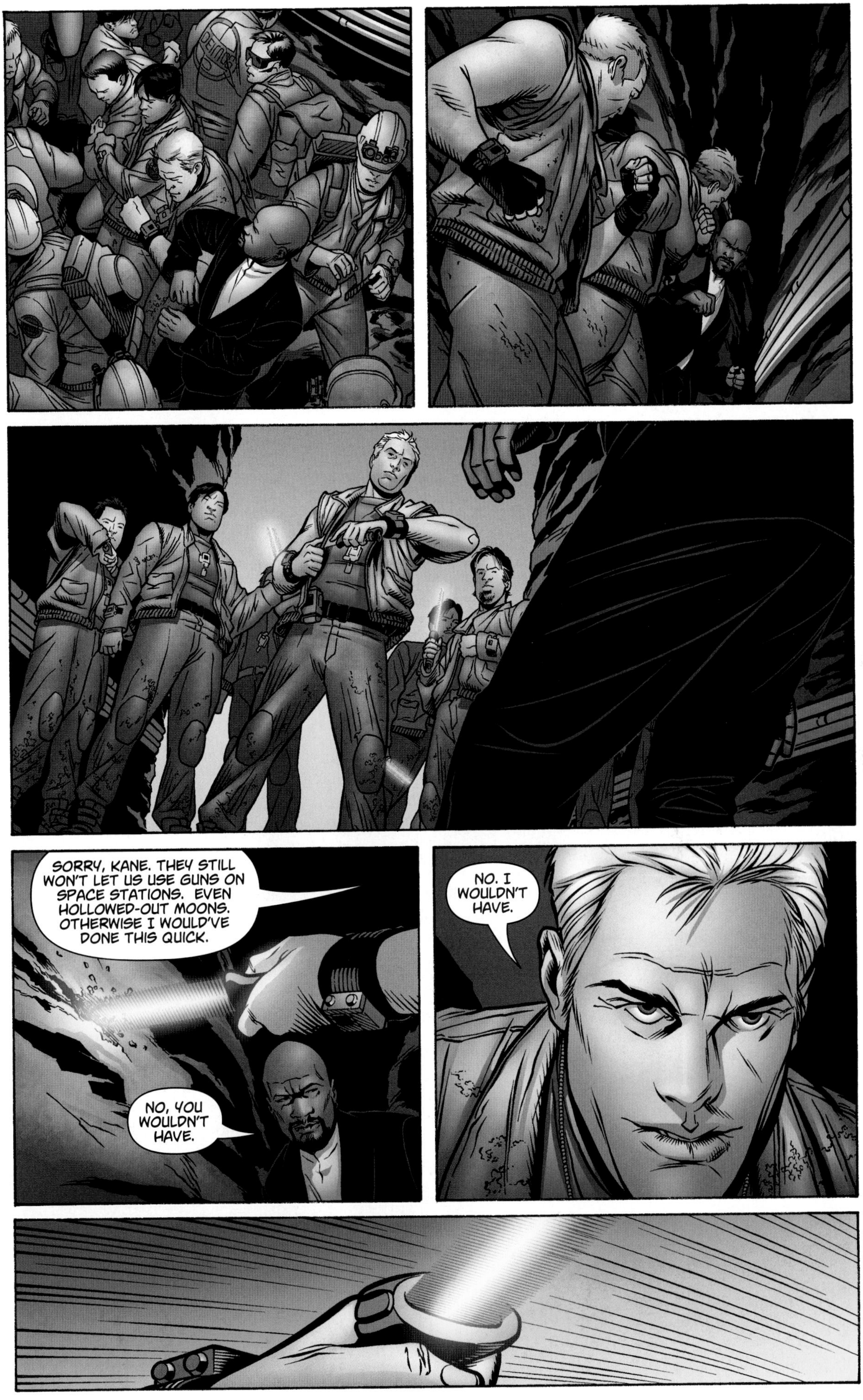
SORRY, KANE. THEY STILL WON'T LET US USE GUNS ON SPACE STATIONS. EVEN HOLLOWED-OUT MOONS. OTHERWISE I WOULD'VE DONE THIS QUICK.
NO, YOU WOULDN'T HAVE.
NO. I WOULDN'T HAVE.

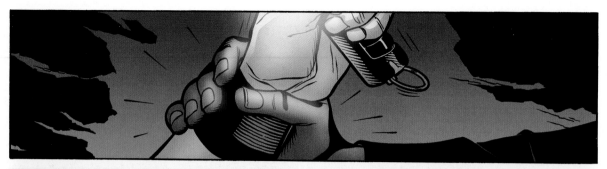

I'M WAITING, LADIES.

CAN I PLEASE GET CHANGED?

YOU LOOK GOOD IN RED. SHUT UP.

TAKE OFF, ROSEWOOD. TAKE PATROL NINE. FORGET EVER SEEING THIS GUY.

I WAS NEVER HERE. SPOOOOOOKY.

NATHAN KANE. SPECIAL WEAPONS INSPECTOR, UNITED NATIONS. COOPERATION FROM ALL POLICE SERVICES MANDATORY. ALL APPLICABLE IMMUNITIES.

WHAT'S THE STORY HERE, INSPECTOR KANE?

STORY IS, I WAS JUMPED.

STEAMER GANG. HAPPENS ALL THE TIME.

WORKERS MUG PEOPLE, EITHER BECAUSE THEY'RE UNDER-PAID AND LOOKING FOR CASH, OR BECAUSE THEY'RE OFF THEIR TITS ON SPEED AND LOOKING FOR SOMEONE TO HURT.

WEREN'T WORKERS. CLEAN HANDS, SMOOTH NAILS.

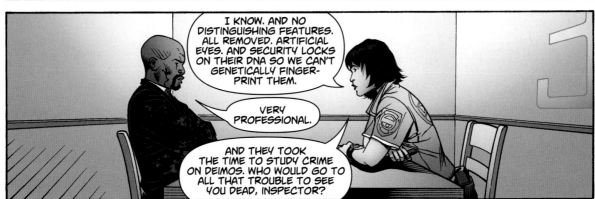

I KNOW. AND NO DISTINGUISHING FEATURES. ALL REMOVED. ARTIFICIAL EYES. AND SECURITY LOCKS ON THEIR DNA SO WE CAN'T GENETICALLY FINGER-PRINT THEM.

VERY PROFESSIONAL.

AND THEY TOOK THE TIME TO STUDY CRIME ON DEIMOS. WHO WOULD GO TO ALL THAT TROUBLE TO SEE YOU DEAD, INSPECTOR?

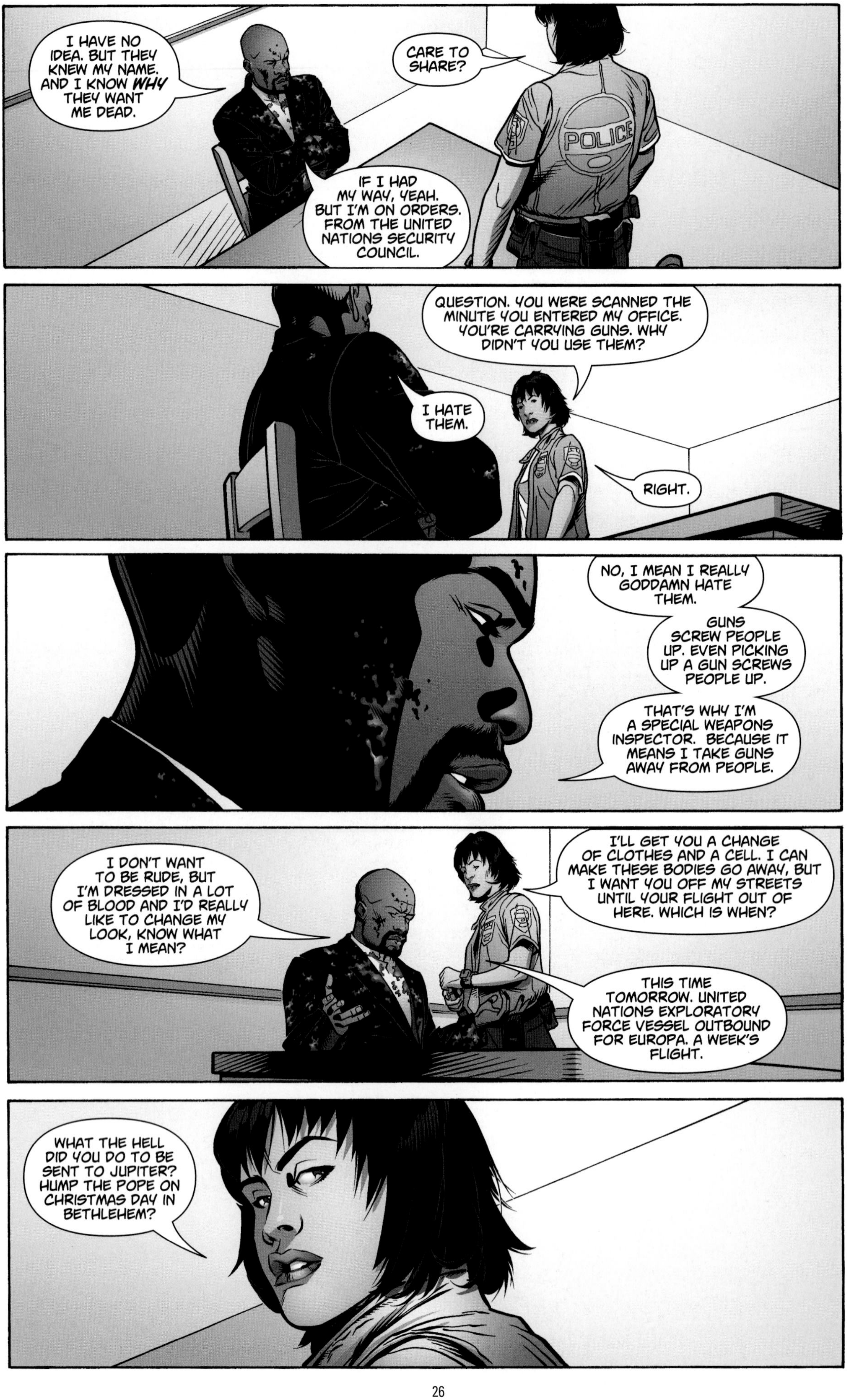
I HAVE NO IDEA. BUT THEY KNEW MY NAME. AND I KNOW *WHY* THEY WANT ME DEAD.
CARE TO SHARE?
IF I HAD MY WAY, YEAH. BUT I'M ON ORDERS. FROM THE UNITED NATIONS SECURITY COUNCIL.
POLICE
QUESTION. YOU WERE SCANNED THE MINUTE YOU ENTERED MY OFFICE. YOU'RE CARRYING GUNS. WHY DIDN'T YOU USE THEM?
I HATE THEM.
RIGHT.
NO, I MEAN I REALLY GODDAMN HATE THEM.
GUNS SCREW PEOPLE UP. EVEN PICKING UP A GUN SCREWS PEOPLE UP.
THAT'S WHY I'M A SPECIAL WEAPONS INSPECTOR. BECAUSE IT MEANS I TAKE GUNS AWAY FROM PEOPLE.
I DON'T WANT TO BE RUDE, BUT I'M DRESSED IN A LOT OF BLOOD AND I'D REALLY LIKE TO CHANGE MY LOOK, KNOW WHAT I MEAN?
I'LL GET YOU A CHANGE OF CLOTHES AND A CELL. I CAN MAKE THESE BODIES GO AWAY, BUT I WANT YOU OFF MY STREETS UNTIL YOUR FLIGHT OUT OF HERE. WHICH IS WHEN?
THIS TIME TOMORROW. UNITED NATIONS EXPLORATORY FORCE VESSEL OUTBOUND FOR EUROPA. A WEEK'S FLIGHT.
WHAT THE HELL DID YOU DO TO BE SENT TO JUPITER? HUMP THE POPE ON CHRISTMAS DAY IN BETHLEHEM?

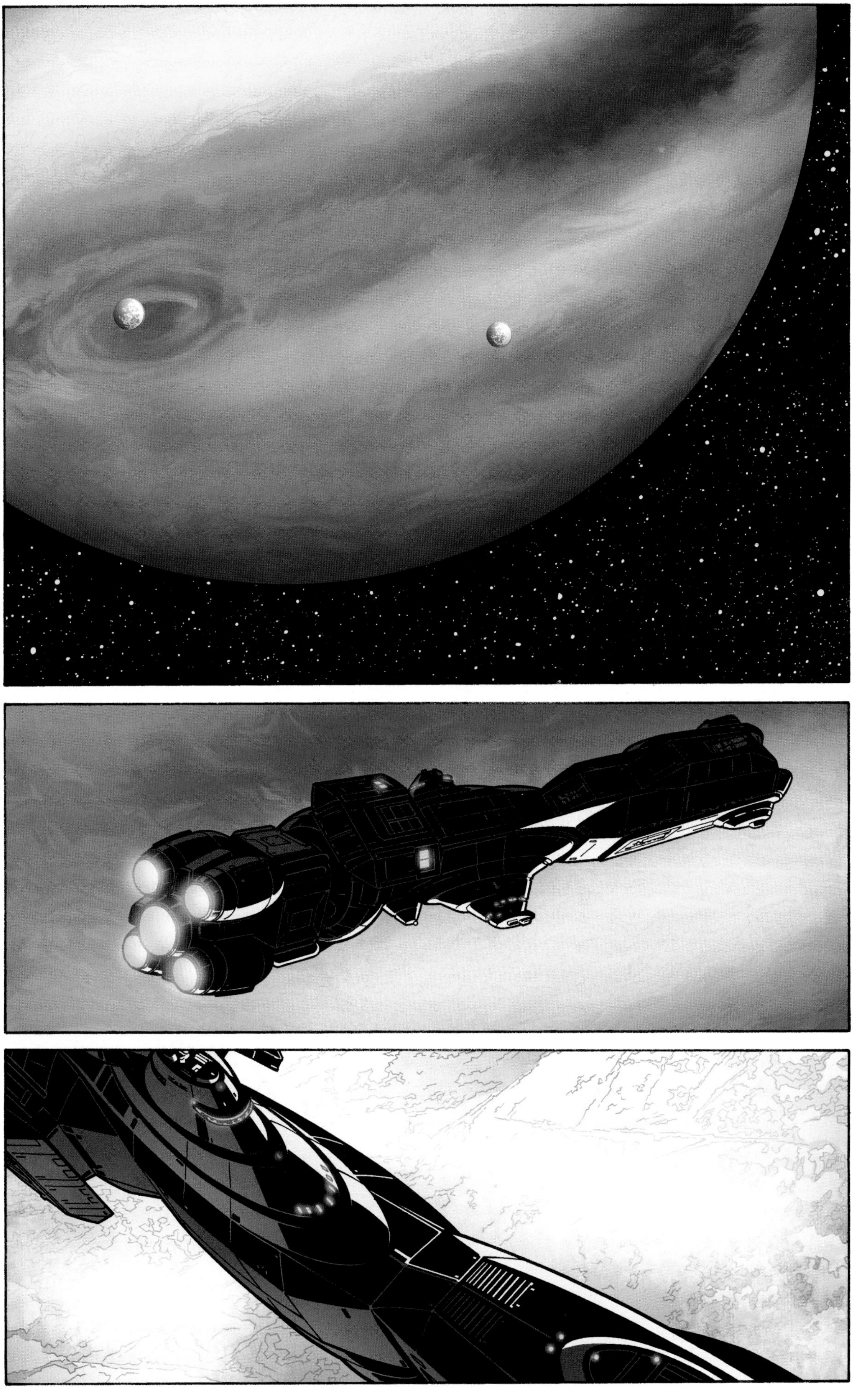

WOULD YOU LOOK AT THAT.

EUROPA. ONLY GENUINE OCEAN PLANET WE KNOW OF. IF IT WERE ANYWHERE ELSE, IT *WOULD* BE A PLANET.

BUT NEXT TO JUPITER, IT'S JUST A MOON. HELL, NEXT TO THAT, *EARTH* WOULD BE A MOON.

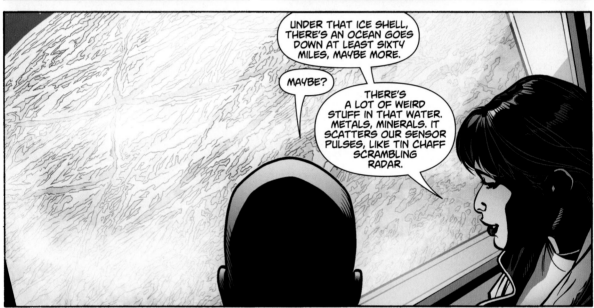

UNDER THAT ICE SHELL, THERE'S AN OCEAN GOES DOWN AT LEAST SIXTY MILES, MAYBE MORE.

MAYBE?

THERE'S A LOT OF WEIRD STUFF IN THAT WATER. METALS, MINERALS. IT SCATTERS OUR SENSOR PULSES, LIKE TIN CHAFF SCRAMBLING RADAR.

THAT'S THE EXPLORATORY FORCE'S PERMANENT EUROPA STATION: COLD HARBOR.

BEEN HERE THREE YEARS. FIRST MAJOR STATION WE'VE HAD IN THE JUPITER SYSTEM.

28

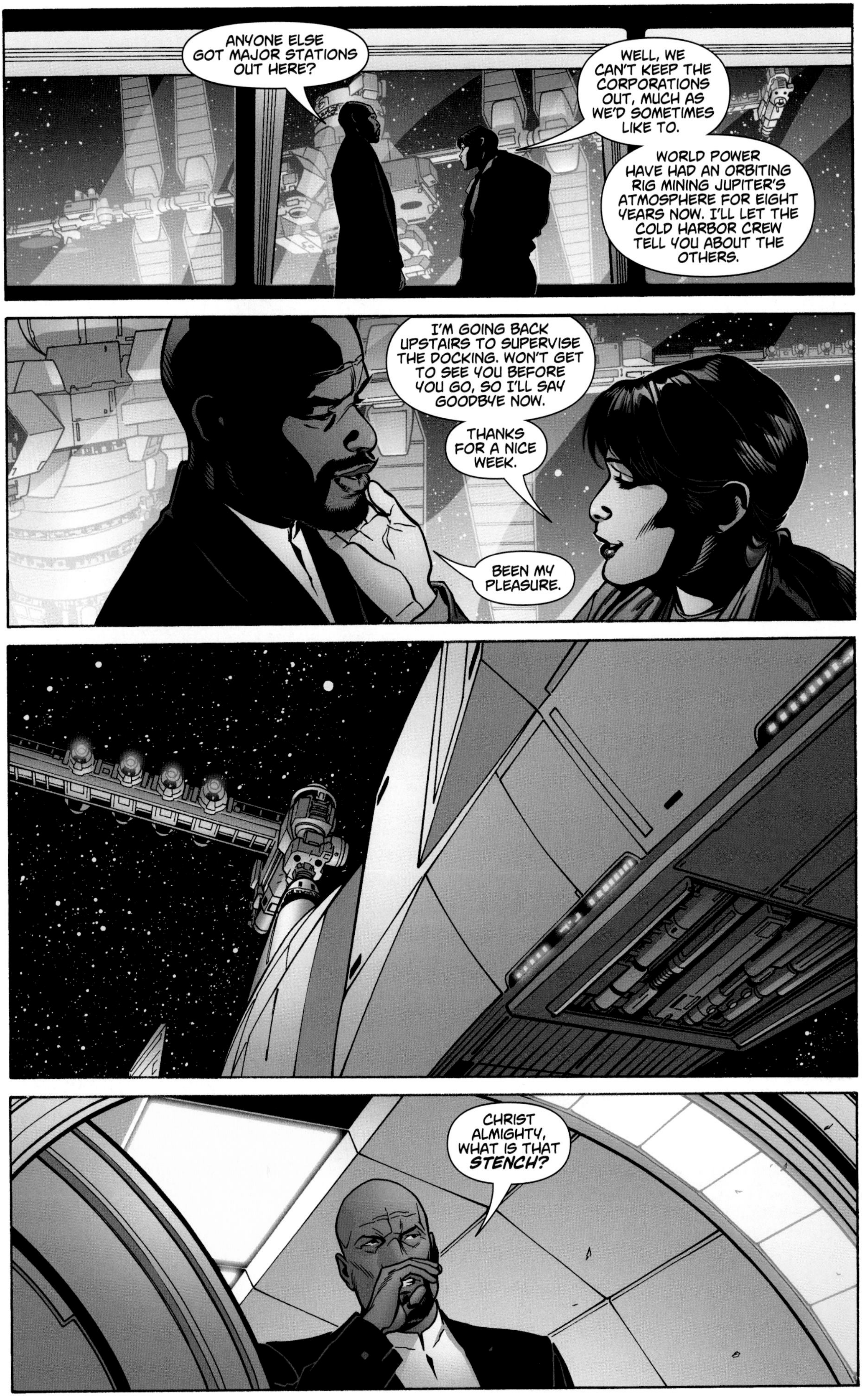
ANYONE ELSE GOT MAJOR STATIONS OUT HERE?
WELL, WE CAN'T KEEP THE CORPORATIONS OUT, MUCH AS WE'D SOMETIMES LIKE TO.
WORLD POWER HAVE HAD AN ORBITING RIG MINING JUPITER'S ATMOSPHERE FOR EIGHT YEARS NOW. I'LL LET THE COLD HARBOR CREW TELL YOU ABOUT THE OTHERS.
I'M GOING BACK UPSTAIRS TO SUPERVISE THE DOCKING. WON'T GET TO SEE YOU BEFORE YOU GO, SO I'LL SAY GOODBYE NOW.
THANKS FOR A NICE WEEK.
BEEN MY PLEASURE.
CHRIST ALMIGHTY, WHAT IS THAT *STENCH?*

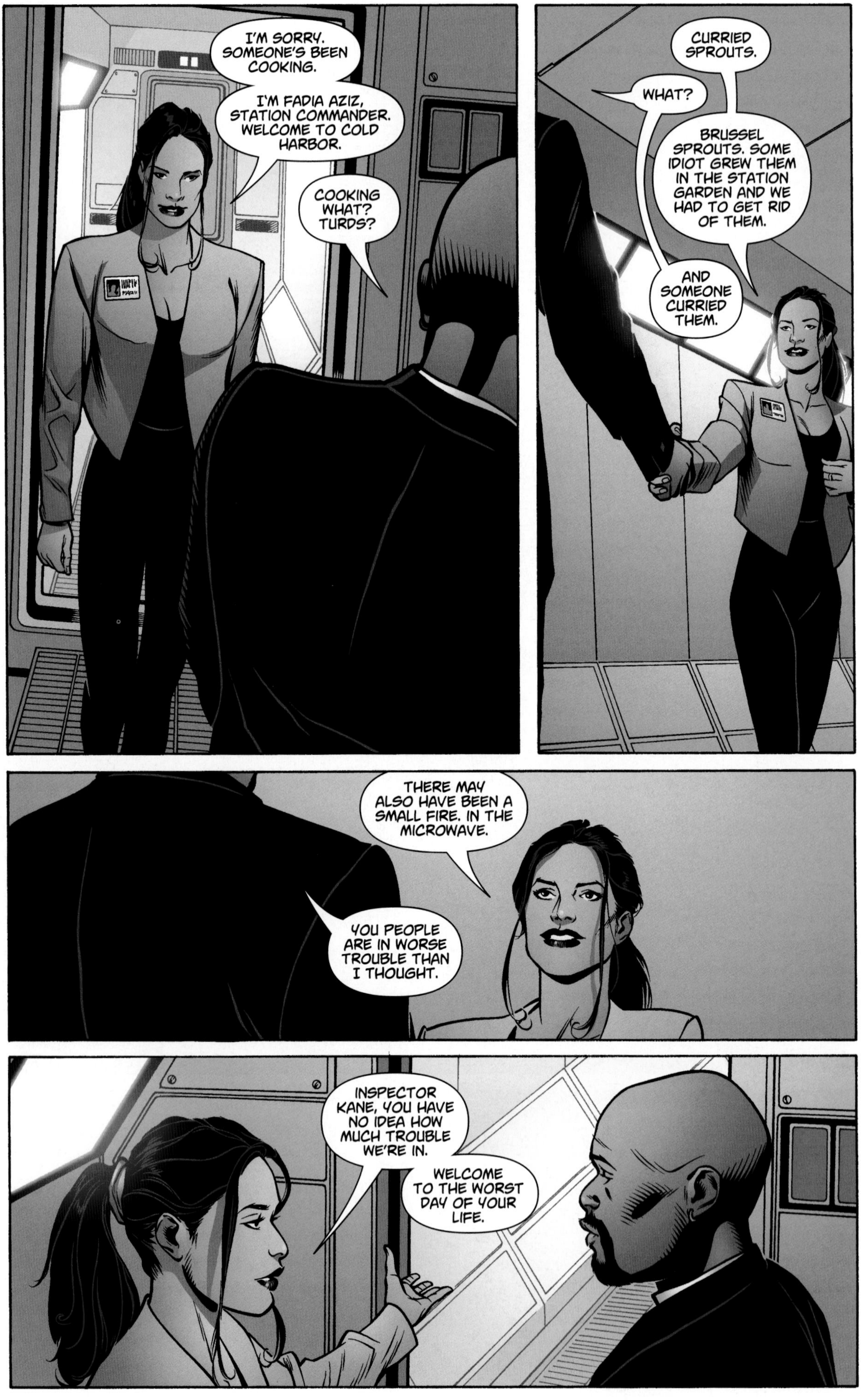
I'M SORRY. SOMEONE'S BEEN COOKING.
I'M FADIA AZIZ, STATION COMMANDER. WELCOME TO COLD HARBOR.
COOKING WHAT? TURDS?
CURRIED SPROUTS.
WHAT?
BRUSSEL SPROUTS. SOME IDIOT GREW THEM IN THE STATION GARDEN AND WE HAD TO GET RID OF THEM.
AND SOMEONE CURRIED THEM.
THERE MAY ALSO HAVE BEEN A SMALL FIRE. IN THE MICROWAVE.
YOU PEOPLE ARE IN WORSE TROUBLE THAN I THOUGHT.
INSPECTOR KANE, YOU HAVE NO IDEA HOW MUCH TROUBLE WE'RE IN.
WELCOME TO THE WORST DAY OF YOUR LIFE.

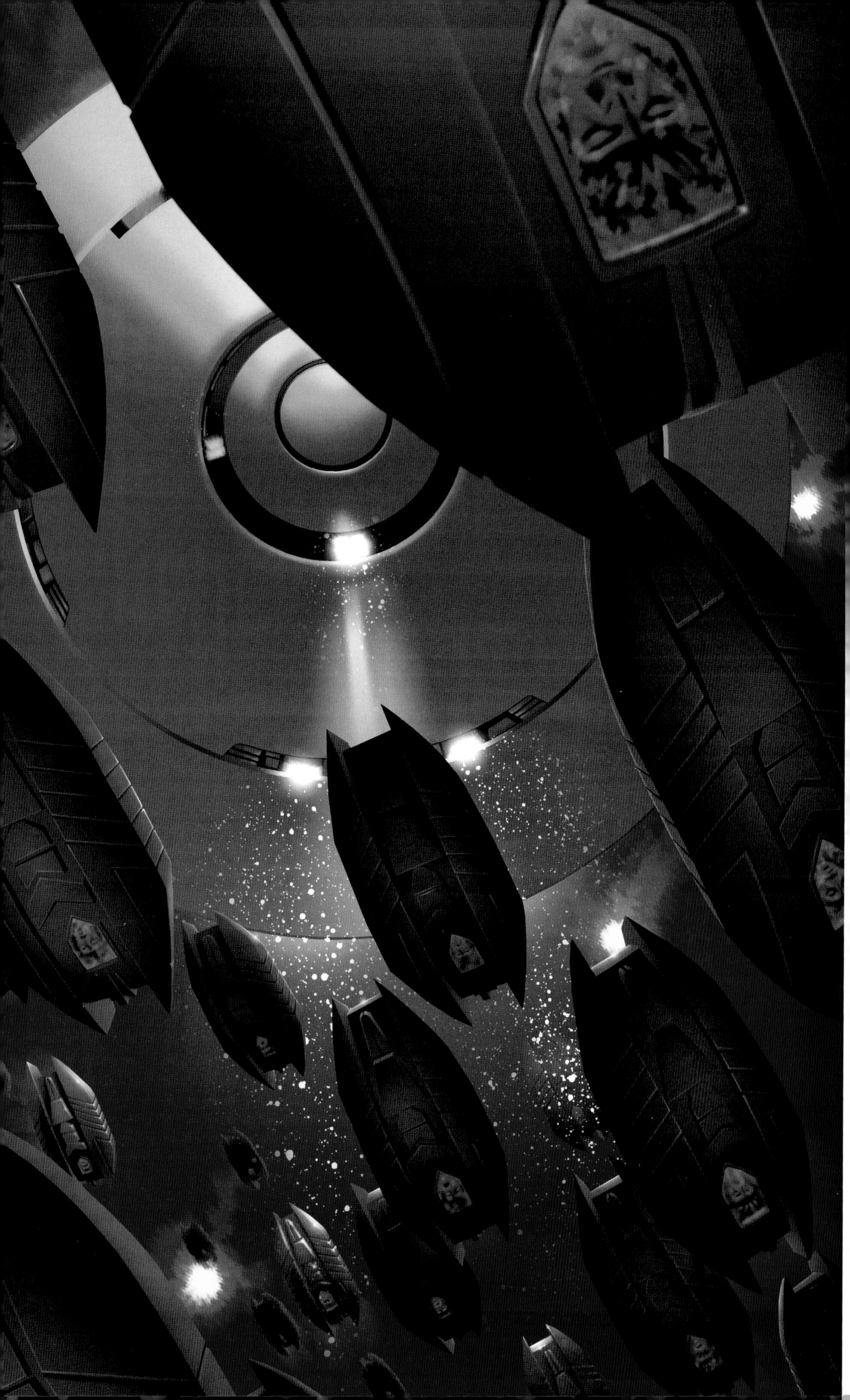

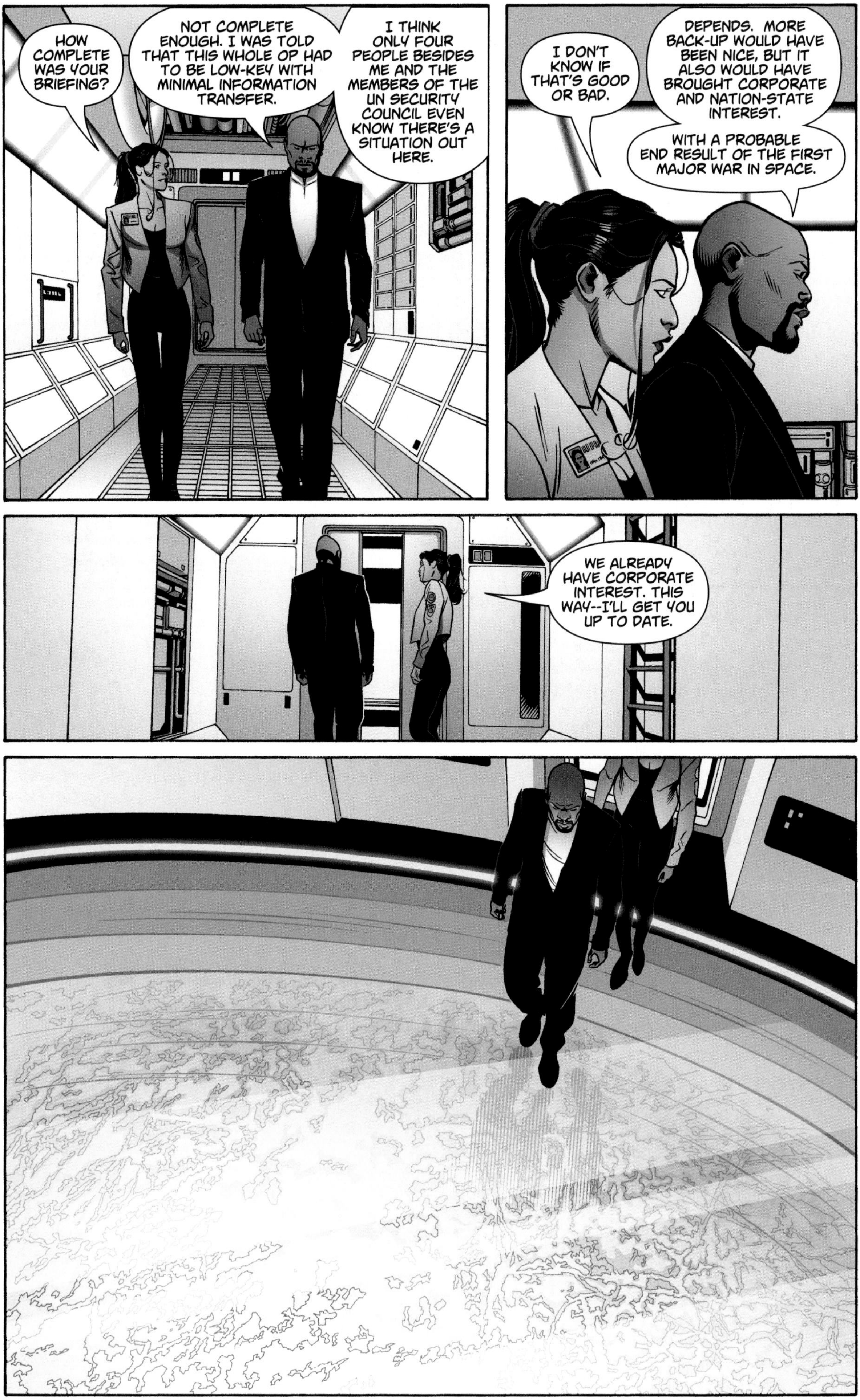
HOW COMPLETE WAS YOUR BRIEFING?
NOT COMPLETE ENOUGH. I WAS TOLD THAT THIS WHOLE OP HAD TO BE LOW-KEY WITH MINIMAL INFORMATION TRANSFER.
I THINK ONLY FOUR PEOPLE BESIDES ME AND THE MEMBERS OF THE UN SECURITY COUNCIL EVEN KNOW THERE'S A SITUATION OUT HERE.
I DON'T KNOW IF THAT'S GOOD OR BAD.
DEPENDS. MORE BACK-UP WOULD HAVE BEEN NICE, BUT IT ALSO WOULD HAVE BROUGHT CORPORATE AND NATION-STATE INTEREST.
WITH A PROBABLE END RESULT OF THE FIRST MAJOR WAR IN SPACE.
WE ALREADY HAVE CORPORATE INTEREST. THIS WAY--I'LL GET YOU UP TO DATE.

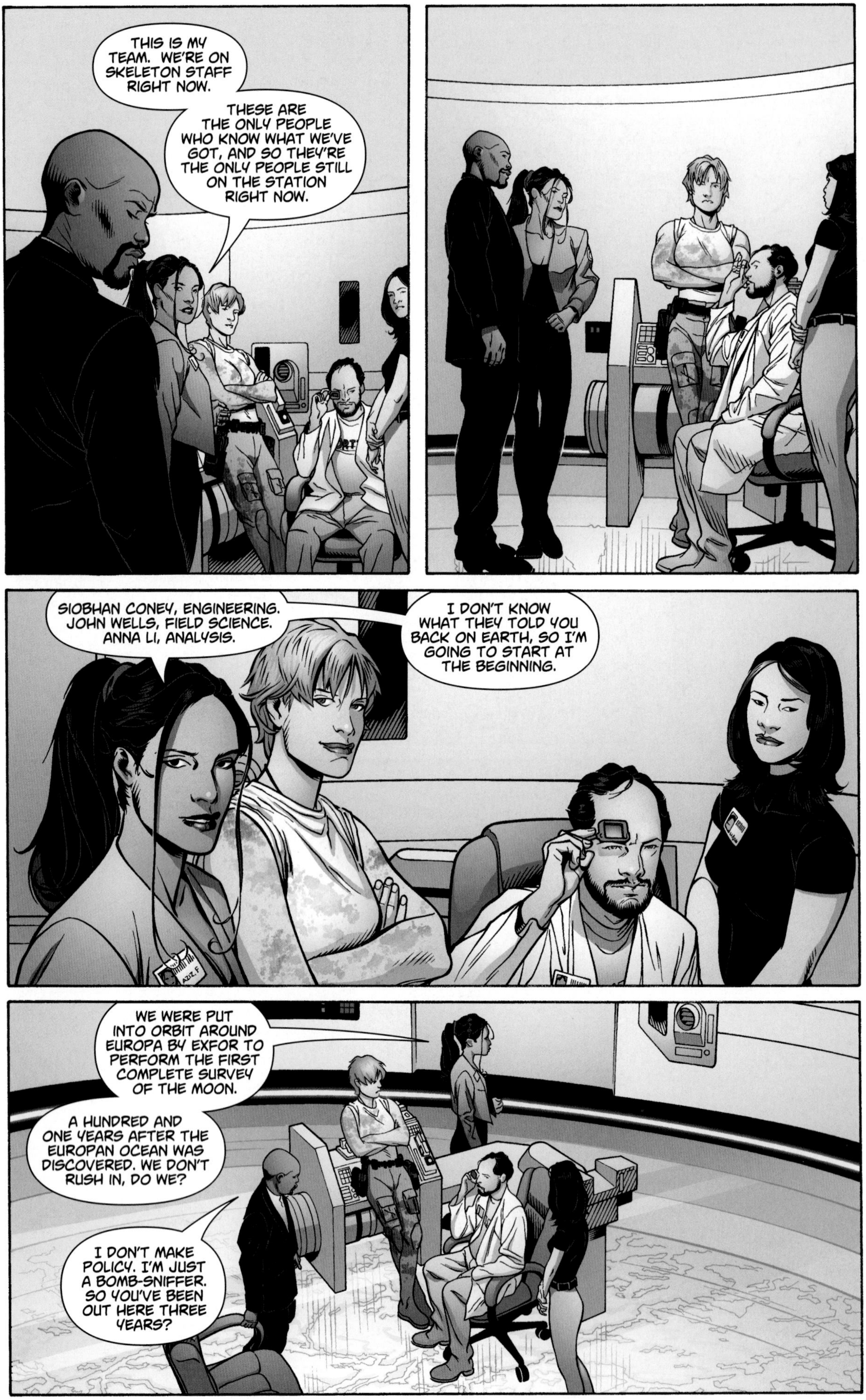
THIS IS MY TEAM. WE'RE ON SKELETON STAFF RIGHT NOW.
THESE ARE THE ONLY PEOPLE WHO KNOW WHAT WE'VE GOT, AND SO THEY'RE THE ONLY PEOPLE STILL ON THE STATION RIGHT NOW.
SIOBHAN CONEY, ENGINEERING. JOHN WELLS, FIELD SCIENCE. ANNA LI, ANALYSIS.
I DON'T KNOW WHAT THEY TOLD YOU BACK ON EARTH, SO I'M GOING TO START AT THE BEGINNING.
WE WERE PUT INTO ORBIT AROUND EUROPA BY EXFOR TO PERFORM THE FIRST COMPLETE SURVEY OF THE MOON.
A HUNDRED AND ONE YEARS AFTER THE EUROPAN OCEAN WAS DISCOVERED. WE DON'T RUSH IN, DO WE?
I DON'T MAKE POLICY. I'M JUST A BOMB-SNIFFER. SO YOU'VE BEEN OUT HERE THREE YEARS?

RIGHT. THE FIRST TWO AND A HALF YEARS WE SPENT UP HERE, WE GOT NOWHERE. WE ESTABLISHED THE PRESENCE OF ACTUAL WATER UNDER THE ICE.

WAS THAT EVER IN QUESTION?

HEY, JUST BECAUSE SOMETHING COMES OUT OF OUR GALLEY ON A PLATE, DOESN'T MEAN IT'S FOOD.

CURRYING THE SPROUTS SEEMED LIKE A GOOD IDEA AT THE TIME. I SAID I WAS SORRY.

NO APOLOGY COVERS THE DAMAGE YOU DID TO OUR ENVIRONMENT.

I'M GOING TO HAVE TO HAVE NEW LUNGS GROWN WHEN WE GET HOME.

IF WE GET HOME.

POINT BEING-- ONCE YOU'RE OFF EARTH, YOU CAN'T MAKE ASSUMPTIONS ABOUT ANYTHING.

SO. WATER. DOES THAT MEAN THERE'S LIFE OUT HERE?

HELL, THREE WEEKS AGO I COULDN'T HAVE TOLD YOU HOW DEEP THE OCEAN IS. ALL THE CRAP IN THE WATER WAS SCATTERING OUR DETECTION PULSES.

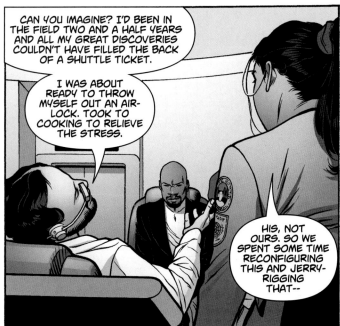

CAN YOU IMAGINE? I'D BEEN IN THE FIELD TWO AND A HALF YEARS AND ALL MY GREAT DISCOVERIES COULDN'T HAVE FILLED THE BACK OF A SHUTTLE TICKET.

I WAS ABOUT READY TO THROW MYSELF OUT AN AIR-LOCK. TOOK TO COOKING TO RELIEVE THE STRESS.

HIS, NOT OURS. SO WE SPENT SOME TIME RECONFIGURING THIS AND JERRY-RIGGING THAT--

"WE?"

--AND THEN SENT DOWN A NEW DETECTION ARRAY THAT WOULD DO THE JOB.

AND OUR FIRST PROPER LOOK AT THE OCEAN DEPTHS, WELL...

LOOK AT THIS. SIOBHAN, SWITCH THE FLOOR TO REMOTE DISPLAY. HOOK INTO OCEAN CAM 01.

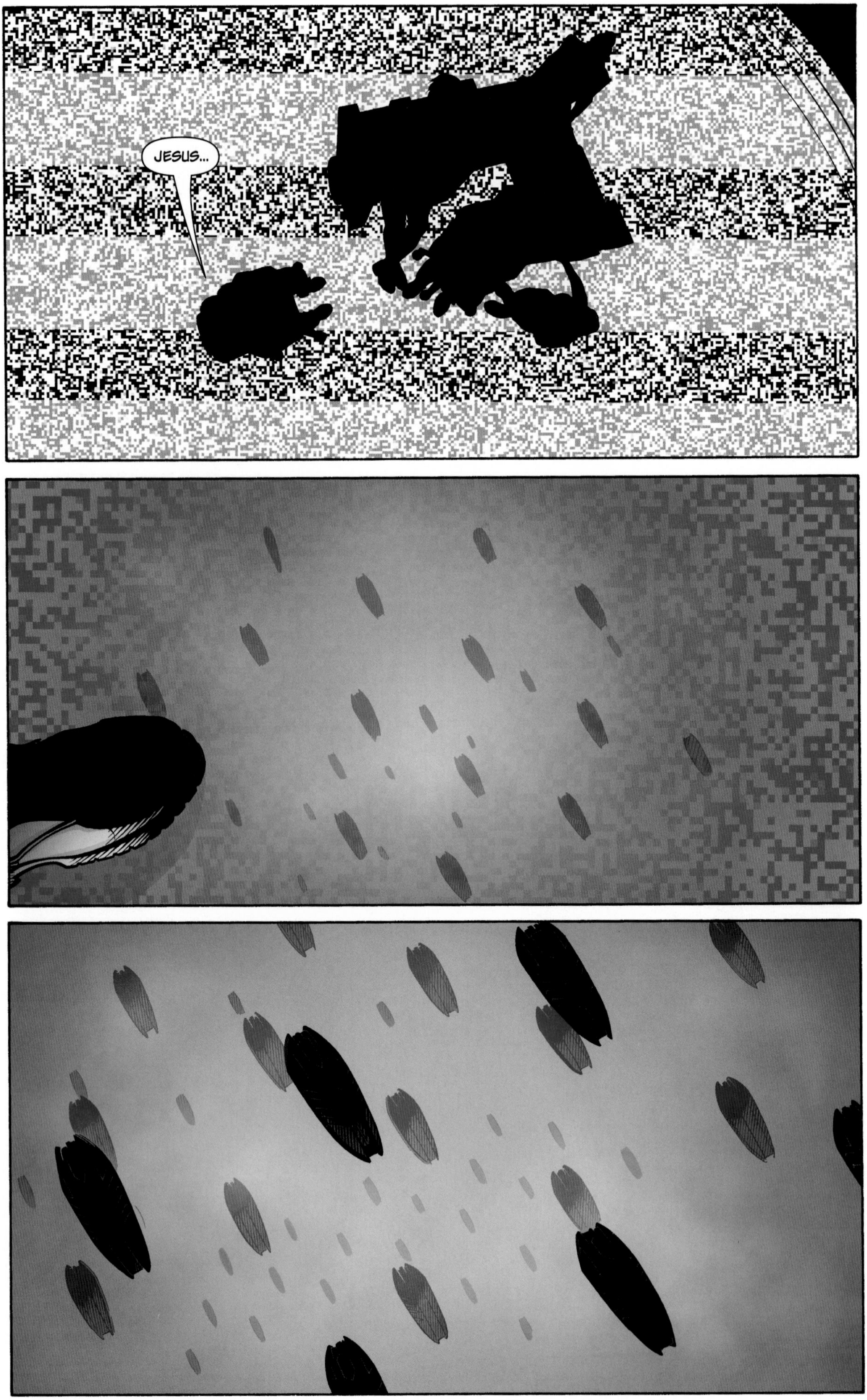
JESUS...

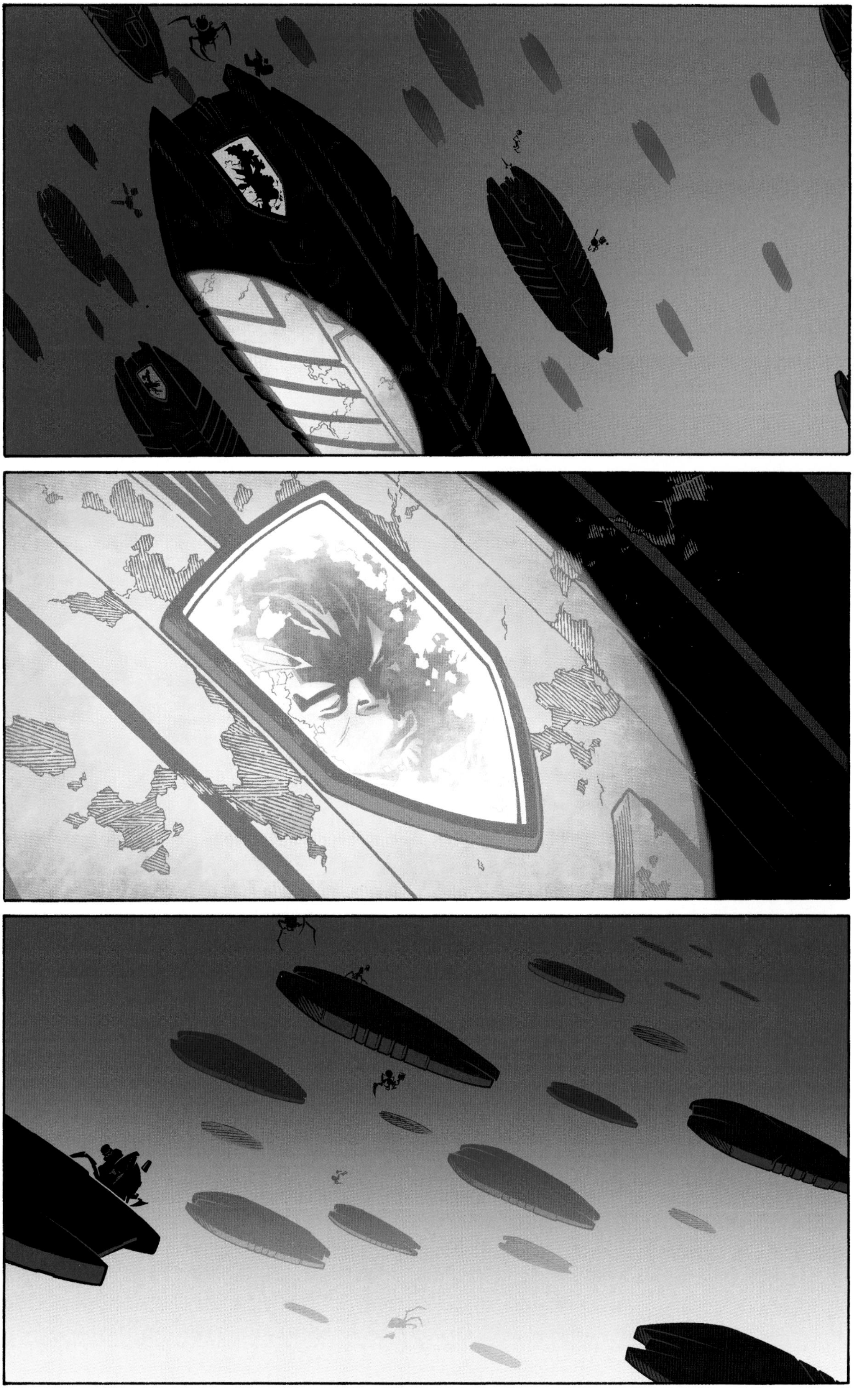

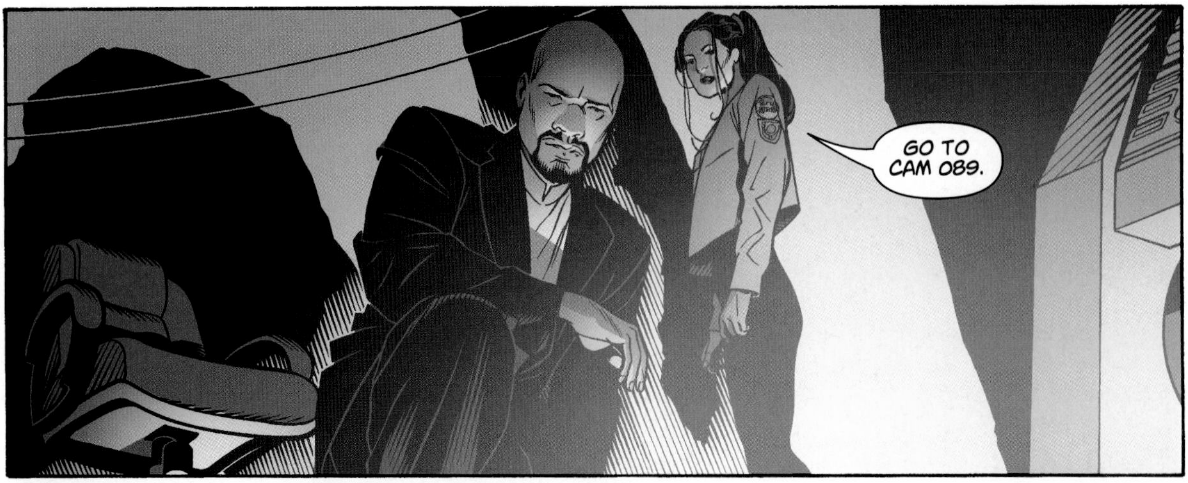
GO TO CAM 089.

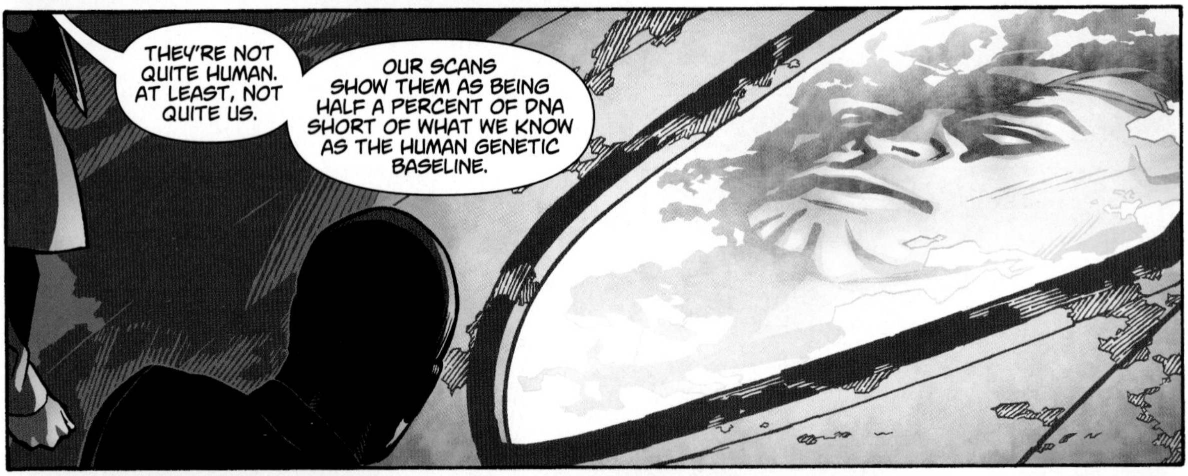
THEY'RE NOT QUITE HUMAN. AT LEAST, NOT QUITE US.
OUR SCANS SHOW THEM AS BEING HALF A PERCENT OF DNA SHORT OF WHAT WE KNOW AS THE HUMAN GENETIC BASELINE.

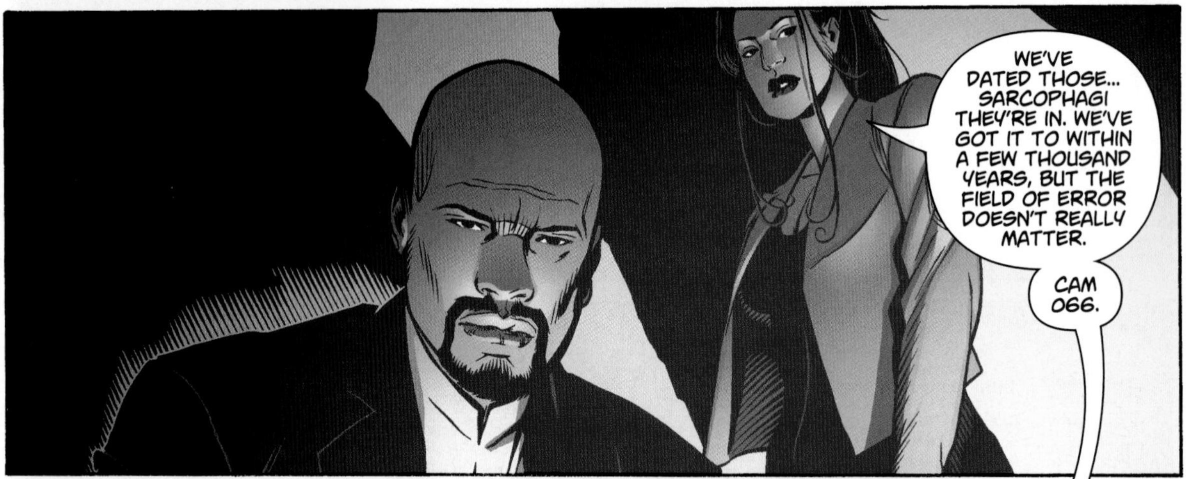
WE'VE DATED THOSE... SARCOPHAGI THEY'RE IN. WE'VE GOT IT TO WITHIN A FEW THOUSAND YEARS, BUT THE FIELD OF ERROR DOESN'T REALLY MATTER.
CAM 066.

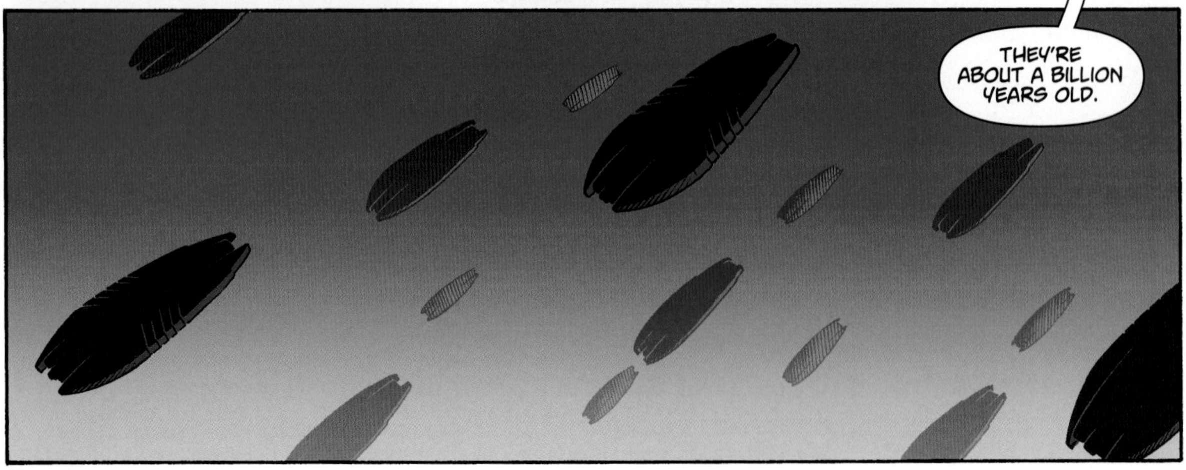
THEY'RE ABOUT A BILLION YEARS OLD.

YOU DON'T CURRY THE COFFEE TOO, DO YOU?

RELAX. I TOLD JOHN THAT IF HE COMES IN HERE WITH INTENT TO COMMIT FOOD CRIME AGAIN I'M GOING TO STRAP HIM TO A DESCENT DISK AND DROP HIM.

HE MIGHT THANK YOU FOR THAT. WHERE IS HE?

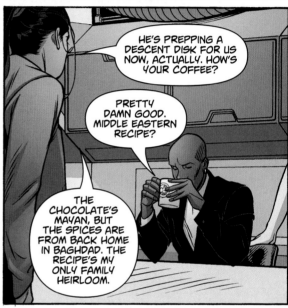

HE'S PREPPING A DESCENT DISK FOR US NOW, ACTUALLY. HOW'S YOUR COFFEE?

PRETTY DAMN GOOD. MIDDLE EASTERN RECIPE?

THE CHOCOLATE'S MAYAN, BUT THE SPICES ARE FROM BACK HOME IN BAGHDAD. THE RECIPE'S MY ONLY FAMILY HEIRLOOM.

CONSIDER YOURSELF HONORED. WE PRACTICALLY HAVE TO DRUG HER TO GET HER TO MAKE IT FOR US.

I SPAT IN THAT.

I DON'T CARE. IT'S THE FIRST DECENT COFFEE I'VE HAD SINCE I LEFT MANHATTAN AND I AIN'T GIVING IT UP. YOU'LL JUST HAVE TO DRUG HER.

I PEED IN IT TOO.

YOU PEOPLE HAVE BEEN OUT HERE WAY TOO LONG.

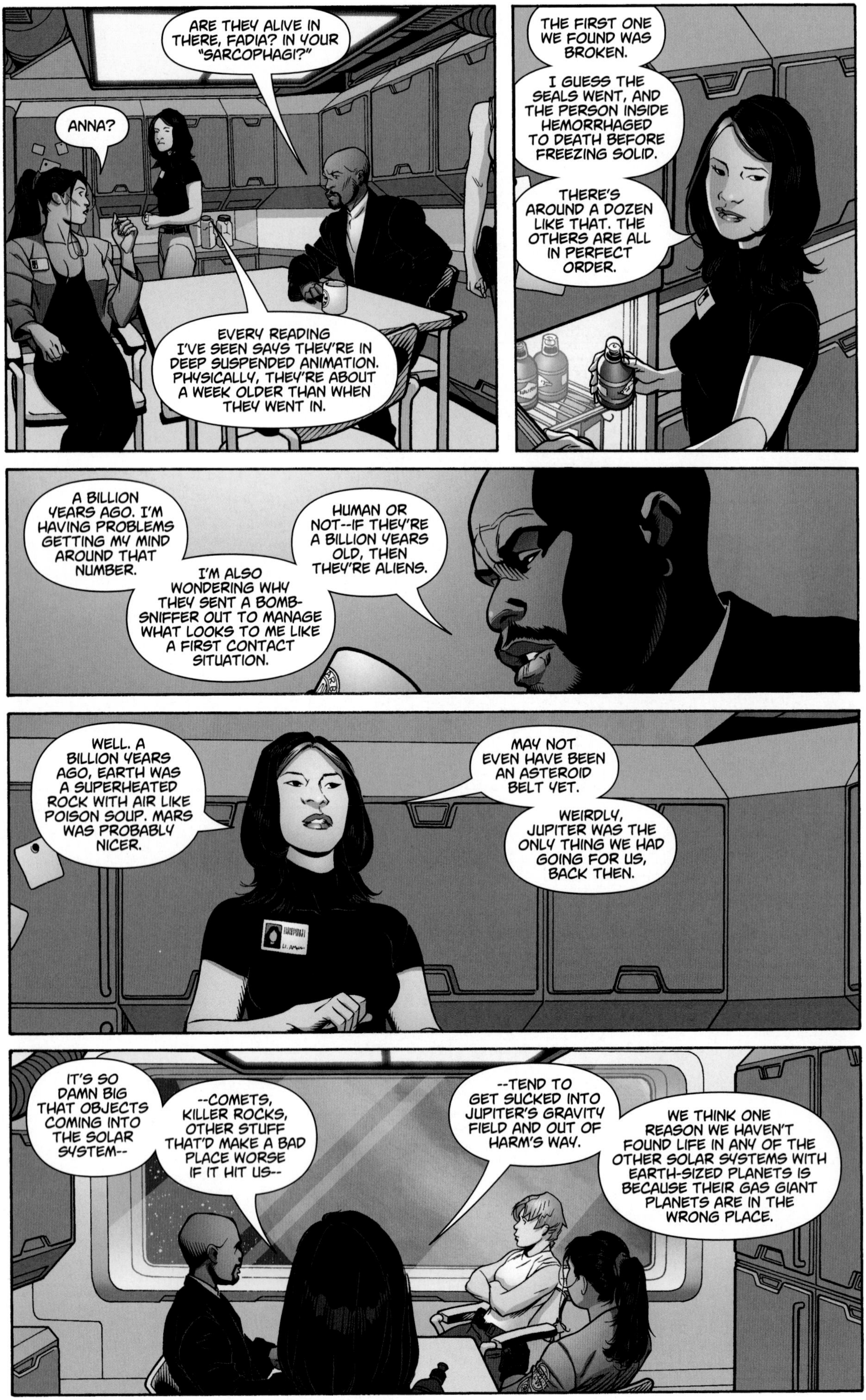
ARE THEY ALIVE IN THERE, FADIA? IN YOUR "SARCOPHAGI?"
ANNA?
EVERY READING I'VE SEEN SAYS THEY'RE IN DEEP SUSPENDED ANIMATION. PHYSICALLY, THEY'RE ABOUT A WEEK OLDER THAN WHEN THEY WENT IN.
THE FIRST ONE WE FOUND WAS BROKEN.
I GUESS THE SEALS WENT, AND THE PERSON INSIDE HEMORRHAGED TO DEATH BEFORE FREEZING SOLID.
THERE'S AROUND A DOZEN LIKE THAT. THE OTHERS ARE ALL IN PERFECT ORDER.
A BILLION YEARS AGO. I'M HAVING PROBLEMS GETTING MY MIND AROUND THAT NUMBER.
I'M ALSO WONDERING WHY THEY SENT A BOMB-SNIFFER OUT TO MANAGE WHAT LOOKS TO ME LIKE A FIRST CONTACT SITUATION.
HUMAN OR NOT--IF THEY'RE A BILLION YEARS OLD, THEN THEY'RE ALIENS.
WELL. A BILLION YEARS AGO, EARTH WAS A SUPERHEATED ROCK WITH AIR LIKE POISON SOUP. MARS WAS PROBABLY NICER.
MAY NOT EVEN HAVE BEEN AN ASTEROID BELT YET.
WEIRDLY, JUPITER WAS THE ONLY THING WE HAD GOING FOR US, BACK THEN.
IT'S SO DAMN BIG THAT OBJECTS COMING INTO THE SOLAR SYSTEM--
--COMETS, KILLER ROCKS, OTHER STUFF THAT'D MAKE A BAD PLACE WORSE IF IT HIT US--
--TEND TO GET SUCKED INTO JUPITER'S GRAVITY FIELD AND OUT OF HARM'S WAY.
WE THINK ONE REASON WE HAVEN'T FOUND LIFE IN ANY OF THE OTHER SOLAR SYSTEMS WITH EARTH-SIZED PLANETS IS BECAUSE THEIR GAS GIANT PLANETS ARE IN THE WRONG PLACE.

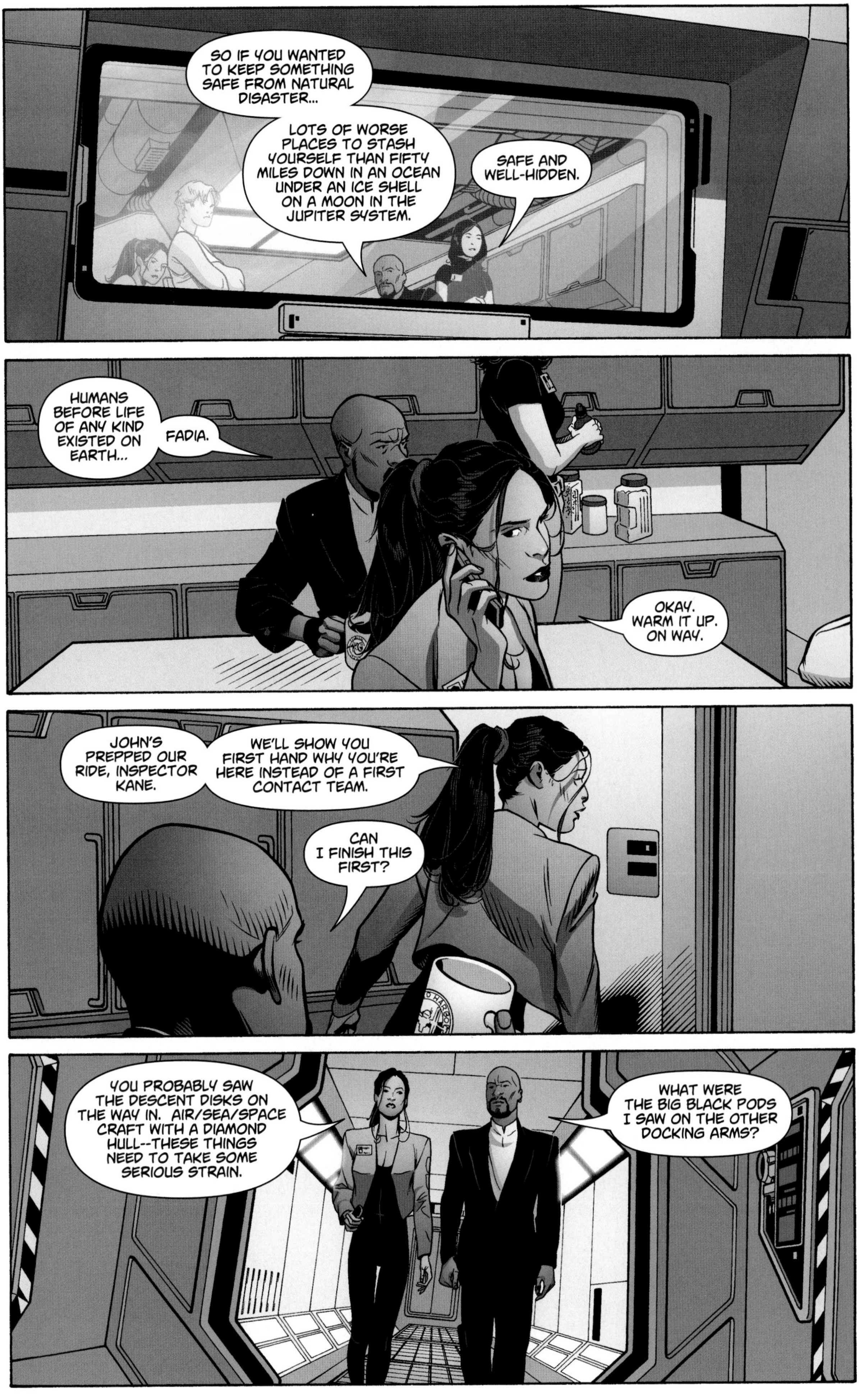
SO IF YOU WANTED TO KEEP SOMETHING SAFE FROM NATURAL DISASTER...
LOTS OF WORSE PLACES TO STASH YOURSELF THAN FIFTY MILES DOWN IN AN OCEAN UNDER AN ICE SHELL ON A MOON IN THE JUPITER SYSTEM.
SAFE AND WELL-HIDDEN.
HUMANS BEFORE LIFE OF ANY KIND EXISTED ON EARTH...
FADIA.
OKAY. WARM IT UP. ON WAY.
JOHN'S PREPPED OUR RIDE, INSPECTOR KANE.
WE'LL SHOW YOU FIRST HAND WHY YOU'RE HERE INSTEAD OF A FIRST CONTACT TEAM.
CAN I FINISH THIS FIRST?
YOU PROBABLY SAW THE DESCENT DISKS ON THE WAY IN. AIR/SEA/SPACE CRAFT WITH A DIAMOND HULL--THESE THINGS NEED TO TAKE SOME SERIOUS STRAIN.
WHAT WERE THE BIG BLACK PODS I SAW ON THE OTHER DOCKING ARMS?

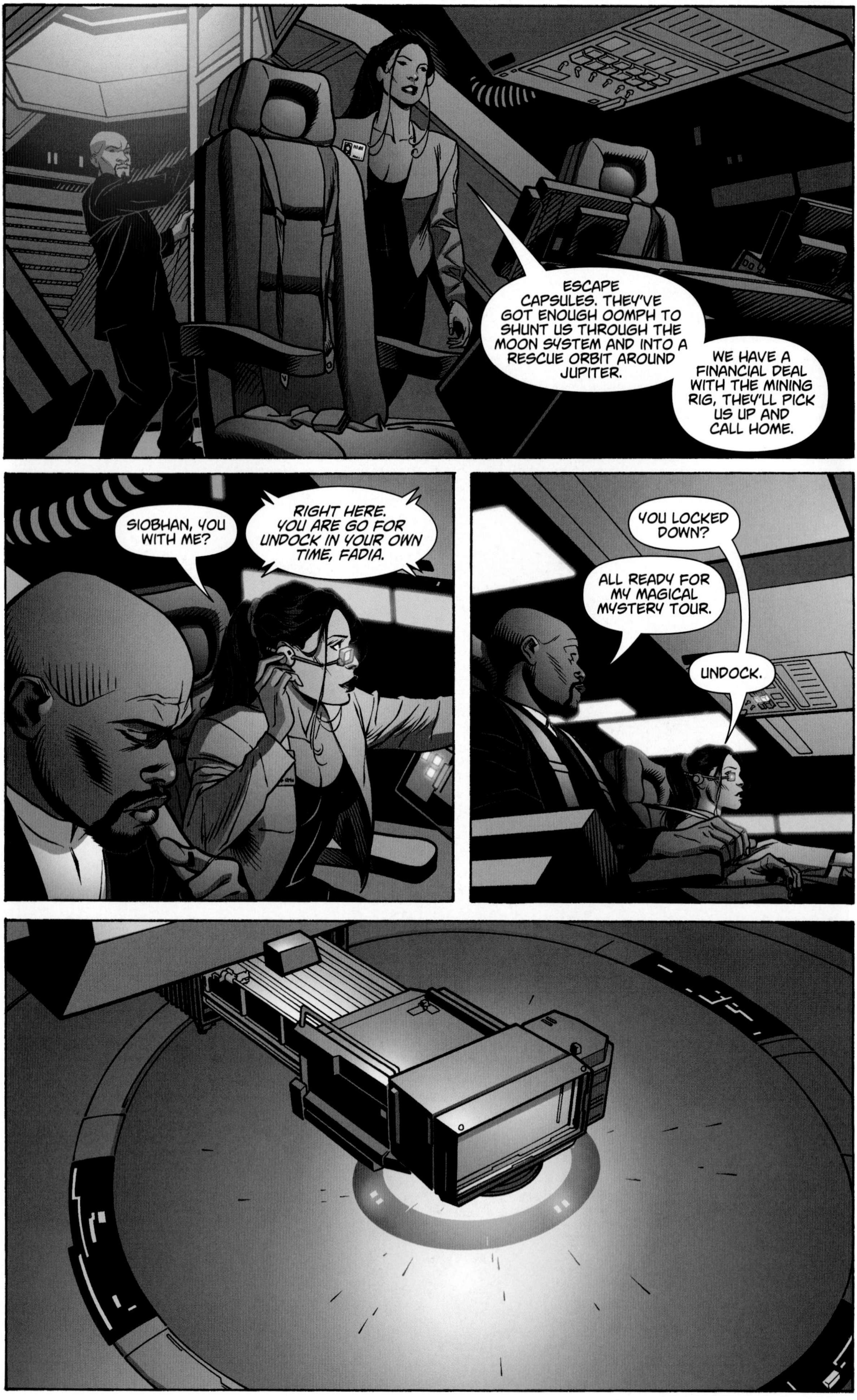
ESCAPE CAPSULES. THEY'VE GOT ENOUGH OOMPH TO SHUNT US THROUGH THE MOON SYSTEM AND INTO A RESCUE ORBIT AROUND JUPITER.
WE HAVE A FINANCIAL DEAL WITH THE MINING RIG, THEY'LL PICK US UP AND CALL HOME.
SIOBHAN, YOU WITH ME?
RIGHT HERE. YOU ARE GO FOR UNDOCK IN YOUR OWN TIME, FADIA.
YOU LOCKED DOWN?
ALL READY FOR MY MAGICAL MYSTERY TOUR.
UNDOCK.

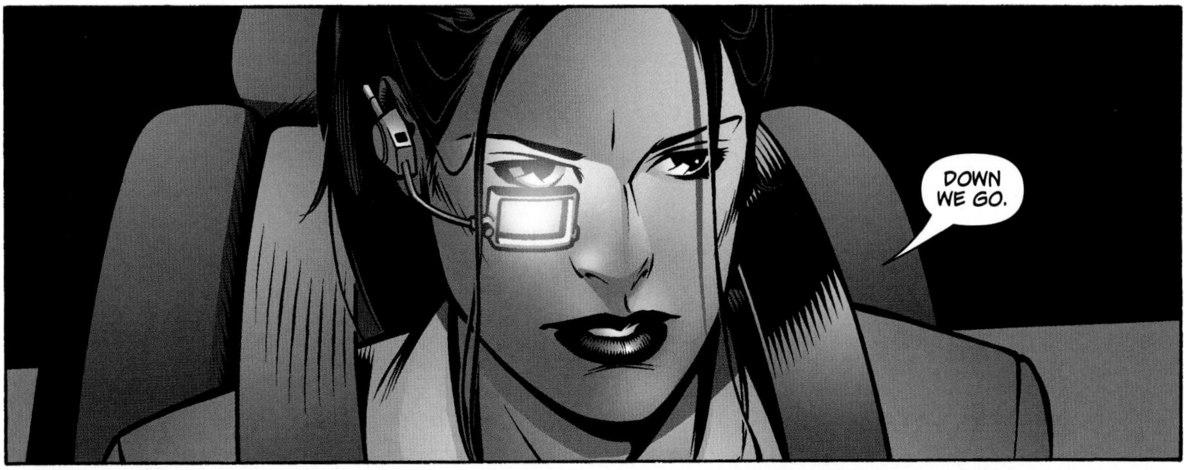
DOWN WE GO.

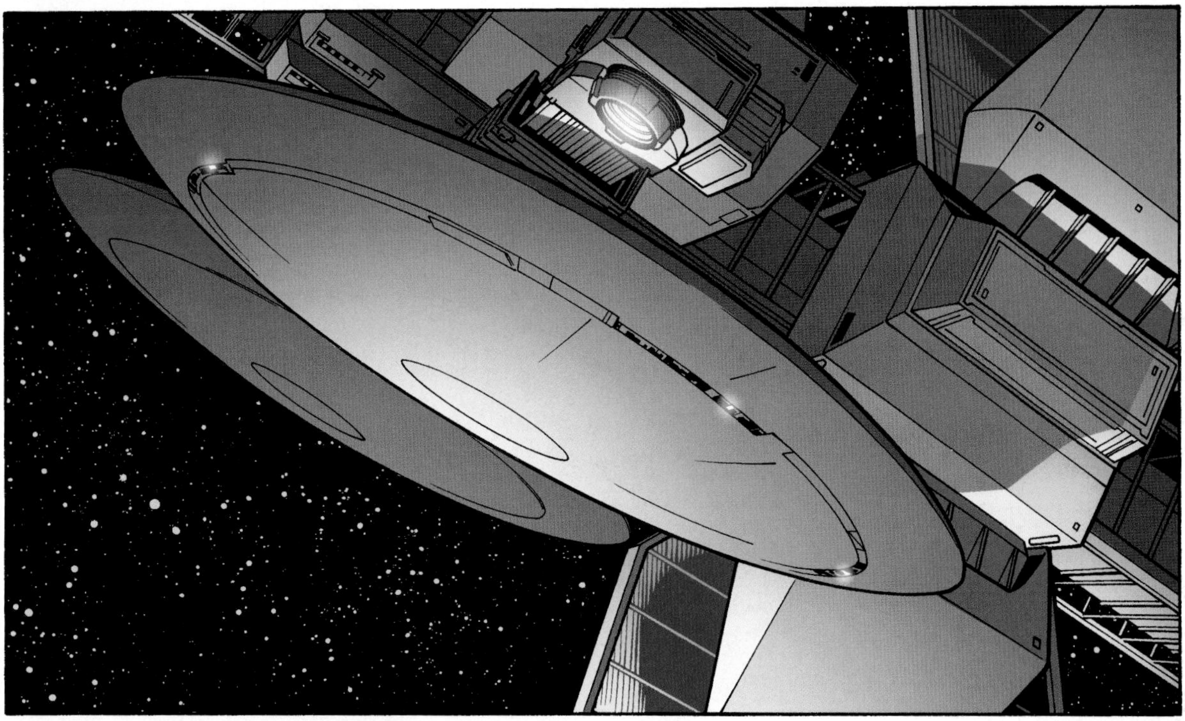

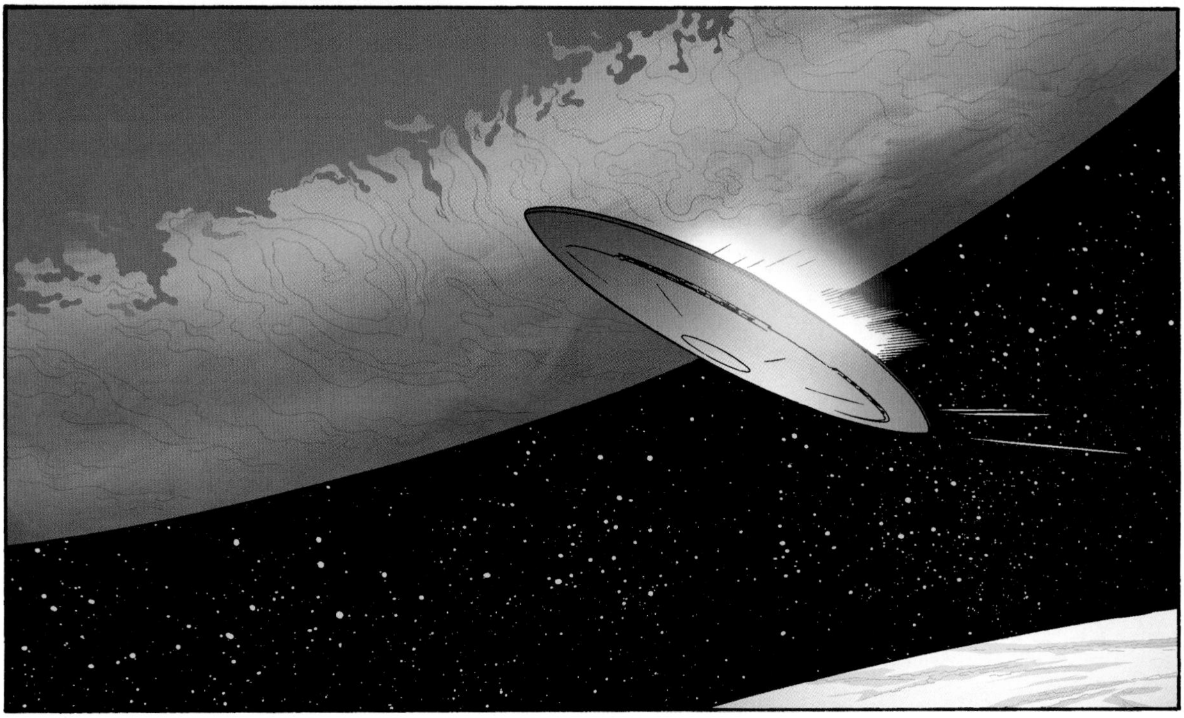

WHAT ARE THOSE LINES? NEVER SEEN ANYTHING LIKE THEM.

REGELATION MARKS.

THE OCEAN HAS JUPITER AND SEVENTEEN OTHER MOONS ACTING ON IT, SO ITS INTERNAL TIDES ARE WEIRD AND STRONG.

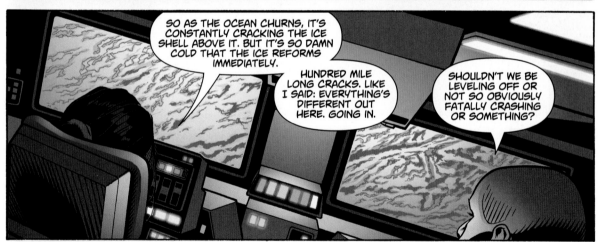

SO AS THE OCEAN CHURNS, IT'S CONSTANTLY CRACKING THE ICE SHELL ABOVE IT. BUT IT'S SO DAMN COLD THAT THE ICE REFORMS IMMEDIATELY.

HUNDRED MILE LONG CRACKS. LIKE I SAID: EVERYTHING'S DIFFERENT OUT HERE. GOING IN.

SHOULDN'T WE BE LEVELING OFF OR NOT SO OBVIOUSLY FATALLY CRASHING OR SOMETHING?

44

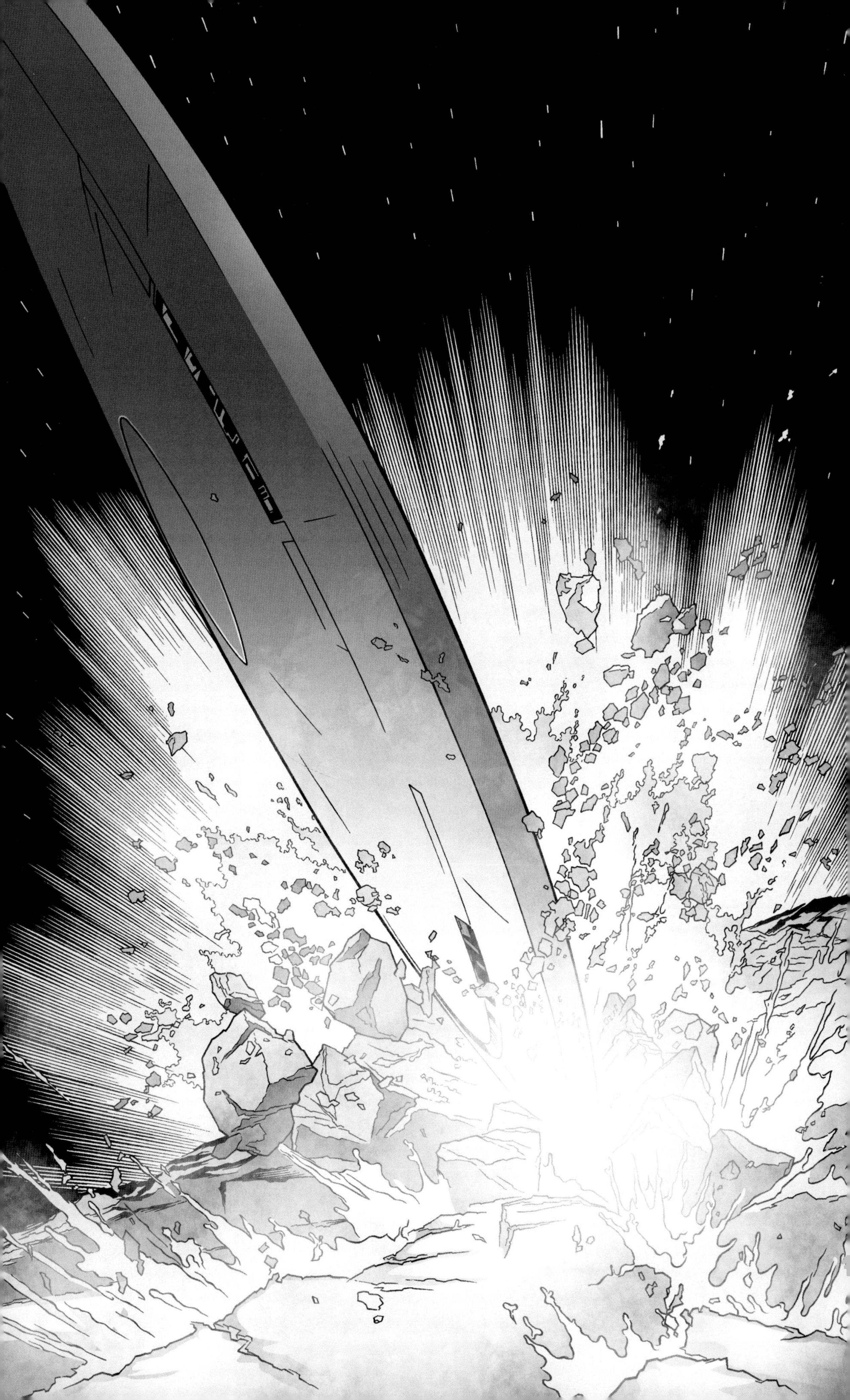

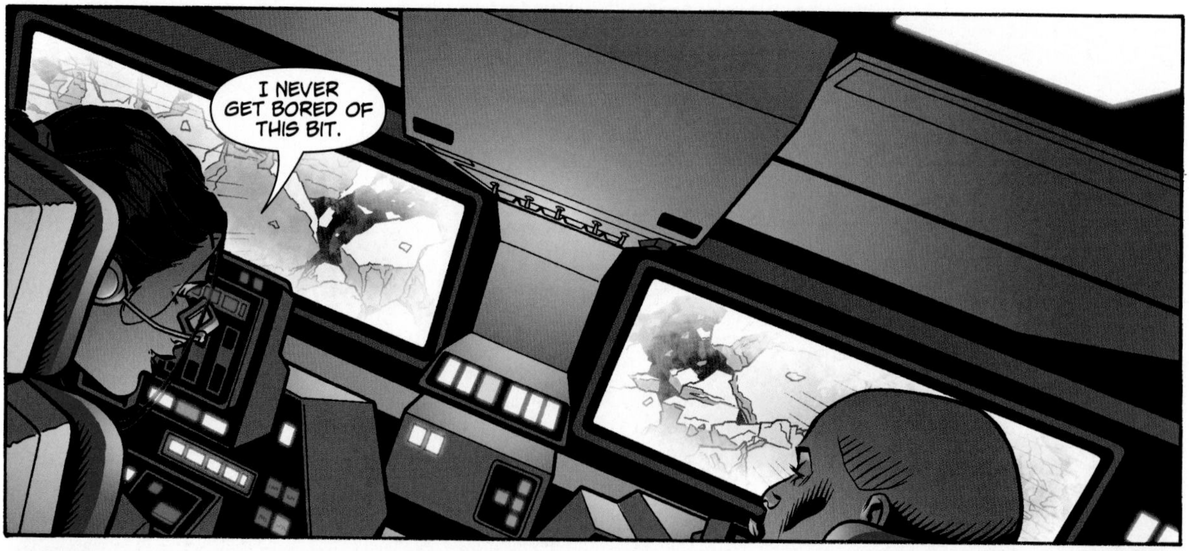
I NEVER GET BORED OF THIS BIT.

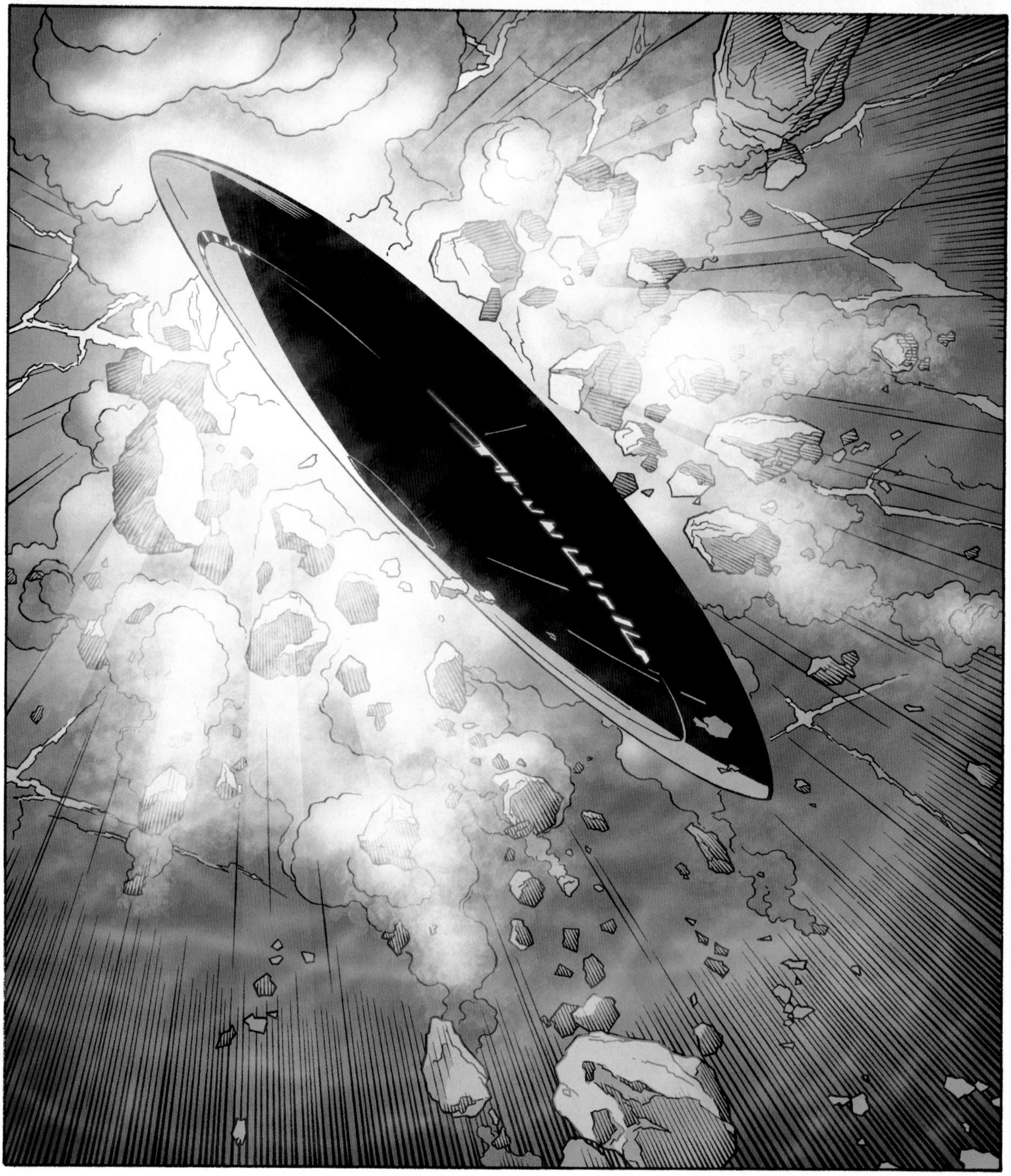

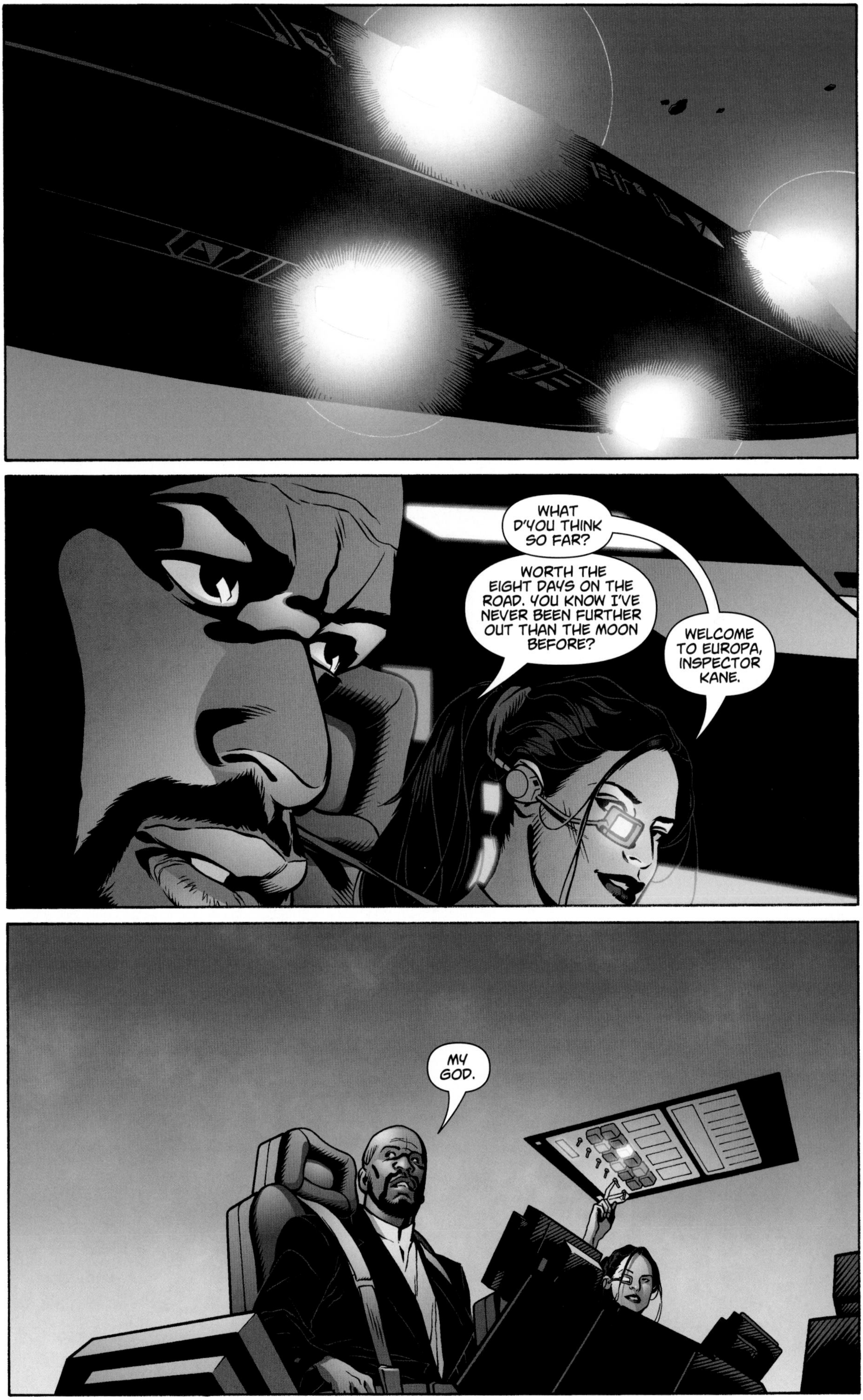
WHAT D'YOU THINK SO FAR?
WORTH THE EIGHT DAYS ON THE ROAD. YOU KNOW I'VE NEVER BEEN FURTHER OUT THAN THE MOON BEFORE?
WELCOME TO EUROPA, INSPECTOR KANE.
MY GOD.

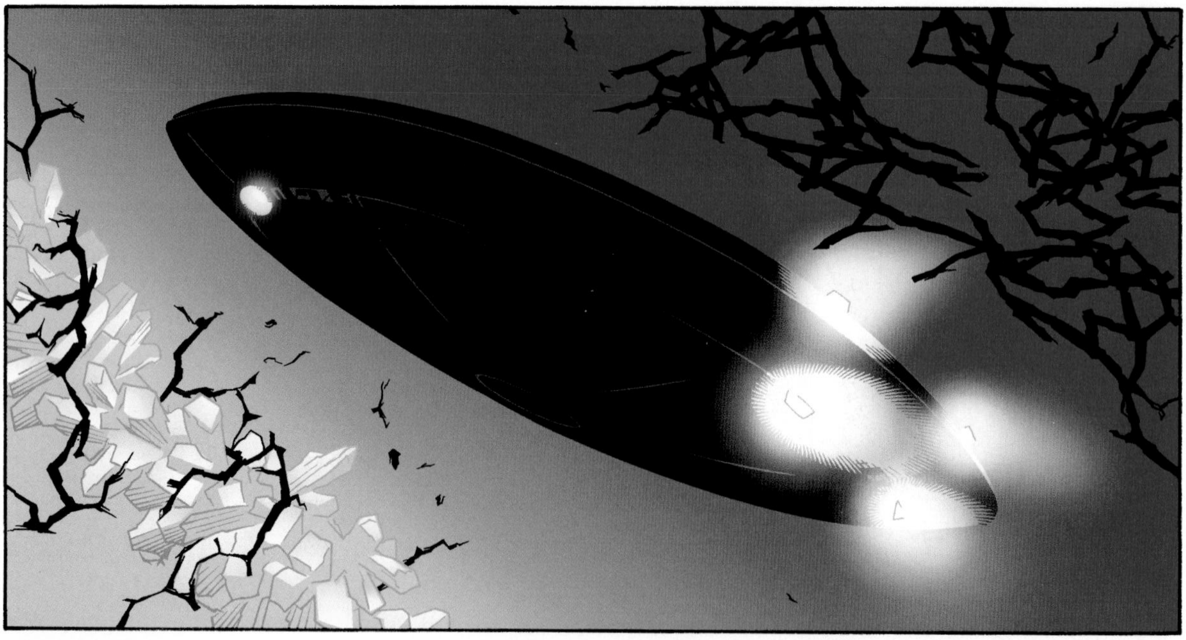

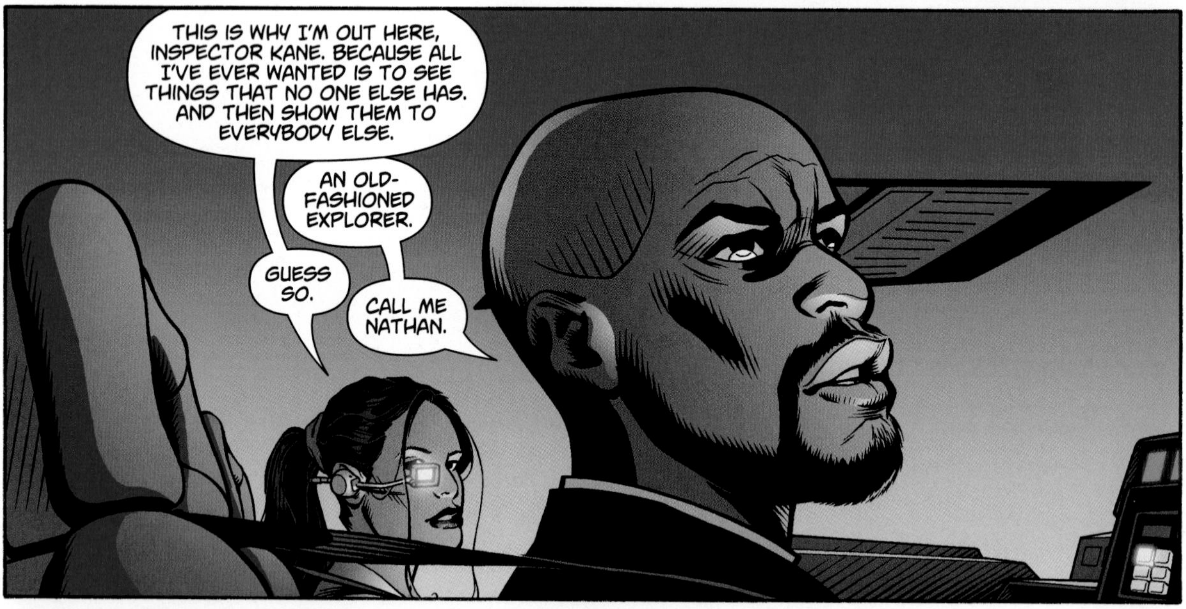
THIS IS WHY I'M OUT HERE, INSPECTOR KANE. BECAUSE ALL I'VE EVER WANTED IS TO SEE THINGS THAT NO ONE ELSE HAS. AND THEN SHOW THEM TO EVERYBODY ELSE.
AN OLD-FASHIONED EXPLORER.
GUESS SO.
CALL ME NATHAN.

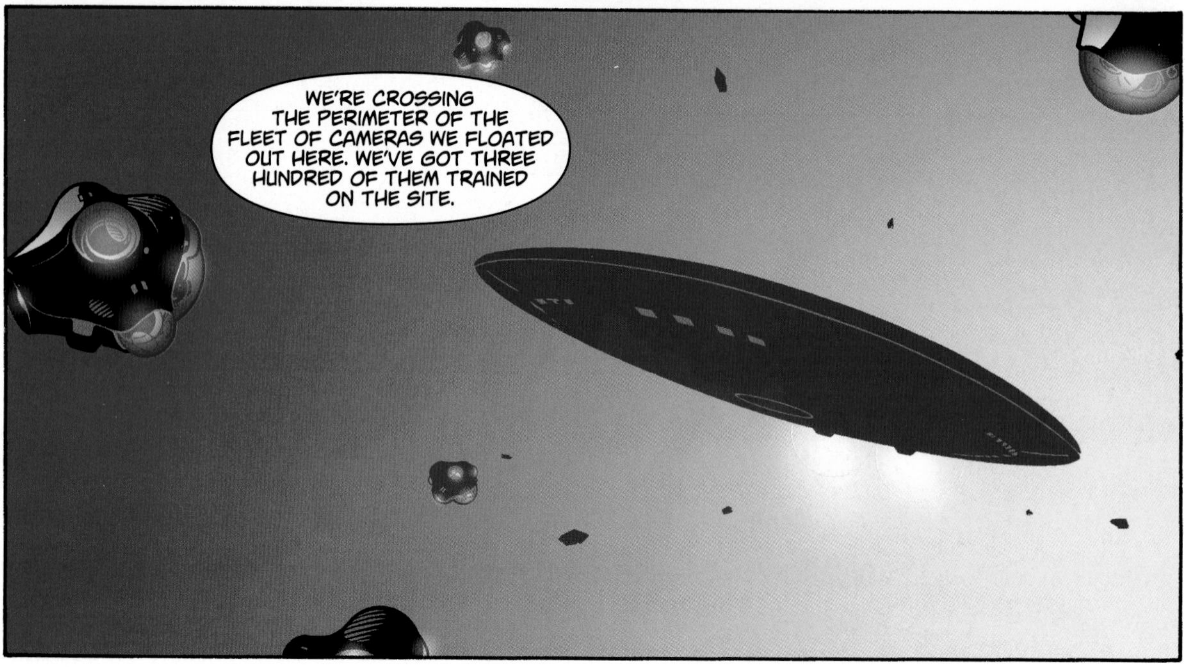
WE'RE CROSSING THE PERIMETER OF THE FLEET OF CAMERAS WE FLOATED OUT HERE. WE'VE GOT THREE HUNDRED OF THEM TRAINED ON THE SITE.

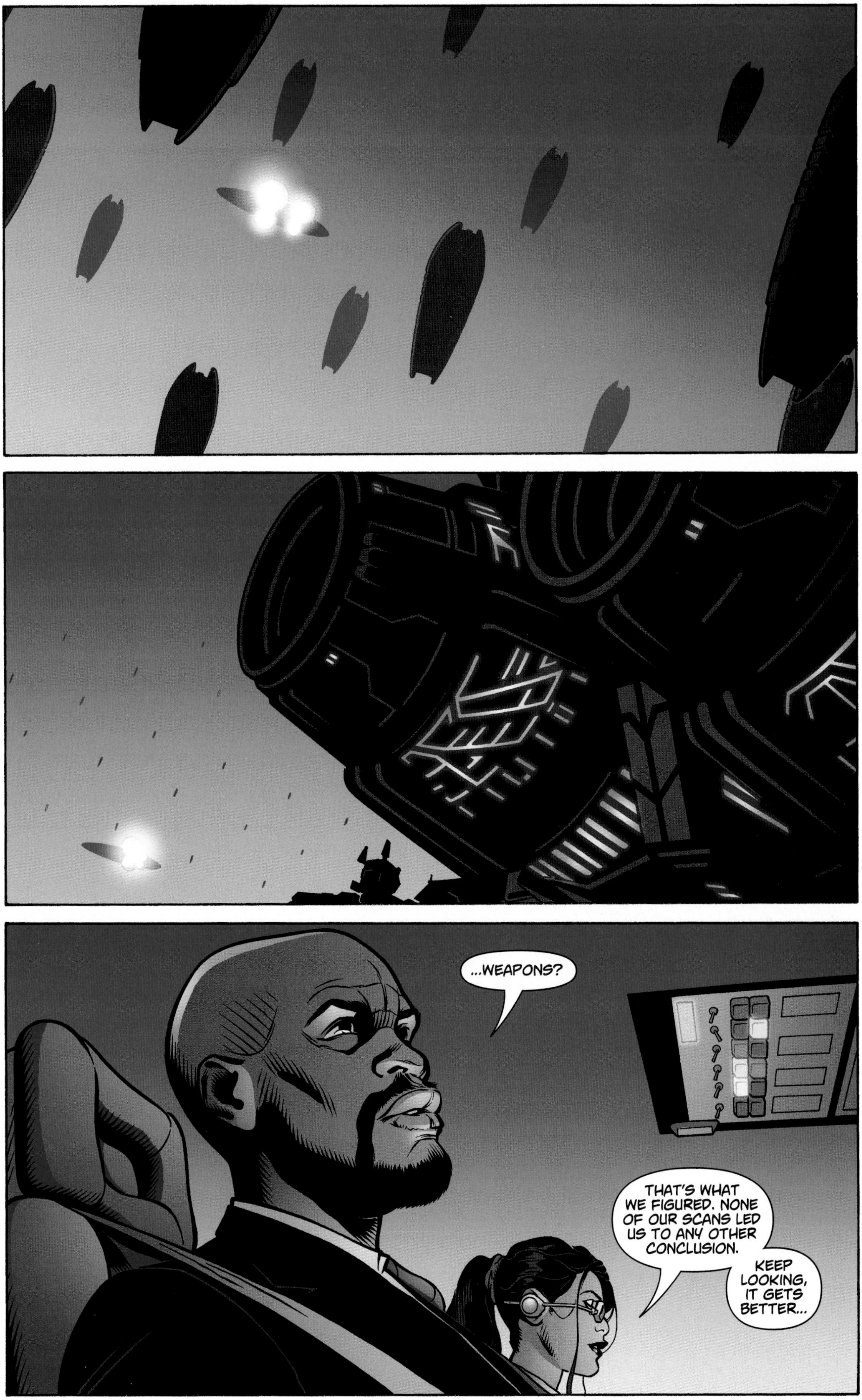
...WEAPONS?
THAT'S WHAT WE FIGURED. NONE OF OUR SCANS LED US TO ANY OTHER CONCLUSION.
KEEP LOOKING, IT GETS BETTER...

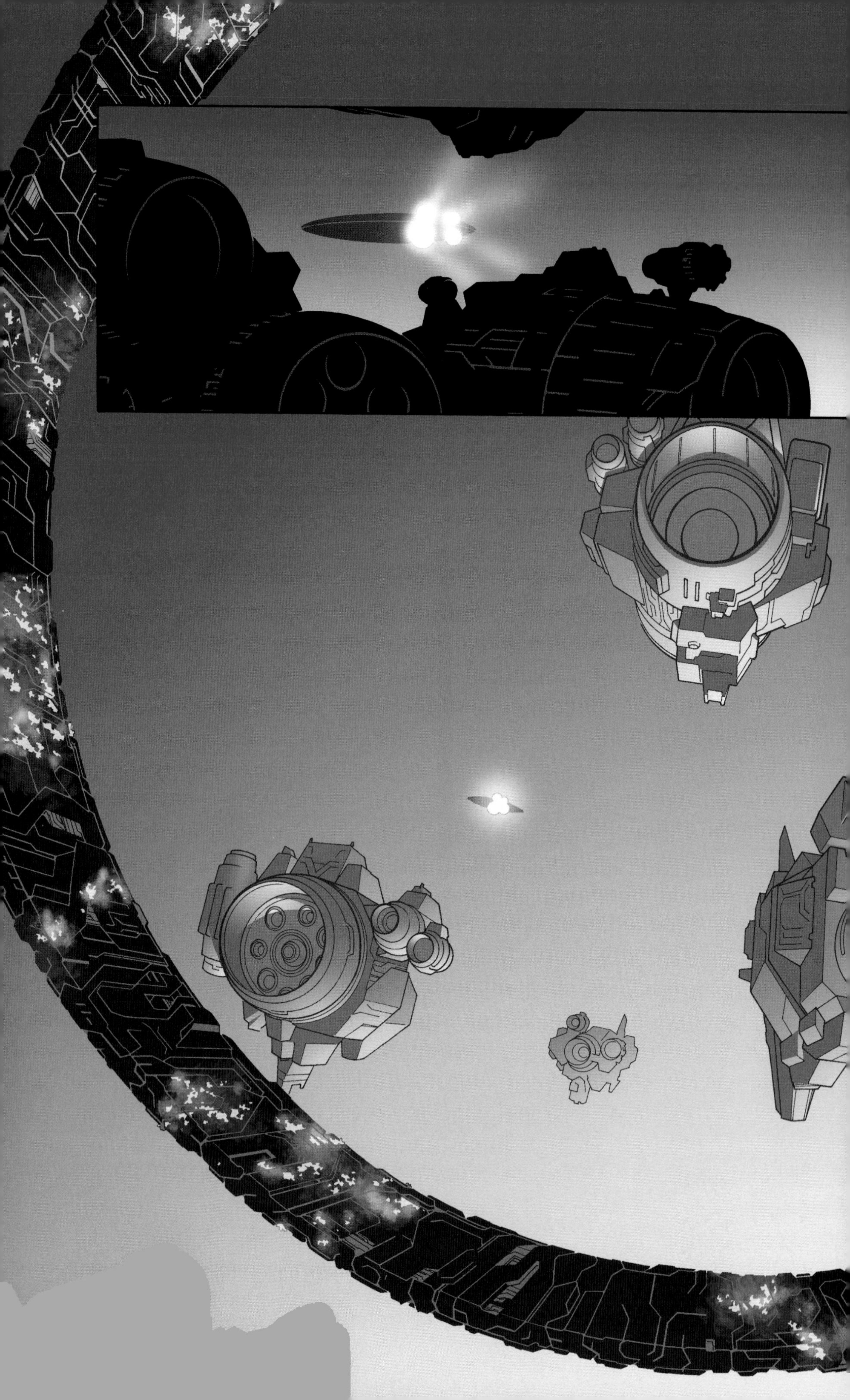

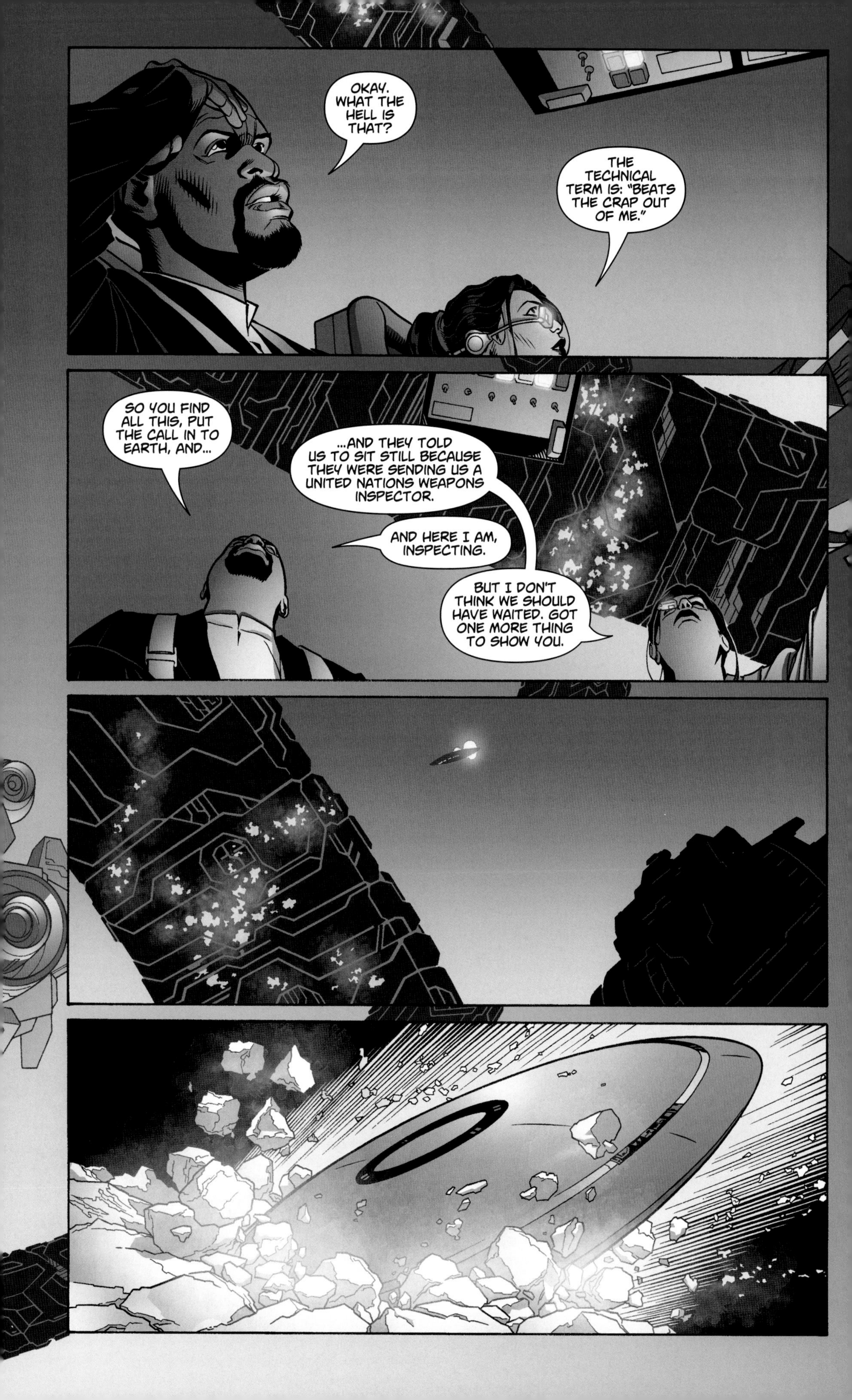
OKAY. WHAT THE HELL IS THAT?
THE TECHNICAL TERM IS: "BEATS THE CRAP OUT OF ME."
SO YOU FIND ALL THIS, PUT THE CALL IN TO EARTH, AND...
...AND THEY TOLD US TO SIT STILL BECAUSE THEY WERE SENDING US A UNITED NATIONS WEAPONS INSPECTOR.
AND HERE I AM, INSPECTING.
BUT I DON'T THINK WE SHOULD HAVE WAITED. GOT ONE MORE THING TO SHOW YOU.

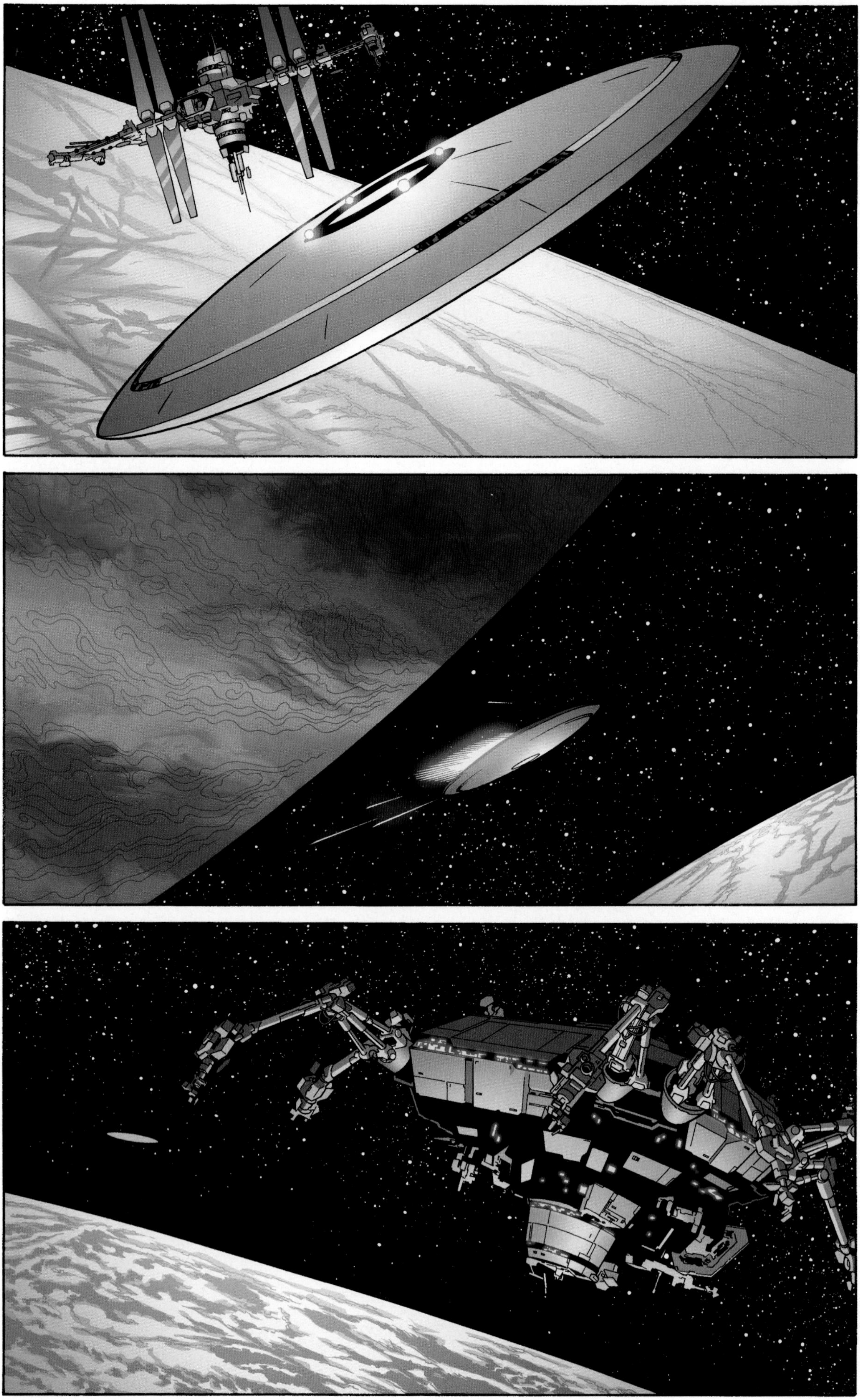

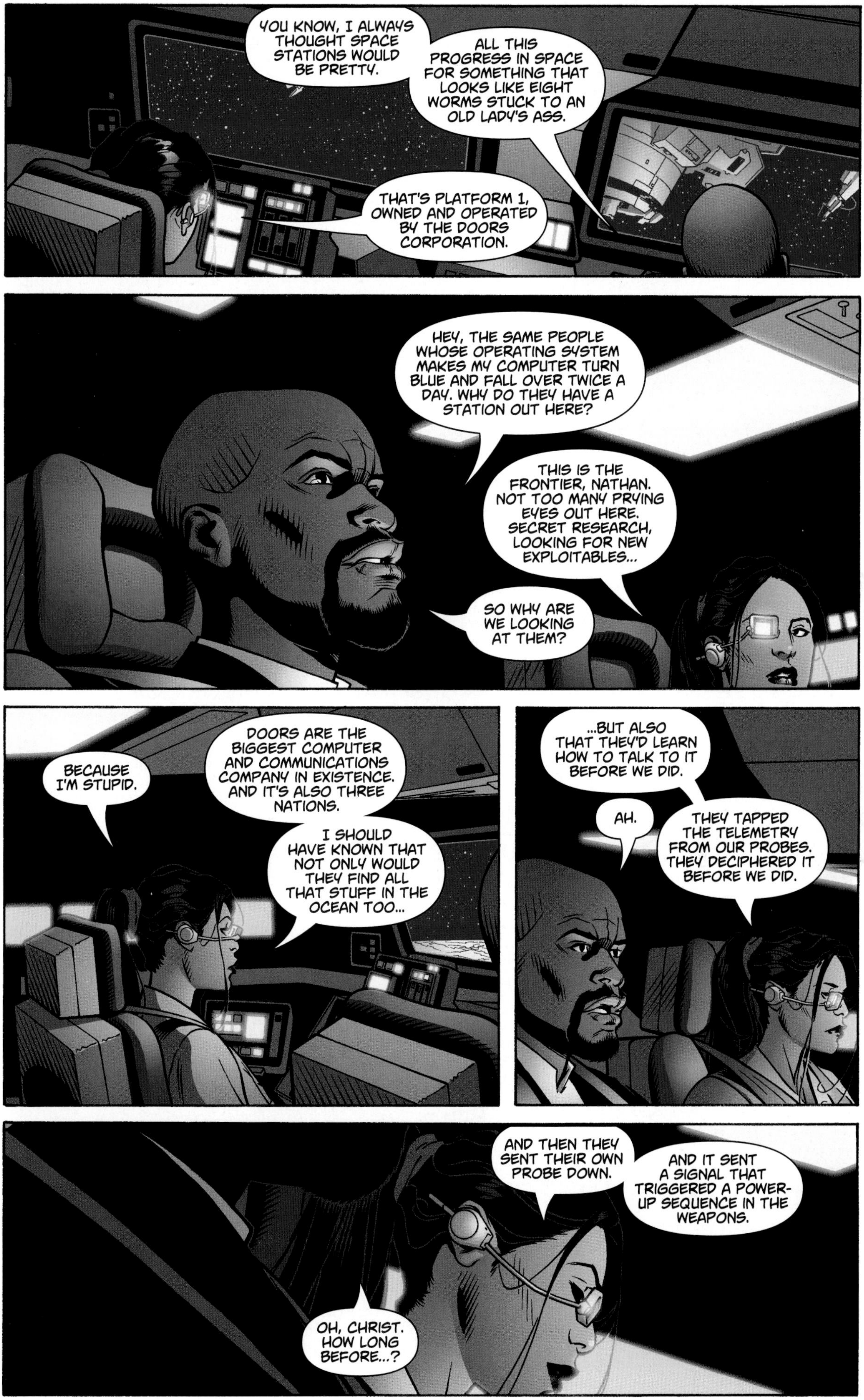
YOU KNOW, I ALWAYS THOUGHT SPACE STATIONS WOULD BE PRETTY.
ALL THIS PROGRESS IN SPACE FOR SOMETHING THAT LOOKS LIKE EIGHT WORMS STUCK TO AN OLD LADY'S ASS.
THAT'S PLATFORM 1, OWNED AND OPERATED BY THE DOORS CORPORATION.
HEY, THE SAME PEOPLE WHOSE OPERATING SYSTEM MAKES MY COMPUTER TURN BLUE AND FALL OVER TWICE A DAY. WHY DO THEY HAVE A STATION OUT HERE?
THIS IS THE FRONTIER, NATHAN. NOT TOO MANY PRYING EYES OUT HERE. SECRET RESEARCH, LOOKING FOR NEW EXPLOITABLES...
SO WHY ARE WE LOOKING AT THEM?
BECAUSE I'M STUPID.
DOORS ARE THE BIGGEST COMPUTER AND COMMUNICATIONS COMPANY IN EXISTENCE. AND IT'S ALSO THREE NATIONS.
I SHOULD HAVE KNOWN THAT NOT ONLY WOULD THEY FIND ALL THAT STUFF IN THE OCEAN TOO...
...BUT ALSO THAT THEY'D LEARN HOW TO TALK TO IT BEFORE WE DID.
AH.
THEY TAPPED THE TELEMETRY FROM OUR PROBES. THEY DECIPHERED IT BEFORE WE DID.
AND THEN THEY SENT THEIR OWN PROBE DOWN.
AND IT SENT A SIGNAL THAT TRIGGERED A POWER-UP SEQUENCE IN THE WEAPONS.
OH, CHRIST. HOW LONG BEFORE...?

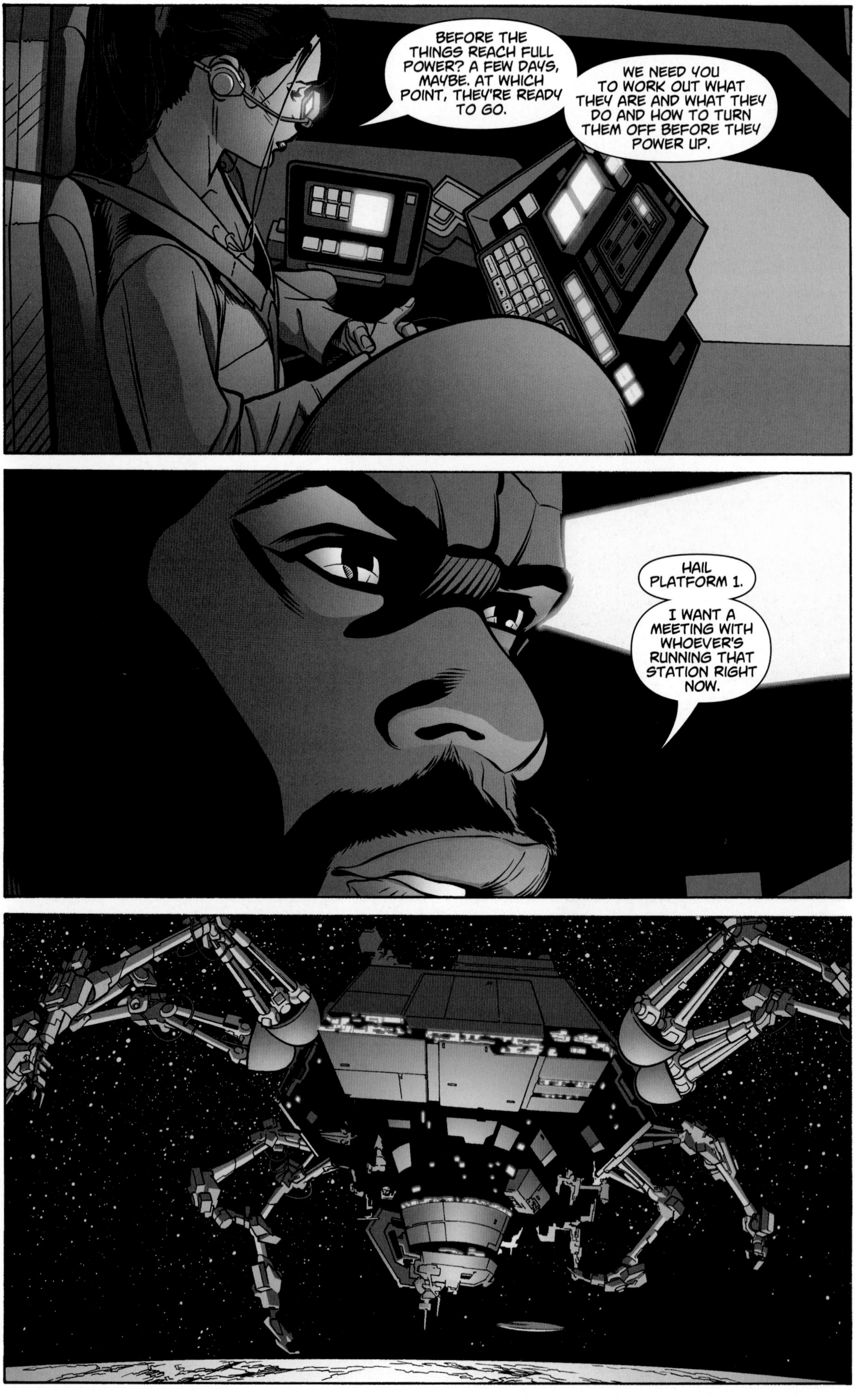
BEFORE THE THINGS REACH FULL POWER? A FEW DAYS, MAYBE. AT WHICH POINT, THEY'RE READY TO GO.
WE NEED YOU TO WORK OUT WHAT THEY ARE AND WHAT THEY DO AND HOW TO TURN THEM OFF BEFORE THEY POWER UP.
HAIL PLATFORM 1.
I WANT A MEETING WITH WHOEVER'S RUNNING THAT STATION RIGHT NOW.

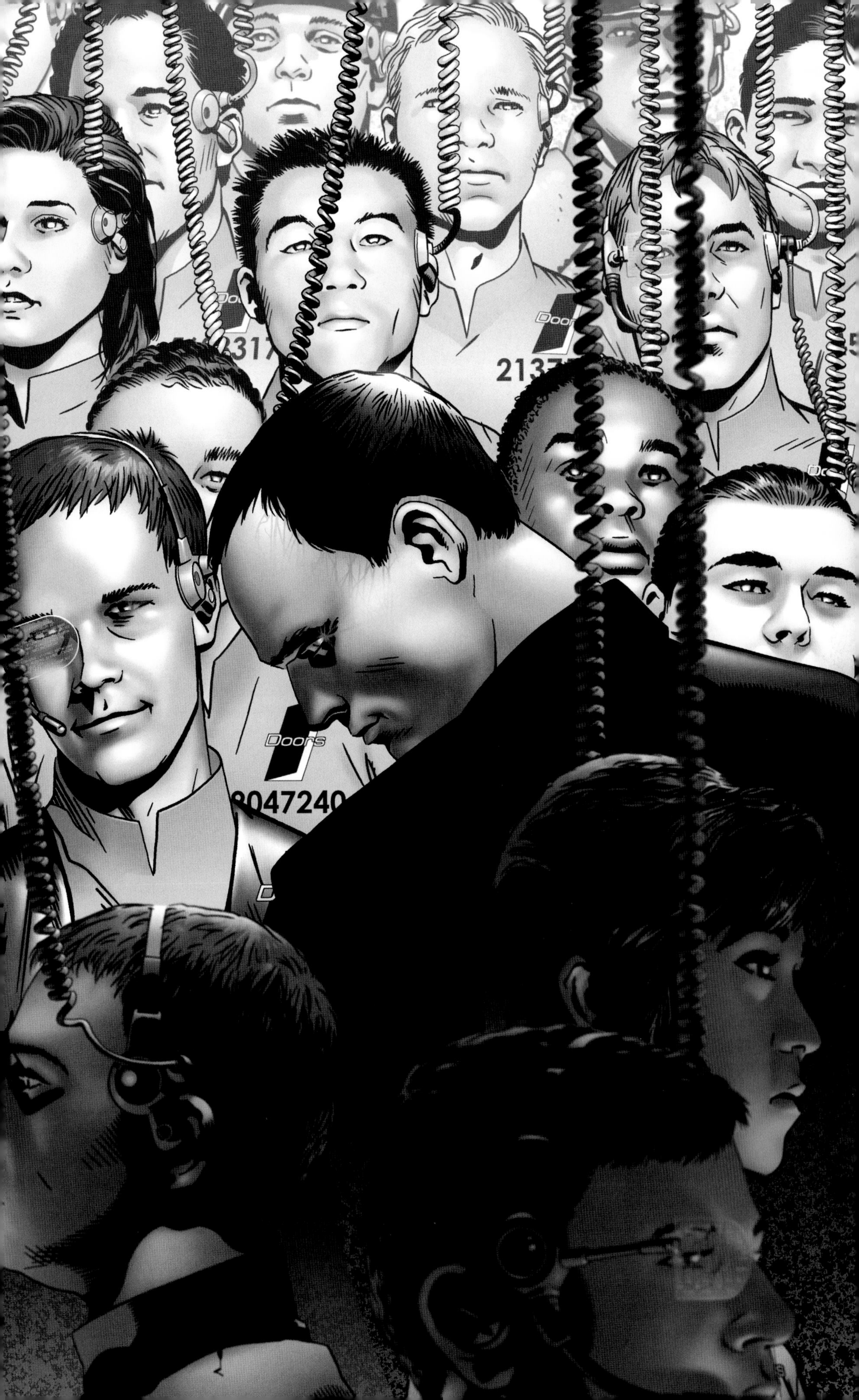

Doors
Doors
8047240

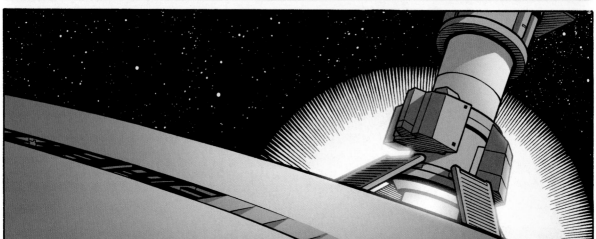

NATHAN KANE, UNITED NATIONS WEAPONS INSPECTORATE. THIS IS FADIA AZIZ, COMMANDING COLD HARBOR.

WE'VE ARRANGED TO SEE THE STATION MANAGER.

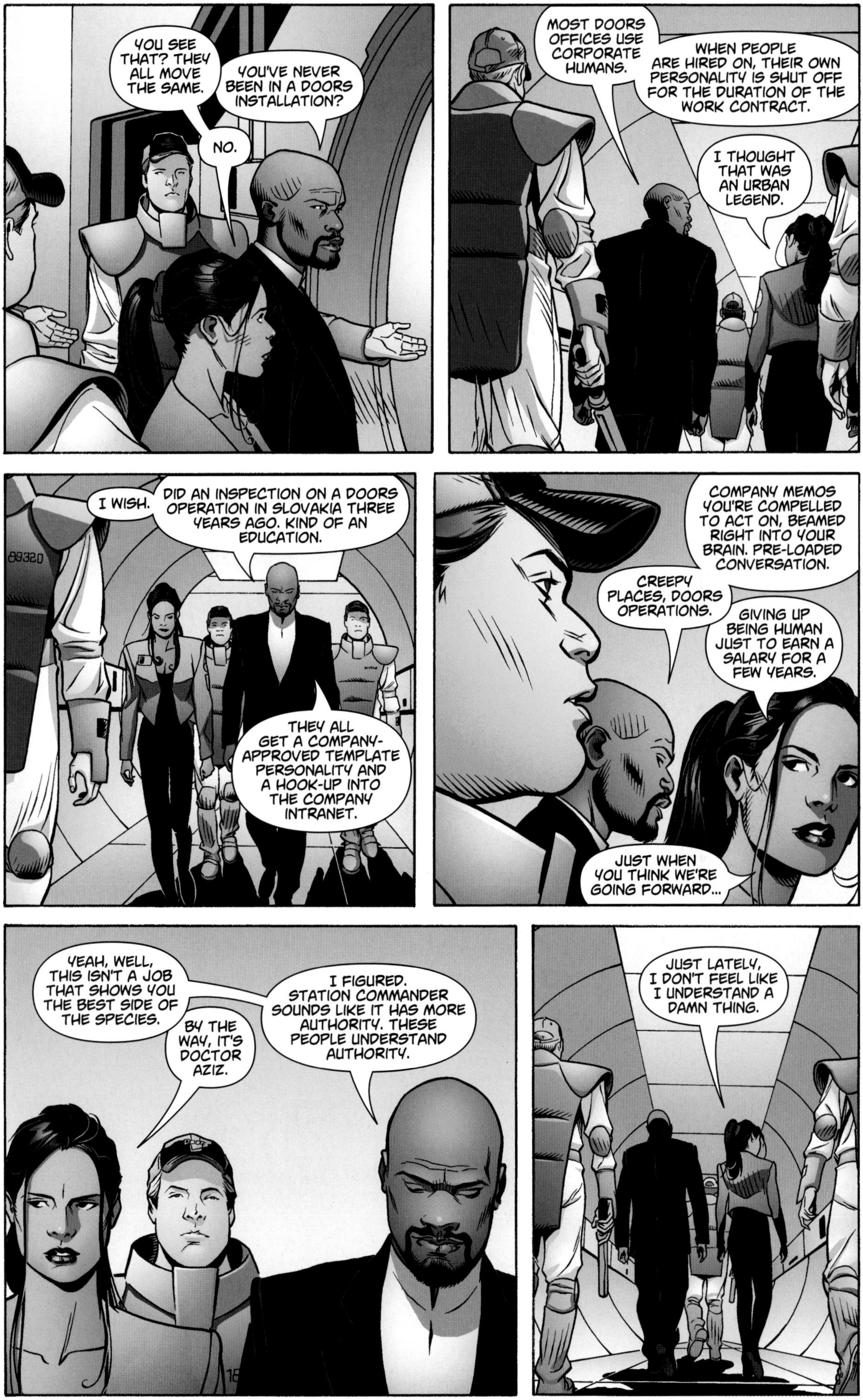
YOU SEE THAT? THEY ALL MOVE THE SAME.
YOU'VE NEVER BEEN IN A DOORS INSTALLATION?
NO.
MOST DOORS OFFICES USE CORPORATE HUMANS.
WHEN PEOPLE ARE HIRED ON, THEIR OWN PERSONALITY IS SHUT OFF FOR THE DURATION OF THE WORK CONTRACT.
I THOUGHT THAT WAS AN URBAN LEGEND.
I WISH.
DID AN INSPECTION ON A DOORS OPERATION IN SLOVAKIA THREE YEARS AGO. KIND OF AN EDUCATION.
THEY ALL GET A COMPANY-APPROVED TEMPLATE PERSONALITY AND A HOOK-UP INTO THE COMPANY INTRANET.
COMPANY MEMOS YOU'RE COMPELLED TO ACT ON, BEAMED RIGHT INTO YOUR BRAIN. PRE-LOADED CONVERSATION.
CREEPY PLACES, DOORS OPERATIONS.
GIVING UP BEING HUMAN JUST TO EARN A SALARY FOR A FEW YEARS.
JUST WHEN YOU THINK WE'RE GOING FORWARD...
YEAH, WELL, THIS ISN'T A JOB THAT SHOWS YOU THE BEST SIDE OF THE SPECIES.
BY THE WAY, IT'S DOCTOR AZIZ.
I FIGURED. STATION COMMANDER SOUNDS LIKE IT HAS MORE AUTHORITY. THESE PEOPLE UNDERSTAND AUTHORITY.
JUST LATELY, I DON'T FEEL LIKE I UNDERSTAND A DAMN THING.

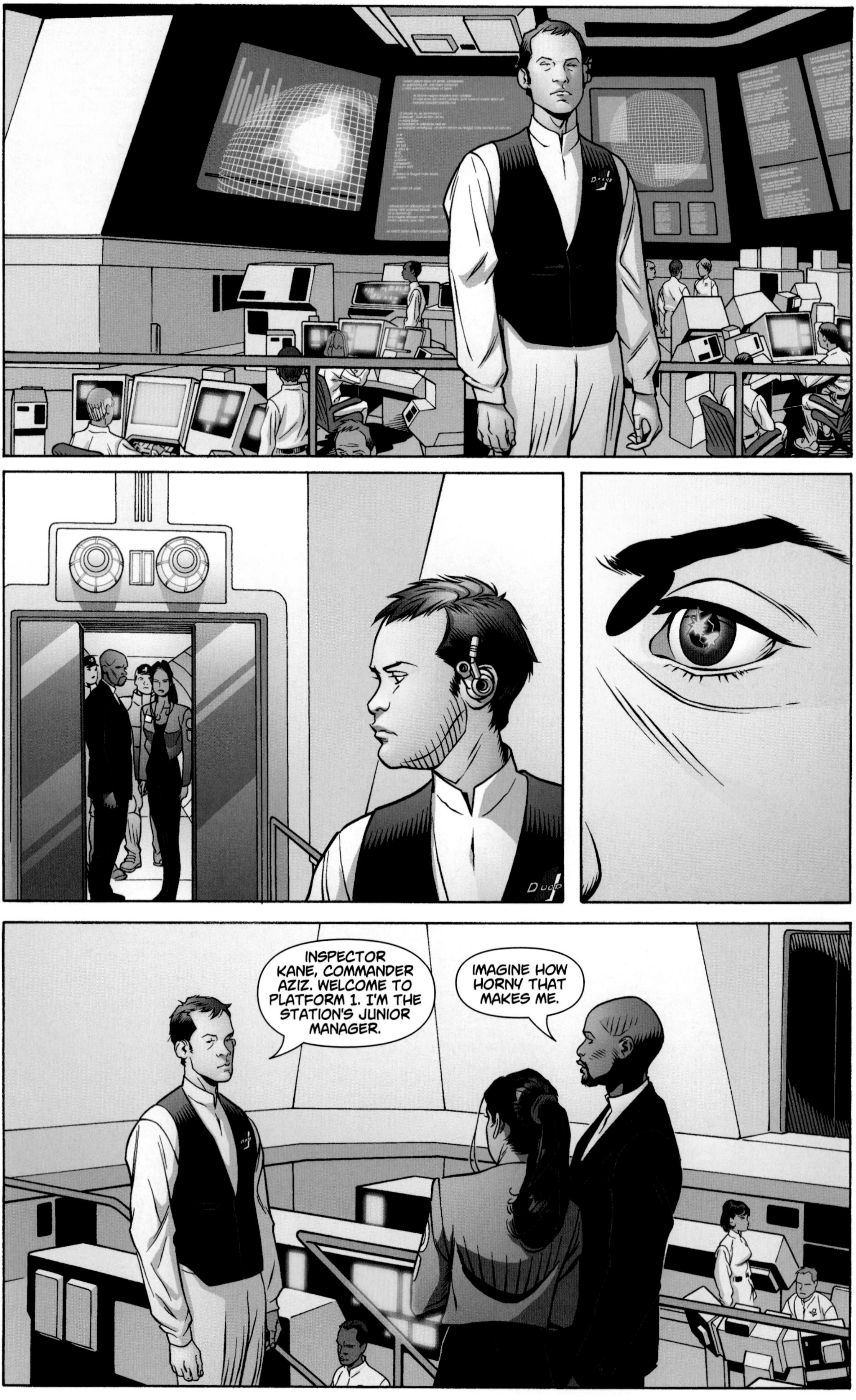
INSPECTOR KANE, COMMANDER AZIZ. WELCOME TO PLATFORM 1. I'M THE STATION'S JUNIOR MANAGER.
IMAGINE HOW HORNY THAT MAKES ME.

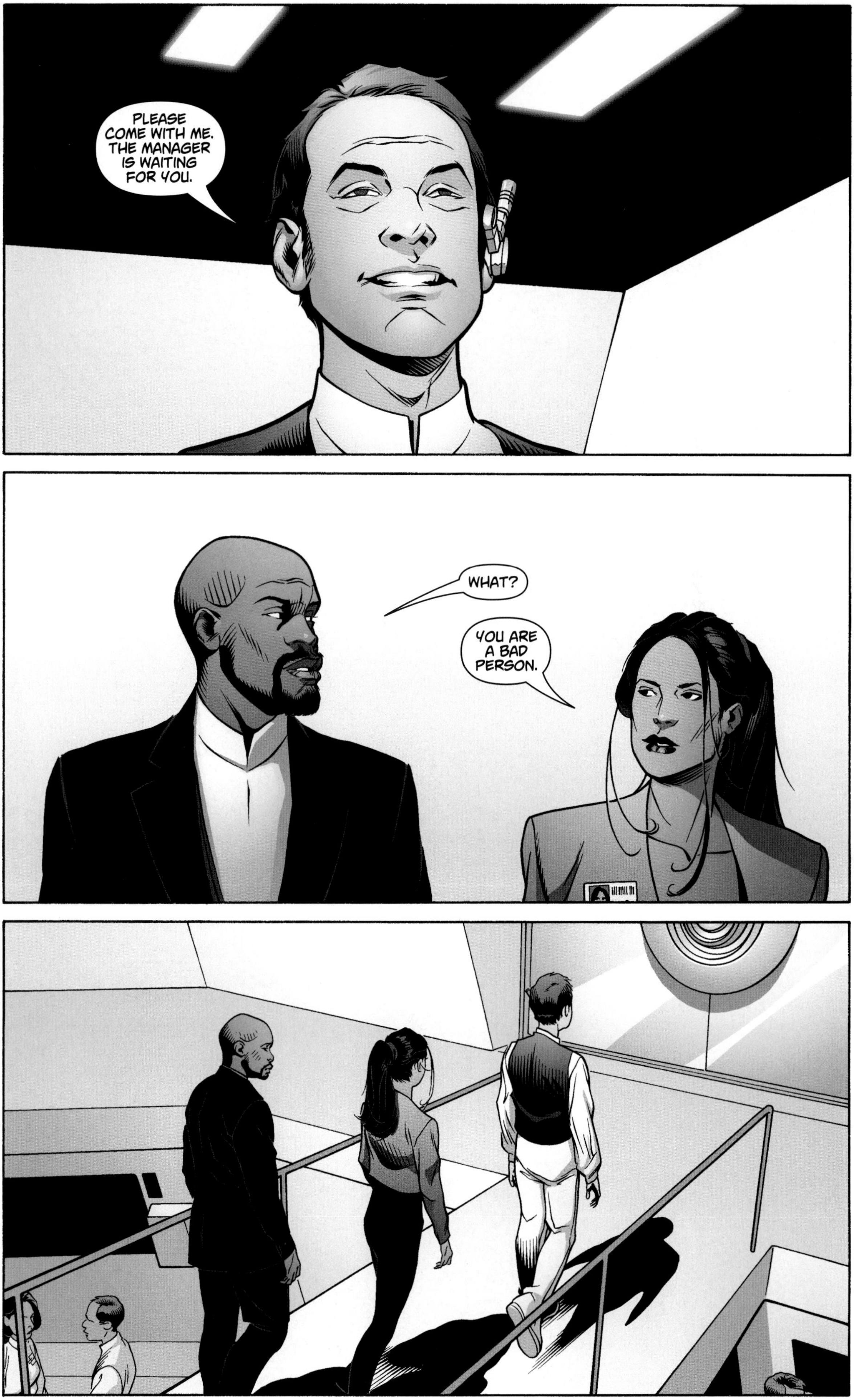
PLEASE COME WITH ME. THE MANAGER IS WAITING FOR YOU.
WHAT?
YOU ARE A BAD PERSON.

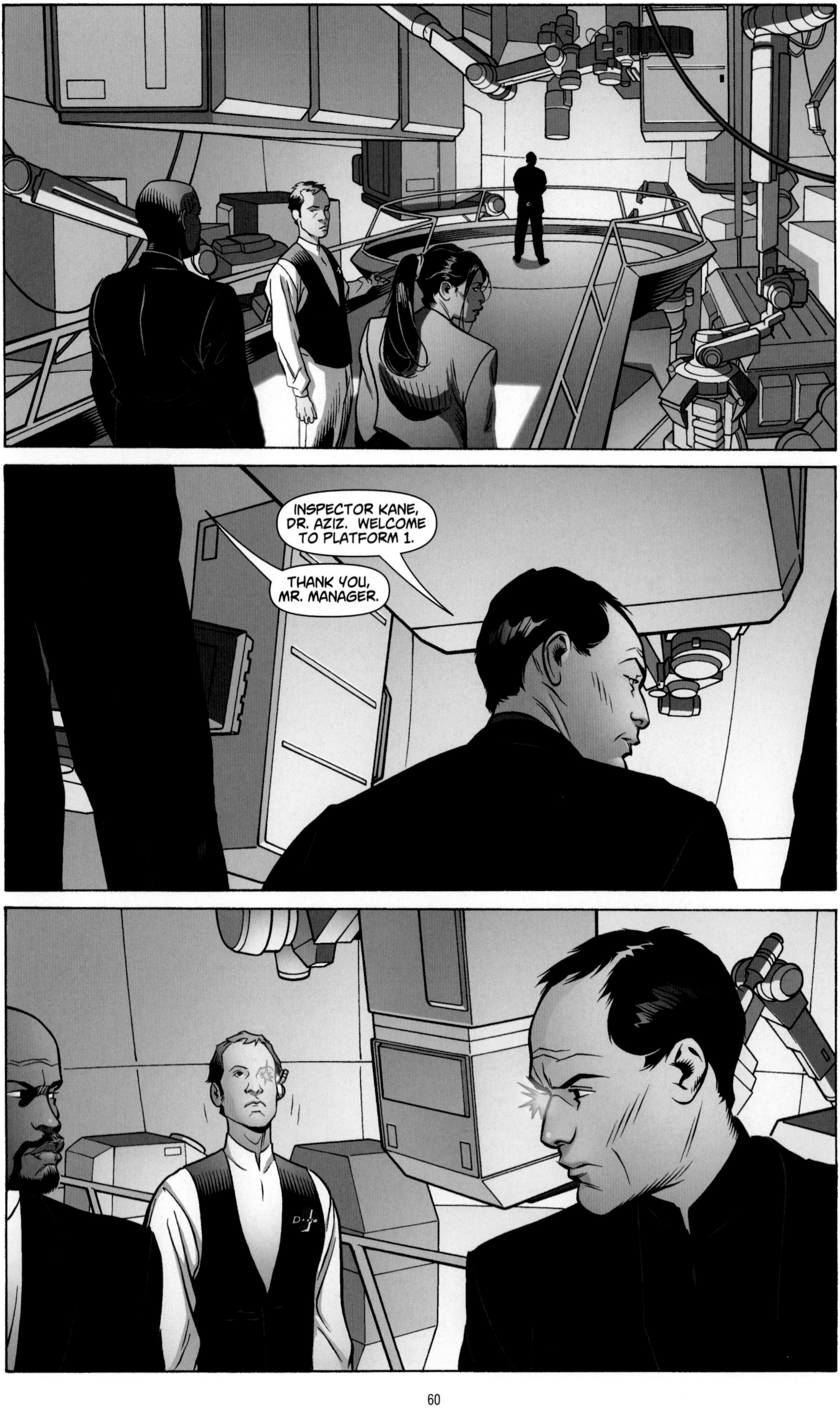
INSPECTOR KANE, DR. AZIZ. WELCOME TO PLATFORM 1.
THANK YOU, MR. MANAGER.

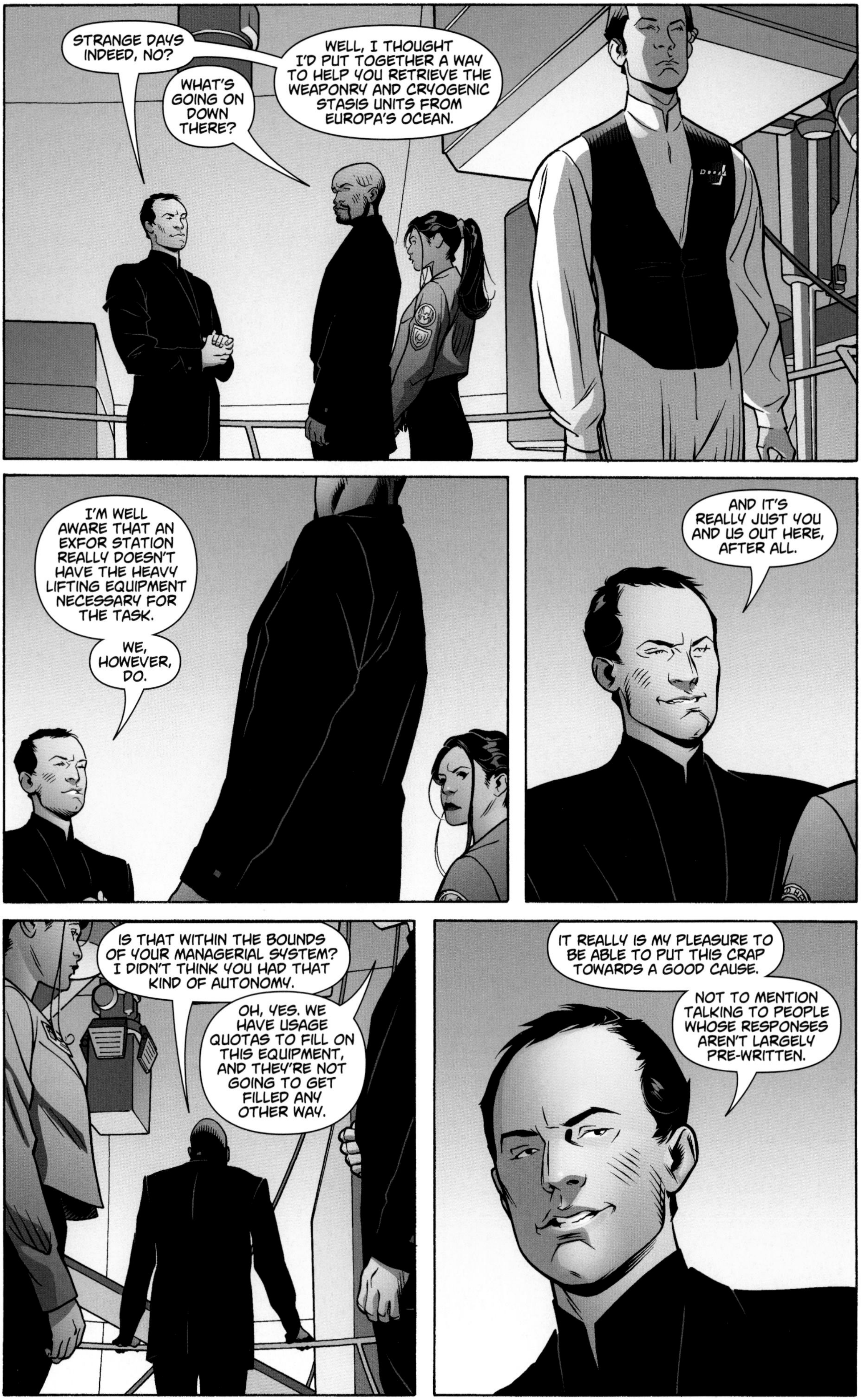
STRANGE DAYS INDEED, NO?
WHAT'S GOING ON DOWN THERE?
WELL, I THOUGHT I'D PUT TOGETHER A WAY TO HELP YOU RETRIEVE THE WEAPONRY AND CRYOGENIC STASIS UNITS FROM EUROPA'S OCEAN.
I'M WELL AWARE THAT AN EXFOR STATION REALLY DOESN'T HAVE THE HEAVY LIFTING EQUIPMENT NECESSARY FOR THE TASK.
WE, HOWEVER, DO.
AND IT'S REALLY JUST YOU AND US OUT HERE, AFTER ALL.
IS THAT WITHIN THE BOUNDS OF YOUR MANAGERIAL SYSTEM? I DIDN'T THINK YOU HAD THAT KIND OF AUTONOMY.
OH, YES. WE HAVE USAGE QUOTAS TO FILL ON THIS EQUIPMENT, AND THEY'RE NOT GOING TO GET FILLED ANY OTHER WAY.
IT REALLY IS MY PLEASURE TO BE ABLE TO PUT THIS CRAP TOWARDS A GOOD CAUSE.
NOT TO MENTION TALKING TO PEOPLE WHOSE RESPONSES AREN'T LARGELY PRE-WRITTEN.

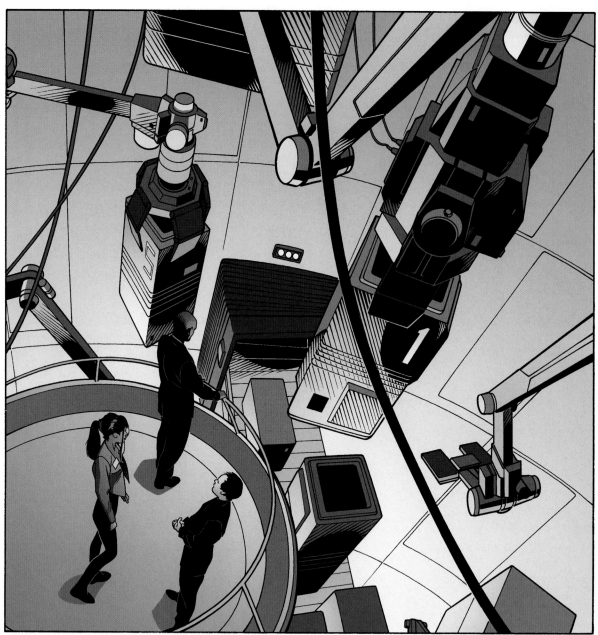

YOU KNOW WHY I'M HERE, OF COURSE.

OH, YES. I'M GLAD TO HELP. WE HAVE NO ISSUE WITH THE UNITED NATIONS.

THIS STATION IS VERY MUCH ON THE EDGE OF THE CORPORATION'S INTEREST IN ANY CASE.

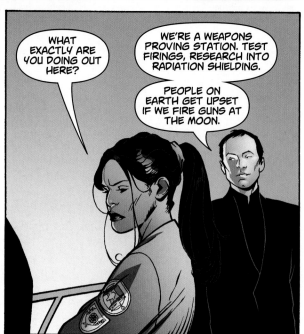

WHAT EXACTLY ARE YOU DOING OUT HERE?

WE'RE A WEAPONS PROVING STATION. TEST FIRINGS, RESEARCH INTO RADIATION SHIELDING.

PEOPLE ON EARTH GET UPSET IF WE FIRE GUNS AT THE MOON.

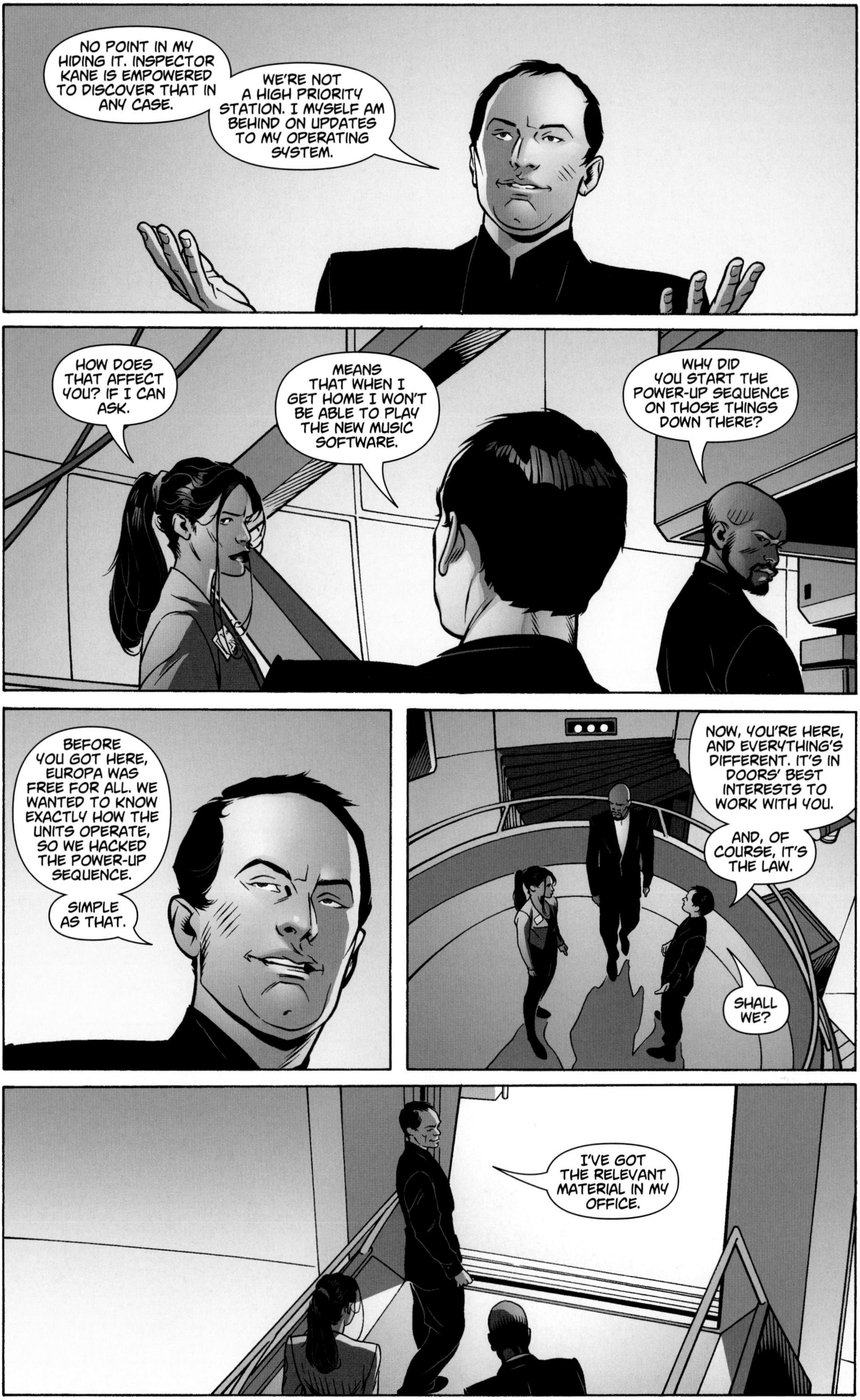
NO POINT IN MY HIDING IT. INSPECTOR KANE IS EMPOWERED TO DISCOVER THAT IN ANY CASE.
WE'RE NOT A HIGH PRIORITY STATION. I MYSELF AM BEHIND ON UPDATES TO MY OPERATING SYSTEM.
HOW DOES THAT AFFECT YOU? IF I CAN ASK.
MEANS THAT WHEN I GET HOME I WON'T BE ABLE TO PLAY THE NEW MUSIC SOFTWARE.
WHY DID YOU START THE POWER-UP SEQUENCE ON THOSE THINGS DOWN THERE?
BEFORE YOU GOT HERE, EUROPA WAS FREE FOR ALL. WE WANTED TO KNOW EXACTLY HOW THE UNITS OPERATE, SO WE HACKED THE POWER-UP SEQUENCE.
SIMPLE AS THAT.
NOW, YOU'RE HERE, AND EVERYTHING'S DIFFERENT. IT'S IN DOORS' BEST INTERESTS TO WORK WITH YOU.
AND, OF COURSE, IT'S THE LAW.
SHALL WE?
I'VE GOT THE RELEVANT MATERIAL IN MY OFFICE.

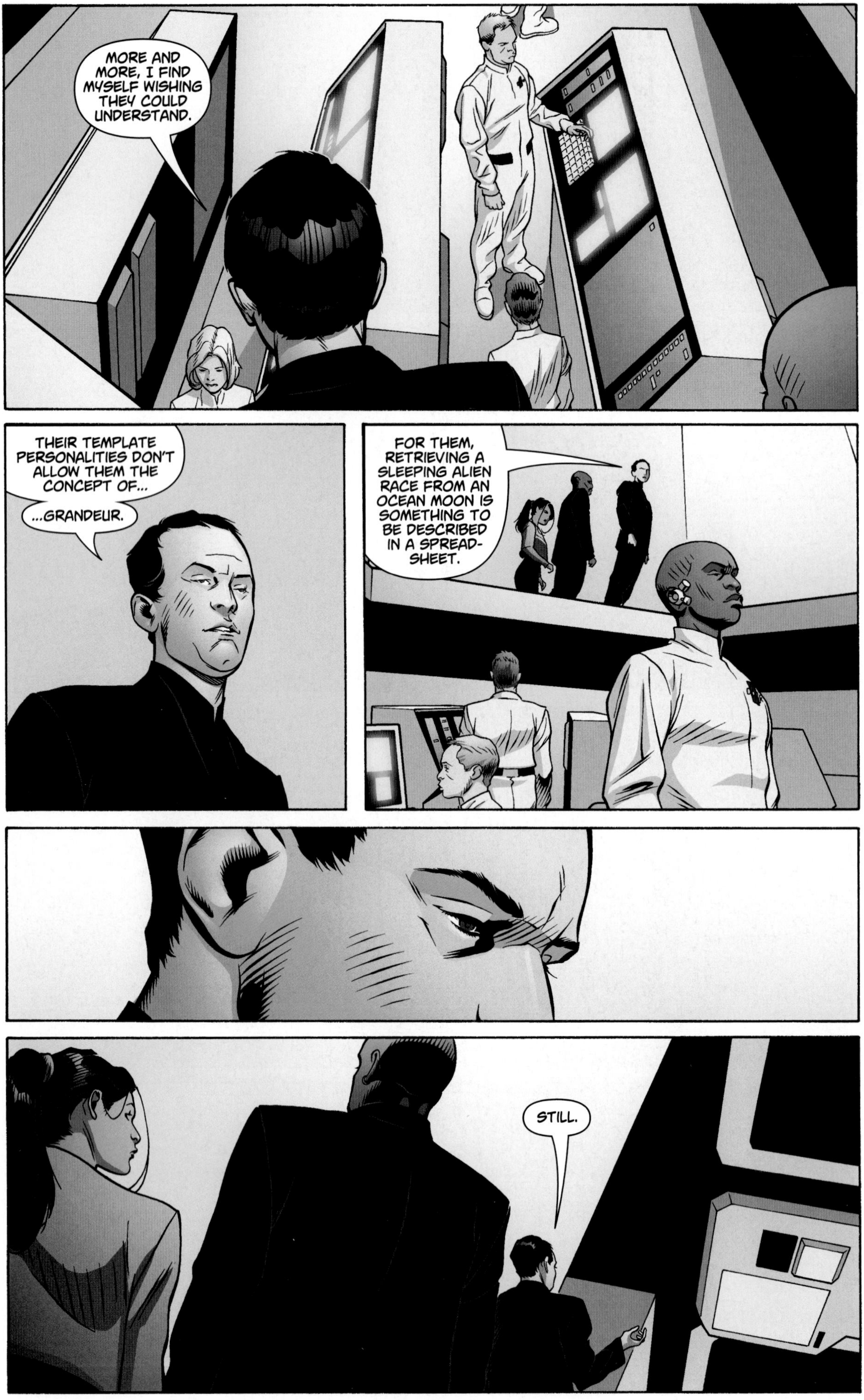
MORE AND MORE, I FIND MYSELF WISHING THEY COULD UNDERSTAND.
THEIR TEMPLATE PERSONALITIES DON'T ALLOW THEM THE CONCEPT OF...
...GRANDEUR.
FOR THEM, RETRIEVING A SLEEPING ALIEN RACE FROM AN OCEAN MOON IS SOMETHING TO BE DESCRIBED IN A SPREAD-SHEET.
STILL.

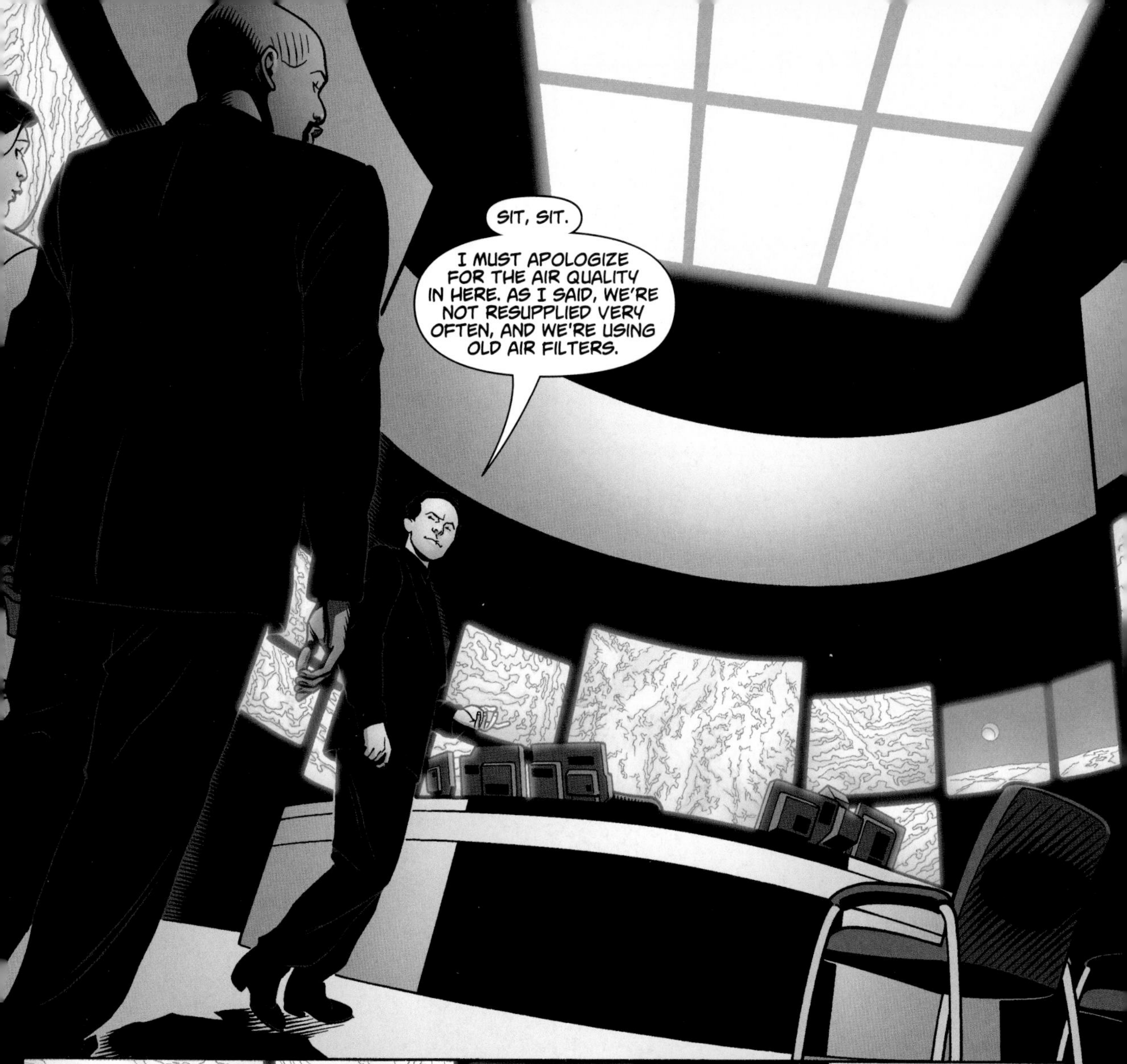
SIT, SIT.
I MUST APOLOGIZE FOR THE AIR QUALITY IN HERE. AS I SAID, WE'RE NOT RESUPPLIED VERY OFTEN, AND WE'RE USING OLD AIR FILTERS.

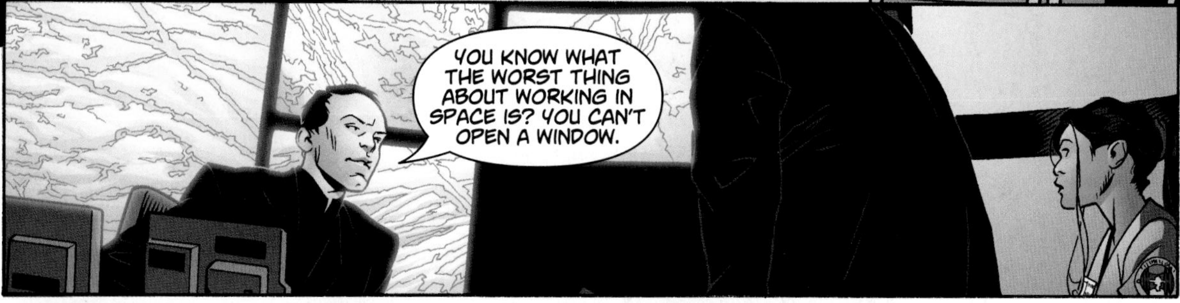
YOU KNOW WHAT THE WORST THING ABOUT WORKING IN SPACE IS? YOU CAN'T OPEN A WINDOW.

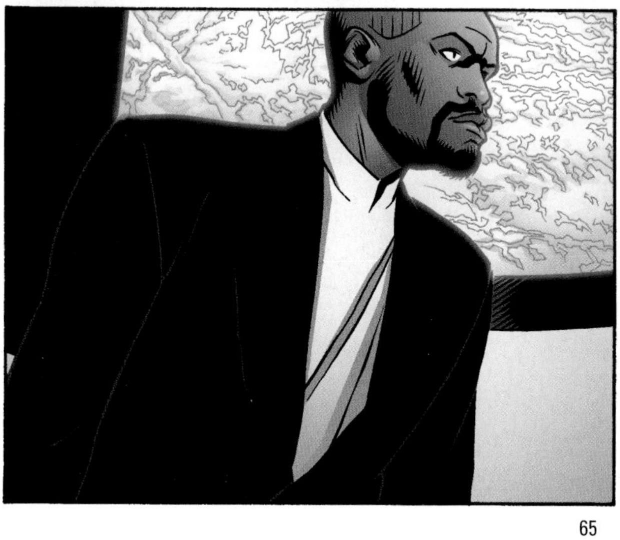

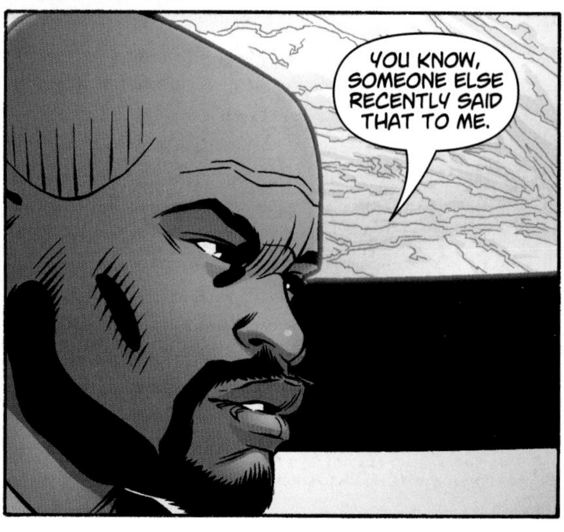
YOU KNOW, SOMEONE ELSE RECENTLY SAID THAT TO ME.

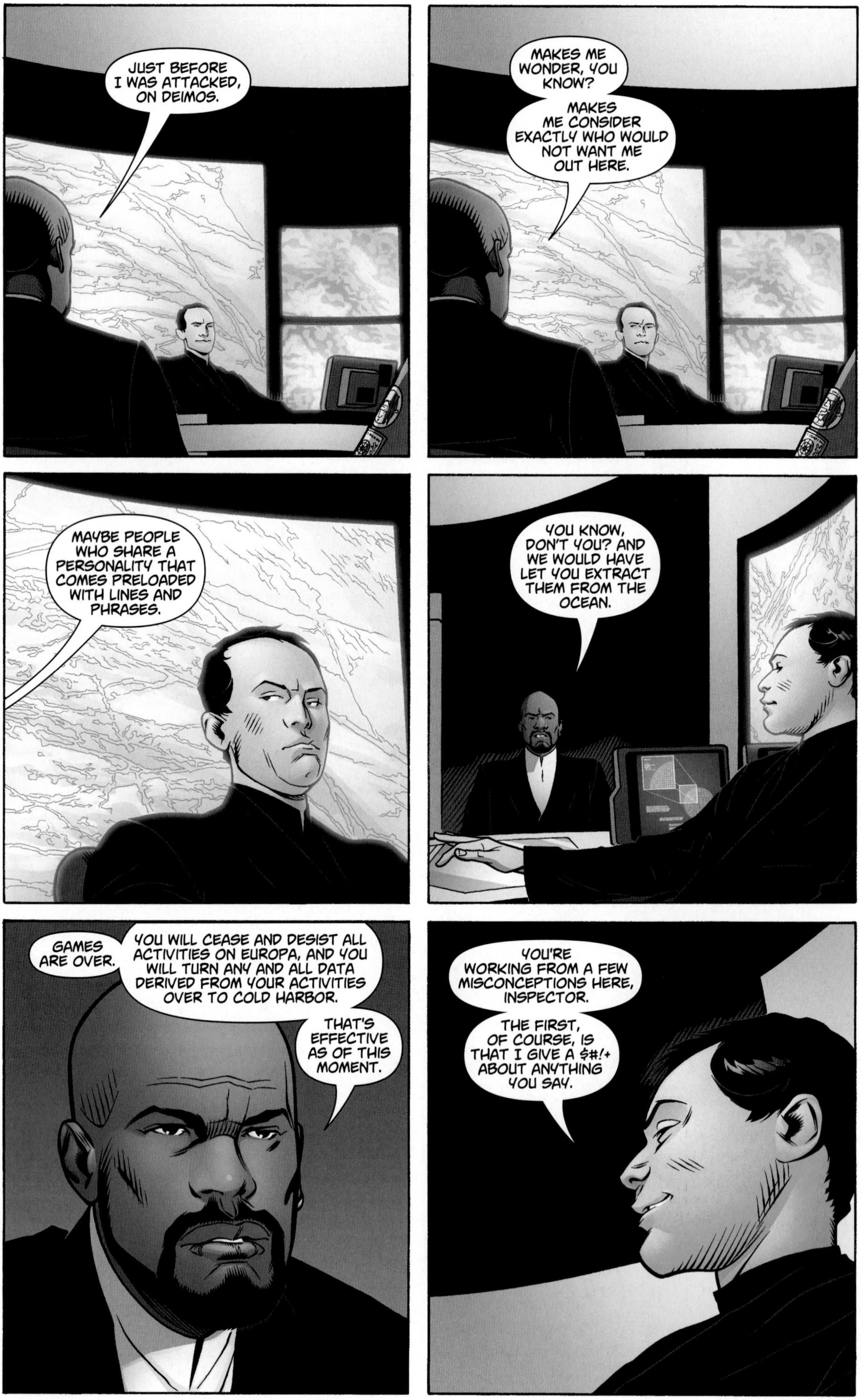
JUST BEFORE I WAS ATTACKED, ON DEIMOS.
MAKES ME WONDER, YOU KNOW?
MAKES ME CONSIDER EXACTLY WHO WOULD NOT WANT ME OUT HERE.
MAYBE PEOPLE WHO SHARE A PERSONALITY THAT COMES PRELOADED WITH LINES AND PHRASES.
YOU KNOW, DON'T YOU? AND WE WOULD HAVE LET YOU EXTRACT THEM FROM THE OCEAN.
GAMES ARE OVER.
YOU WILL CEASE AND DESIST ALL ACTIVITIES ON EUROPA, AND YOU WILL TURN ANY AND ALL DATA DERIVED FROM YOUR ACTIVITIES OVER TO COLD HARBOR.
THAT'S EFFECTIVE AS OF THIS MOMENT.
YOU'RE WORKING FROM A FEW MISCONCEPTIONS HERE, INSPECTOR.
THE FIRST, OF COURSE, IS THAT I GIVE A $#!+ ABOUT ANYTHING YOU SAY.

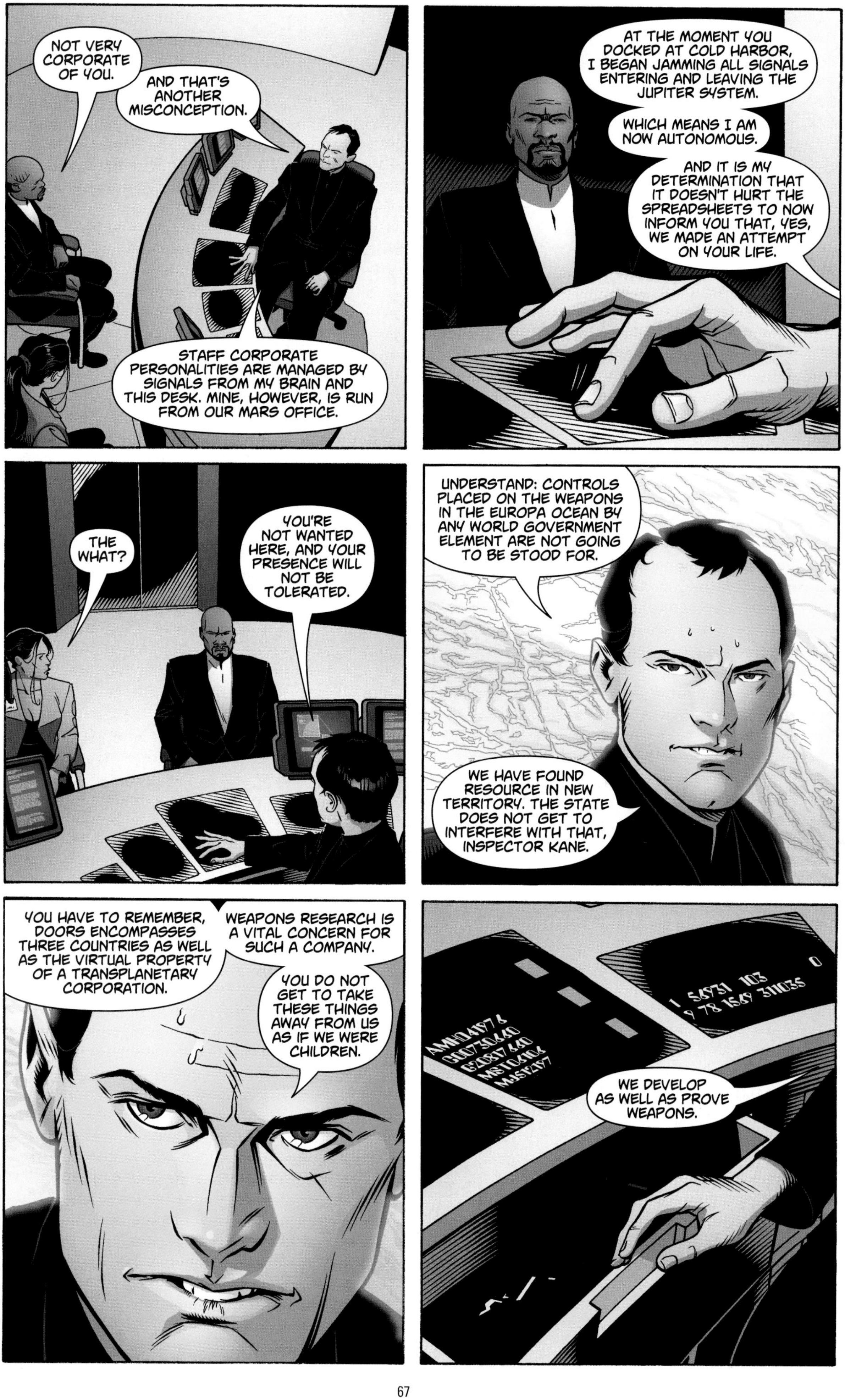
NOT VERY CORPORATE OF YOU.
AND THAT'S ANOTHER MISCONCEPTION.
STAFF CORPORATE PERSONALITIES ARE MANAGED BY SIGNALS FROM MY BRAIN AND THIS DESK. MINE, HOWEVER, IS RUN FROM OUR MARS OFFICE.
AT THE MOMENT YOU DOCKED AT COLD HARBOR, I BEGAN JAMMING ALL SIGNALS ENTERING AND LEAVING THE JUPITER SYSTEM.
WHICH MEANS I AM NOW AUTONOMOUS.
AND IT IS MY DETERMINATION THAT IT DOESN'T HURT THE SPREADSHEETS TO NOW INFORM YOU THAT, YES, WE MADE AN ATTEMPT ON YOUR LIFE.
THE WHAT?
YOU'RE NOT WANTED HERE, AND YOUR PRESENCE WILL NOT BE TOLERATED.
UNDERSTAND: CONTROLS PLACED ON THE WEAPONS IN THE EUROPA OCEAN BY ANY WORLD GOVERNMENT ELEMENT ARE NOT GOING TO BE STOOD FOR.
WE HAVE FOUND RESOURCE IN NEW TERRITORY. THE STATE DOES NOT GET TO INTERFERE WITH THAT, INSPECTOR KANE.
YOU HAVE TO REMEMBER, DOORS ENCOMPASSES THREE COUNTRIES AS WELL AS THE VIRTUAL PROPERTY OF A TRANSPLANETARY CORPORATION.
WEAPONS RESEARCH IS A VITAL CONCERN FOR SUCH A COMPANY.
YOU DO NOT GET TO TAKE THESE THINGS AWAY FROM US AS IF WE WERE CHILDREN.
WE DEVELOP AS WELL AS PROVE WEAPONS.

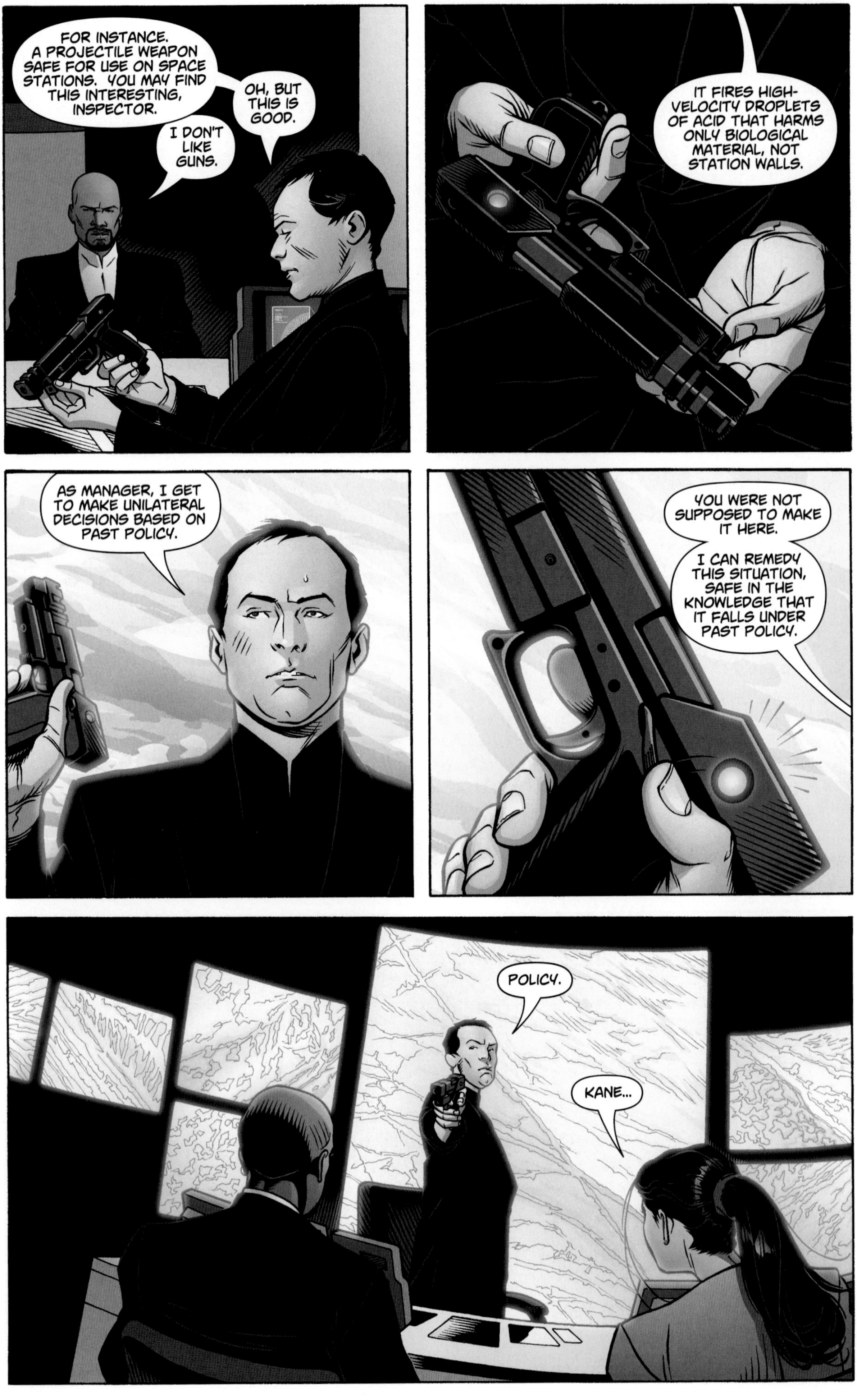
FOR INSTANCE. A PROJECTILE WEAPON SAFE FOR USE ON SPACE STATIONS. YOU MAY FIND THIS INTERESTING, INSPECTOR.
I DON'T LIKE GUNS.
OH, BUT THIS IS GOOD.
IT FIRES HIGH-VELOCITY DROPLETS OF ACID THAT HARMS ONLY BIOLOGICAL MATERIAL, NOT STATION WALLS.
AS MANAGER, I GET TO MAKE UNILATERAL DECISIONS BASED ON PAST POLICY.
YOU WERE NOT SUPPOSED TO MAKE IT HERE.
I CAN REMEDY THIS SITUATION, SAFE IN THE KNOWLEDGE THAT IT FALLS UNDER PAST POLICY.
POLICY.
KANE...

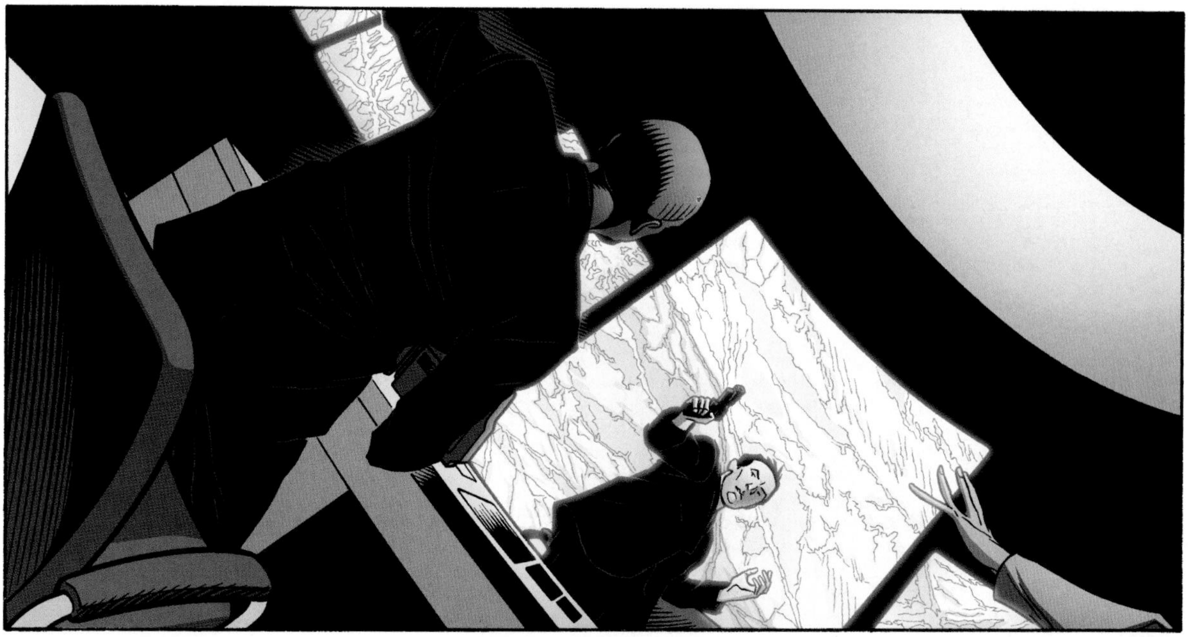

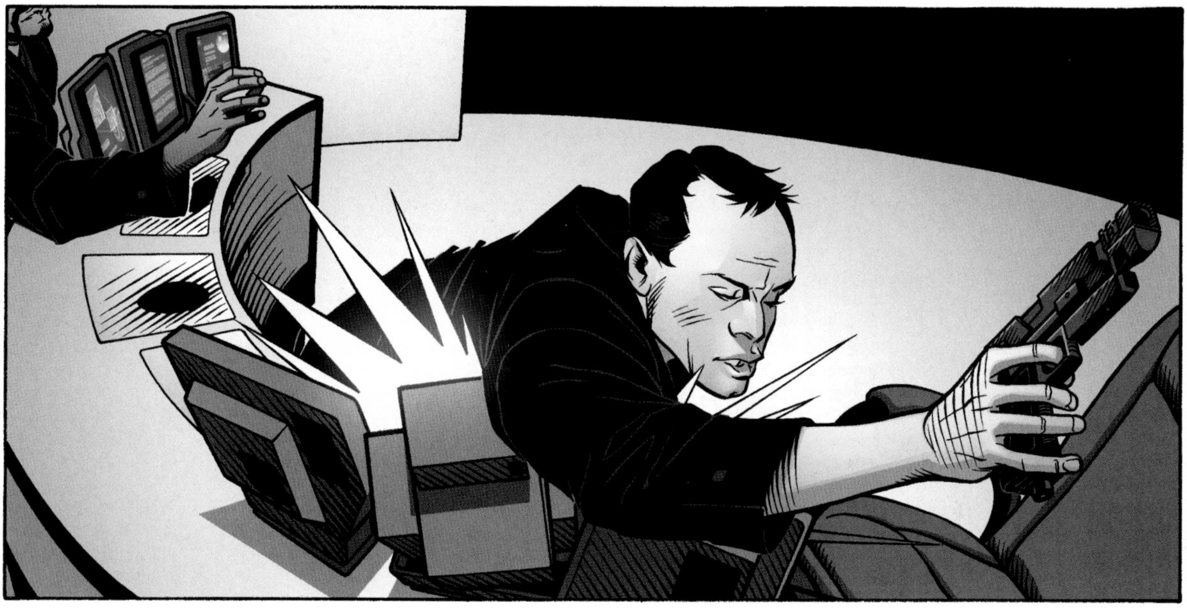

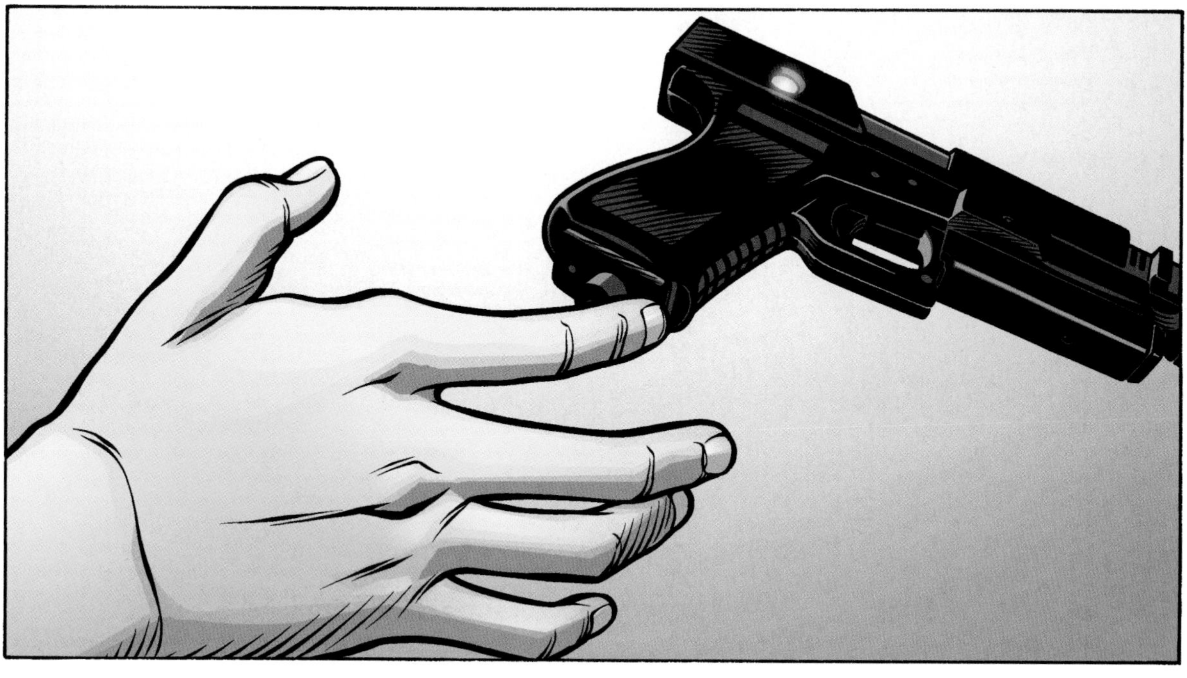

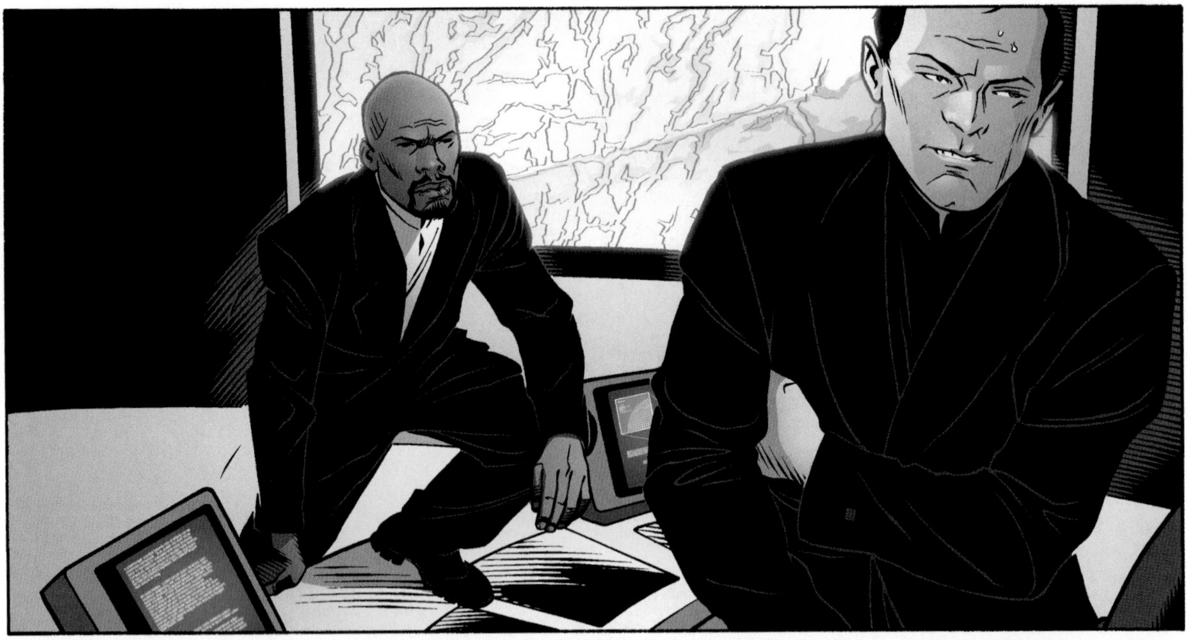

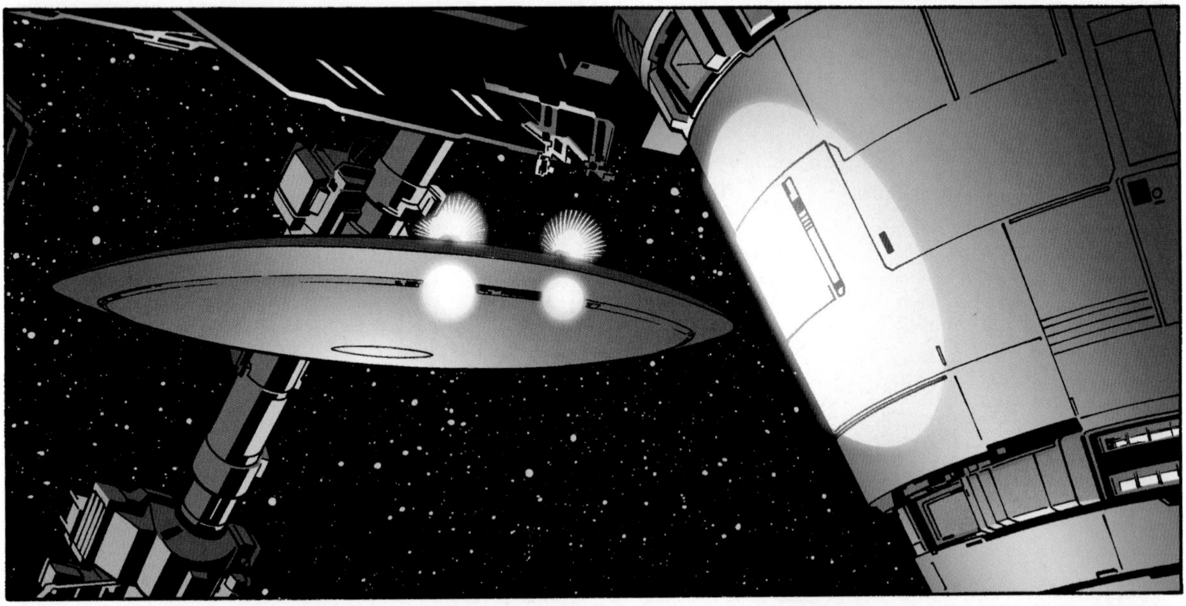

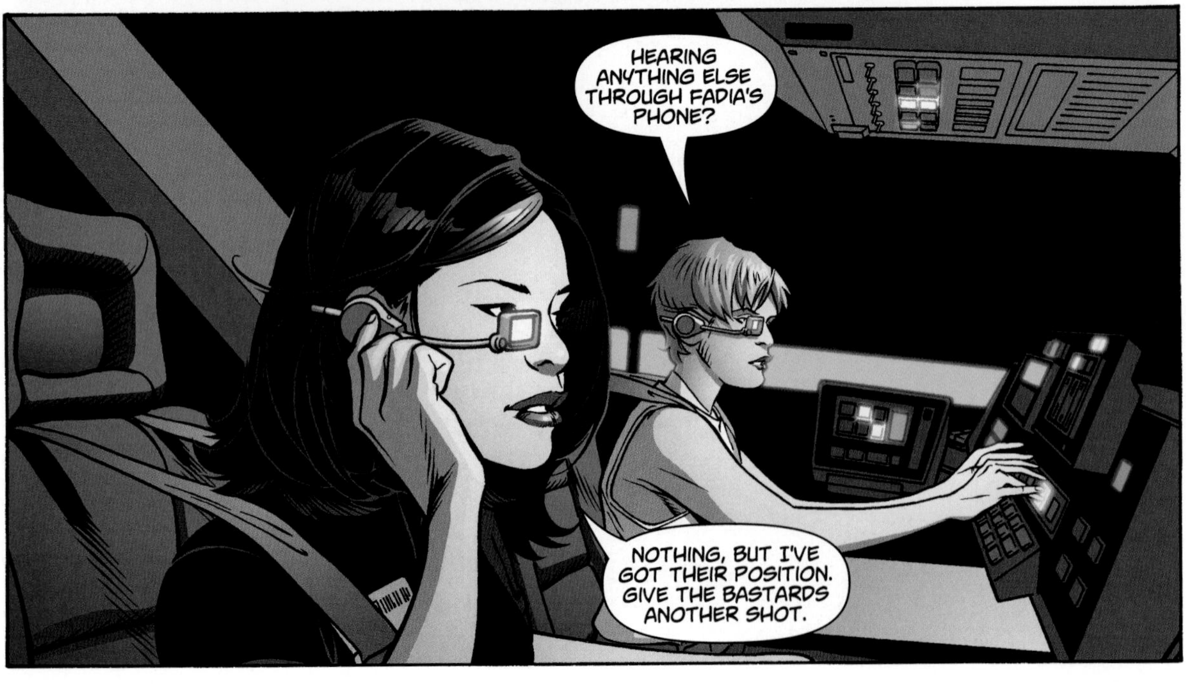
HEARING ANYTHING ELSE THROUGH FADIA'S PHONE?
NOTHING, BUT I'VE GOT THEIR POSITION. GIVE THE BASTARDS ANOTHER SHOT.

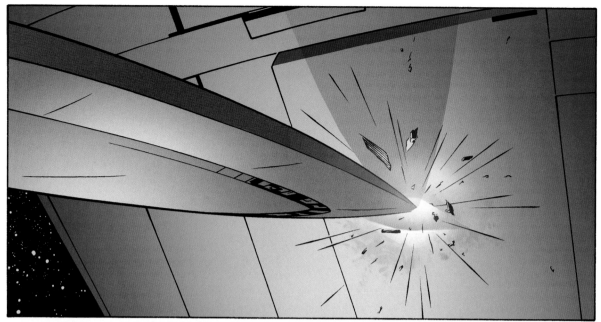

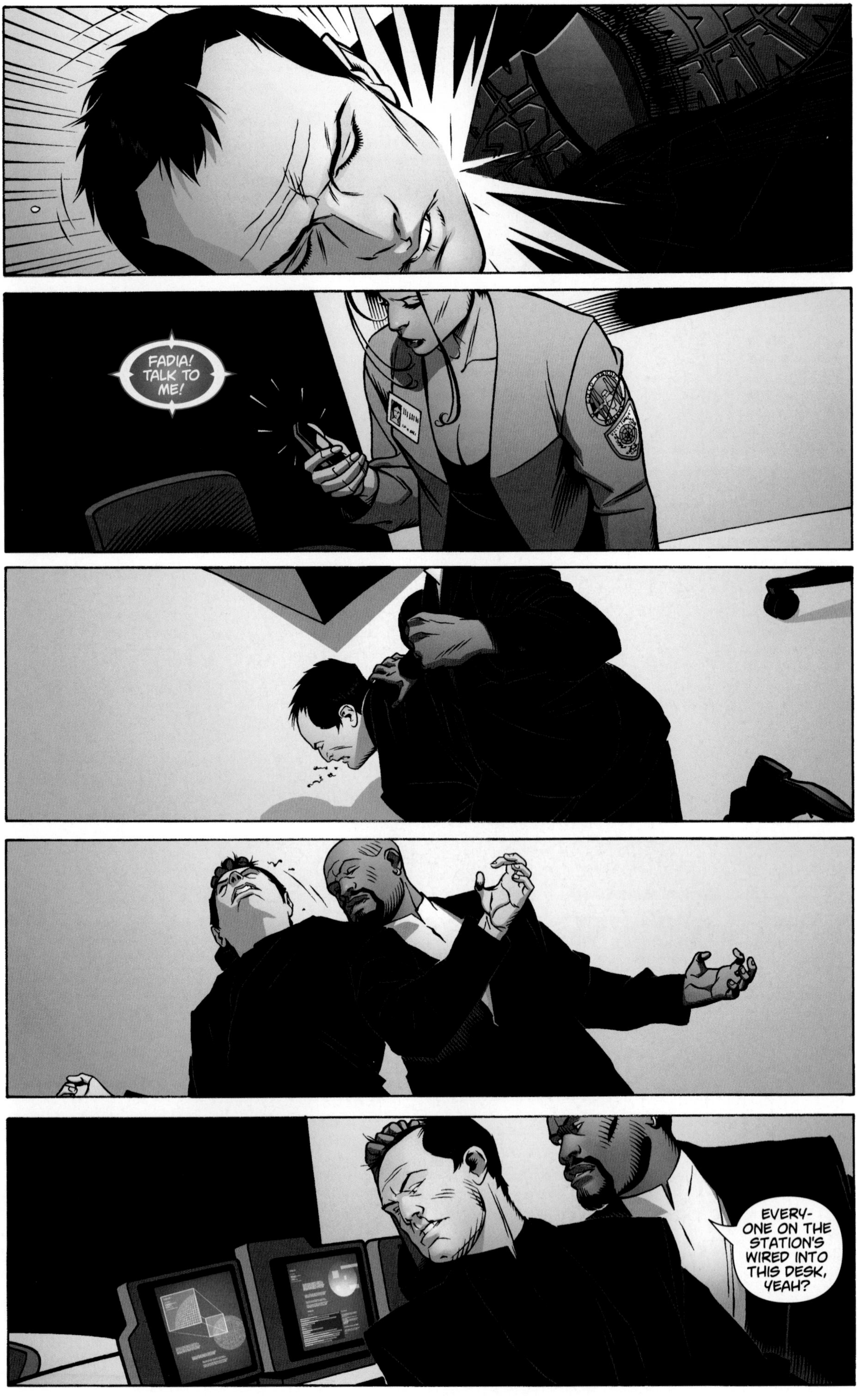
FADIA! TALK TO ME!
EVERY-ONE ON THE STATION'S WIRED INTO THIS DESK, YEAH?

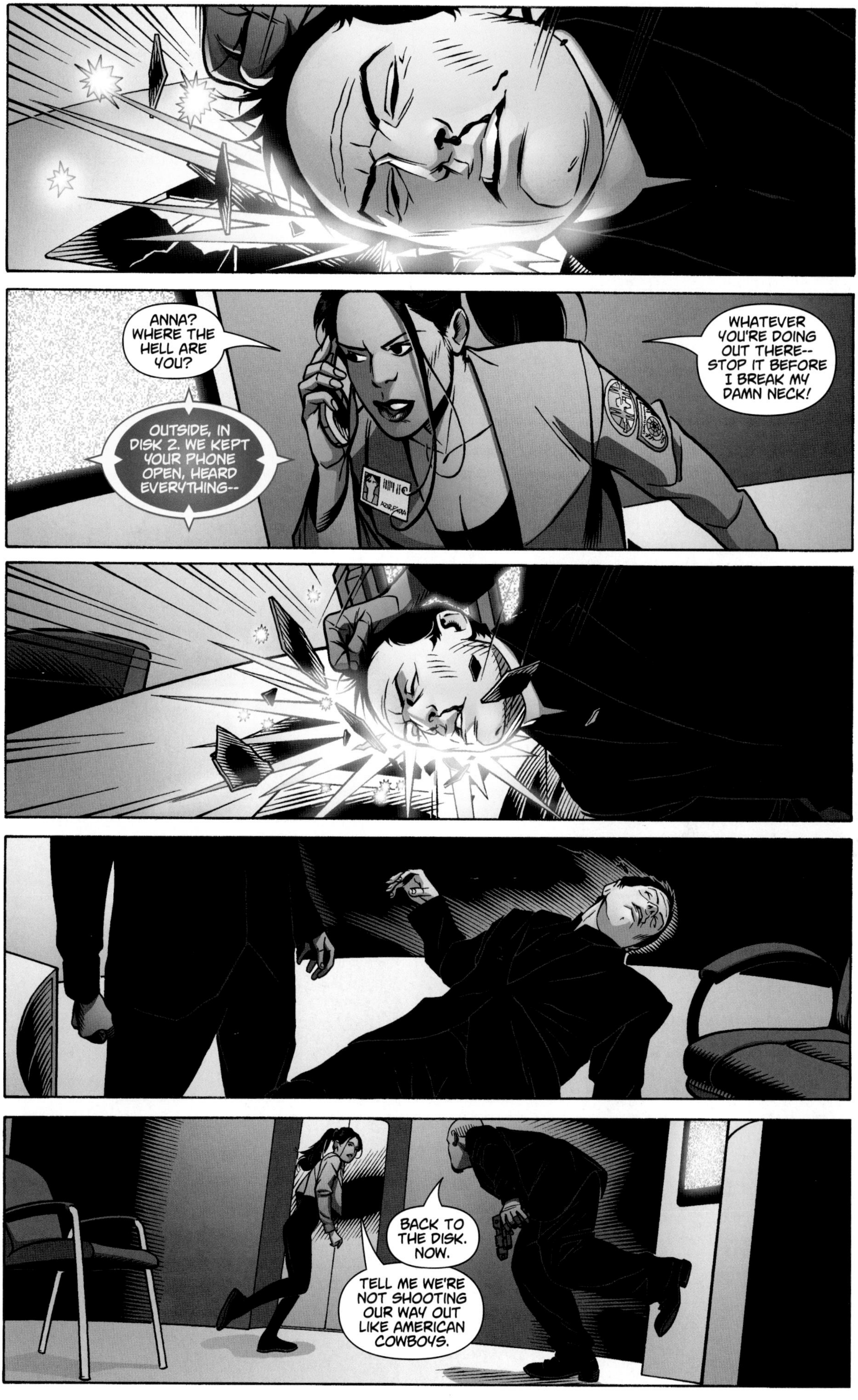
ANNA? WHERE THE HELL ARE YOU?
OUTSIDE, IN DISK 2. WE KEPT YOUR PHONE OPEN, HEARD EVERYTHING--
WHATEVER YOU'RE DOING OUT THERE-- STOP IT BEFORE I BREAK MY DAMN NECK!
BACK TO THE DISK. NOW.
TELL ME WE'RE NOT SHOOTING OUR WAY OUT LIKE AMERICAN COWBOYS.

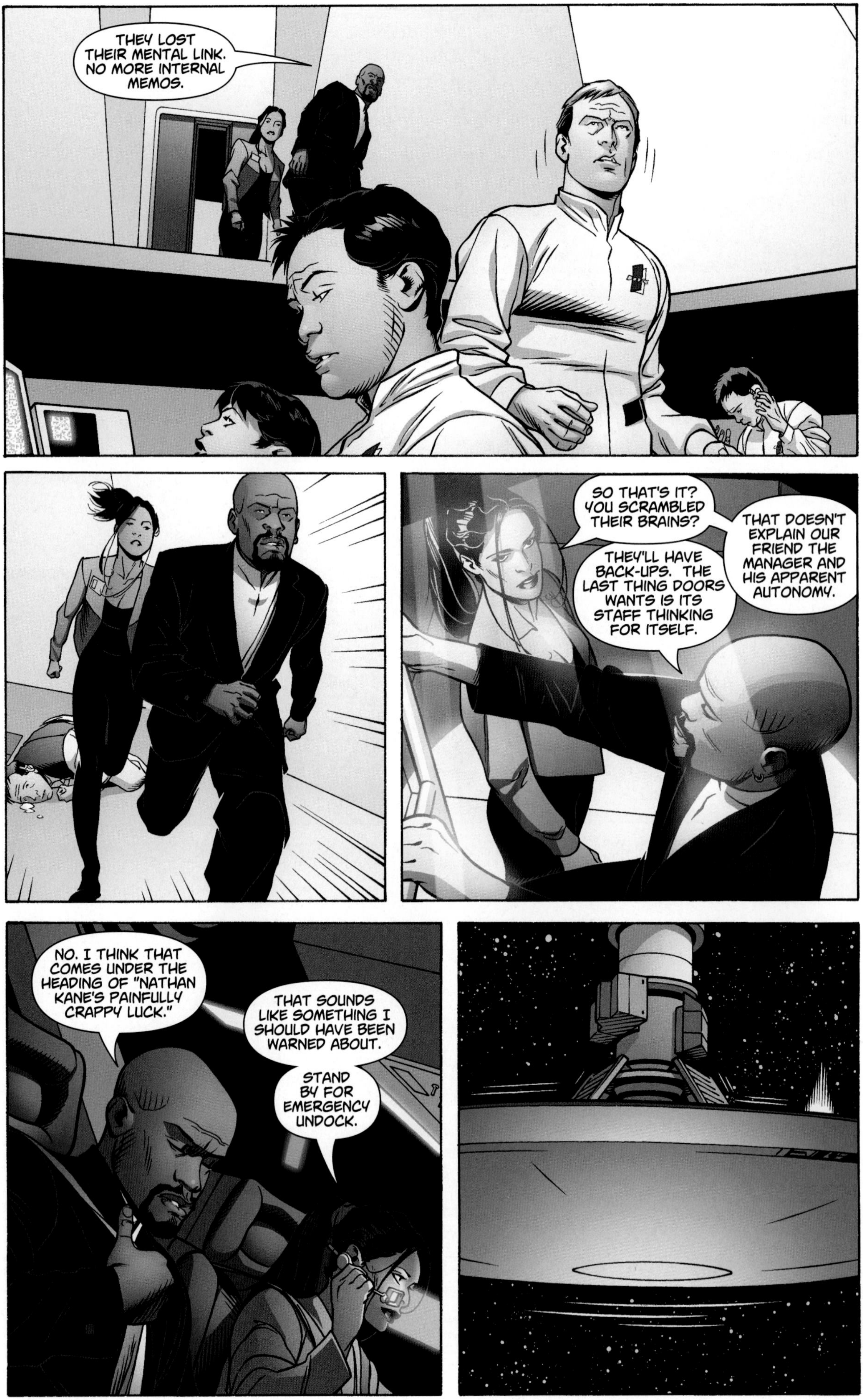
THEY LOST THEIR MENTAL LINK. NO MORE INTERNAL MEMOS.
SO THAT'S IT? YOU SCRAMBLED THEIR BRAINS?
THEY'LL HAVE BACK-UPS. THE LAST THING DOORS WANTS IS ITS STAFF THINKING FOR ITSELF.
THAT DOESN'T EXPLAIN OUR FRIEND THE MANAGER AND HIS APPARENT AUTONOMY.
NO. I THINK THAT COMES UNDER THE HEADING OF "NATHAN KANE'S PAINFULLY CRAPPY LUCK."
THAT SOUNDS LIKE SOMETHING I SHOULD HAVE BEEN WARNED ABOUT.
STAND BY FOR EMERGENCY UNDOCK.

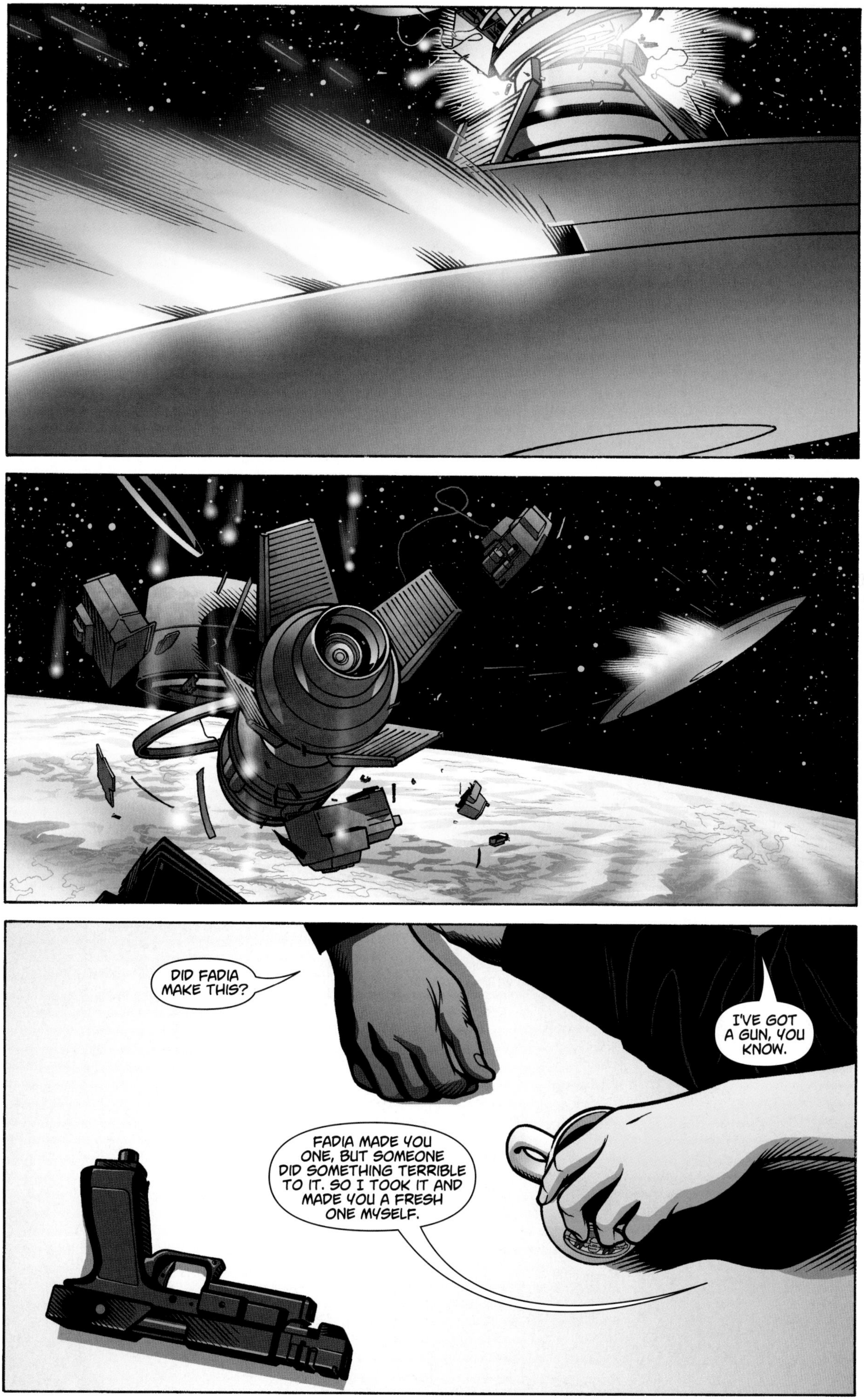
DID FADIA MAKE THIS?
I'VE GOT A GUN, YOU KNOW.
FADIA MADE YOU ONE, BUT SOMEONE DID SOMETHING TERRIBLE TO IT. SO I TOOK IT AND MADE YOU A FRESH ONE MYSELF.

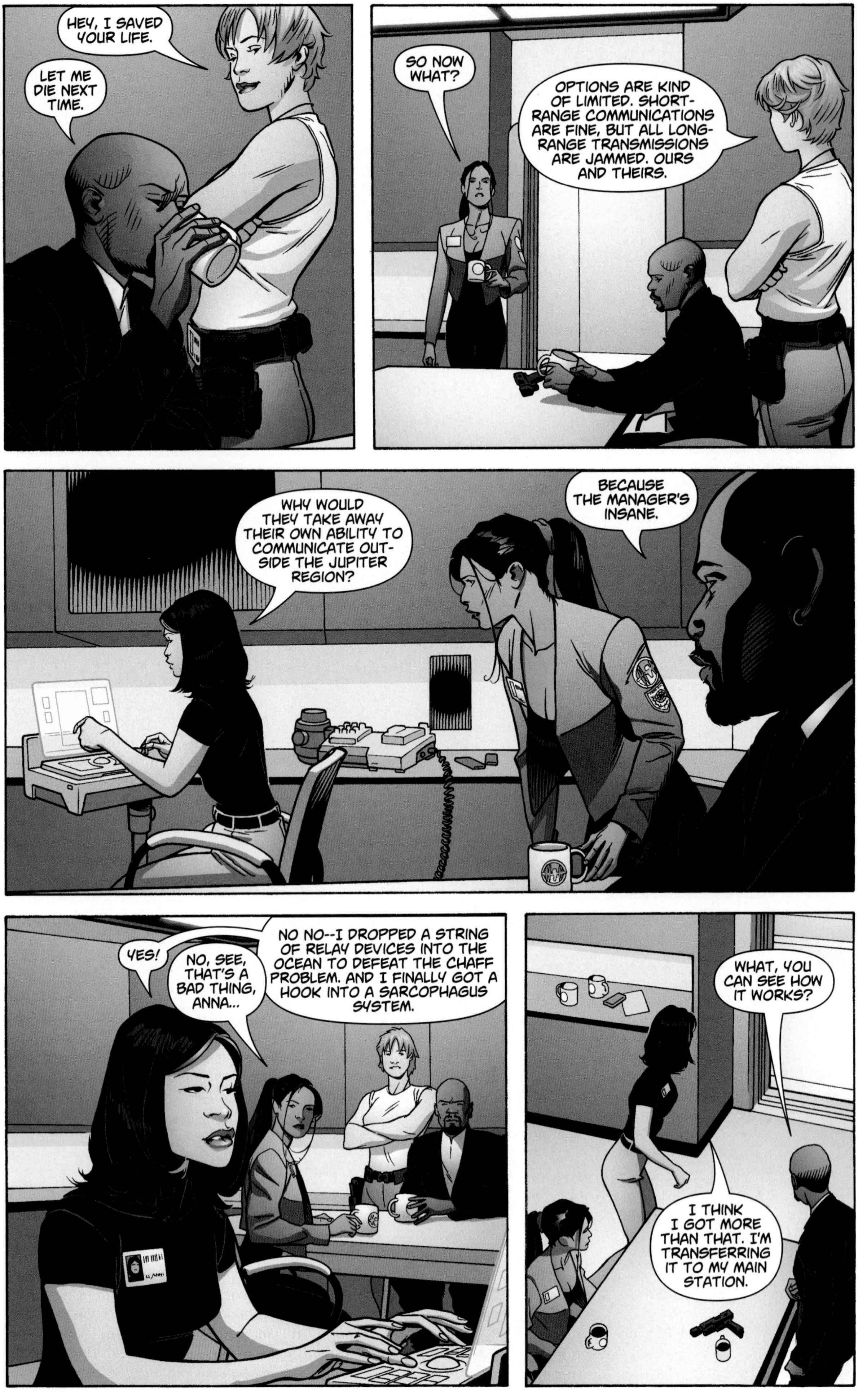
HEY, I SAVED YOUR LIFE.
LET ME DIE NEXT TIME.
SO NOW WHAT?
OPTIONS ARE KIND OF LIMITED. SHORT-RANGE COMMUNICATIONS ARE FINE, BUT ALL LONG-RANGE TRANSMISSIONS ARE JAMMED. OURS AND THEIRS.
WHY WOULD THEY TAKE AWAY THEIR OWN ABILITY TO COMMUNICATE OUTSIDE THE JUPITER REGION?
BECAUSE THE MANAGER'S INSANE.
YES!
NO, SEE, THAT'S A BAD THING, ANNA...
NO NO--I DROPPED A STRING OF RELAY DEVICES INTO THE OCEAN TO DEFEAT THE CHAFF PROBLEM. AND I FINALLY GOT A HOOK INTO A SARCOPHAGUS SYSTEM.
WHAT, YOU CAN SEE HOW IT WORKS?
I THINK I GOT MORE THAN THAT. I'M TRANSFERRING IT TO MY MAIN STATION.

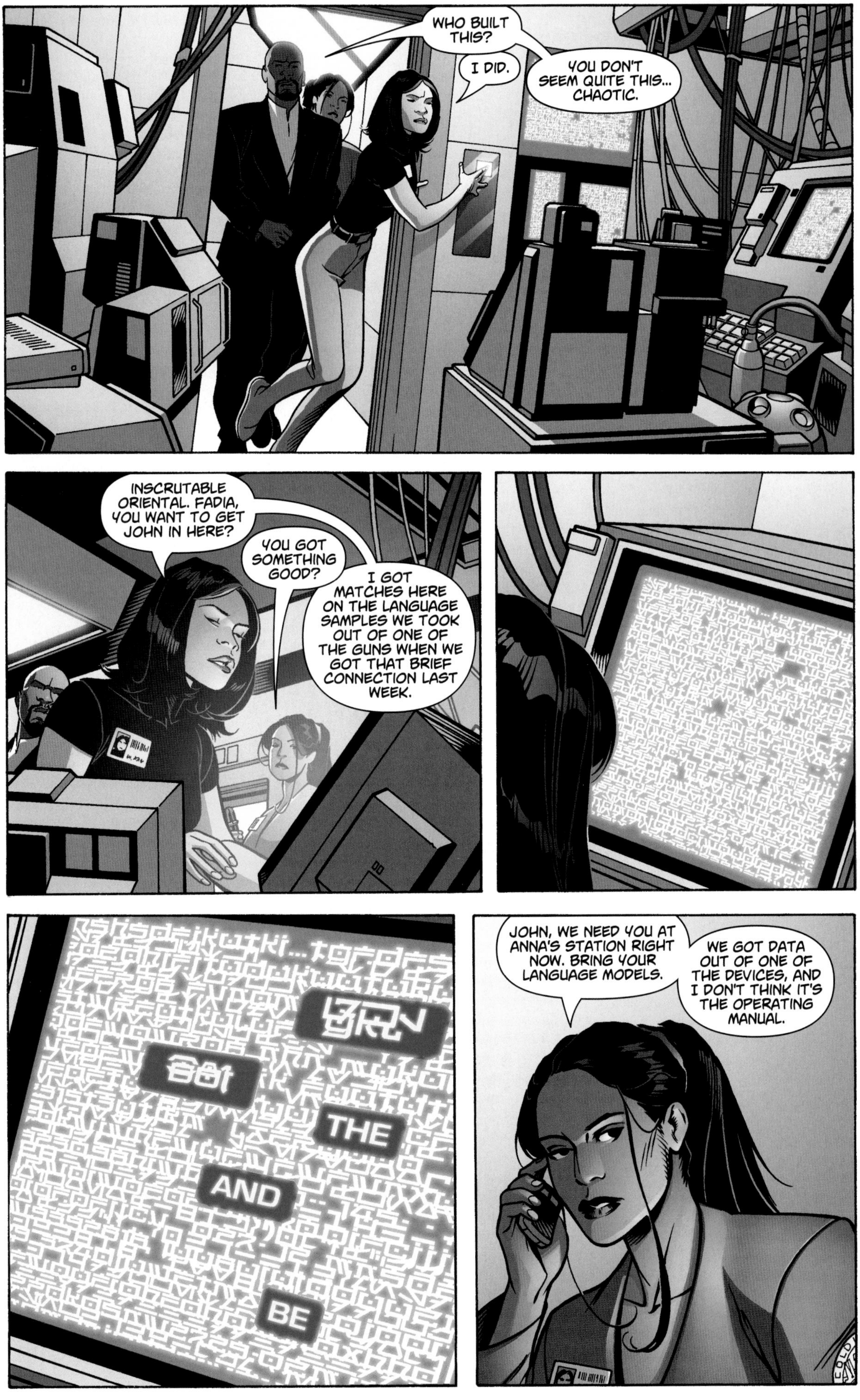
WHO BUILT THIS?
I DID.
YOU DON'T SEEM QUITE THIS... CHAOTIC.
INSCRUTABLE ORIENTAL. FADIA, YOU WANT TO GET JOHN IN HERE?
YOU GOT SOMETHING GOOD?
I GOT MATCHES HERE ON THE LANGUAGE SAMPLES WE TOOK OUT OF ONE OF THE GUNS WHEN WE GOT THAT BRIEF CONNECTION LAST WEEK.
THE
AND
BE
JOHN, WE NEED YOU AT ANNA'S STATION RIGHT NOW. BRING YOUR LANGUAGE MODELS.
WE GOT DATA OUT OF ONE OF THE DEVICES, AND I DON'T THINK IT'S THE OPERATING MANUAL.

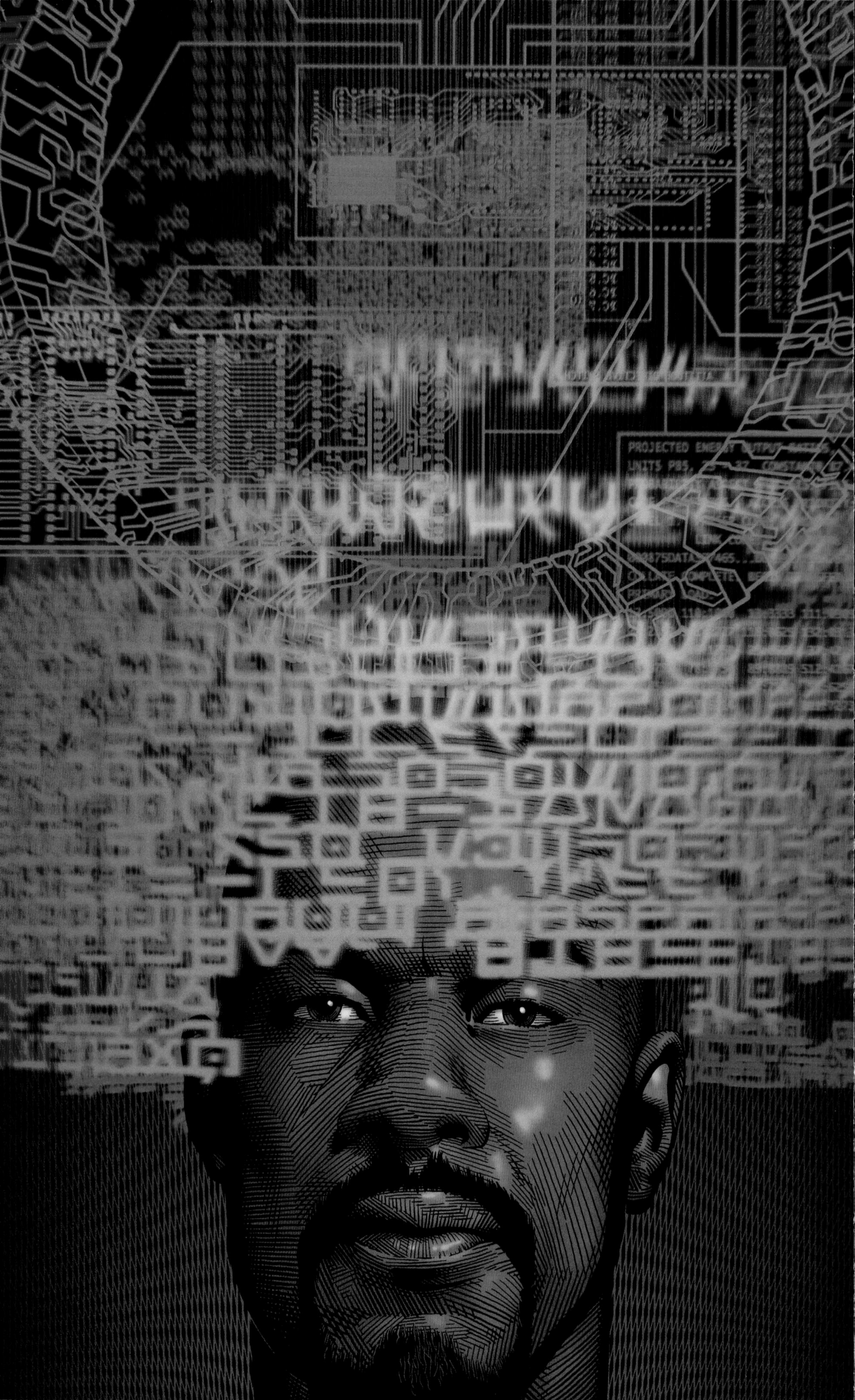

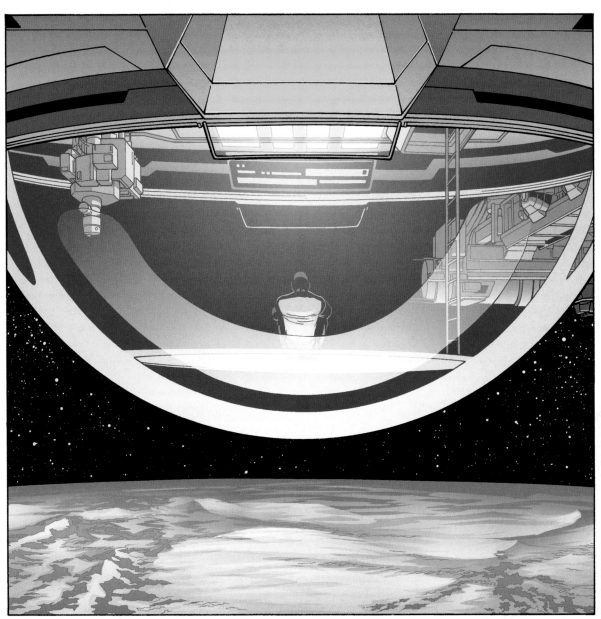

IT'S LATE.

I CAN NEVER TELL. MY BODYCLOCK NEVER ADJUSTS TO SPACE STATION TIME.

I CAN GET YOU SOME MEDS FOR THAT.

NAH. BEING UNSLEPT AND CRANKY KIND OF SUITS ME TO THE JOB AT HAND.

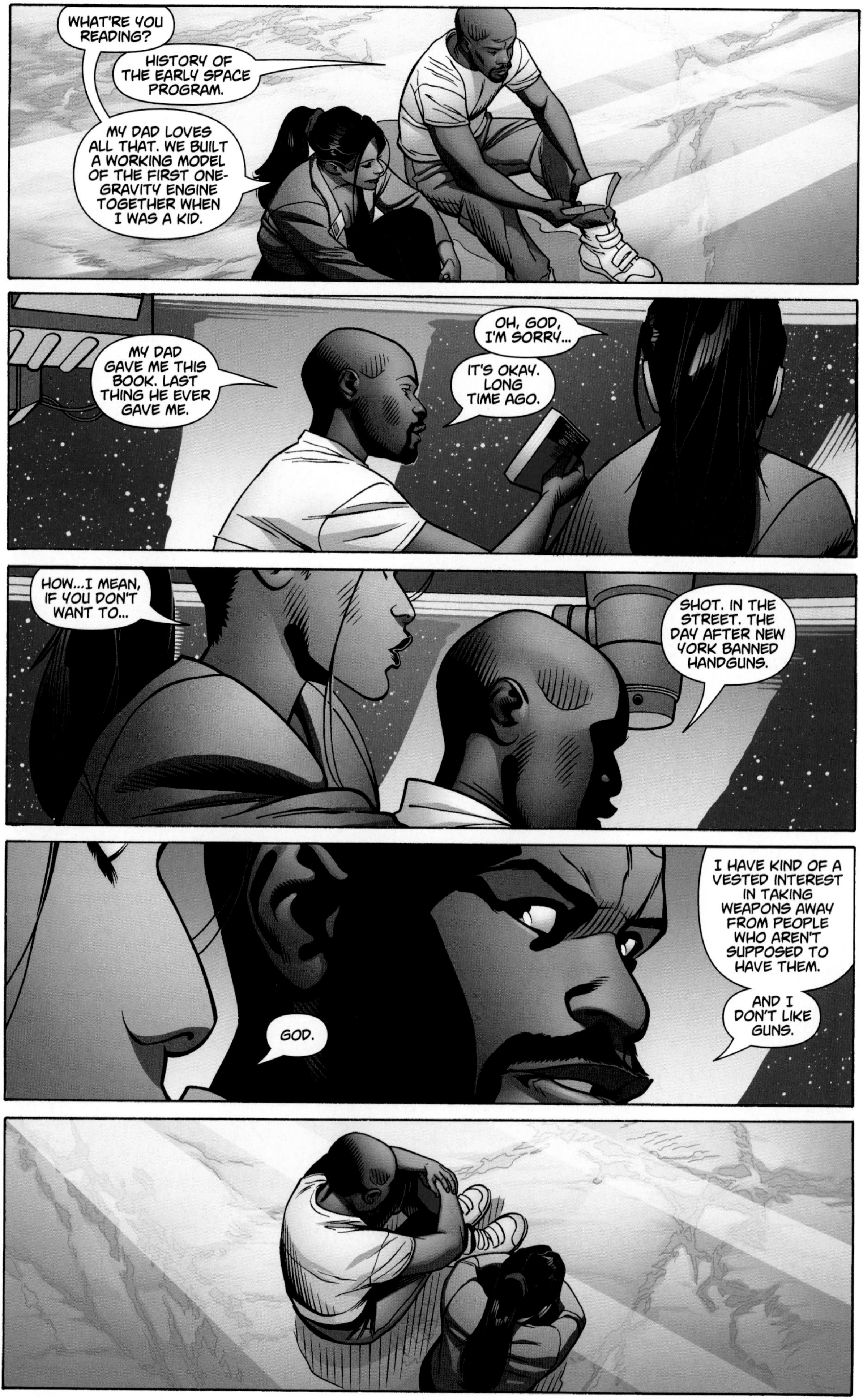
WHAT'RE YOU READING?
HISTORY OF THE EARLY SPACE PROGRAM.
MY DAD LOVES ALL THAT. WE BUILT A WORKING MODEL OF THE FIRST ONE-GRAVITY ENGINE TOGETHER WHEN I WAS A KID.
MY DAD GAVE ME THIS BOOK. LAST THING HE EVER GAVE ME.
OH, GOD, I'M SORRY...
IT'S OKAY. LONG TIME AGO.
HOW...I MEAN, IF YOU DON'T WANT TO...
SHOT. IN THE STREET. THE DAY AFTER NEW YORK BANNED HANDGUNS.
I HAVE KIND OF A VESTED INTEREST IN TAKING WEAPONS AWAY FROM PEOPLE WHO AREN'T SUPPOSED TO HAVE THEM.
AND I DON'T LIKE GUNS.
GOD.

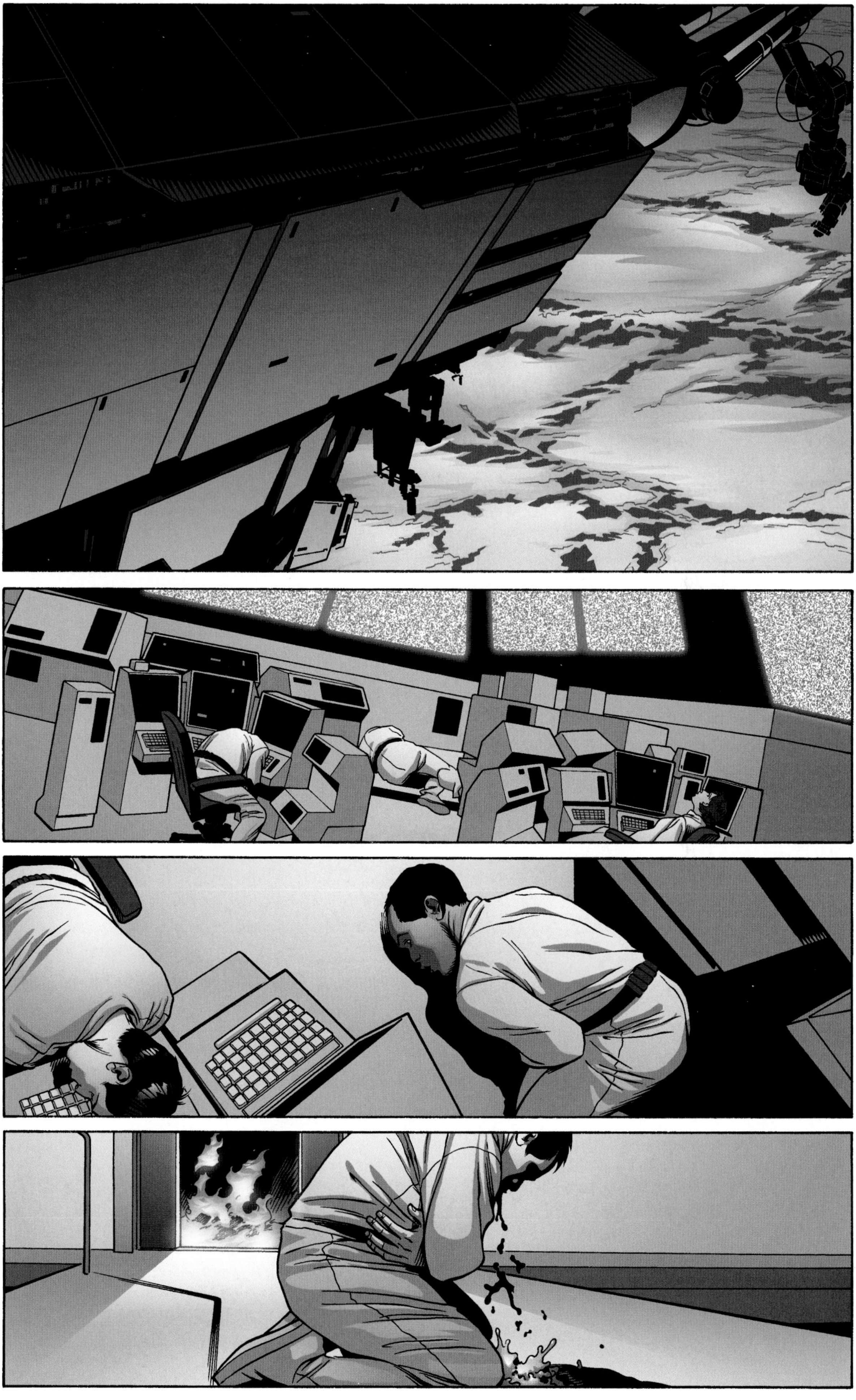

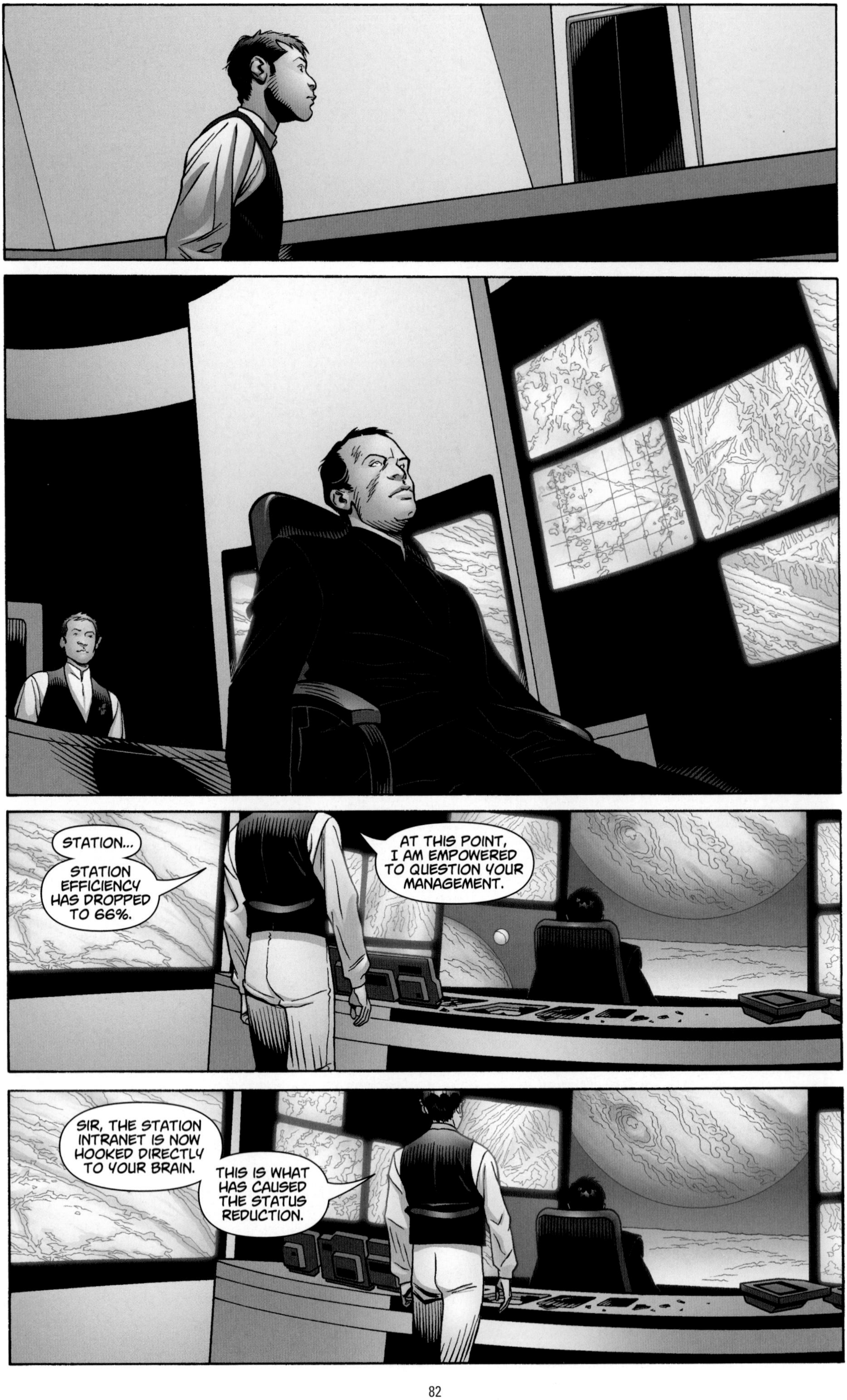
STATION...
STATION EFFICIENCY HAS DROPPED TO 66%.
AT THIS POINT, I AM EMPOWERED TO QUESTION YOUR MANAGEMENT.
SIR, THE STATION INTRANET IS NOW HOOKED DIRECTLY TO YOUR BRAIN.
THIS IS WHAT HAS CAUSED THE STATUS REDUCTION.

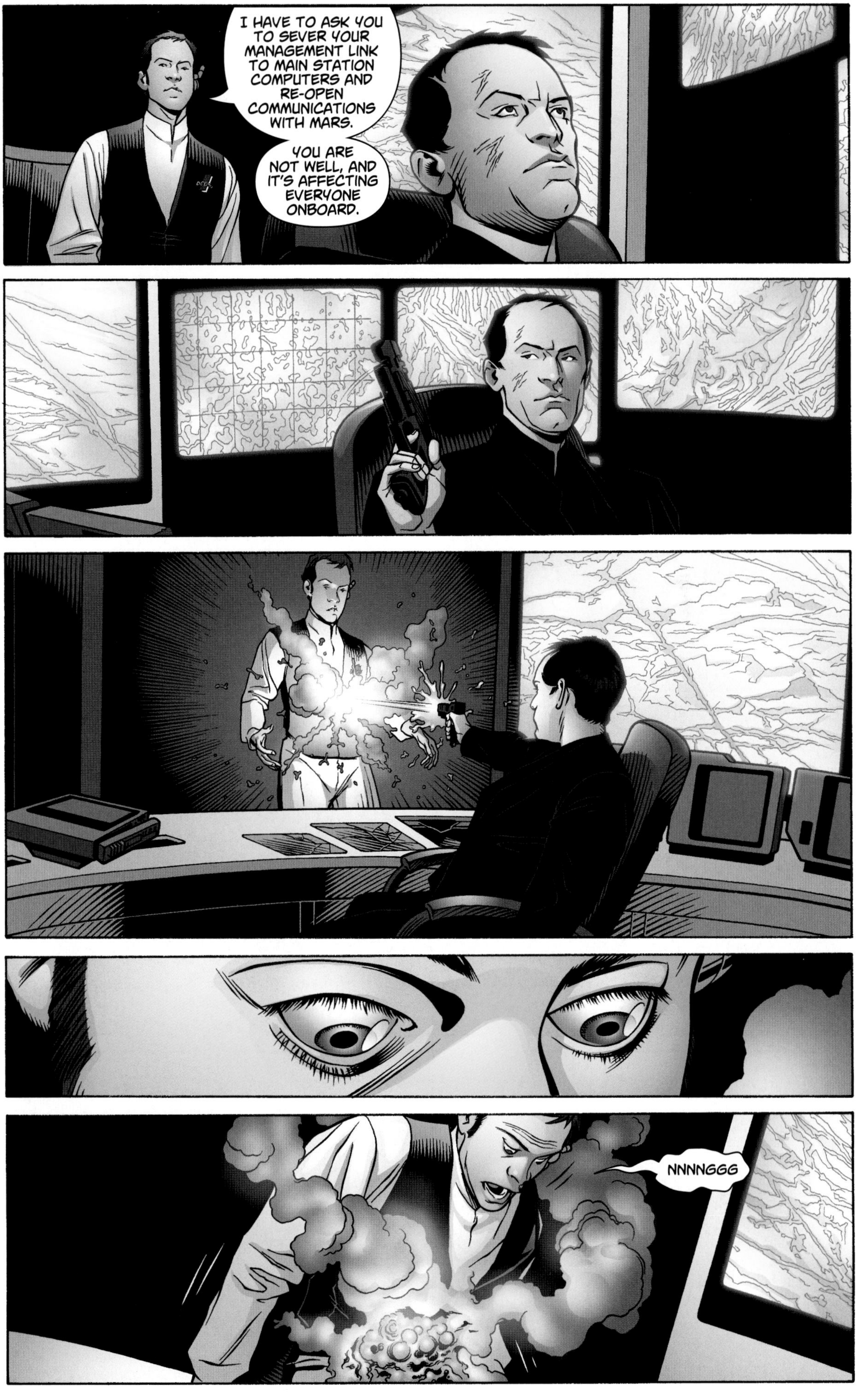
I HAVE TO ASK YOU TO SEVER YOUR MANAGEMENT LINK TO MAIN STATION COMPUTERS AND RE-OPEN COMMUNICATIONS WITH MARS.
YOU ARE NOT WELL, AND IT'S AFFECTING EVERYONE ONBOARD.
NNNNGGG

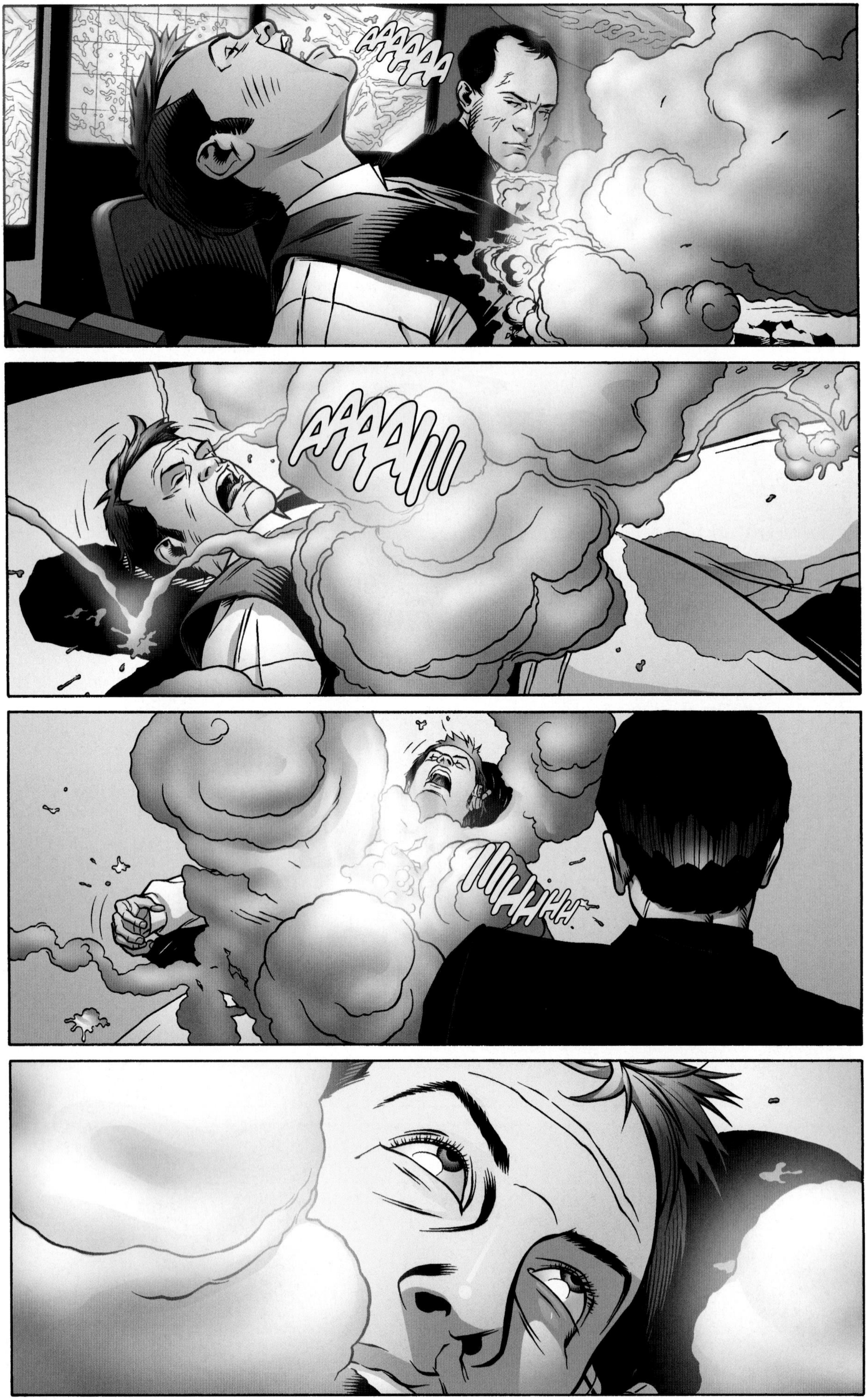
AAAAAA
AAAAIIII
IIIIHHHH

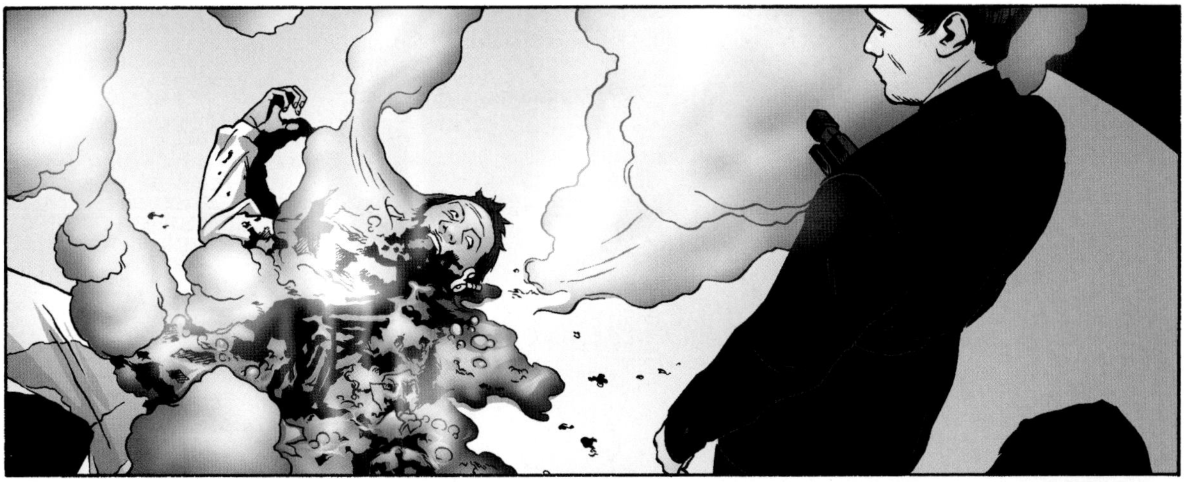

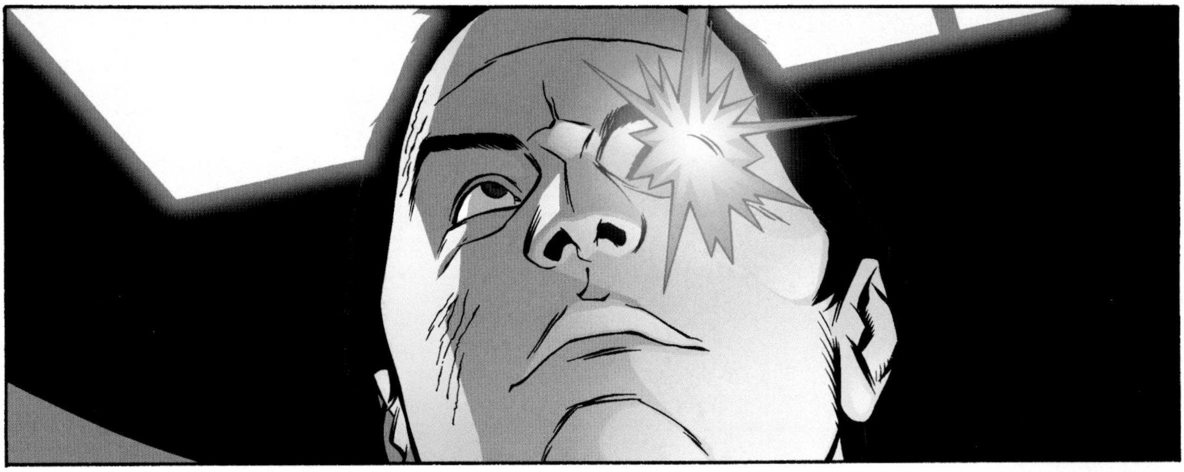

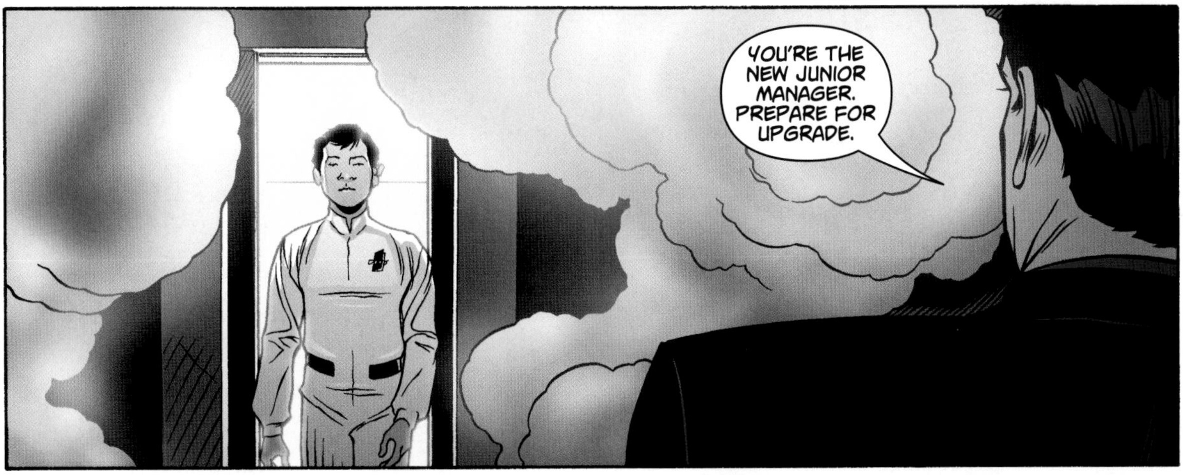
YOU'RE THE NEW JUNIOR MANAGER. PREPARE FOR UPGRADE.

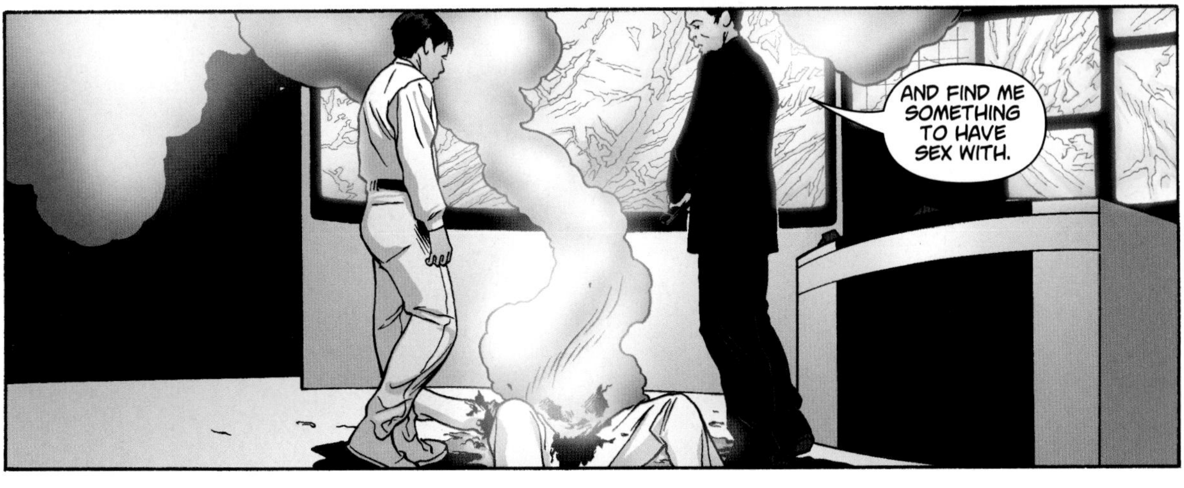
AND FIND ME SOMETHING TO HAVE SEX WITH.

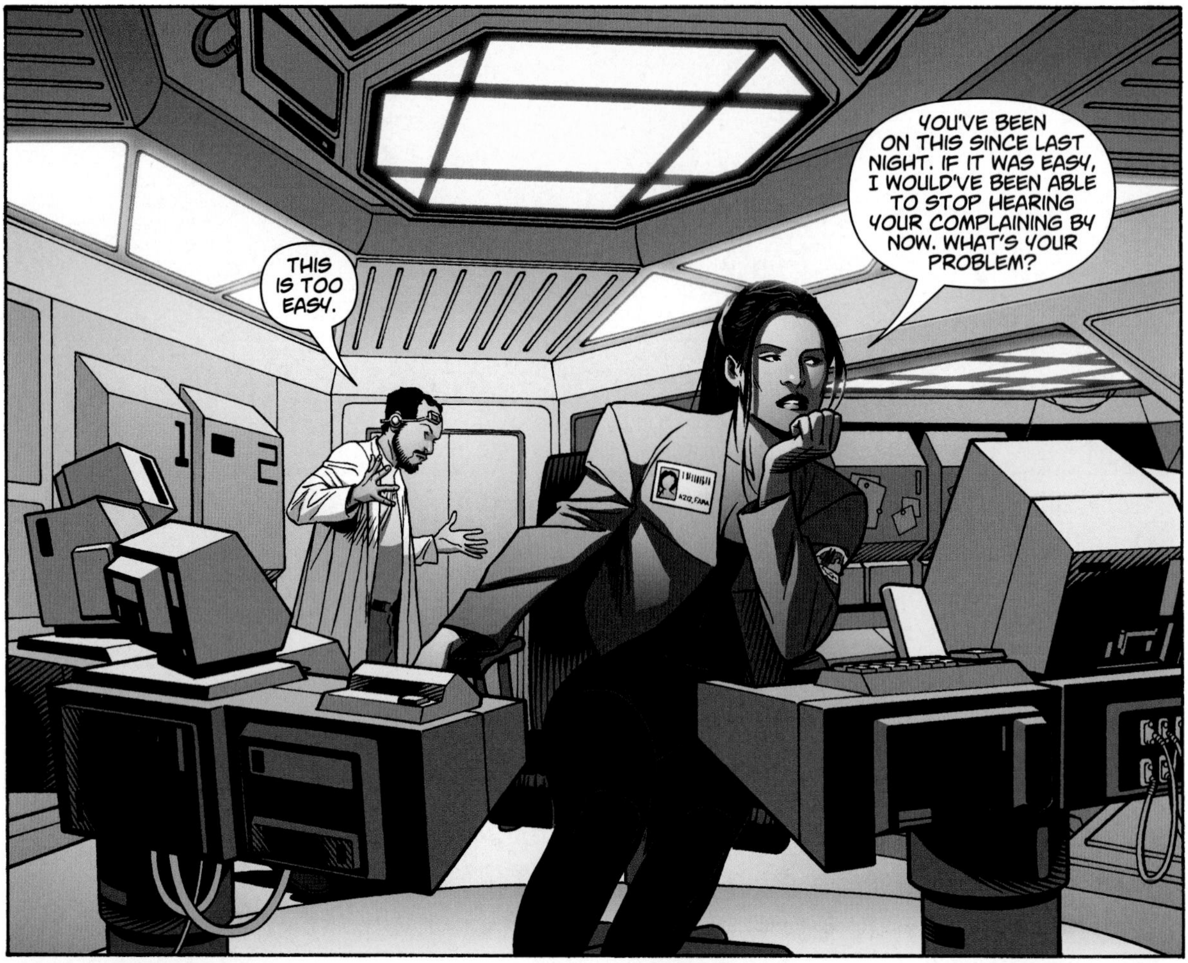
THIS IS TOO EASY.
YOU'VE BEEN ON THIS SINCE LAST NIGHT. IF IT WAS EASY, I WOULD'VE BEEN ABLE TO STOP HEARING YOUR COMPLAINING BY NOW. WHAT'S YOUR PROBLEM?

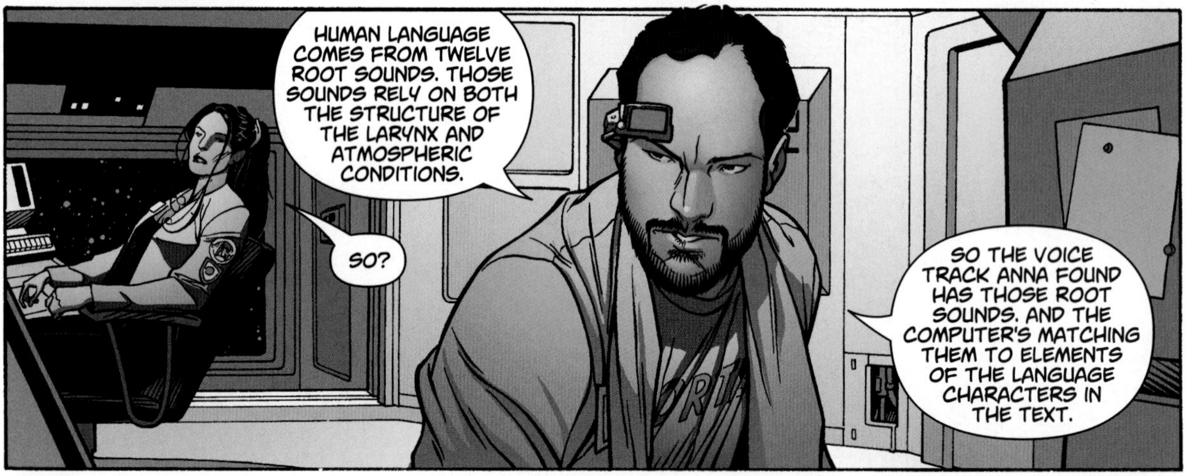
HUMAN LANGUAGE COMES FROM TWELVE ROOT SOUNDS. THOSE SOUNDS RELY ON BOTH THE STRUCTURE OF THE LARYNX AND ATMOSPHERIC CONDITIONS.
SO?
SO THE VOICE TRACK ANNA FOUND HAS THOSE ROOT SOUNDS. AND THE COMPUTER'S MATCHING THEM TO ELEMENTS OF THE LANGUAGE CHARACTERS IN THE TEXT.

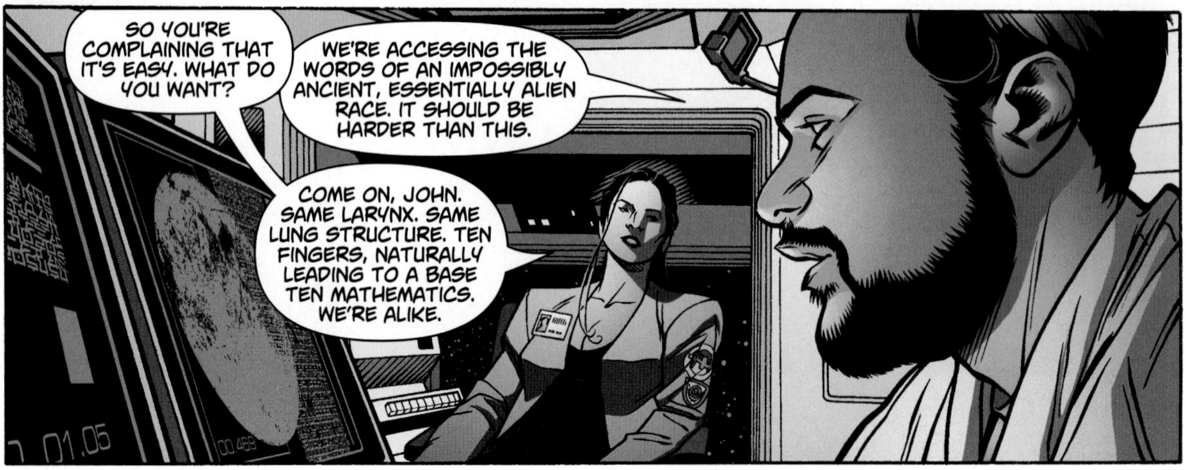
SO YOU'RE COMPLAINING THAT IT'S EASY. WHAT DO YOU WANT?
WE'RE ACCESSING THE WORDS OF AN IMPOSSIBLY ANCIENT, ESSENTIALLY ALIEN RACE. IT SHOULD BE HARDER THAN THIS.
COME ON, JOHN. SAME LARYNX. SAME LUNG STRUCTURE. TEN FINGERS, NATURALLY LEADING TO A BASE TEN MATHEMATICS. WE'RE ALIKE.

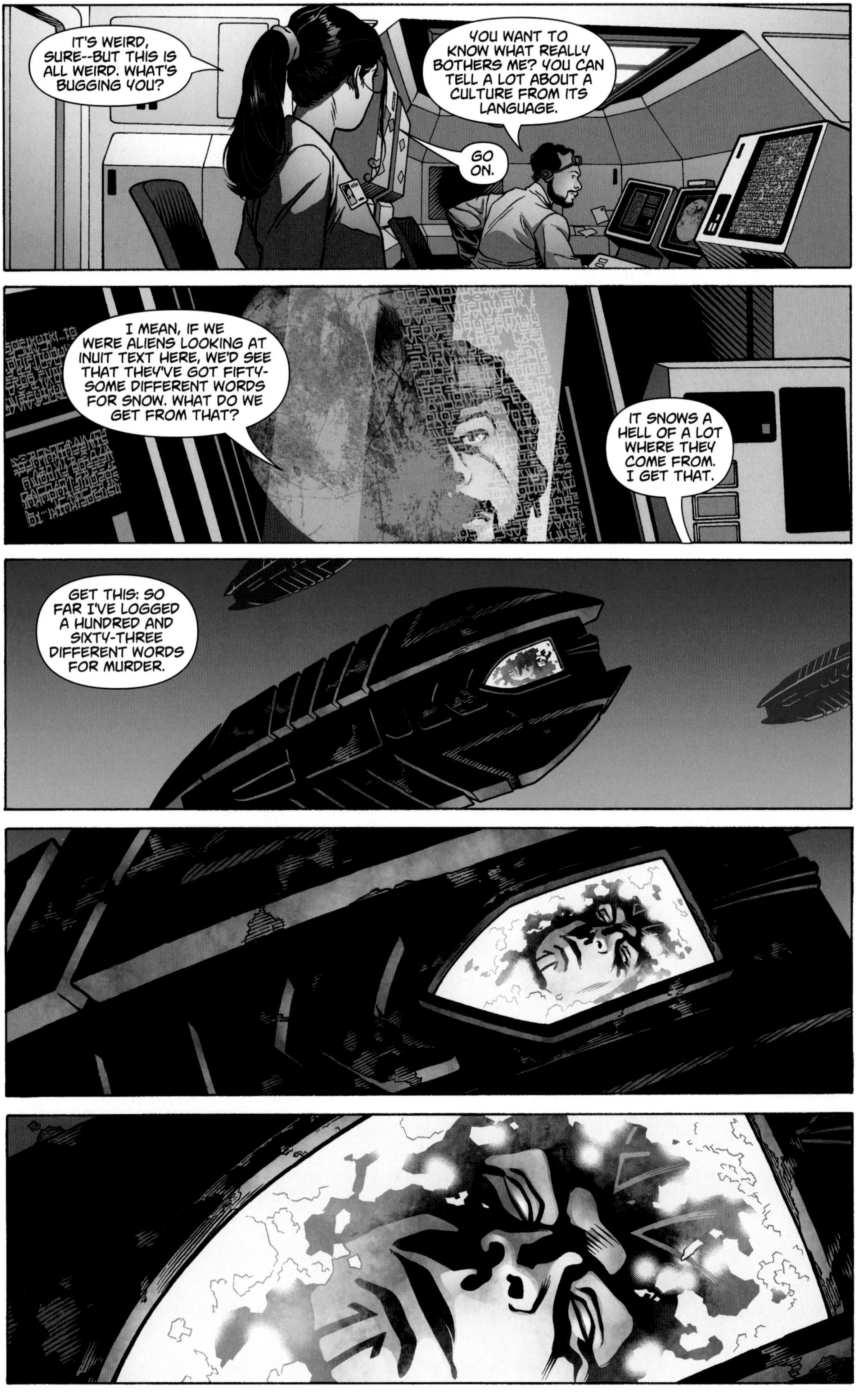
IT'S WEIRD, SURE--BUT THIS IS ALL WEIRD. WHAT'S BUGGING YOU?
YOU WANT TO KNOW WHAT REALLY BOTHERS ME? YOU CAN TELL A LOT ABOUT A CULTURE FROM ITS LANGUAGE.
GO ON.
I MEAN, IF WE WERE ALIENS LOOKING AT INUIT TEXT HERE, WE'D SEE THAT THEY'VE GOT FIFTY-SOME DIFFERENT WORDS FOR SNOW. WHAT DO WE GET FROM THAT?
IT SNOWS A HELL OF A LOT WHERE THEY COME FROM. I GET THAT.
GET THIS: SO FAR I'VE LOGGED A HUNDRED AND SIXTY-THREE DIFFERENT WORDS FOR MURDER.

AIR-TO-GROUND WEAPON. OR AIR-TO-AIR.

SPACE-TO-SPACE, MAYBE? BUT WHERE ARE THE SPACE VEHICLES TO MOUNT THEM ON?

THE HELL WITH IT. SHOW ME ITS PROJECTED POWER FLOW SYSTEM.

ISOLATE POWER GENERATORS...

DAMN IT. TOO MANY, TOO FAR INSIDE. NO CHANCE OF KNOCKING THEM OUT IF SOMEONE DECIDES TO USE THEM.

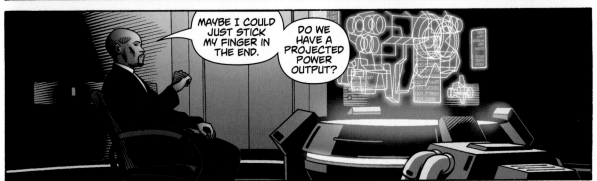

MAYBE I COULD JUST STICK MY FINGER IN THE END.

DO WE HAVE A PROJECTED POWER OUTPUT?

NO. NONONONO.

THIS HAS TO BE WRONG.

YES, NATHAN.

THE POWER OUTPUT PROJECTIONS ON THE GUNS ARE ALL SCREWY, AND THE SCREEN'S GIVING ME A CALLOUT ABOUT "ZERO POINT ENERGY." WHAT'S THE STORY HERE?

88

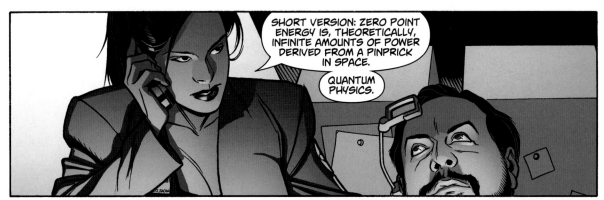

SHORT VERSION: ZERO POINT ENERGY IS, THEORETICALLY, INFINITE AMOUNTS OF POWER DERIVED FROM A PINPRICK IN SPACE.

QUANTUM PHYSICS.

THEN HERE'S THE NEWS.

ONE OF THESE GUNS THROWS OUT ENOUGH POWER TO SET A PLANET ON FIRE.

DOOR LOCK.

HELLO?

BUSY. WHO IS IT?

IT WAS UNLOCKED.

NO IT DAMN WELL WASN'T.

YOUR DOORLOCK'S BROKEN. I'M THE MECHANIC. I'M HERE TO FIX IT. WANT A BEER?

WHAT'S THIS?

MY LUGGAGE.

YOU TRAVEL LIGHT.

OOH, GUNS.

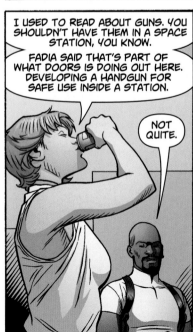

I USED TO READ ABOUT GUNS. YOU SHOULDN'T HAVE THEM IN A SPACE STATION, YOU KNOW.

FADIA SAID THAT'S PART OF WHAT DOORS IS DOING OUT HERE. DEVELOPING A HANDGUN FOR SAFE USE INSIDE A STATION.

NOT QUITE.

THESE ARE DESIGNED FOR USE IN SPACE. THEY HAVE NO RECOIL. GAS-FIRED.

SO IF YOU'RE IN A ZERO-GRAVITY SITUATION, FIRING THEM WON'T SEND YOU FLYING BACK-WARD AT SEVEN HUNDRED MILES AN HOUR.

I CAN SEE WHERE THAT WOULD BE USEFUL.

FIRST TIME I WAS ON THE MOON, I HAD TO USE A PISTOL ON THE SURFACE.

THE RECOIL SENT ME SHOOTING OFF AT ESCAPE VELOCITY.

MOONBASE ALPHA HAD TO SCRAMBLE A SHUTTLE TO CATCH ME.

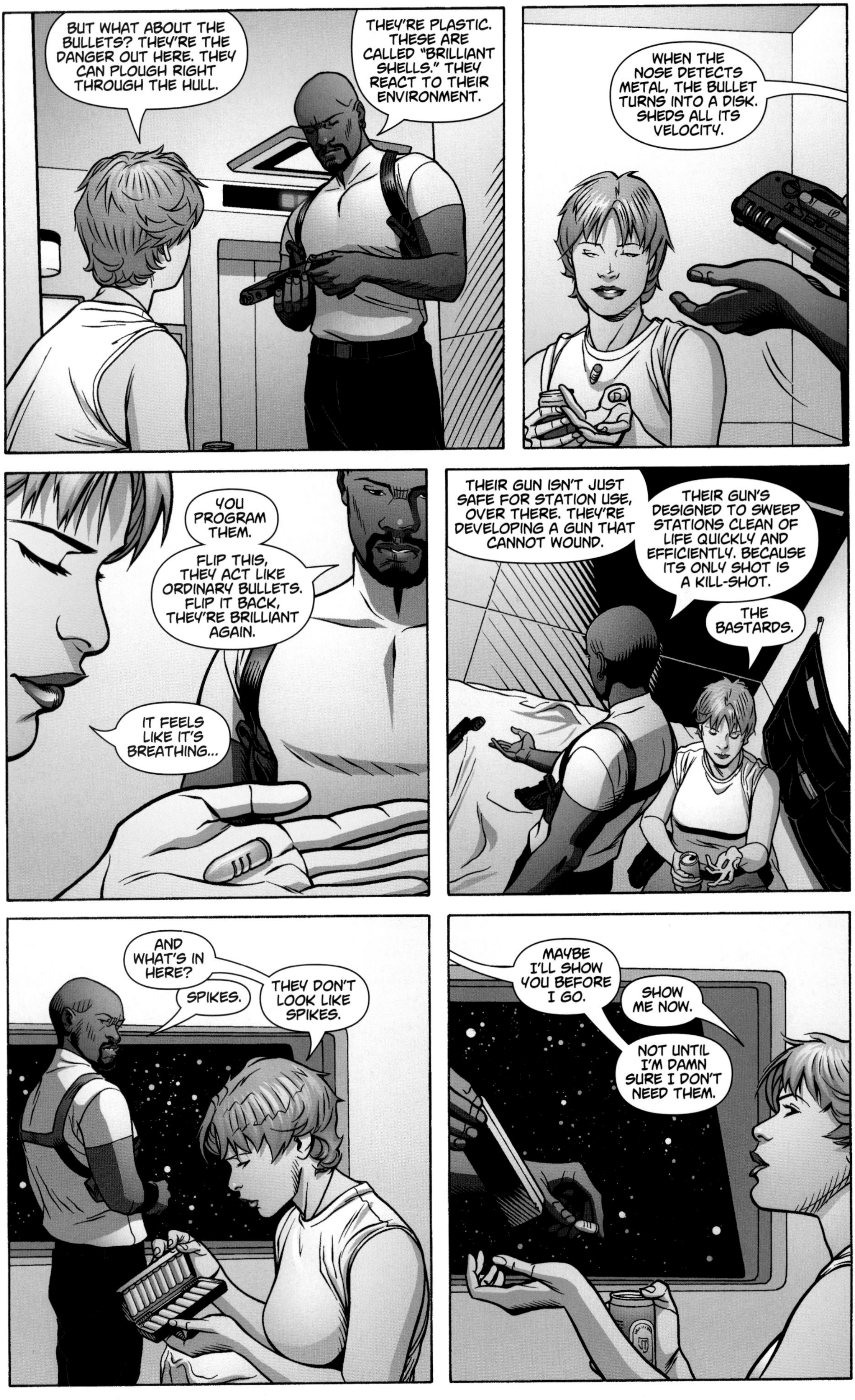
BUT WHAT ABOUT THE BULLETS? THEY'RE THE DANGER OUT HERE. THEY CAN PLOUGH RIGHT THROUGH THE HULL.
THEY'RE PLASTIC. THESE ARE CALLED "BRILLIANT SHELLS." THEY REACT TO THEIR ENVIRONMENT.
WHEN THE NOSE DETECTS METAL, THE BULLET TURNS INTO A DISK. SHEDS ALL ITS VELOCITY.
YOU PROGRAM THEM.
FLIP THIS, THEY ACT LIKE ORDINARY BULLETS. FLIP IT BACK, THEY'RE BRILLIANT AGAIN.
IT FEELS LIKE IT'S BREATHING...
THEIR GUN ISN'T JUST SAFE FOR STATION USE, OVER THERE. THEY'RE DEVELOPING A GUN THAT CANNOT WOUND.
THEIR GUN'S DESIGNED TO SWEEP STATIONS CLEAN OF LIFE QUICKLY AND EFFICIENTLY. BECAUSE ITS ONLY SHOT IS A KILL-SHOT.
THE BASTARDS.
AND WHAT'S IN HERE?
SPIKES.
THEY DON'T LOOK LIKE SPIKES.
MAYBE I'LL SHOW YOU BEFORE I GO.
SHOW ME NOW.
NOT UNTIL I'M DAMN SURE I DON'T NEED THEM.

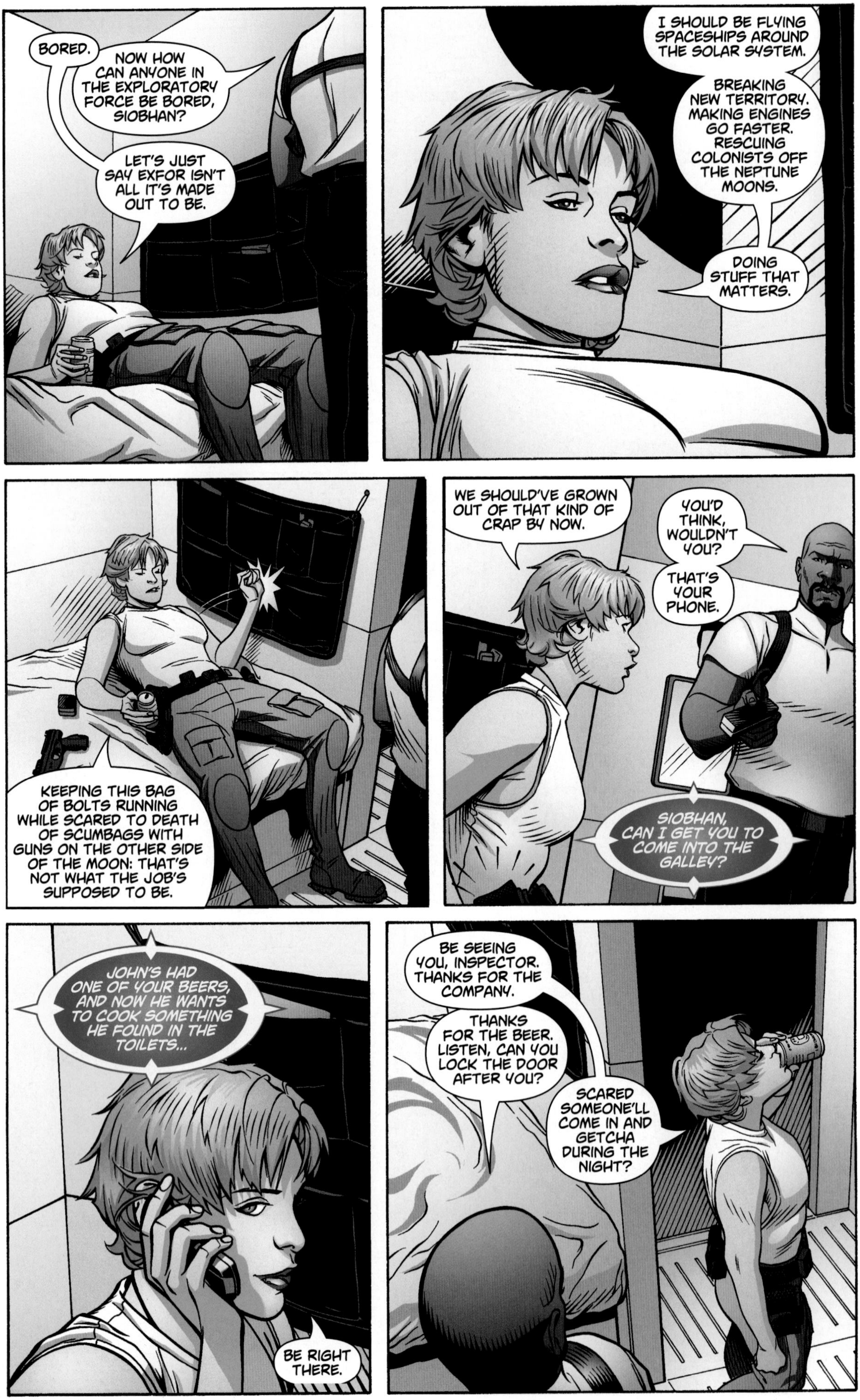

BORED.
NOW HOW CAN ANYONE IN THE EXPLORATORY FORCE BE BORED, SIOBHAN?
LET'S JUST SAY EXFOR ISN'T ALL IT'S MADE OUT TO BE.
I SHOULD BE FLYING SPACESHIPS AROUND THE SOLAR SYSTEM.
BREAKING NEW TERRITORY. MAKING ENGINES GO FASTER. RESCUING COLONISTS OFF THE NEPTUNE MOONS.
DOING STUFF THAT MATTERS.
KEEPING THIS BAG OF BOLTS RUNNING WHILE SCARED TO DEATH OF SCUMBAGS WITH GUNS ON THE OTHER SIDE OF THE MOON: THAT'S NOT WHAT THE JOB'S SUPPOSED TO BE.
WE SHOULD'VE GROWN OUT OF THAT KIND OF CRAP BY NOW.
YOU'D THINK, WOULDN'T YOU?
THAT'S YOUR PHONE.
SIOBHAN, CAN I GET YOU TO COME INTO THE GALLEY?
JOHN'S HAD ONE OF YOUR BEERS, AND NOW HE WANTS TO COOK SOMETHING HE FOUND IN THE TOILETS...
BE RIGHT THERE.
BE SEEING YOU, INSPECTOR. THANKS FOR THE COMPANY.
THANKS FOR THE BEER. LISTEN, CAN YOU LOCK THE DOOR AFTER YOU?
SCARED SOMEONE'LL COME IN AND GETCHA DURING THE NIGHT?

CALL ME A HEALTHY PARANOID.

PARANOIDS ARE JUST PEOPLE WITH ALL THE FACTS. G'NIGHT.

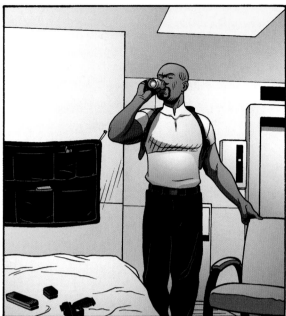

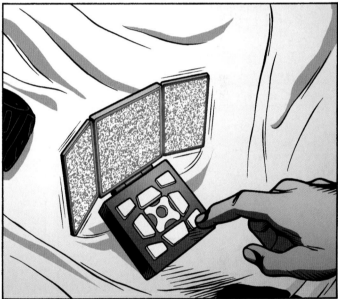

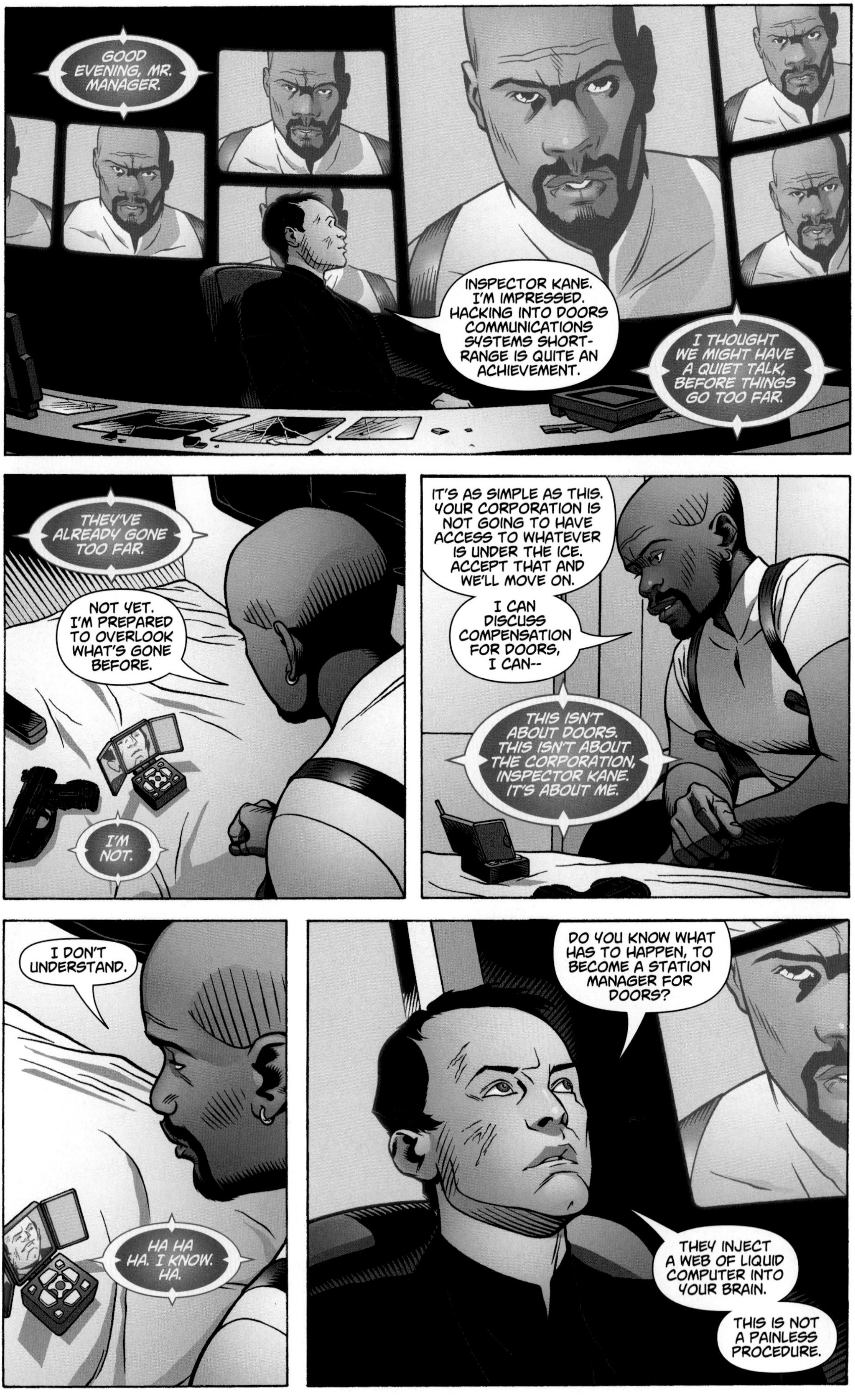

GOOD EVENING, MR. MANAGER.
INSPECTOR KANE. I'M IMPRESSED. HACKING INTO DOORS COMMUNICATIONS SYSTEMS SHORT-RANGE IS QUITE AN ACHIEVEMENT.
I THOUGHT WE MIGHT HAVE A QUIET TALK, BEFORE THINGS GO TOO FAR.
THEY'VE ALREADY GONE TOO FAR.
NOT YET. I'M PREPARED TO OVERLOOK WHAT'S GONE BEFORE.
I'M NOT.
IT'S AS SIMPLE AS THIS. YOUR CORPORATION IS NOT GOING TO HAVE ACCESS TO WHATEVER IS UNDER THE ICE. ACCEPT THAT AND WE'LL MOVE ON.
I CAN DISCUSS COMPENSATION FOR DOORS, I CAN--
THIS ISN'T ABOUT DOORS. THIS ISN'T ABOUT THE CORPORATION, INSPECTOR KANE. IT'S ABOUT ME.
I DON'T UNDERSTAND.
HA HA HA. I KNOW. HA.
DO YOU KNOW WHAT HAS TO HAPPEN, TO BECOME A STATION MANAGER FOR DOORS?
THEY INJECT A WEB OF LIQUID COMPUTER INTO YOUR BRAIN.
THIS IS NOT A PAINLESS PROCEDURE.

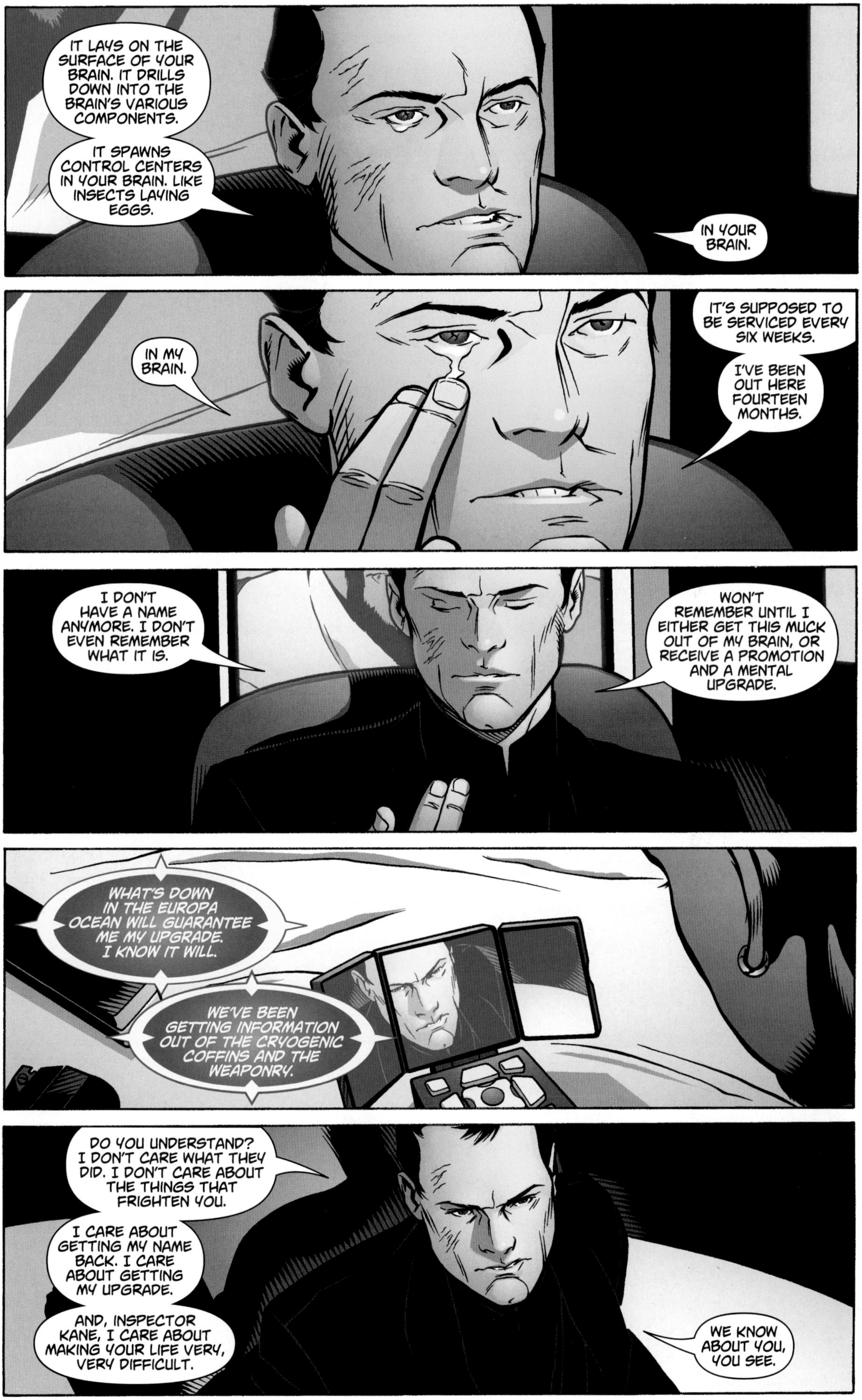
IT LAYS ON THE SURFACE OF YOUR BRAIN. IT DRILLS DOWN INTO THE BRAIN'S VARIOUS COMPONENTS.
IT SPAWNS CONTROL CENTERS IN YOUR BRAIN. LIKE INSECTS LAYING EGGS.
IN YOUR BRAIN.
IN MY BRAIN.
IT'S SUPPOSED TO BE SERVICED EVERY SIX WEEKS.
I'VE BEEN OUT HERE FOURTEEN MONTHS.
I DON'T HAVE A NAME ANYMORE. I DON'T EVEN REMEMBER WHAT IT IS.
WON'T REMEMBER UNTIL I EITHER GET THIS MUCK OUT OF MY BRAIN, OR RECEIVE A PROMOTION AND A MENTAL UPGRADE.
WHAT'S DOWN IN THE EUROPA OCEAN WILL GUARANTEE ME MY UPGRADE. I KNOW IT WILL.
WE'VE BEEN GETTING INFORMATION OUT OF THE CRYOGENIC COFFINS AND THE WEAPONRY.
DO YOU UNDERSTAND? I DON'T CARE WHAT THEY DID. I DON'T CARE ABOUT THE THINGS THAT FRIGHTEN YOU.
I CARE ABOUT GETTING MY NAME BACK. I CARE ABOUT GETTING MY UPGRADE.
AND, INSPECTOR KANE, I CARE ABOUT MAKING YOUR LIFE VERY, VERY DIFFICULT.
WE KNOW ABOUT YOU, YOU SEE.

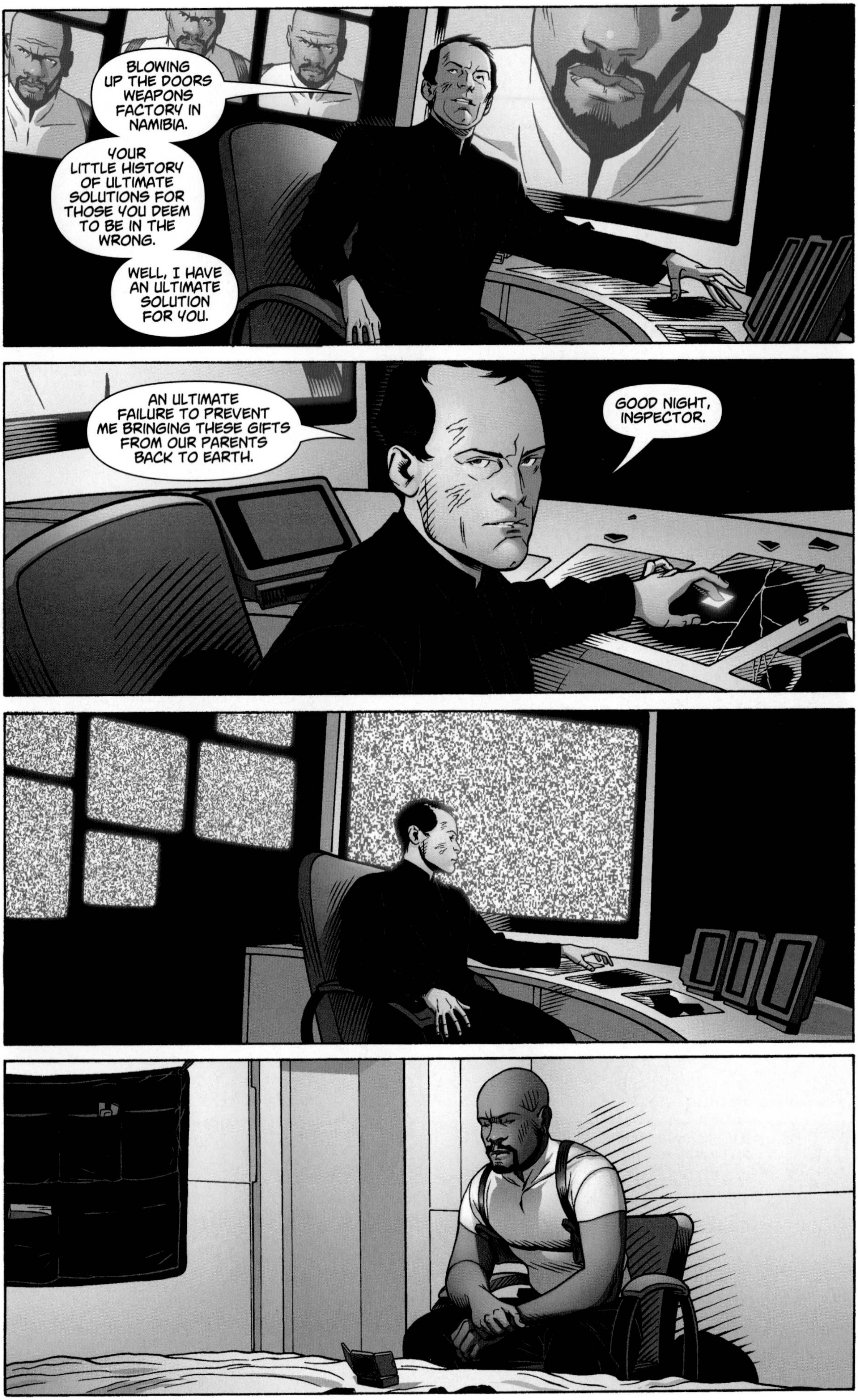
BLOWING UP THE DOORS WEAPONS FACTORY IN NAMIBIA.
YOUR LITTLE HISTORY OF ULTIMATE SOLUTIONS FOR THOSE YOU DEEM TO BE IN THE WRONG.
WELL, I HAVE AN ULTIMATE SOLUTION FOR YOU.
AN ULTIMATE FAILURE TO PREVENT ME BRINGING THESE GIFTS FROM OUR PARENTS BACK TO EARTH.
GOOD NIGHT, INSPECTOR.

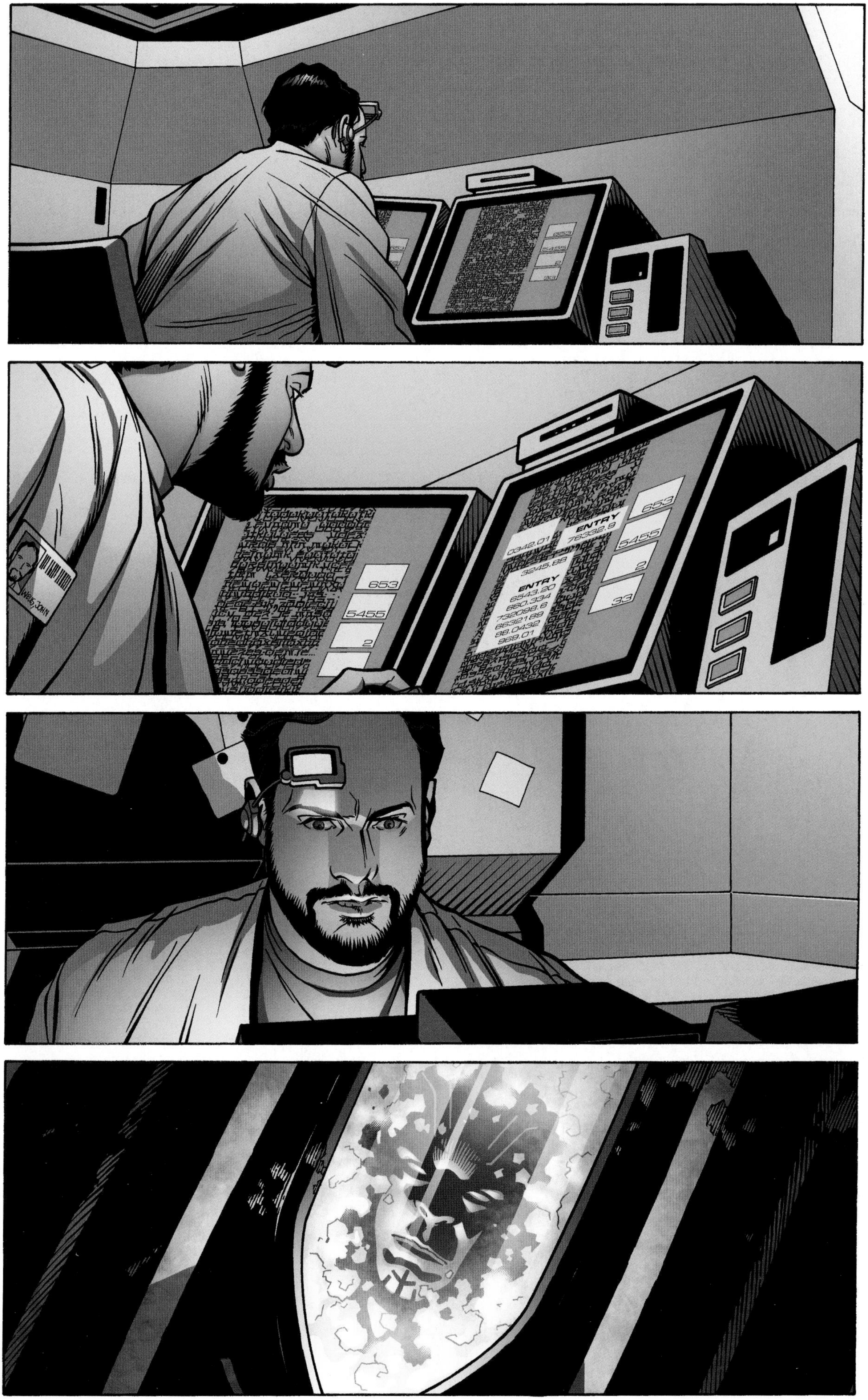
653
5455
2
ENTRY
76332.9
0342.01
3245.88
ENTRY
6543.20
660.334
732098.6
6632189
88.0432
969.01
653
5455
2
33

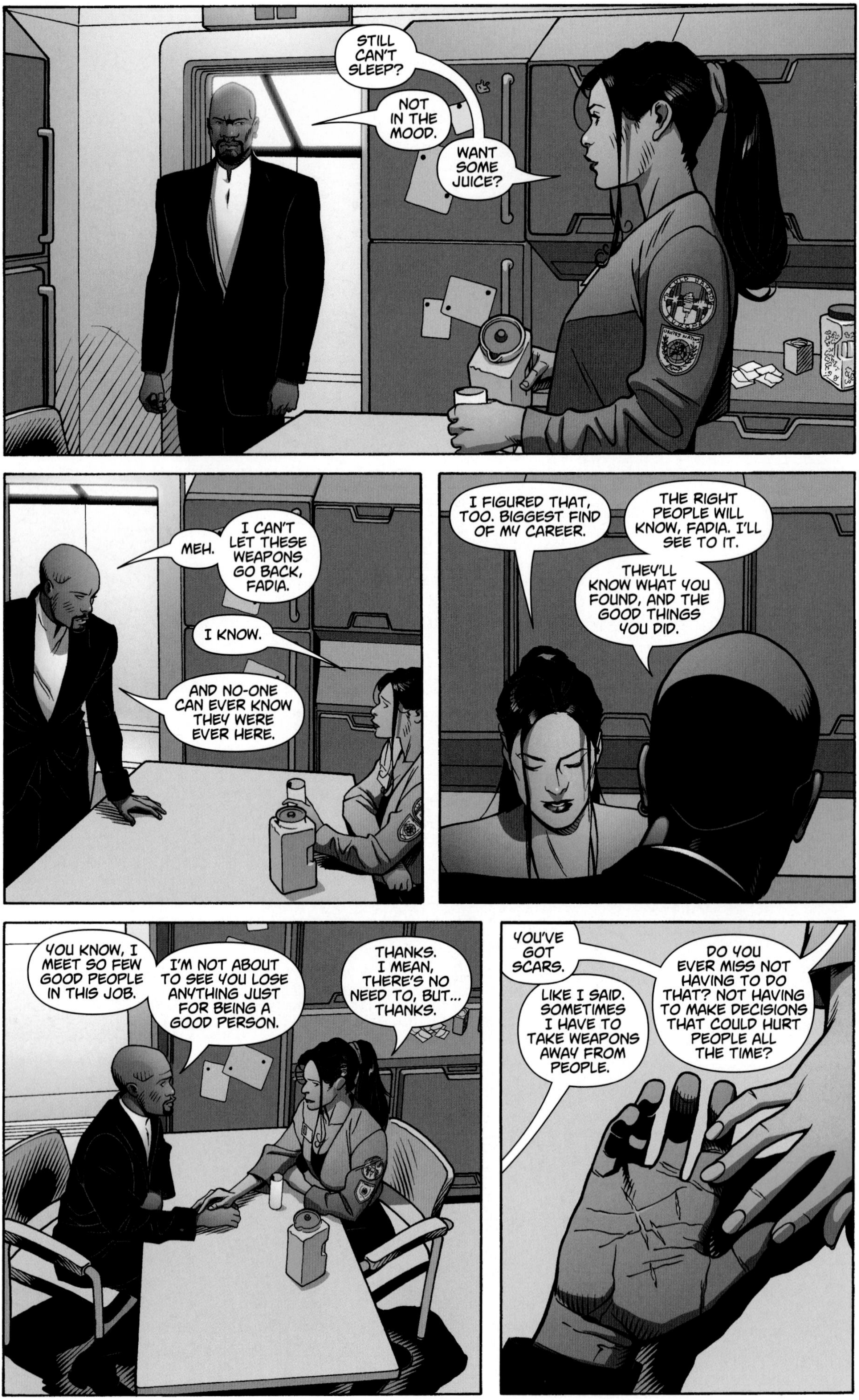
STILL CAN'T SLEEP?
NOT IN THE MOOD.
WANT SOME JUICE?
MEH.
I CAN'T LET THESE WEAPONS GO BACK, FADIA.
I KNOW.
AND NO-ONE CAN EVER KNOW THEY WERE EVER HERE.
I FIGURED THAT, TOO. BIGGEST FIND OF MY CAREER.
THE RIGHT PEOPLE WILL KNOW, FADIA. I'LL SEE TO IT.
THEY'LL KNOW WHAT YOU FOUND, AND THE GOOD THINGS YOU DID.
YOU KNOW, I MEET SO FEW GOOD PEOPLE IN THIS JOB.
I'M NOT ABOUT TO SEE YOU LOSE ANYTHING JUST FOR BEING A GOOD PERSON.
THANKS. I MEAN, THERE'S NO NEED TO, BUT... THANKS.
YOU'VE GOT SCARS.
LIKE I SAID. SOMETIMES I HAVE TO TAKE WEAPONS AWAY FROM PEOPLE.
DO YOU EVER MISS NOT HAVING TO DO THAT? NOT HAVING TO MAKE DECISIONS THAT COULD HURT PEOPLE ALL THE TIME?

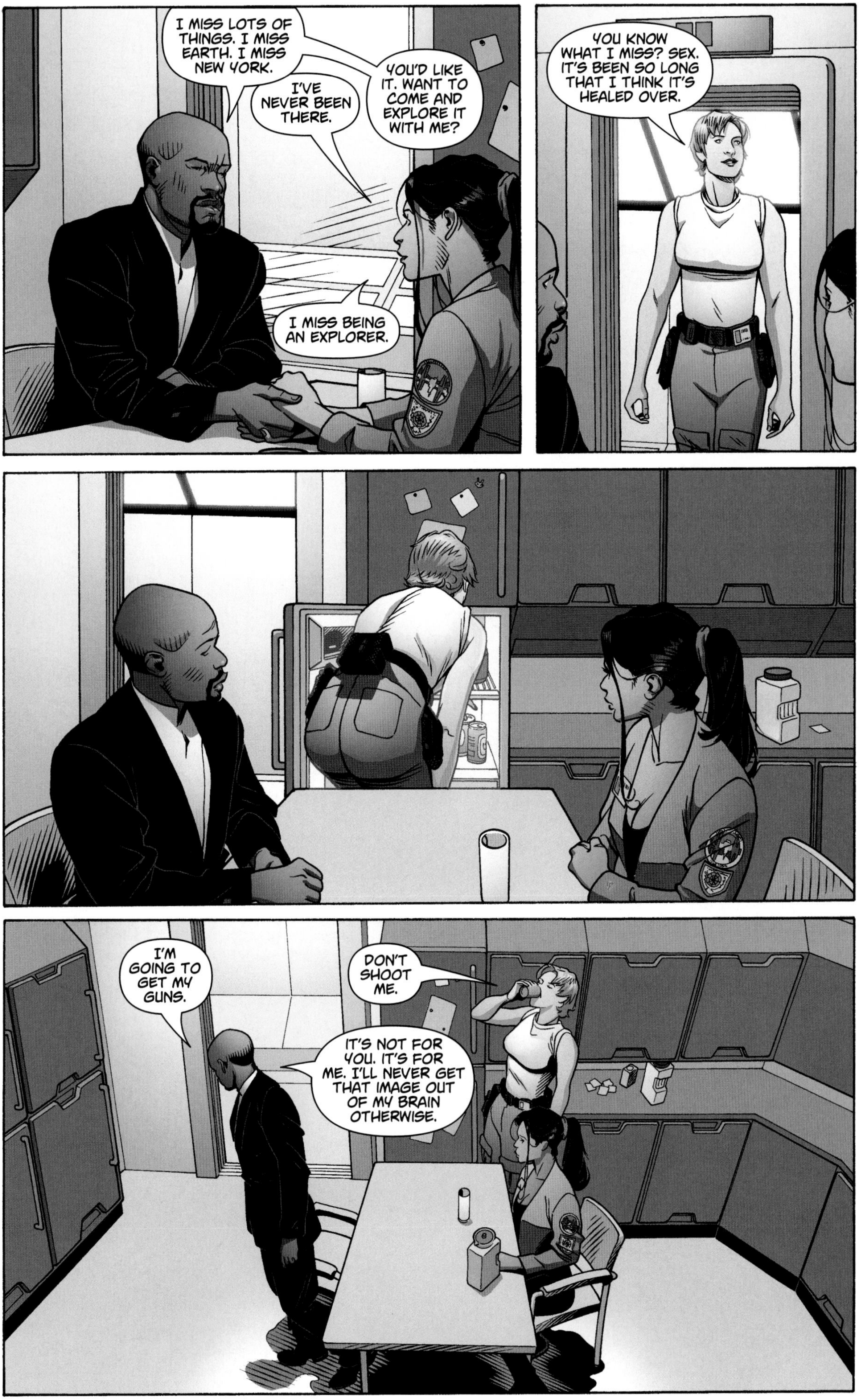
I MISS LOTS OF THINGS. I MISS EARTH. I MISS NEW YORK.
I'VE NEVER BEEN THERE.
YOU'D LIKE IT. WANT TO COME AND EXPLORE IT WITH ME?
I MISS BEING AN EXPLORER.
YOU KNOW WHAT I MISS? SEX. IT'S BEEN SO LONG THAT I THINK IT'S HEALED OVER.
I'M GOING TO GET MY GUNS.
DON'T SHOOT ME.
IT'S NOT FOR YOU. IT'S FOR ME. I'LL NEVER GET THAT IMAGE OUT OF MY BRAIN OTHERWISE.

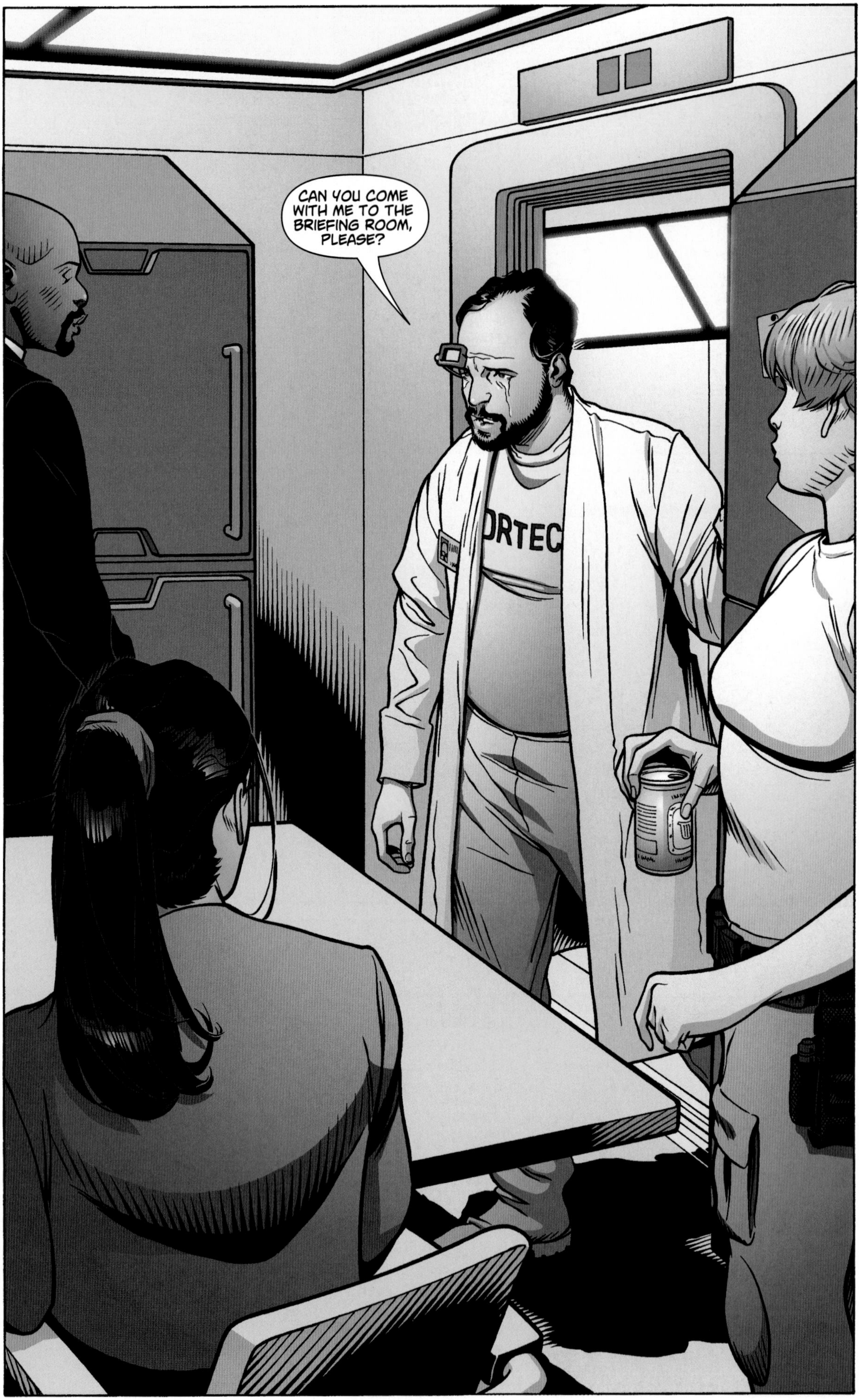
CAN YOU COME WITH ME TO THE BRIEFING ROOM, PLEASE?
ORTEC

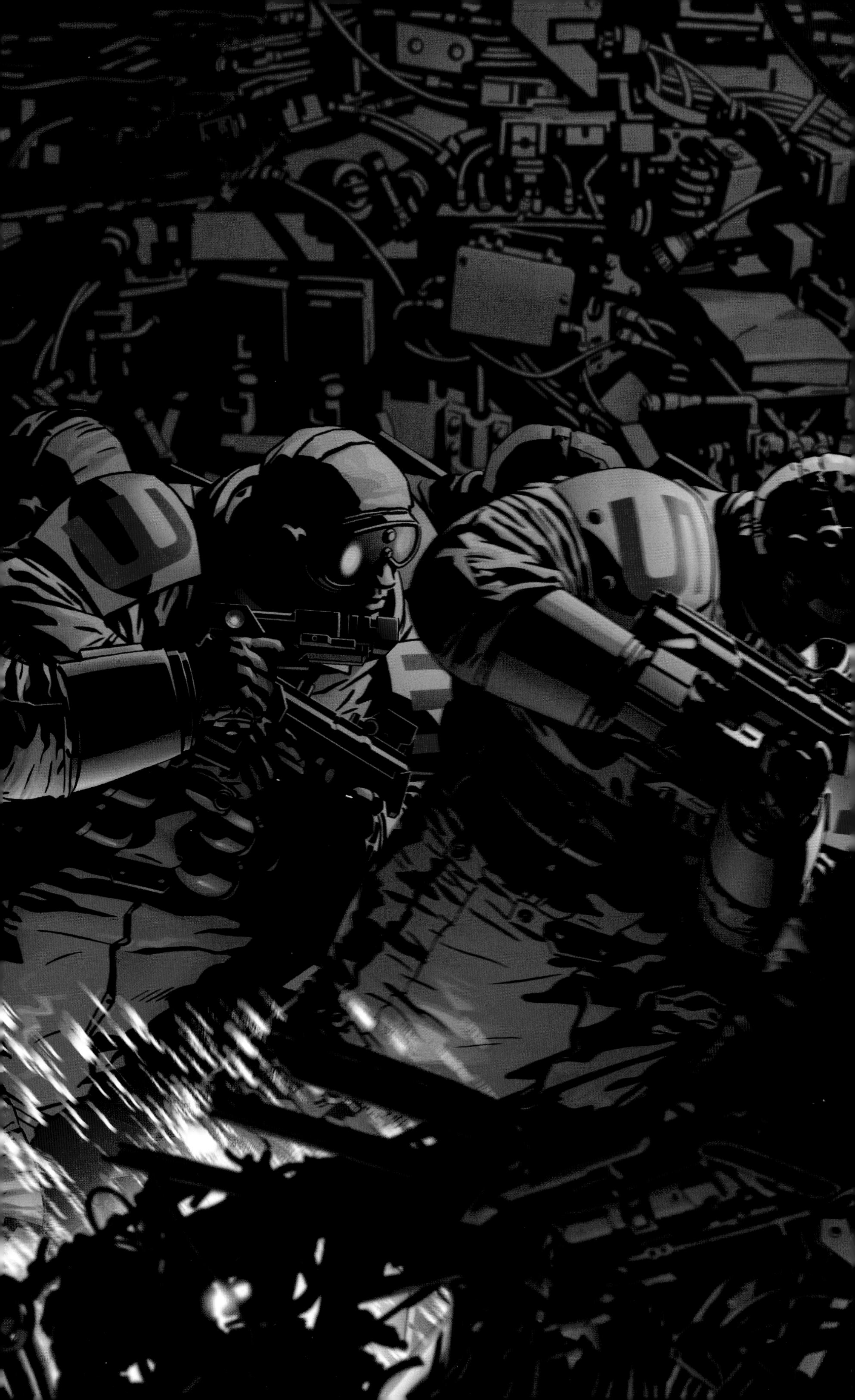

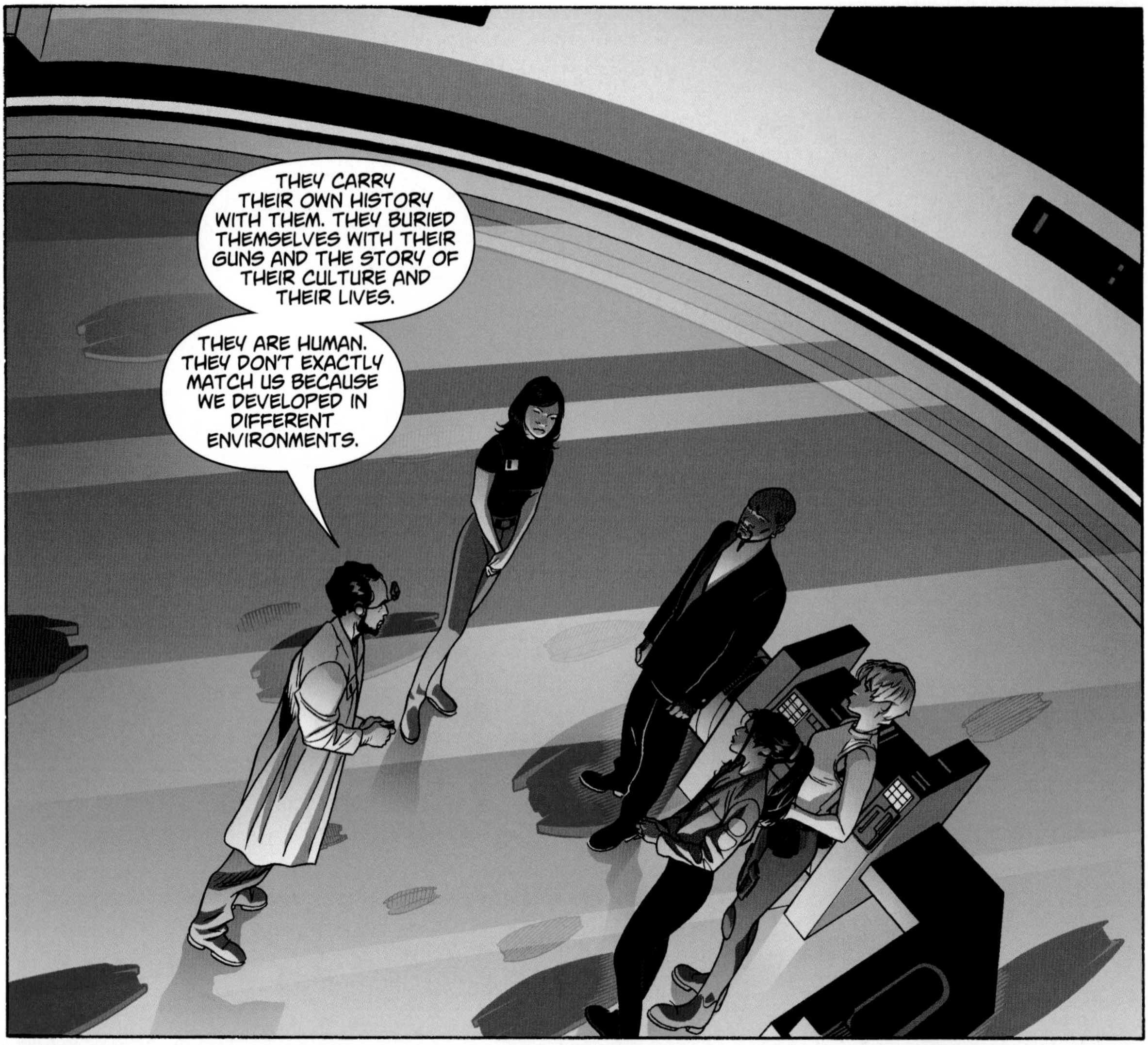
THEY CARRY THEIR OWN HISTORY WITH THEM. THEY BURIED THEMSELVES WITH THEIR GUNS AND THE STORY OF THEIR CULTURE AND THEIR LIVES.
THEY ARE HUMAN. THEY DON'T EXACTLY MATCH US BECAUSE WE DEVELOPED IN DIFFERENT ENVIRONMENTS.

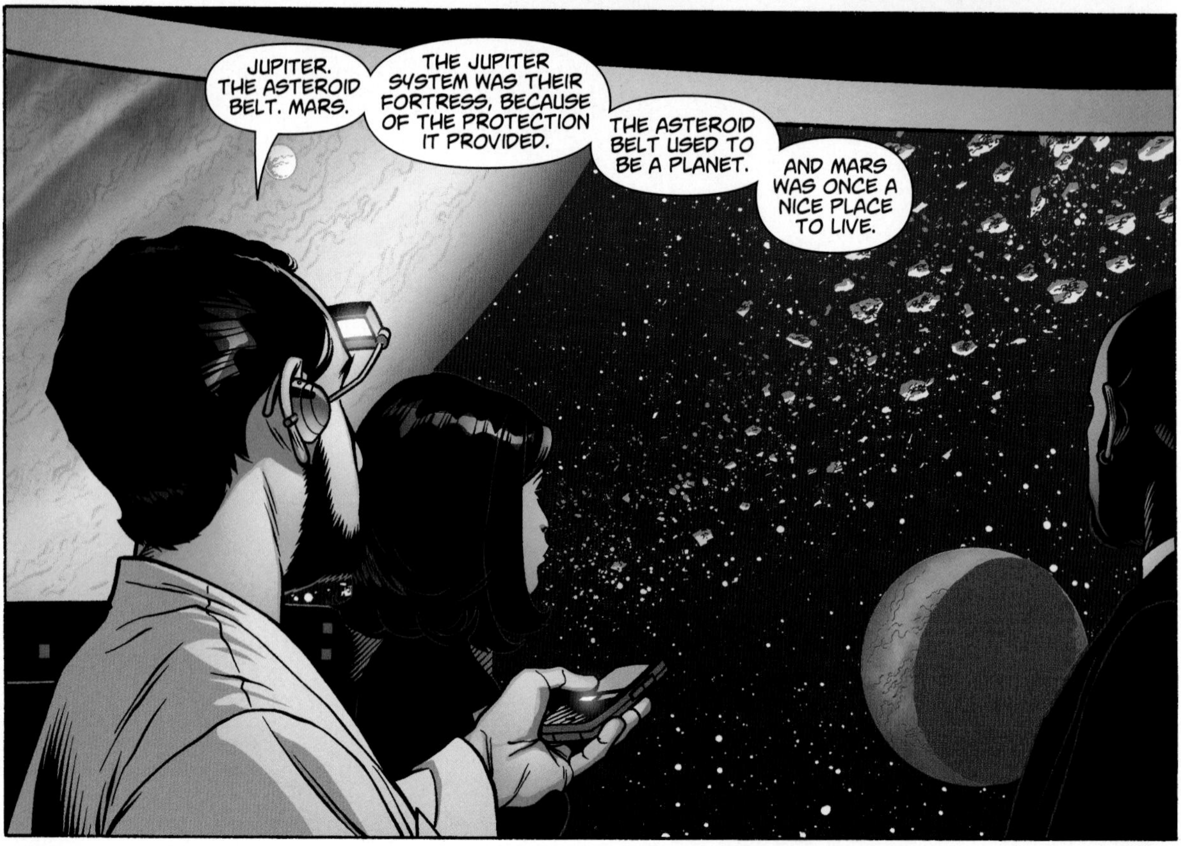
JUPITER. THE ASTEROID BELT. MARS.
THE JUPITER SYSTEM WAS THEIR FORTRESS, BECAUSE OF THE PROTECTION IT PROVIDED.
THE ASTEROID BELT USED TO BE A PLANET.
AND MARS WAS ONCE A NICE PLACE TO LIVE.

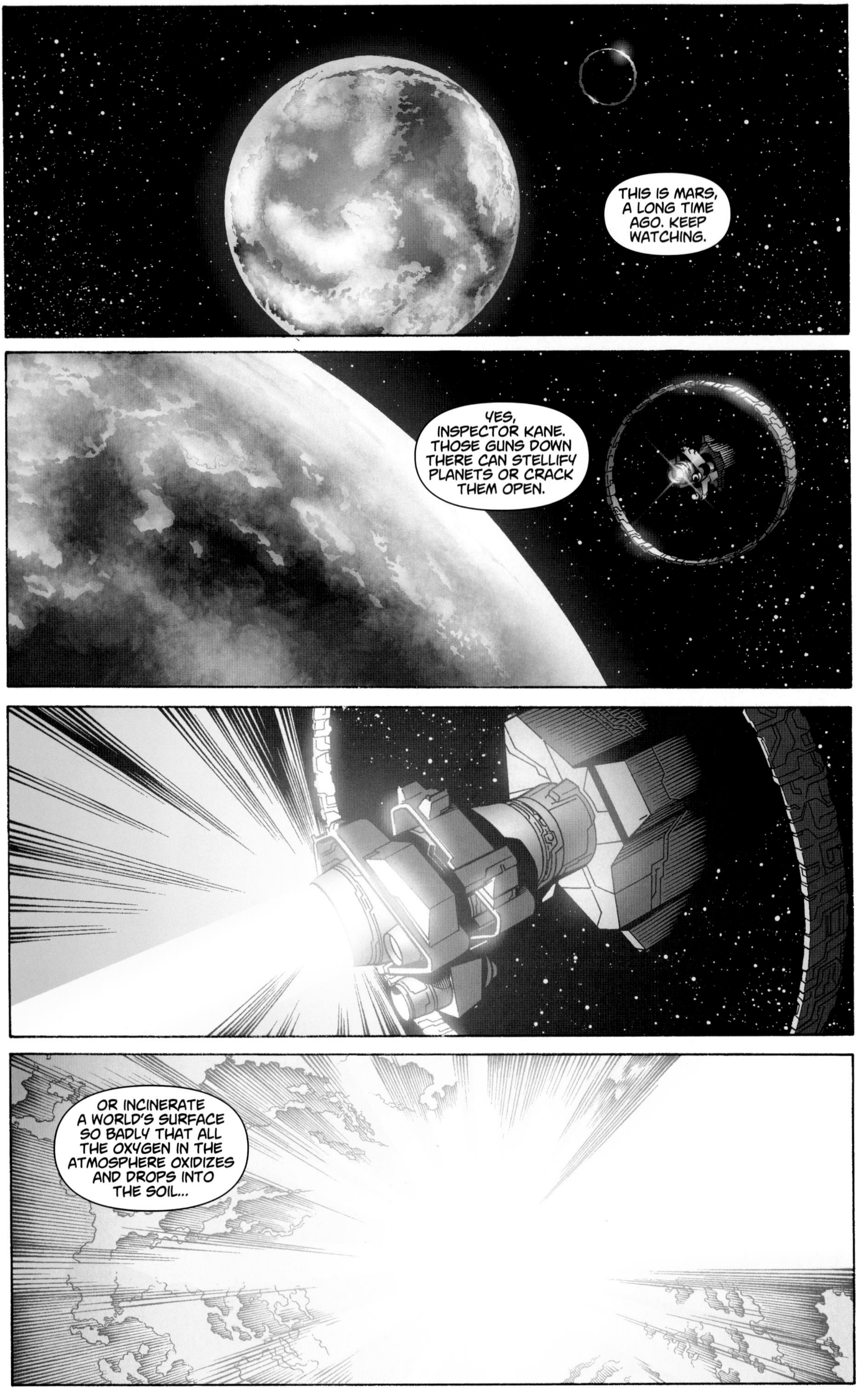
THIS IS MARS, A LONG TIME AGO. KEEP WATCHING.
YES, INSPECTOR KANE. THOSE GUNS DOWN THERE CAN STELLIFY PLANETS OR CRACK THEM OPEN.
OR INCINERATE A WORLD'S SURFACE SO BADLY THAT ALL THE OXYGEN IN THE ATMOSPHERE OXIDIZES AND DROPS INTO THE SOIL...

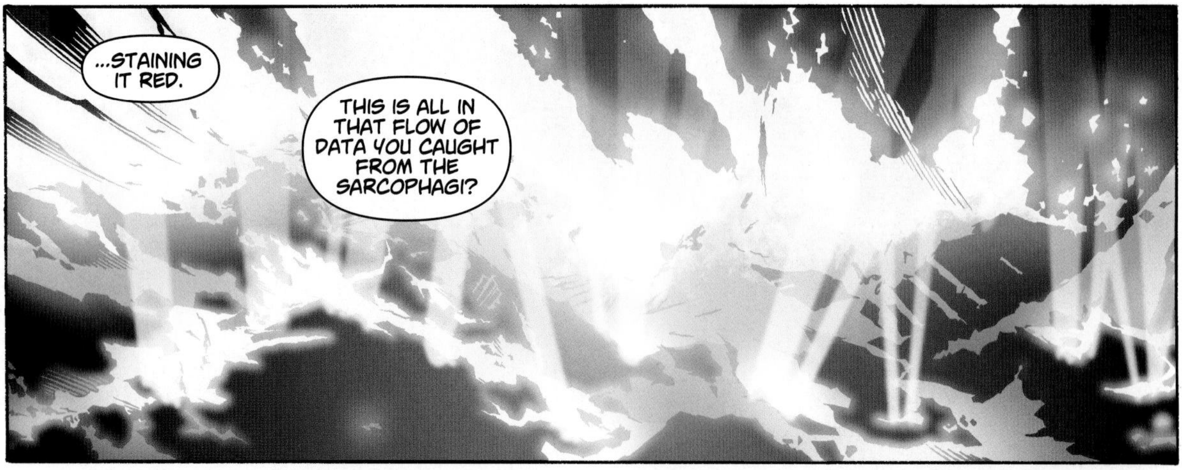
...STAINING IT RED.
THIS IS ALL IN THAT FLOW OF DATA YOU CAUGHT FROM THE SARCOPHAGI?

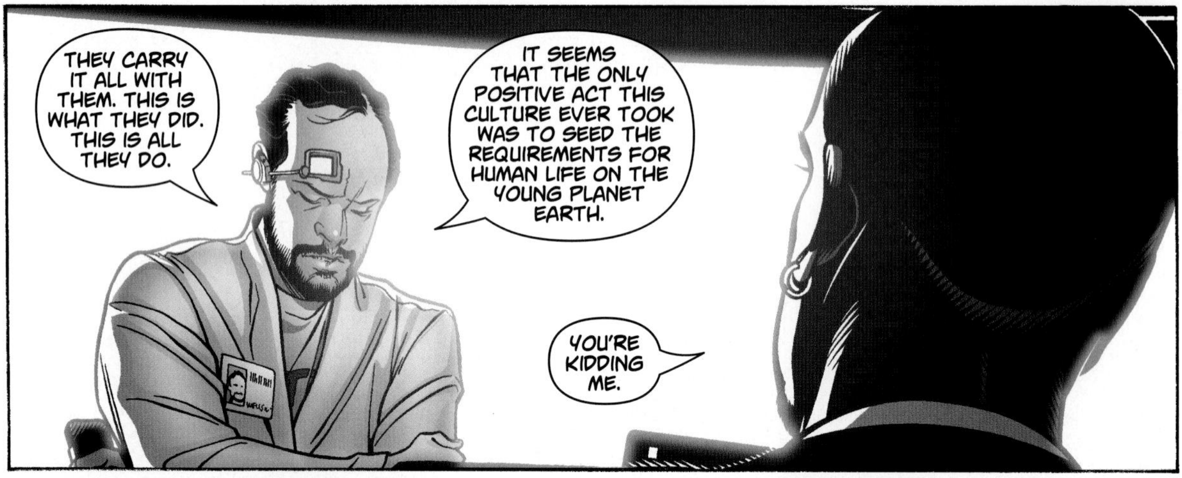
THEY CARRY IT ALL WITH THEM. THIS IS WHAT THEY DID. THIS IS ALL THEY DO.
IT SEEMS THAT THE ONLY POSITIVE ACT THIS CULTURE EVER TOOK WAS TO SEED THE REQUIREMENTS FOR HUMAN LIFE ON THE YOUNG PLANET EARTH.
YOU'RE KIDDING ME.

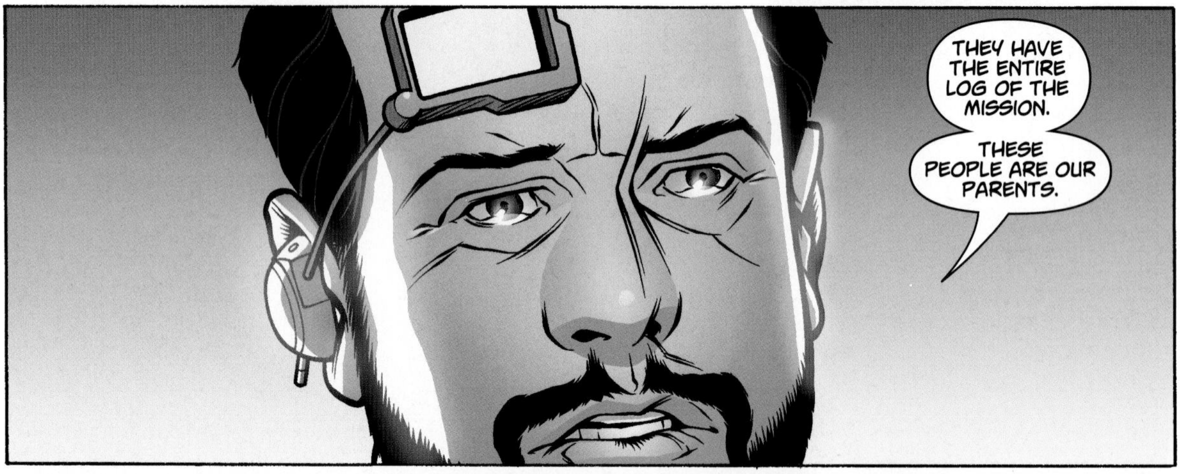
THEY HAVE THE ENTIRE LOG OF THE MISSION.
THESE PEOPLE ARE OUR PARENTS.

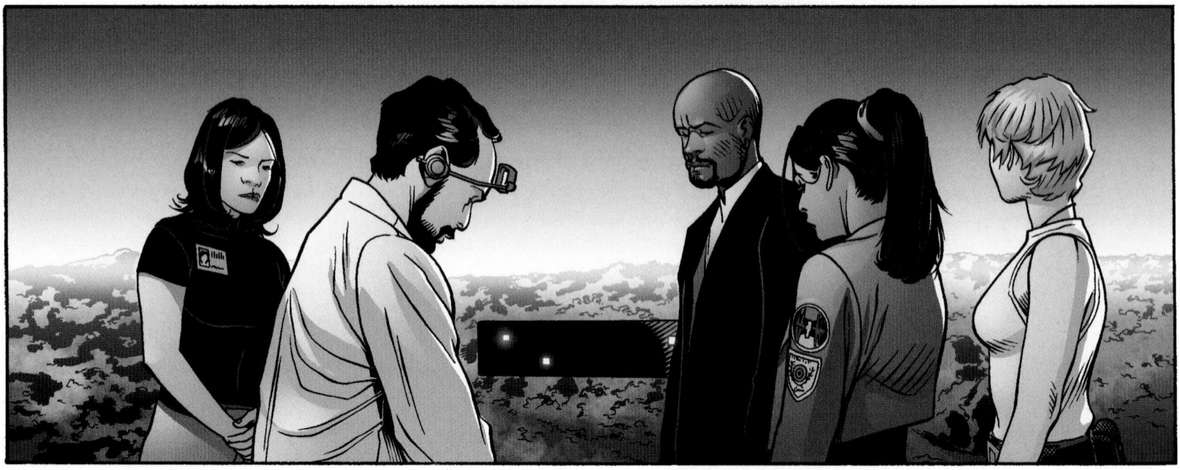

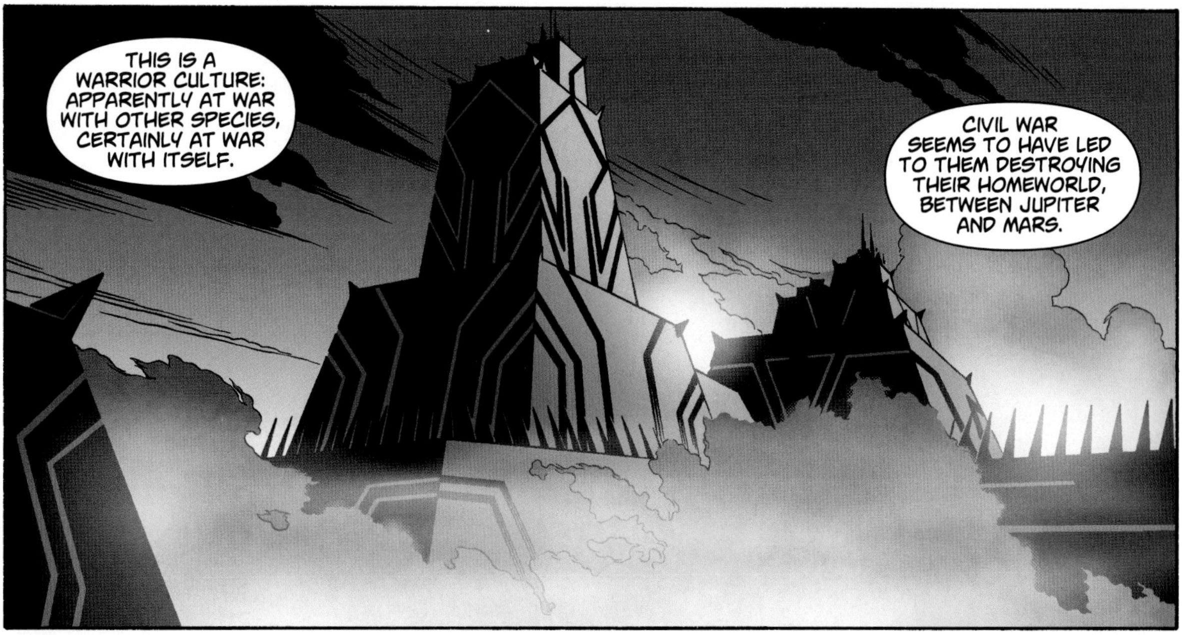
THIS IS A WARRIOR CULTURE: APPARENTLY AT WAR WITH OTHER SPECIES, CERTAINLY AT WAR WITH ITSELF.
CIVIL WAR SEEMS TO HAVE LED TO THEM DESTROYING THEIR HOMEWORLD, BETWEEN JUPITER AND MARS.
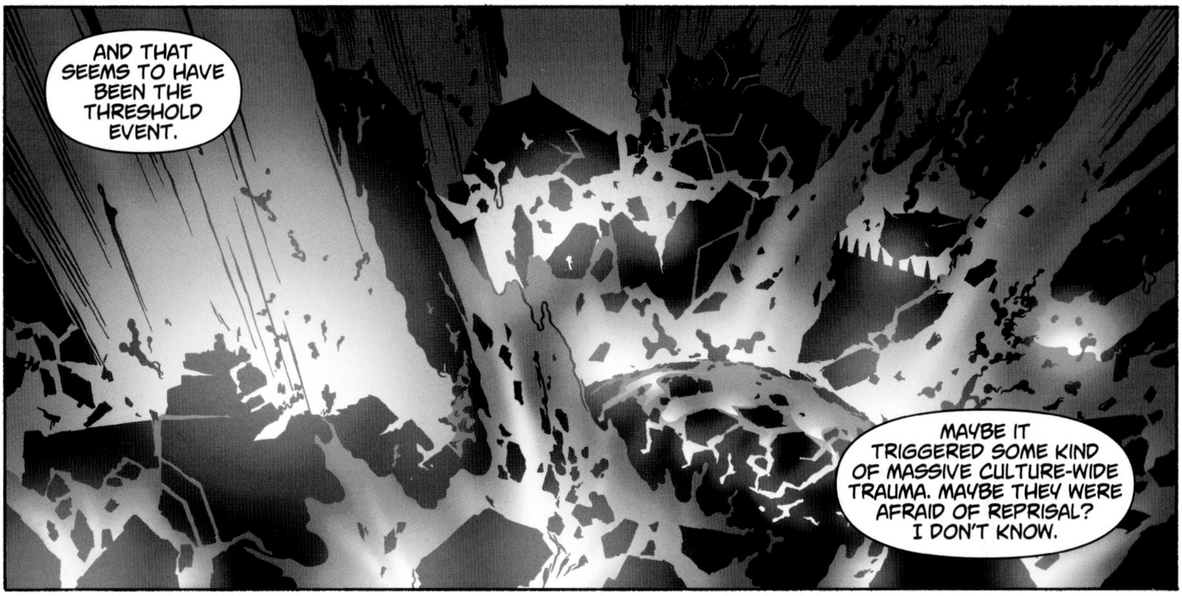
AND THAT SEEMS TO HAVE BEEN THE THRESHOLD EVENT.
MAYBE IT TRIGGERED SOME KIND OF MASSIVE CULTURE-WIDE TRAUMA. MAYBE THEY WERE AFRAID OF REPRISAL? I DON'T KNOW.
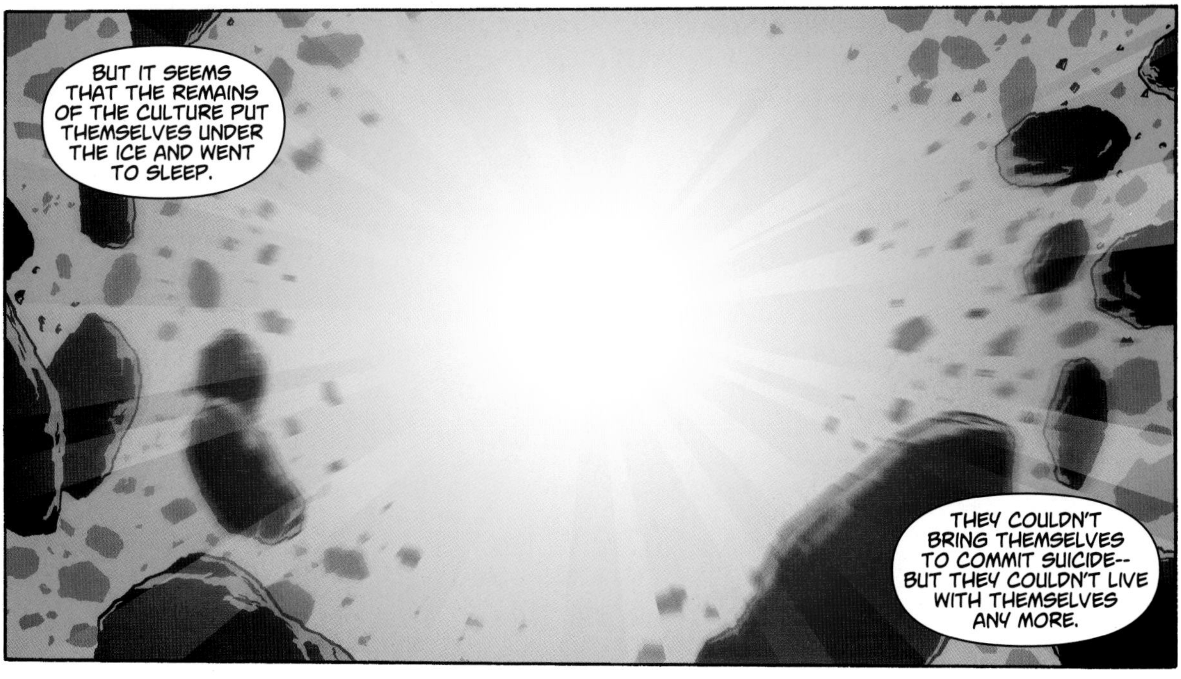
BUT IT SEEMS THAT THE REMAINS OF THE CULTURE PUT THEMSELVES UNDER THE ICE AND WENT TO SLEEP.
THEY COULDN'T BRING THEMSELVES TO COMMIT SUICIDE-- BUT THEY COULDN'T LIVE WITH THEMSELVES ANY MORE.

YOU KNOW WHAT BOTHERS ME MOST? WHATEVER'S IN THEM IS IN US. WE ARE THEIR CHILDREN.

WELL, I GUESS WHAT THEY SAY IS TRUE. YOU DON'T GET TO CHOOSE YOUR FAMILY.

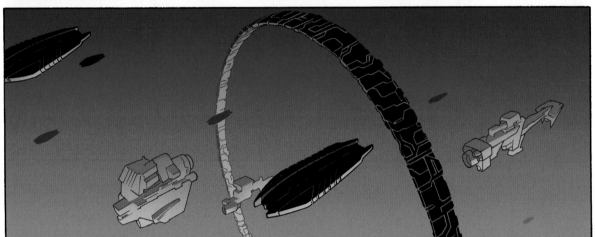

DAMN. MY STATION, RIGHT NOW.

WHAT'S HAPPENING?

THE TORUS JUST DEVELOPED A POWER FIELD.

IT MUST BE HOOKED INTO THE OVERALL POWER-UP SEQUENCE.

TALK TO ME. WHAT'S IT DOING?

OH, THIS IS GOOD.

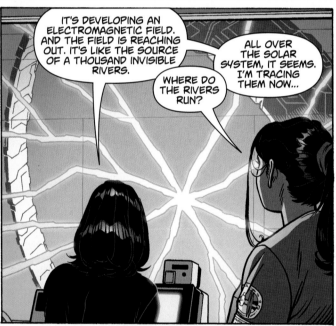

IT'S DEVELOPING AN ELECTROMAGNETIC FIELD. AND THE FIELD IS REACHING OUT. IT'S LIKE THE SOURCE OF A THOUSAND INVISIBLE RIVERS.

ALL OVER THE SOLAR SYSTEM, IT SEEMS. I'M TRACING THEM NOW...

WHERE DO THE RIVERS RUN?

ALL OVER? YOU HAVE NO IDEA HOW MUCH I HATE THE SOUND OF THAT.

WITH GOOD REASON, INSPECTOR KANE. AT LEAST ONE OF THEM REACHES OUT TO TRANSLUNAR SPACE--

--WITHIN A QUARTER MILLION MILES OF EARTH.

LI, ANNA

PROGRAMMED ALERT ONE TRIGGERED.

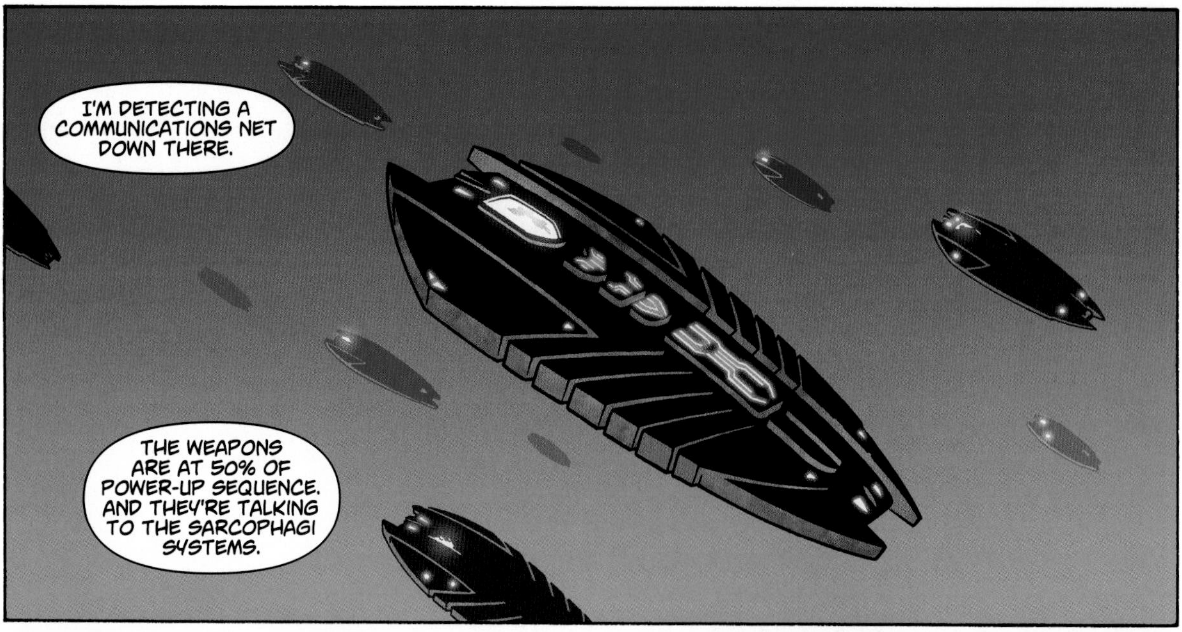
I'M DETECTING A COMMUNICATIONS NET DOWN THERE.
THE WEAPONS ARE AT 50% OF POWER-UP SEQUENCE. AND THEY'RE TALKING TO THE SARCOPHAGI SYSTEMS.

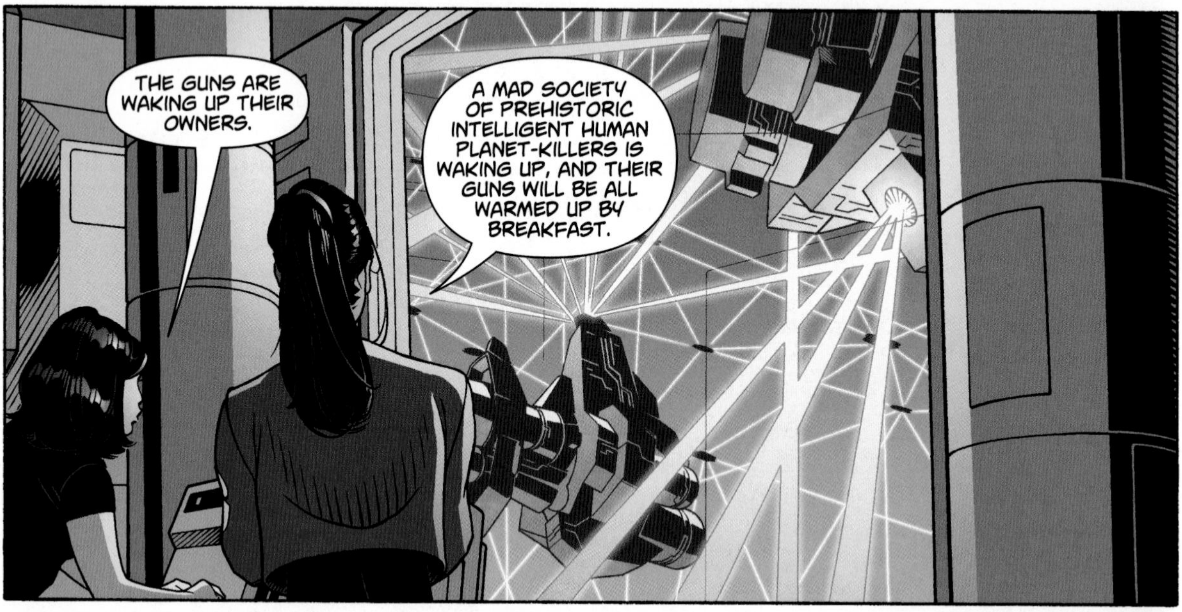
THE GUNS ARE WAKING UP THEIR OWNERS.
A MAD SOCIETY OF PREHISTORIC INTELLIGENT HUMAN PLANET-KILLERS IS WAKING UP, AND THEIR GUNS WILL BE ALL WARMED UP BY BREAKFAST.

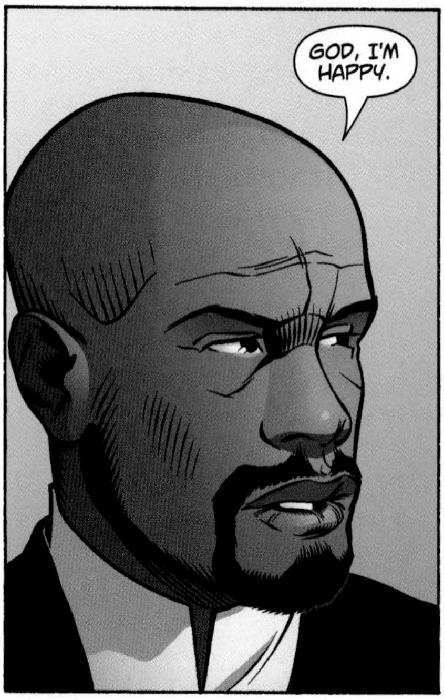
GOD, I'M HAPPY.

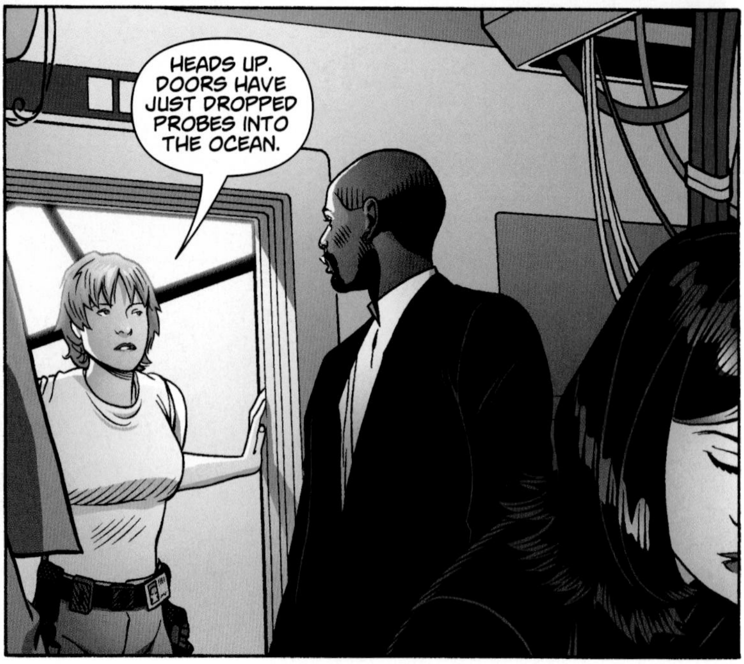
HEADS UP. DOORS HAVE JUST DROPPED PROBES INTO THE OCEAN.

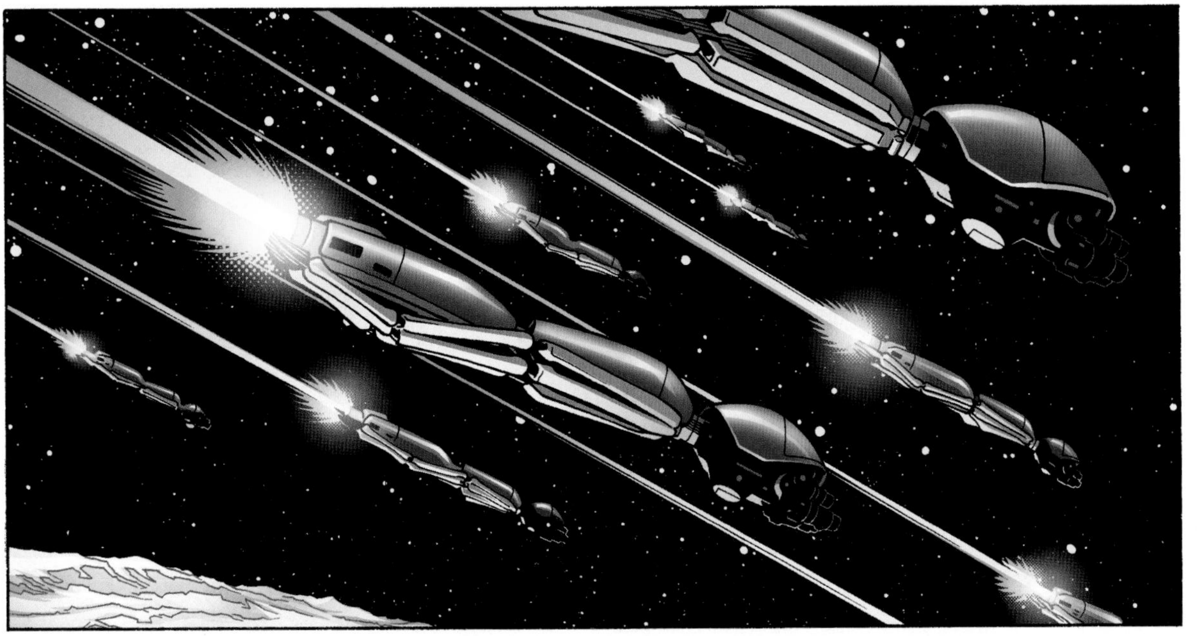

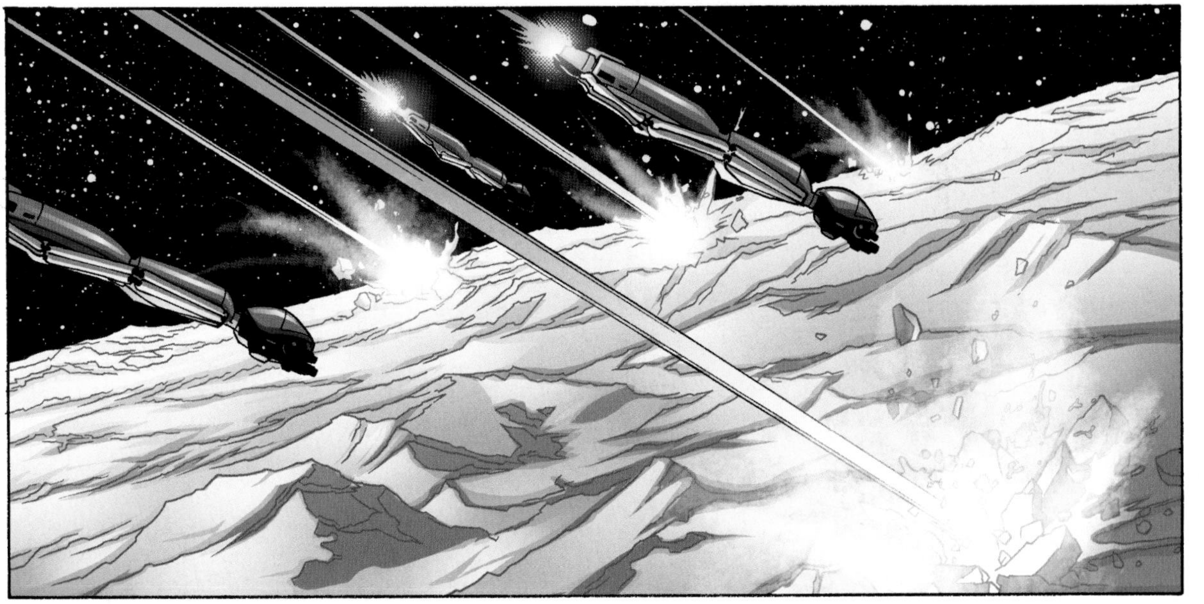

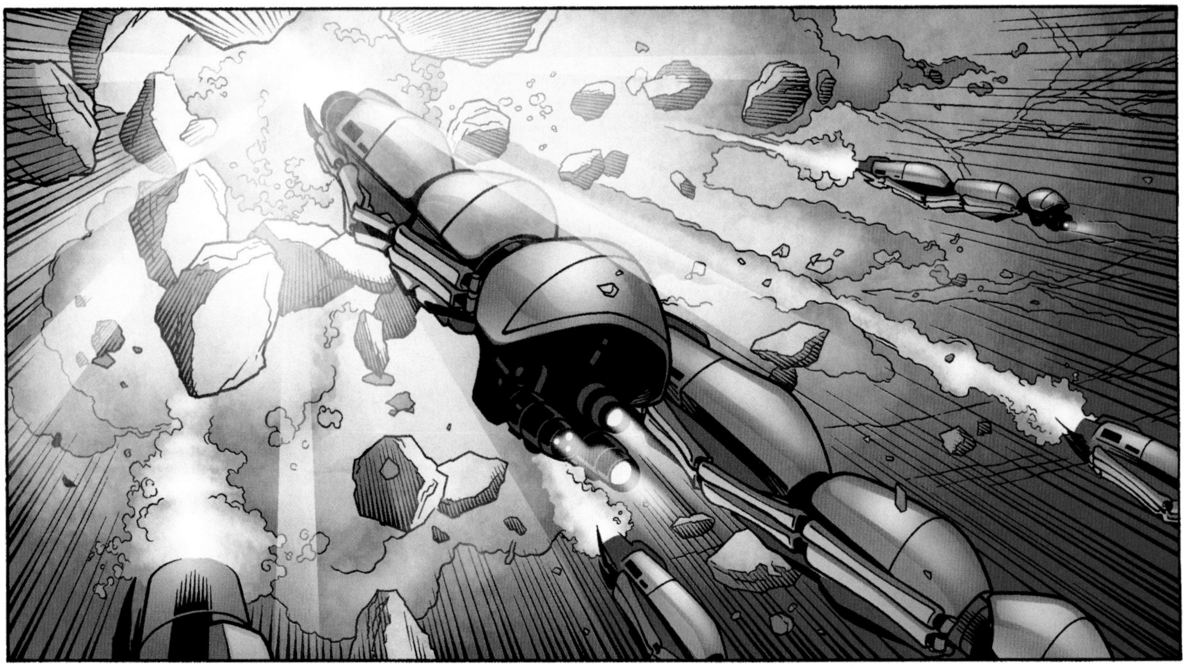

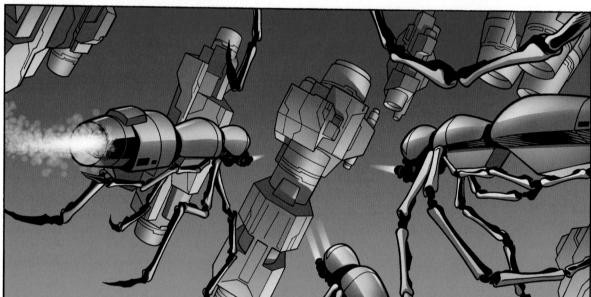

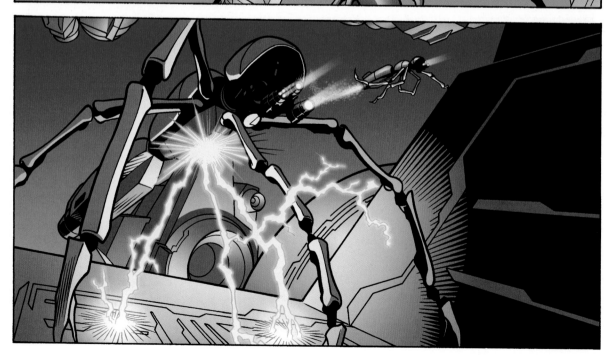

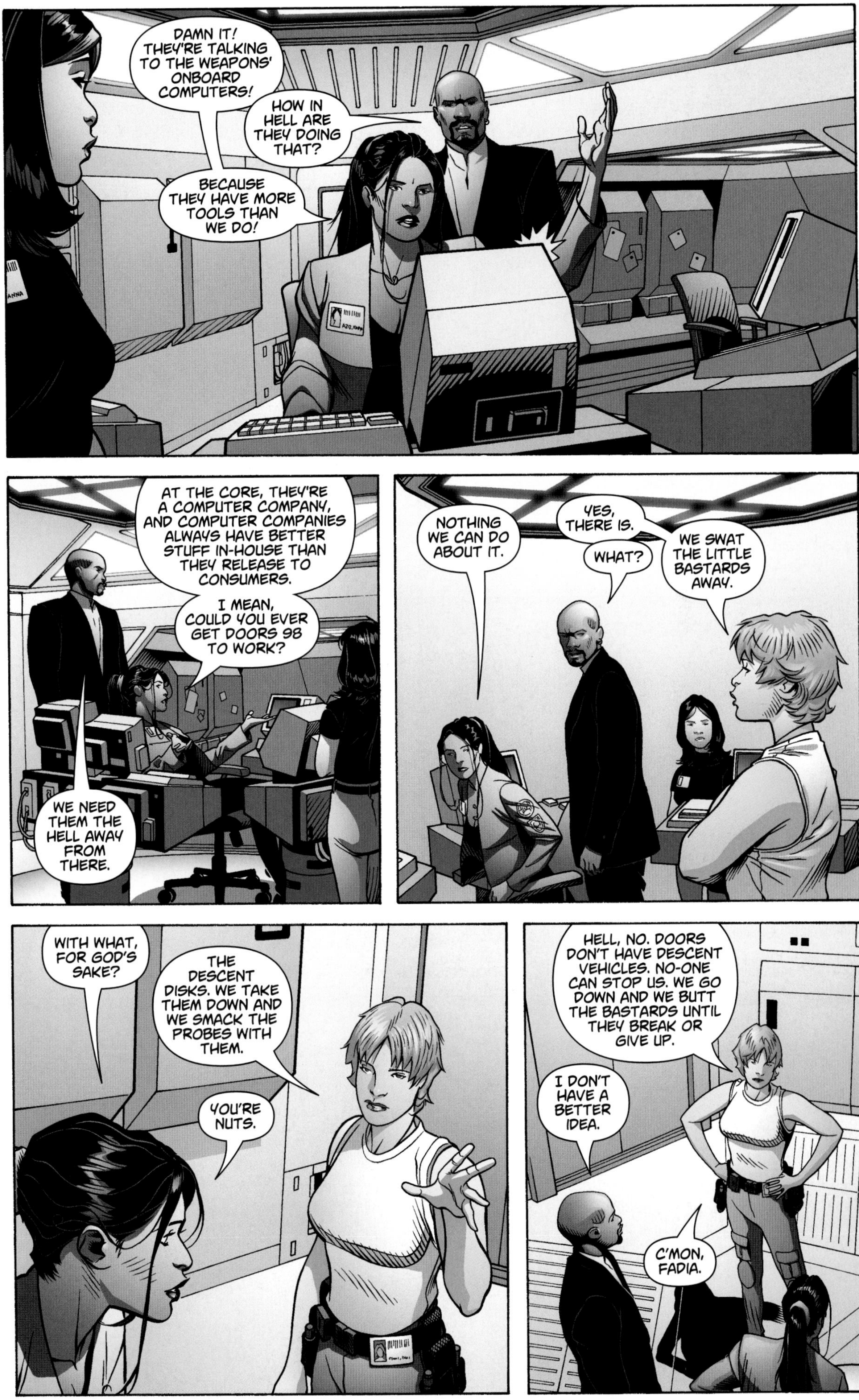
DAMN IT! THEY'RE TALKING TO THE WEAPONS' ONBOARD COMPUTERS!
HOW IN HELL ARE THEY DOING THAT?
BECAUSE THEY HAVE MORE TOOLS THAN WE DO!
AT THE CORE, THEY'RE A COMPUTER COMPANY, AND COMPUTER COMPANIES ALWAYS HAVE BETTER STUFF IN-HOUSE THAN THEY RELEASE TO CONSUMERS.
I MEAN, COULD YOU EVER GET DOORS 98 TO WORK?
WE NEED THEM THE HELL AWAY FROM THERE.
NOTHING WE CAN DO ABOUT IT.
YES, THERE IS.
WHAT?
WE SWAT THE LITTLE BASTARDS AWAY.
WITH WHAT, FOR GOD'S SAKE?
THE DESCENT DISKS. WE TAKE THEM DOWN AND WE SMACK THE PROBES WITH THEM.
YOU'RE NUTS.
HELL, NO. DOORS DON'T HAVE DESCENT VEHICLES. NO-ONE CAN STOP US. WE GO DOWN AND WE BUTT THE BASTARDS UNTIL THEY BREAK OR GIVE UP.
I DON'T HAVE A BETTER IDEA.
C'MON, FADIA.

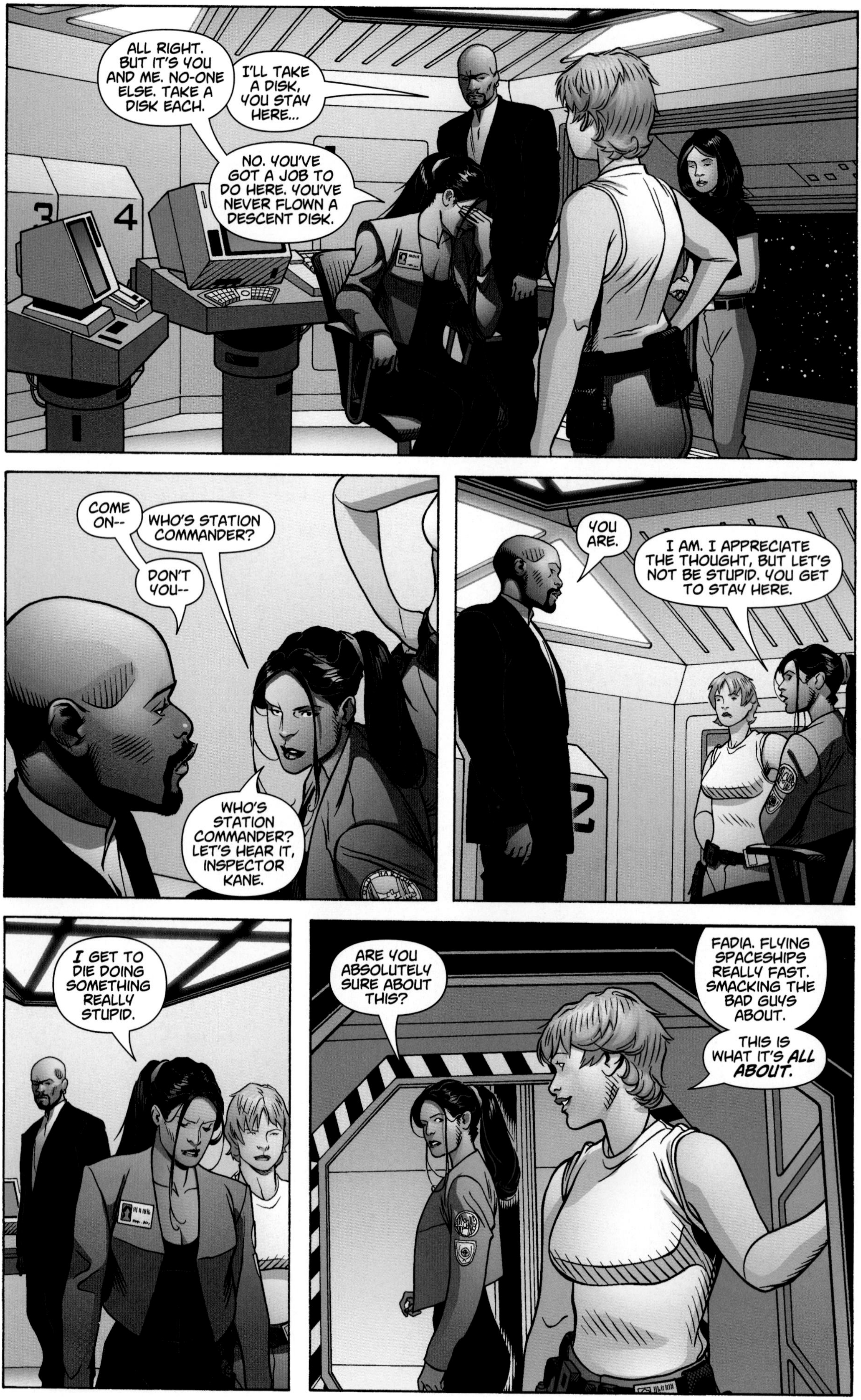
ALL RIGHT. BUT IT'S YOU AND ME. NO-ONE ELSE. TAKE A DISK EACH.
I'LL TAKE A DISK, YOU STAY HERE...
NO. YOU'VE GOT A JOB TO DO HERE. YOU'VE NEVER FLOWN A DESCENT DISK.
COME ON--
WHO'S STATION COMMANDER?
DON'T YOU--
WHO'S STATION COMMANDER? LET'S HEAR IT, INSPECTOR KANE.
YOU ARE.
I AM. I APPRECIATE THE THOUGHT, BUT LET'S NOT BE STUPID. YOU GET TO STAY HERE.
I GET TO DIE DOING SOMETHING REALLY STUPID.
ARE YOU ABSOLUTELY SURE ABOUT THIS?
FADIA. FLYING SPACESHIPS REALLY FAST. SMACKING THE BAD GUYS ABOUT.
THIS IS WHAT IT'S ***ALL ABOUT.***

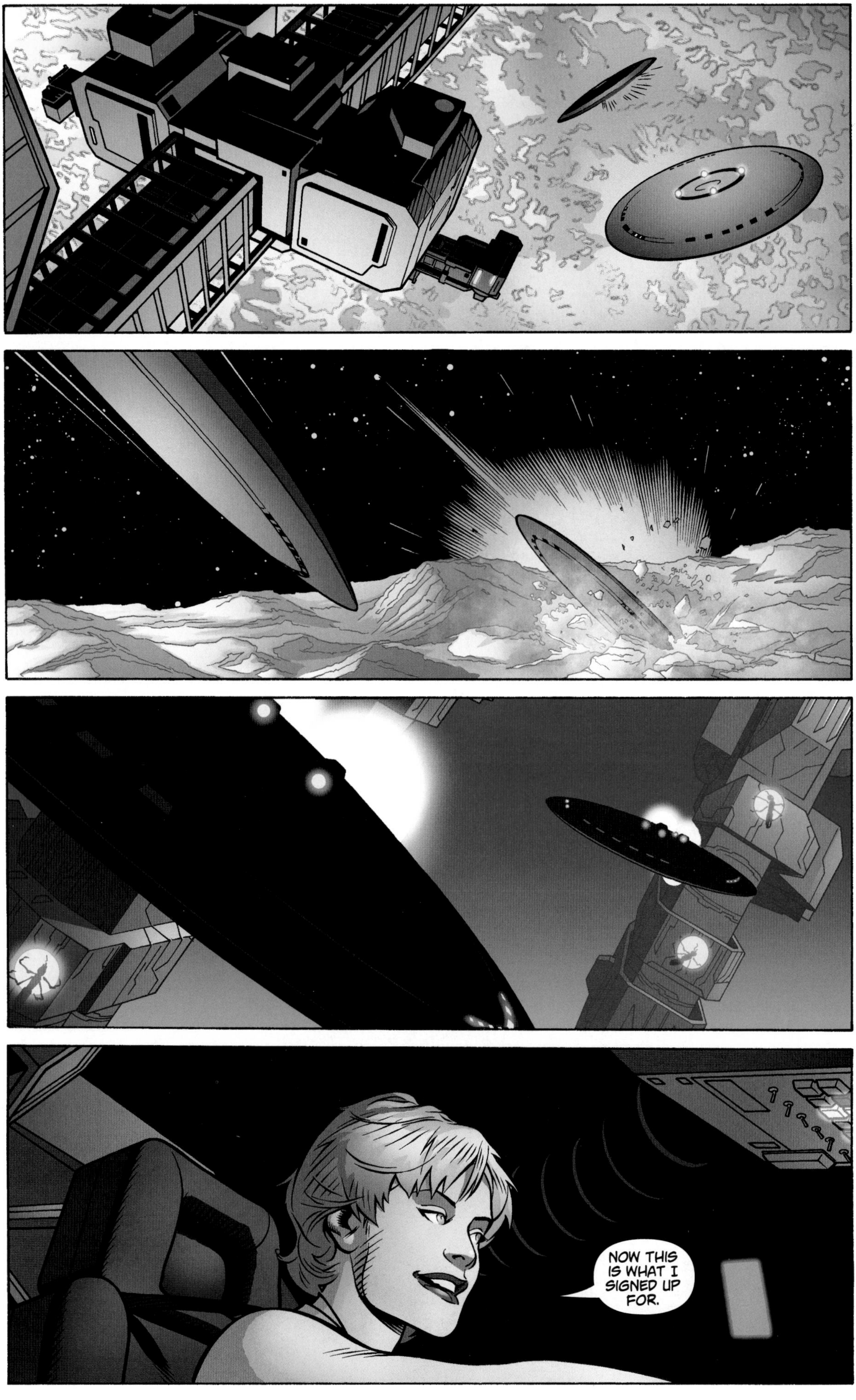
NOW THIS IS WHAT I SIGNED UP FOR.

ANNA, DO WE STILL HAVE OUR OWN PROBES DOWN THERE?

YES. WHY?

IF I CAN USE THEM TO HACK INTO ONE OF THEIR PROBES, I CAN RIDE THEIR COMMUNICATIONS BEAMS RIGHT INTO THE CONTROL SYSTEM OF ONE OF THOSE GUNS.

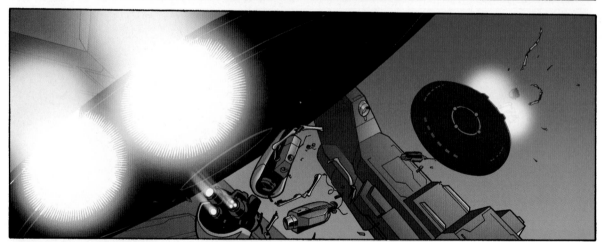

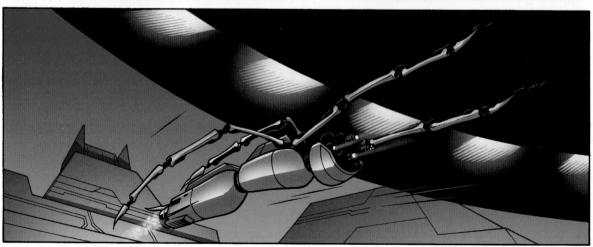

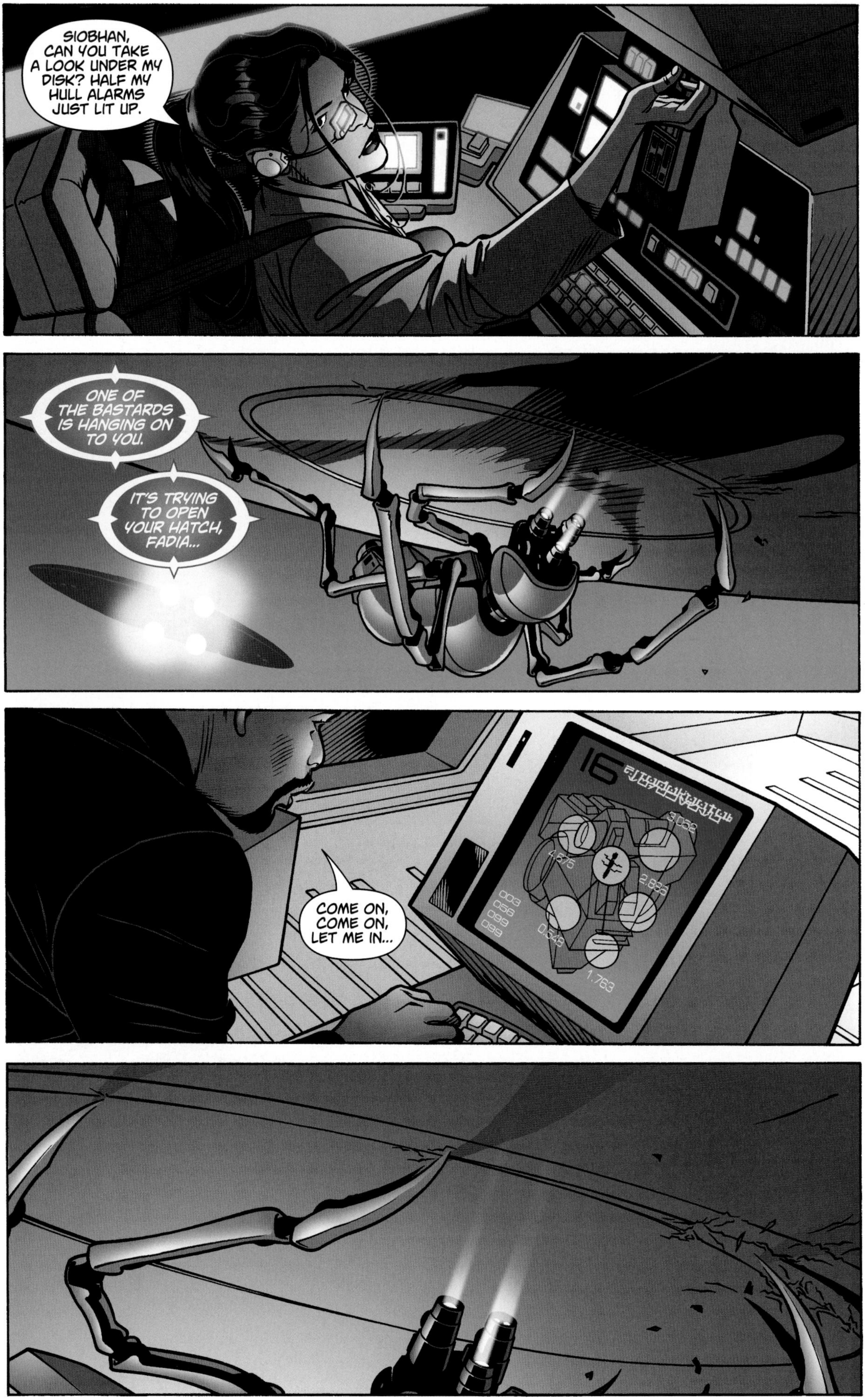
SIOBHAN, CAN YOU TAKE A LOOK UNDER MY DISK? HALF MY HULL ALARMS JUST LIT UP.
ONE OF THE BASTARDS IS HANGING ON TO YOU.
IT'S TRYING TO OPEN YOUR HATCH, FADIA...
COME ON, COME ON, LET ME IN...

RIGHT.
RUN COMMAND PROGRAM
KANE-1
SIOBHAN...
I'M ON IT.

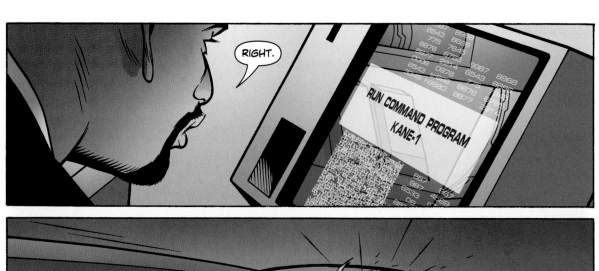

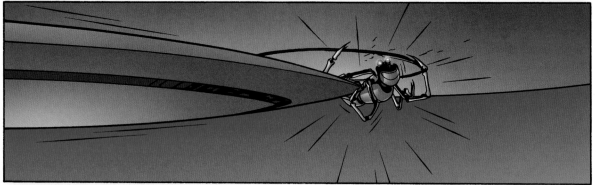

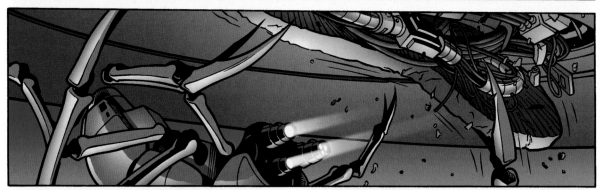

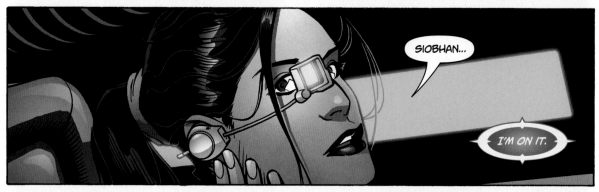

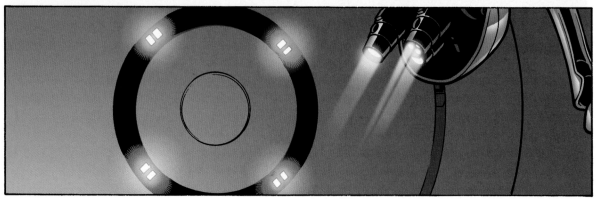

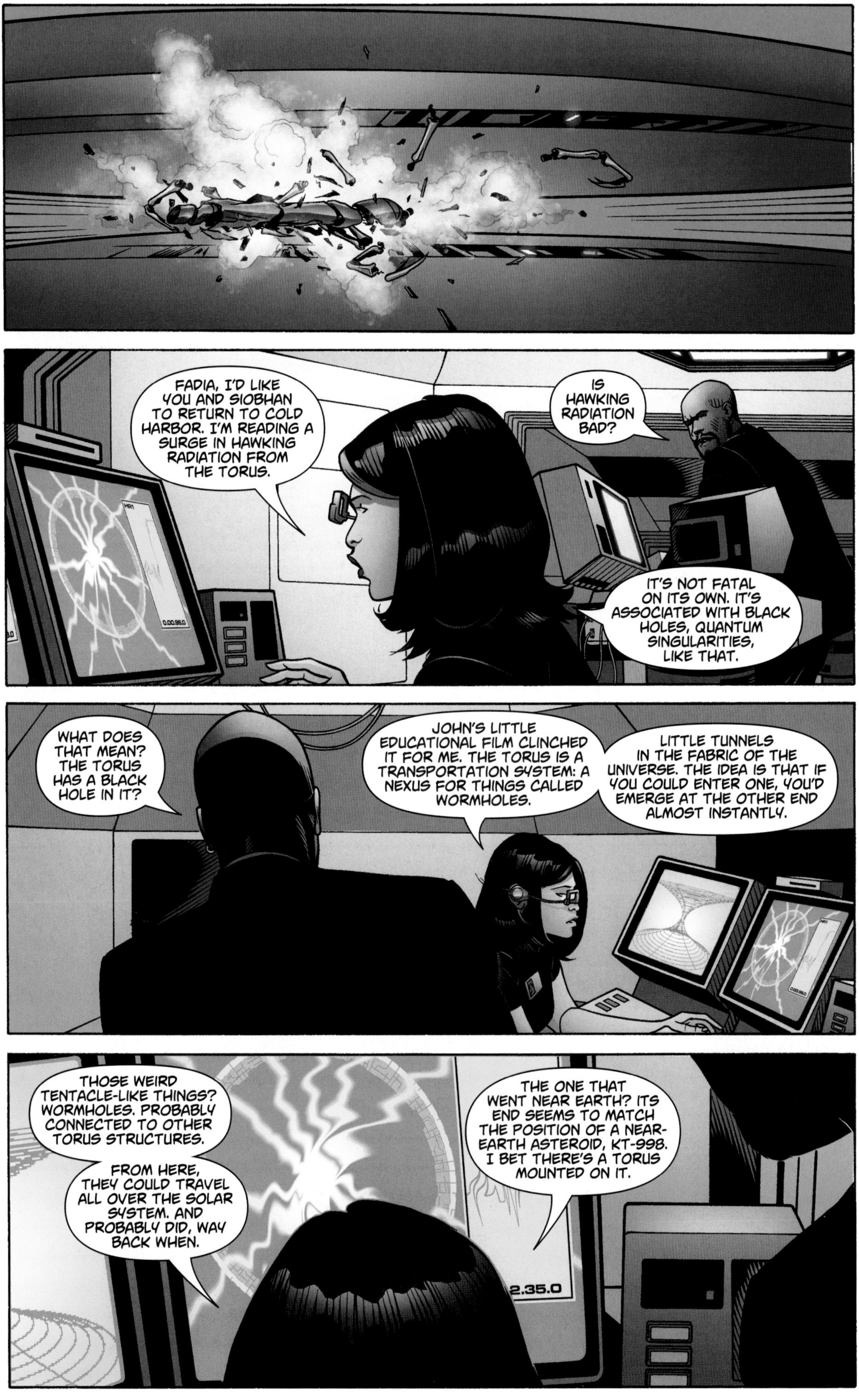
FADIA, I'D LIKE YOU AND SIOBHAN TO RETURN TO COLD HARBOR. I'M READING A SURGE IN HAWKING RADIATION FROM THE TORUS.
IS HAWKING RADIATION BAD?
IT'S NOT FATAL ON ITS OWN. IT'S ASSOCIATED WITH BLACK HOLES, QUANTUM SINGULARITIES, LIKE THAT.
WHAT DOES THAT MEAN? THE TORUS HAS A BLACK HOLE IN IT?
JOHN'S LITTLE EDUCATIONAL FILM CLINCHED IT FOR ME. THE TORUS IS A TRANSPORTATION SYSTEM: A NEXUS FOR THINGS CALLED WORMHOLES.
LITTLE TUNNELS IN THE FABRIC OF THE UNIVERSE. THE IDEA IS THAT IF YOU COULD ENTER ONE, YOU'D EMERGE AT THE OTHER END ALMOST INSTANTLY.
THOSE WEIRD TENTACLE-LIKE THINGS? WORMHOLES. PROBABLY CONNECTED TO OTHER TORUS STRUCTURES.
FROM HERE, THEY COULD TRAVEL ALL OVER THE SOLAR SYSTEM. AND PROBABLY DID, WAY BACK WHEN.
THE ONE THAT WENT NEAR EARTH? ITS END SEEMS TO MATCH THE POSITION OF A NEAR-EARTH ASTEROID, KT-998. I BET THERE'S A TORUS MOUNTED ON IT.
2.35.0

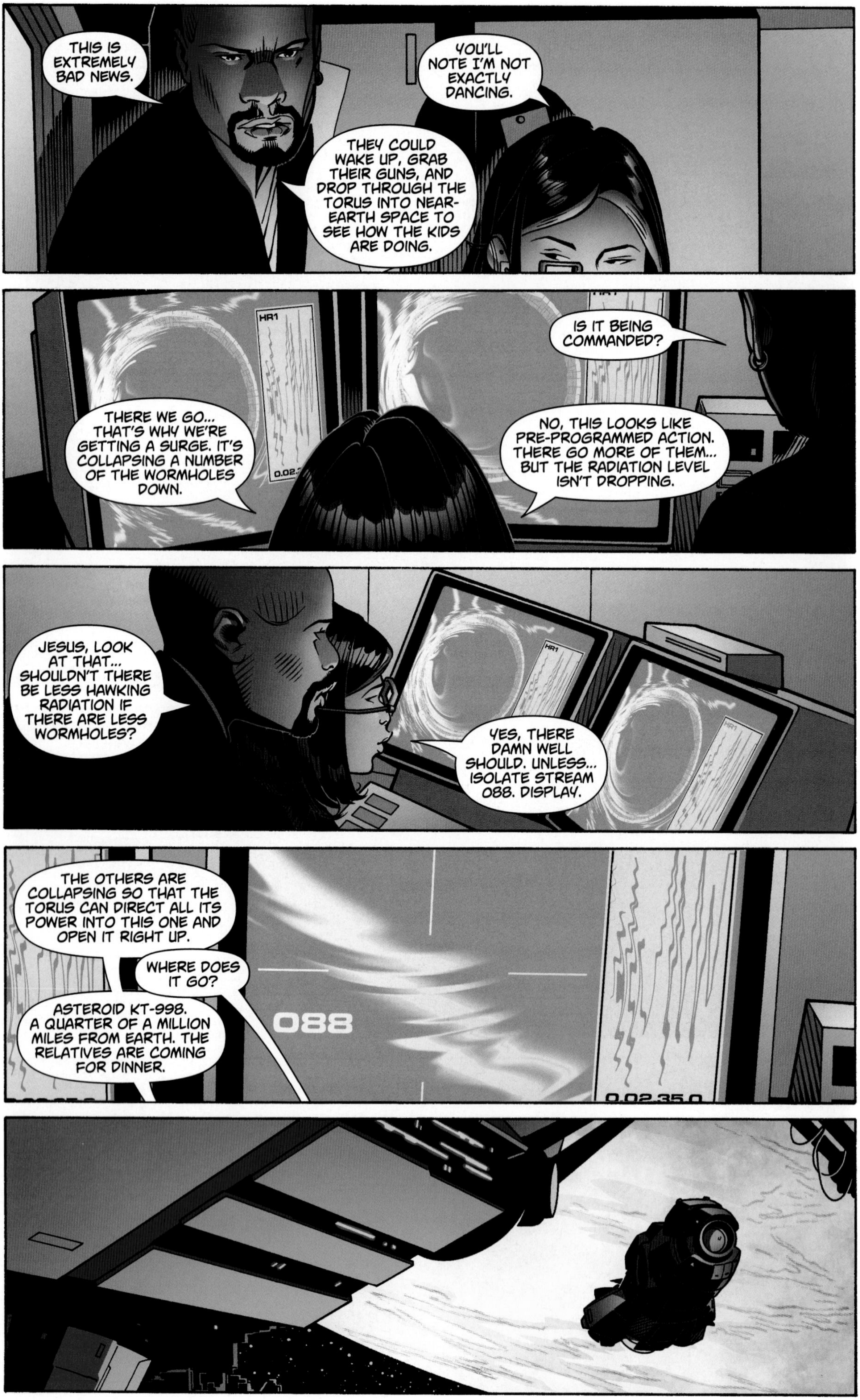
THIS IS EXTREMELY BAD NEWS.
YOU'LL NOTE I'M NOT EXACTLY DANCING.
THEY COULD WAKE UP, GRAB THEIR GUNS, AND DROP THROUGH THE TORUS INTO NEAR-EARTH SPACE TO SEE HOW THE KIDS ARE DOING.
IS IT BEING COMMANDED?
THERE WE GO... THAT'S WHY WE'RE GETTING A SURGE. IT'S COLLAPSING A NUMBER OF THE WORMHOLES DOWN.
NO, THIS LOOKS LIKE PRE-PROGRAMMED ACTION. THERE GO MORE OF THEM... BUT THE RADIATION LEVEL ISN'T DROPPING.
JESUS, LOOK AT THAT... SHOULDN'T THERE BE LESS HAWKING RADIATION IF THERE ARE LESS WORMHOLES?
YES, THERE DAMN WELL SHOULD. UNLESS... ISOLATE STREAM 088. DISPLAY.
THE OTHERS ARE COLLAPSING SO THAT THE TORUS CAN DIRECT ALL ITS POWER INTO THIS ONE AND OPEN IT RIGHT UP.
WHERE DOES IT GO?
ASTEROID KT-998. A QUARTER OF A MILLION MILES FROM EARTH. THE RELATIVES ARE COMING FOR DINNER.
088

YOU
OKAY?

I'M
ALIVE.

SIOBHAN?

WEIRDLY
HORNY.

WHAT?

WE'VE GOT
A HULL BREACH
ON THE NORTH
SIDE.

THE
BASTARDS ARE
CUTTING THEIR
WAY IN.

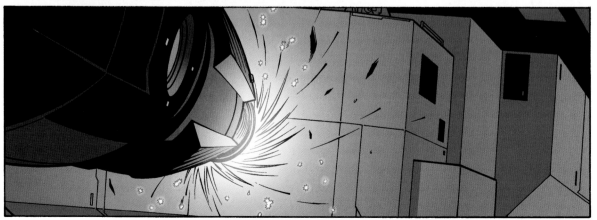

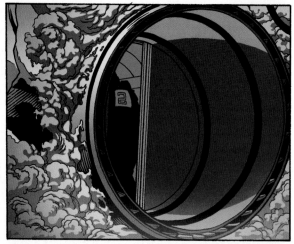

KILL EVERYTHING YOU SEE.

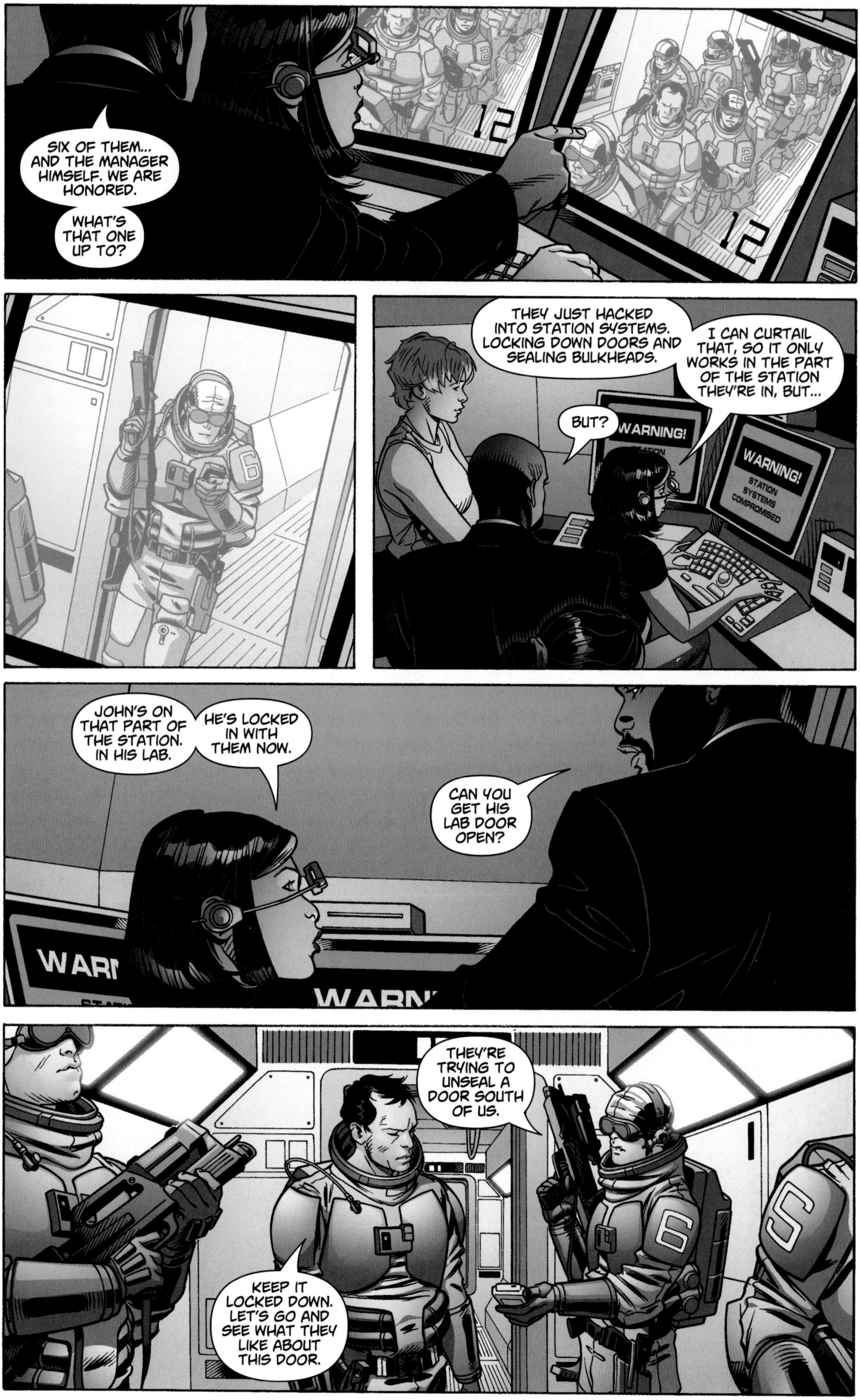
SIX OF THEM... AND THE MANAGER HIMSELF. WE ARE HONORED.
WHAT'S THAT ONE UP TO?
12
12
THEY JUST HACKED INTO STATION SYSTEMS. LOCKING DOWN DOORS AND SEALING BULKHEADS.
I CAN CURTAIL THAT, SO IT ONLY WORKS IN THE PART OF THE STATION THEY'RE IN, BUT...
BUT?
WARNING!
WARNING! STATION SYSTEMS COMPROMISED
JOHN'S ON THAT PART OF THE STATION. IN HIS LAB.
HE'S LOCKED IN WITH THEM NOW.
CAN YOU GET HIS LAB DOOR OPEN?
THEY'RE TRYING TO UNSEAL A DOOR SOUTH OF US.
KEEP IT LOCKED DOWN. LET'S GO AND SEE WHAT THEY LIKE ABOUT THIS DOOR.

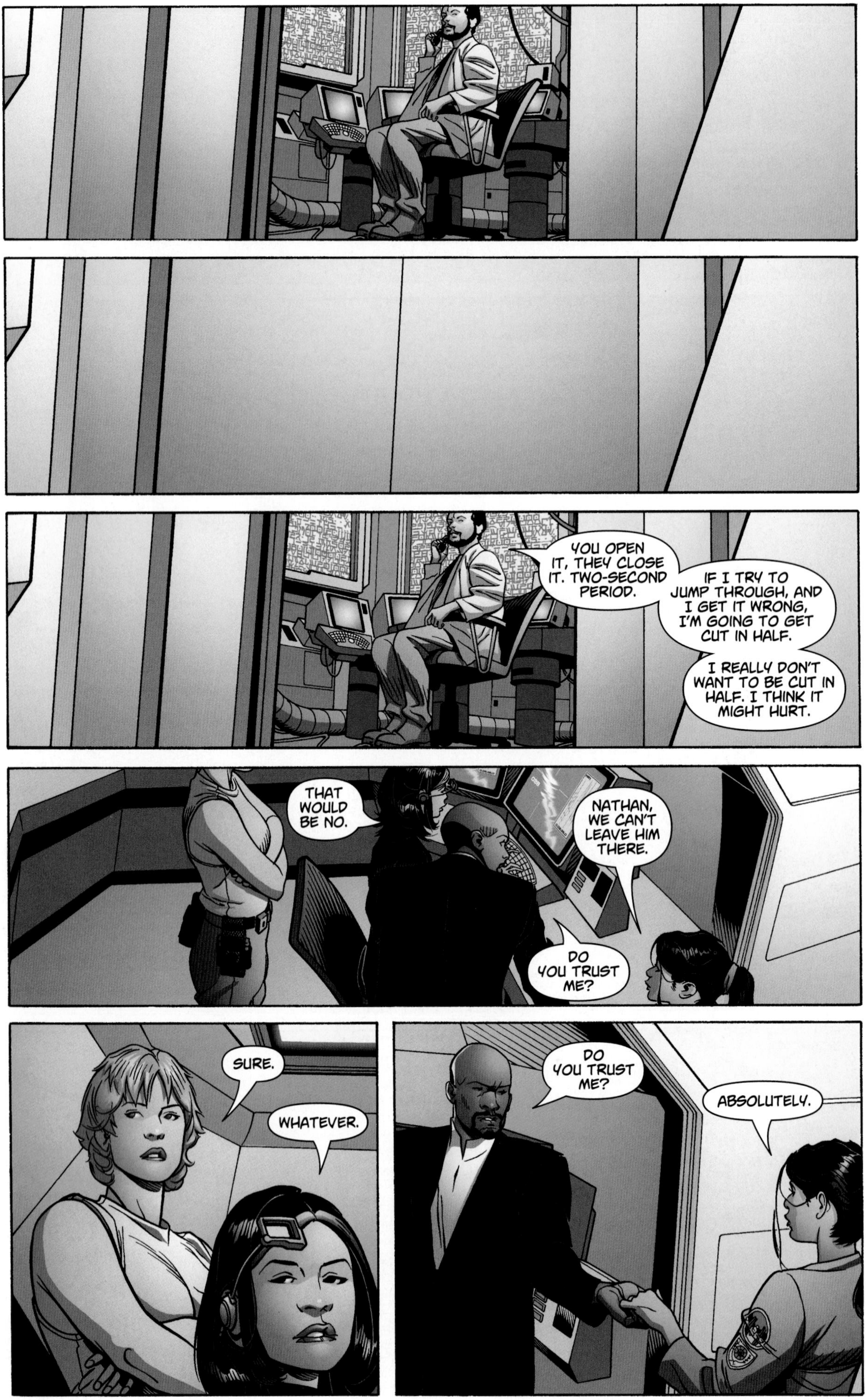

YOU OPEN IT, THEY CLOSE IT. TWO-SECOND PERIOD.
IF I TRY TO JUMP THROUGH, AND I GET IT WRONG, I'M GOING TO GET CUT IN HALF.
I REALLY DON'T WANT TO BE CUT IN HALF. I THINK IT MIGHT HURT.
THAT WOULD BE NO.
NATHAN, WE CAN'T LEAVE HIM THERE.
DO YOU TRUST ME?
SURE.
WHATEVER.
DO YOU TRUST ME?
ABSOLUTELY.

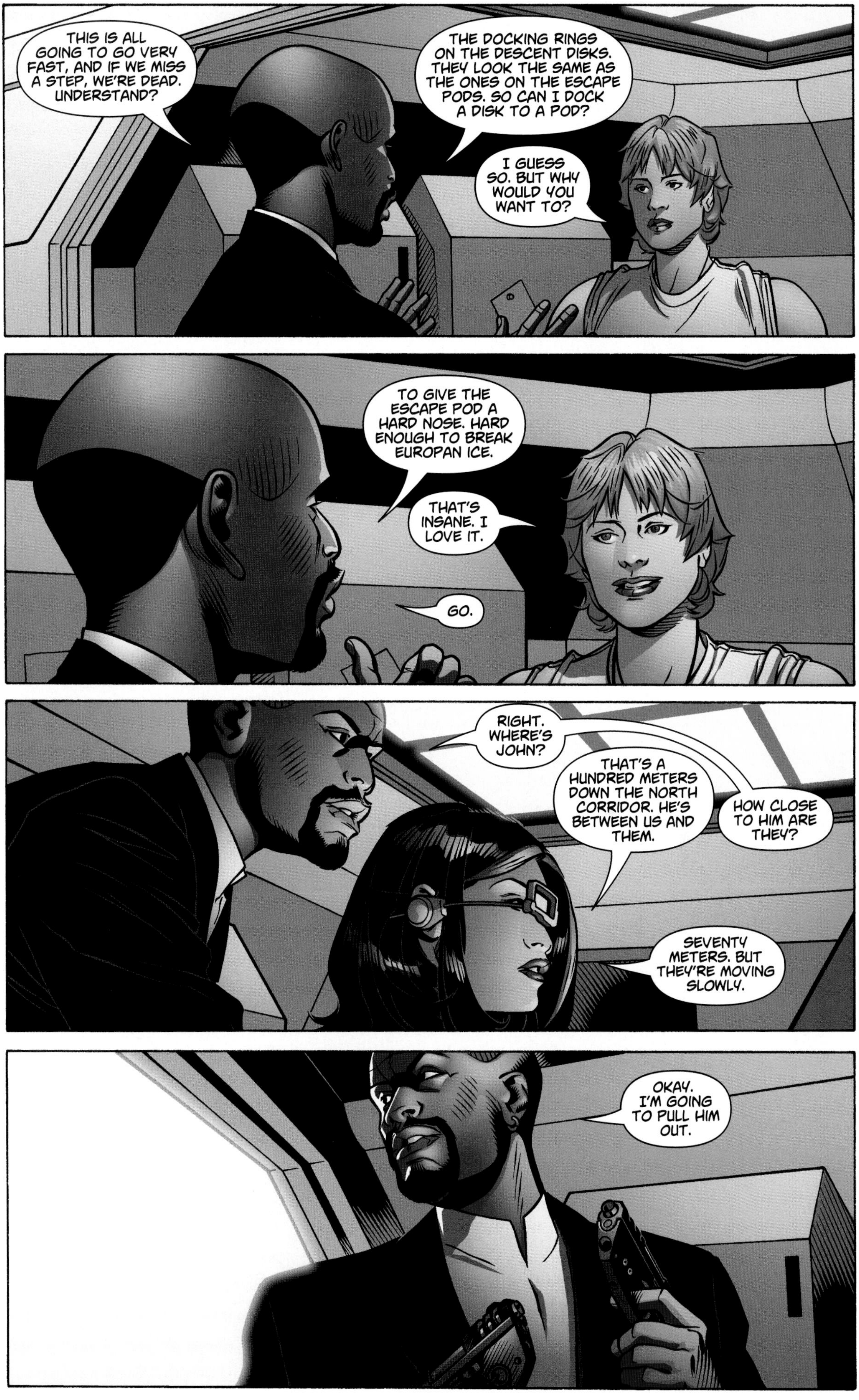
THIS IS ALL GOING TO GO VERY FAST, AND IF WE MISS A STEP, WE'RE DEAD. UNDERSTAND?
THE DOCKING RINGS ON THE DESCENT DISKS. THEY LOOK THE SAME AS THE ONES ON THE ESCAPE PODS. SO CAN I DOCK A DISK TO A POD?
I GUESS SO. BUT WHY WOULD YOU WANT TO?
TO GIVE THE ESCAPE POD A HARD NOSE. HARD ENOUGH TO BREAK EUROPAN ICE.
THAT'S INSANE. I LOVE IT.
GO.
RIGHT. WHERE'S JOHN?
THAT'S A HUNDRED METERS DOWN THE NORTH CORRIDOR. HE'S BETWEEN US AND THEM.
HOW CLOSE TO HIM ARE THEY?
SEVENTY METERS. BUT THEY'RE MOVING SLOWLY.
OKAY. I'M GOING TO PULL HIM OUT.

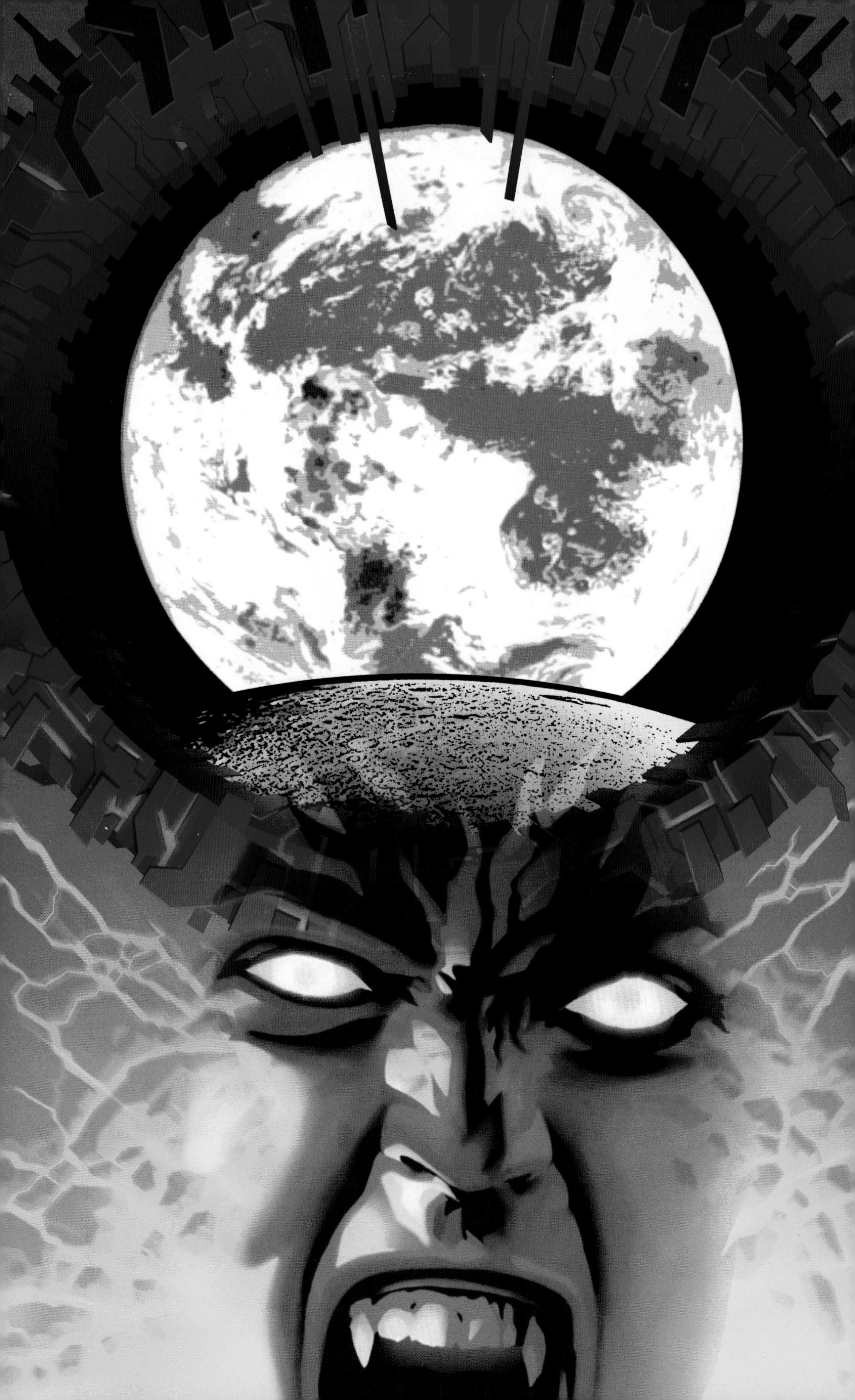

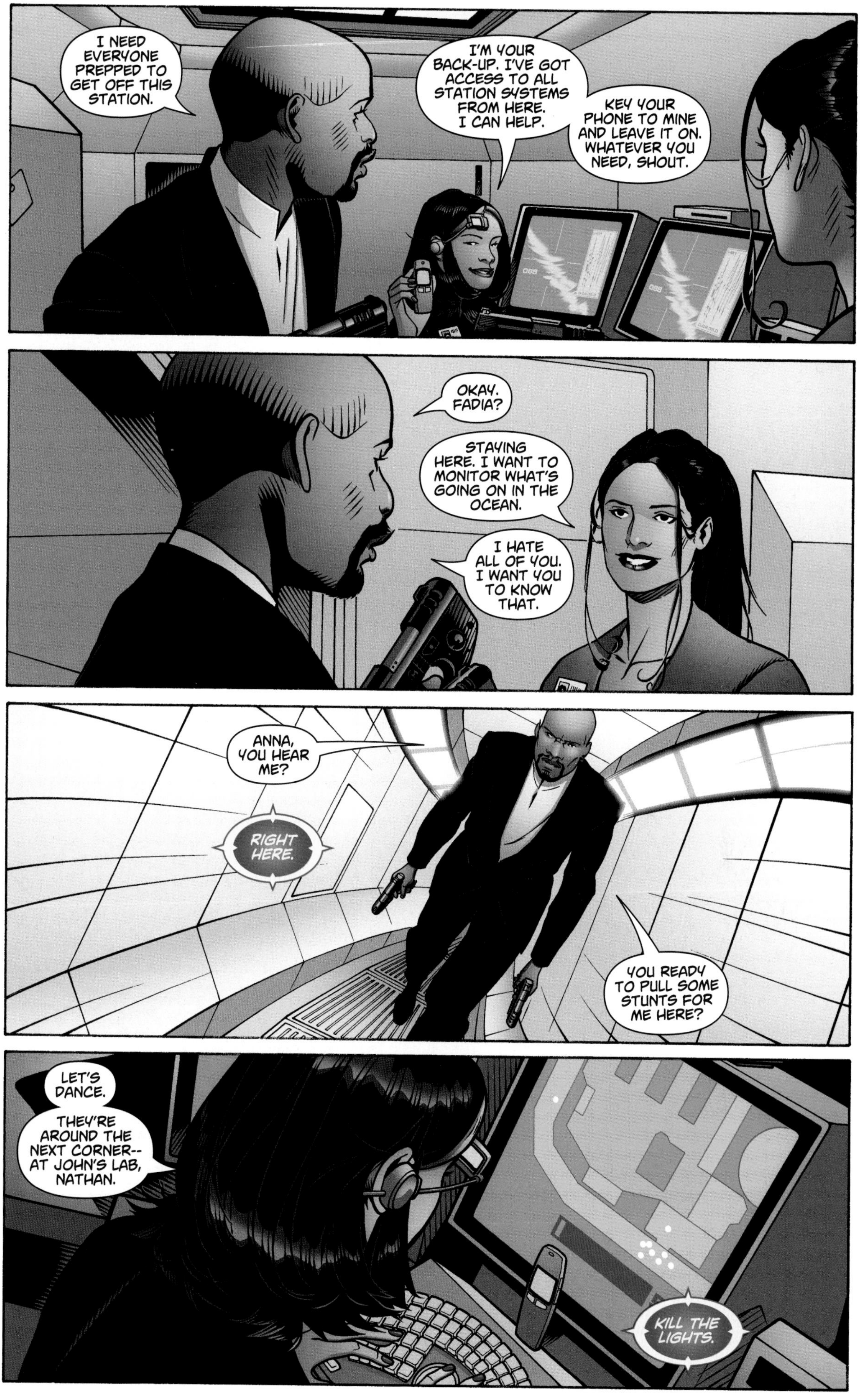
I NEED EVERYONE PREPPED TO GET OFF THIS STATION.
I'M YOUR BACK-UP. I'VE GOT ACCESS TO ALL STATION SYSTEMS FROM HERE. I CAN HELP.
KEY YOUR PHONE TO MINE AND LEAVE IT ON. WHATEVER YOU NEED, SHOUT.
OKAY. FADIA?
STAYING HERE. I WANT TO MONITOR WHAT'S GOING ON IN THE OCEAN.
I HATE ALL OF YOU. I WANT YOU TO KNOW THAT.
ANNA, YOU HEAR ME?
RIGHT HERE.
YOU READY TO PULL SOME STUNTS FOR ME HERE?
LET'S DANCE.
THEY'RE AROUND THE NEXT CORNER-- AT JOHN'S LAB, NATHAN.
KILL THE LIGHTS.

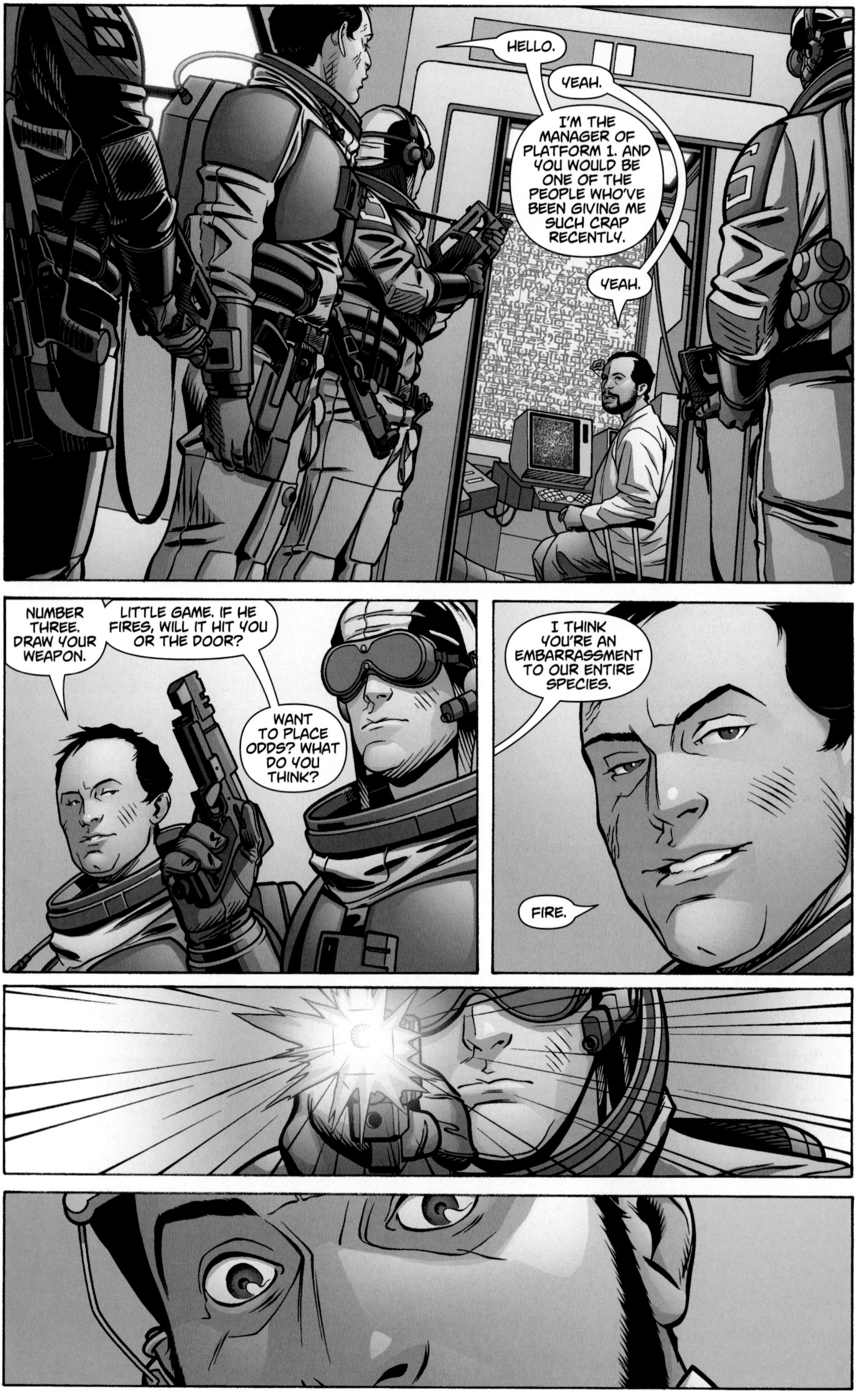

HELLO.
YEAH.
I'M THE MANAGER OF PLATFORM 1. AND YOU WOULD BE ONE OF THE PEOPLE WHO'VE BEEN GIVING ME SUCH CRAP RECENTLY.
YEAH.
NUMBER THREE. DRAW YOUR WEAPON.
LITTLE GAME. IF HE FIRES, WILL IT HIT YOU OR THE DOOR?
WANT TO PLACE ODDS? WHAT DO YOU THINK?
I THINK YOU'RE AN EMBARRASSMENT TO OUR ENTIRE SPECIES.
FIRE.

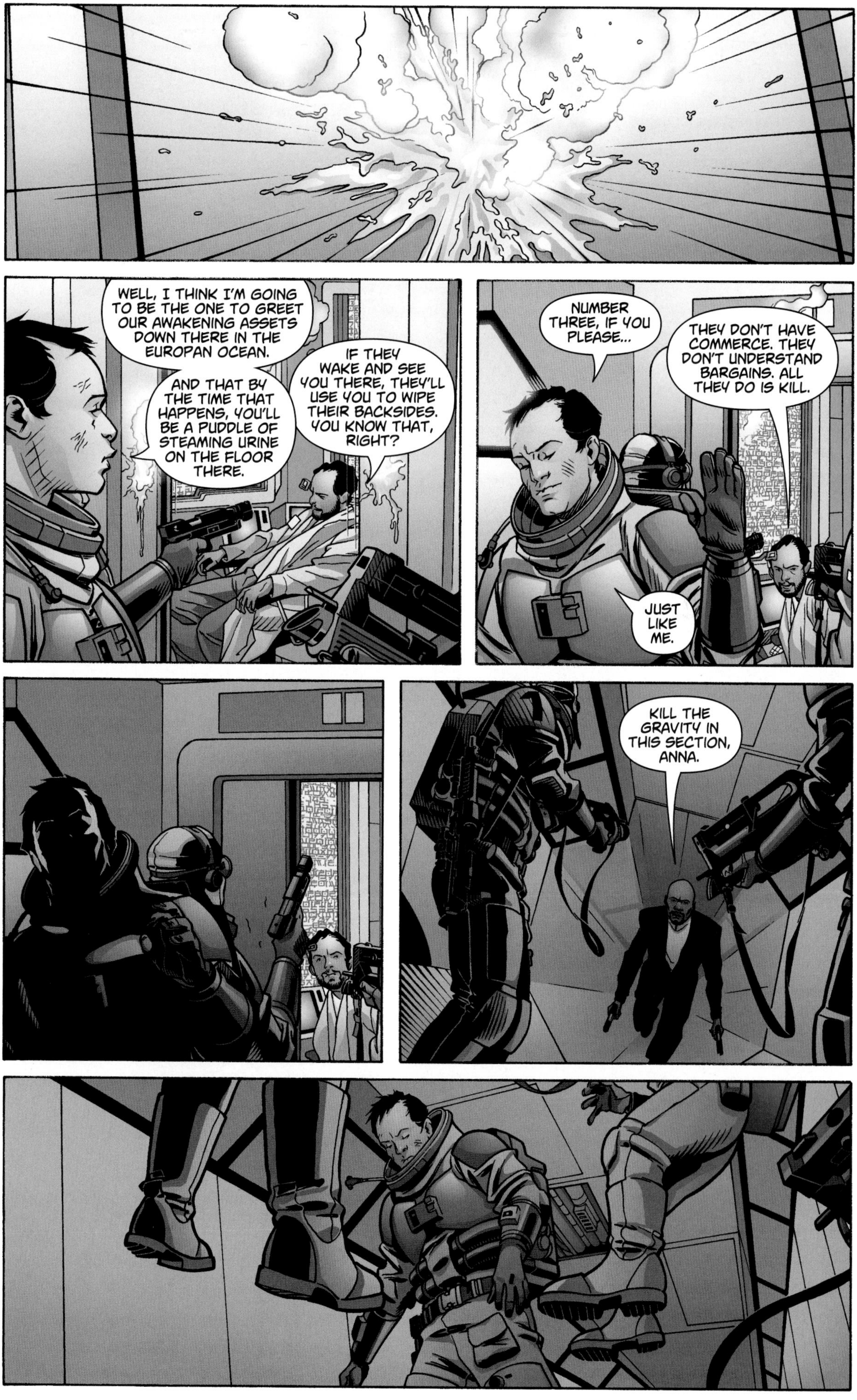
WELL, I THINK I'M GOING TO BE THE ONE TO GREET OUR AWAKENING ASSETS DOWN THERE IN THE EUROPAN OCEAN.
AND THAT BY THE TIME THAT HAPPENS, YOU'LL BE A PUDDLE OF STEAMING URINE ON THE FLOOR THERE.
IF THEY WAKE AND SEE YOU THERE, THEY'LL USE YOU TO WIPE THEIR BACKSIDES. YOU KNOW THAT, RIGHT?
NUMBER THREE, IF YOU PLEASE...
THEY DON'T HAVE COMMERCE. THEY DON'T UNDERSTAND BARGAINS. ALL THEY DO IS KILL.
JUST LIKE ME.
KILL THE GRAVITY IN THIS SECTION, ANNA.

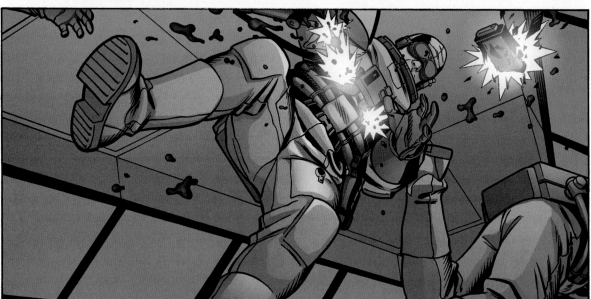

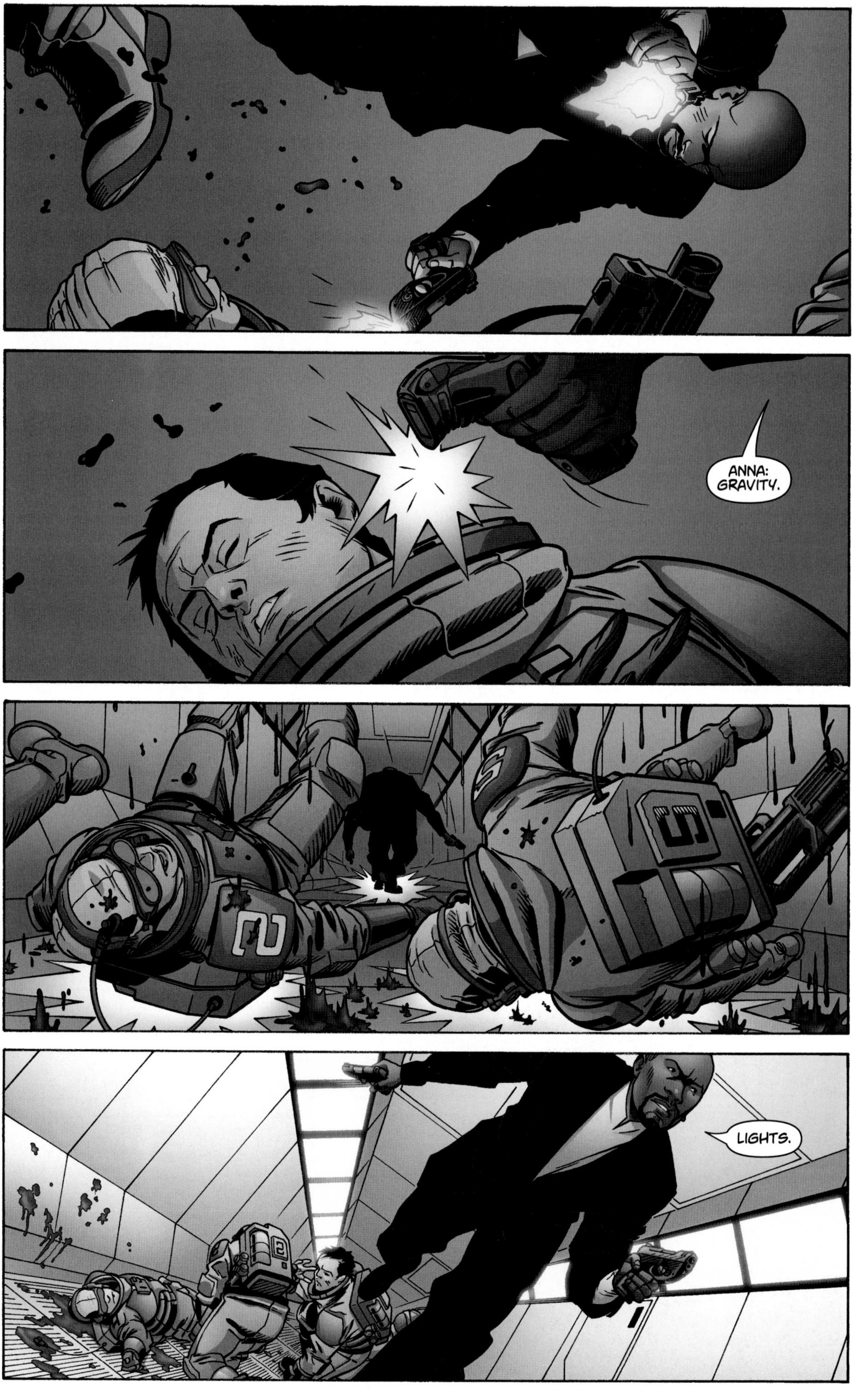
ANNA: GRAVITY.
LIGHTS.

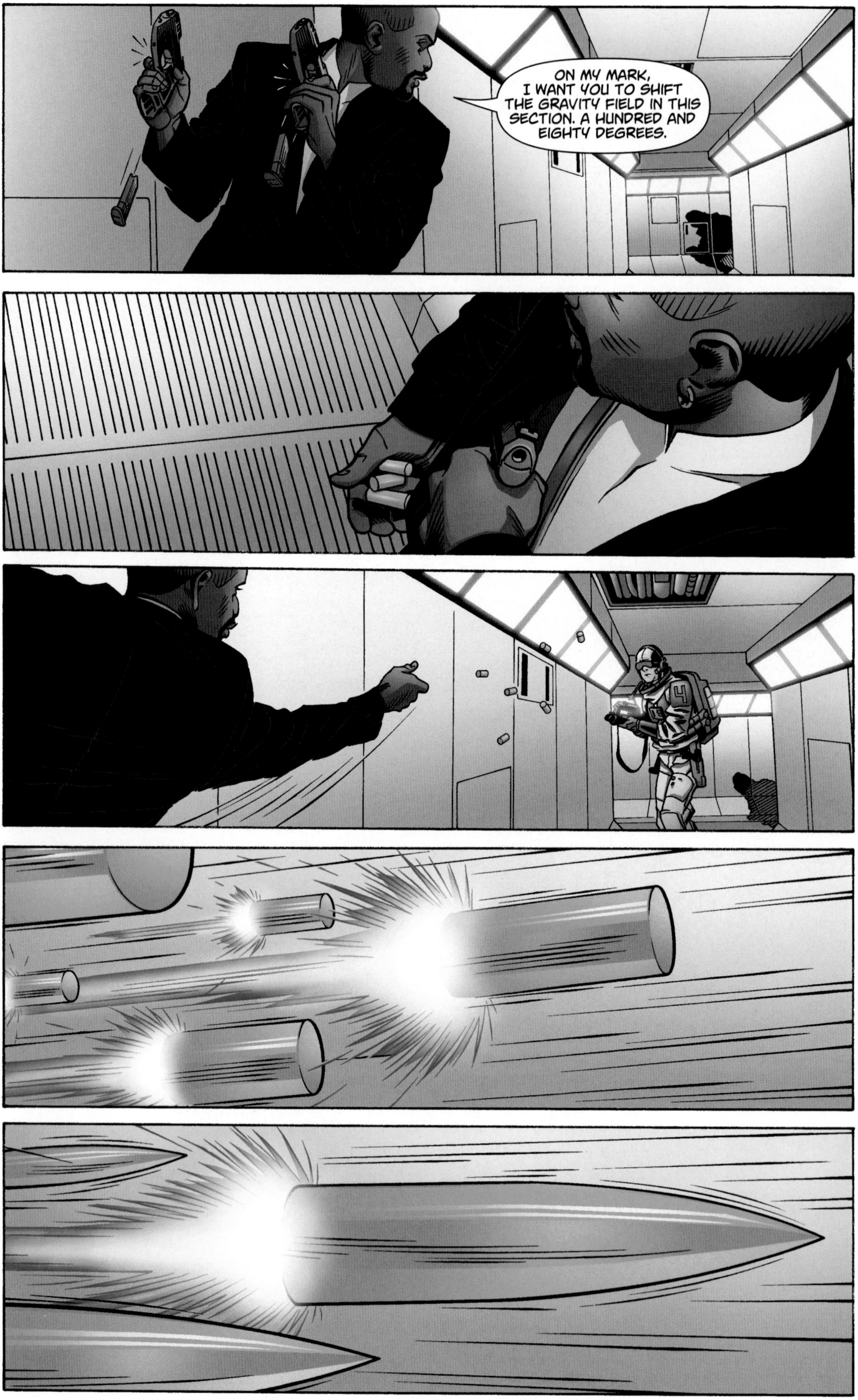
ON MY MARK, I WANT YOU TO SHIFT THE GRAVITY FIELD IN THIS SECTION. A HUNDRED AND EIGHTY DEGREES.

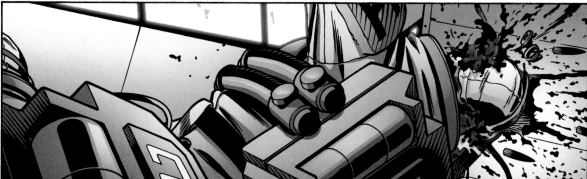

MARK.

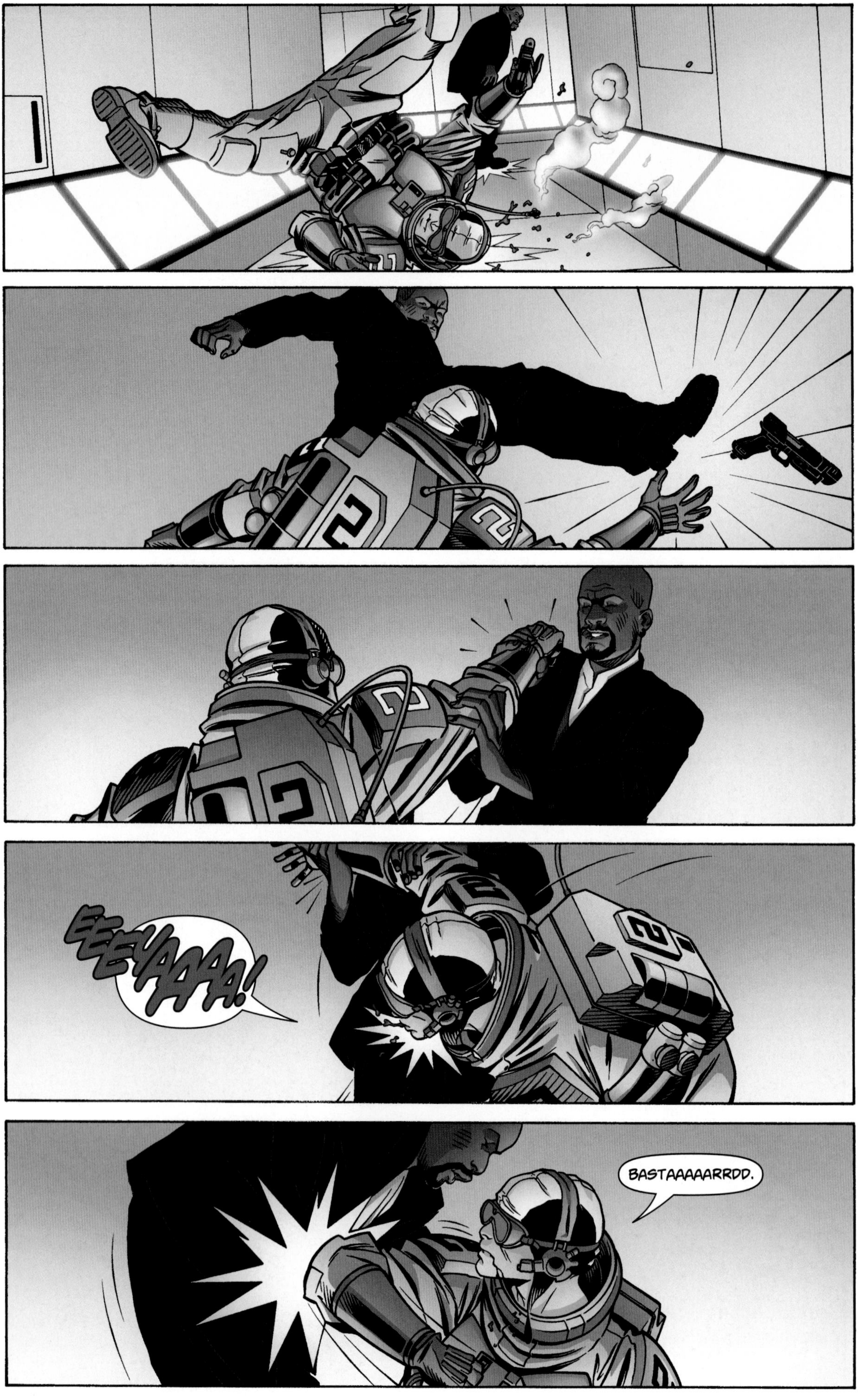
EEEYAAAA!
BASTAAAAARRDD.

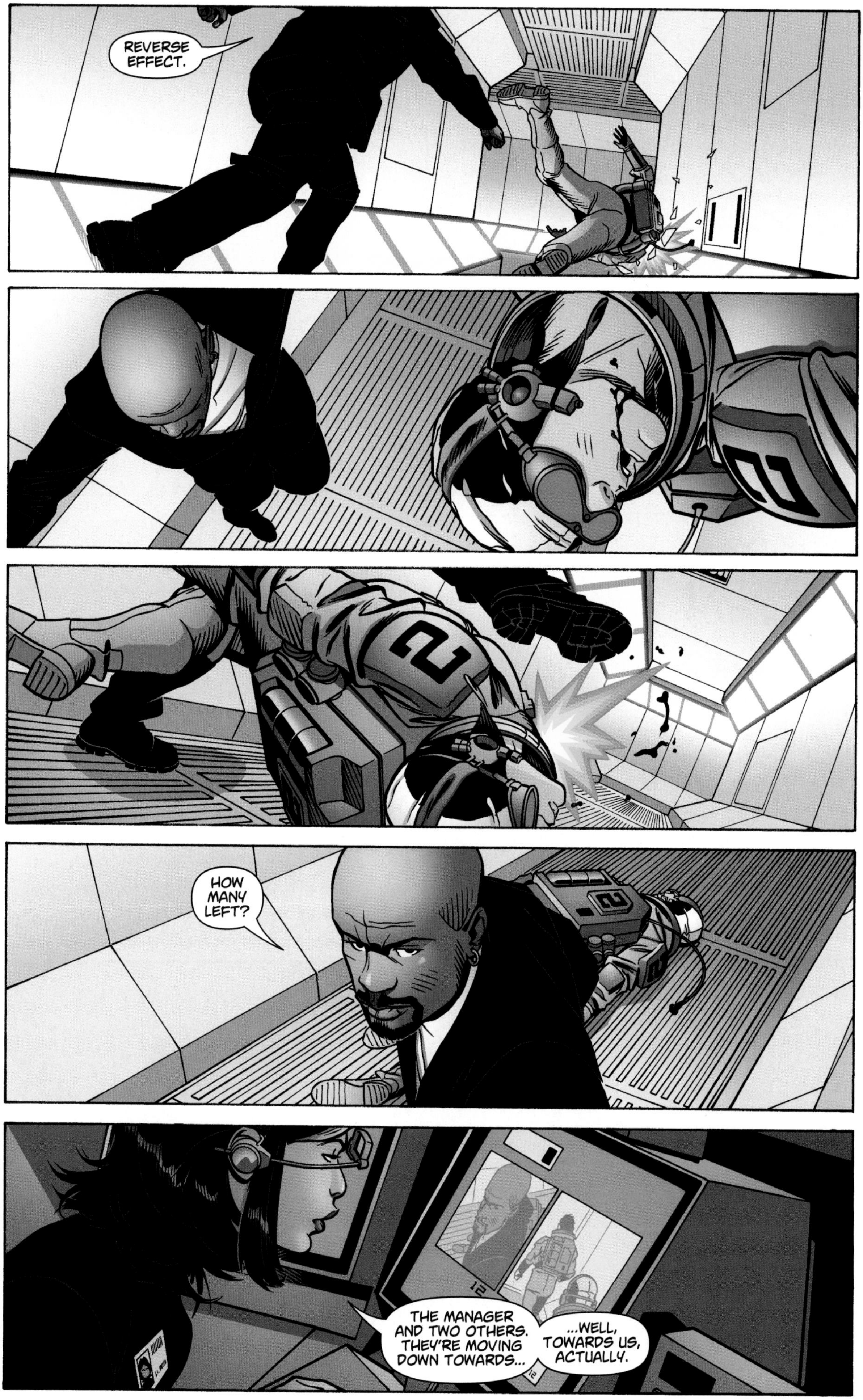
REVERSE EFFECT.
HOW MANY LEFT?
THE MANAGER AND TWO OTHERS. THEY'RE MOVING DOWN TOWARDS...
...WELL, TOWARDS US, ACTUALLY.

TAKE A COUPLE OF STEPS BACK, JOHN.

NOW WHAT?

NOW WE TRY NOT TO DIE SOME MORE.

NATHAN; THE GUNS ARE POWERED UP.

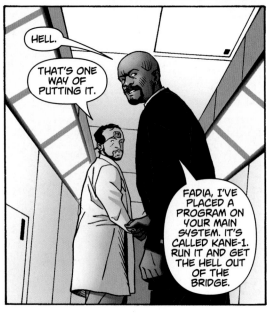

HELL.

THAT'S ONE WAY OF PUTTING IT.

FADIA, I'VE PLACED A PROGRAM ON YOUR MAIN SYSTEM. IT'S CALLED KANE-1. RUN IT AND GET THE HELL OUT OF THE BRIDGE.

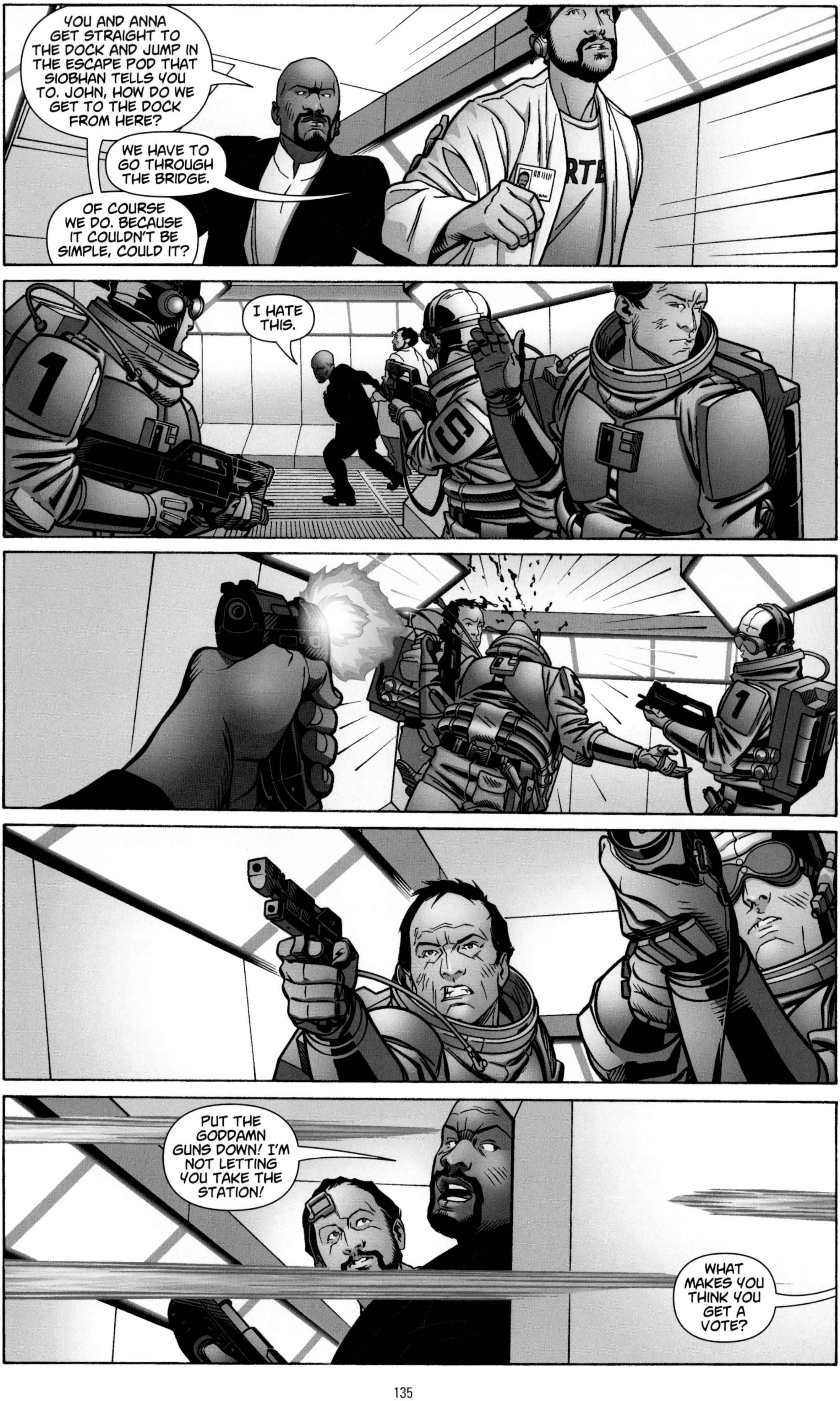
YOU AND ANNA GET STRAIGHT TO THE DOCK AND JUMP IN THE ESCAPE POD THAT SIOBHAN TELLS YOU TO. JOHN, HOW DO WE GET TO THE DOCK FROM HERE?
WE HAVE TO GO THROUGH THE BRIDGE.
OF COURSE WE DO. BECAUSE IT COULDN'T BE SIMPLE, COULD IT?
I HATE THIS.
PUT THE GODDAMN GUNS DOWN! I'M NOT LETTING YOU TAKE THE STATION!
WHAT MAKES YOU THINK YOU GET A VOTE?

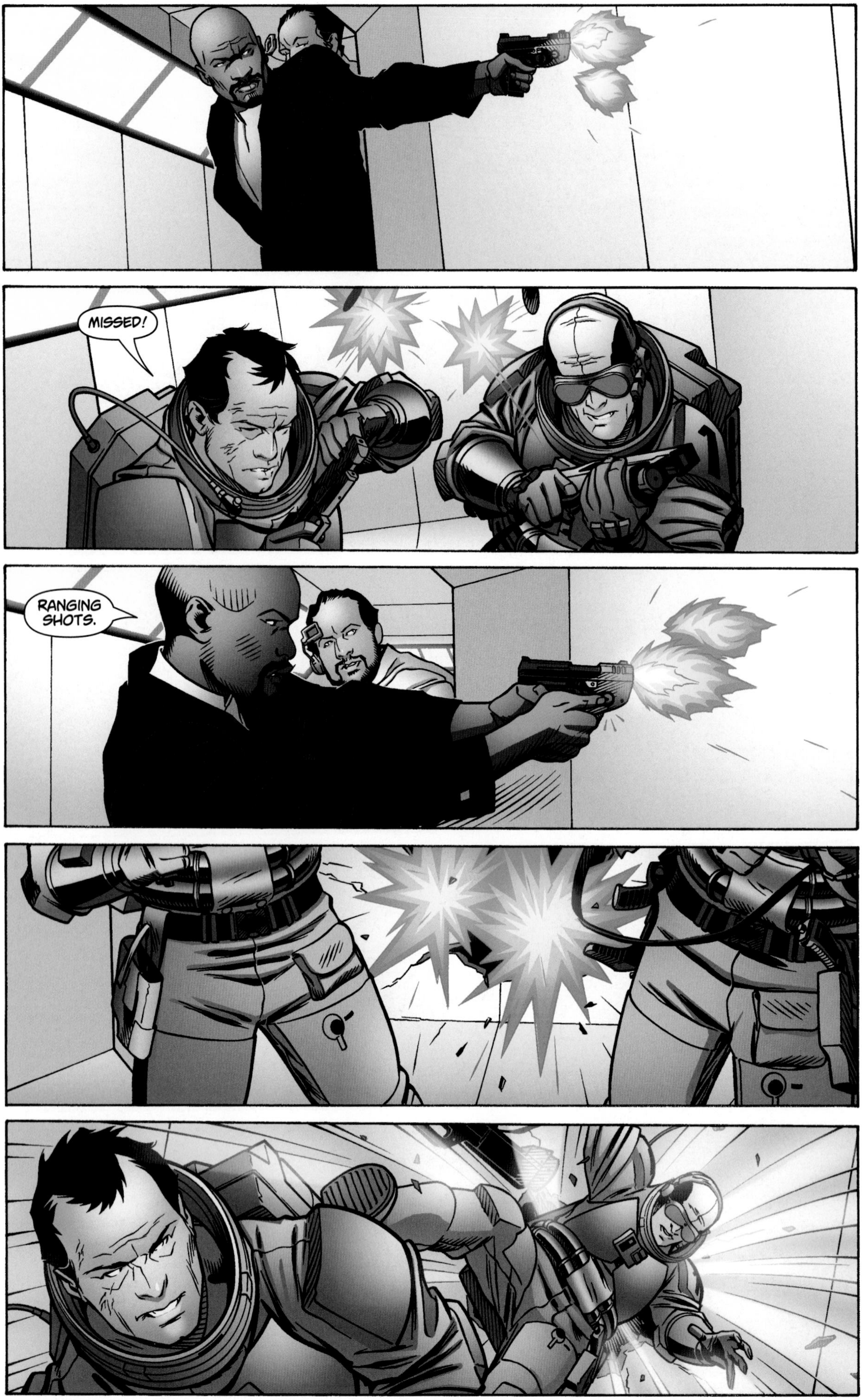
MISSED!
RANGING SHOTS.

PLEASE... I CAN FEEL THE COLD BURNING MY SKIN OFF...

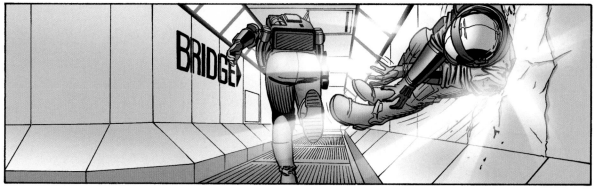

BRIDGE

GOD, I'M SORRY.

ANNA, SEAL THE HULL BREACH ON THIS CORRIDOR. AND GET OUT OF THE GODDAMN BRIDGE.

HOW DID YOU KNOW I WAS STILL HERE?

BECAUSE NO-ONE ON THIS STATION EVER DOES AS THEY'RE TOLD.

ALL RIGHT, YOU--

OKAY, GO--

YOU BASTARD!

ANNA, GET TO THE ESCAPE POD! NOW!

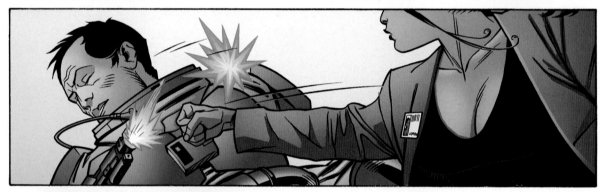

THIS IS GOING TO HURT.

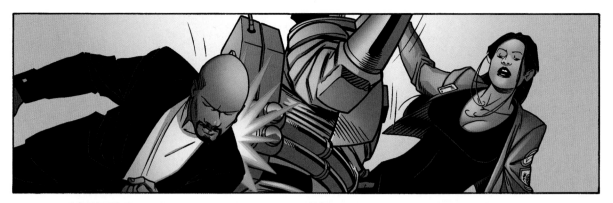

GO!

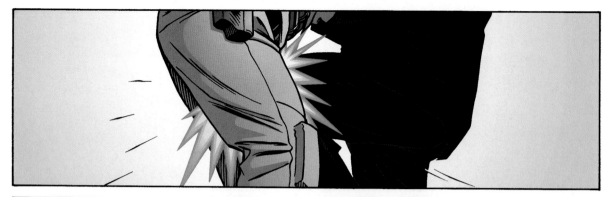

THOSE GUNS ARE MINE, KANE. THEY'RE OURS.

THEY BELONG TO US BY RIGHT OF INHERITANCE, DAMMIT.

KANE-1

PRESS

ENTER

TO COMMIT

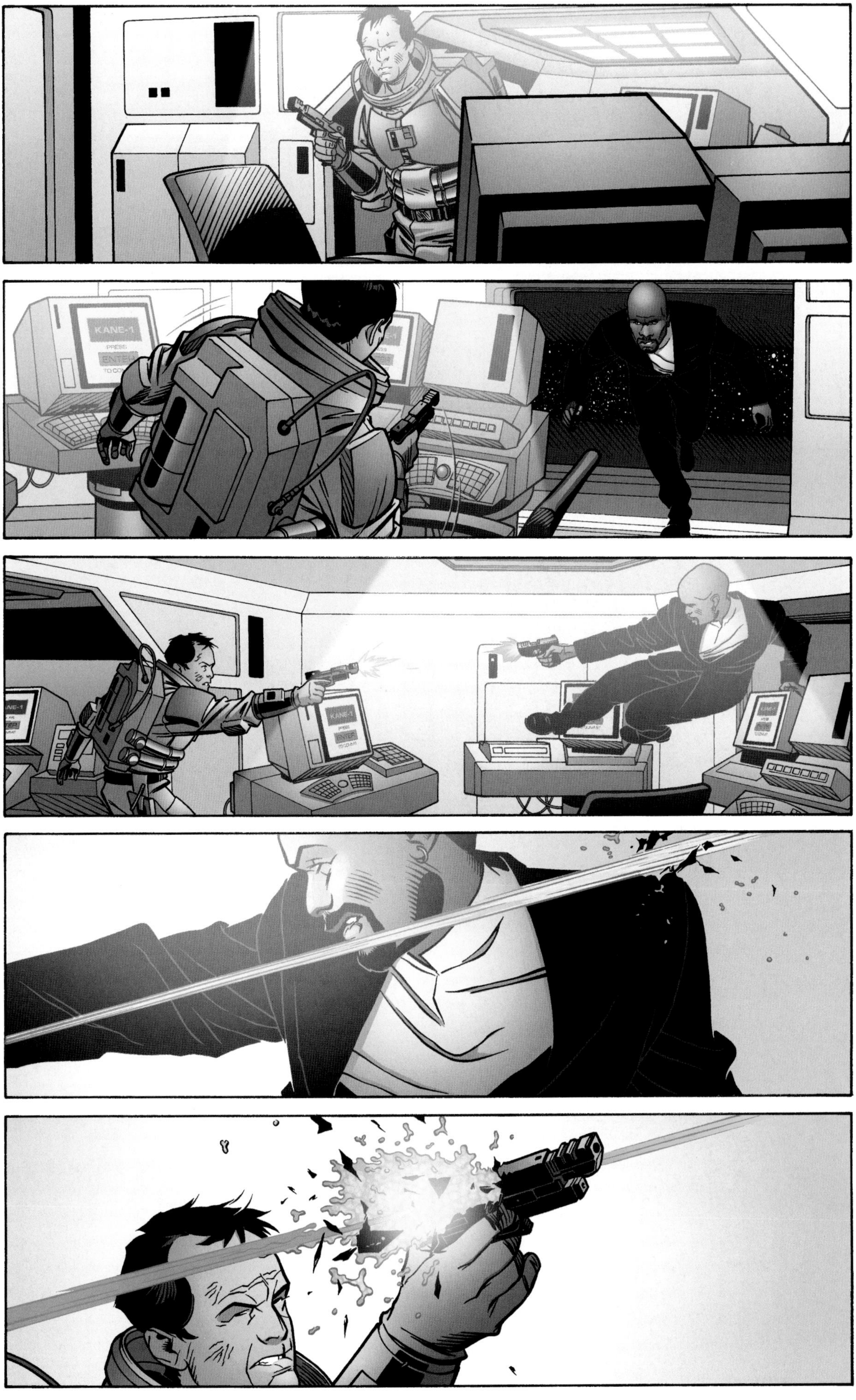
KANE-1
PRESS
ENTER
KANE-1
PRESS
ENTER

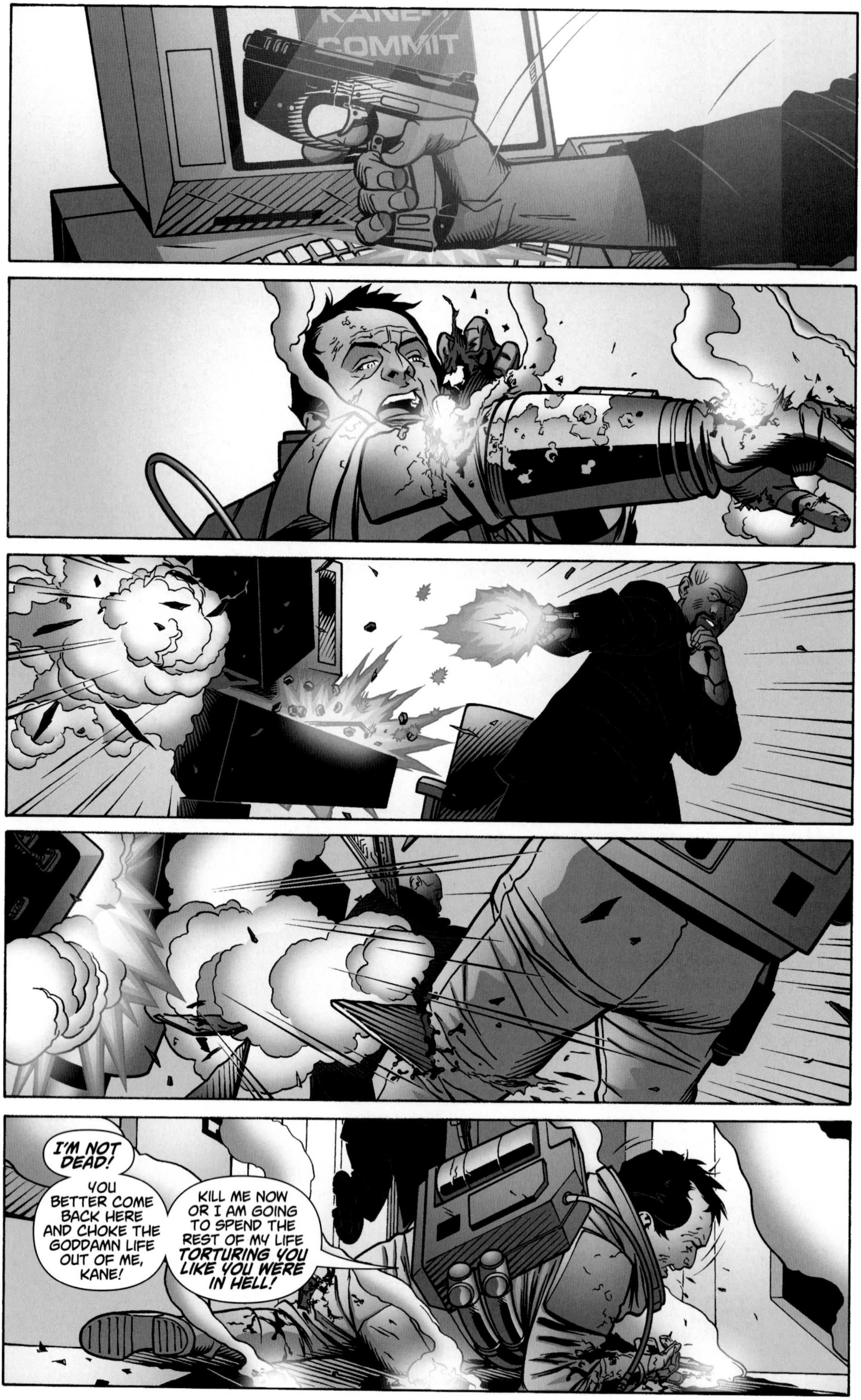
COMMIT
I'M NOT DEAD!
YOU BETTER COME BACK HERE AND CHOKE THE GODDAMN LIFE OUT OF ME, KANE!
KILL ME NOW OR I AM GOING TO SPEND THE REST OF MY LIFE TORTURING YOU LIKE YOU WERE IN HELL!

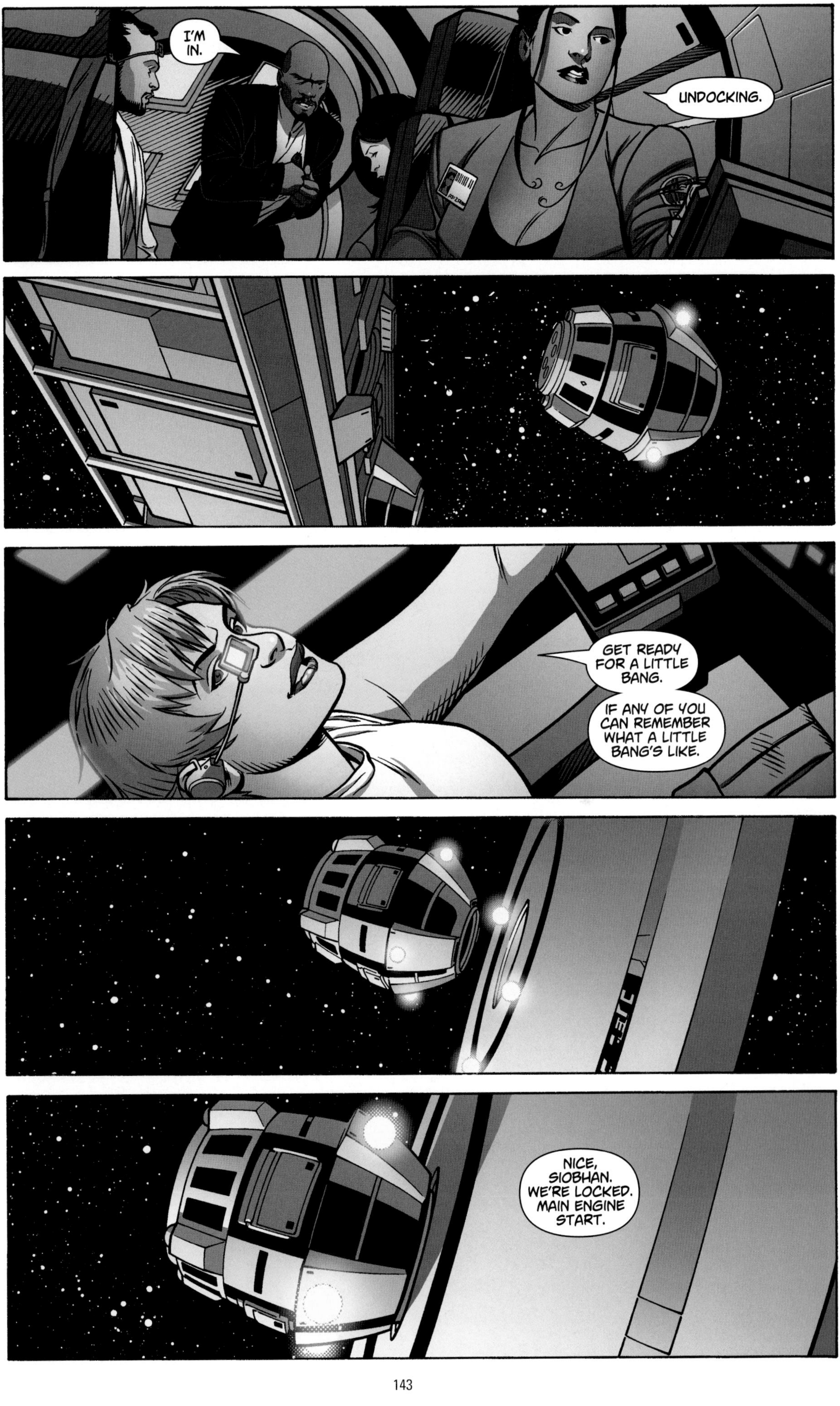
I'M IN.
UNDOCKING.
GET READY FOR A LITTLE BANG.
IF ANY OF YOU CAN REMEMBER WHAT A LITTLE BANG'S LIKE.
NICE, SIOBHAN. WE'RE LOCKED. MAIN ENGINE START.

POINT US AT EUROPA. I'VE KIND OF DONE SOMETHING BAD AND WE NEED TO MOVE VERY FAST.

OH, GOD.

LOSERS.

LEFT ME HERE TO MEET THEM. AND WITH ALL YOUR RESEARCH.

LOSERS.

KANE-1 COMMIT

WHAT?

KANE-1 COMMIT

WEAPON FIRING

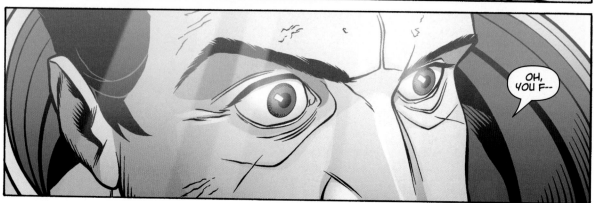

OH, YOU F--

WHAT DID YOU DO?

I HACKED INTO THE BIGGEST GUN I COULD FIND, MADE IT TURN AROUND SO THAT IT'S POINTING AT EUROPA'S CORE, AND...

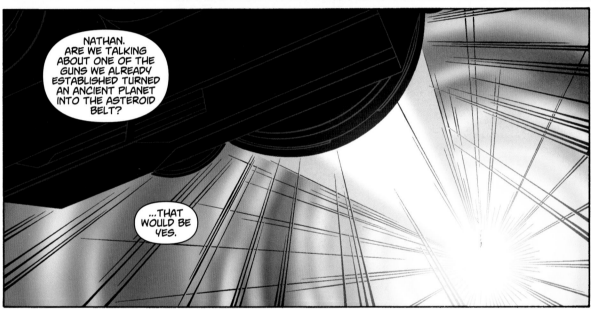

NATHAN. ARE WE TALKING ABOUT ONE OF THE GUNS WE ALREADY ESTABLISHED TURNED AN ANCIENT PLANET INTO THE ASTEROID BELT?

...THAT WOULD BE YES.

I'VE BASICALLY STELLIFIED EUROPA.

ITS CORE IS BEING TURNED INTO A SMALL, SHORT-LIVED SUN RIGHT ABOUT...

NOW.

IT'S REALLY NOT AS BAD AS IT SOUNDS.

EXCEPT THAT WE HAVE LESS THAN TWO MINUTES TO REACH THE TORUS BEFORE WE ALL DIE.

STRAP YOURSELF DOWN QUICKLY. THIS IS GOING TO BE EXTRAORDINARILY PAINFUL.

WILL THE STRAPS HELP WITH THAT?

NO.

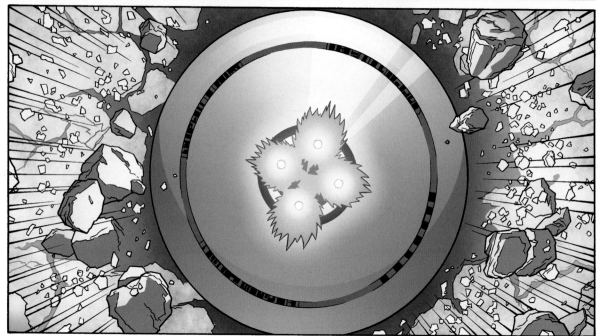

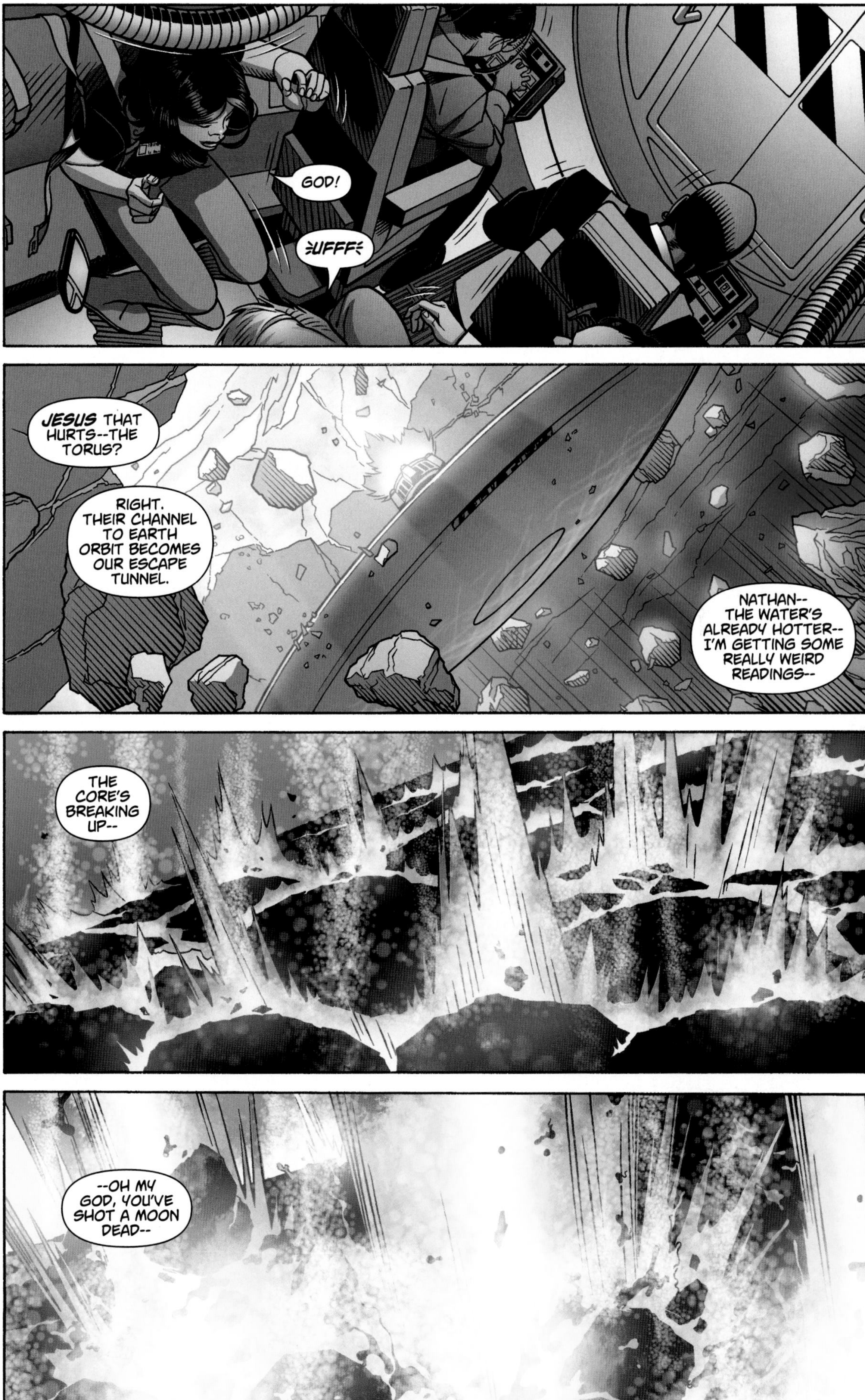
GOD!
UFFF
JESUS THAT HURTS--THE TORUS?
RIGHT. THEIR CHANNEL TO EARTH ORBIT BECOMES OUR ESCAPE TUNNEL.
NATHAN-- THE WATER'S ALREADY HOTTER-- I'M GETTING SOME REALLY WEIRD READINGS--
THE CORE'S BREAKING UP--
--OH MY GOD, YOU'VE SHOT A MOON DEAD--

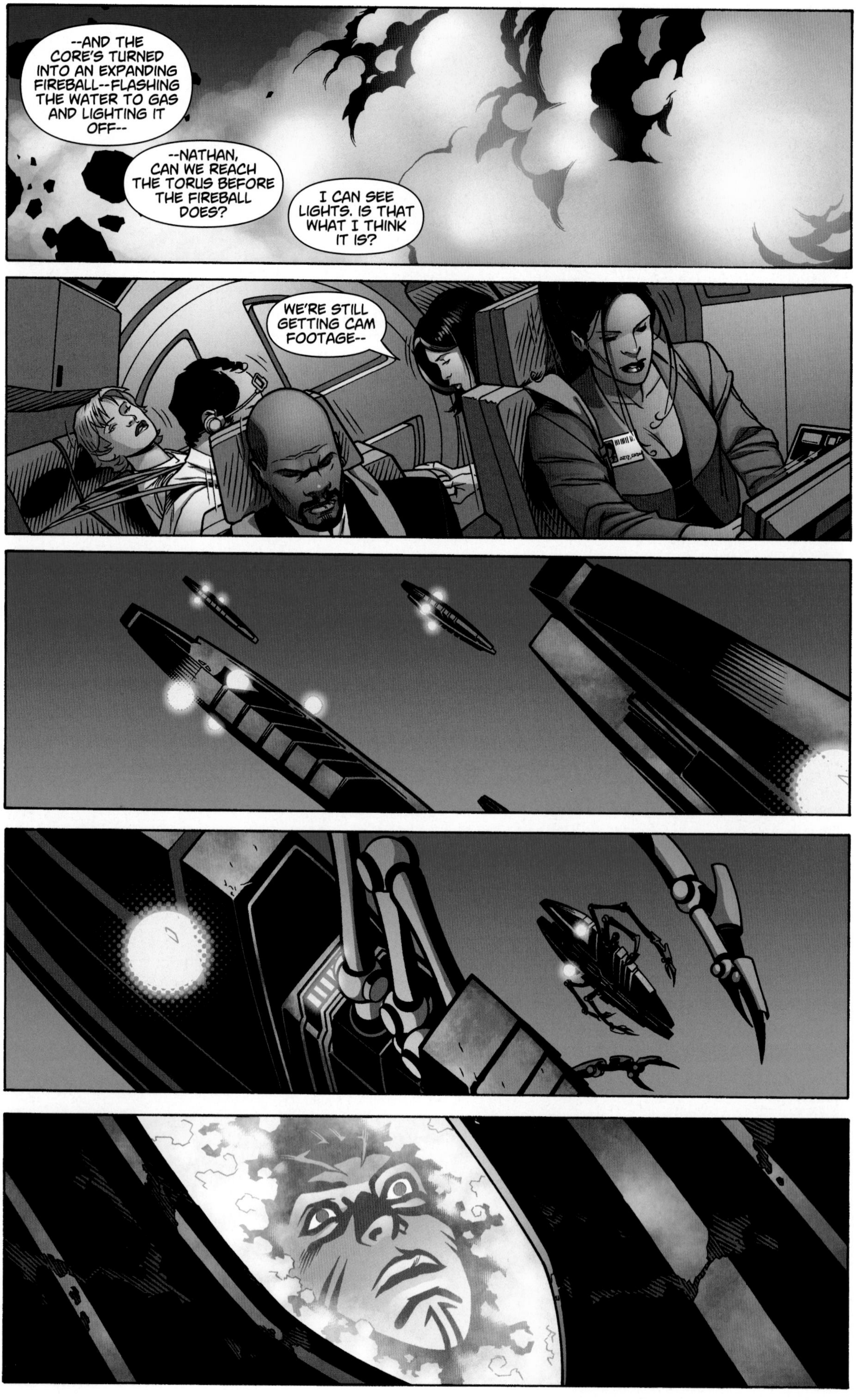
--AND THE CORE'S TURNED INTO AN EXPANDING FIREBALL--FLASHING THE WATER TO GAS AND LIGHTING IT OFF--
--NATHAN, CAN WE REACH THE TORUS BEFORE THE FIREBALL DOES?
I CAN SEE LIGHTS. IS THAT WHAT I THINK IT IS?
WE'RE STILL GETTING CAM FOOTAGE--

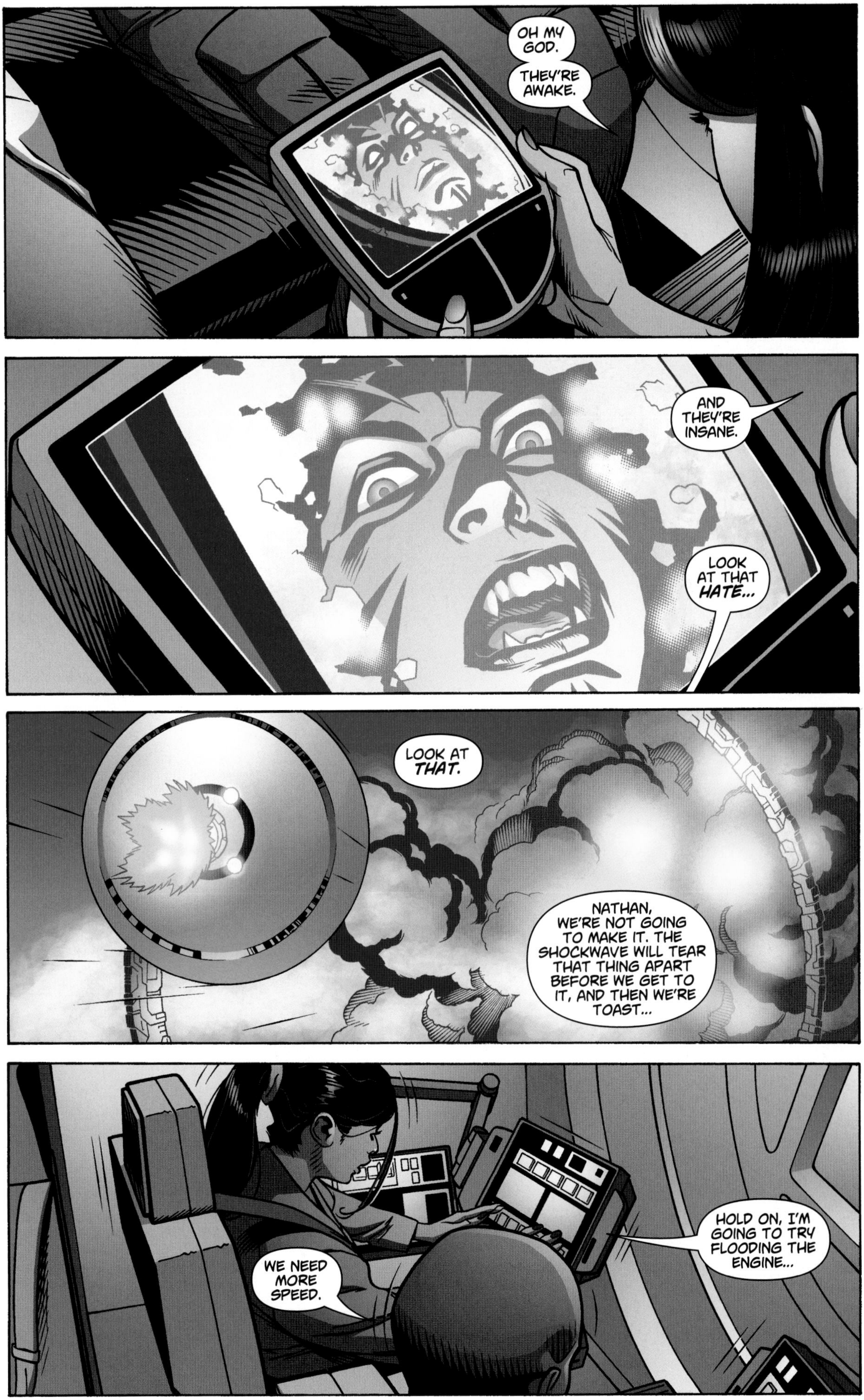
OH MY GOD.
THEY'RE AWAKE.
AND THEY'RE INSANE.
LOOK AT THAT *HATE...*
LOOK AT *THAT.*
NATHAN, WE'RE NOT GOING TO MAKE IT. THE SHOCKWAVE WILL TEAR THAT THING APART BEFORE WE GET TO IT, AND THEN WE'RE TOAST...
HOLD ON, I'M GOING TO TRY FLOODING THE ENGINE...
WE NEED MORE SPEED.

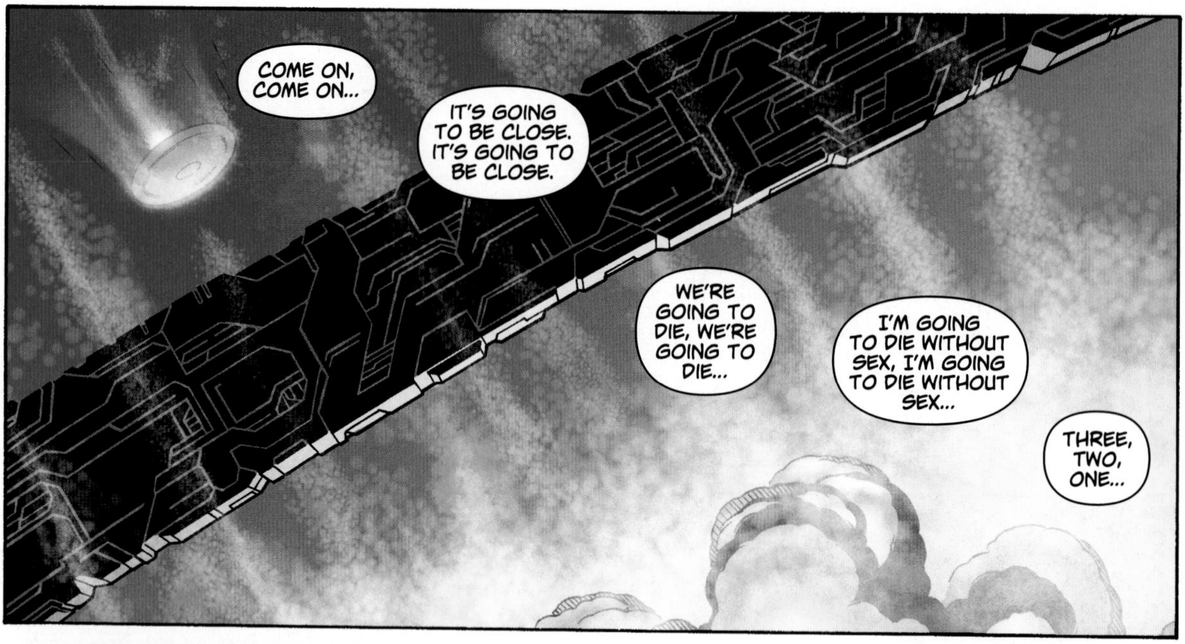
COME ON, COME ON...
IT'S GOING TO BE CLOSE. IT'S GOING TO BE CLOSE.
WE'RE GOING TO DIE, WE'RE GOING TO DIE...
I'M GOING TO DIE WITHOUT SEX, I'M GOING TO DIE WITHOUT SEX...
THREE, TWO, ONE...

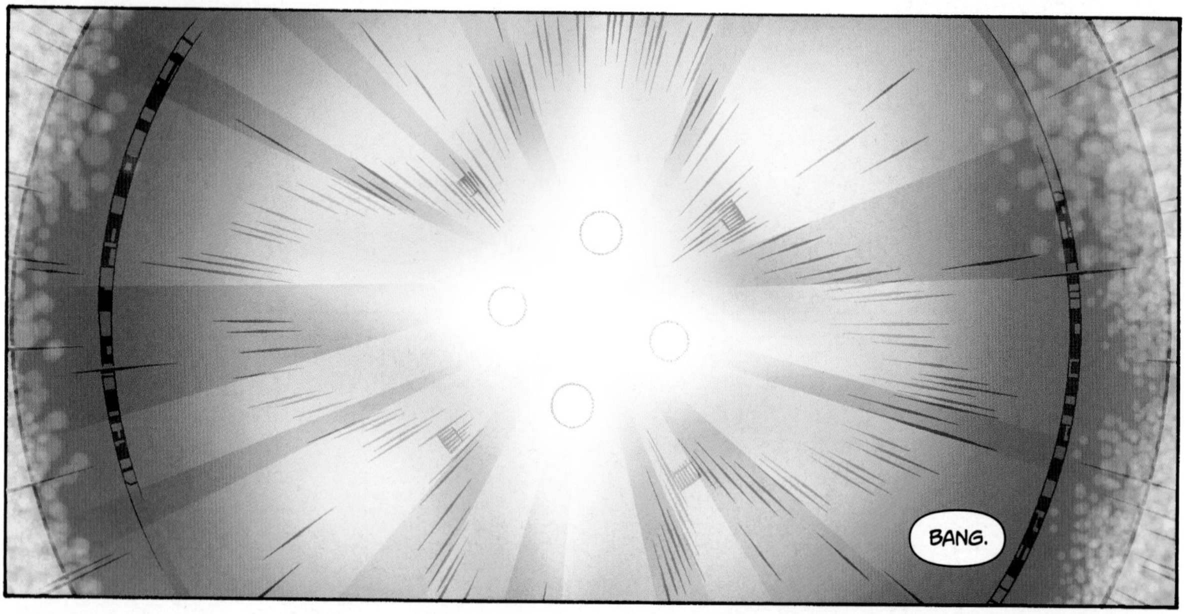
BANG.

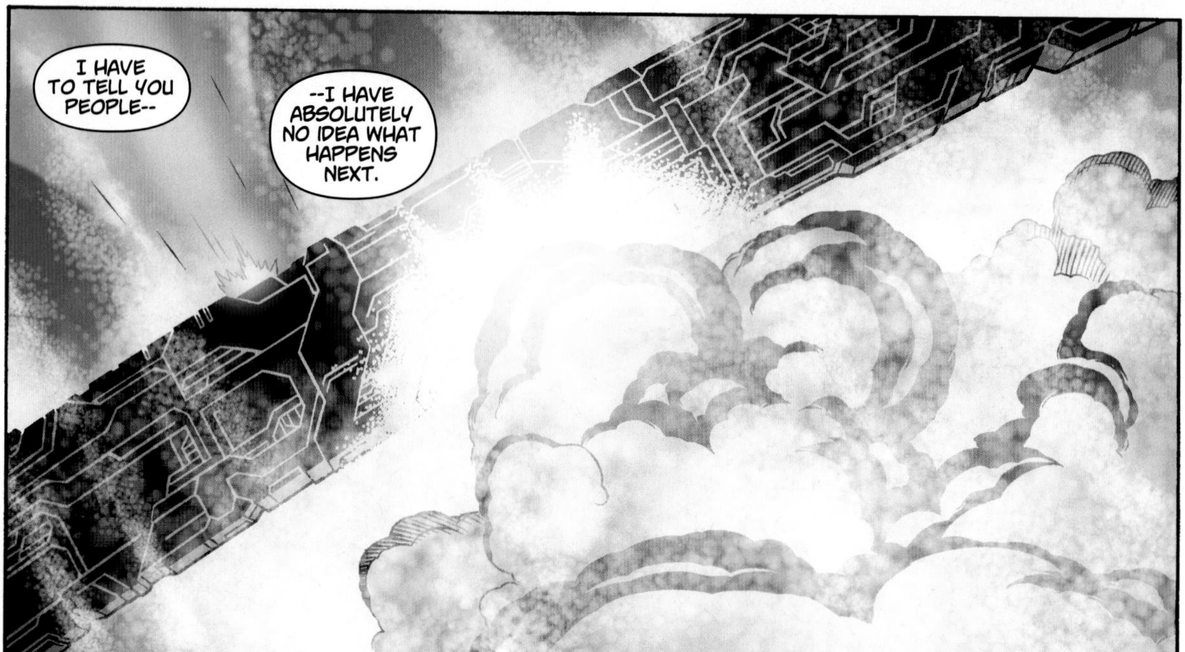
I HAVE TO TELL YOU PEOPLE--
--I HAVE ABSOLUTELY NO IDEA WHAT HAPPENS NEXT.

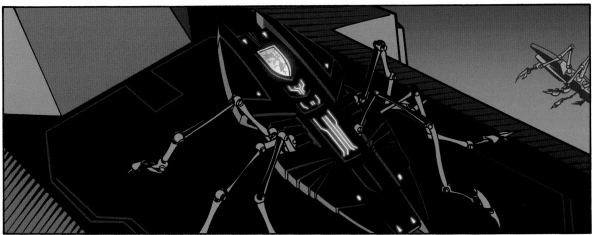

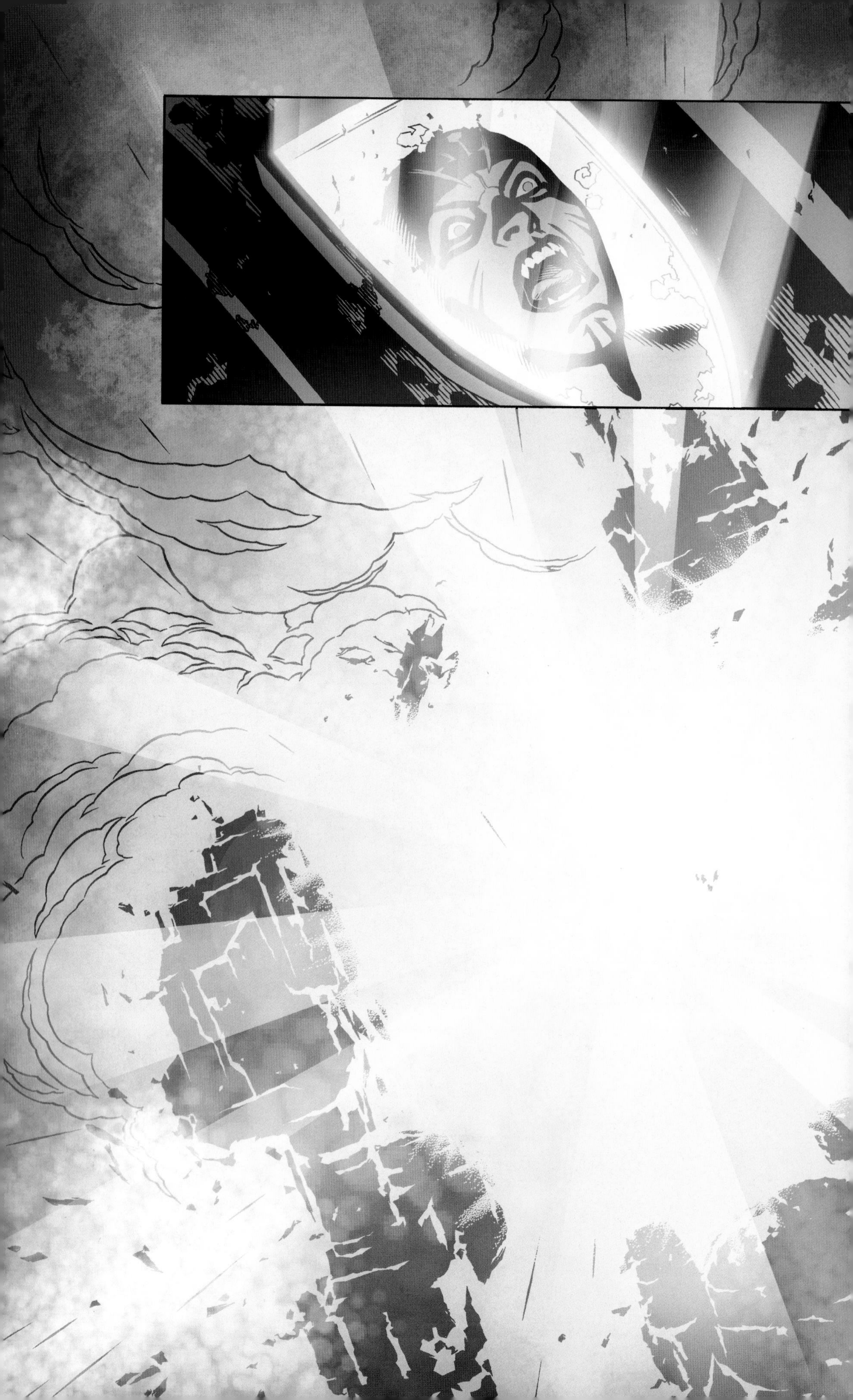

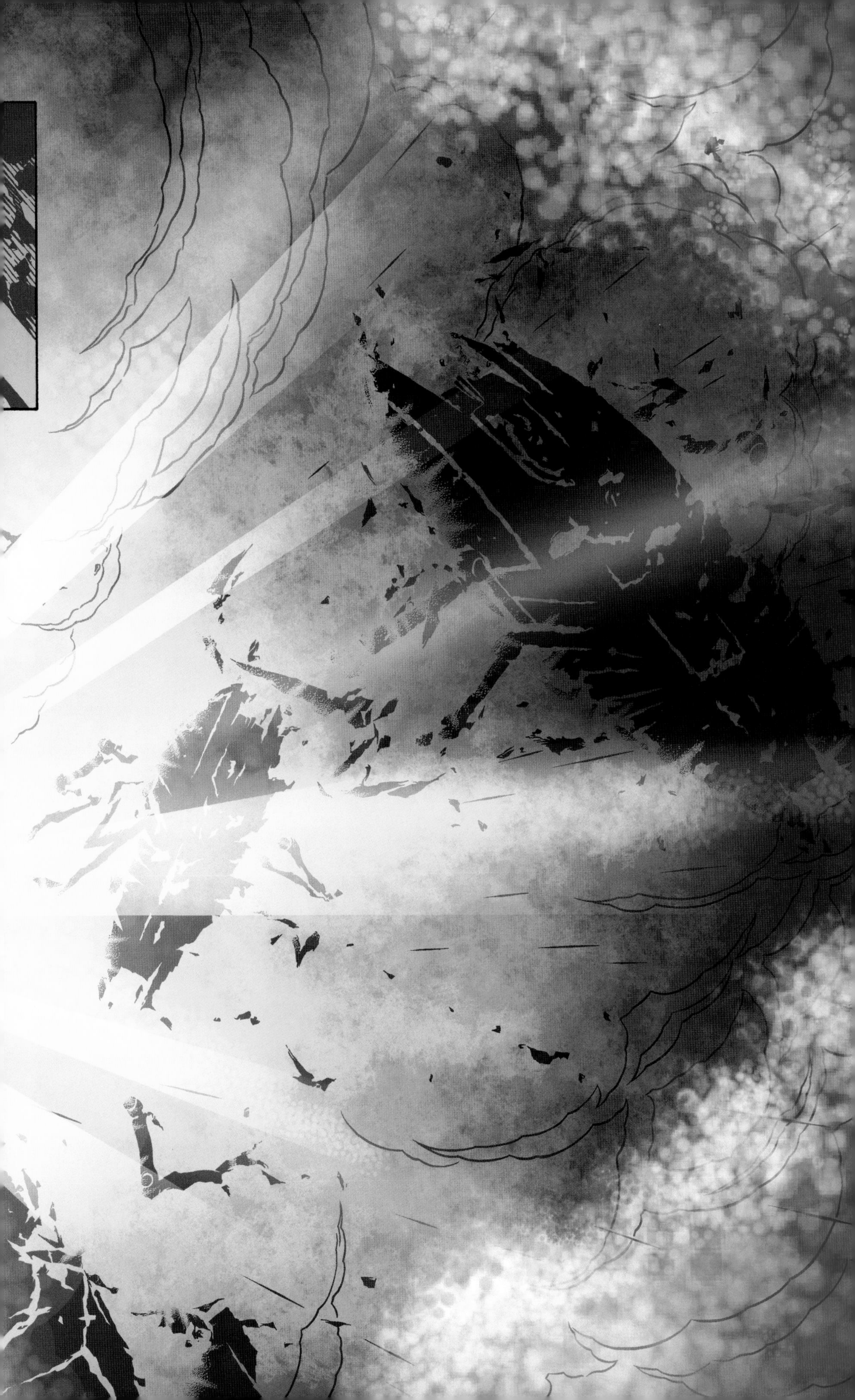

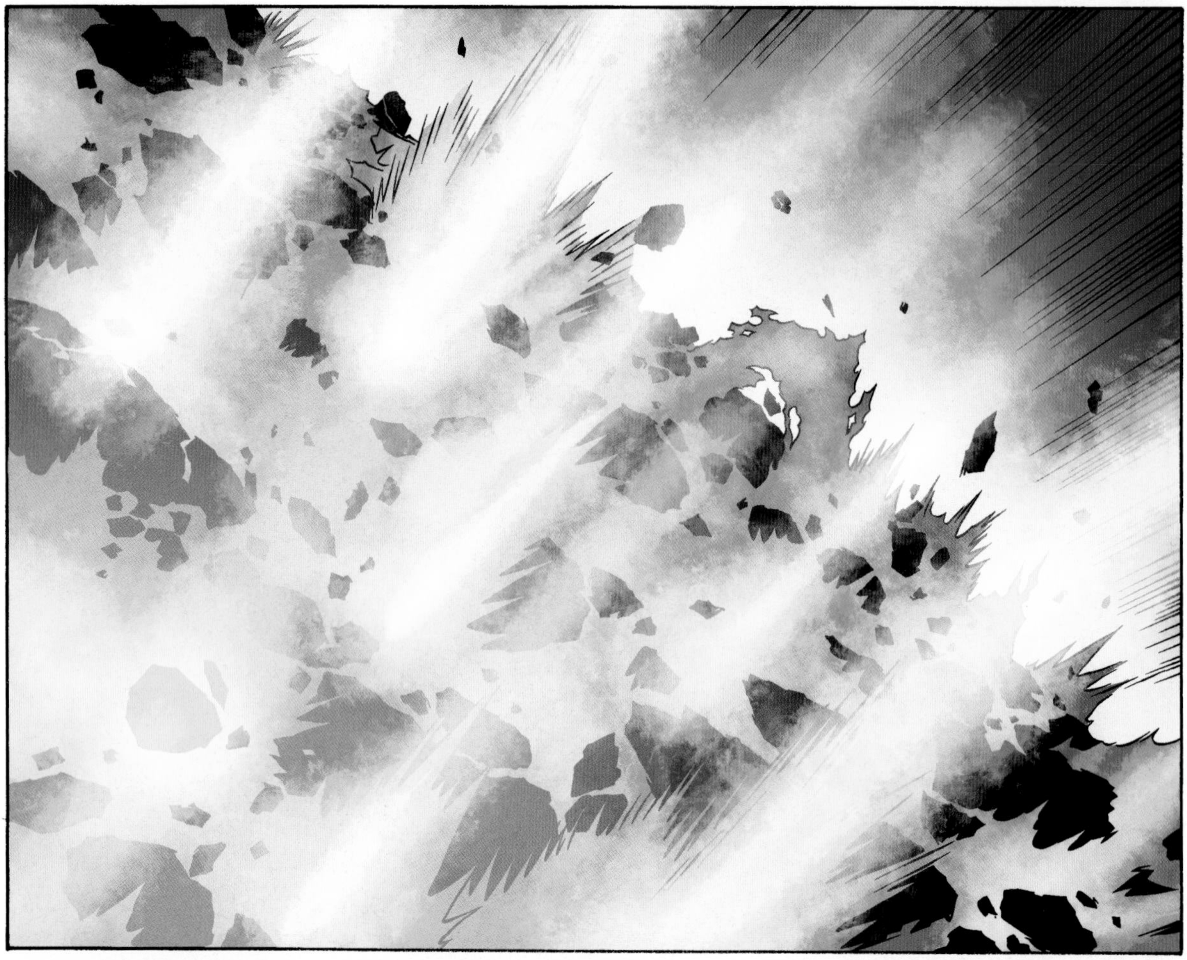

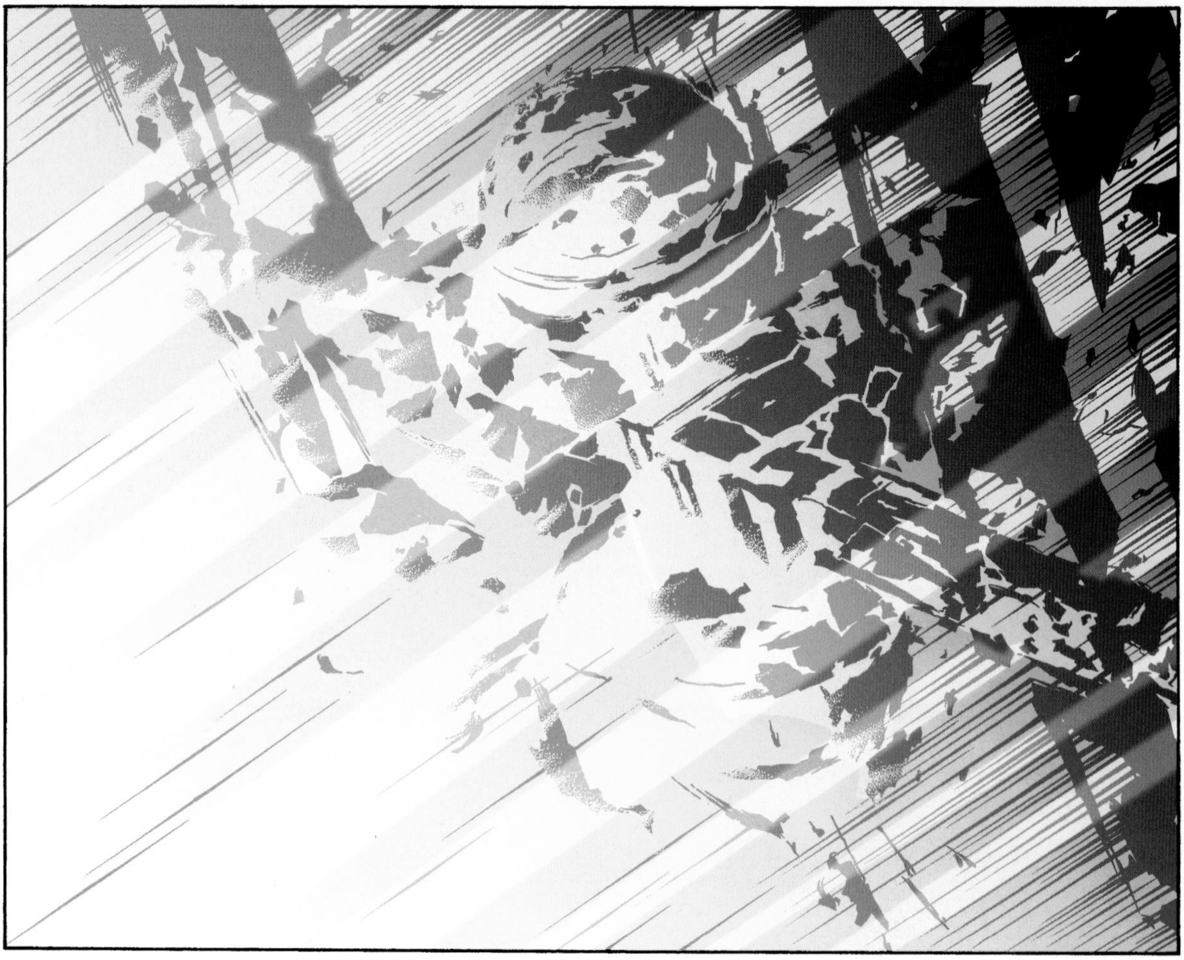

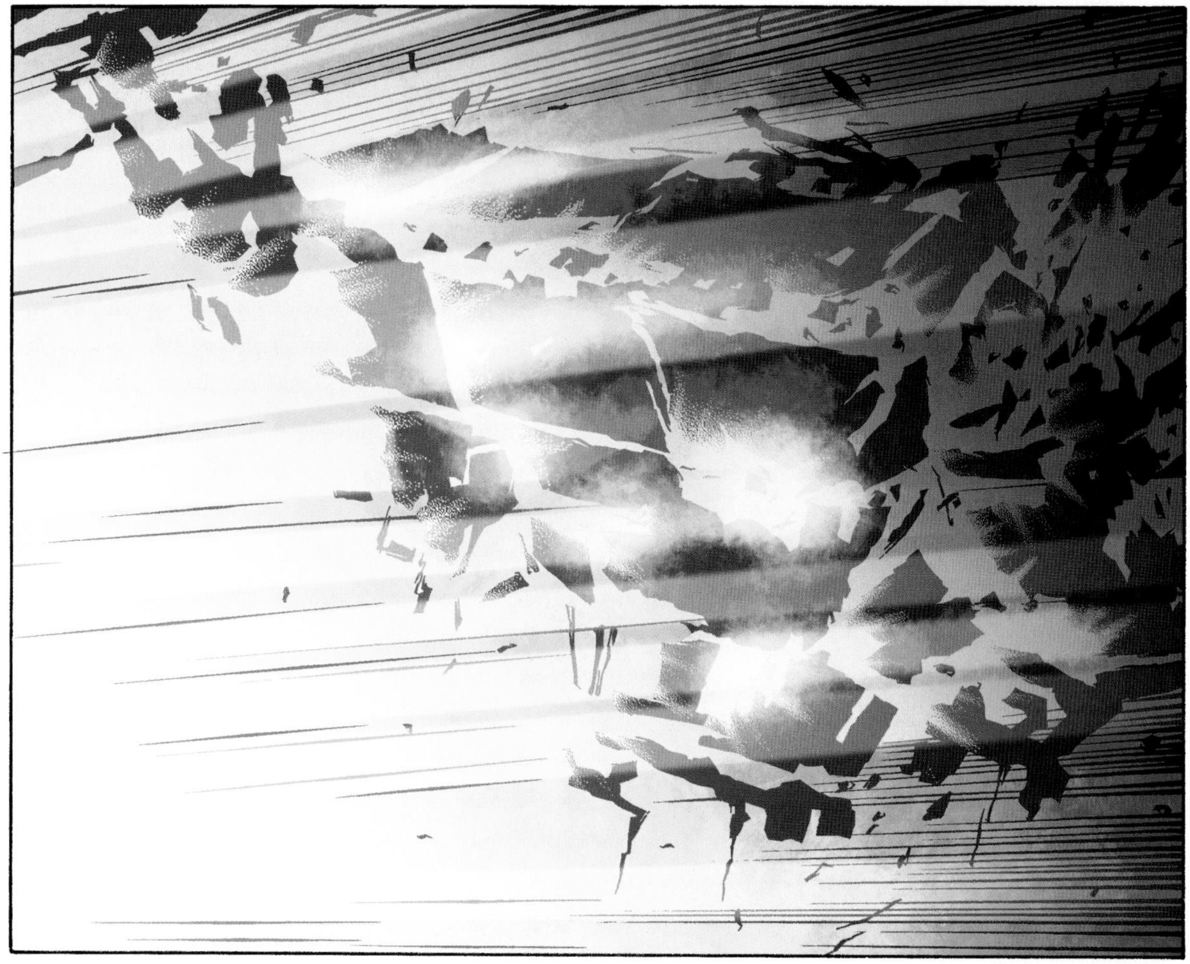

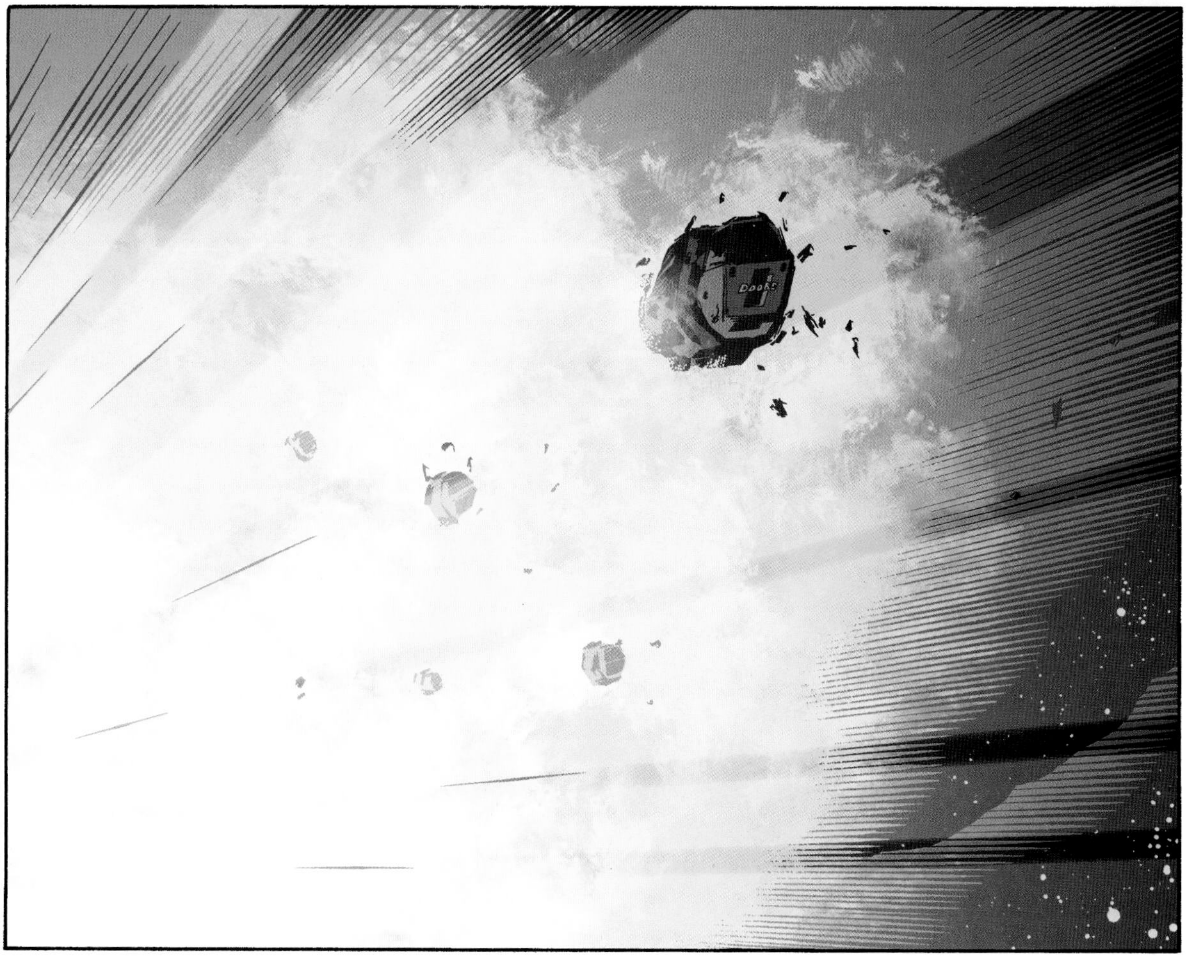
DOORS

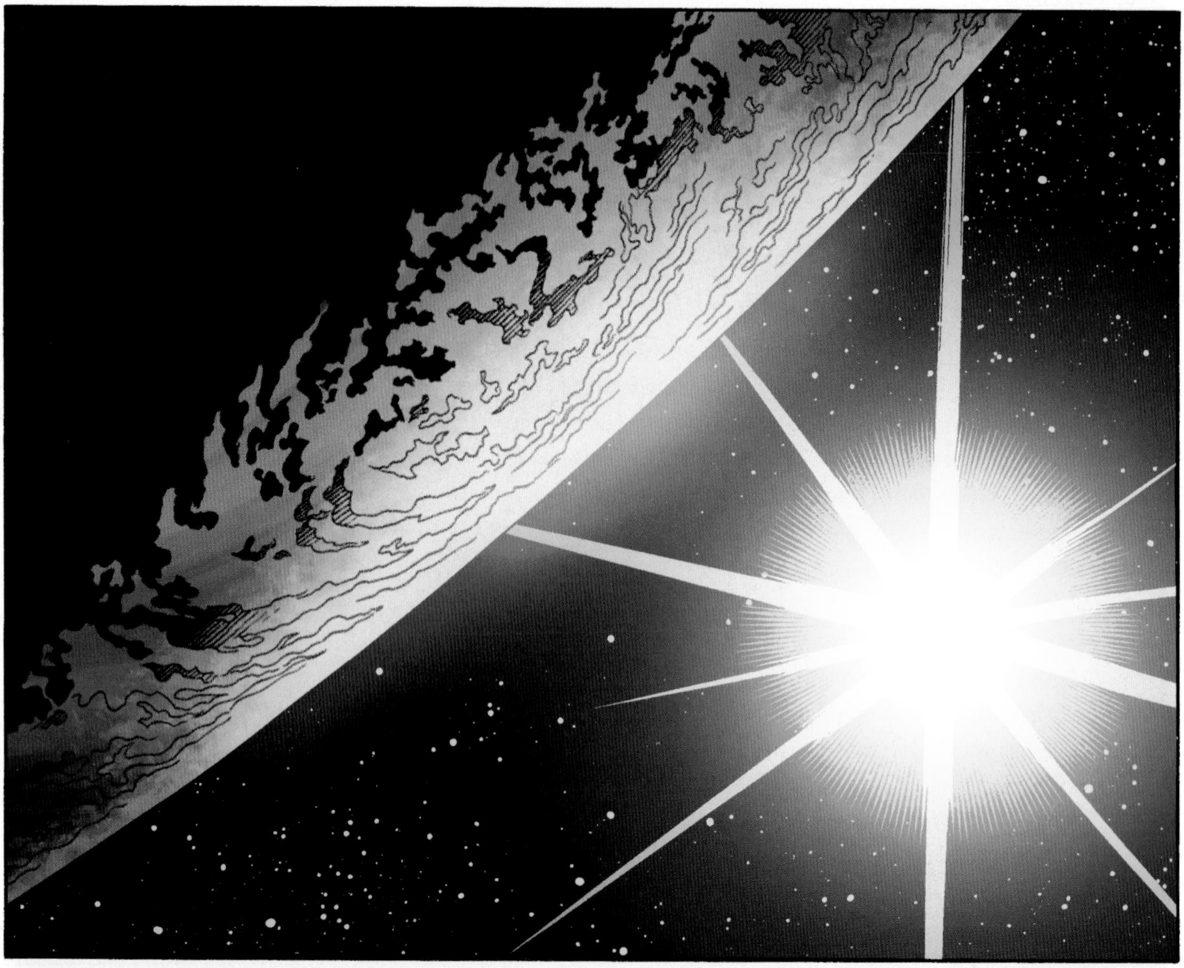

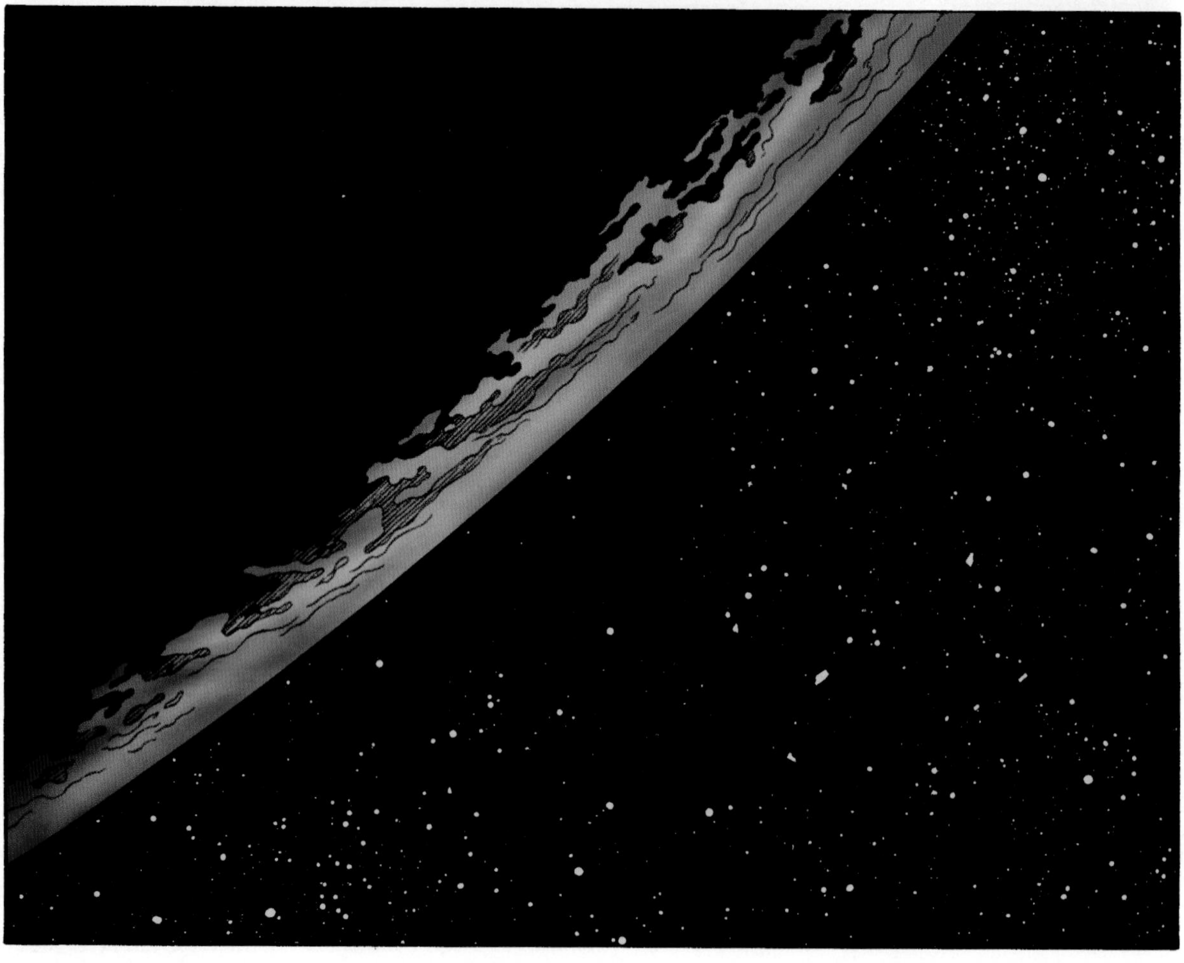

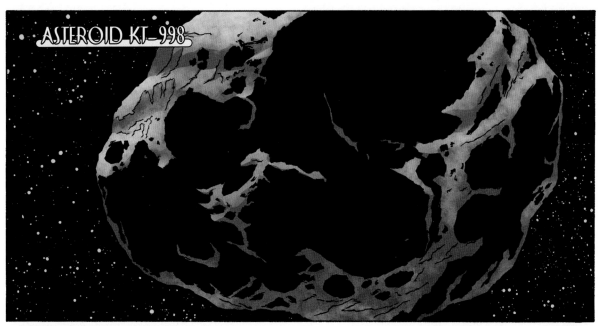

ASTEROID KT-998

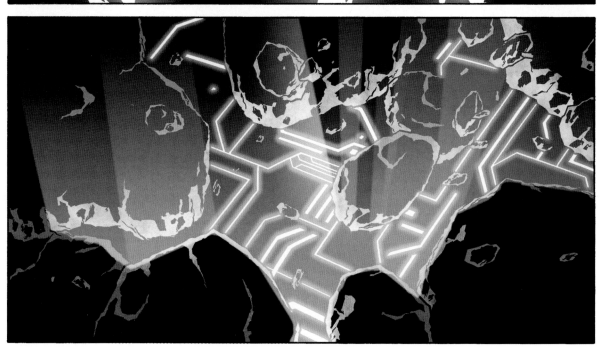

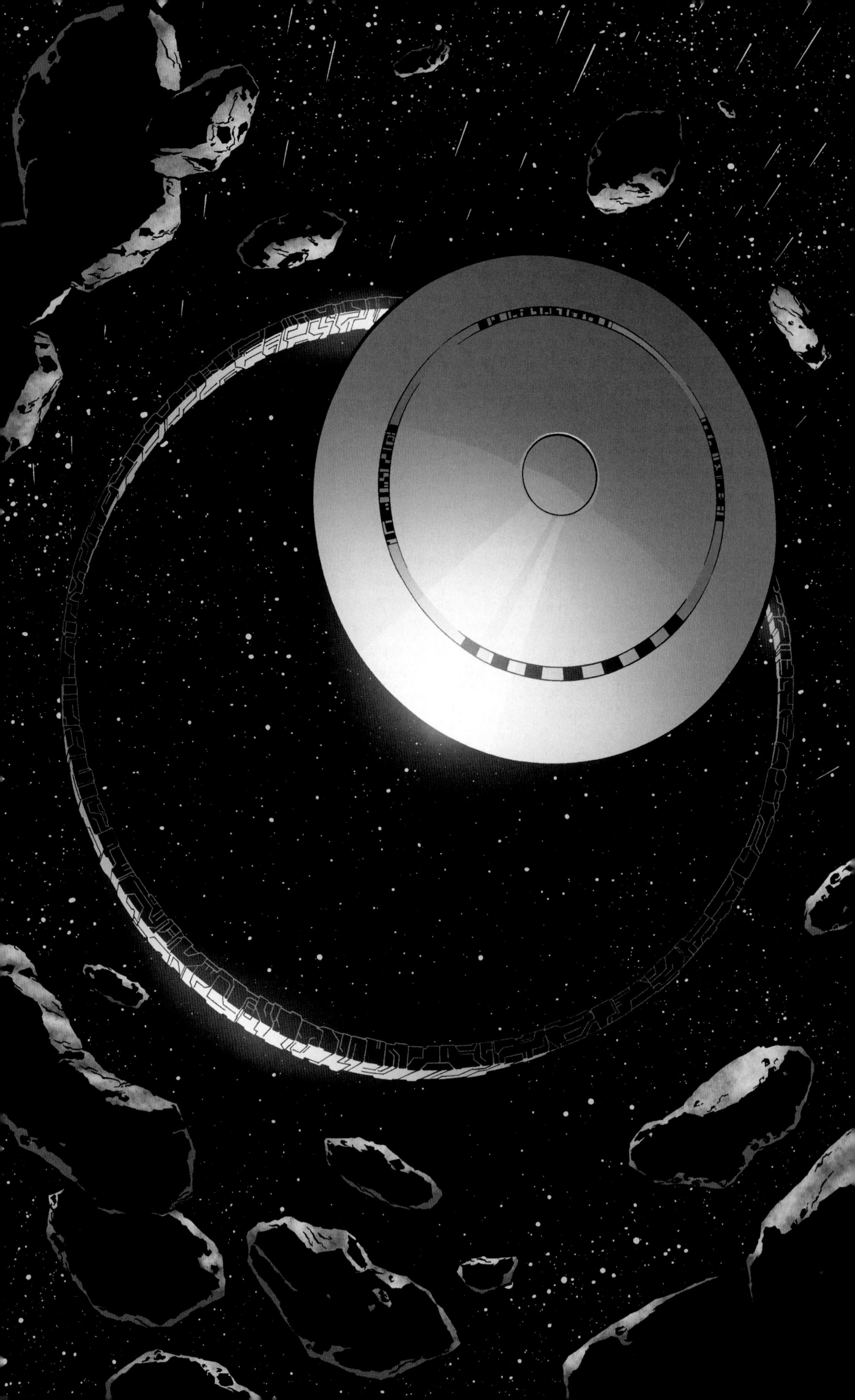

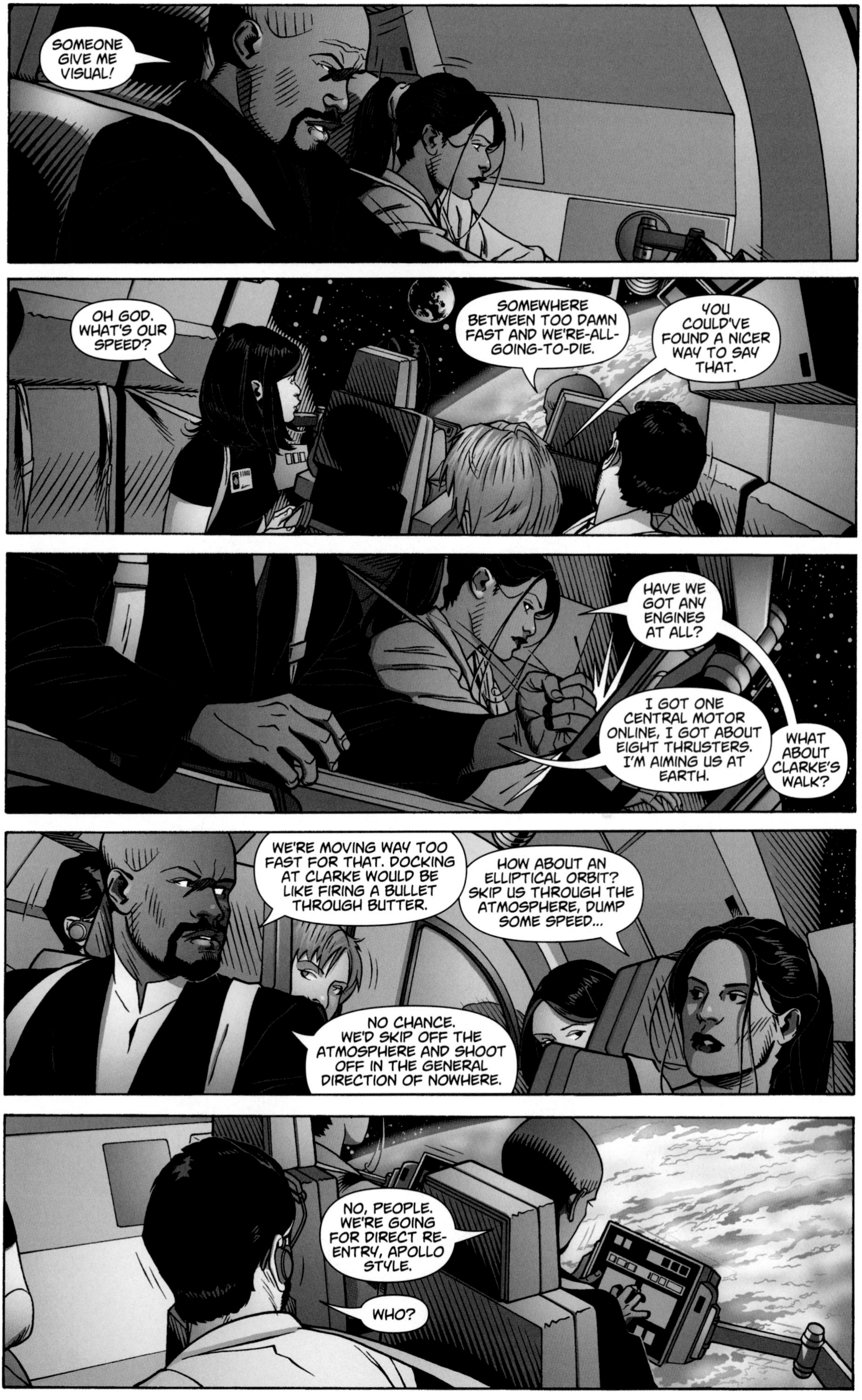
SOMEONE GIVE ME VISUAL!
OH GOD. WHAT'S OUR SPEED?
SOMEWHERE BETWEEN TOO DAMN FAST AND WE'RE-ALL-GOING-TO-DIE.
YOU COULD'VE FOUND A NICER WAY TO SAY THAT.
HAVE WE GOT ANY ENGINES AT ALL?
I GOT ONE CENTRAL MOTOR ONLINE, I GOT ABOUT EIGHT THRUSTERS. I'M AIMING US AT EARTH.
WHAT ABOUT CLARKE'S WALK?
WE'RE MOVING WAY TOO FAST FOR THAT. DOCKING AT CLARKE WOULD BE LIKE FIRING A BULLET THROUGH BUTTER.
HOW ABOUT AN ELLIPTICAL ORBIT? SKIP US THROUGH THE ATMOSPHERE, DUMP SOME SPEED...
NO CHANCE. WE'D SKIP OFF THE ATMOSPHERE AND SHOOT OFF IN THE GENERAL DIRECTION OF NOWHERE.
NO, PEOPLE. WE'RE GOING FOR DIRECT RE-ENTRY, APOLLO STYLE.
WHO?

WE LOST RADAR, WE LOST MAPPING, WE LOST COMMS...

WE DON'T NEED THEM. BACK IN THE OLD DAYS, THEY DID RE-ENTRY WITH A COMPUTER DUMBER THAN MY WATCH AND A COUPLE OF PARACHUTES.

WE DON'T HAVE ANY PARACHUTES.

SHUT UP.

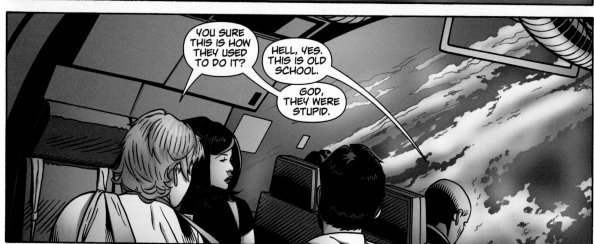

YOU SURE THIS IS HOW THEY USED TO DO IT?

HELL, YES. THIS IS OLD SCHOOL.

GOD, THEY WERE STUPID.

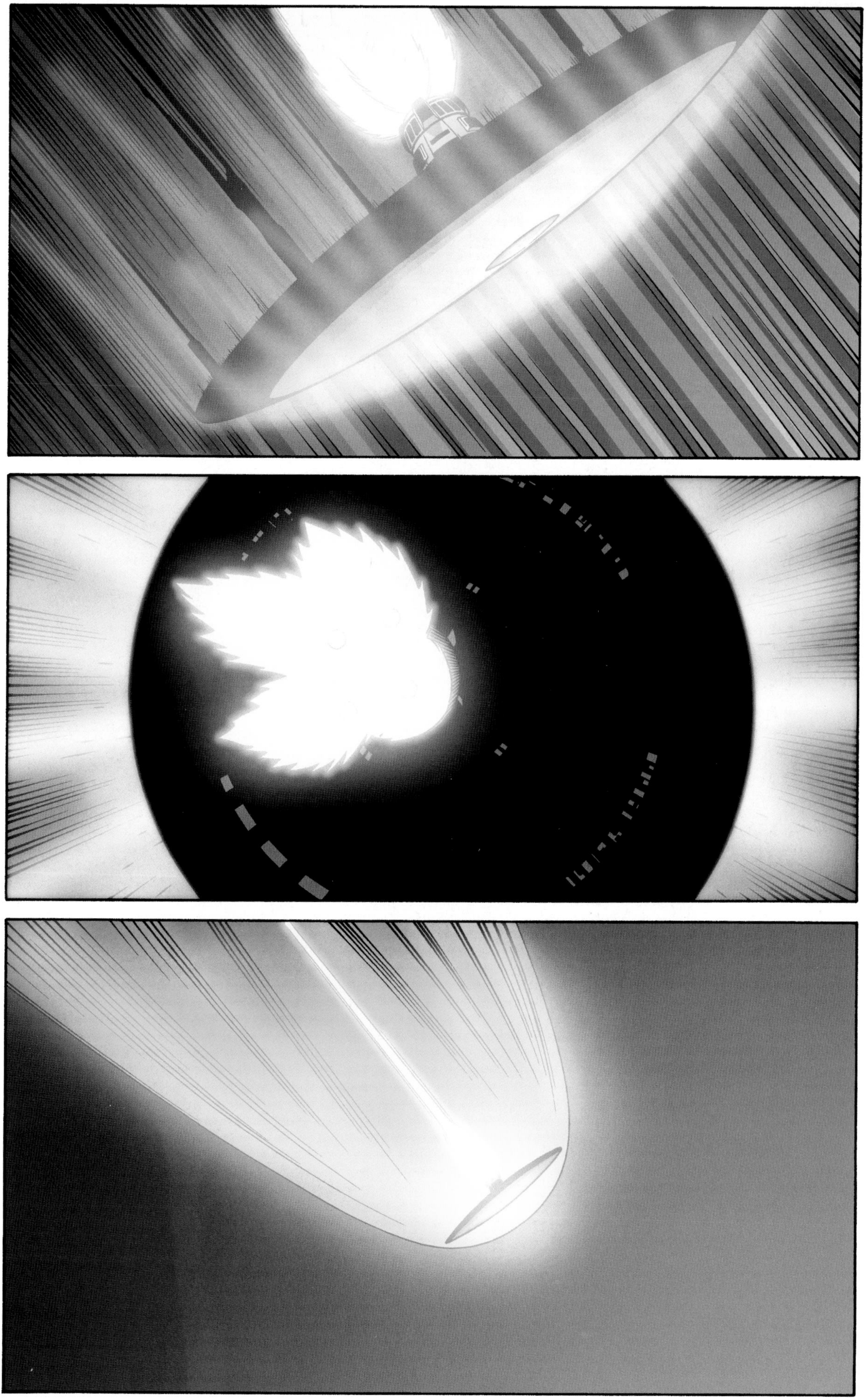

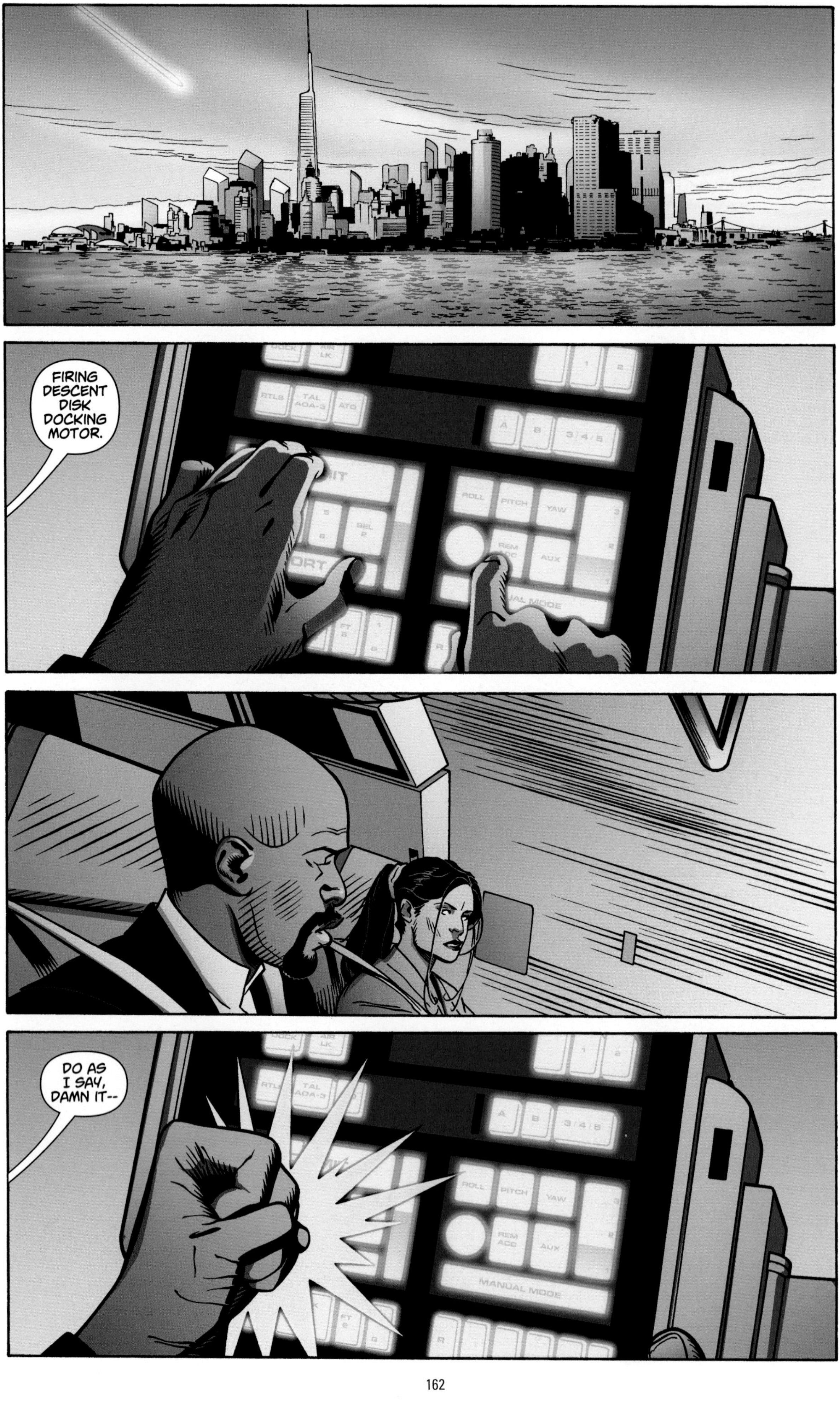
FIRING DESCENT DISK DOCKING MOTOR.
DO AS I SAY, DAMN IT--

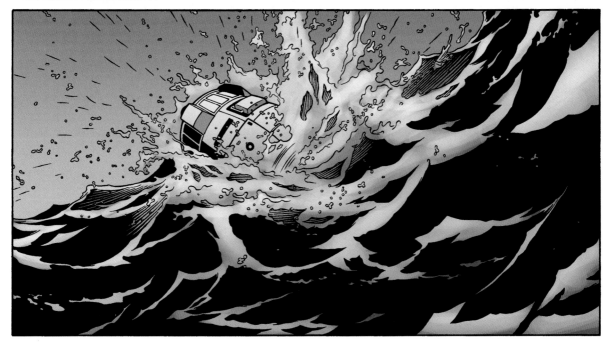

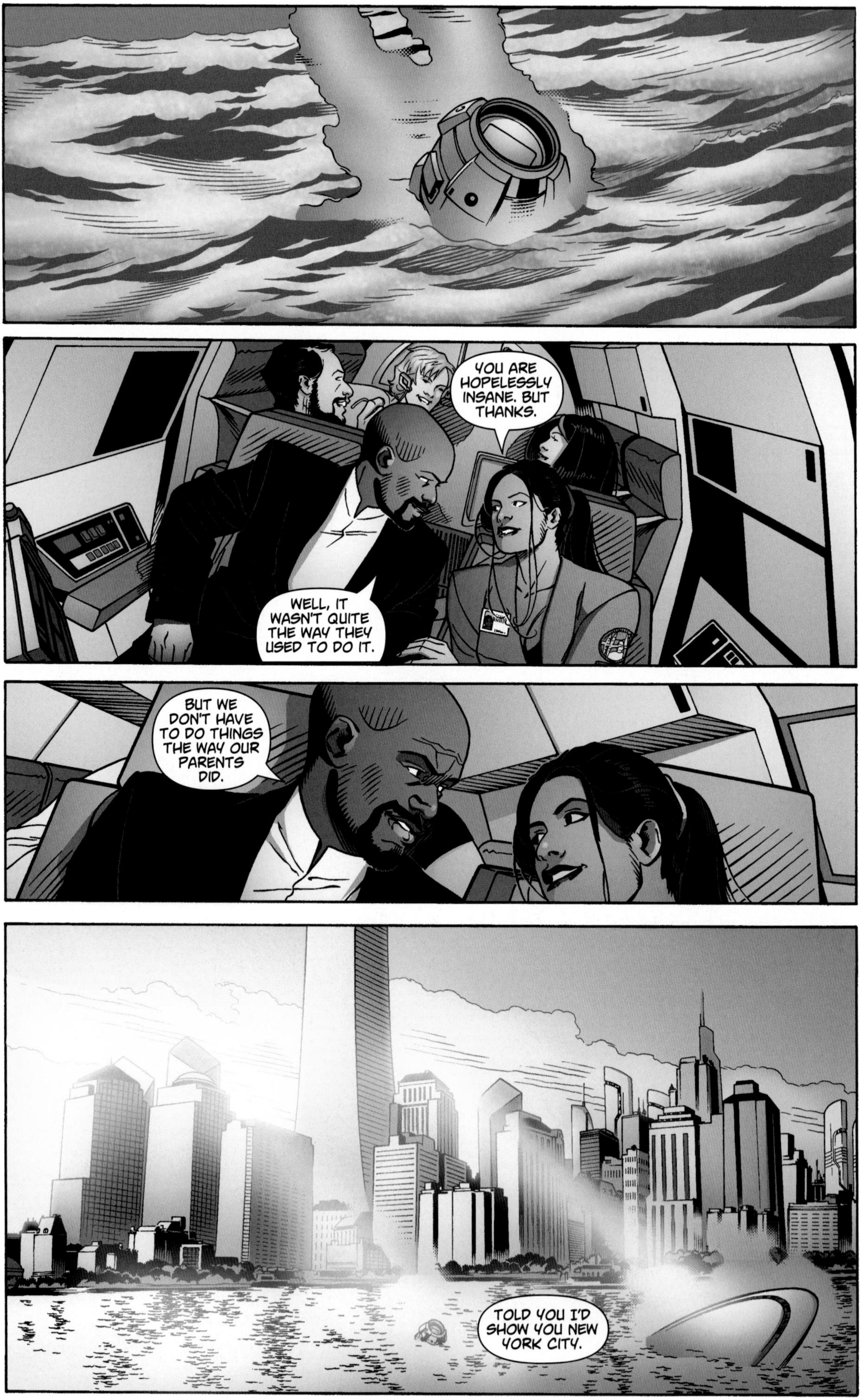

YOU ARE HOPELESSLY INSANE. BUT THANKS.
WELL, IT WASN'T QUITE THE WAY THEY USED TO DO IT.
BUT WE DON'T HAVE TO DO THINGS THE WAY OUR PARENTS DID.
TOLD YOU I'D SHOW YOU NEW YORK CITY.

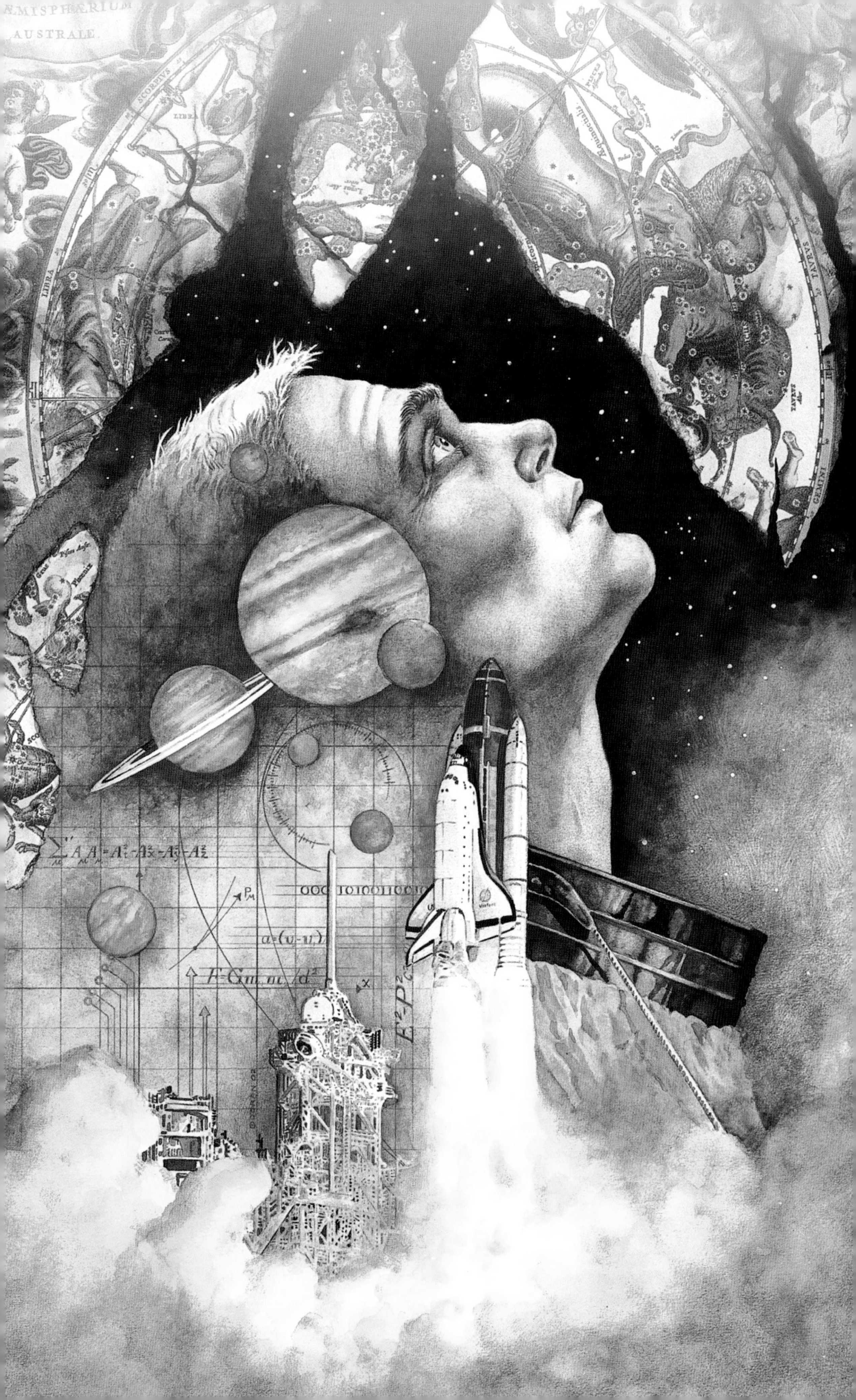
AUSTRALE
SCORPIUS
LIBRA
TAURUS
GEMINI

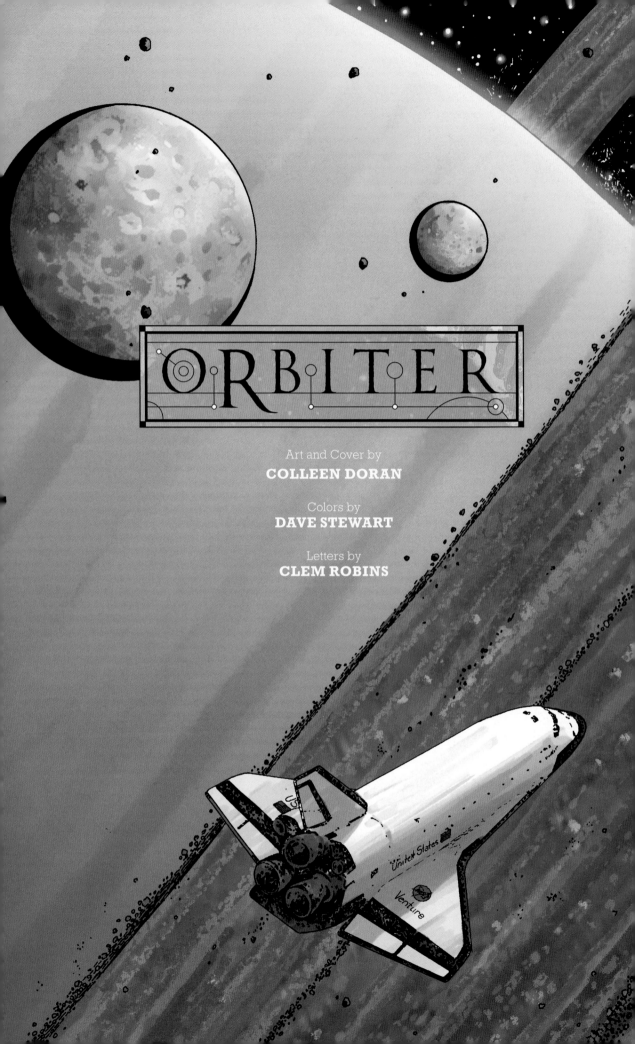

ORBITER

Art and Cover by
COLLEEN DORAN

Colors by
DAVE STEWART

Letters by
CLEM ROBINS

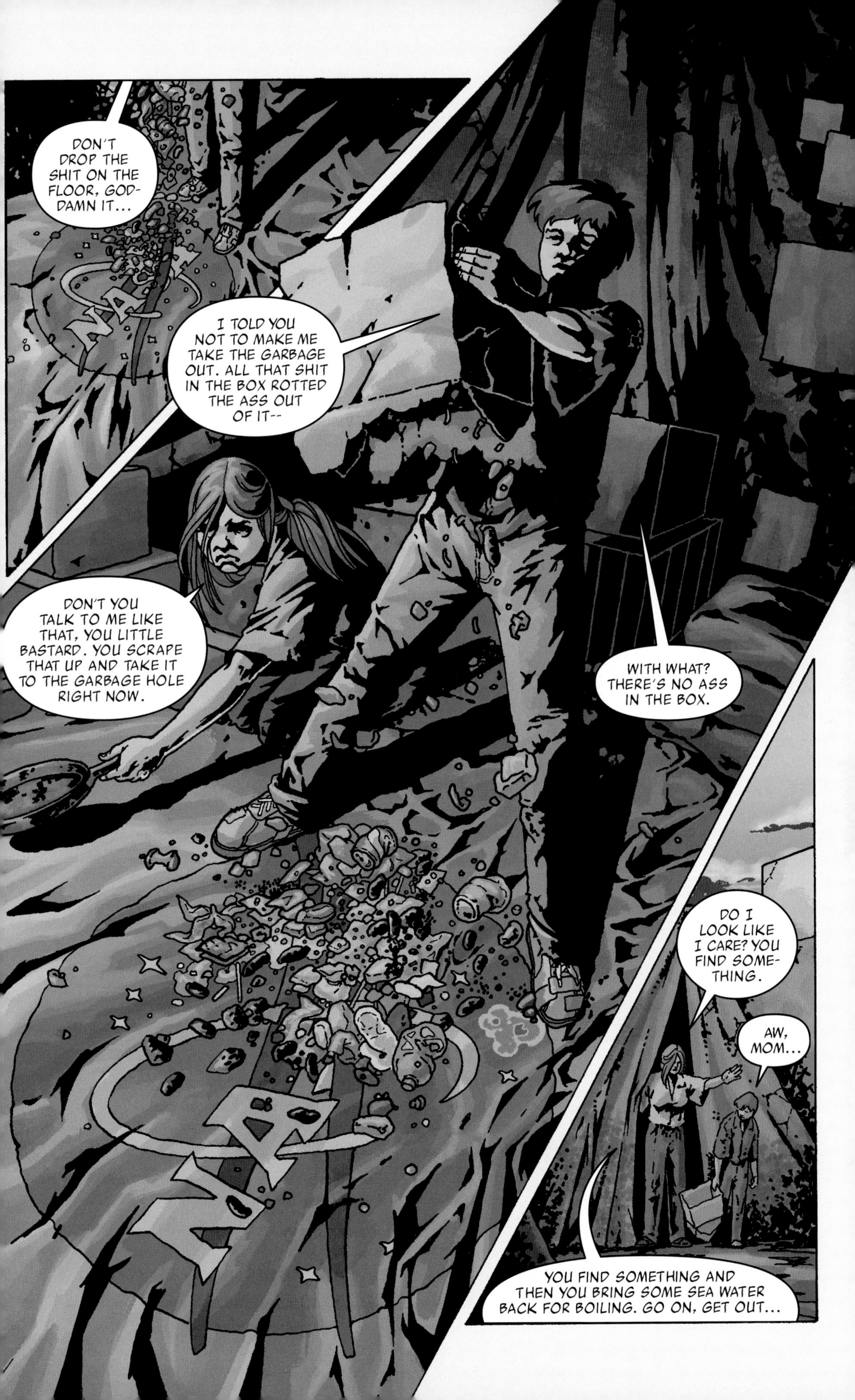
DON'T DROP THE SHIT ON THE FLOOR, GOD-DAMN IT...
I TOLD YOU NOT TO MAKE ME TAKE THE GARBAGE OUT. ALL THAT SHIT IN THE BOX ROTTED THE ASS OUT OF IT--
DON'T YOU TALK TO ME LIKE THAT, YOU LITTLE BASTARD. YOU SCRAPE THAT UP AND TAKE IT TO THE GARBAGE HOLE RIGHT NOW.
WITH WHAT? THERE'S NO ASS IN THE BOX.
DO I LOOK LIKE I CARE? YOU FIND SOME-THING.
AW, MOM...
YOU FIND SOMETHING AND THEN YOU BRING SOME SEA WATER BACK FOR BOILING. GO ON, GET OUT...

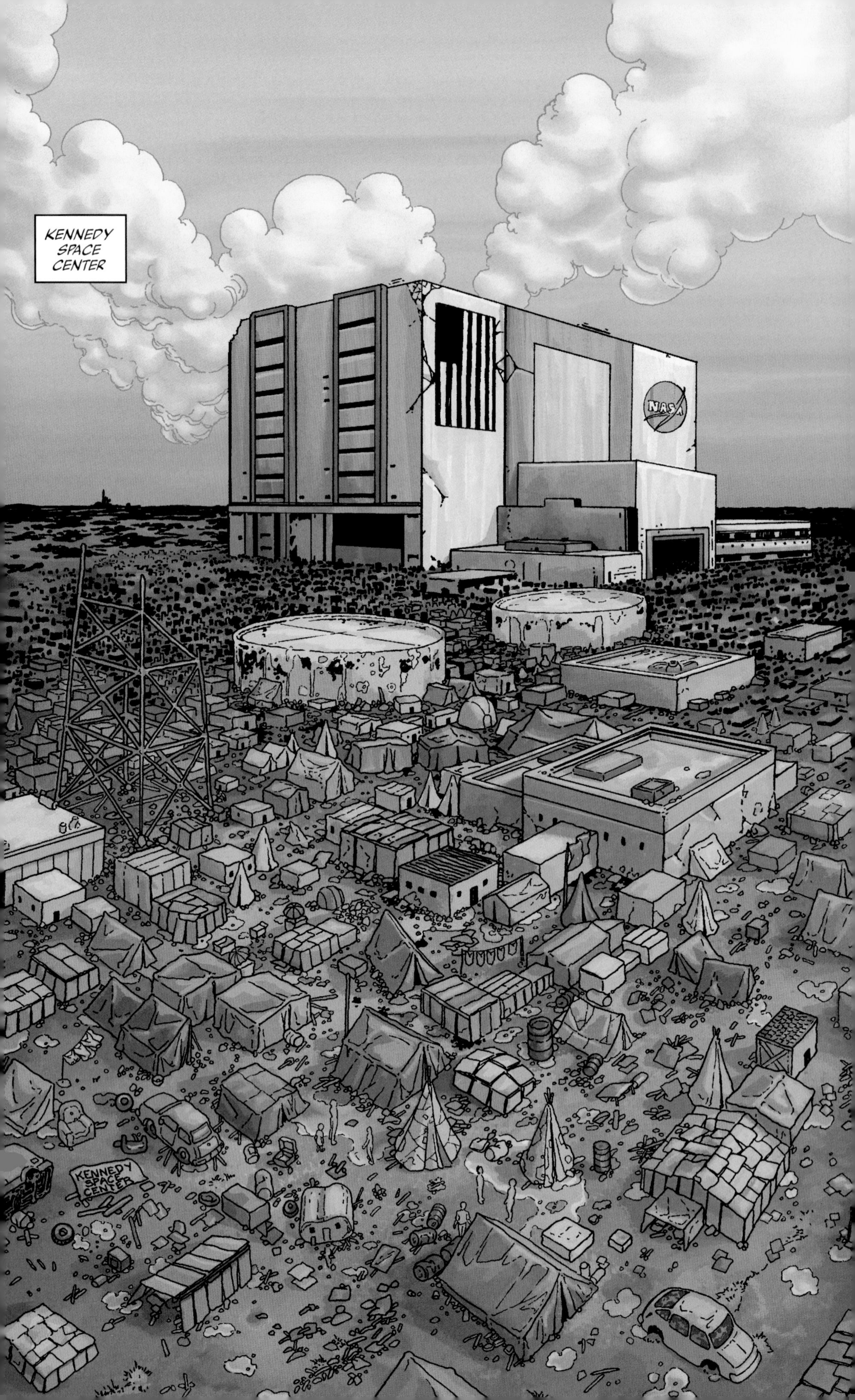
KENNEDY SPACE CENTER
NASA
KENNEDY SPACE CENTER

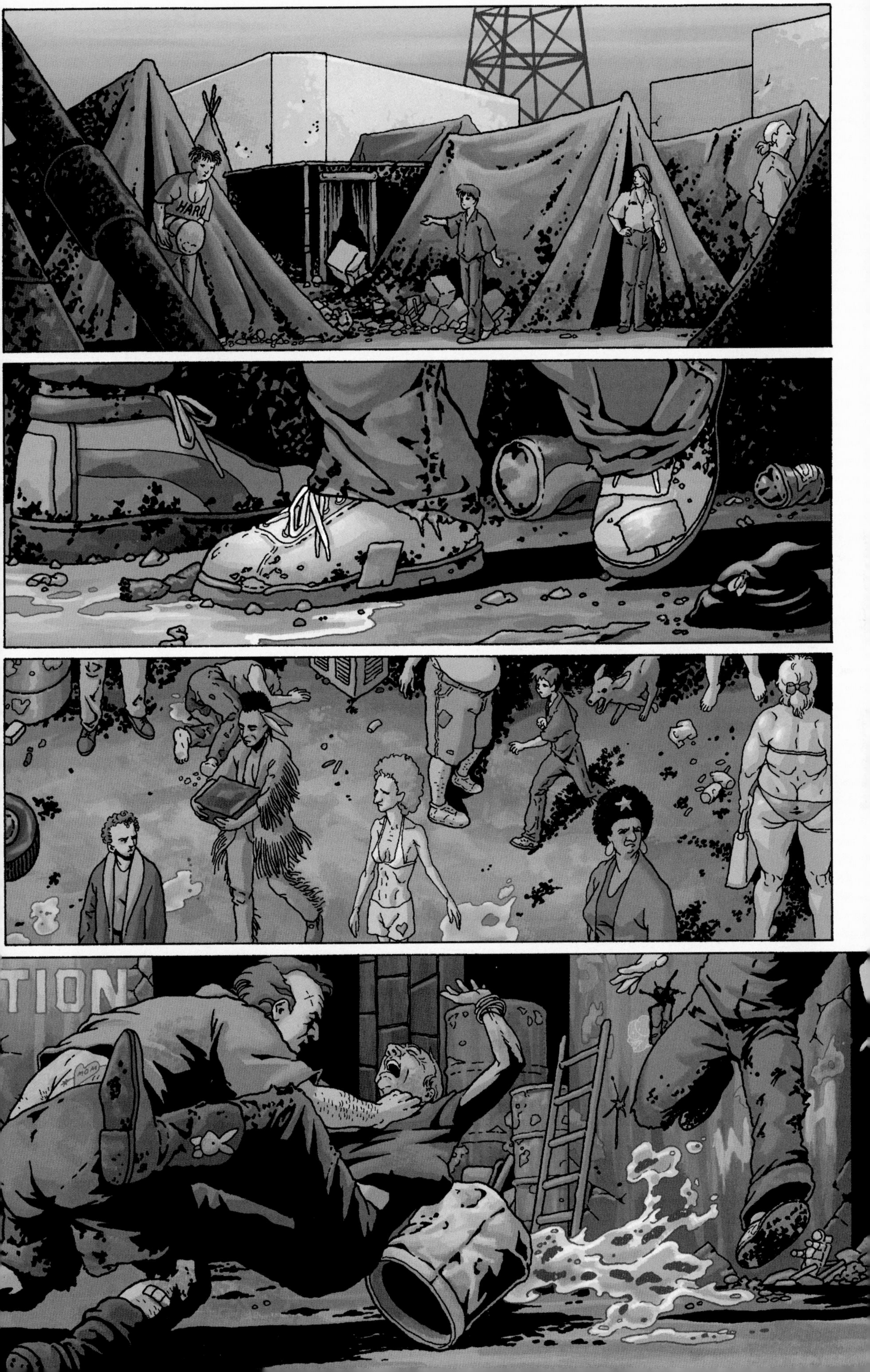
TION

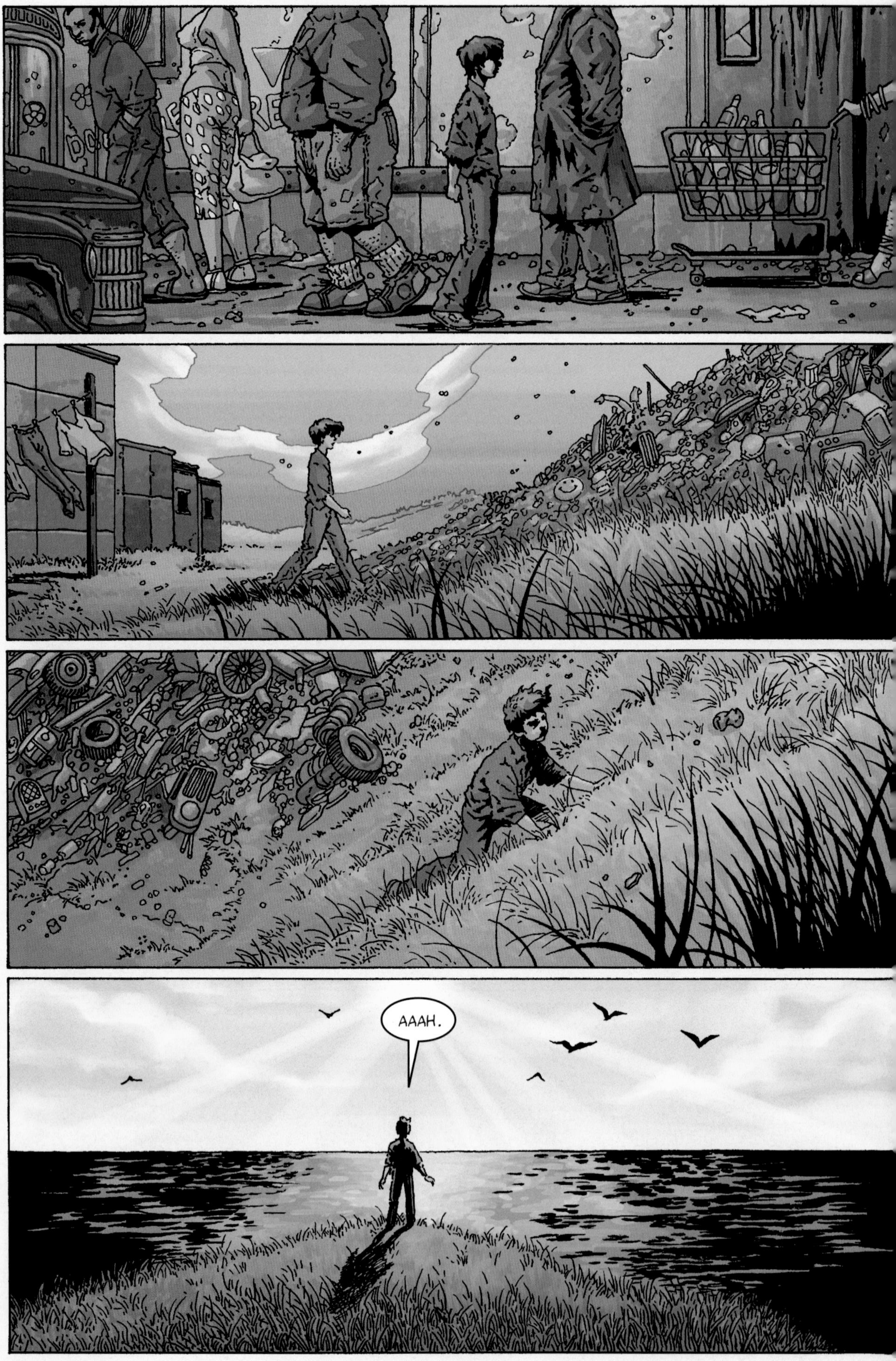
AAAH.

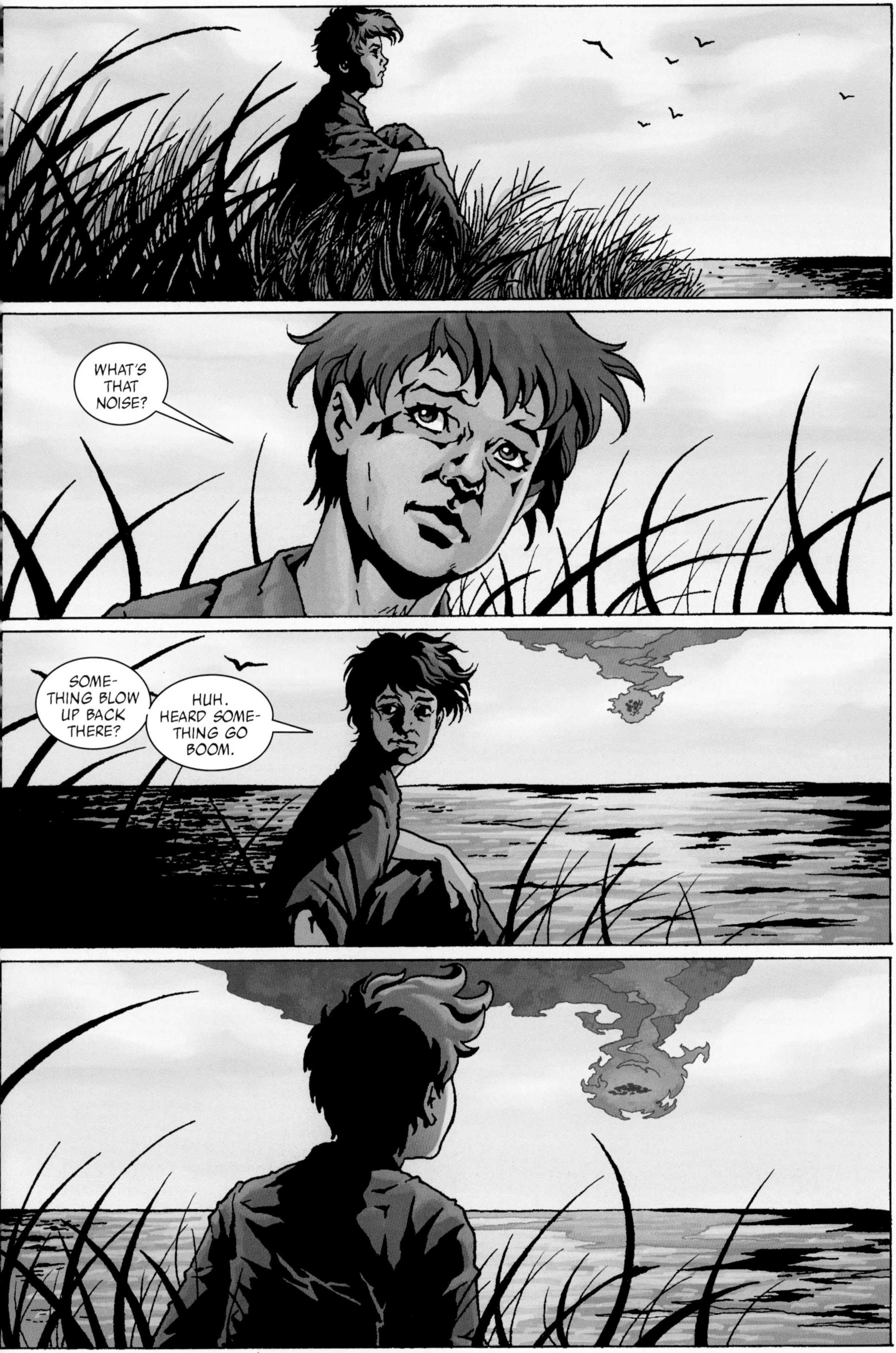
WHAT'S THAT NOISE?
SOME-THING BLOW UP BACK THERE?
HUH. HEARD SOME-THING GO BOOM.

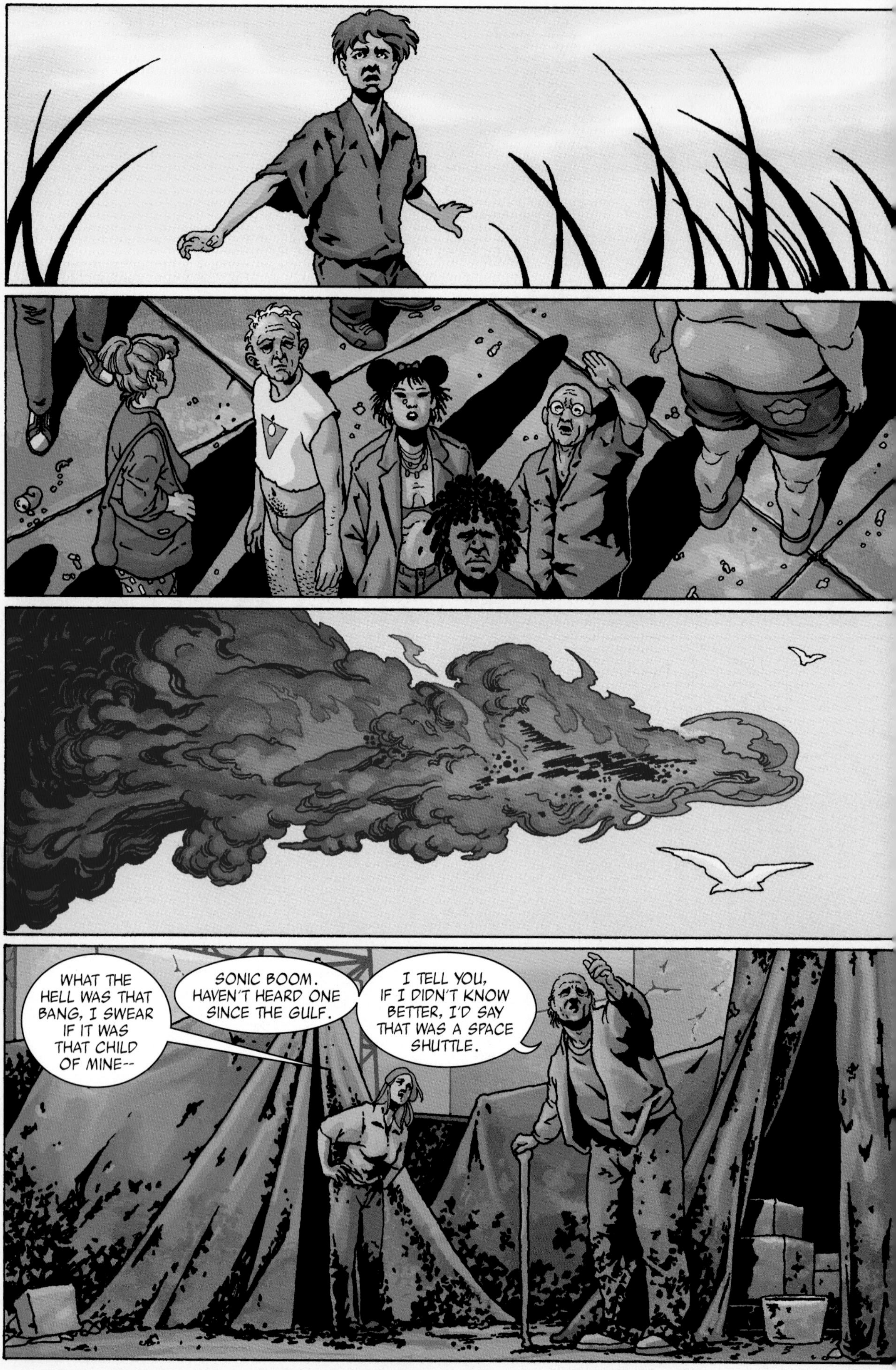
WHAT THE HELL WAS THAT BANG, I SWEAR IF IT WAS THAT CHILD OF MINE--
SONIC BOOM. HAVEN'T HEARD ONE SINCE THE GULF.
I TELL YOU, IF I DIDN'T KNOW BETTER, I'D SAY THAT WAS A SPACE SHUTTLE.

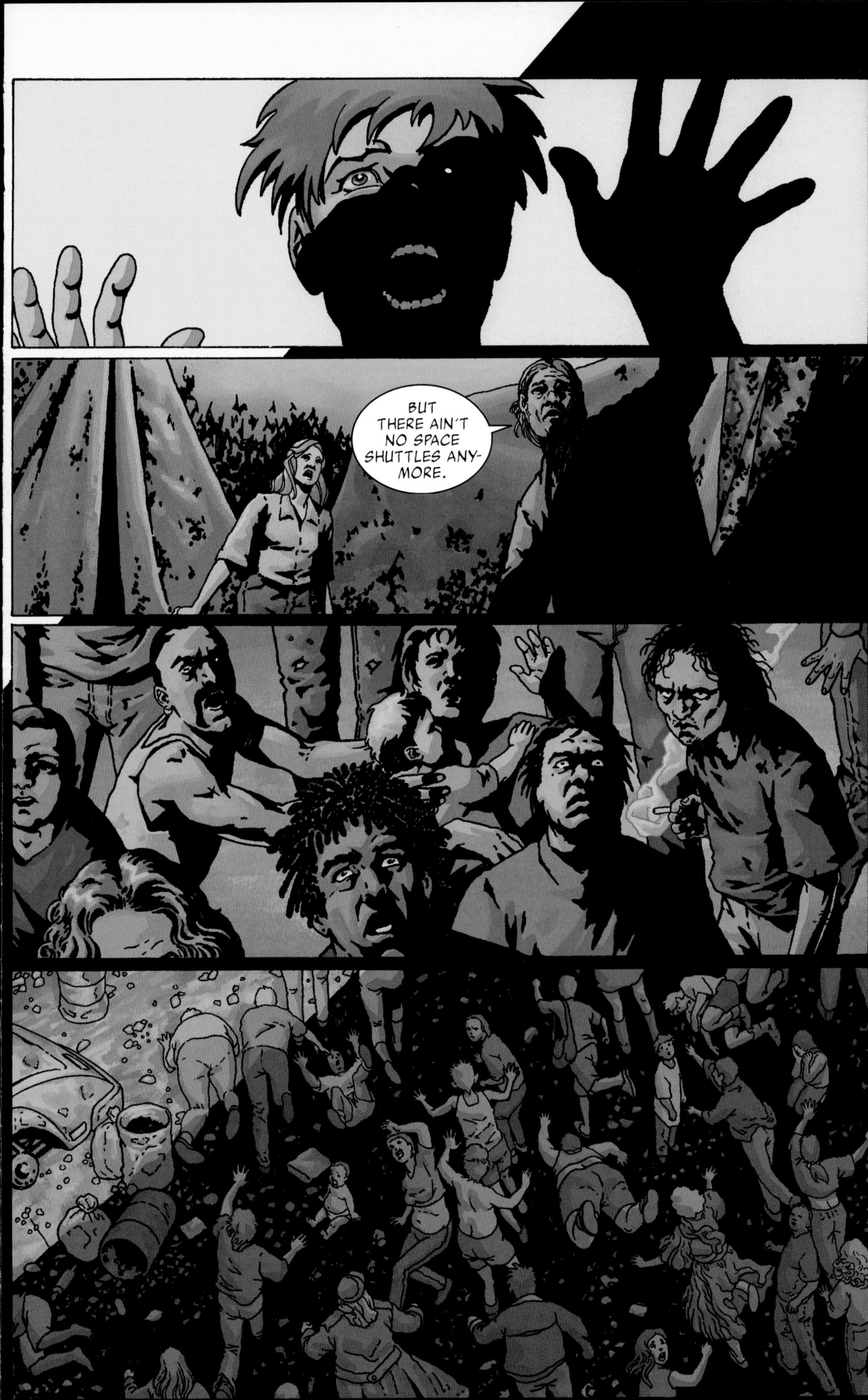
BUT THERE AIN'T NO SPACE SHUTTLES ANY-MORE.

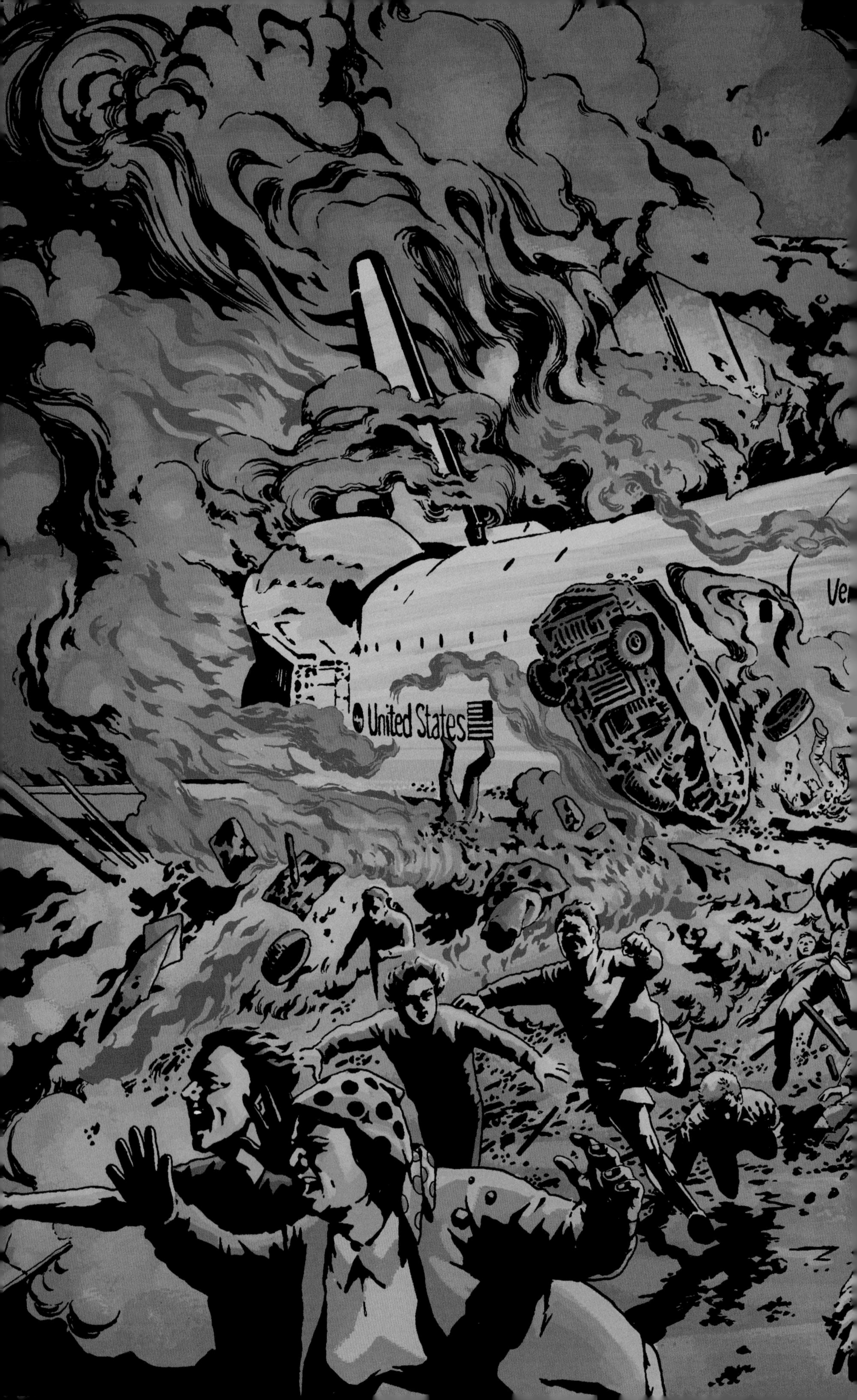
United States

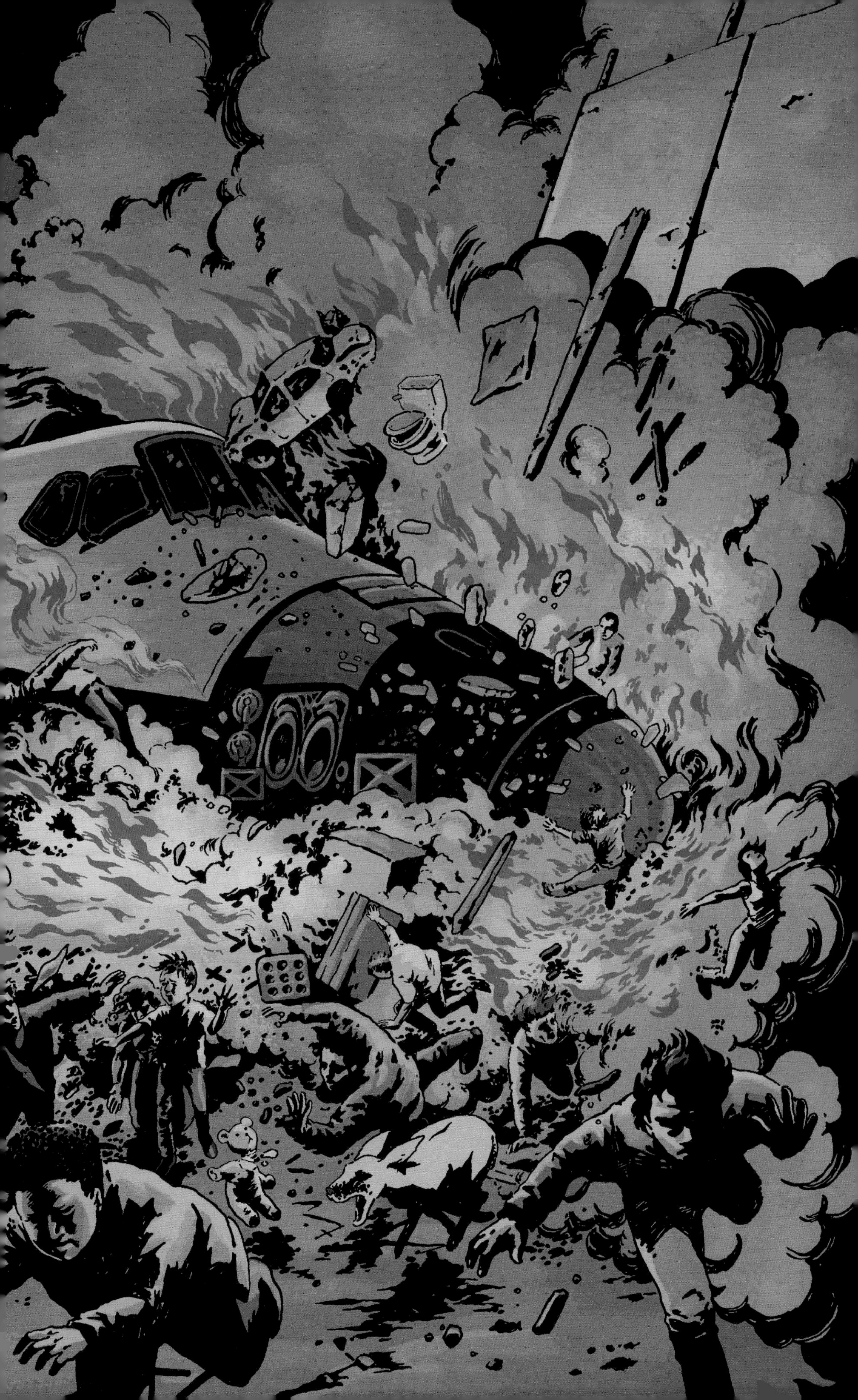

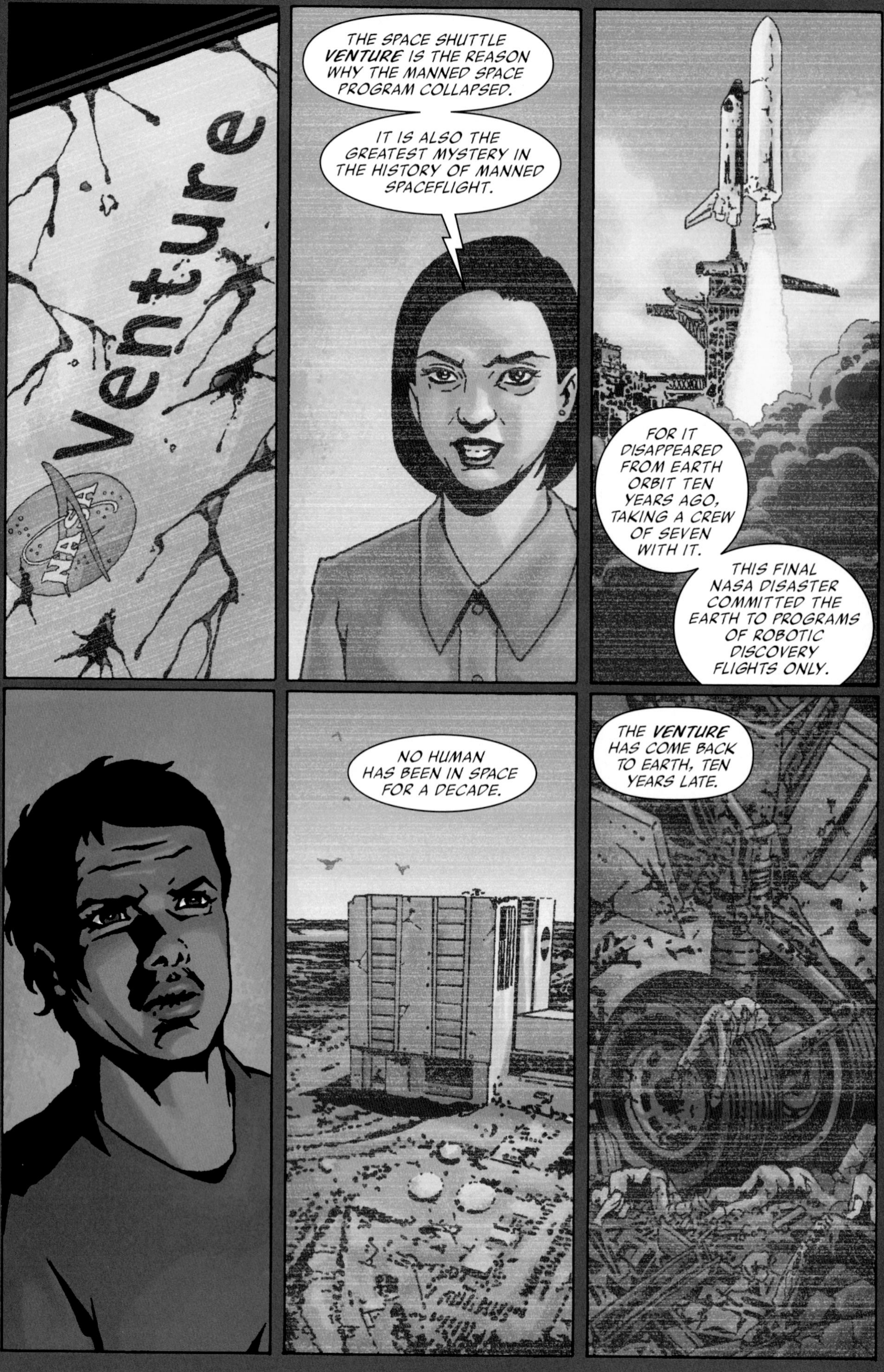

Venture
NASA
THE SPACE SHUTTLE VENTURE IS THE REASON WHY THE MANNED SPACE PROGRAM COLLAPSED.
IT IS ALSO THE GREATEST MYSTERY IN THE HISTORY OF MANNED SPACEFLIGHT.
FOR IT DISAPPEARED FROM EARTH ORBIT TEN YEARS AGO, TAKING A CREW OF SEVEN WITH IT.
THIS FINAL NASA DISASTER COMMITTED THE EARTH TO PROGRAMS OF ROBOTIC DISCOVERY FLIGHTS ONLY.
NO HUMAN HAS BEEN IN SPACE FOR A DECADE.
THE VENTURE HAS COME BACK TO EARTH, TEN YEARS LATE.

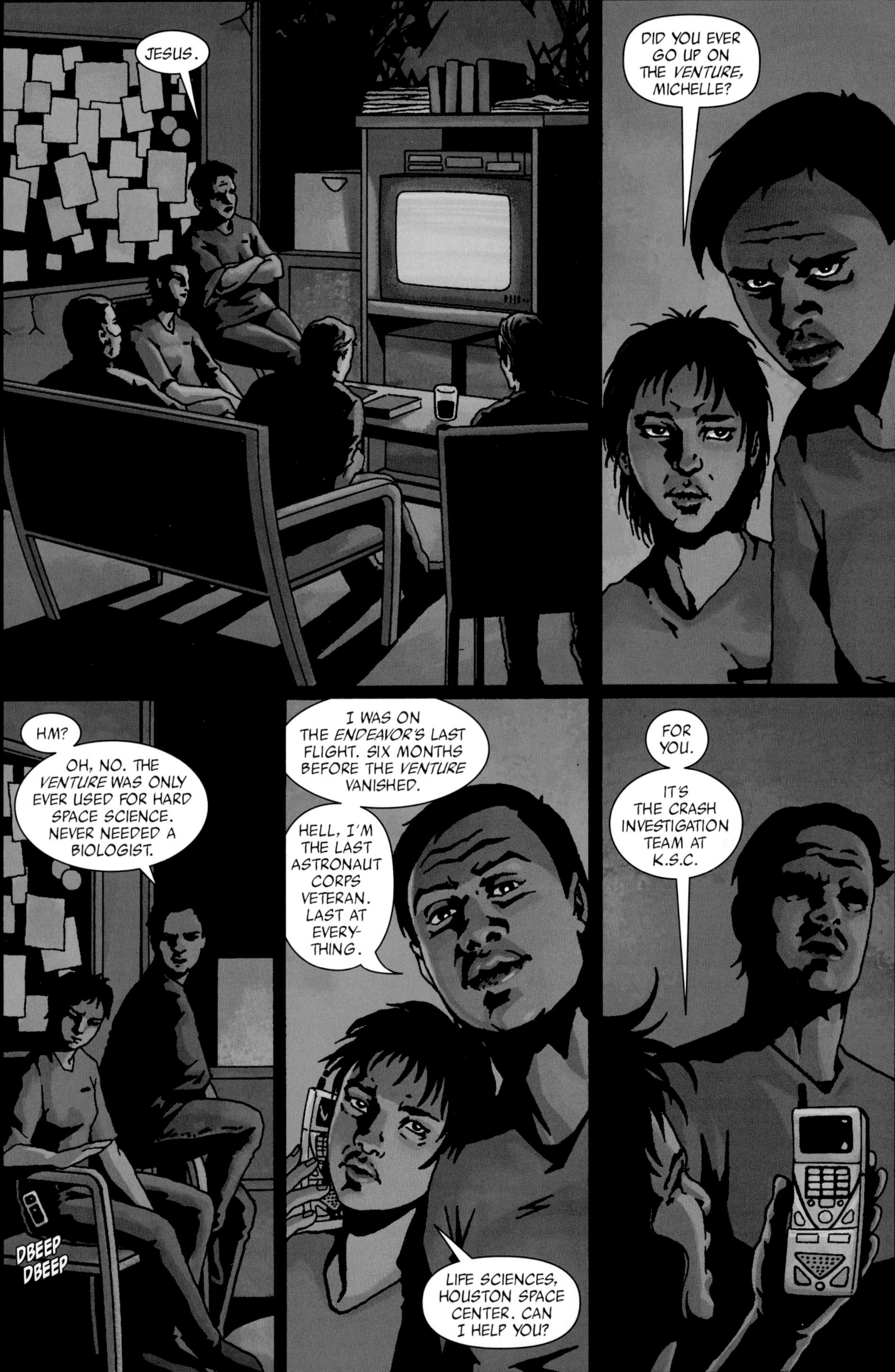
JESUS.
DID YOU EVER GO UP ON THE *VENTURE*, MICHELLE?
HM?
OH, NO. THE *VENTURE* WAS ONLY EVER USED FOR HARD SPACE SCIENCE. NEVER NEEDED A BIOLOGIST.
DBEEP DBEEP
I WAS ON THE *ENDEAVOR'S* LAST FLIGHT. SIX MONTHS BEFORE THE *VENTURE* VANISHED.
HELL, I'M THE LAST ASTRONAUT CORPS VETERAN. LAST AT EVERY-THING.
LIFE SCIENCES, HOUSTON SPACE CENTER. CAN I HELP YOU?
FOR YOU.
IT'S THE CRASH INVESTIGATION TEAM AT K.S.C.

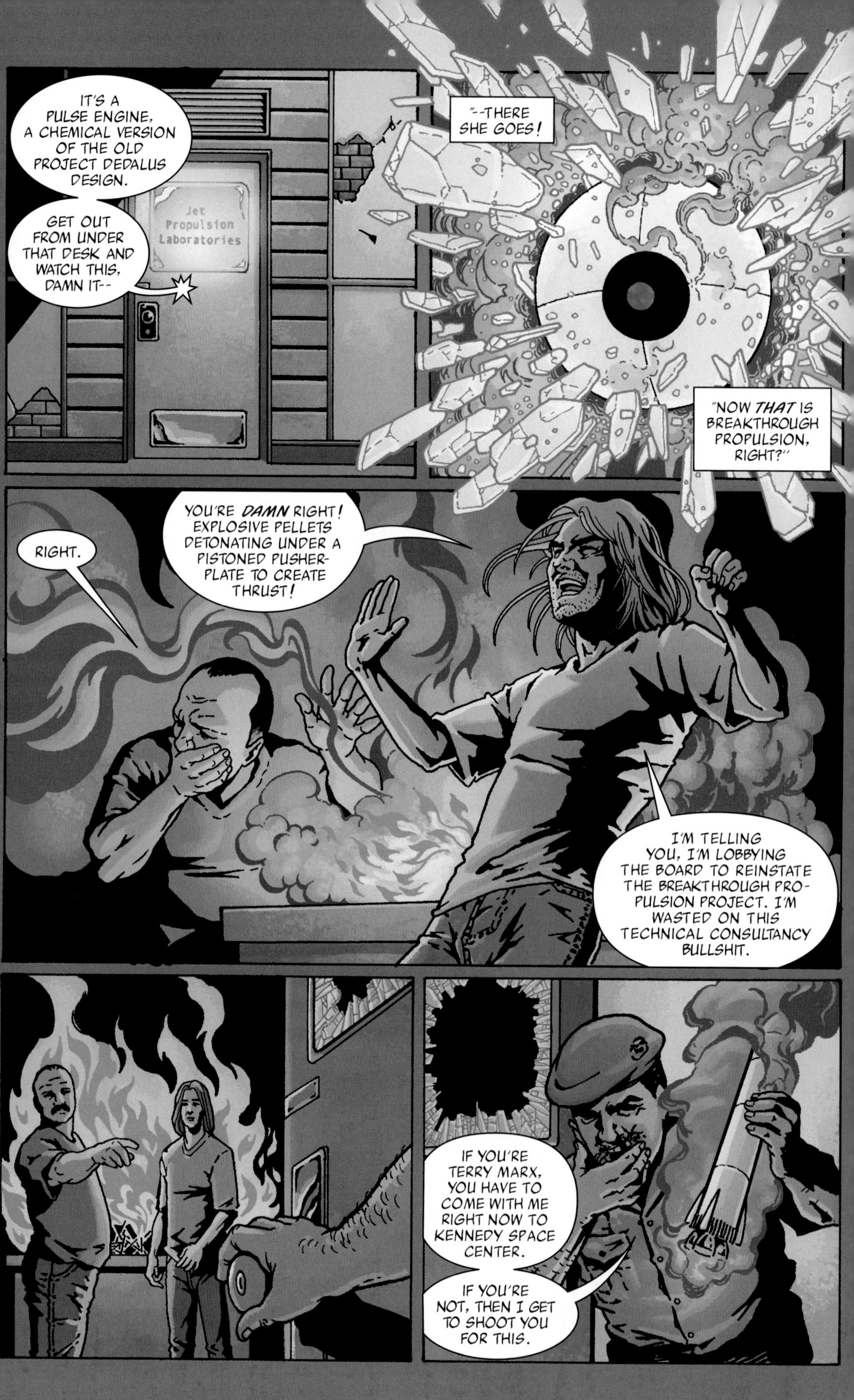
IT'S A PULSE ENGINE, A CHEMICAL VERSION OF THE OLD PROJECT DEDALUS DESIGN.
GET OUT FROM UNDER THAT DESK AND WATCH THIS, DAMN IT--
Jet Propulsion Laboratories
"--THERE SHE GOES!
"NOW THAT IS BREAKTHROUGH PROPULSION, RIGHT?"
RIGHT.
YOU'RE DAMN RIGHT! EXPLOSIVE PELLETS DETONATING UNDER A PISTONED PUSHER-PLATE TO CREATE THRUST!
I'M TELLING YOU, I'M LOBBYING THE BOARD TO REINSTATE THE BREAKTHROUGH PRO-PULSION PROJECT. I'M WASTED ON THIS TECHNICAL CONSULTANCY BULLSHIT.
IF YOU'RE TERRY MARX, YOU HAVE TO COME WITH ME RIGHT NOW TO KENNEDY SPACE CENTER.
IF YOU'RE NOT, THEN I GET TO SHOOT YOU FOR THIS.

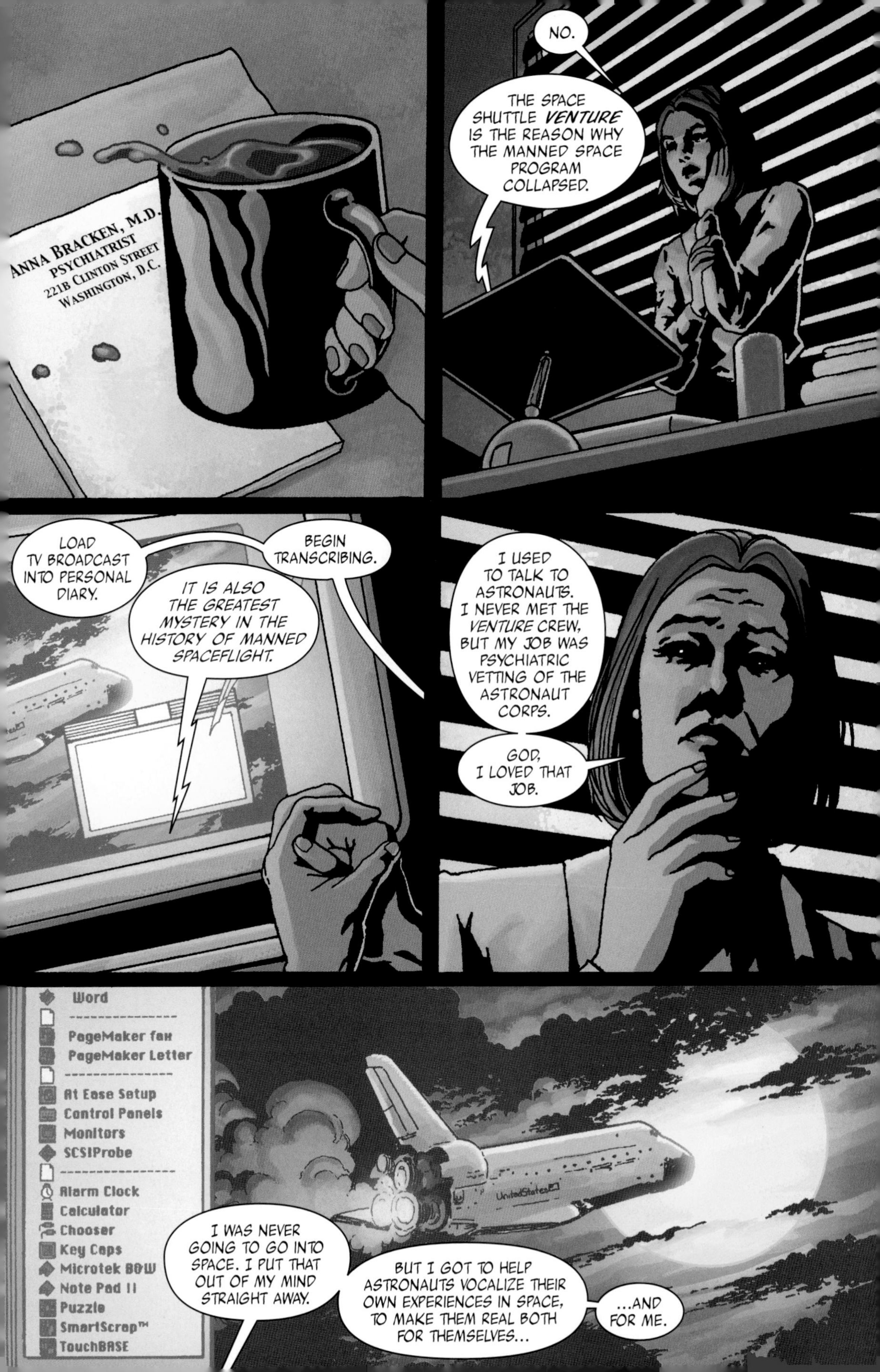

ANNA BRACKEN, M.D.
PSYCHIATRIST
221B CLINTON STREET
WASHINGTON, D.C.
NO.
THE SPACE SHUTTLE VENTURE IS THE REASON WHY THE MANNED SPACE PROGRAM COLLAPSED.
LOAD TV BROADCAST INTO PERSONAL DIARY.
BEGIN TRANSCRIBING.
IT IS ALSO THE GREATEST MYSTERY IN THE HISTORY OF MANNED SPACEFLIGHT.
I USED TO TALK TO ASTRONAUTS. I NEVER MET THE VENTURE CREW, BUT MY JOB WAS PSYCHIATRIC VETTING OF THE ASTRONAUT CORPS.
GOD, I LOVED THAT JOB.
Word
PageMaker fax
PageMaker Letter
At Ease Setup
Control Panels
Monitors
SCSIProbe
Alarm Clock
Calculator
Chooser
Key Caps
Microtek B&W
Note Pad II
Puzzle
SmartScrap™
TouchBASE
United States
I WAS NEVER GOING TO GO INTO SPACE. I PUT THAT OUT OF MY MIND STRAIGHT AWAY.
BUT I GOT TO HELP ASTRONAUTS VOCALIZE THEIR OWN EXPERIENCES IN SPACE, TO MAKE THEM REAL BOTH FOR THEMSELVES...
...AND FOR ME.

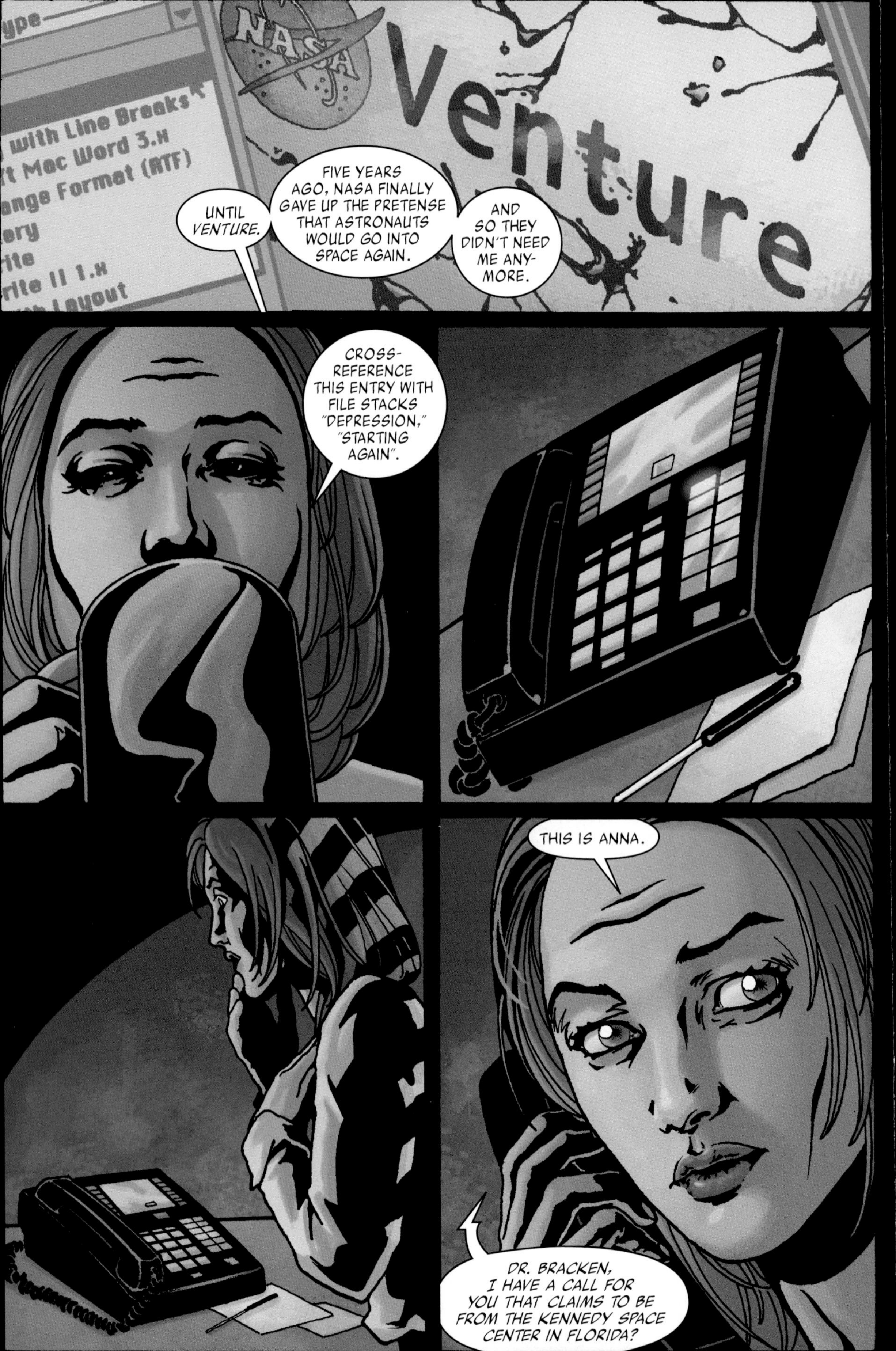
Venture
UNTIL VENTURE.
FIVE YEARS AGO, NASA FINALLY GAVE UP THE PRETENSE THAT ASTRONAUTS WOULD GO INTO SPACE AGAIN.
AND SO THEY DIDN'T NEED ME ANYMORE.
CROSS-REFERENCE THIS ENTRY WITH FILE STACKS "DEPRESSION," "STARTING AGAIN".
THIS IS ANNA.
DR. BRACKEN, I HAVE A CALL FOR YOU THAT CLAIMS TO BE FROM THE KENNEDY SPACE CENTER IN FLORIDA?

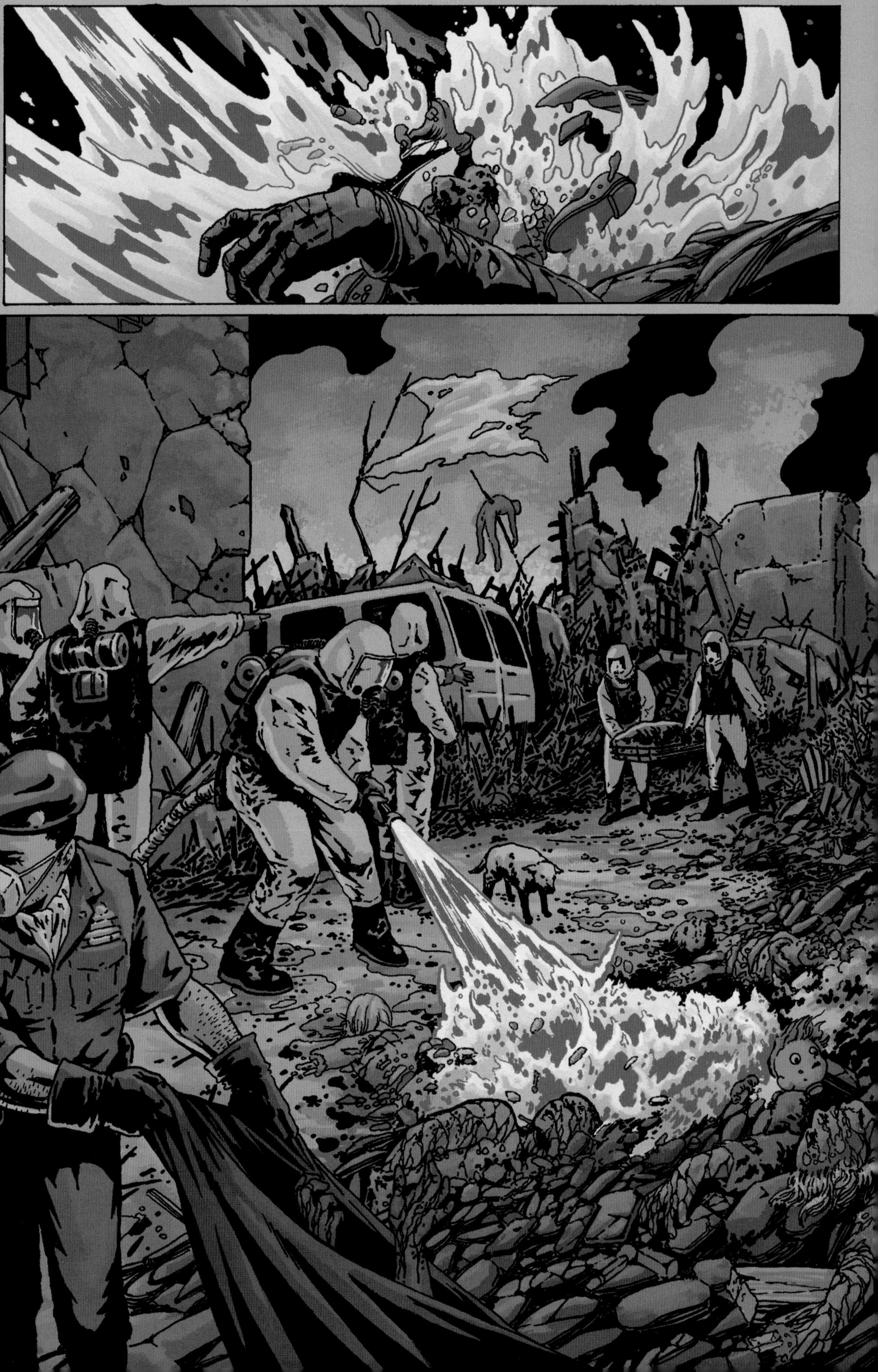

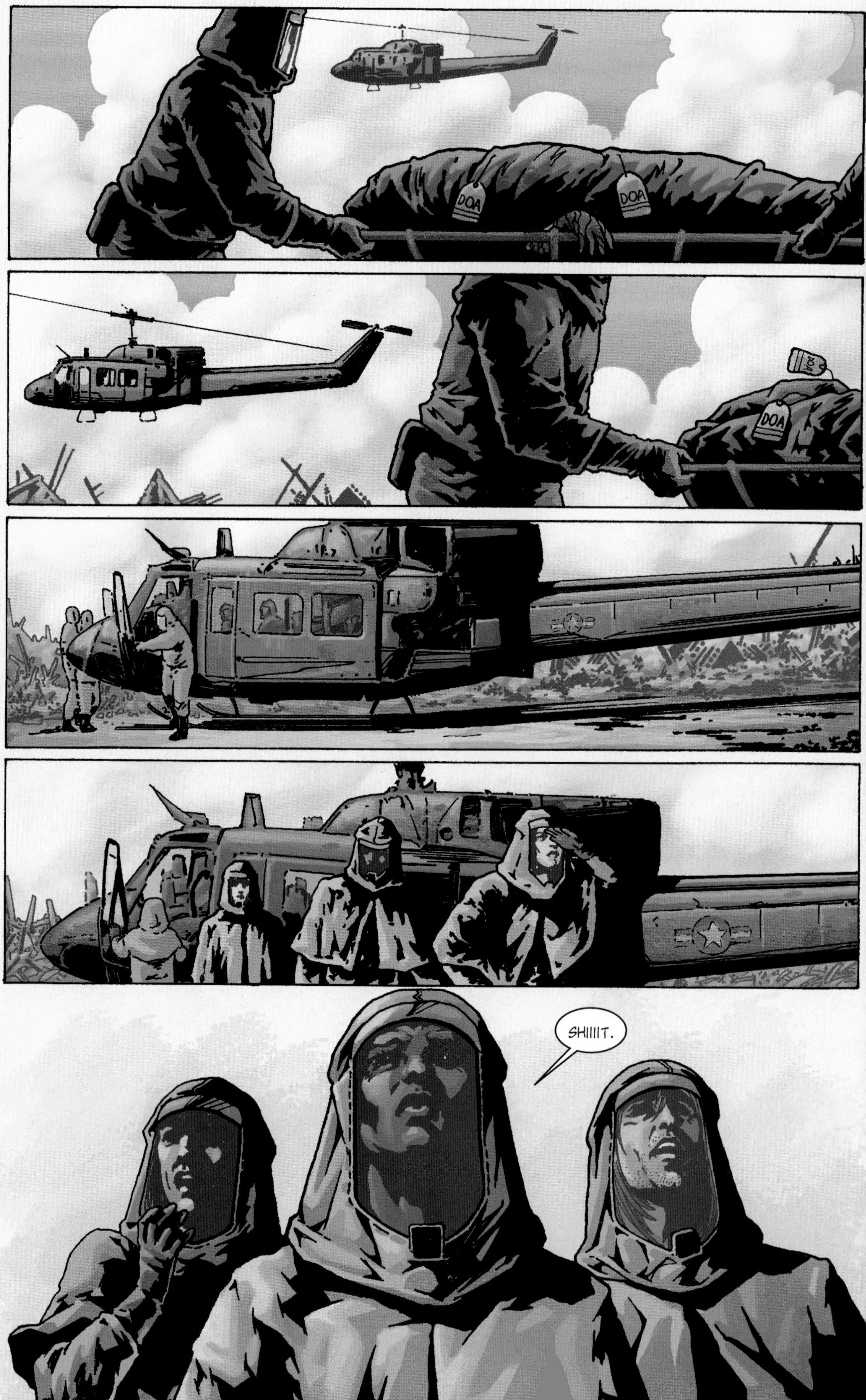
DOA
DOA
DOA
DOA
DOA
SHIIIIT.

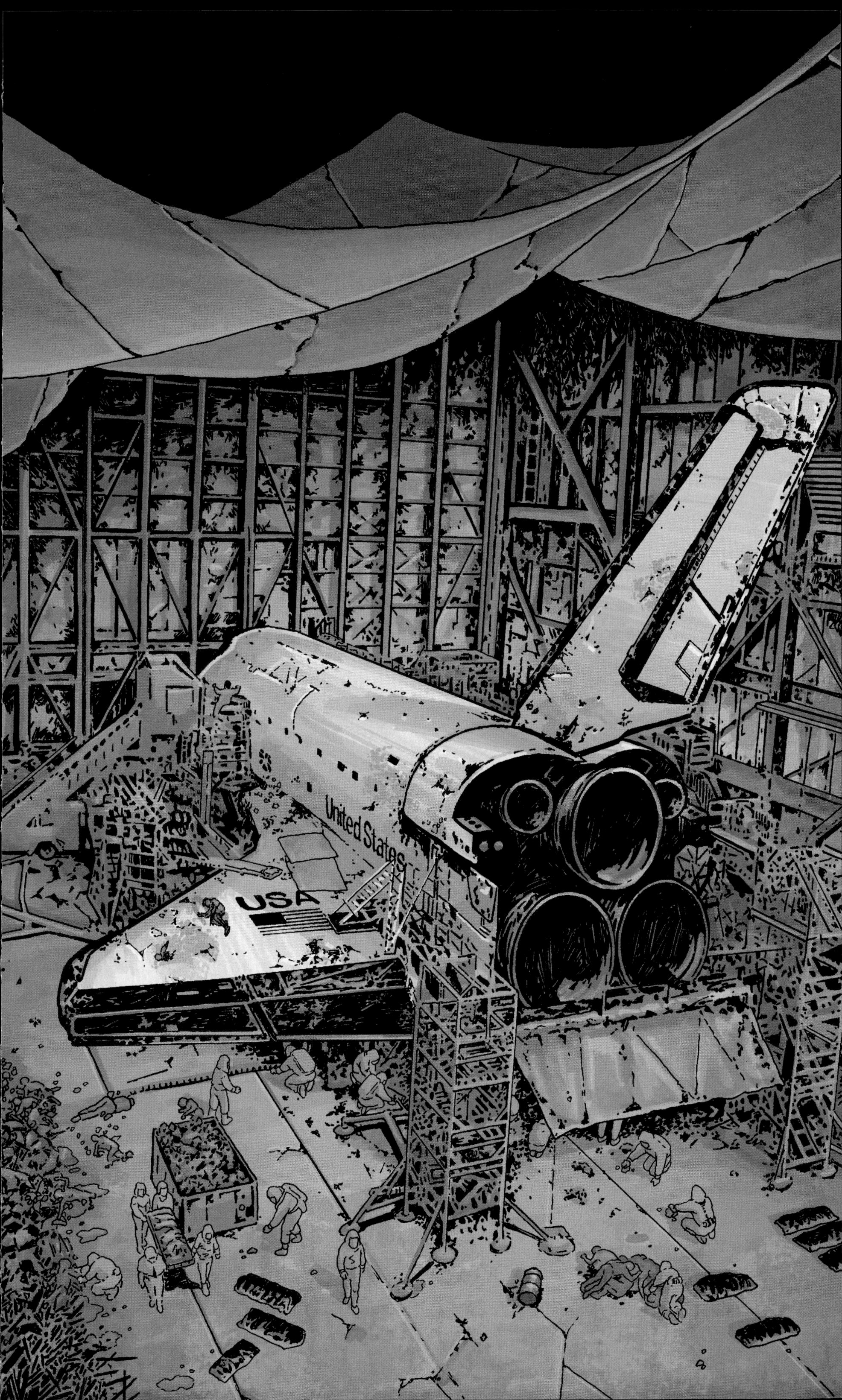
United States
USA

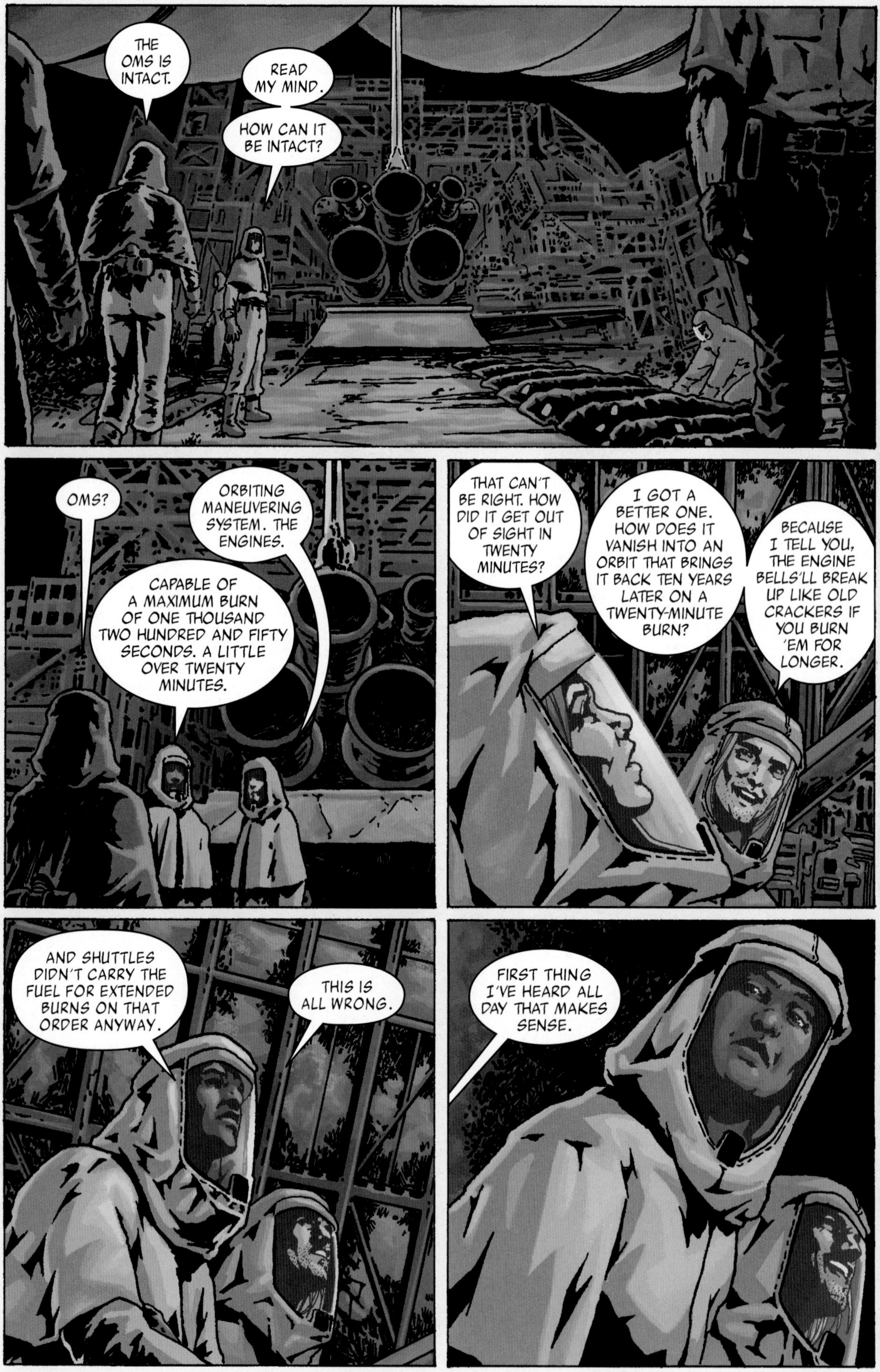
THE OMS IS INTACT.
READ MY MIND.
HOW CAN IT BE INTACT?
OMS?
ORBITING MANEUVERING SYSTEM. THE ENGINES.
CAPABLE OF A MAXIMUM BURN OF ONE THOUSAND TWO HUNDRED AND FIFTY SECONDS. A LITTLE OVER TWENTY MINUTES.
THAT CAN'T BE RIGHT. HOW DID IT GET OUT OF SIGHT IN TWENTY MINUTES?
I GOT A BETTER ONE. HOW DOES IT VANISH INTO AN ORBIT THAT BRINGS IT BACK TEN YEARS LATER ON A TWENTY-MINUTE BURN?
BECAUSE I TELL YOU, THE ENGINE BELLS'LL BREAK UP LIKE OLD CRACKERS IF YOU BURN 'EM FOR LONGER.
AND SHUTTLES DIDN'T CARRY THE FUEL FOR EXTENDED BURNS ON THAT ORDER ANYWAY.
THIS IS ALL WRONG.
FIRST THING I'VE HEARD ALL DAY THAT MAKES SENSE.

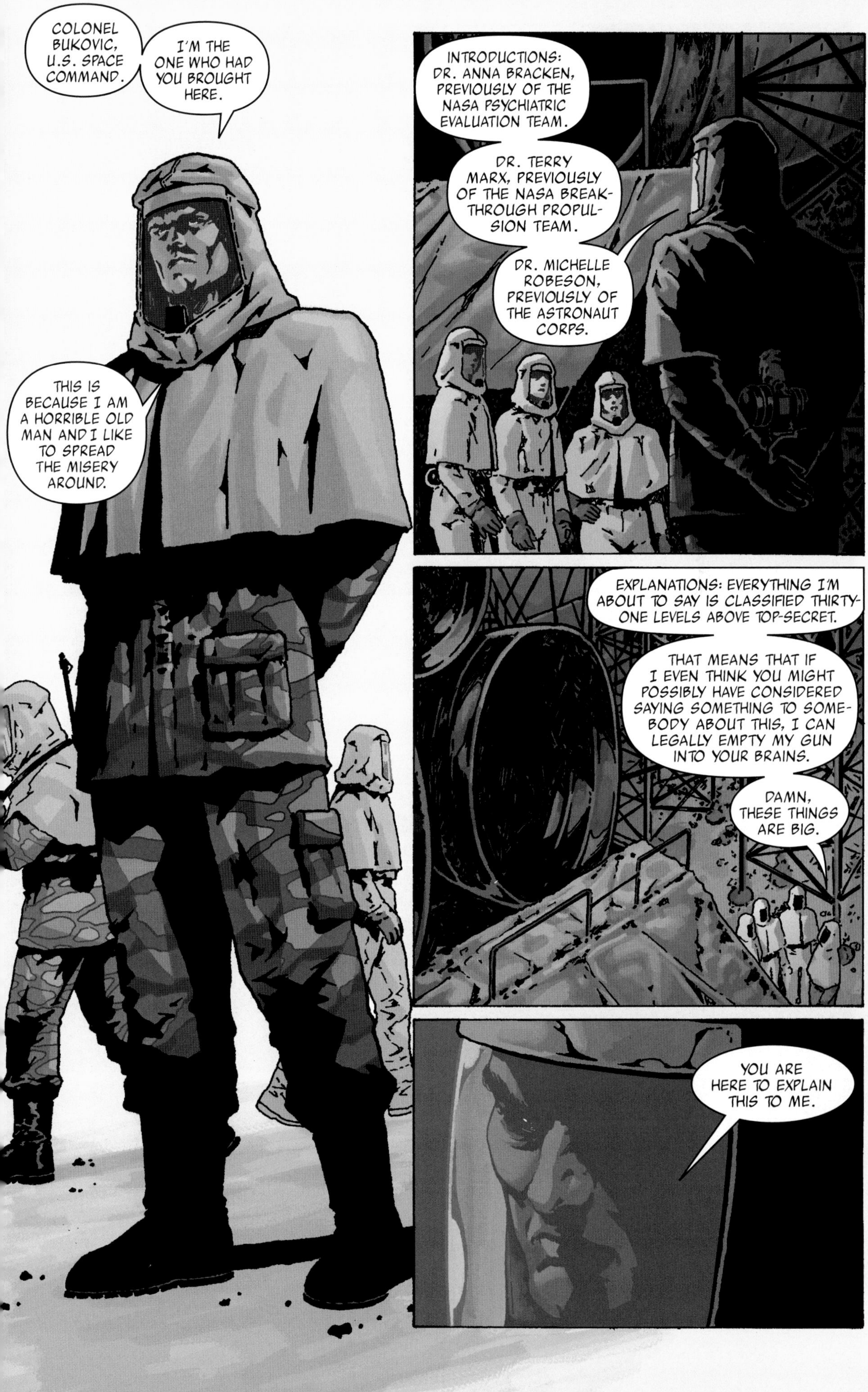
COLONEL BUKOVIC, U.S. SPACE COMMAND.
I'M THE ONE WHO HAD YOU BROUGHT HERE.
THIS IS BECAUSE I AM A HORRIBLE OLD MAN AND I LIKE TO SPREAD THE MISERY AROUND.
INTRODUCTIONS: DR. ANNA BRACKEN, PREVIOUSLY OF THE NASA PSYCHIATRIC EVALUATION TEAM.
DR. TERRY MARX, PREVIOUSLY OF THE NASA BREAK-THROUGH PROPUL-SION TEAM.
DR. MICHELLE ROBESON, PREVIOUSLY OF THE ASTRONAUT CORPS.
EXPLANATIONS: EVERYTHING I'M ABOUT TO SAY IS CLASSIFIED THIRTY-ONE LEVELS ABOVE TOP-SECRET.
THAT MEANS THAT IF I EVEN THINK YOU MIGHT POSSIBLY HAVE CONSIDERED SAYING SOMETHING TO SOME-BODY ABOUT THIS, I CAN LEGALLY EMPTY MY GUN INTO YOUR BRAINS.
DAMN, THESE THINGS ARE BIG.
YOU ARE HERE TO EXPLAIN THIS TO ME.

DR. ROBESON, YOU'RE PROBABLY THE MOST FAMILIAR WITH THE SHUTTLE. TELL ME, DO YOU NOTICE ANYTHING IMMEDIATELY DIFFERENT ABOUT IT?

ASIDE FROM THE FACT THAT IT'S HERE?

NOTHING UNUSUAL. SOME STAINING AND DISCOLORATION, BUT THAT'S ONLY TO BE EXPECTED AFTER TEN YEARS IN COLD SOAK AND A REENTRY.

TOUCH IT.

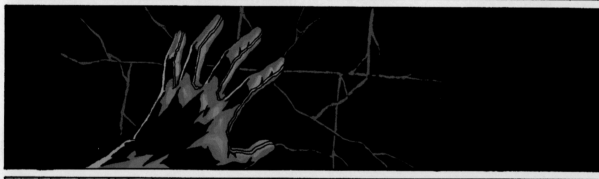

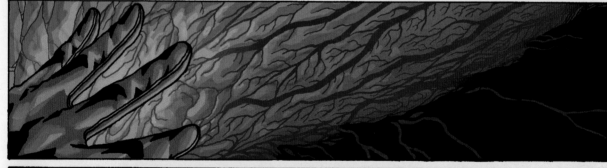

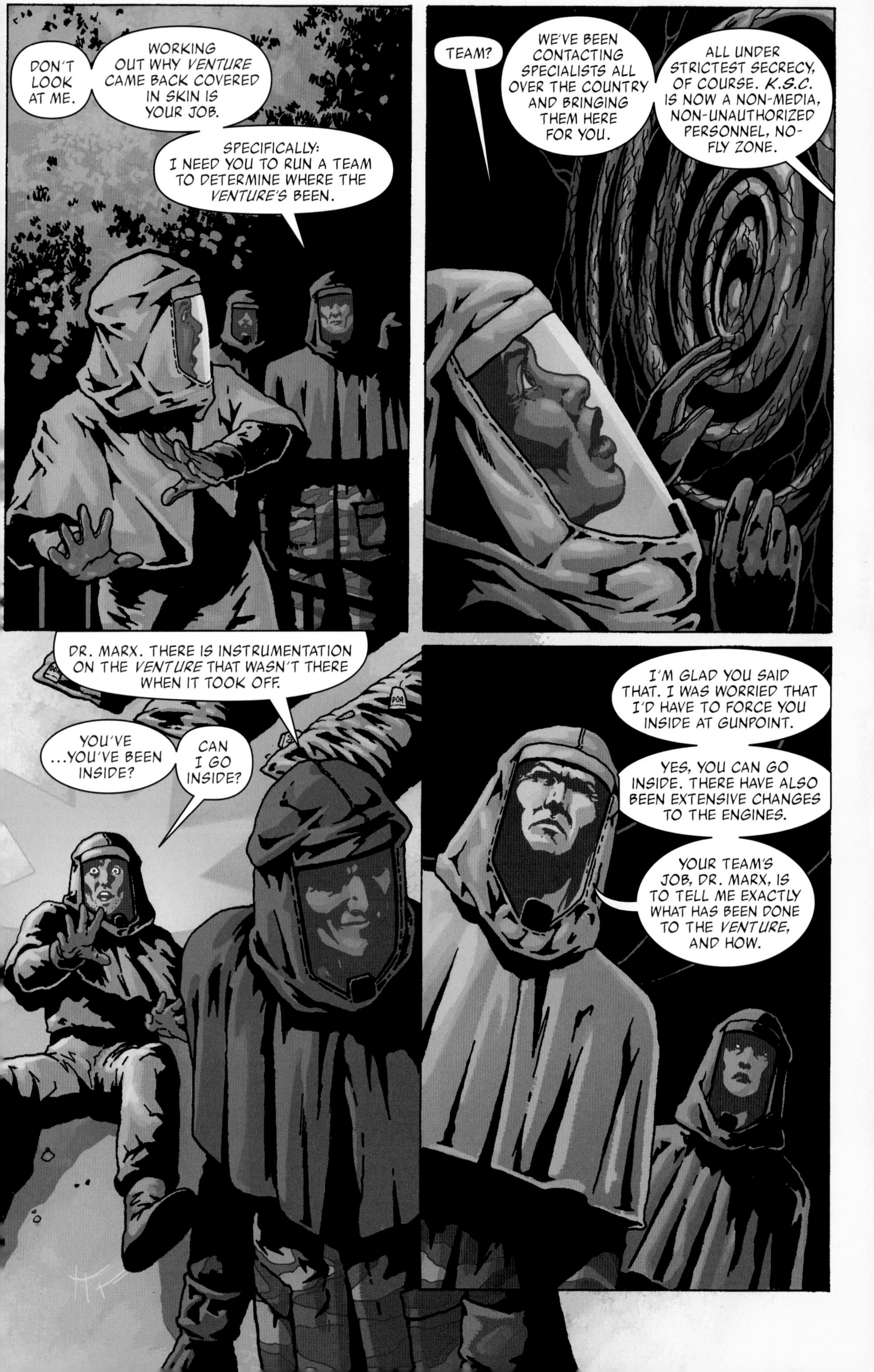
DON'T LOOK AT ME.
WORKING OUT WHY VENTURE CAME BACK COVERED IN SKIN IS YOUR JOB.
SPECIFICALLY: I NEED YOU TO RUN A TEAM TO DETERMINE WHERE THE VENTURE'S BEEN.
TEAM?
WE'VE BEEN CONTACTING SPECIALISTS ALL OVER THE COUNTRY AND BRINGING THEM HERE FOR YOU.
ALL UNDER STRICTEST SECRECY, OF COURSE. K.S.C. IS NOW A NON-MEDIA, NON-UNAUTHORIZED PERSONNEL, NO-FLY ZONE.
DR. MARX. THERE IS INSTRUMENTATION ON THE VENTURE THAT WASN'T THERE WHEN IT TOOK OFF.
YOU'VE ...YOU'VE BEEN INSIDE?
CAN I GO INSIDE?
I'M GLAD YOU SAID THAT. I WAS WORRIED THAT I'D HAVE TO FORCE YOU INSIDE AT GUNPOINT.
YES, YOU CAN GO INSIDE. THERE HAVE ALSO BEEN EXTENSIVE CHANGES TO THE ENGINES.
YOUR TEAM'S JOB, DR. MARX, IS TO TELL ME EXACTLY WHAT HAS BEEN DONE TO THE VENTURE, AND HOW.

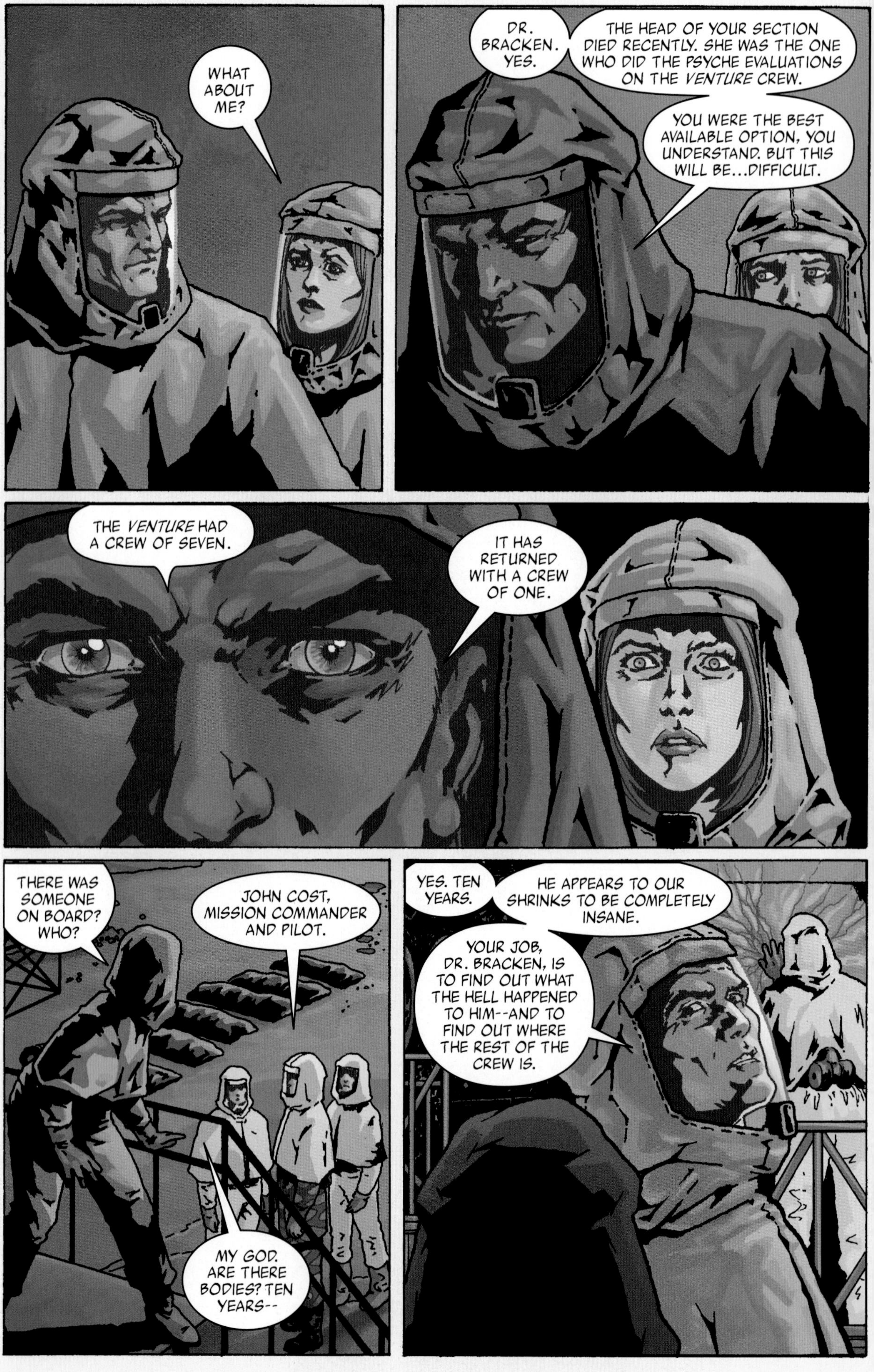
WHAT ABOUT ME?
DR. BRACKEN. YES.
THE HEAD OF YOUR SECTION DIED RECENTLY. SHE WAS THE ONE WHO DID THE PSYCHE EVALUATIONS ON THE *VENTURE* CREW.
YOU WERE THE BEST AVAILABLE OPTION, YOU UNDERSTAND. BUT THIS WILL BE...DIFFICULT.
THE *VENTURE* HAD A CREW OF SEVEN.
IT HAS RETURNED WITH A CREW OF ONE.
THERE WAS SOMEONE ON BOARD? WHO?
JOHN COST, MISSION COMMANDER AND PILOT.
MY GOD. ARE THERE BODIES? TEN YEARS--
YES. TEN YEARS.
HE APPEARS TO OUR SHRINKS TO BE COMPLETELY INSANE.
YOUR JOB, DR. BRACKEN, IS TO FIND OUT WHAT THE HELL HAPPENED TO HIM--AND TO FIND OUT WHERE THE REST OF THE CREW IS.

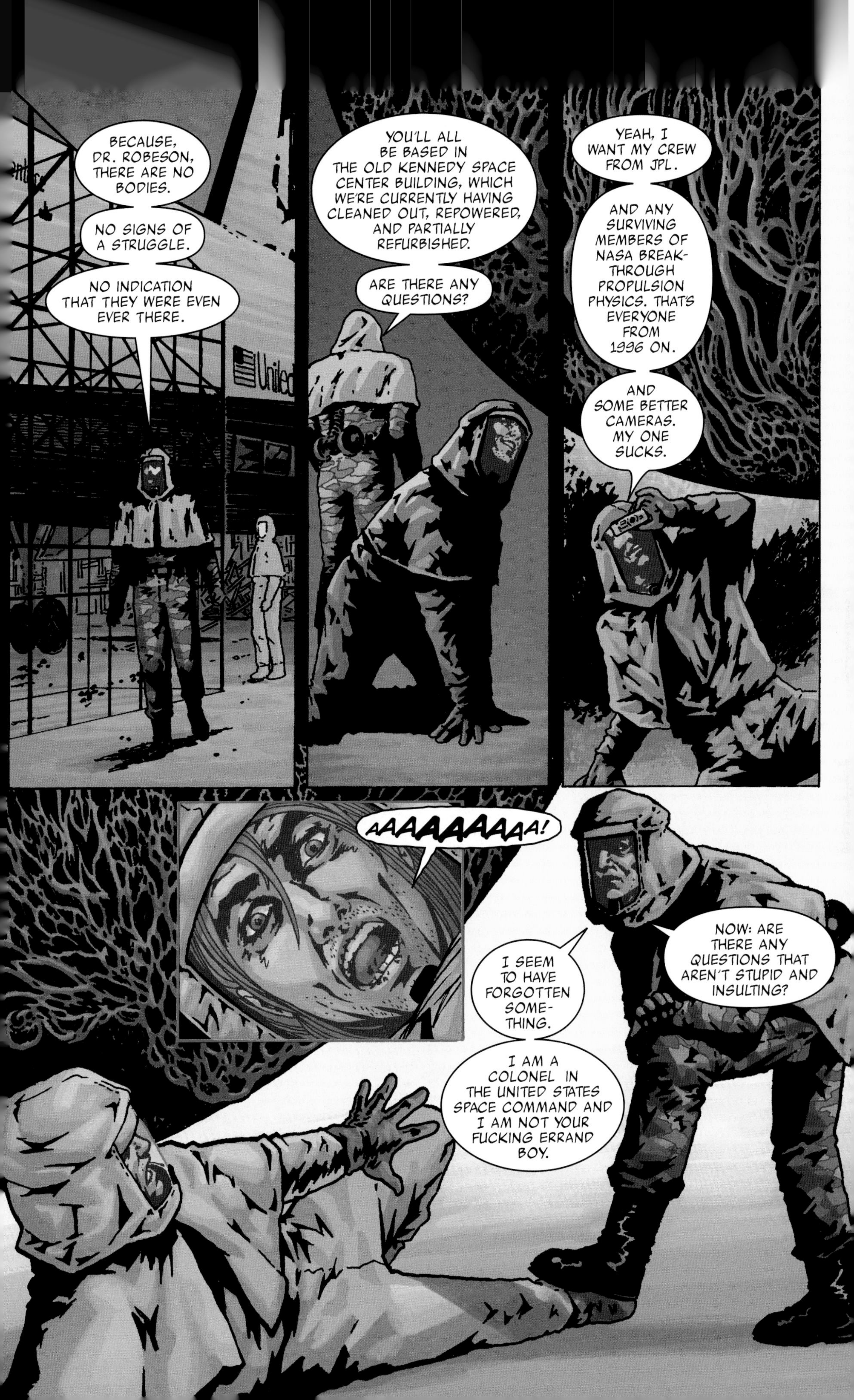
BECAUSE, DR. ROBESON, THERE ARE NO BODIES.
NO SIGNS OF A STRUGGLE.
NO INDICATION THAT THEY WERE EVEN EVER THERE.
YOU'LL ALL BE BASED IN THE OLD KENNEDY SPACE CENTER BUILDING, WHICH WE'RE CURRENTLY HAVING CLEANED OUT, REPOWERED, AND PARTIALLY REFURBISHED.
ARE THERE ANY QUESTIONS?
YEAH, I WANT MY CREW FROM JPL.
AND ANY SURVIVING MEMBERS OF NASA BREAK-THROUGH PROPULSION PHYSICS. THAT'S EVERYONE FROM 1996 ON.
AND SOME BETTER CAMERAS. MY ONE SUCKS.
AAAAAAAAA!
I SEEM TO HAVE FORGOTTEN SOME-THING.
I AM A COLONEL IN THE UNITED STATES SPACE COMMAND AND I AM NOT YOUR FUCKING ERRAND BOY.
NOW: ARE THERE ANY QUESTIONS THAT AREN'T STUPID AND INSULTING?

THIS IS UNREAL.

I'M GUESSING YOUR NUMBERS ON THIS THING COME FROM SPACE COMMAND, NOT CORE NASA IN HOUSTON.

HOW FAR DO YOUR BOYS THINK IT'S GONE?

OH, I'M GLAD YOU ASKED ME THAT.

IN THE FIRST STAGE OF THE CLEAN-UP OPERATION HERE, ONE OF MY MEN NOTICED DETRITUS HIGH IN THE FORWARD WHEEL HOUSING.

HE WAS HOSING SOME CHILDREN OFF THE WHEEL AT THE TIME--YOU CAN UNDERSTAND HIM NOT WANTING TO LOOK.

MY MAN HAD A COUPLE OF SPECIALISTS RETRIEVE A SAMPLE OF THE DETRITUS, AND IT WAS CHOPPERED OUT FOR ANALYSIS.

THE ANALYSTS PROMPTLY CALLED FOR MY MAN'S HEAD.

THEY ASSUMED IT WAS SOME KIND OF SICK JOKE--NOT KNOWING, OF COURSE, THAT I HAVE ABSOLUTELY NO SENSE OF HUMOR.

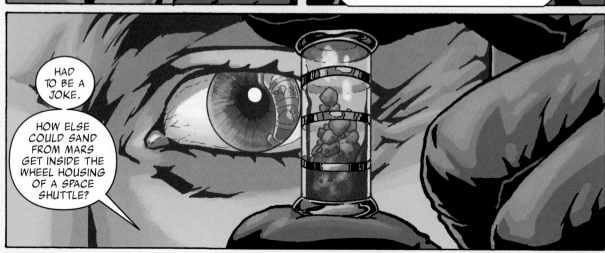

HAD TO BE A JOKE.

HOW ELSE COULD SAND FROM MARS GET INSIDE THE WHEEL HOUSING OF A SPACE SHUTTLE?

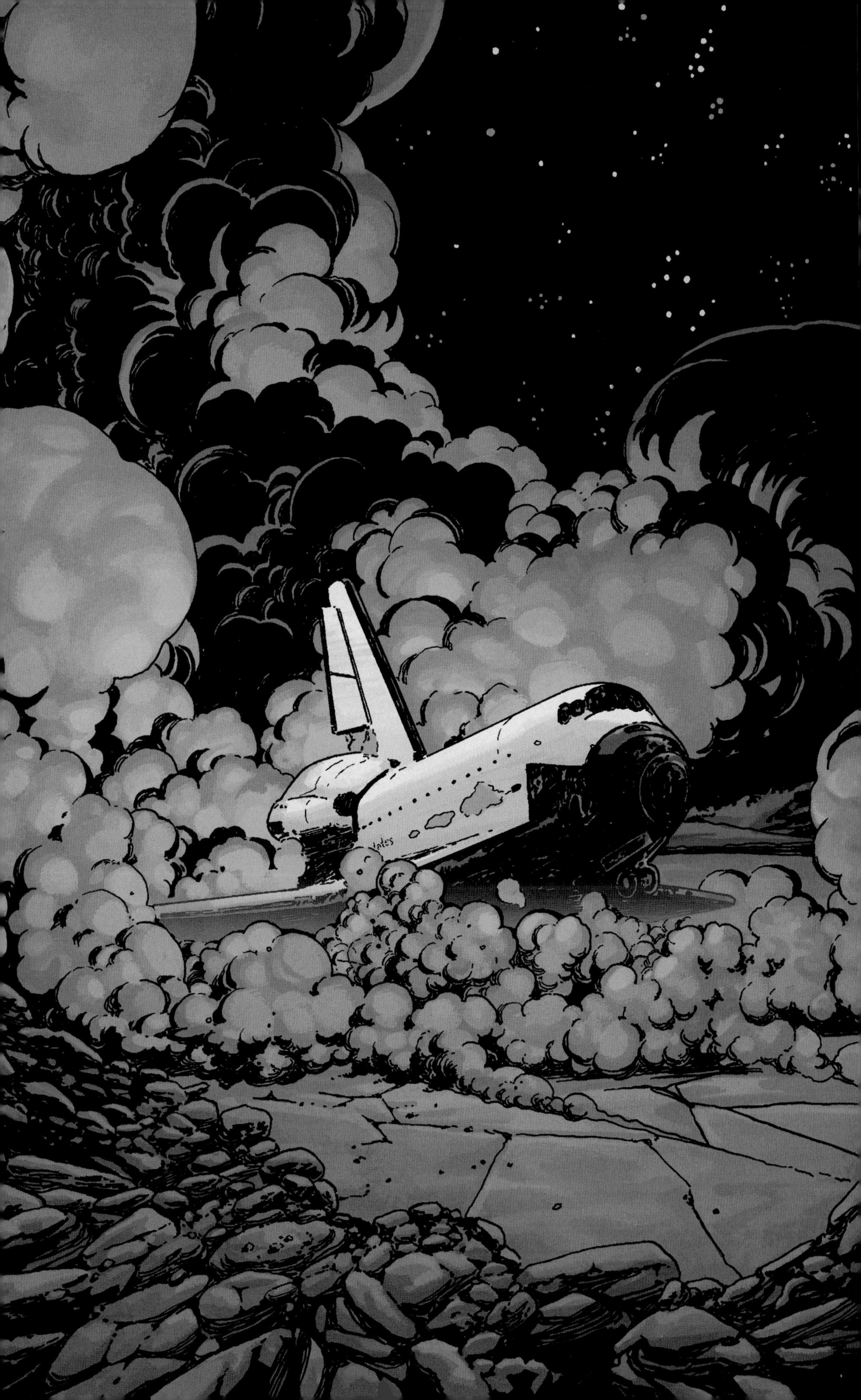
Yates

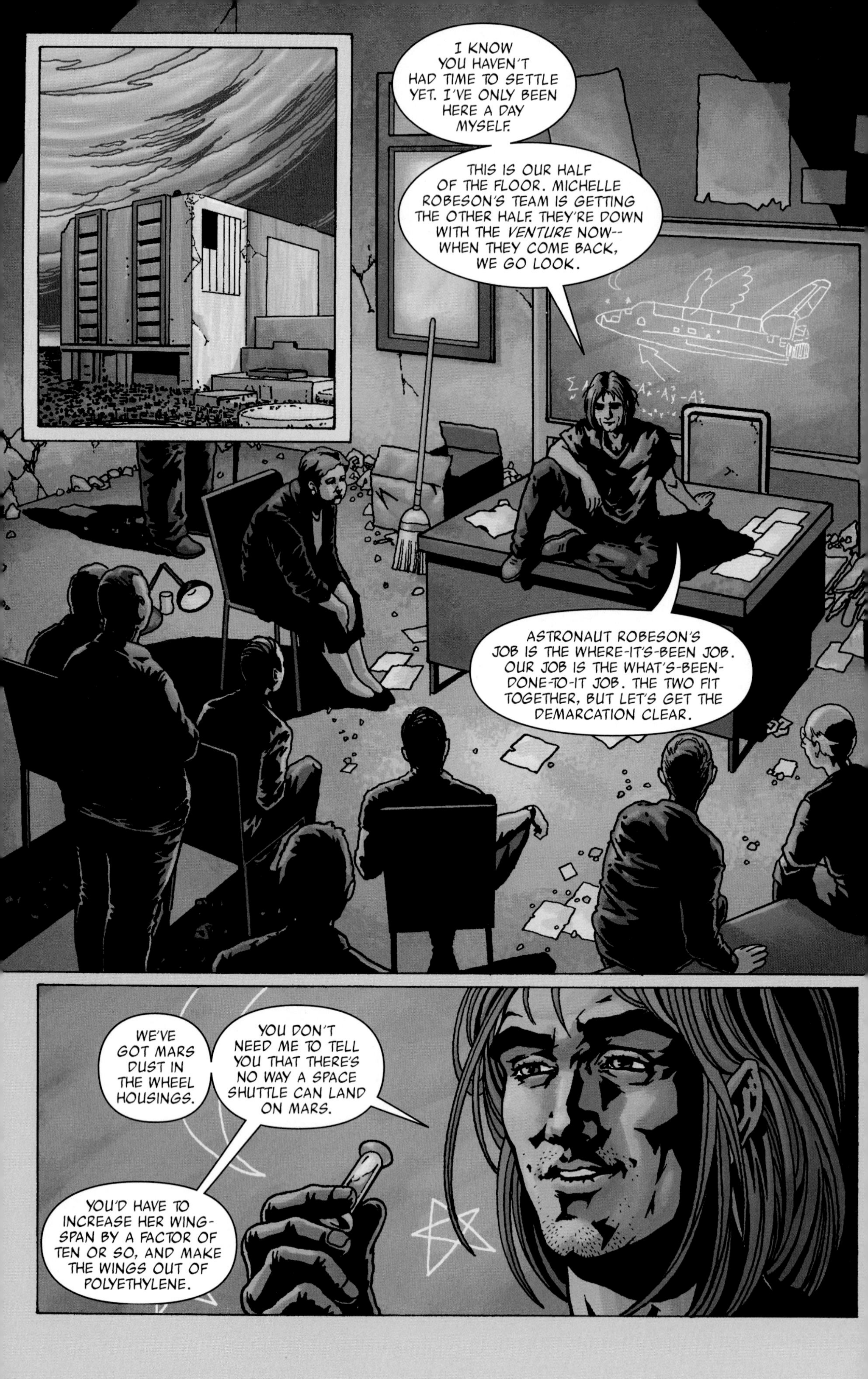
I KNOW YOU HAVEN'T HAD TIME TO SETTLE YET. I'VE ONLY BEEN HERE A DAY MYSELF.
THIS IS OUR HALF OF THE FLOOR. MICHELLE ROBESON'S TEAM IS GETTING THE OTHER HALF. THEY'RE DOWN WITH THE *VENTURE* NOW-- WHEN THEY COME BACK, WE GO LOOK.
ASTRONAUT ROBESON'S JOB IS THE WHERE-IT'S-BEEN JOB. OUR JOB IS THE WHAT'S-BEEN-DONE-TO-IT JOB. THE TWO FIT TOGETHER, BUT LET'S GET THE DEMARCATION CLEAR.
WE'VE GOT MARS DUST IN THE WHEEL HOUSINGS.
YOU DON'T NEED ME TO TELL YOU THAT THERE'S NO WAY A SPACE SHUTTLE CAN LAND ON MARS.
YOU'D HAVE TO INCREASE HER WING-SPAN BY A FACTOR OF TEN OR SO, AND MAKE THE WINGS OUT OF POLYETHYLENE.

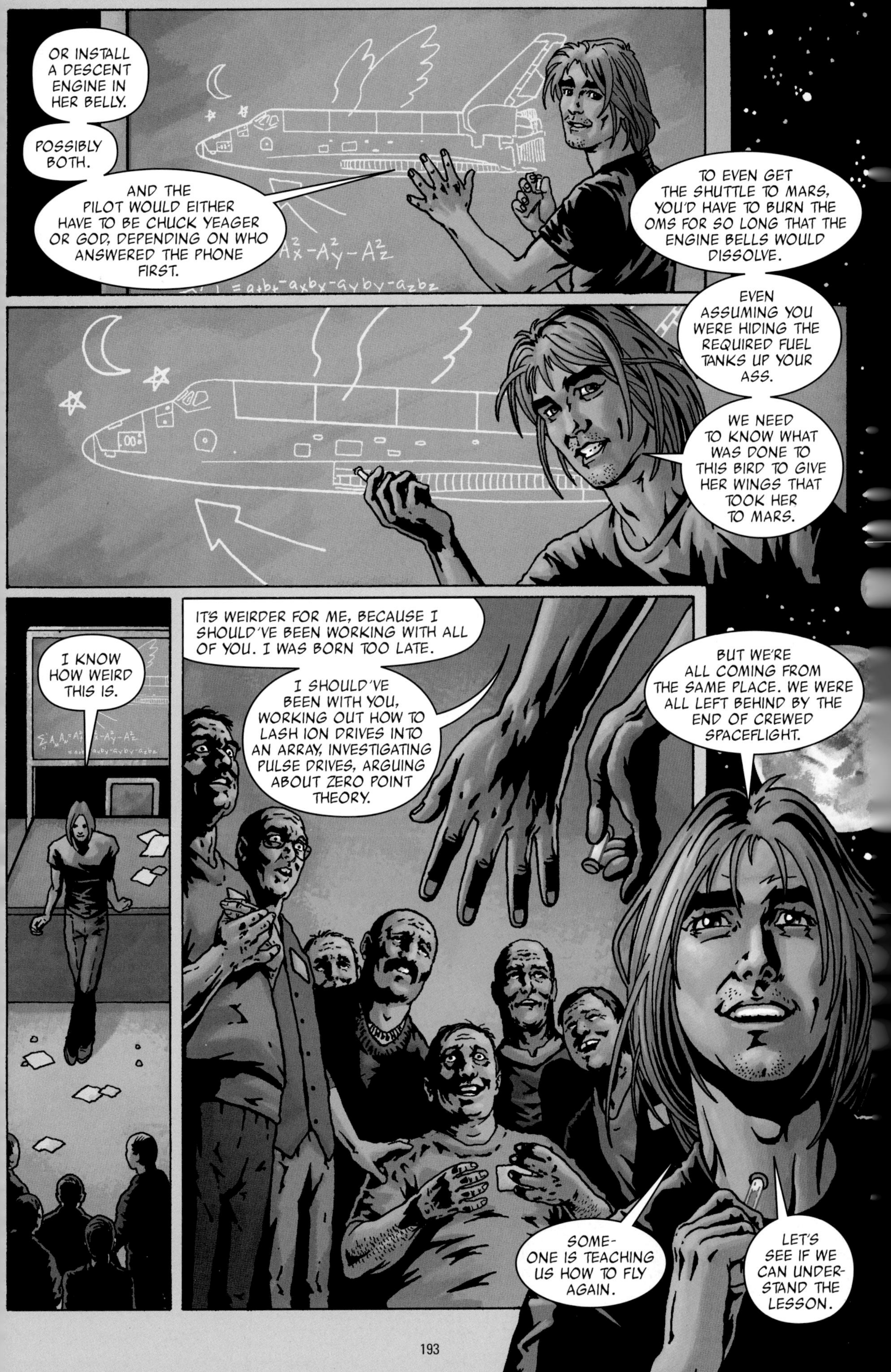
OR INSTALL A DESCENT ENGINE IN HER BELLY.
POSSIBLY BOTH.
AND THE PILOT WOULD EITHER HAVE TO BE CHUCK YEAGER OR GOD, DEPENDING ON WHO ANSWERED THE PHONE FIRST.
TO EVEN GET THE SHUTTLE TO MARS, YOU'D HAVE TO BURN THE OMS FOR SO LONG THAT THE ENGINE BELLS WOULD DISSOLVE.
EVEN ASSUMING YOU WERE HIDING THE REQUIRED FUEL TANKS UP YOUR ASS.
WE NEED TO KNOW WHAT WAS DONE TO THIS BIRD TO GIVE HER WINGS THAT TOOK HER TO MARS.
I KNOW HOW WEIRD THIS IS.
IT'S WEIRDER FOR ME, BECAUSE I SHOULD'VE BEEN WORKING WITH ALL OF YOU. I WAS BORN TOO LATE.
I SHOULD'VE BEEN WITH YOU, WORKING OUT HOW TO LASH ION DRIVES INTO AN ARRAY, INVESTIGATING PULSE DRIVES, ARGUING ABOUT ZERO POINT THEORY.
BUT WE'RE ALL COMING FROM THE SAME PLACE. WE WERE ALL LEFT BEHIND BY THE END OF CREWED SPACEFLIGHT.
SOME-ONE IS TEACHING US HOW TO FLY AGAIN.
LET'S SEE IF WE CAN UNDER-STAND THE LESSON.

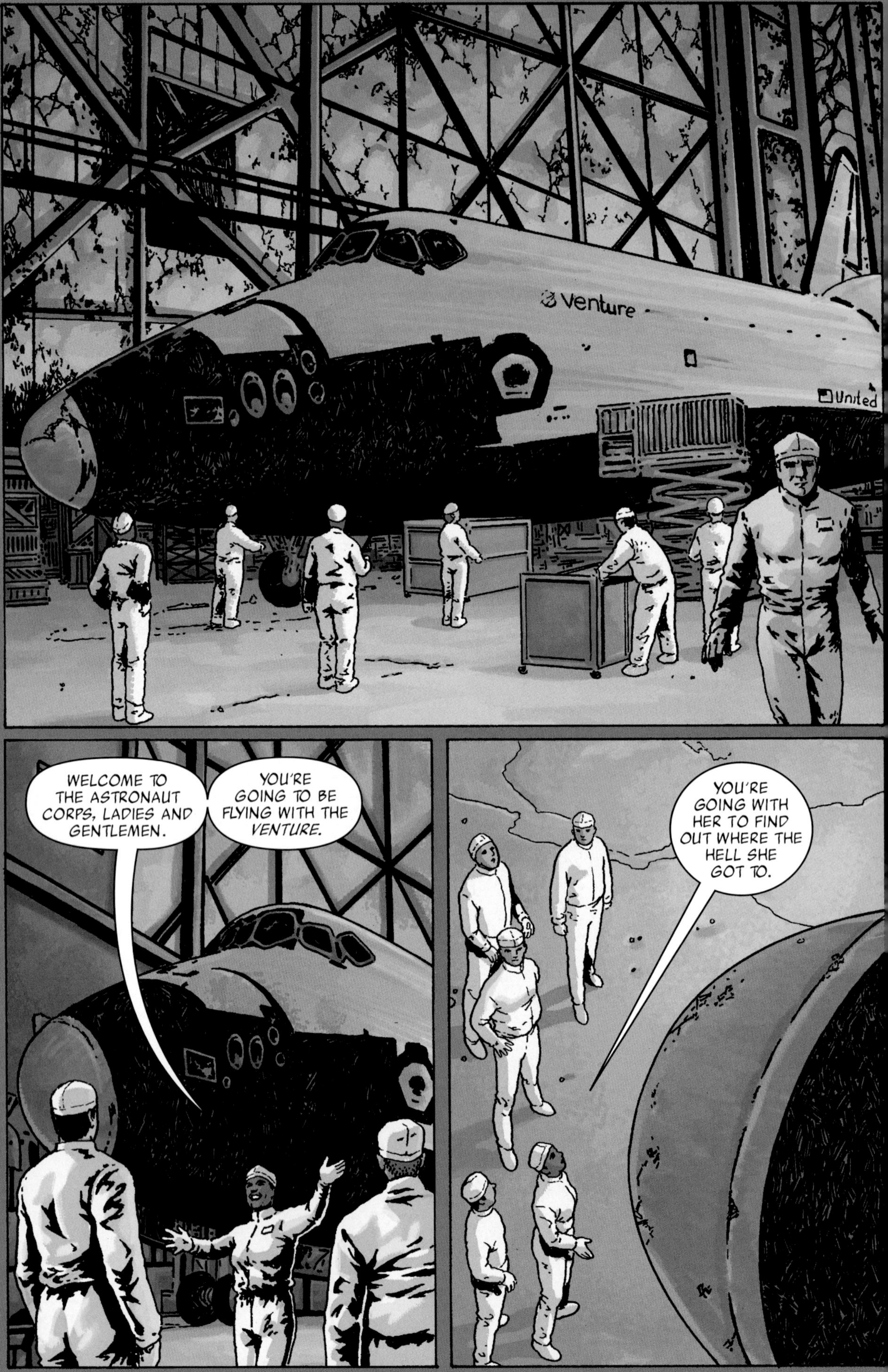
Venture
United
WELCOME TO THE ASTRONAUT CORPS, LADIES AND GENTLEMEN.
YOU'RE GOING TO BE FLYING WITH THE *VENTURE*.
YOU'RE GOING WITH HER TO FIND OUT WHERE THE HELL SHE GOT TO.

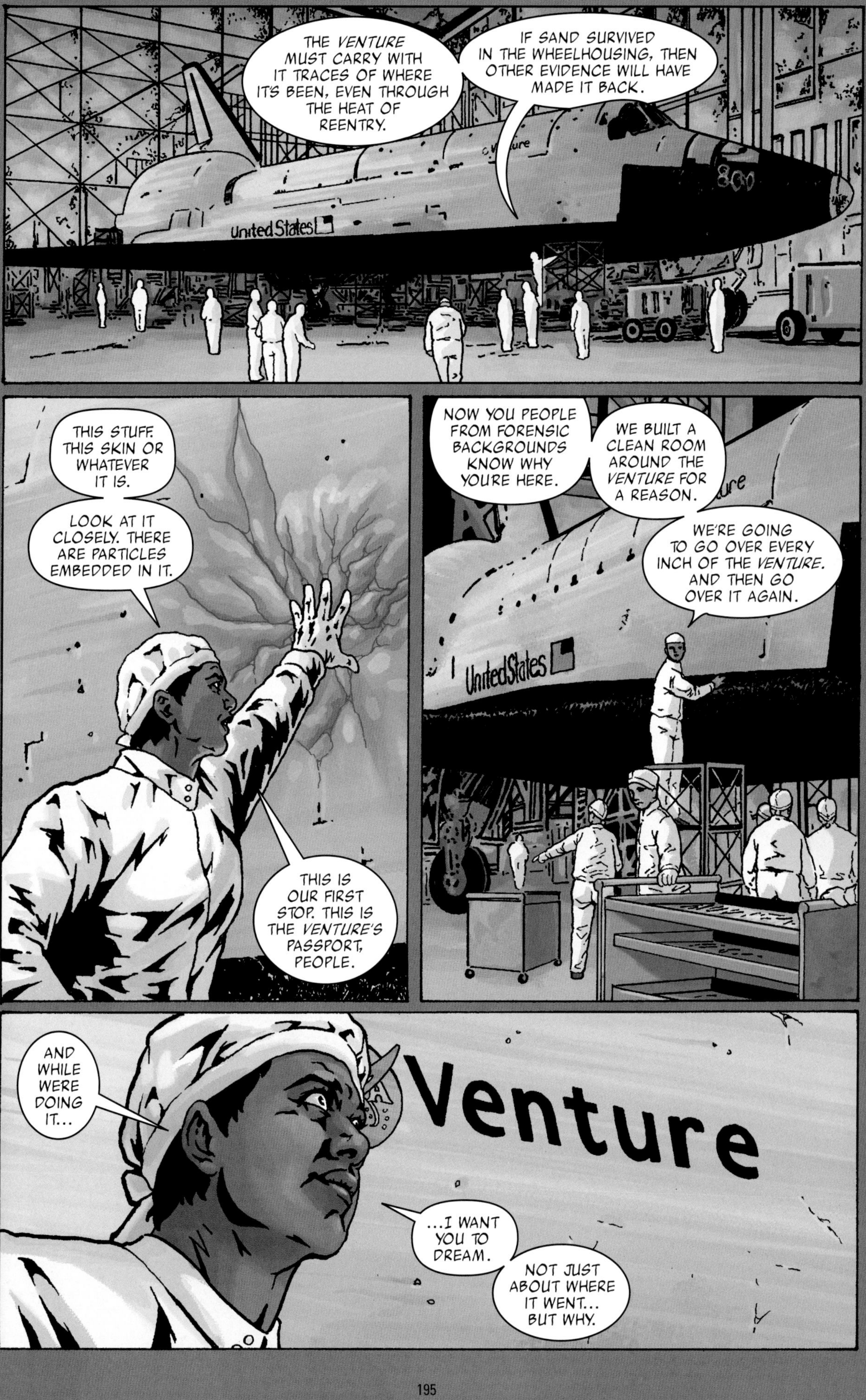

THE *VENTURE* MUST CARRY WITH IT TRACES OF WHERE IT'S BEEN, EVEN THROUGH THE HEAT OF REENTRY.
IF SAND SURVIVED IN THE WHEELHOUSING, THEN OTHER EVIDENCE WILL HAVE MADE IT BACK.
United States
THIS STUFF. THIS SKIN OR WHATEVER IT IS.
LOOK AT IT CLOSELY. THERE ARE PARTICLES EMBEDDED IN IT.
THIS IS OUR FIRST STOP. THIS IS THE *VENTURE'S* PASSPORT, PEOPLE.
NOW YOU PEOPLE FROM FORENSIC BACKGROUNDS KNOW WHY YOU'RE HERE.
WE BUILT A CLEAN ROOM AROUND THE *VENTURE* FOR A REASON.
WE'RE GOING TO GO OVER EVERY INCH OF THE *VENTURE*. AND THEN GO OVER IT AGAIN.
United States
AND WHILE WERE DOING IT...
Venture
...I WANT YOU TO DREAM.
NOT JUST ABOUT WHERE IT WENT... BUT WHY.

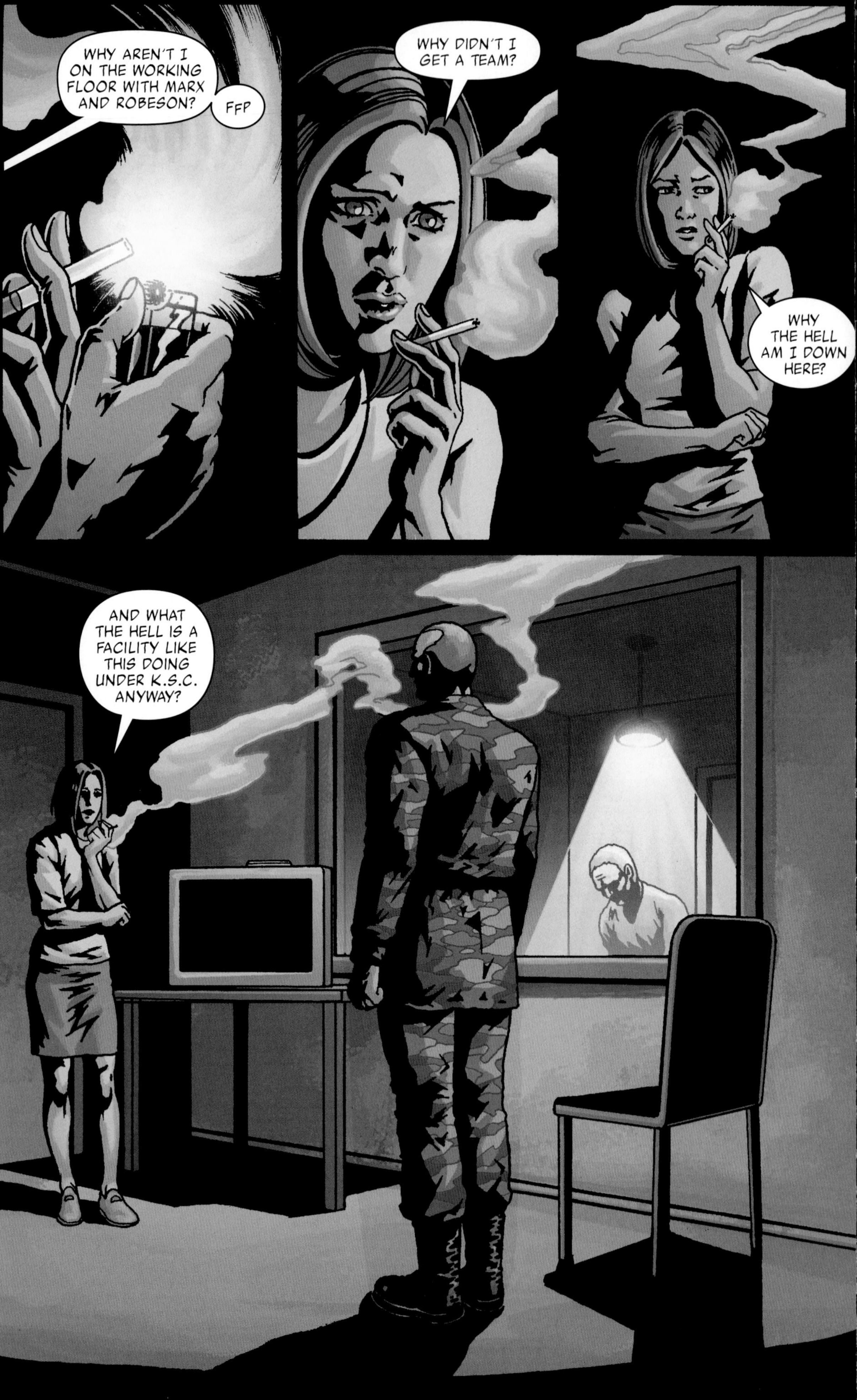
WHY AREN'T I ON THE WORKING FLOOR WITH MARX AND ROBESON?
FFP
WHY DIDN'T I GET A TEAM?
WHY THE HELL AM I DOWN HERE?
AND WHAT THE HELL IS A FACILITY LIKE THIS DOING UNDER K.S.C. ANYWAY?

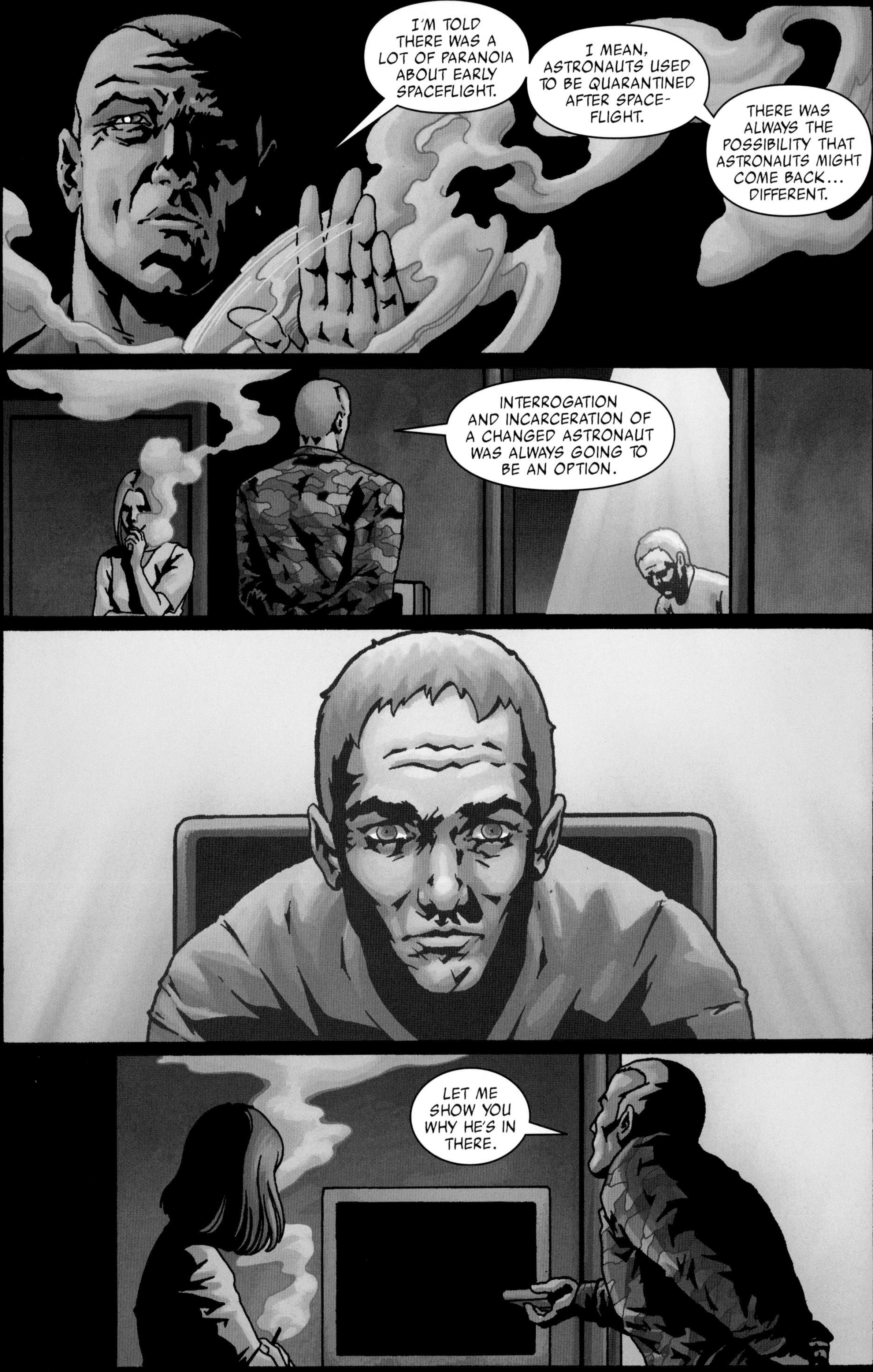
I'M TOLD THERE WAS A LOT OF PARANOIA ABOUT EARLY SPACEFLIGHT.
I MEAN, ASTRONAUTS USED TO BE QUARANTINED AFTER SPACE-FLIGHT.
THERE WAS ALWAYS THE POSSIBILITY THAT ASTRONAUTS MIGHT COME BACK... DIFFERENT.
INTERROGATION AND INCARCERATION OF A CHANGED ASTRONAUT WAS ALWAYS GOING TO BE AN OPTION.
LET ME SHOW YOU WHY HE'S IN THERE.

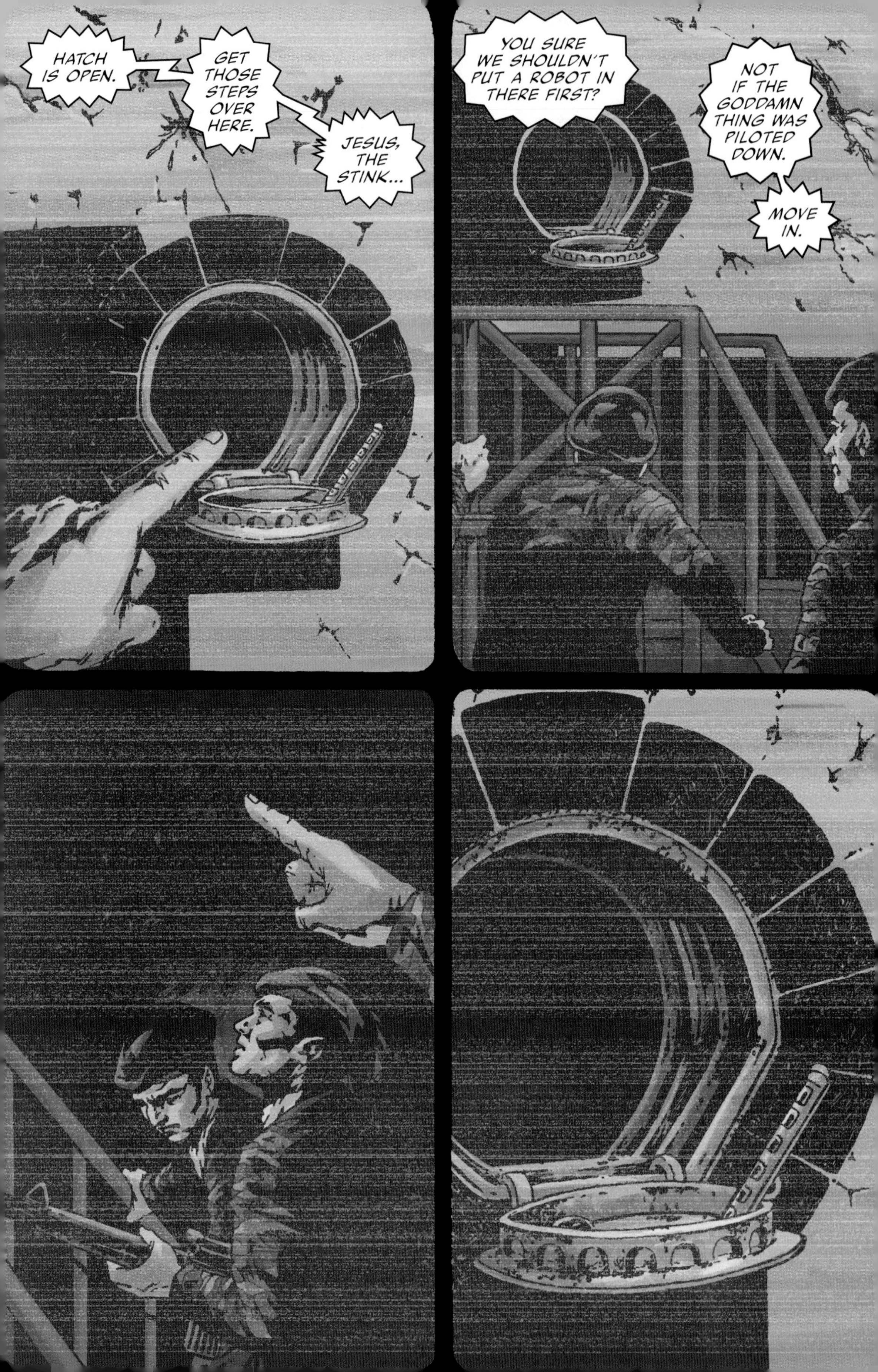
HATCH IS OPEN.
GET THOSE STEPS OVER HERE.
JESUS, THE STINK...
YOU SURE WE SHOULDN'T PUT A ROBOT IN THERE FIRST?
NOT IF THE GODDAMN THING WAS PILOTED DOWN.
MOVE IN.

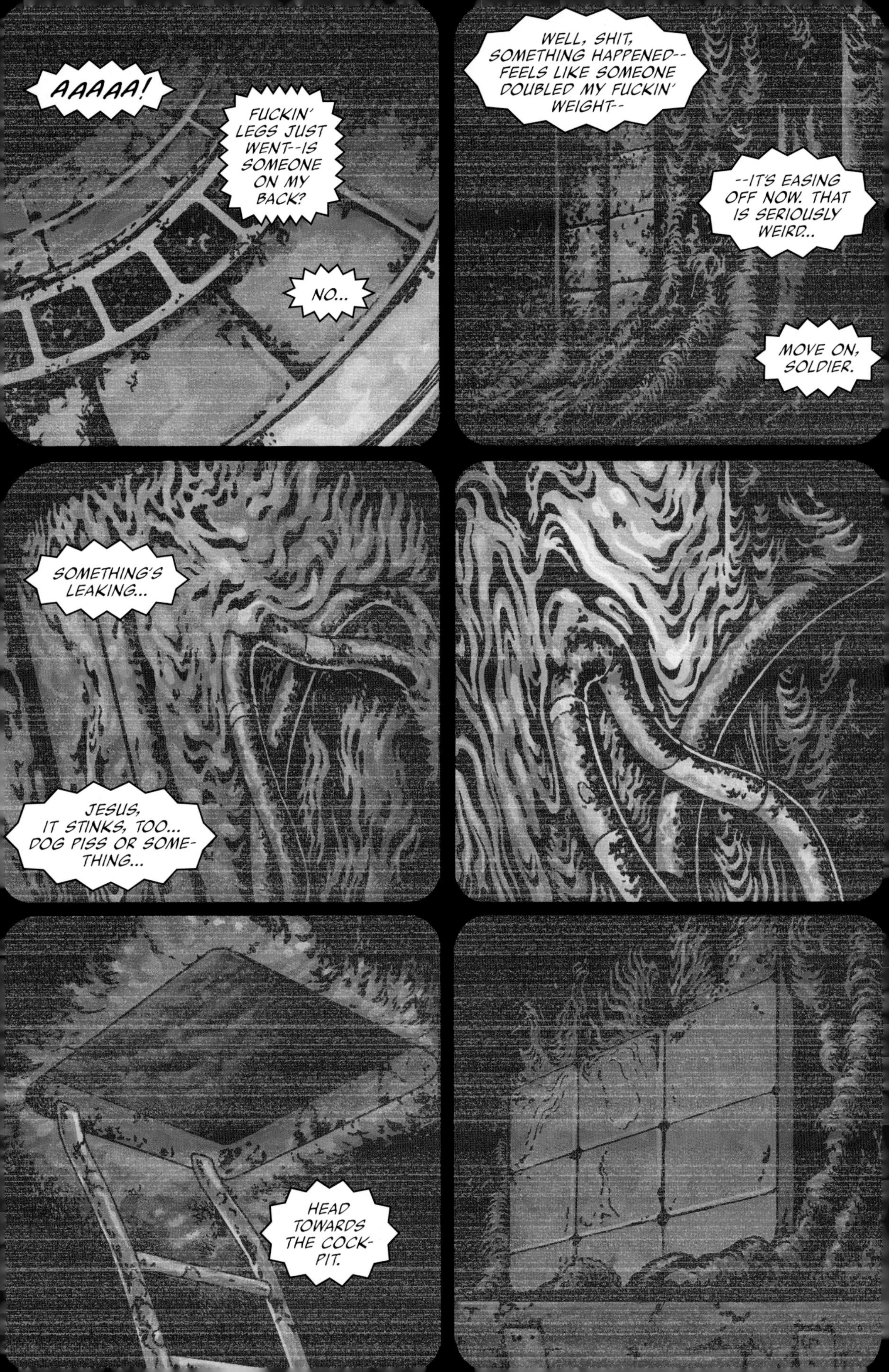
AAAAA!
FUCKIN' LEGS JUST WENT--IS SOMEONE ON MY BACK?
NO...
WELL, SHIT, SOMETHING HAPPENED--FEELS LIKE SOMEONE DOUBLED MY FUCKIN' WEIGHT--
--IT'S EASING OFF NOW. THAT IS SERIOUSLY WEIRD...
MOVE ON, SOLDIER.
SOMETHING'S LEAKING...
JESUS, IT STINKS, TOO... DOG PISS OR SOME-THING...
HEAD TOWARDS THE COCK-PIT.

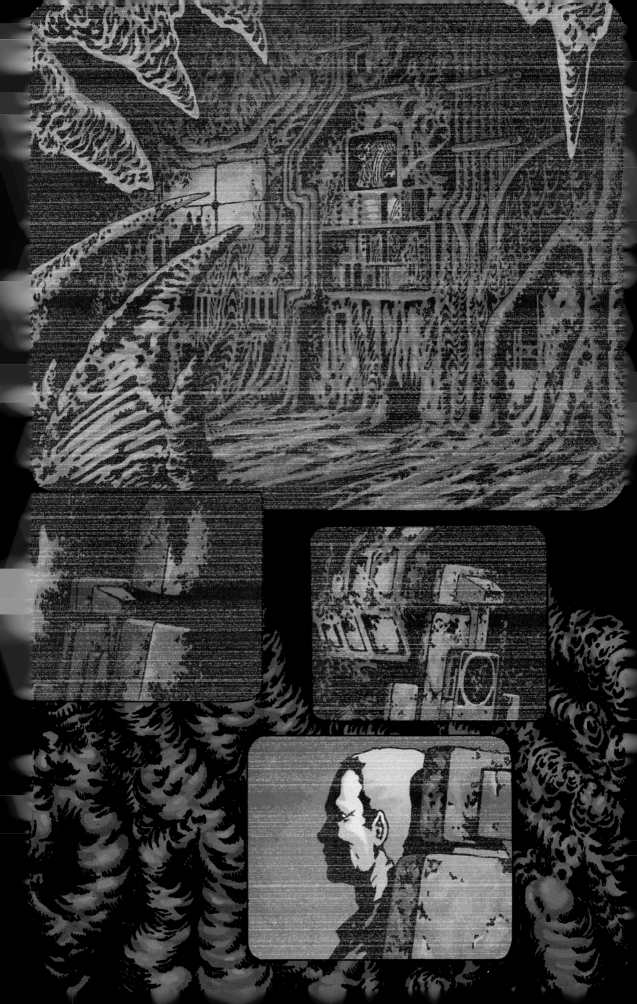

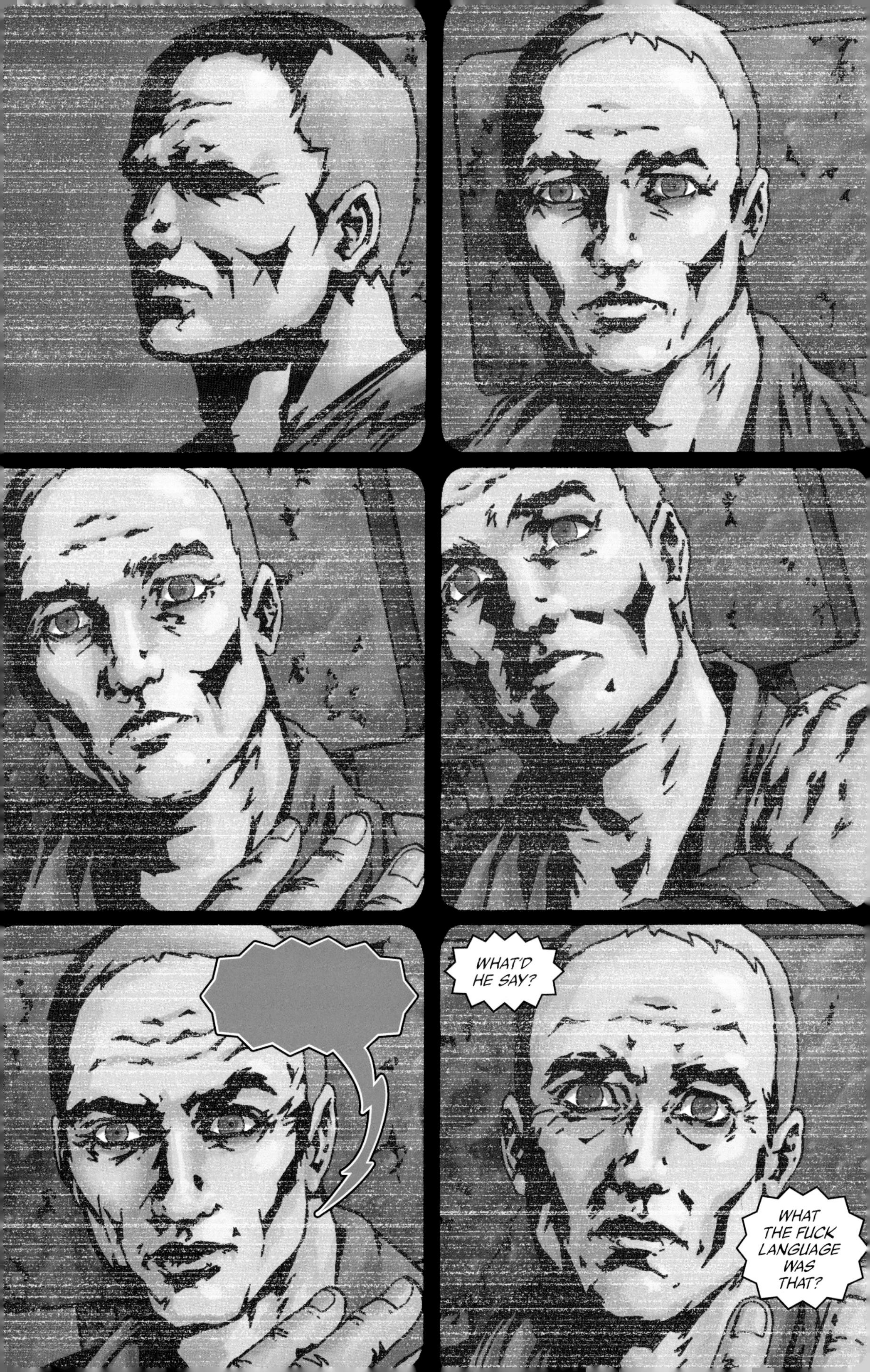
WHAT'D HE SAY?
WHAT THE FUCK LANGUAGE WAS THAT?

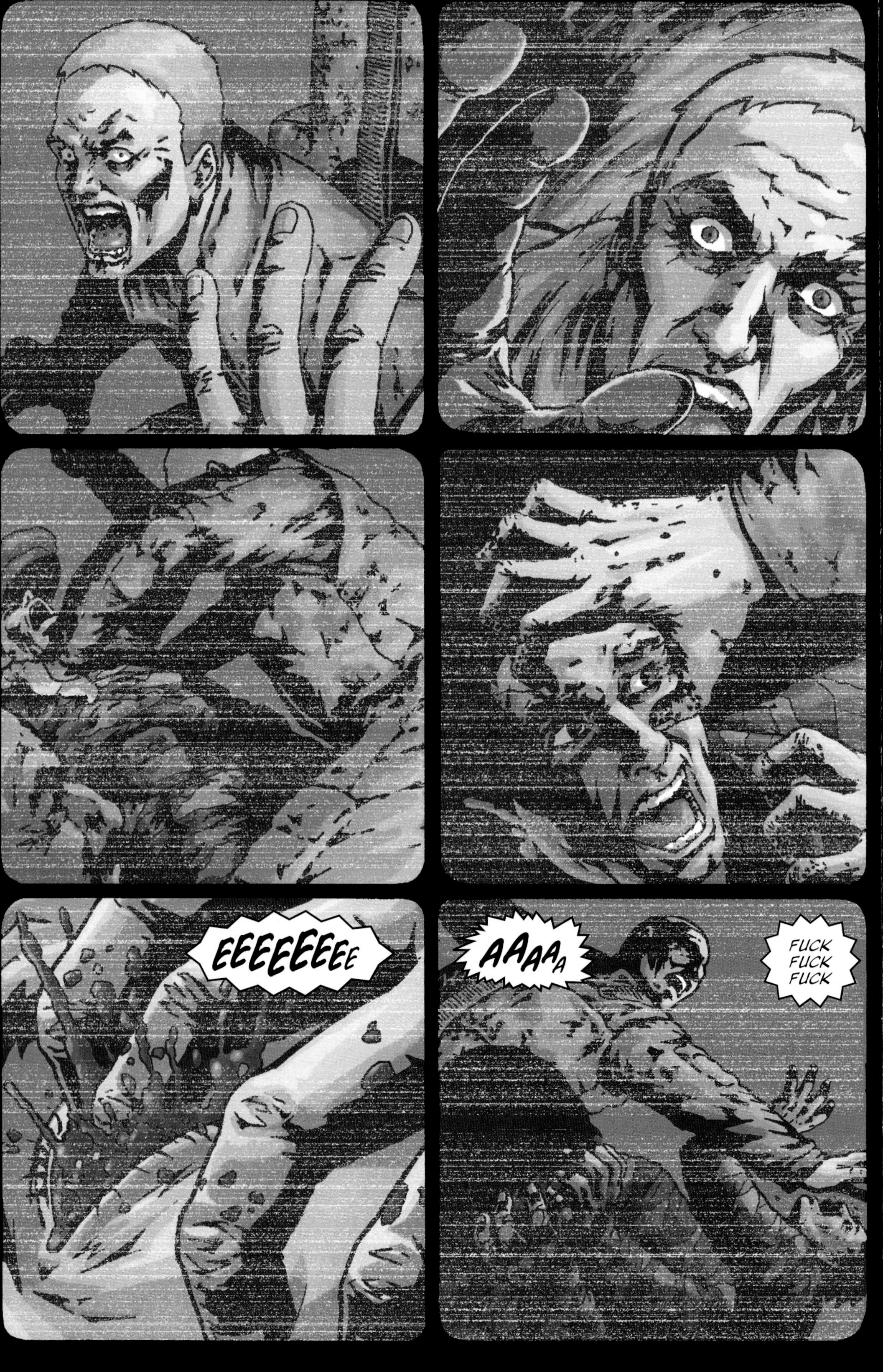
EEEEEEEEE
AAAAA
FUCK
FUCK
FUCK

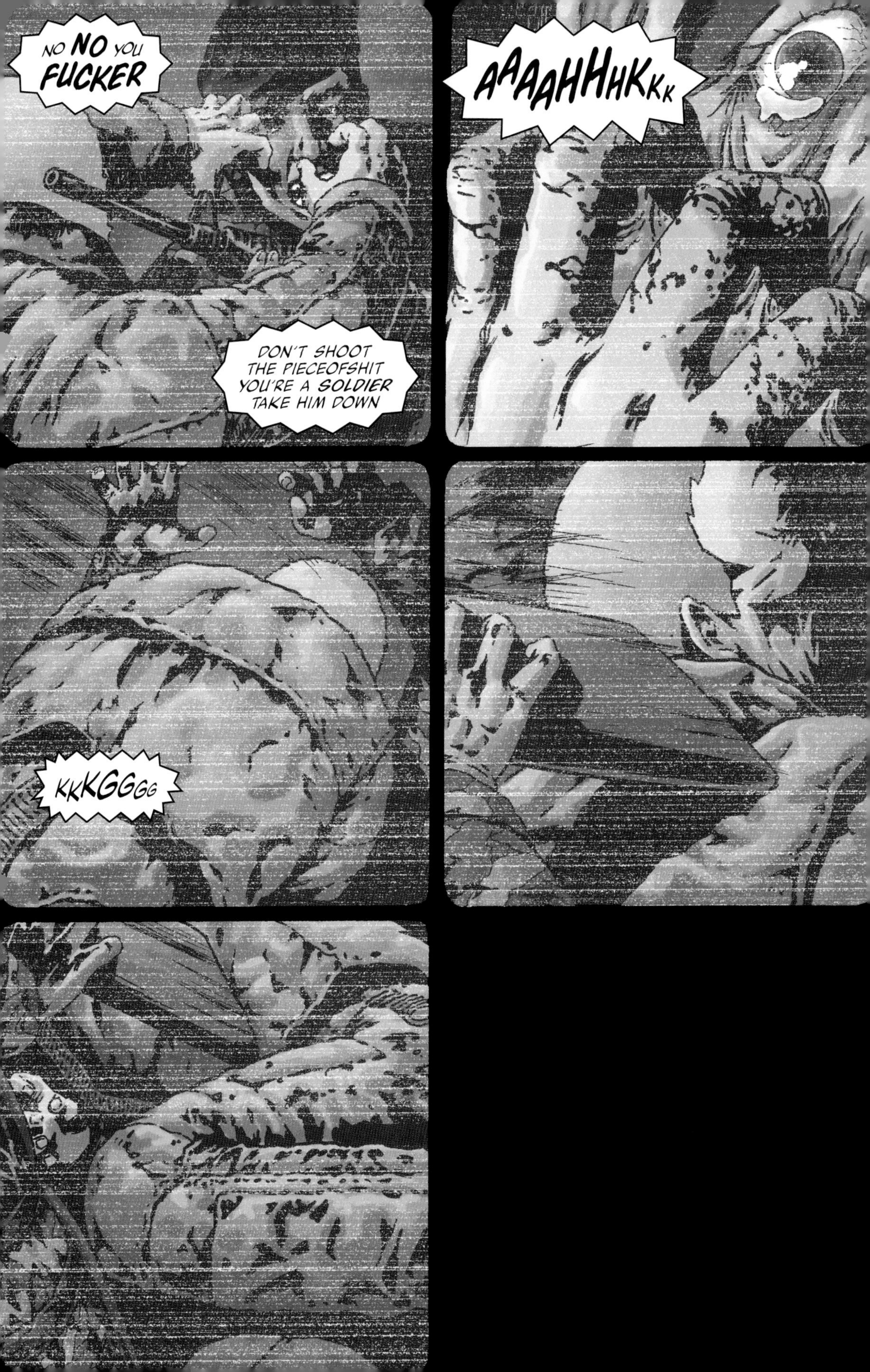
NO NO YOU FUCKER
DON'T SHOOT THE PIECEOFSHIT YOU'RE A SOLDIER TAKE HIM DOWN
AAAAHHHKKK
KKKGGGG

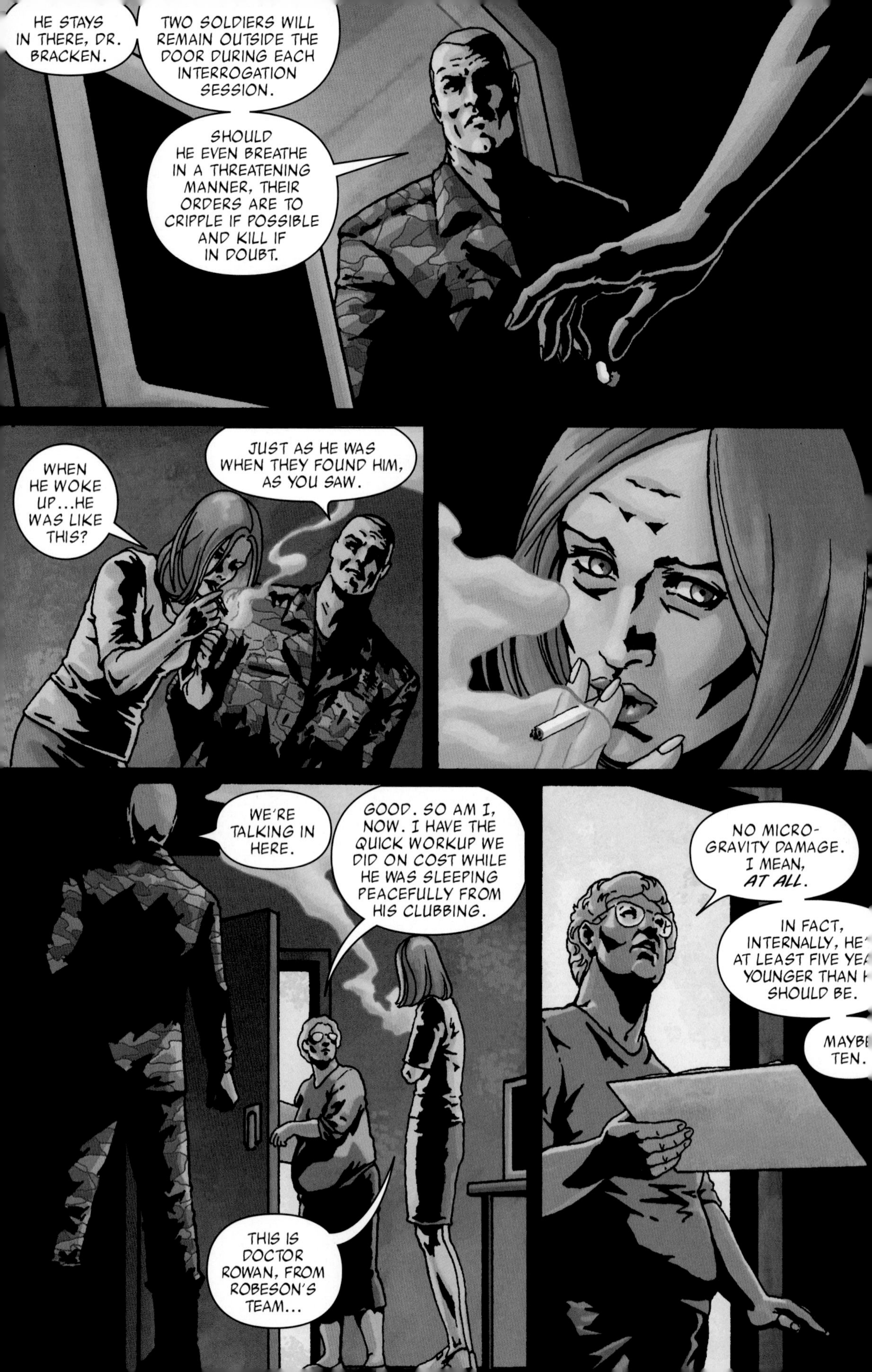
HE STAYS IN THERE, DR. BRACKEN.
TWO SOLDIERS WILL REMAIN OUTSIDE THE DOOR DURING EACH INTERROGATION SESSION.
SHOULD HE EVEN BREATHE IN A THREATENING MANNER, THEIR ORDERS ARE TO CRIPPLE IF POSSIBLE AND KILL IF IN DOUBT.
WHEN HE WOKE UP...HE WAS LIKE THIS?
JUST AS HE WAS WHEN THEY FOUND HIM, AS YOU SAW.
WE'RE TALKING IN HERE.
GOOD. SO AM I, NOW. I HAVE THE QUICK WORKUP WE DID ON COST WHILE HE WAS SLEEPING PEACEFULLY FROM HIS CLUBBING.
THIS IS DOCTOR ROWAN, FROM ROBESON'S TEAM...
NO MICRO-GRAVITY DAMAGE. I MEAN, *AT ALL*.
IN FACT, INTERNALLY, HE' AT LEAST FIVE YEA YOUNGER THAN H SHOULD BE.
MAYBE TEN.

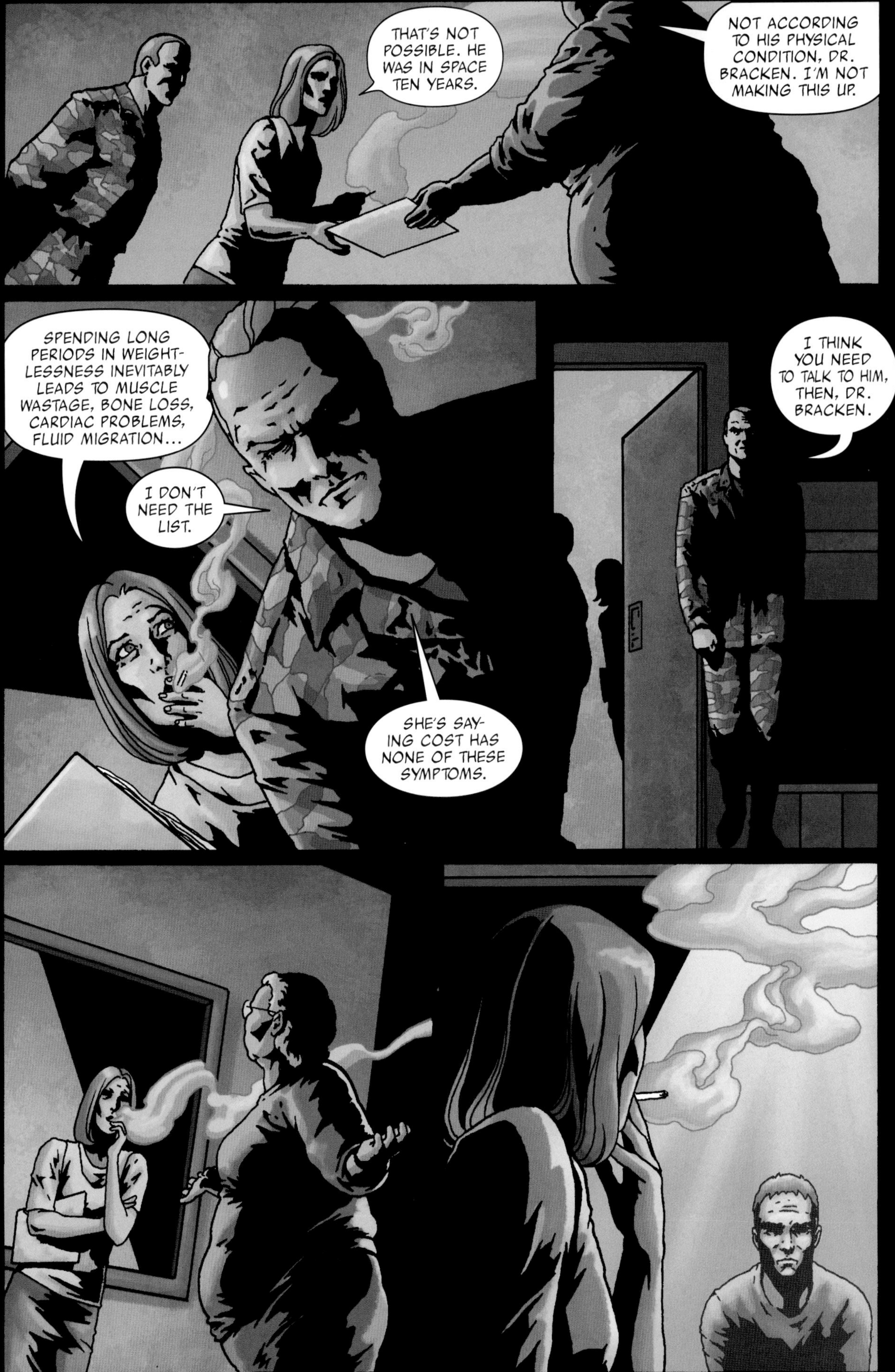
THAT'S NOT POSSIBLE. HE WAS IN SPACE TEN YEARS.
NOT ACCORDING TO HIS PHYSICAL CONDITION, DR. BRACKEN. I'M NOT MAKING THIS UP.
SPENDING LONG PERIODS IN WEIGHT-LESSNESS INEVITABLY LEADS TO MUSCLE WASTAGE, BONE LOSS, CARDIAC PROBLEMS, FLUID MIGRATION...
I DON'T NEED THE LIST.
SHE'S SAYING COST HAS NONE OF THESE SYMPTOMS.
I THINK YOU NEED TO TALK TO HIM, THEN, DR. BRACKEN.

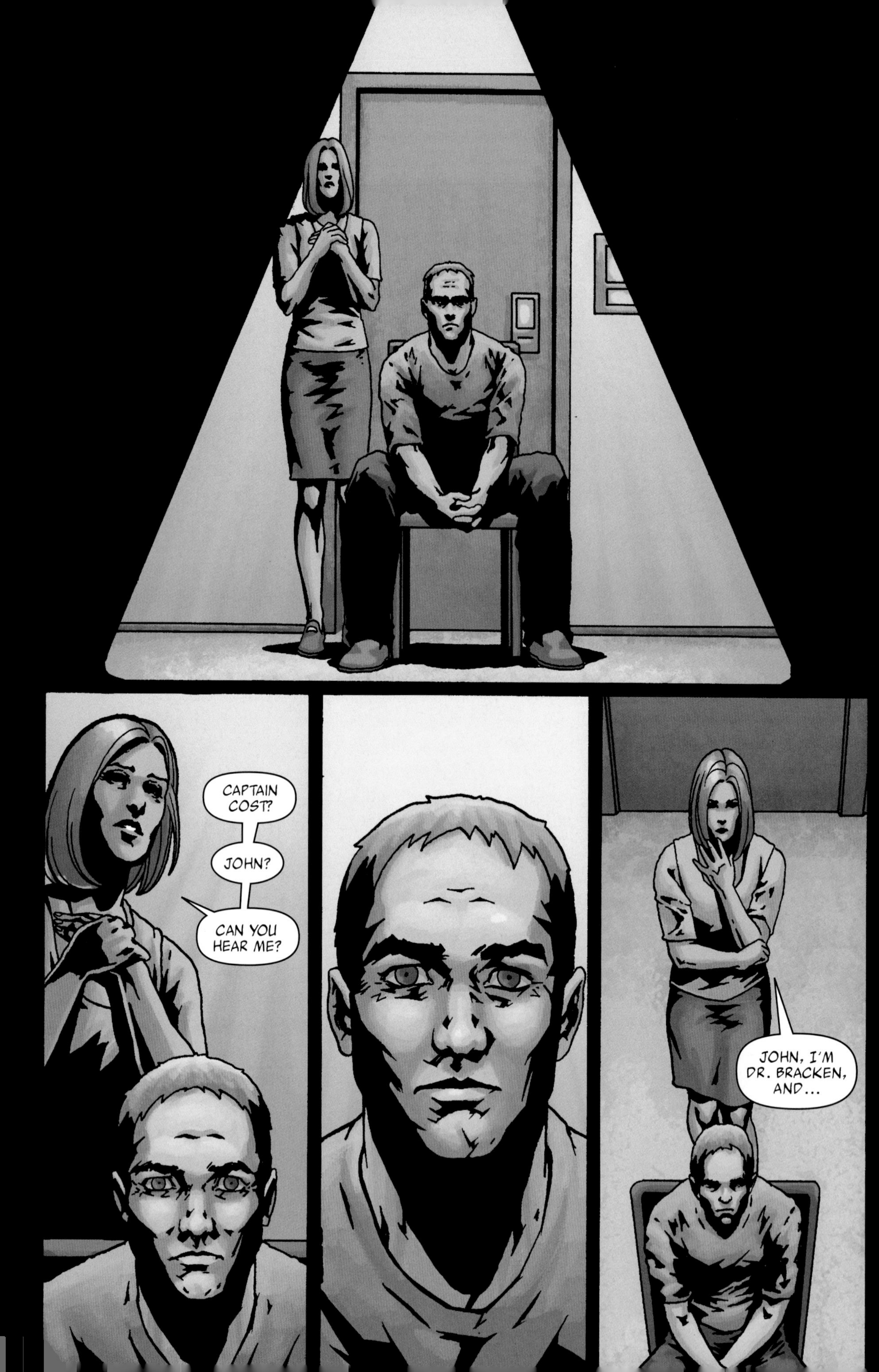
CAPTAIN COST?
JOHN?
CAN YOU HEAR ME?
JOHN, I'M DR. BRACKEN, AND...

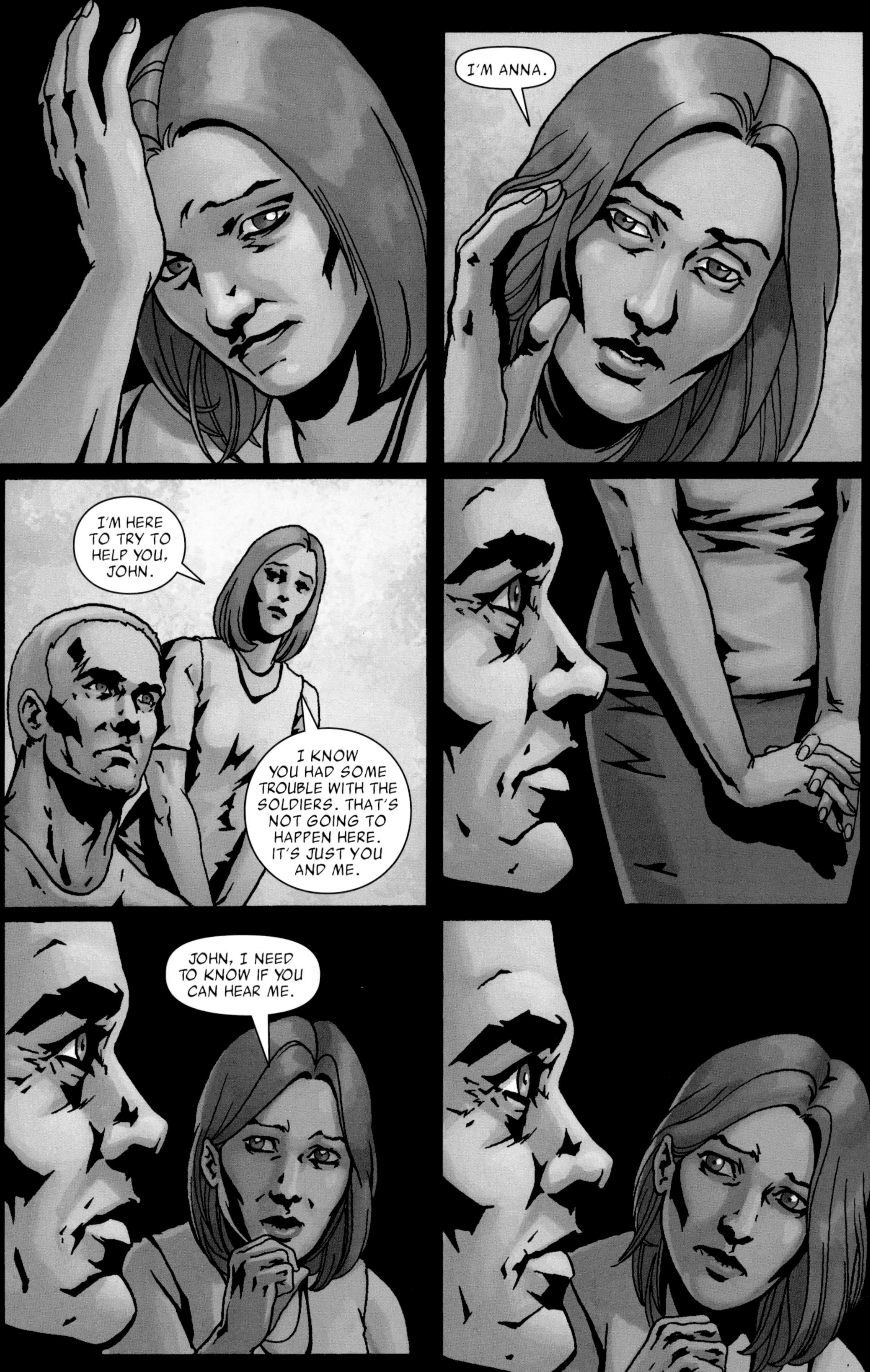
I'M ANNA.
I'M HERE TO TRY TO HELP YOU, JOHN.
I KNOW YOU HAD SOME TROUBLE WITH THE SOLDIERS. THAT'S NOT GOING TO HAPPEN HERE. IT'S JUST YOU AND ME.
JOHN, I NEED TO KNOW IF YOU CAN HEAR ME.

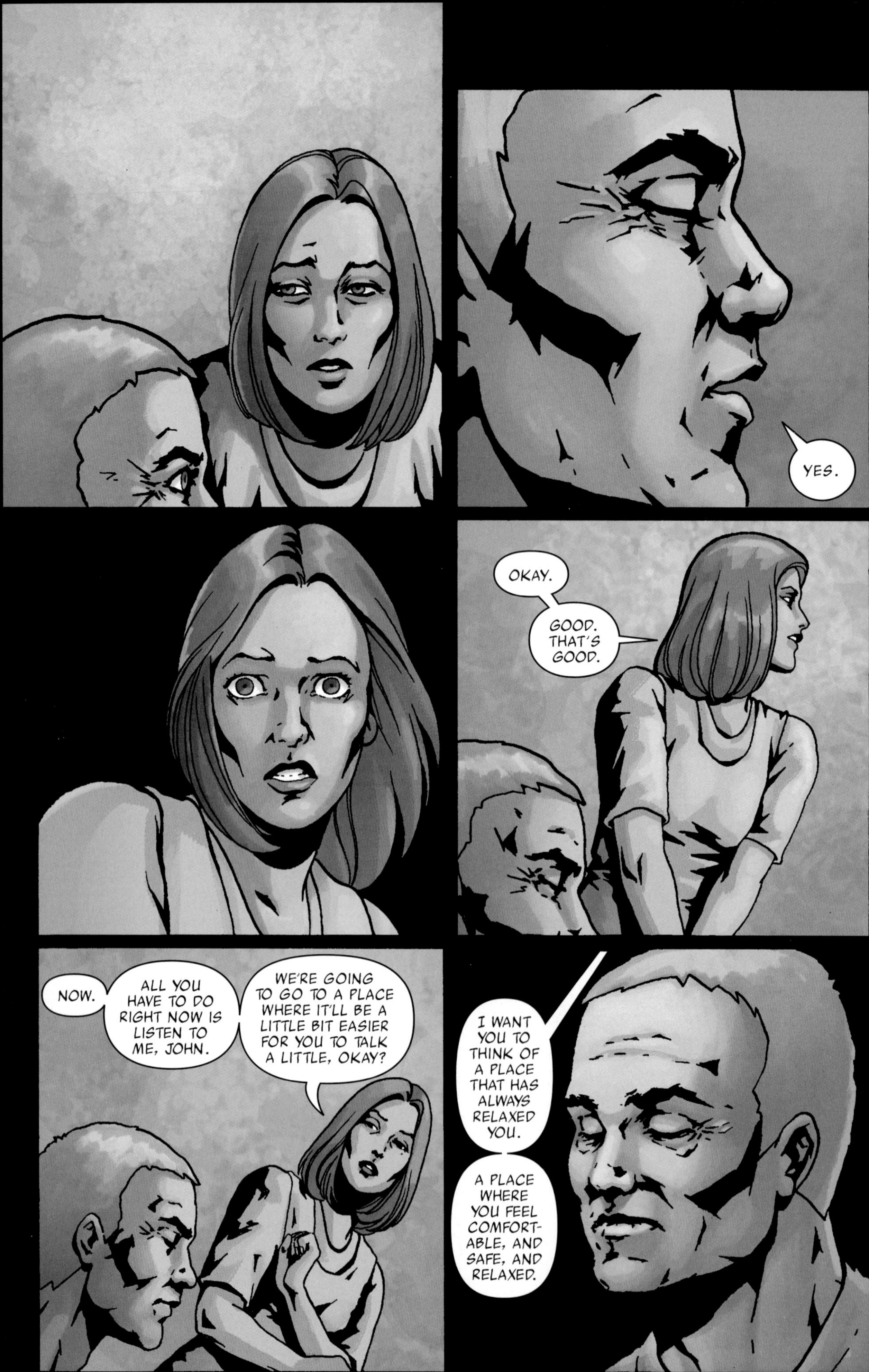
YES.
OKAY.
GOOD. THAT'S GOOD.
NOW.
ALL YOU HAVE TO DO RIGHT NOW IS LISTEN TO ME, JOHN.
WE'RE GOING TO GO TO A PLACE WHERE IT'LL BE A LITTLE BIT EASIER FOR YOU TO TALK A LITTLE, OKAY?
I WANT YOU TO THINK OF A PLACE THAT HAS ALWAYS RELAXED YOU.
A PLACE WHERE YOU FEEL COMFORT-ABLE, AND SAFE, AND RELAXED.

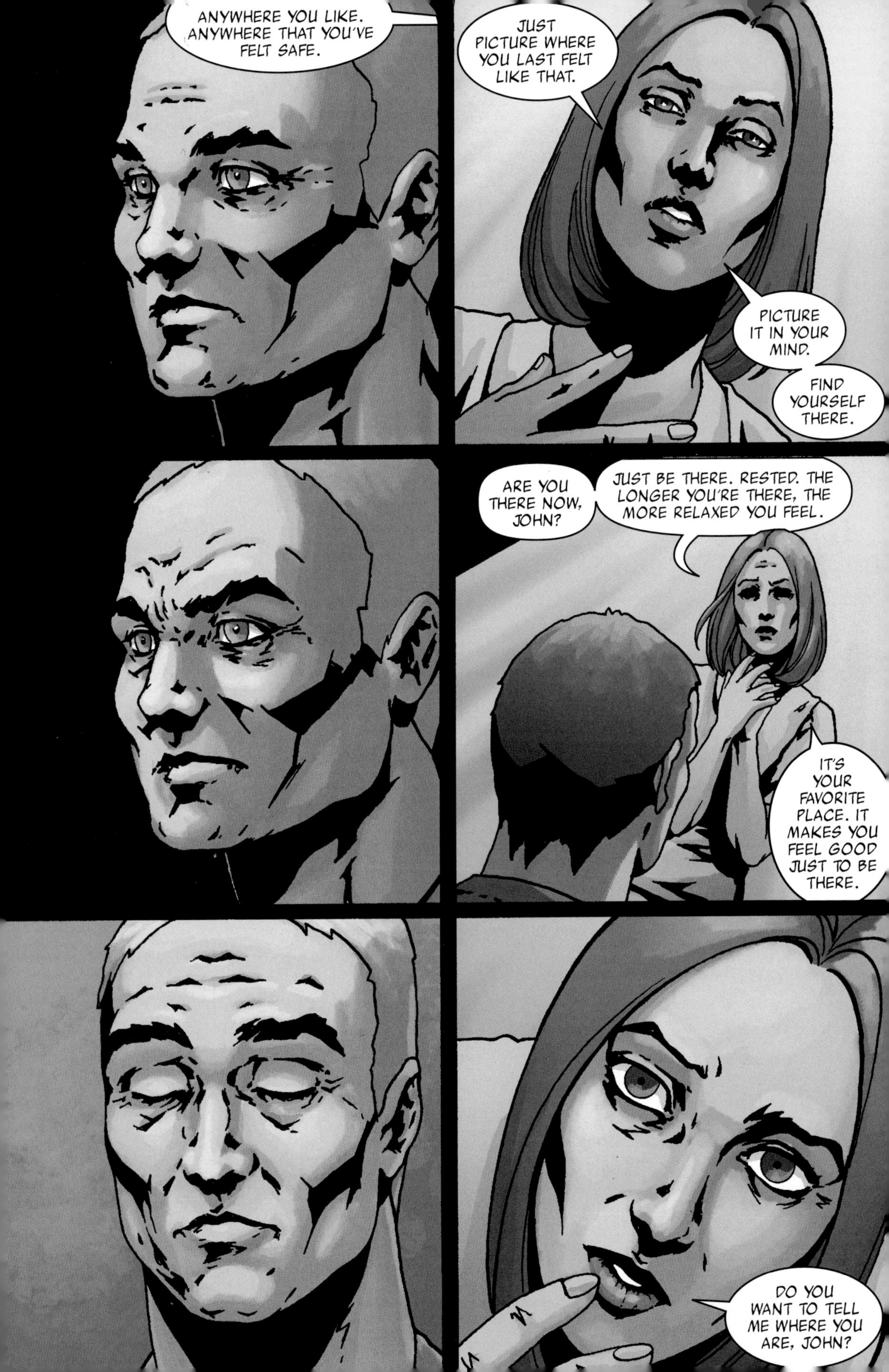
ANYWHERE YOU LIKE. ANYWHERE THAT YOU'VE FELT SAFE.
JUST PICTURE WHERE YOU LAST FELT LIKE THAT.
PICTURE IT IN YOUR MIND.
FIND YOURSELF THERE.
JUST BE THERE. RESTED. THE LONGER YOU'RE THERE, THE MORE RELAXED YOU FEEL.
ARE YOU THERE NOW, JOHN?
IT'S YOUR FAVORITE PLACE. IT MAKES YOU FEEL GOOD JUST TO BE THERE.
DO YOU WANT TO TELL ME WHERE YOU ARE, JOHN?

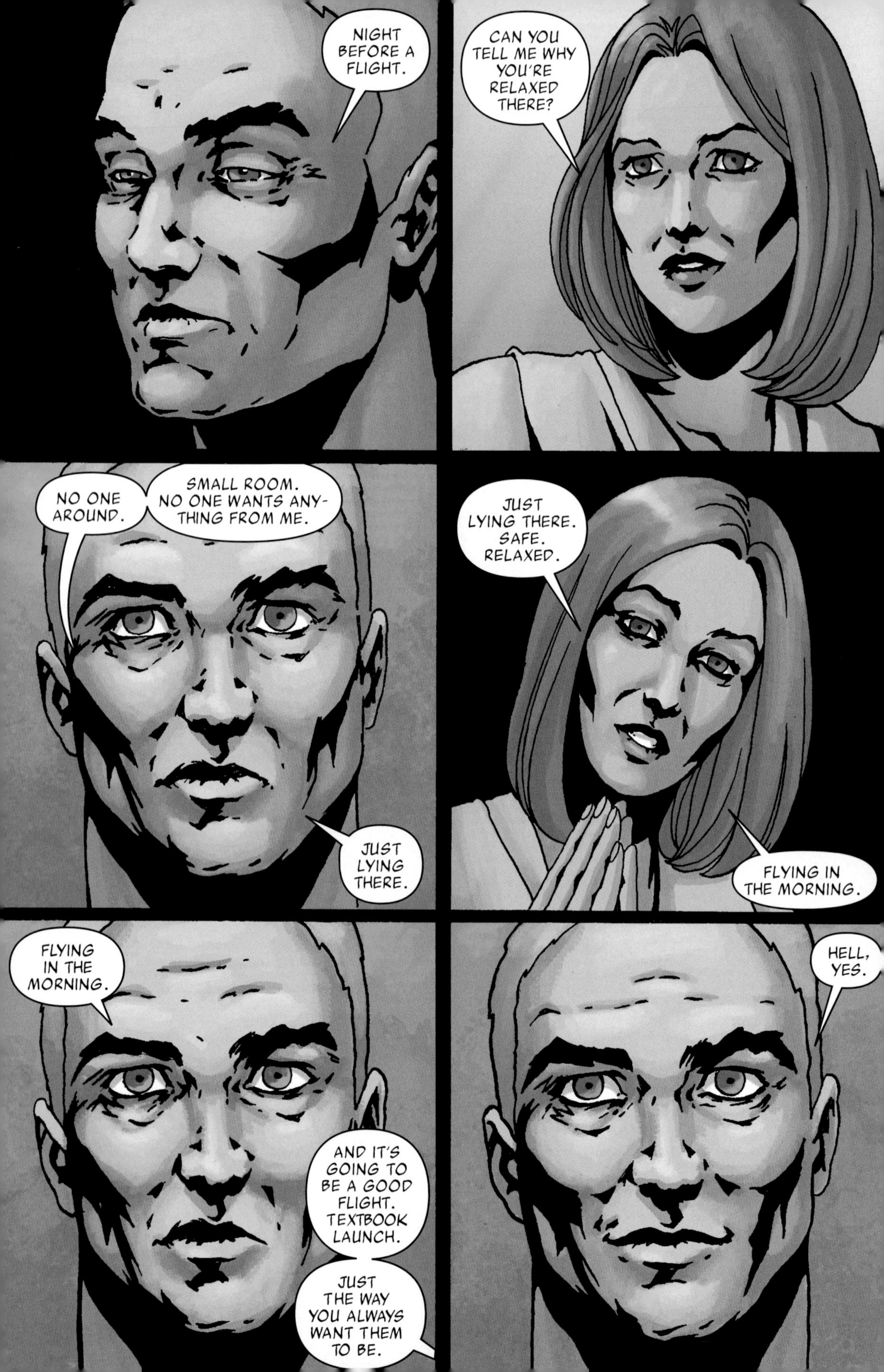
NIGHT BEFORE A FLIGHT.
CAN YOU TELL ME WHY YOU'RE RELAXED THERE?
NO ONE AROUND.
SMALL ROOM. NO ONE WANTS ANY-THING FROM ME.
JUST LYING THERE.
JUST LYING THERE. SAFE. RELAXED.
FLYING IN THE MORNING.
FLYING IN THE MORNING.
AND IT'S GOING TO BE A GOOD FLIGHT. TEXTBOOK LAUNCH.
JUST THE WAY YOU ALWAYS WANT THEM TO BE.
HELL, YES.

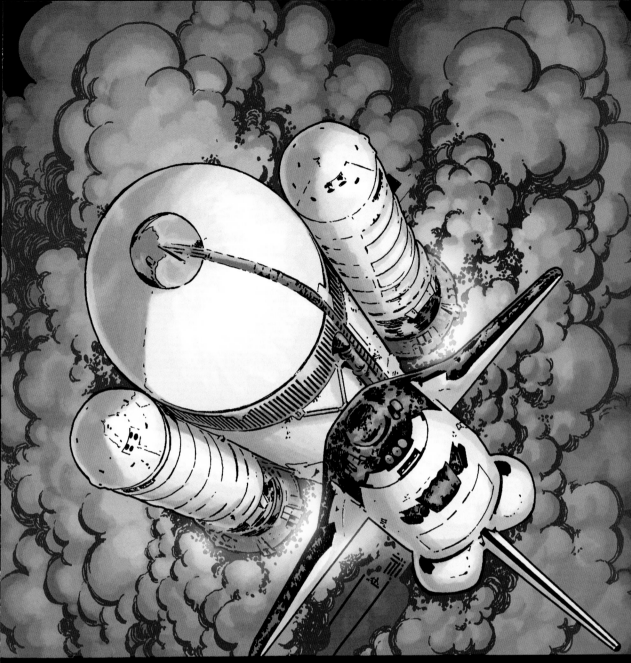

GO FOR THE MAIN ENGINE START. MAIN ENGINE THREE START, TWO START, ONE START, SRB IGNITION...

ON THE WAY.

DO YOU STILL FEEL SAFE?

ALWAYS.

SHE'S A SAFE BIRD.

MAX-Q AT TWENTY-SIX SECONDS, THEN THROTTLE HER UP AT SIXTY, ONE HUNDRED FOUR PERCENT THRUST...

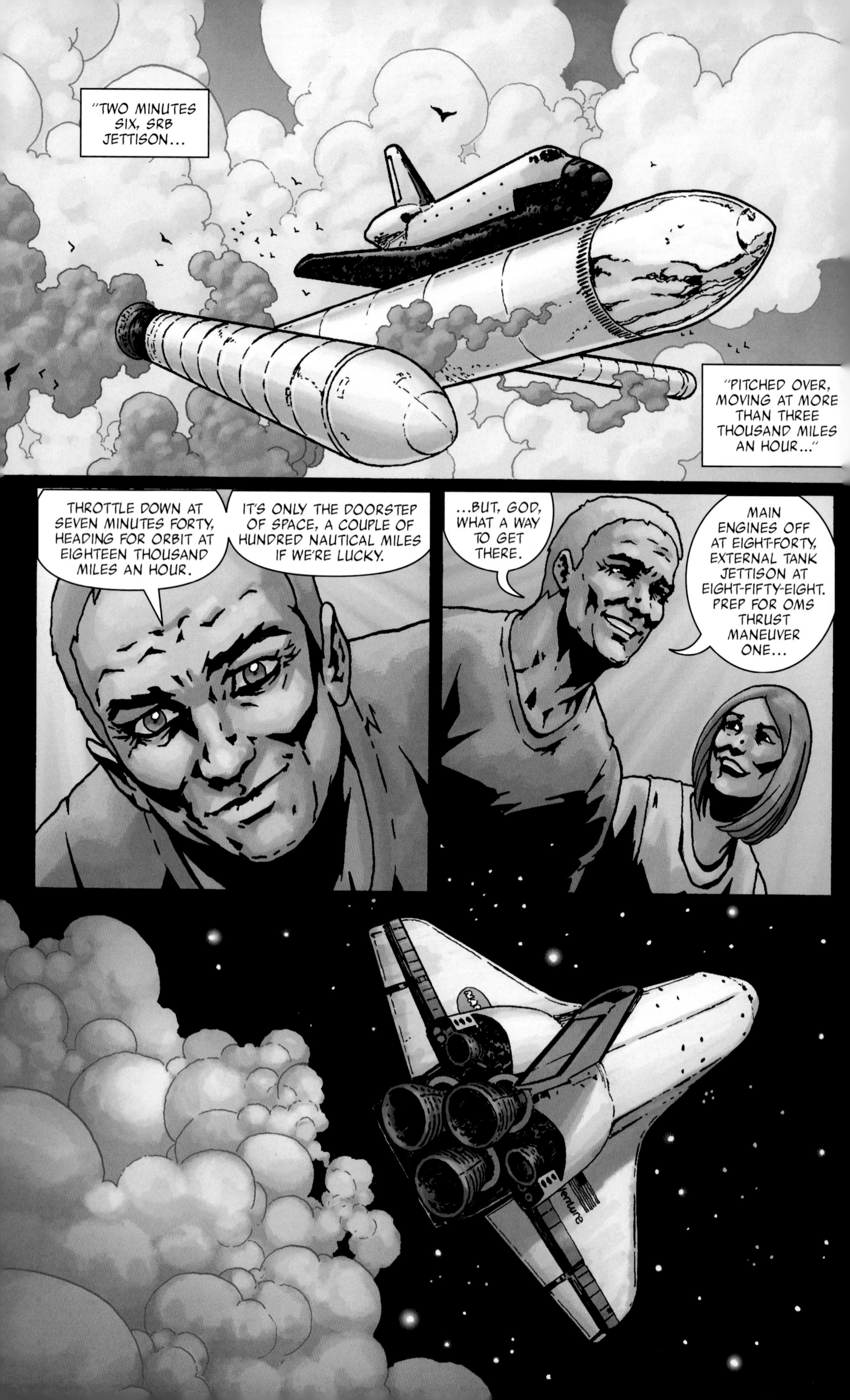
"TWO MINUTES SIX, SRB JETTISON...
"PITCHED OVER, MOVING AT MORE THAN THREE THOUSAND MILES AN HOUR..."
THROTTLE DOWN AT SEVEN MINUTES FORTY, HEADING FOR ORBIT AT EIGHTEEN THOUSAND MILES AN HOUR.
IT'S ONLY THE DOORSTEP OF SPACE, A COUPLE OF HUNDRED NAUTICAL MILES IF WE'RE LUCKY.
...BUT, GOD, WHAT A WAY TO GET THERE.
MAIN ENGINES OFF AT EIGHT-FORTY, EXTERNAL TANK JETTISON AT EIGHT-FIFTY-EIGHT. PREP FOR OMS THRUST MANEUVER ONE...

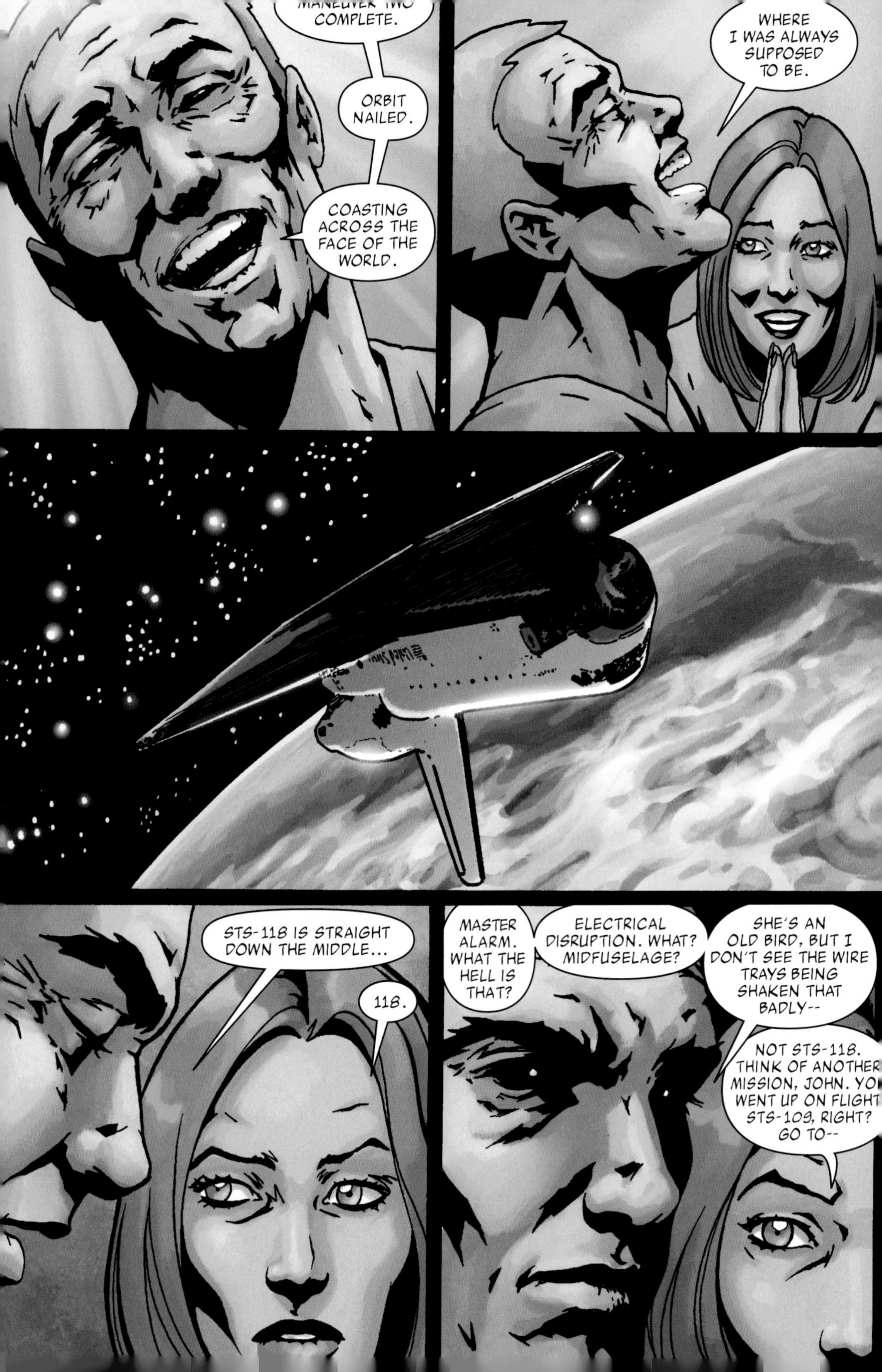
COMPLETE.
ORBIT NAILED.
COASTING ACROSS THE FACE OF THE WORLD.
WHERE I WAS ALWAYS SUPPOSED TO BE.
STS-118 IS STRAIGHT DOWN THE MIDDLE...
118.
MASTER ALARM. WHAT THE HELL IS THAT?
ELECTRICAL DISRUPTION. WHAT? MIDFUSELAGE?
SHE'S AN OLD BIRD, BUT I DON'T SEE THE WIRE TRAYS BEING SHAKEN THAT BADLY--
NOT STS-118. THINK OF ANOTHER MISSION, JOHN. YO WENT UP ON FLIGHT STS-109, RIGHT? GO TO--

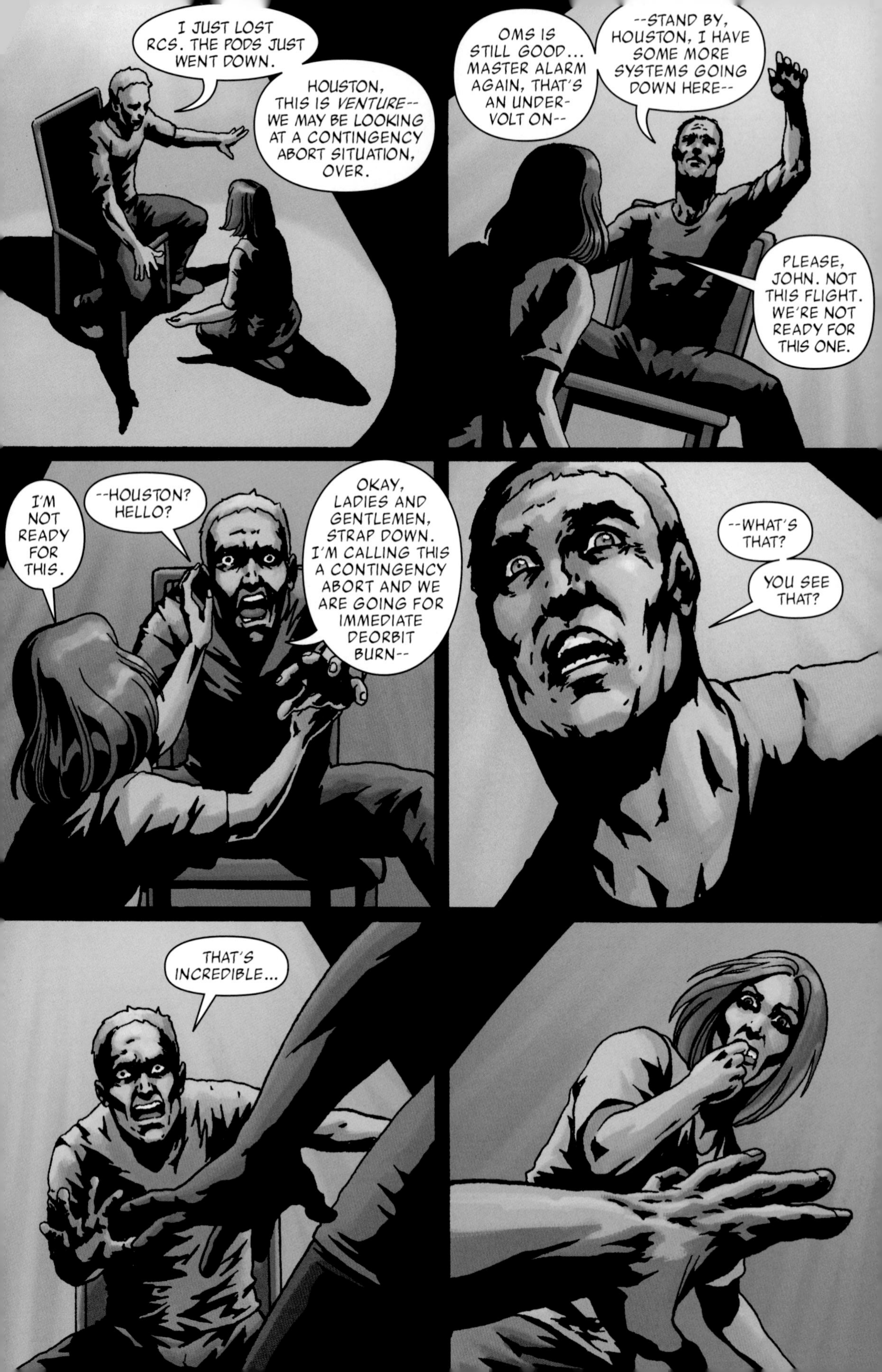
I JUST LOST RCS. THE PODS JUST WENT DOWN.
HOUSTON, THIS IS *VENTURE*-- WE MAY BE LOOKING AT A CONTINGENCY ABORT SITUATION, OVER.
OMS IS STILL GOOD... MASTER ALARM AGAIN, THAT'S AN UNDER-VOLT ON--
--STAND BY, HOUSTON, I HAVE SOME MORE SYSTEMS GOING DOWN HERE--
PLEASE, JOHN. NOT THIS FLIGHT. WE'RE NOT READY FOR THIS ONE.
I'M NOT READY FOR THIS.
--HOUSTON? HELLO?
OKAY, LADIES AND GENTLEMEN, STRAP DOWN. I'M CALLING THIS A CONTINGENCY ABORT AND WE ARE GOING FOR IMMEDIATE DEORBIT BURN--
--WHAT'S THAT?
YOU SEE THAT?
THAT'S INCREDIBLE...

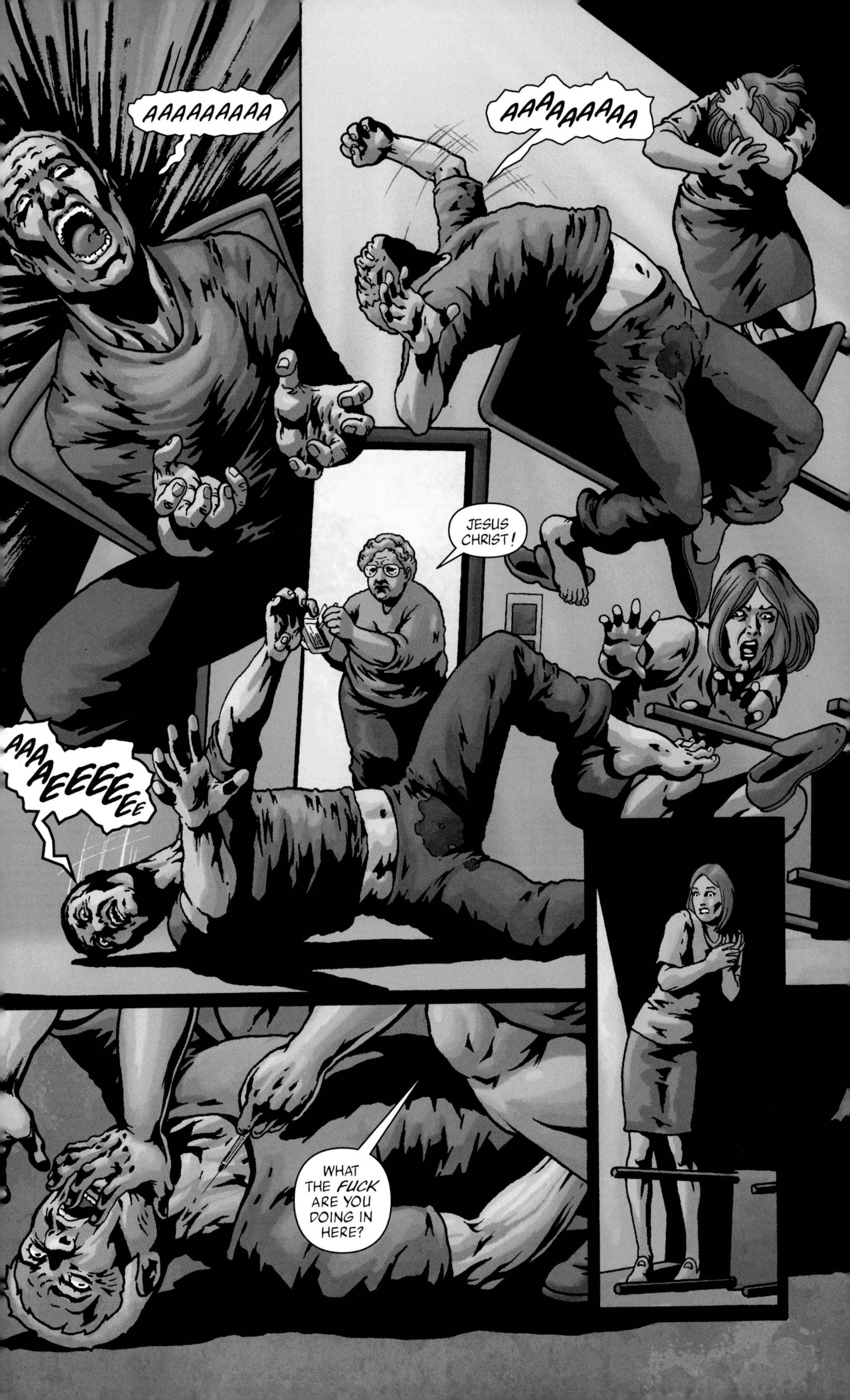
AAAAAAAAA
AAAAAAAA
JESUS CHRIST!
AAAEEEEEEE
WHAT THE FUCK ARE YOU DOING IN HERE?

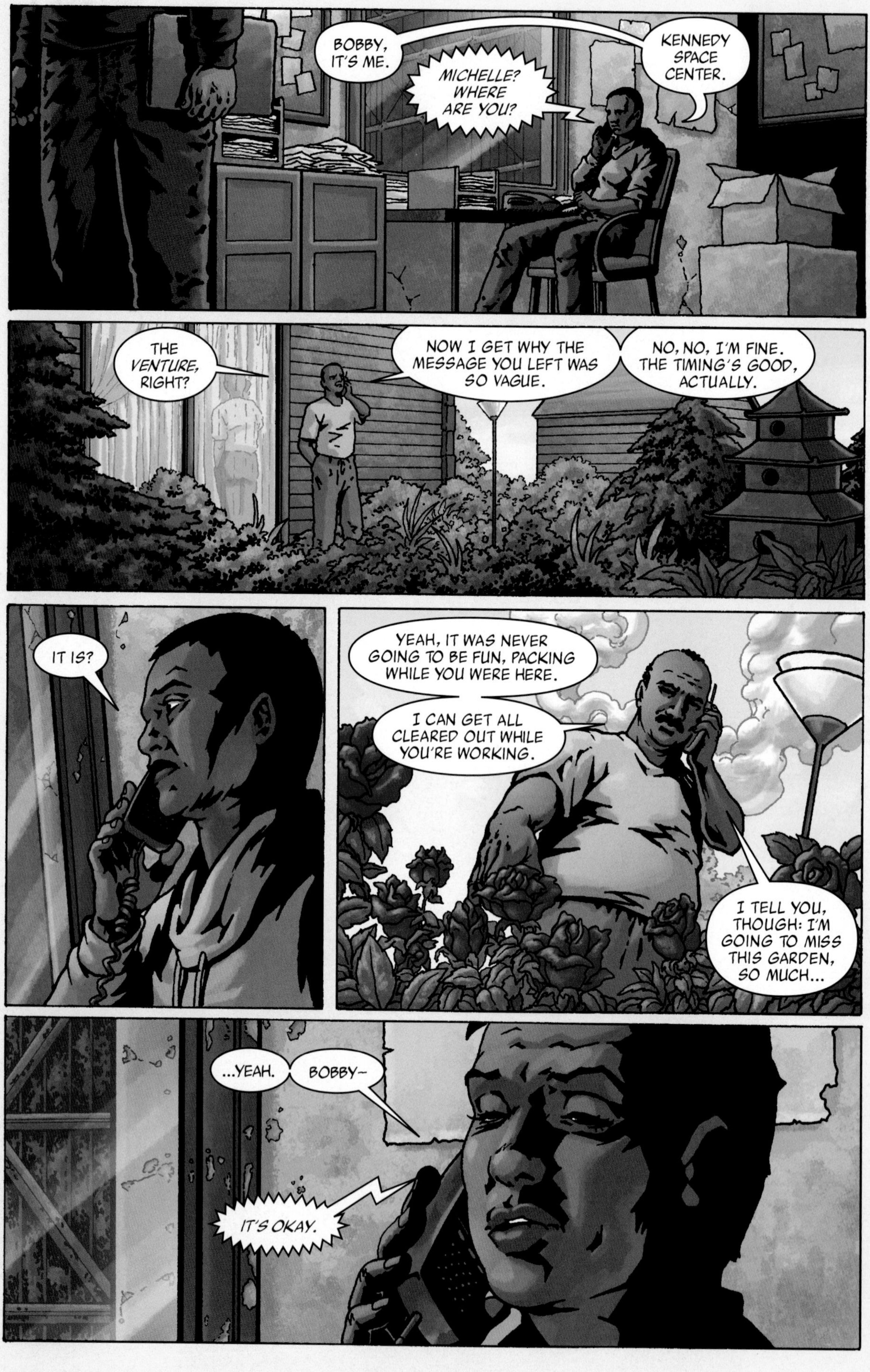
BOBBY, IT'S ME.
MICHELLE? WHERE ARE YOU?
KENNEDY SPACE CENTER.
THE VENTURE, RIGHT?
NOW I GET WHY THE MESSAGE YOU LEFT WAS SO VAGUE.
NO, NO, I'M FINE. THE TIMING'S GOOD, ACTUALLY.
IT IS?
YEAH, IT WAS NEVER GOING TO BE FUN, PACKING WHILE YOU WERE HERE.
I CAN GET ALL CLEARED OUT WHILE YOU'RE WORKING.
I TELL YOU, THOUGH: I'M GOING TO MISS THIS GARDEN, SO MUCH...
...YEAH.
BOBBY–
IT'S OKAY.

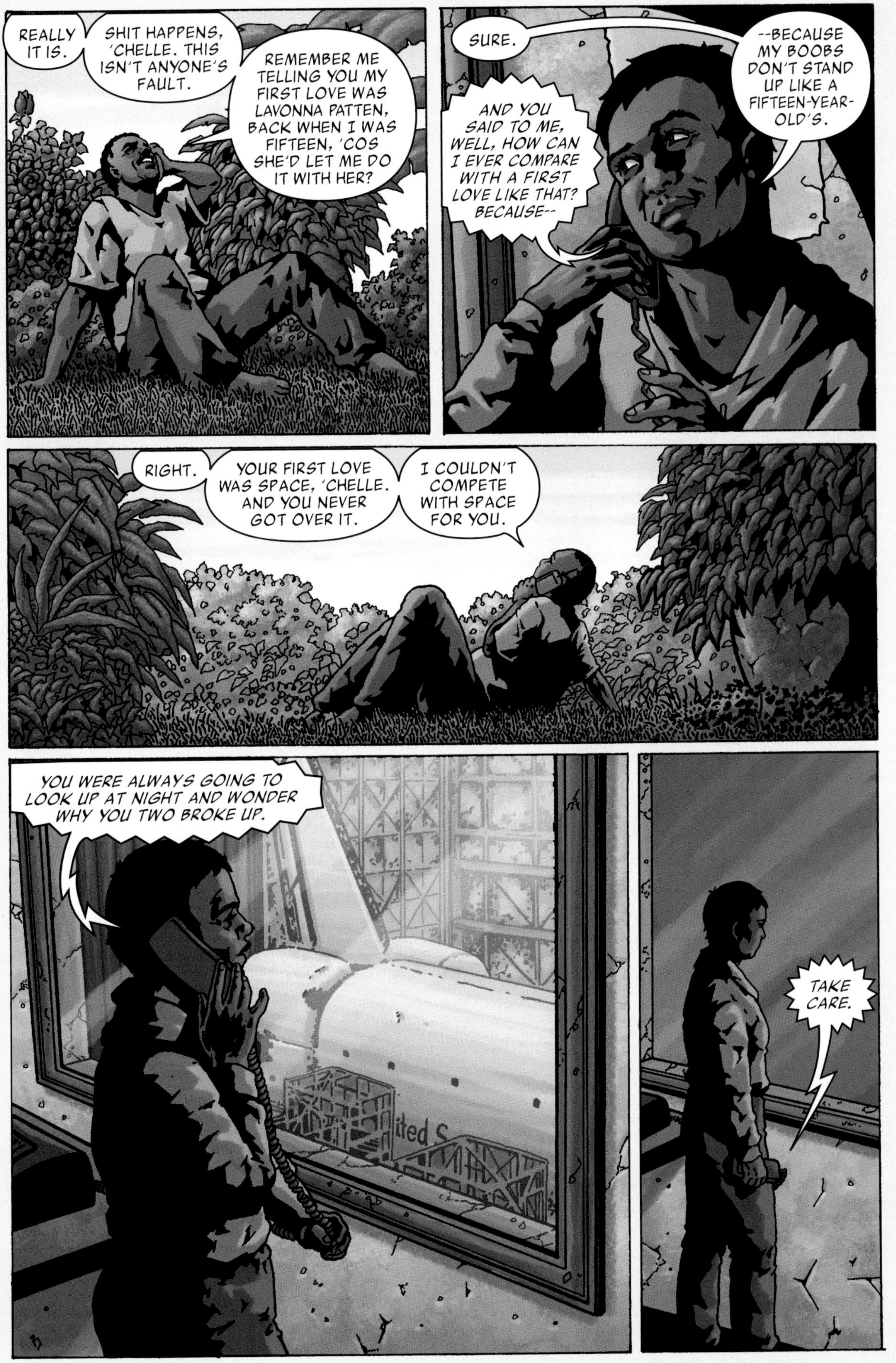
REALLY IT IS.
SHIT HAPPENS, 'CHELLE. THIS ISN'T ANYONE'S FAULT.
REMEMBER ME TELLING YOU MY FIRST LOVE WAS LAVONNA PATTEN, BACK WHEN I WAS FIFTEEN, 'COS SHE'D LET ME DO IT WITH HER?
SURE.
AND YOU SAID TO ME, WELL, HOW CAN I EVER COMPARE WITH A FIRST LOVE LIKE THAT? BECAUSE--
--BECAUSE MY BOOBS DON'T STAND UP LIKE A FIFTEEN-YEAR-OLD'S.
RIGHT.
YOUR FIRST LOVE WAS SPACE, 'CHELLE. AND YOU NEVER GOT OVER IT.
I COULDN'T COMPETE WITH SPACE FOR YOU.
YOU WERE ALWAYS GOING TO LOOK UP AT NIGHT AND WONDER WHY YOU TWO BROKE UP.
TAKE CARE.

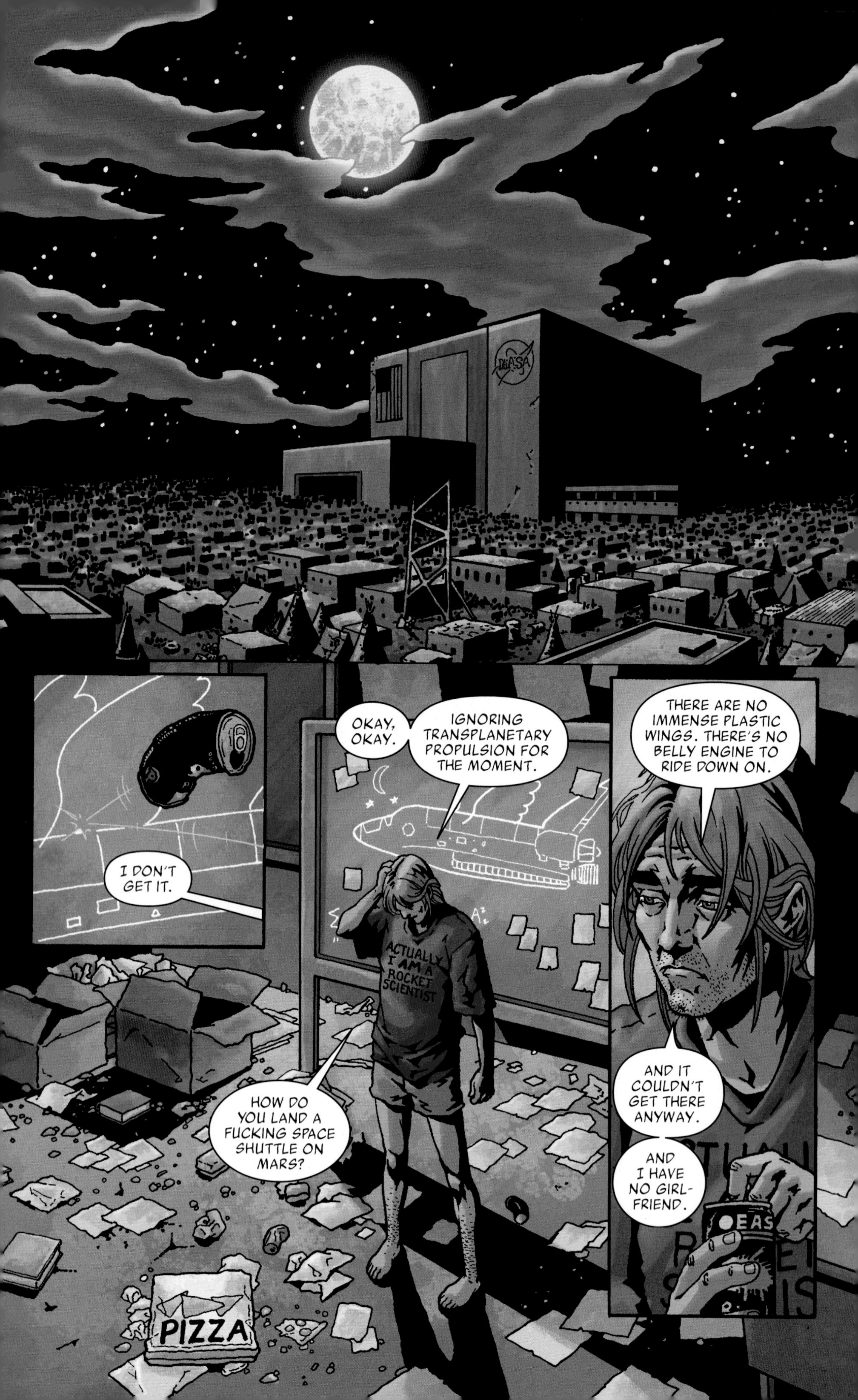
NASA
I DON'T GET IT.
OKAY, OKAY.
IGNORING TRANSPLANETARY PROPULSION FOR THE MOMENT.
HOW DO YOU LAND A FUCKING SPACE SHUTTLE ON MARS?
ACTUALLY I AM A ROCKET SCIENTIST
THERE ARE NO IMMENSE PLASTIC WINGS. THERE'S NO BELLY ENGINE TO RIDE DOWN ON.
AND IT COULDN'T GET THERE ANYWAY.
AND I HAVE NO GIRL-FRIEND.
PIZZA

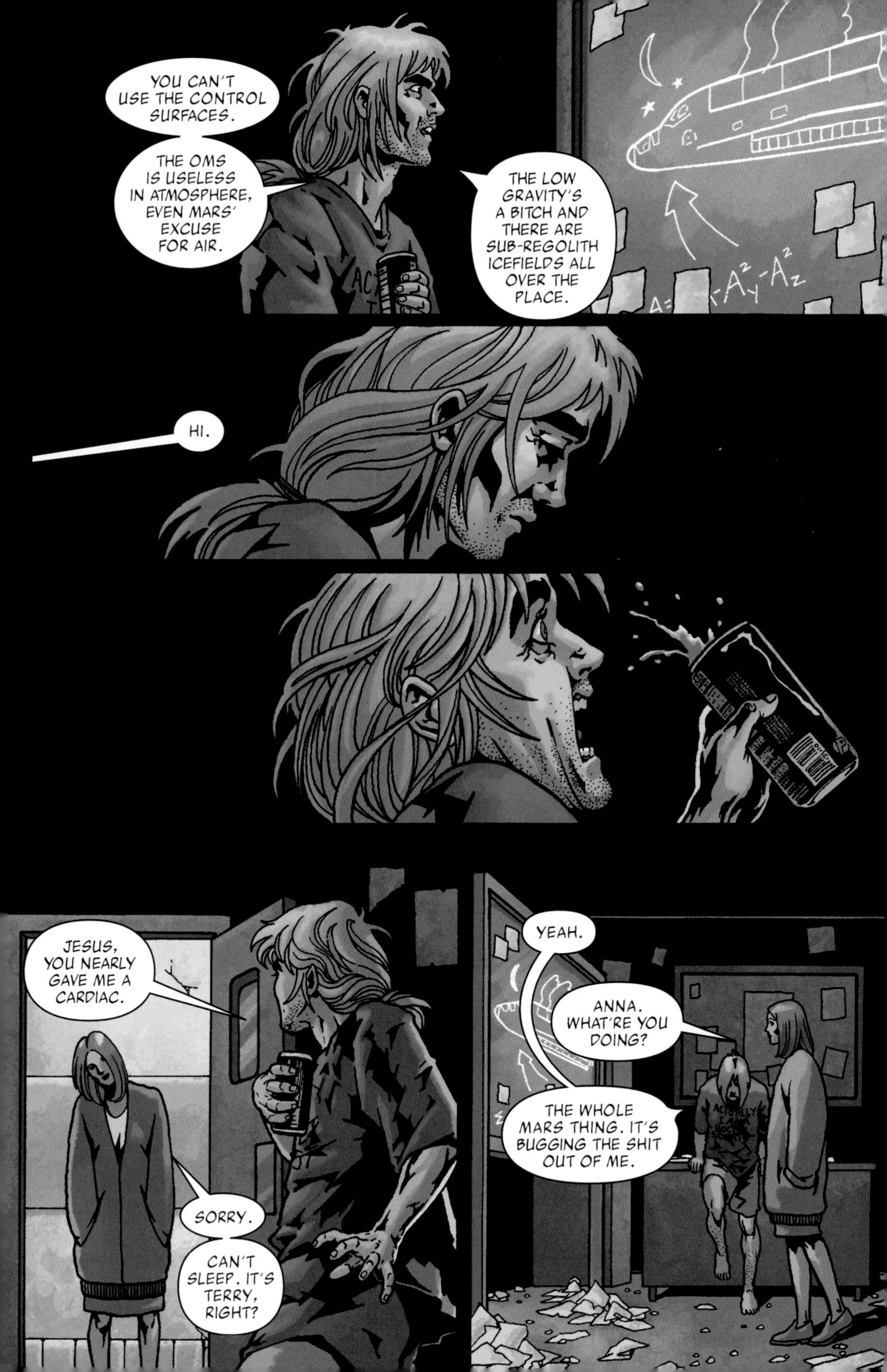
YOU CAN'T USE THE CONTROL SURFACES.
THE OMS IS USELESS IN ATMOSPHERE, EVEN MARS' EXCUSE FOR AIR.
THE LOW GRAVITY'S A BITCH AND THERE ARE SUB-REGOLITH ICEFIELDS ALL OVER THE PLACE.
HI.
JESUS, YOU NEARLY GAVE ME A CARDIAC.
SORRY.
CAN'T SLEEP. IT'S TERRY, RIGHT?
YEAH.
ANNA. WHAT'RE YOU DOING?
THE WHOLE MARS THING. IT'S BUGGING THE SHIT OUT OF ME.

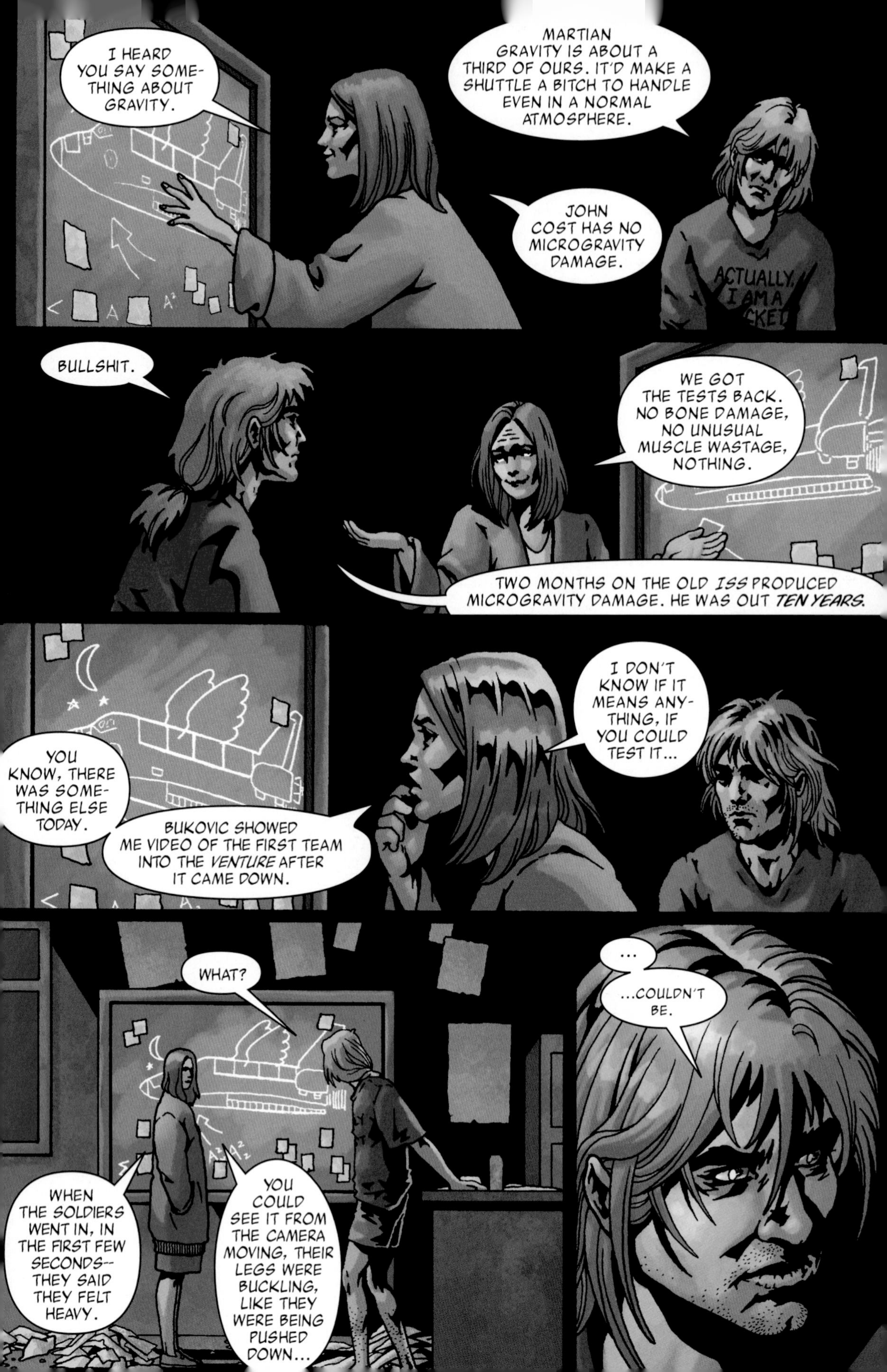
I HEARD YOU SAY SOMETHING ABOUT GRAVITY.
MARTIAN GRAVITY IS ABOUT A THIRD OF OURS. IT'D MAKE A SHUTTLE A BITCH TO HANDLE EVEN IN A NORMAL ATMOSPHERE.
JOHN COST HAS NO MICROGRAVITY DAMAGE.
ACTUALLY, I AM A
BULLSHIT.
WE GOT THE TESTS BACK. NO BONE DAMAGE, NO UNUSUAL MUSCLE WASTAGE, NOTHING.
TWO MONTHS ON THE OLD *ISS* PRODUCED MICROGRAVITY DAMAGE. HE WAS OUT *TEN YEARS.*
YOU KNOW, THERE WAS SOMETHING ELSE TODAY.
BUKOVIC SHOWED ME VIDEO OF THE FIRST TEAM INTO THE *VENTURE* AFTER IT CAME DOWN.
I DON'T KNOW IF IT MEANS ANYTHING, IF YOU COULD TEST IT...
WHAT?
WHEN THE SOLDIERS WENT IN, IN THE FIRST FEW SECONDS-- THEY SAID THEY FELT HEAVY.
YOU COULD SEE IT FROM THE CAMERA MOVING, THEIR LEGS WERE BUCKLING, LIKE THEY WERE BEING PUSHED DOWN...
...
...COULDN'T BE.

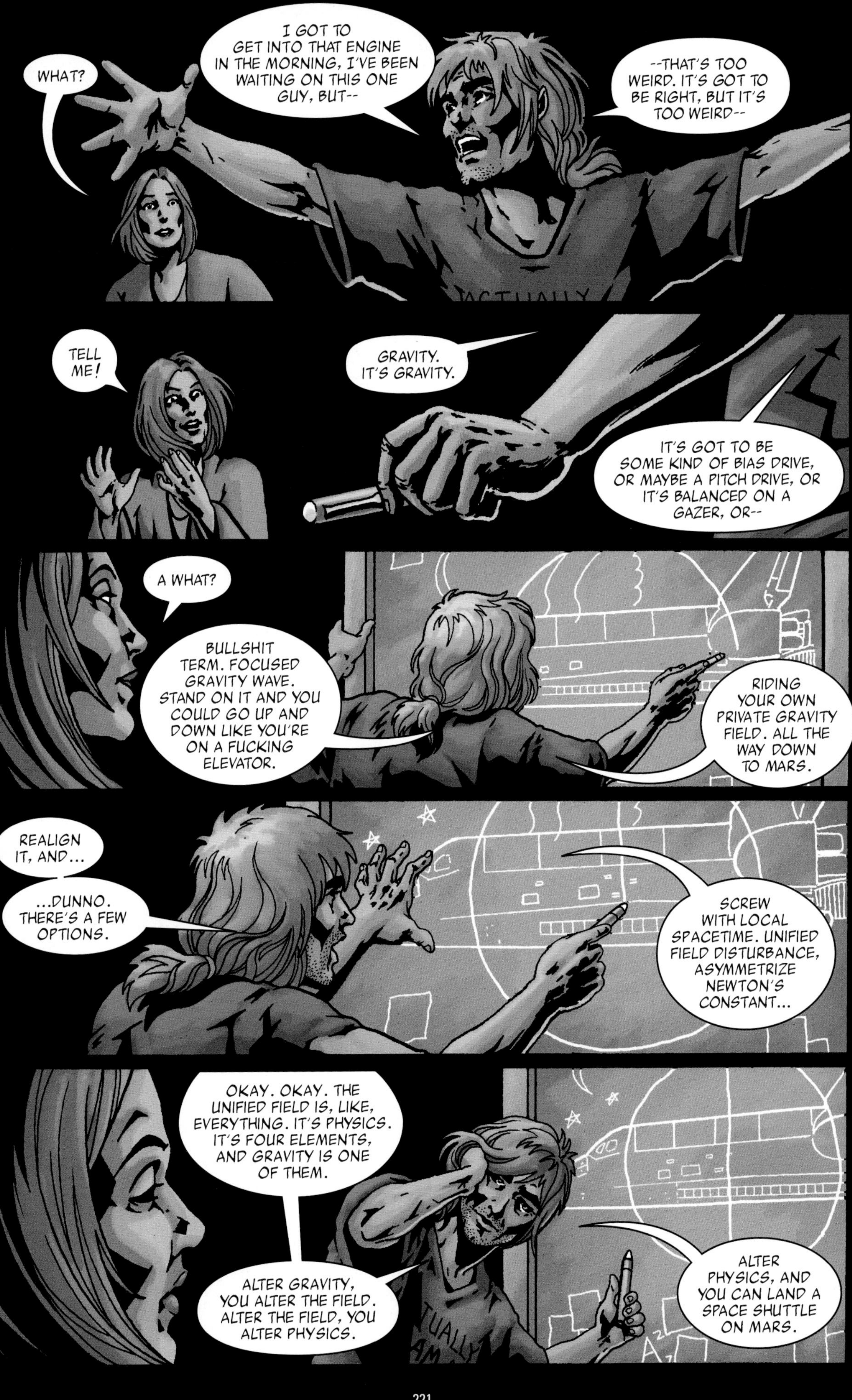
WHAT?
I GOT TO GET INTO THAT ENGINE IN THE MORNING, I'VE BEEN WAITING ON THIS ONE GUY, BUT--
--THAT'S TOO WEIRD. IT'S GOT TO BE RIGHT, BUT IT'S TOO WEIRD--
TELL ME!
GRAVITY. IT'S GRAVITY.
IT'S GOT TO BE SOME KIND OF BIAS DRIVE, OR MAYBE A PITCH DRIVE, OR IT'S BALANCED ON A GAZER, OR--
A WHAT?
BULLSHIT TERM. FOCUSED GRAVITY WAVE. STAND ON IT AND YOU COULD GO UP AND DOWN LIKE YOU'RE ON A FUCKING ELEVATOR.
RIDING YOUR OWN PRIVATE GRAVITY FIELD. ALL THE WAY DOWN TO MARS.
REALIGN IT, AND...
...DUNNO. THERE'S A FEW OPTIONS.
SCREW WITH LOCAL SPACETIME. UNIFIED FIELD DISTURBANCE, ASYMMETRIZE NEWTON'S CONSTANT...
OKAY. OKAY. THE UNIFIED FIELD IS, LIKE, EVERYTHING. IT'S PHYSICS. IT'S FOUR ELEMENTS, AND GRAVITY IS ONE OF THEM.
ALTER GRAVITY, YOU ALTER THE FIELD. ALTER THE FIELD, YOU ALTER PHYSICS.
ALTER PHYSICS, AND YOU CAN LAND A SPACE SHUTTLE ON MARS.

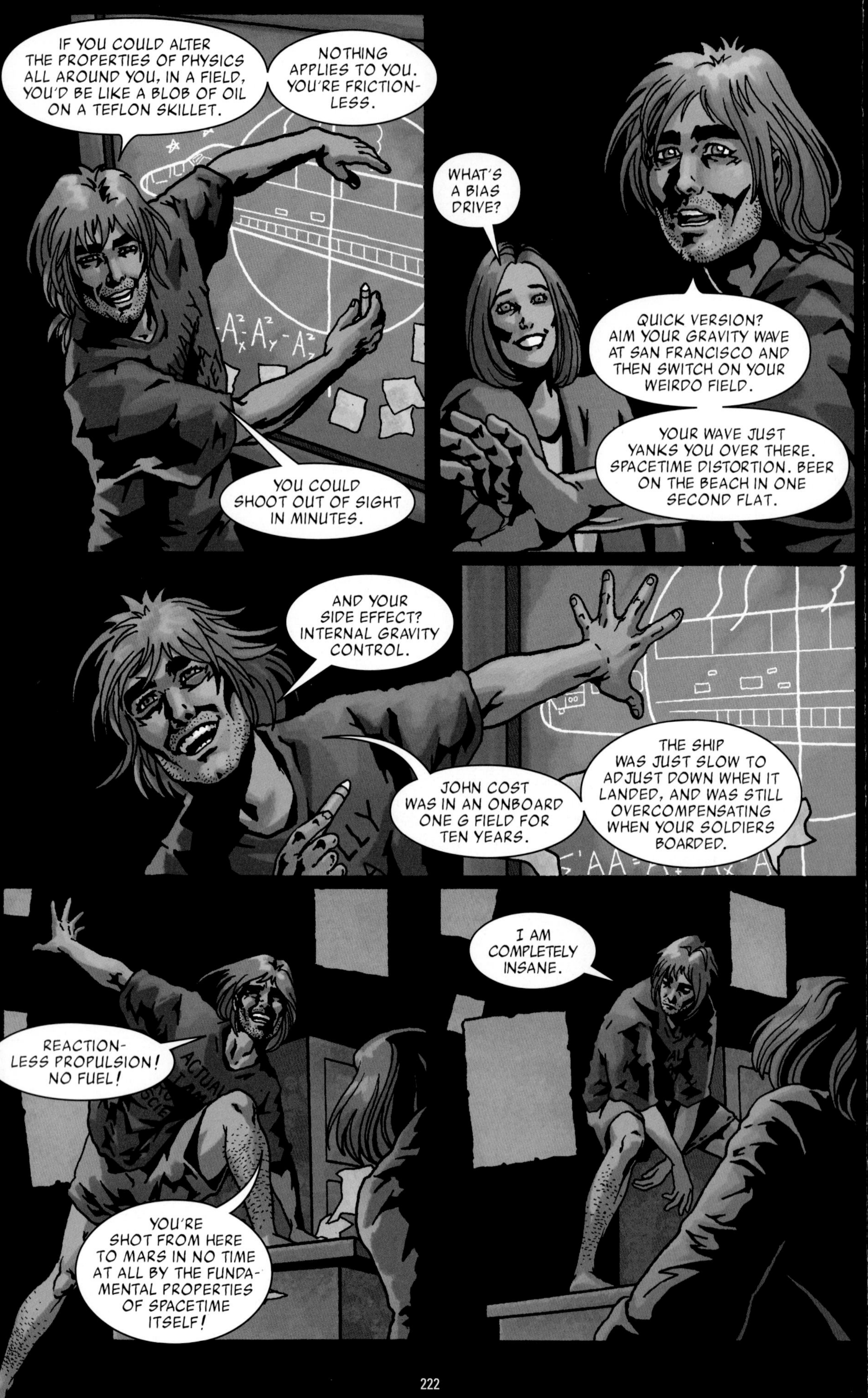
IF YOU COULD ALTER THE PROPERTIES OF PHYSICS ALL AROUND YOU, IN A FIELD, YOU'D BE LIKE A BLOB OF OIL ON A TEFLON SKILLET.
NOTHING APPLIES TO YOU. YOU'RE FRICTION-LESS.
YOU COULD SHOOT OUT OF SIGHT IN MINUTES.
WHAT'S A BIAS DRIVE?
QUICK VERSION? AIM YOUR GRAVITY WAVE AT SAN FRANCISCO AND THEN SWITCH ON YOUR WEIRDO FIELD.
YOUR WAVE JUST YANKS YOU OVER THERE. SPACETIME DISTORTION. BEER ON THE BEACH IN ONE SECOND FLAT.
AND YOUR SIDE EFFECT? INTERNAL GRAVITY CONTROL.
JOHN COST WAS IN AN ONBOARD ONE G FIELD FOR TEN YEARS.
THE SHIP WAS JUST SLOW TO ADJUST DOWN WHEN IT LANDED, AND WAS STILL OVERCOMPENSATING WHEN YOUR SOLDIERS BOARDED.
REACTION-LESS PROPULSION! NO FUEL!
YOU'RE SHOT FROM HERE TO MARS IN NO TIME AT ALL BY THE FUNDA-MENTAL PROPERTIES OF SPACETIME ITSELF!
I AM COMPLETELY INSANE.

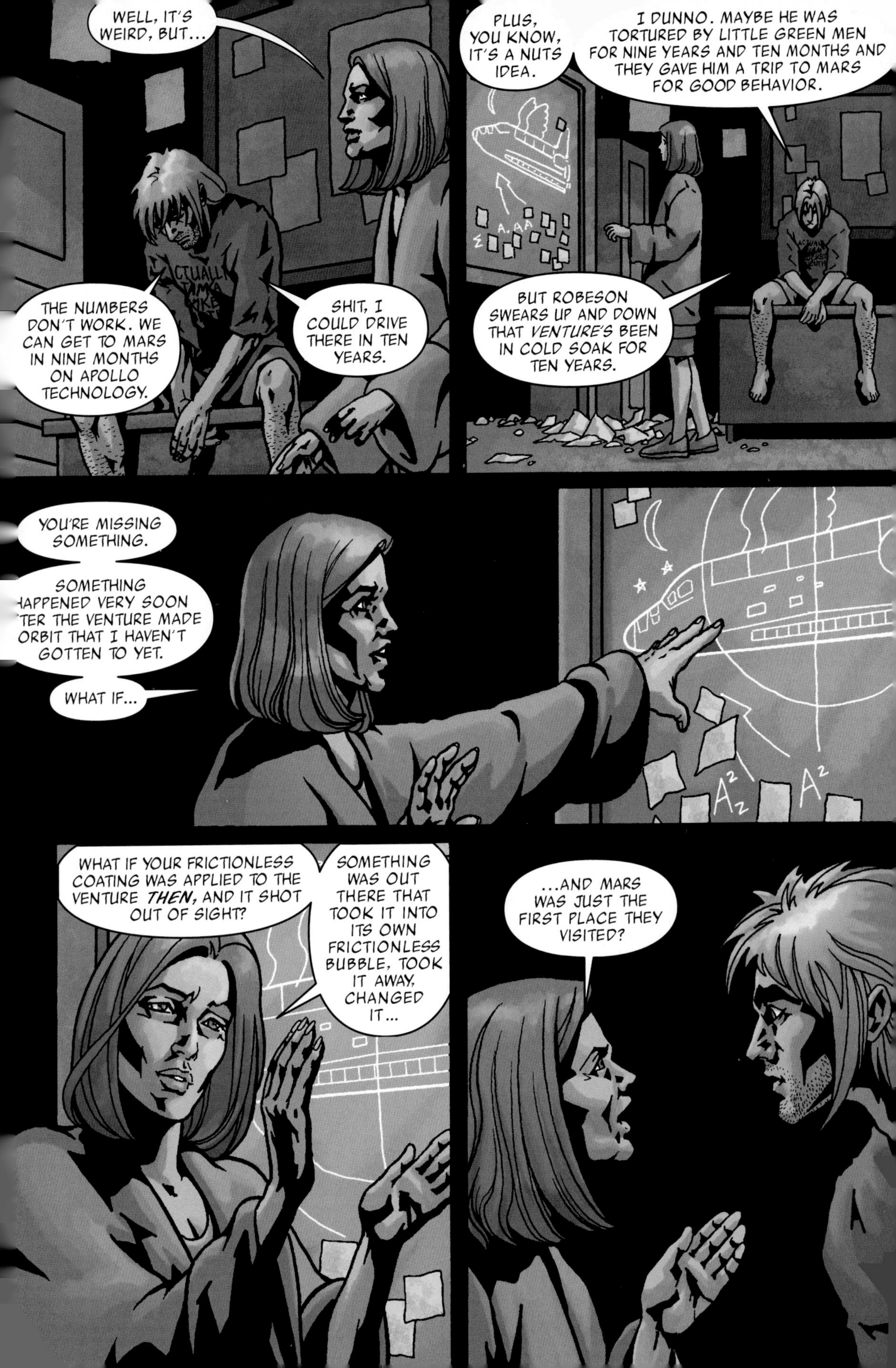
WELL, IT'S WEIRD, BUT...
THE NUMBERS DON'T WORK. WE CAN GET TO MARS IN NINE MONTHS ON APOLLO TECHNOLOGY.
SHIT, I COULD DRIVE THERE IN TEN YEARS.
PLUS, YOU KNOW, IT'S A NUTS IDEA.
I DUNNO. MAYBE HE WAS TORTURED BY LITTLE GREEN MEN FOR NINE YEARS AND TEN MONTHS AND THEY GAVE HIM A TRIP TO MARS FOR GOOD BEHAVIOR.
BUT ROBESON SWEARS UP AND DOWN THAT *VENTURE'S* BEEN IN COLD SOAK FOR TEN YEARS.
YOU'RE MISSING SOMETHING.
SOMETHING APPENED VERY SOON TER THE VENTURE MADE ORBIT THAT I HAVEN'T GOTTEN TO YET.
WHAT IF...
WHAT IF YOUR FRICTIONLESS COATING WAS APPLIED TO THE VENTURE ***THEN***, AND IT SHOT OUT OF SIGHT?
SOMETHING WAS OUT THERE THAT TOOK IT INTO ITS OWN FRICTIONLESS BUBBLE, TOOK IT AWAY, CHANGED IT...
...AND MARS WAS JUST THE FIRST PLACE THEY VISITED?

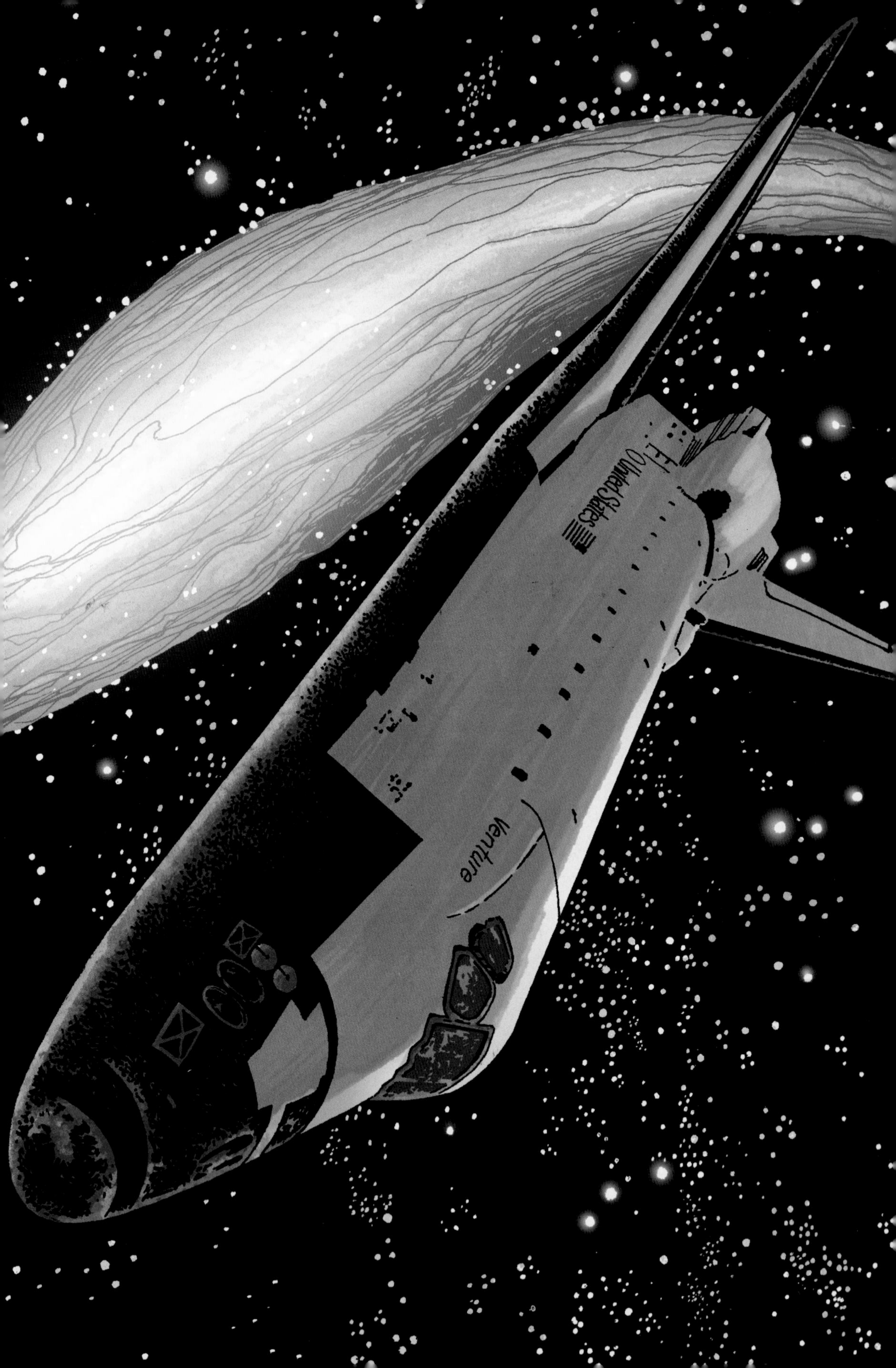
United States
Venture

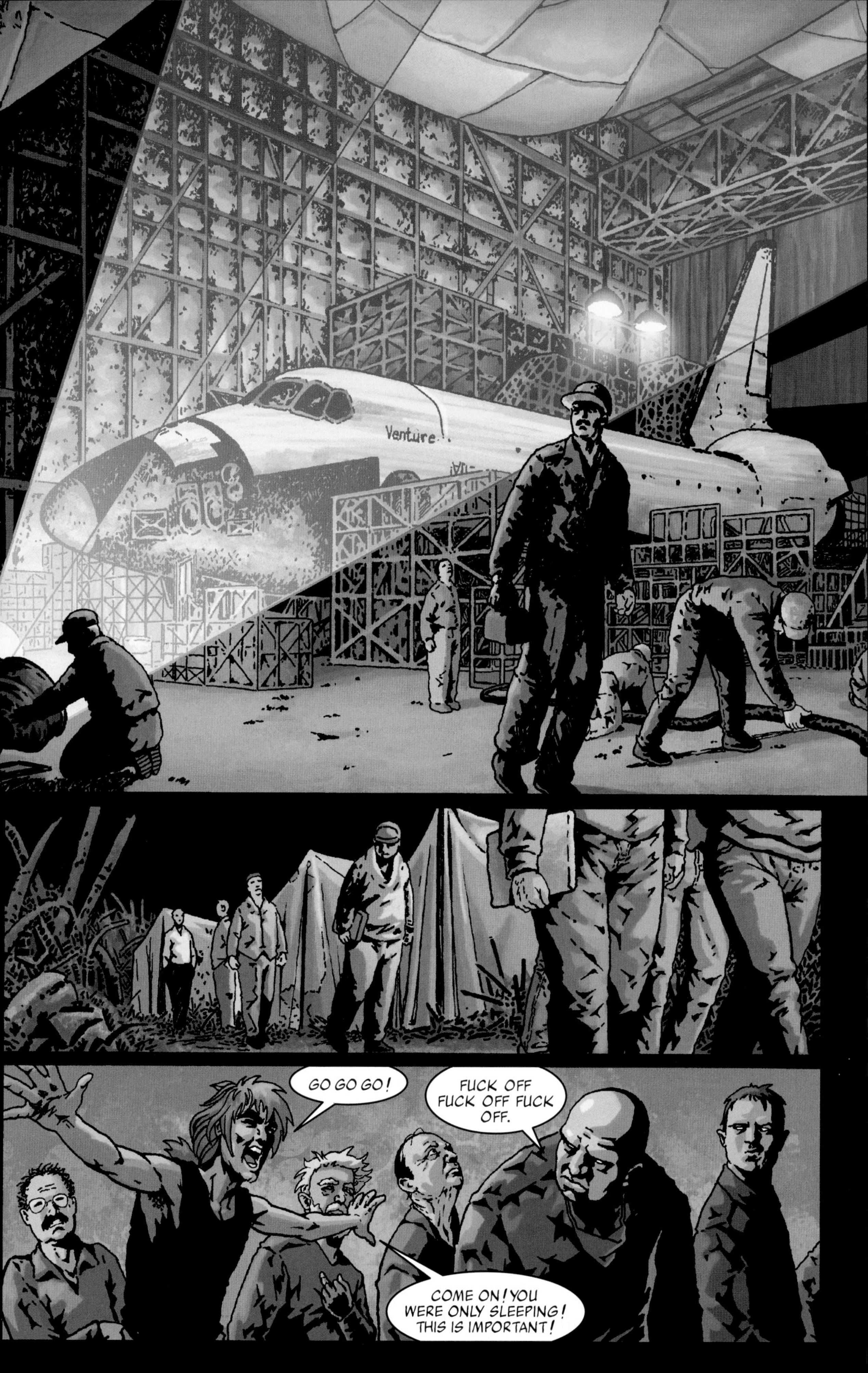
Venture
GO GO GO!
FUCK OFF FUCK OFF FUCK OFF.
COME ON! YOU WERE ONLY SLEEPING! THIS IS IMPORTANT!

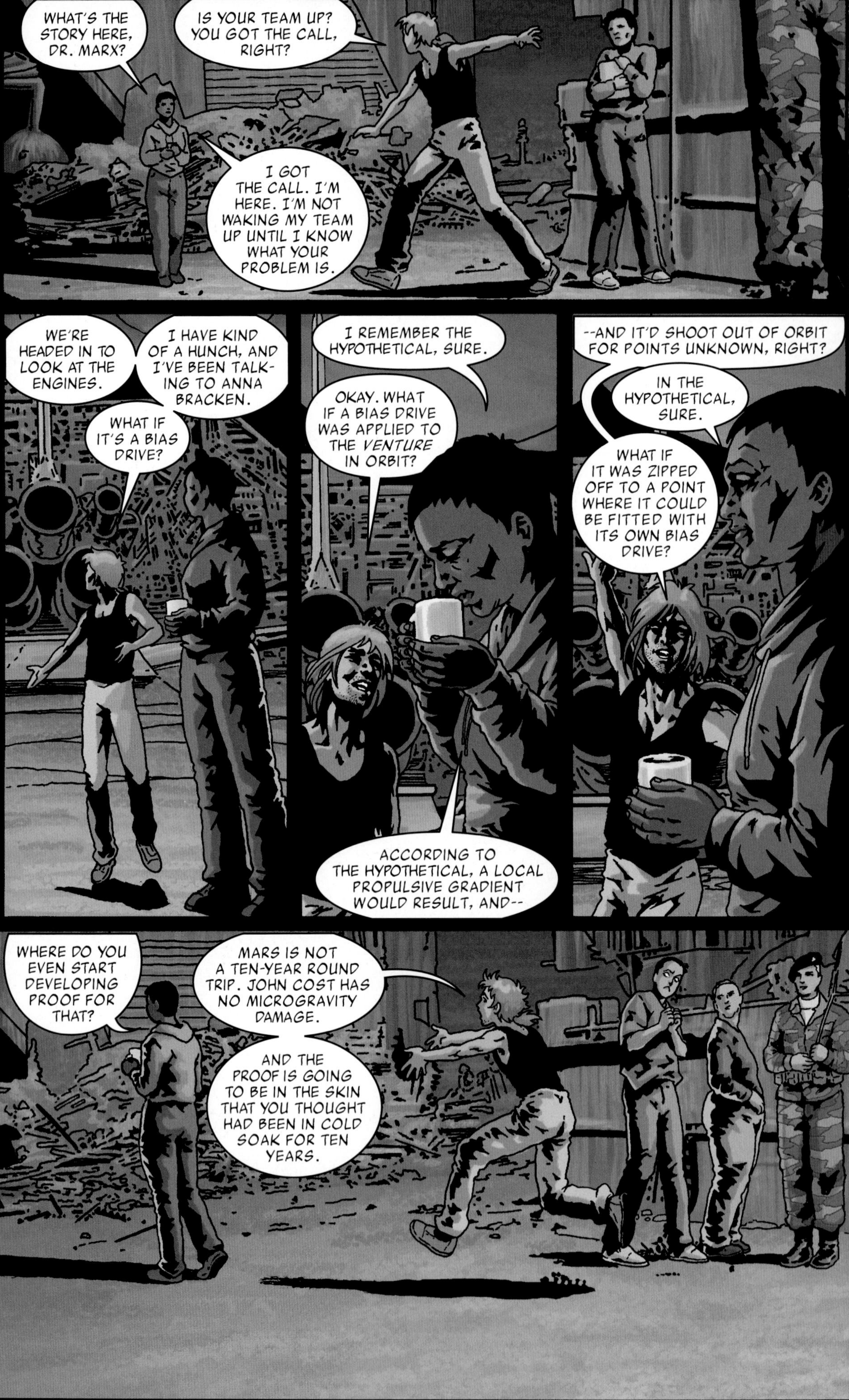
WHAT'S THE STORY HERE, DR. MARX?
IS YOUR TEAM UP? YOU GOT THE CALL, RIGHT?
I GOT THE CALL. I'M HERE. I'M NOT WAKING MY TEAM UP UNTIL I KNOW WHAT YOUR PROBLEM IS.
WE'RE HEADED IN TO LOOK AT THE ENGINES.
I HAVE KIND OF A HUNCH, AND I'VE BEEN TALKING TO ANNA BRACKEN.
WHAT IF IT'S A BIAS DRIVE?
I REMEMBER THE HYPOTHETICAL, SURE.
OKAY. WHAT IF A BIAS DRIVE WAS APPLIED TO THE *VENTURE* IN ORBIT?
ACCORDING TO THE HYPOTHETICAL, A LOCAL PROPULSIVE GRADIENT WOULD RESULT, AND--
--AND IT'D SHOOT OUT OF ORBIT FOR POINTS UNKNOWN, RIGHT?
IN THE HYPOTHETICAL, SURE.
WHAT IF IT WAS ZIPPED OFF TO A POINT WHERE IT COULD BE FITTED WITH ITS OWN BIAS DRIVE?
WHERE DO YOU EVEN START DEVELOPING PROOF FOR THAT?
MARS IS NOT A TEN-YEAR ROUND TRIP. JOHN COST HAS NO MICROGRAVITY DAMAGE.
AND THE PROOF IS GOING TO BE IN THE SKIN THAT YOU THOUGHT HAD BEEN IN COLD SOAK FOR TEN YEARS.

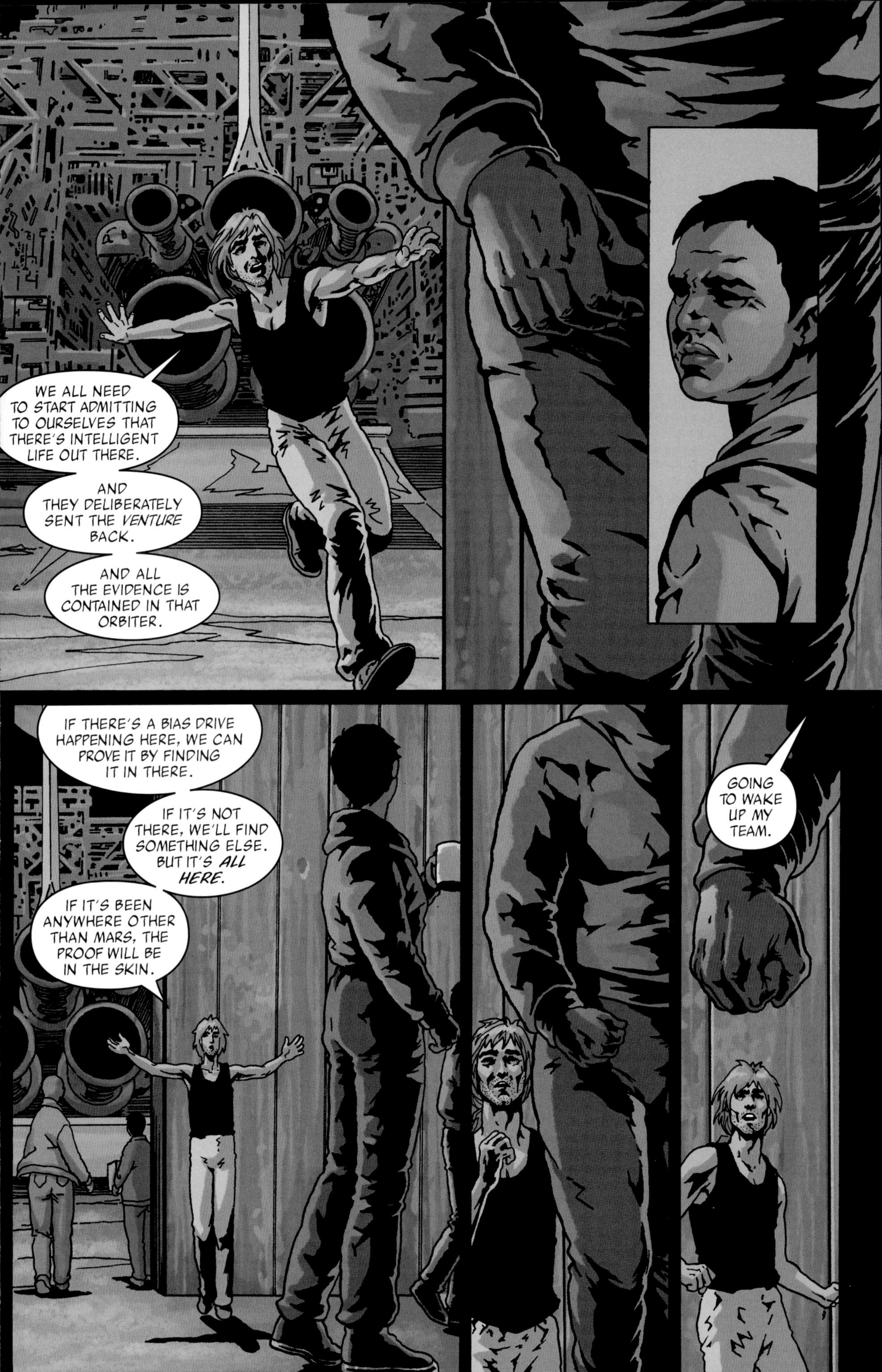
WE ALL NEED TO START ADMITTING TO OURSELVES THAT THERE'S INTELLIGENT LIFE OUT THERE.
AND THEY DELIBERATELY SENT THE *VENTURE* BACK.
AND ALL THE EVIDENCE IS CONTAINED IN THAT ORBITER.
IF THERE'S A BIAS DRIVE HAPPENING HERE, WE CAN PROVE IT BY FINDING IT IN THERE.
IF IT'S NOT THERE, WE'LL FIND SOMETHING ELSE. BUT IT'S ***ALL HERE***.
IF IT'S BEEN ANYWHERE OTHER THAN MARS, THE PROOF WILL BE IN THE SKIN.
GOING TO WAKE UP MY TEAM.

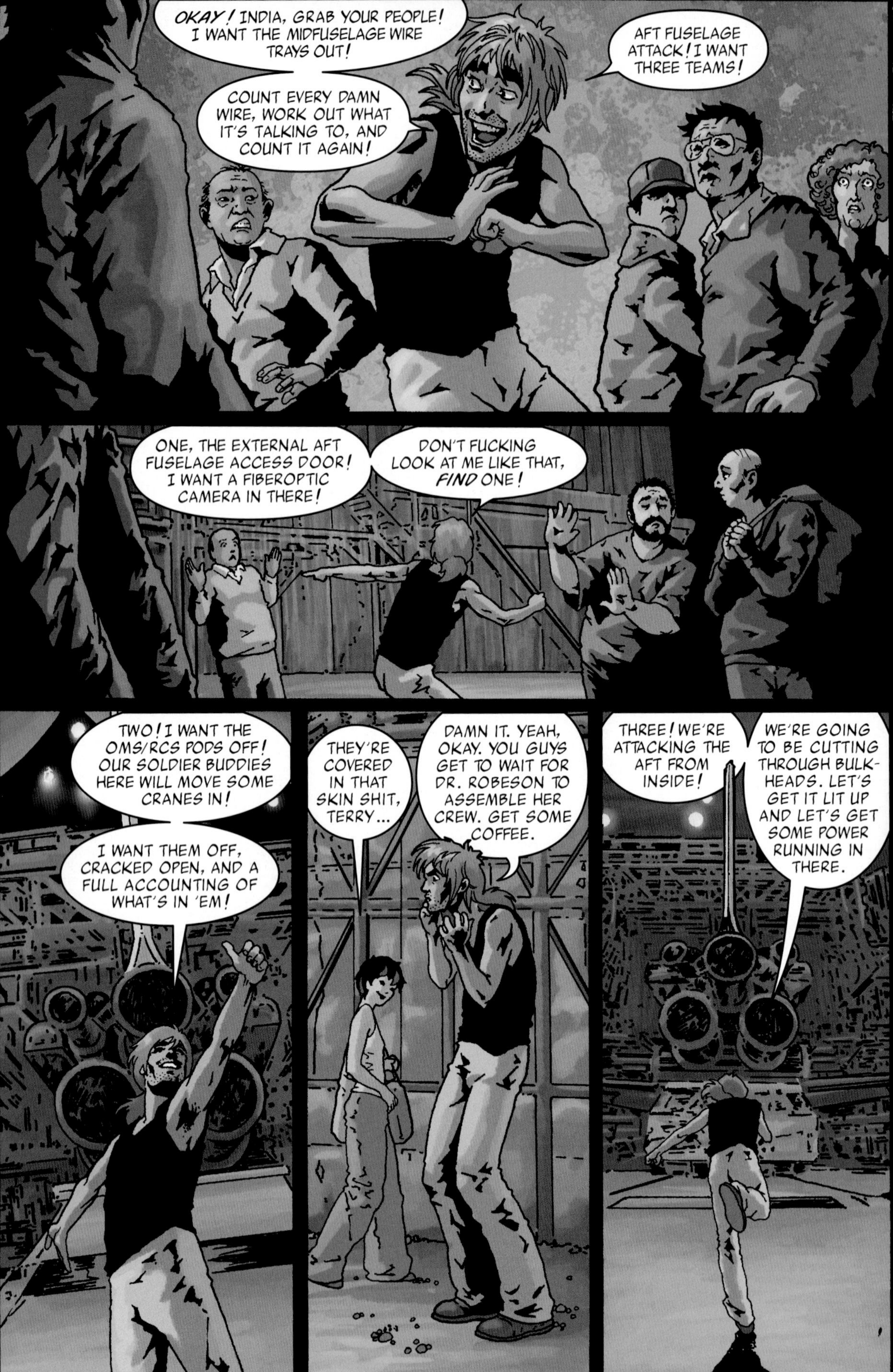
OKAY! INDIA, GRAB YOUR PEOPLE! I WANT THE MIDFUSELAGE WIRE TRAYS OUT!
COUNT EVERY DAMN WIRE, WORK OUT WHAT IT'S TALKING TO, AND COUNT IT AGAIN!
AFT FUSELAGE ATTACK! I WANT THREE TEAMS!
ONE, THE EXTERNAL AFT FUSELAGE ACCESS DOOR! I WANT A FIBEROPTIC CAMERA IN THERE!
DON'T FUCKING LOOK AT ME LIKE THAT, FIND ONE!
TWO! I WANT THE OMS/RCS PODS OFF! OUR SOLDIER BUDDIES HERE WILL MOVE SOME CRANES IN!
I WANT THEM OFF, CRACKED OPEN, AND A FULL ACCOUNTING OF WHAT'S IN 'EM!
THEY'RE COVERED IN THAT SKIN SHIT, TERRY...
DAMN IT. YEAH, OKAY. YOU GUYS GET TO WAIT FOR DR. ROBESON TO ASSEMBLE HER CREW. GET SOME COFFEE.
THREE! WE'RE ATTACKING THE AFT FROM INSIDE!
WE'RE GOING TO BE CUTTING THROUGH BULK-HEADS. LET'S GET IT LIT UP AND LET'S GET SOME POWER RUNNING IN THERE.

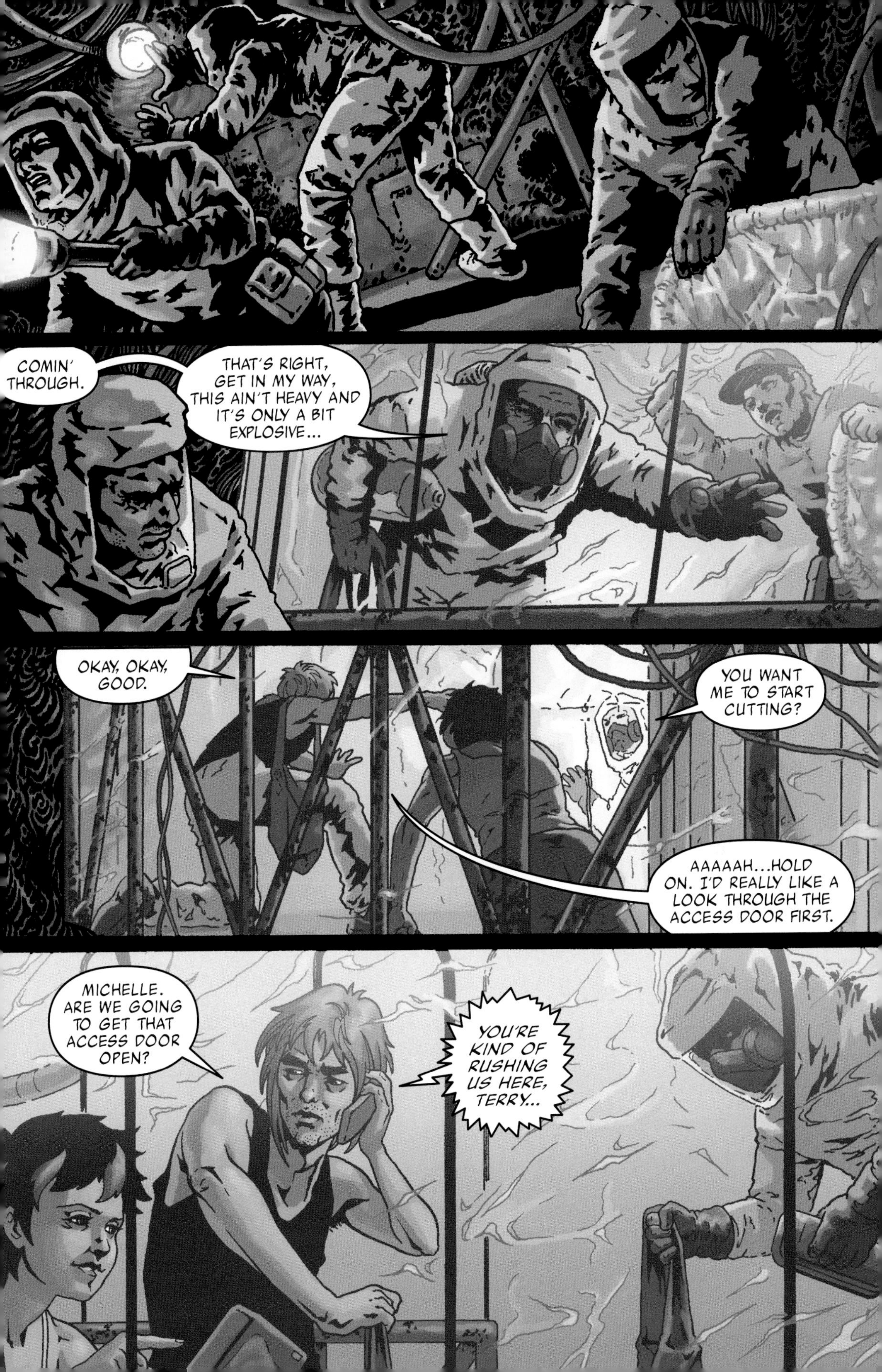
COMIN' THROUGH.
THAT'S RIGHT, GET IN MY WAY, THIS AIN'T HEAVY AND IT'S ONLY A BIT EXPLOSIVE...
OKAY, OKAY, GOOD.
YOU WANT ME TO START CUTTING?
AAAAAH...HOLD ON. I'D REALLY LIKE A LOOK THROUGH THE ACCESS DOOR FIRST.
MICHELLE. ARE WE GOING TO GET THAT ACCESS DOOR OPEN?
YOU'RE KIND OF RUSHING US HERE, TERRY...

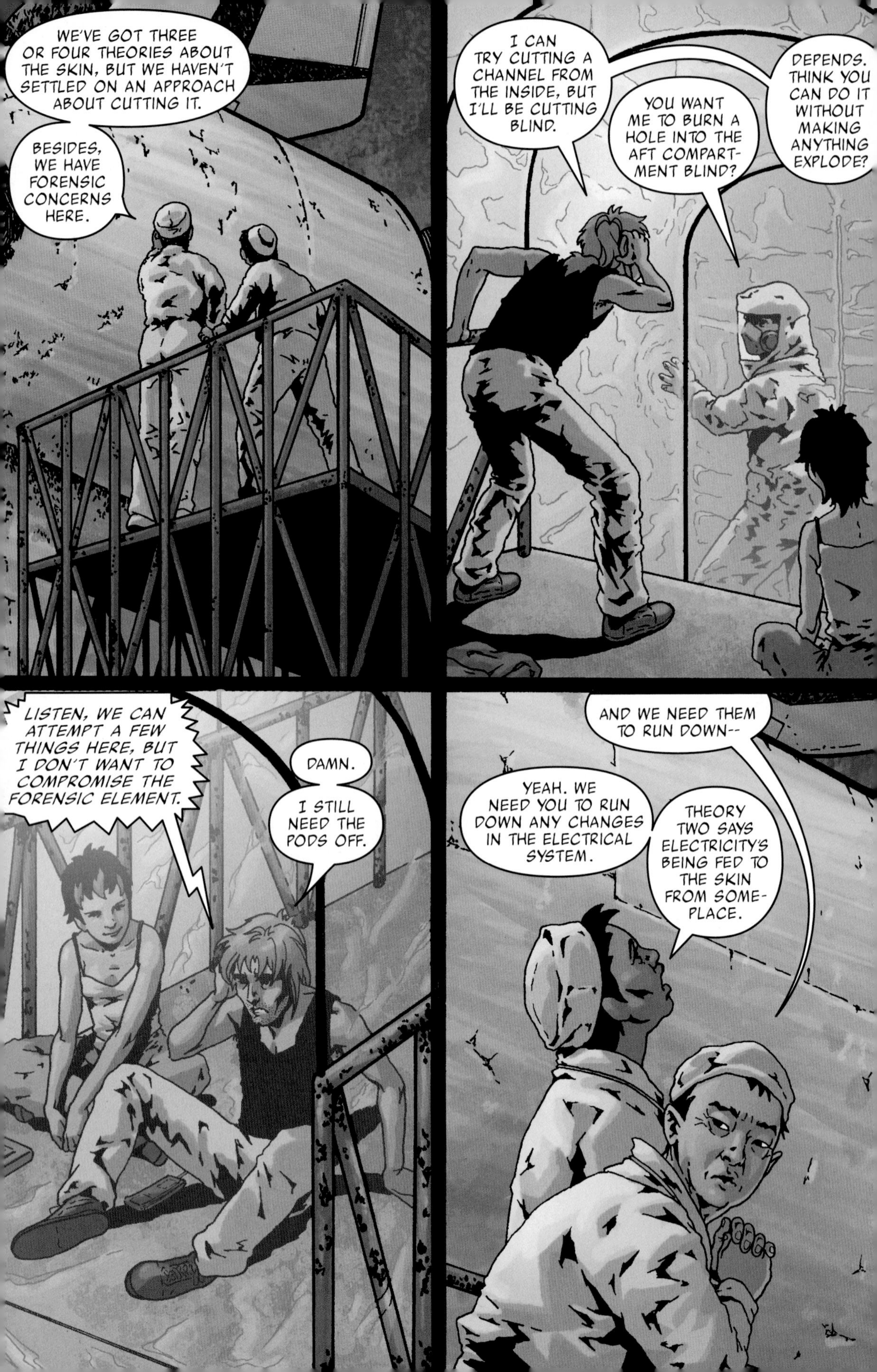
WE'VE GOT THREE OR FOUR THEORIES ABOUT THE SKIN, BUT WE HAVEN'T SETTLED ON AN APPROACH ABOUT CUTTING IT.
BESIDES, WE HAVE FORENSIC CONCERNS HERE.
I CAN TRY CUTTING A CHANNEL FROM THE INSIDE, BUT I'LL BE CUTTING BLIND.
YOU WANT ME TO BURN A HOLE INTO THE AFT COMPARTMENT BLIND?
DEPENDS. THINK YOU CAN DO IT WITHOUT MAKING ANYTHING EXPLODE?
LISTEN, WE CAN ATTEMPT A FEW THINGS HERE, BUT I DON'T WANT TO COMPROMISE THE FORENSIC ELEMENT.
DAMN.
I STILL NEED THE PODS OFF.
AND WE NEED THEM TO RUN DOWN--
YEAH. WE NEED YOU TO RUN DOWN ANY CHANGES IN THE ELECTRICAL SYSTEM.
THEORY TWO SAYS ELECTRICITY'S BEING FED TO THE SKIN FROM SOME-PLACE.

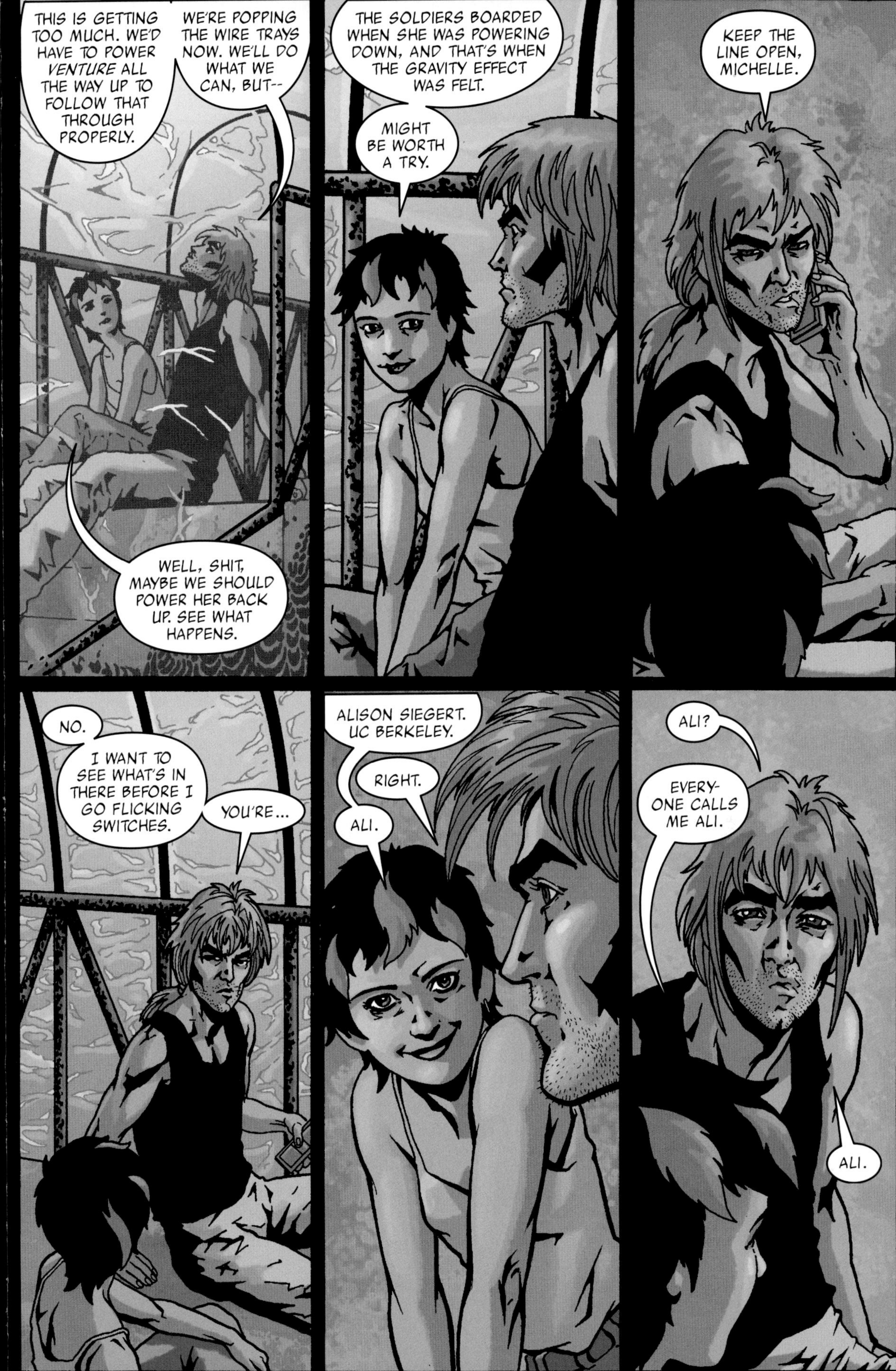
THIS IS GETTING TOO MUCH. WE'D HAVE TO POWER *VENTURE* ALL THE WAY UP TO FOLLOW THAT THROUGH PROPERLY.
WE'RE POPPING THE WIRE TRAYS NOW. WE'LL DO WHAT WE CAN, BUT--
WELL, SHIT, MAYBE WE SHOULD POWER HER BACK UP. SEE WHAT HAPPENS.
THE SOLDIERS BOARDED WHEN SHE WAS POWERING DOWN, AND THAT'S WHEN THE GRAVITY EFFECT WAS FELT.
MIGHT BE WORTH A TRY.
KEEP THE LINE OPEN, MICHELLE.
NO.
I WANT TO SEE WHAT'S IN THERE BEFORE I GO FLICKING SWITCHES.
YOU'RE...
ALISON SIEGERT. UC BERKELEY.
RIGHT.
ALI.
ALI?
EVERY-ONE CALLS ME ALI.
ALI.

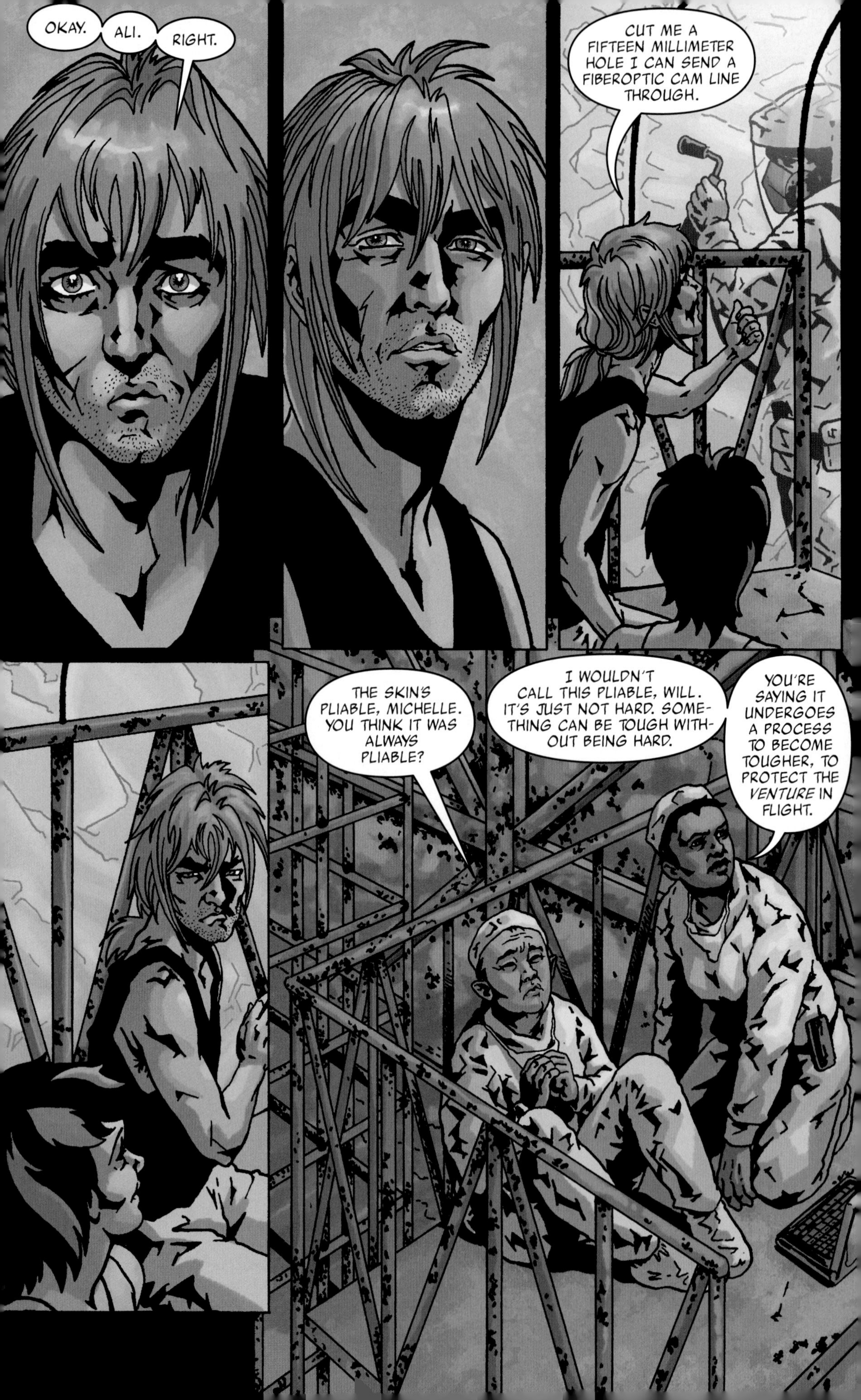
OKAY.
ALI.
RIGHT.
CUT ME A FIFTEEN MILLIMETER HOLE I CAN SEND A FIBEROPTIC CAM LINE THROUGH.
THE SKIN'S PLIABLE, MICHELLE. YOU THINK IT WAS ALWAYS PLIABLE?
I WOULDN'T CALL THIS PLIABLE, WILL. IT'S JUST NOT HARD. SOMETHING CAN BE TOUGH WITHOUT BEING HARD.
YOU'RE SAYING IT UNDERGOES A PROCESS TO BECOME TOUGHER, TO PROTECT THE *VENTURE* IN FLIGHT.

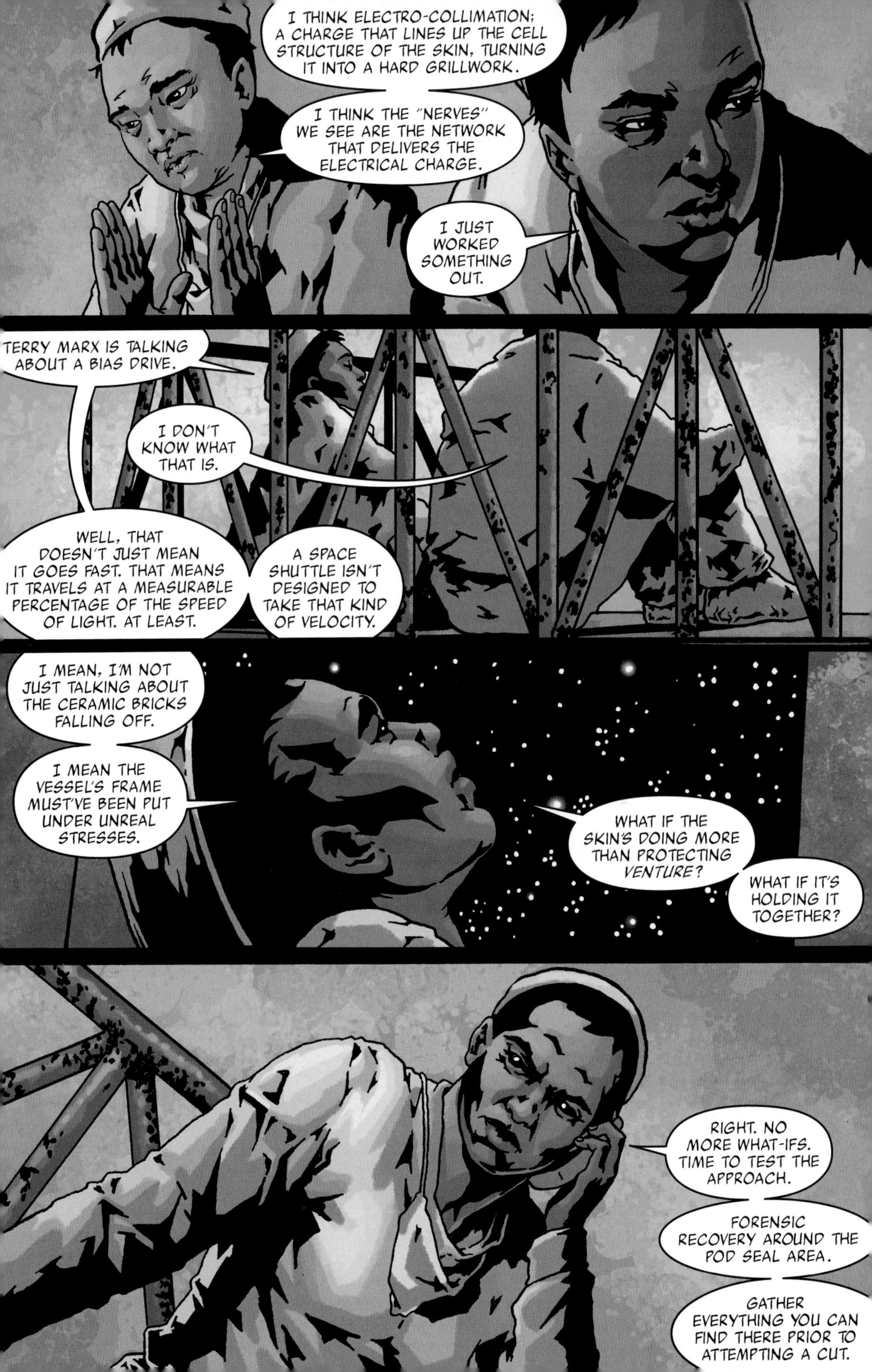
I THINK ELECTRO-COLLIMATION; A CHARGE THAT LINES UP THE CELL STRUCTURE OF THE SKIN, TURNING IT INTO A HARD GRILLWORK.
I THINK THE "NERVES" WE SEE ARE THE NETWORK THAT DELIVERS THE ELECTRICAL CHARGE.
I JUST WORKED SOMETHING OUT.
TERRY MARX IS TALKING ABOUT A BIAS DRIVE.
I DON'T KNOW WHAT THAT IS.
WELL, THAT DOESN'T JUST MEAN IT GOES FAST. THAT MEANS IT TRAVELS AT A MEASURABLE PERCENTAGE OF THE SPEED OF LIGHT. AT LEAST.
A SPACE SHUTTLE ISN'T DESIGNED TO TAKE THAT KIND OF VELOCITY.
I MEAN, I'M NOT JUST TALKING ABOUT THE CERAMIC BRICKS FALLING OFF.
I MEAN THE VESSEL'S FRAME MUST'VE BEEN PUT UNDER UNREAL STRESSES.
WHAT IF THE SKIN'S DOING MORE THAN PROTECTING VENTURE?
WHAT IF IT'S HOLDING IT TOGETHER?
RIGHT. NO MORE WHAT-IFS. TIME TO TEST THE APPROACH.
FORENSIC RECOVERY AROUND THE POD SEAL AREA.
GATHER EVERYTHING YOU CAN FIND THERE PRIOR TO ATTEMPTING A CUT.

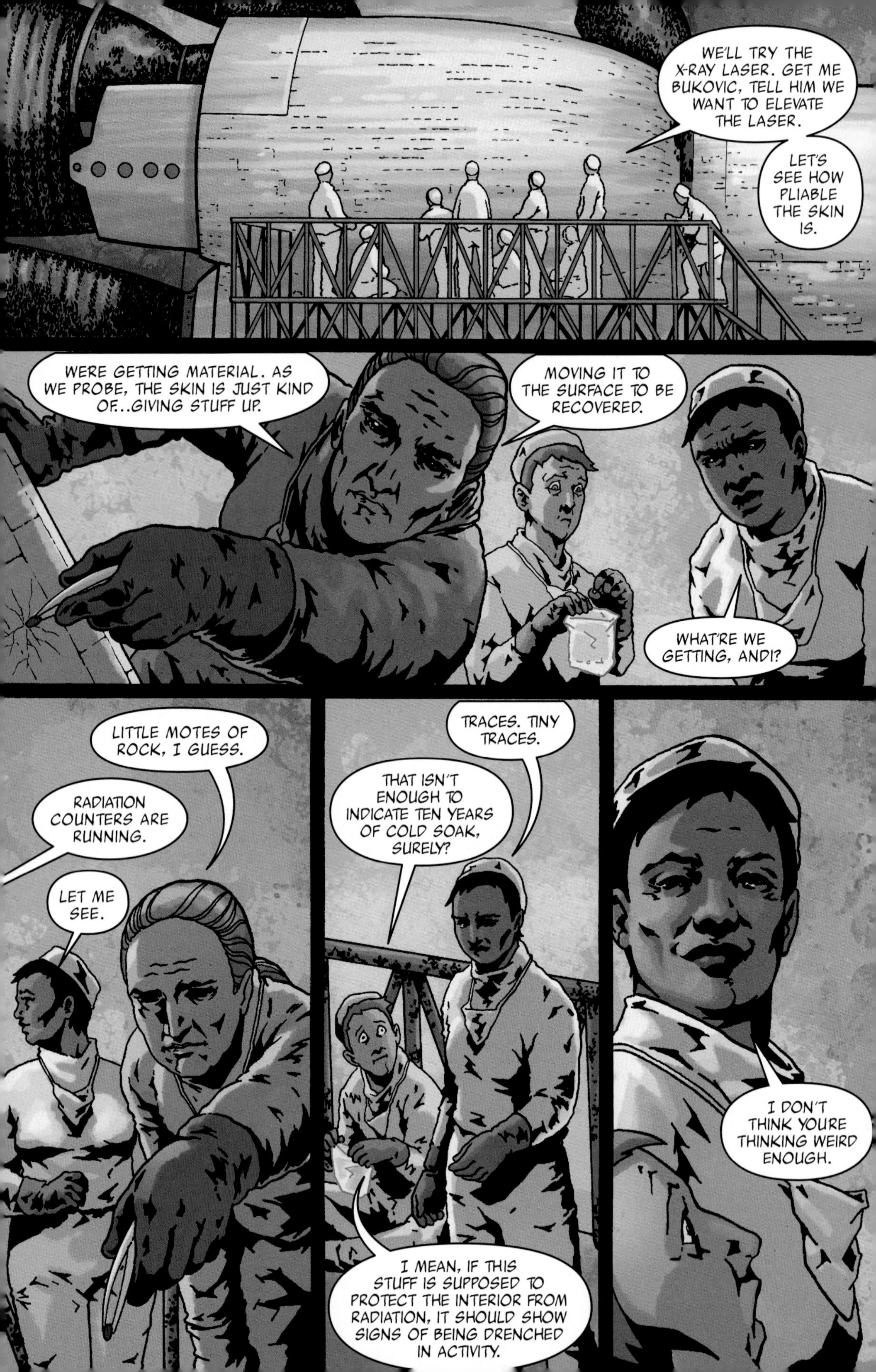
WE'LL TRY THE X-RAY LASER. GET ME BUKOVIC, TELL HIM WE WANT TO ELEVATE THE LASER.
LET'S SEE HOW PLIABLE THE SKIN IS.
WERE GETTING MATERIAL. AS WE PROBE, THE SKIN IS JUST KIND OF...GIVING STUFF UP.
MOVING IT TO THE SURFACE TO BE RECOVERED.
WHAT'RE WE GETTING, ANDI?
LITTLE MOTES OF ROCK, I GUESS.
RADIATION COUNTERS ARE RUNNING.
LET ME SEE.
TRACES. TINY TRACES.
THAT ISN'T ENOUGH TO INDICATE TEN YEARS OF COLD SOAK, SURELY?
I MEAN, IF THIS STUFF IS SUPPOSED TO PROTECT THE INTERIOR FROM RADIATION, IT SHOULD SHOW SIGNS OF BEING DRENCHED IN ACTIVITY.
I DON'T THINK YOURE THINKING WEIRD ENOUGH.

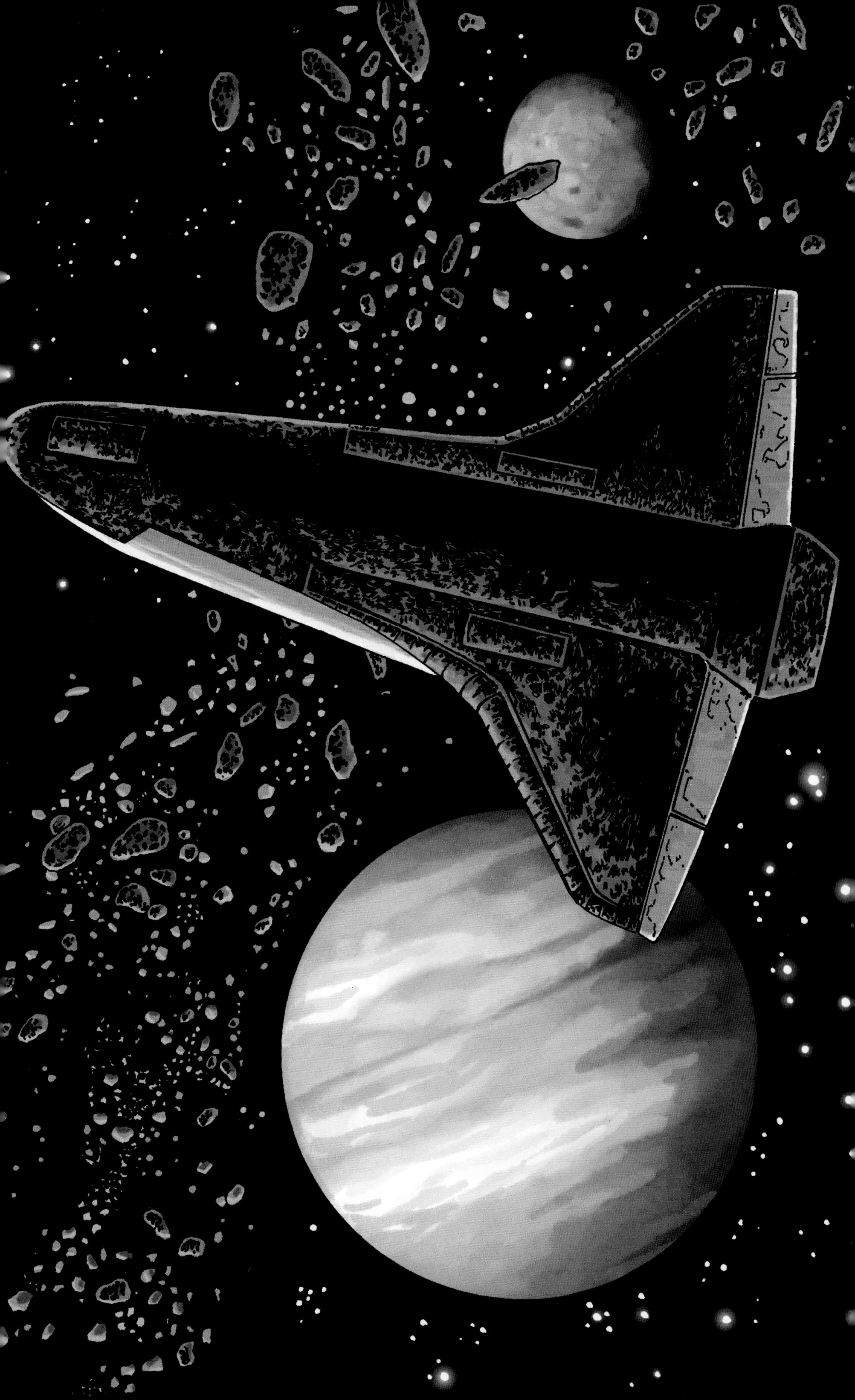

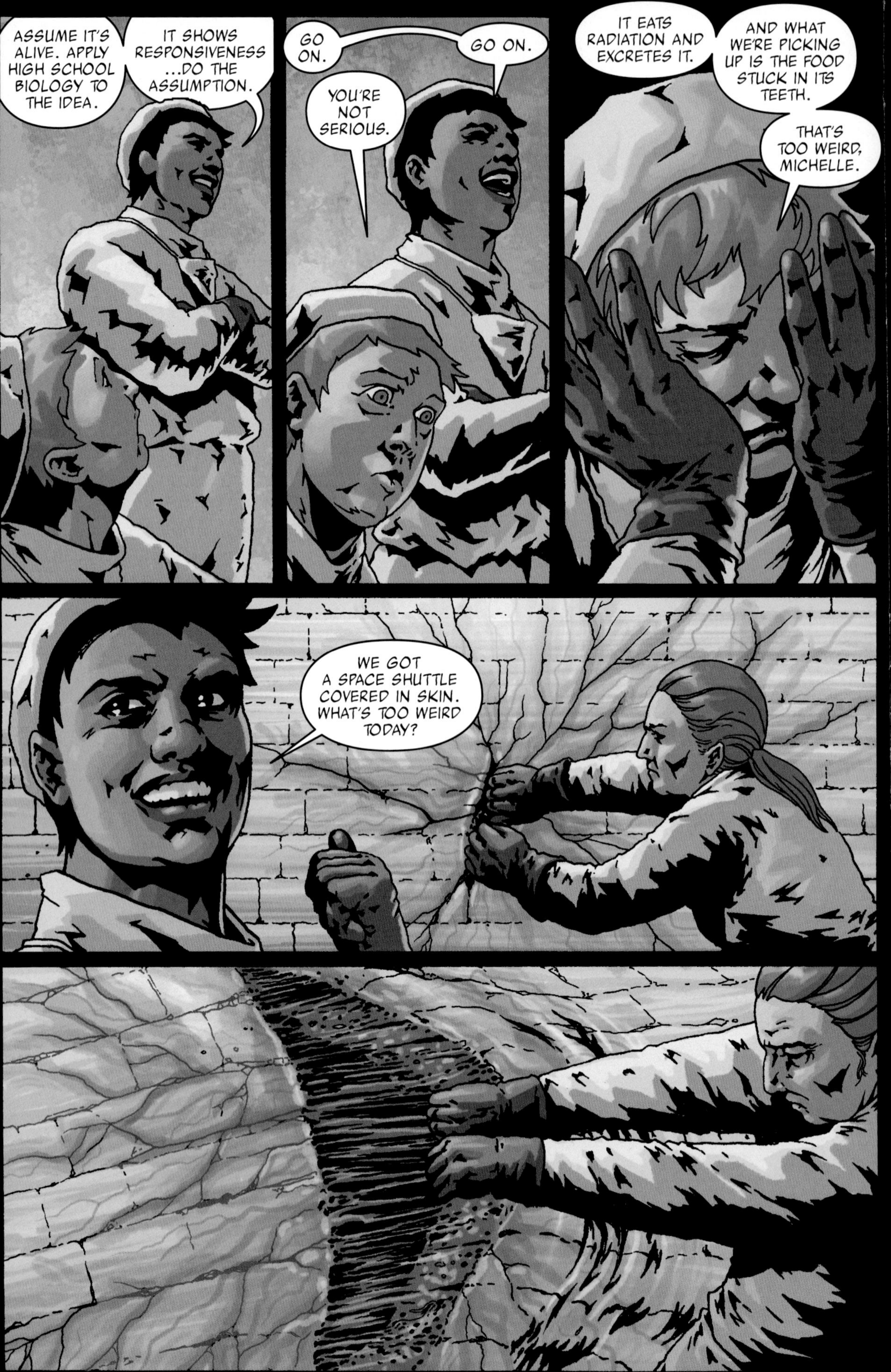
ASSUME IT'S ALIVE. APPLY HIGH SCHOOL BIOLOGY TO THE IDEA.
IT SHOWS RESPONSIVENESS ...DO THE ASSUMPTION.
GO ON.
GO ON.
YOU'RE NOT SERIOUS.
IT EATS RADIATION AND EXCRETES IT.
AND WHAT WE'RE PICKING UP IS THE FOOD STUCK IN ITS TEETH.
THAT'S TOO WEIRD, MICHELLE.
WE GOT A SPACE SHUTTLE COVERED IN SKIN. WHAT'S TOO WEIRD TODAY?

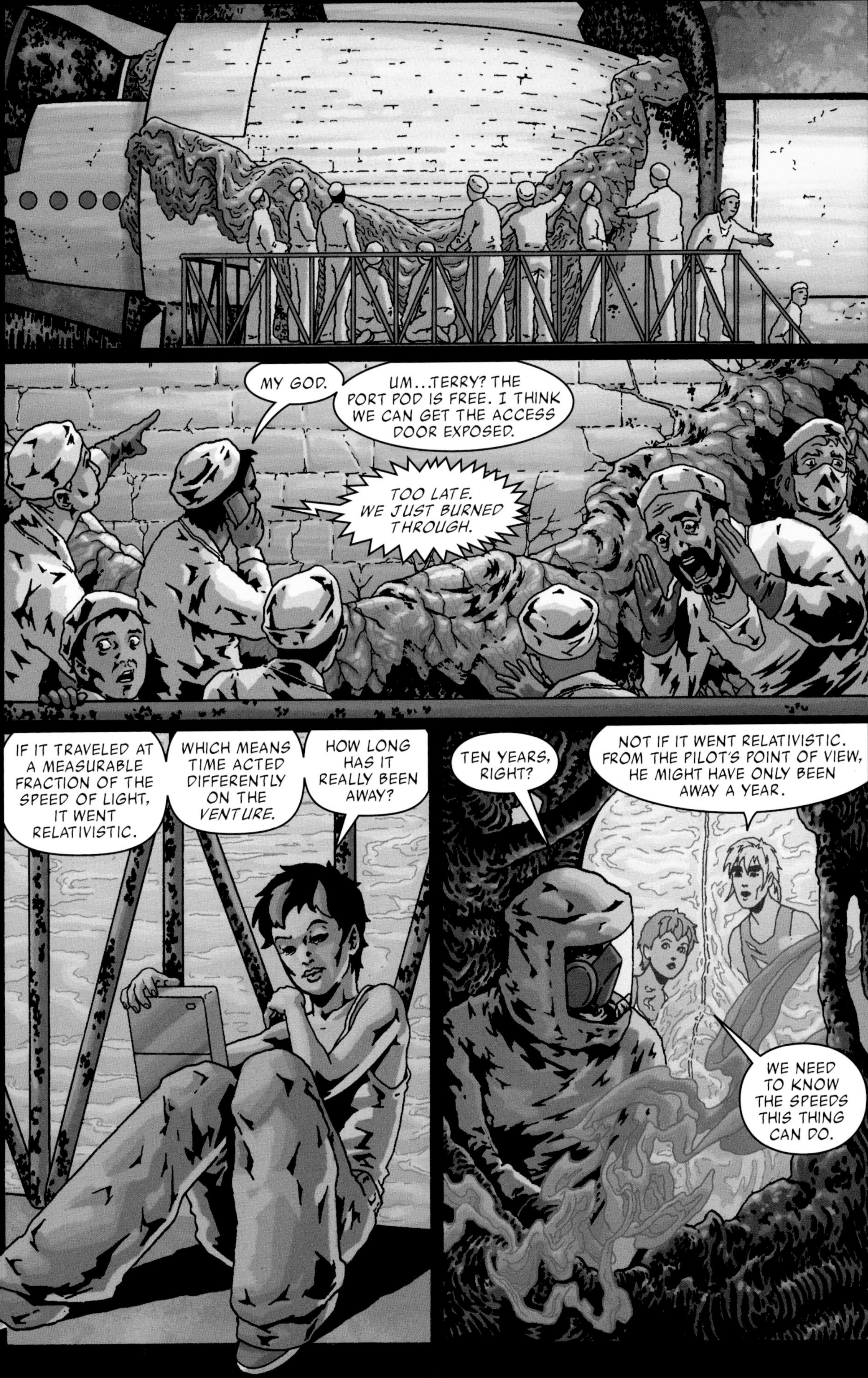
MY GOD.
UM...TERRY? THE PORT POD IS FREE. I THINK WE CAN GET THE ACCESS DOOR EXPOSED.
TOO LATE. WE JUST BURNED THROUGH.
IF IT TRAVELED AT A MEASURABLE FRACTION OF THE SPEED OF LIGHT, IT WENT RELATIVISTIC.
WHICH MEANS TIME ACTED DIFFERENTLY ON THE *VENTURE*.
HOW LONG HAS IT REALLY BEEN AWAY?
TEN YEARS, RIGHT?
NOT IF IT WENT RELATIVISTIC. FROM THE PILOT'S POINT OF VIEW, HE MIGHT HAVE ONLY BEEN AWAY A YEAR.
WE NEED TO KNOW THE SPEEDS THIS THING CAN DO.

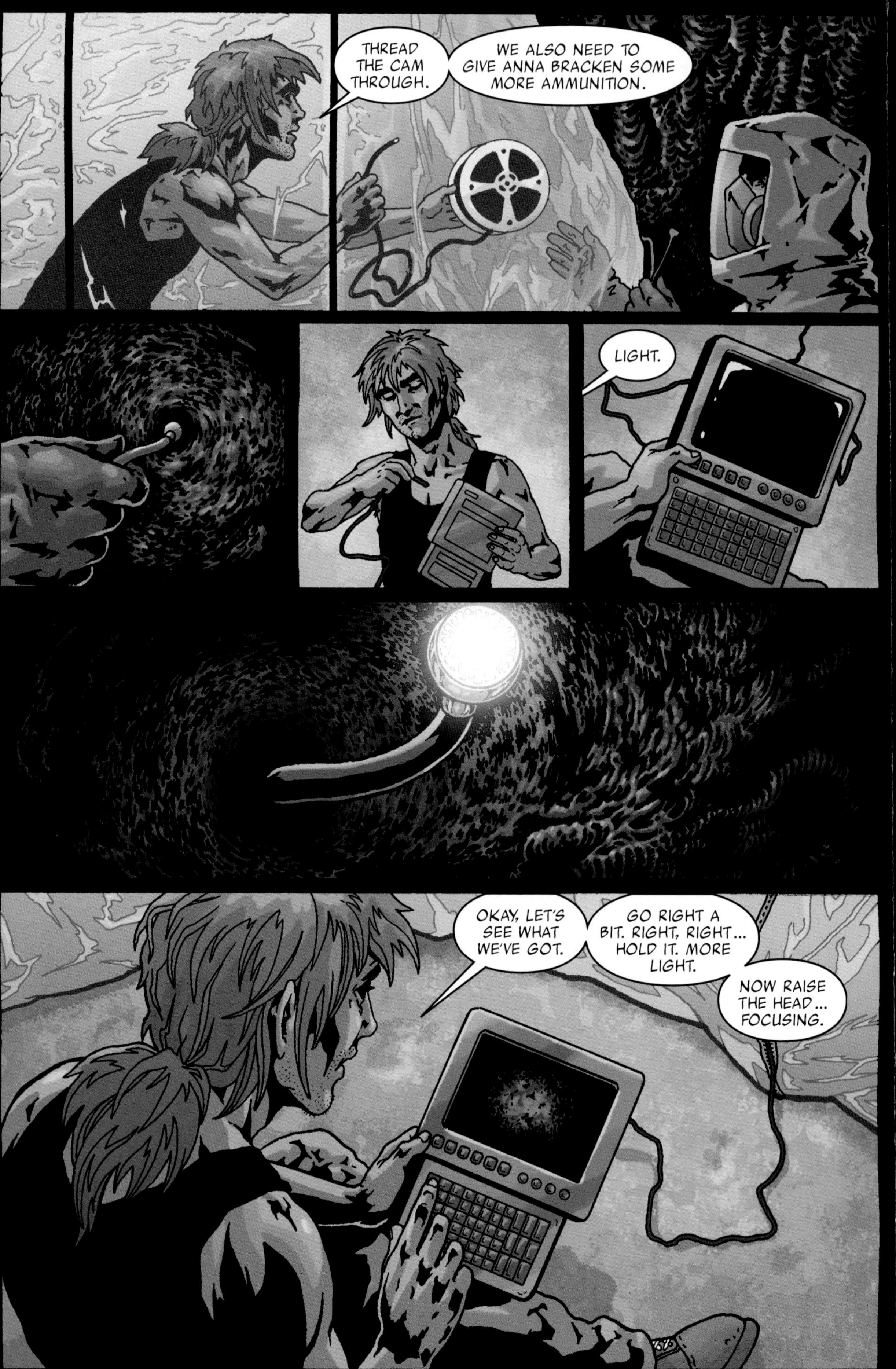
THREAD THE CAM THROUGH.
WE ALSO NEED TO GIVE ANNA BRACKEN SOME MORE AMMUNITION.
LIGHT.
OKAY, LET'S SEE WHAT WE'VE GOT.
GO RIGHT A BIT. RIGHT, RIGHT... HOLD IT. MORE LIGHT.
NOW RAISE THE HEAD... FOCUSING.

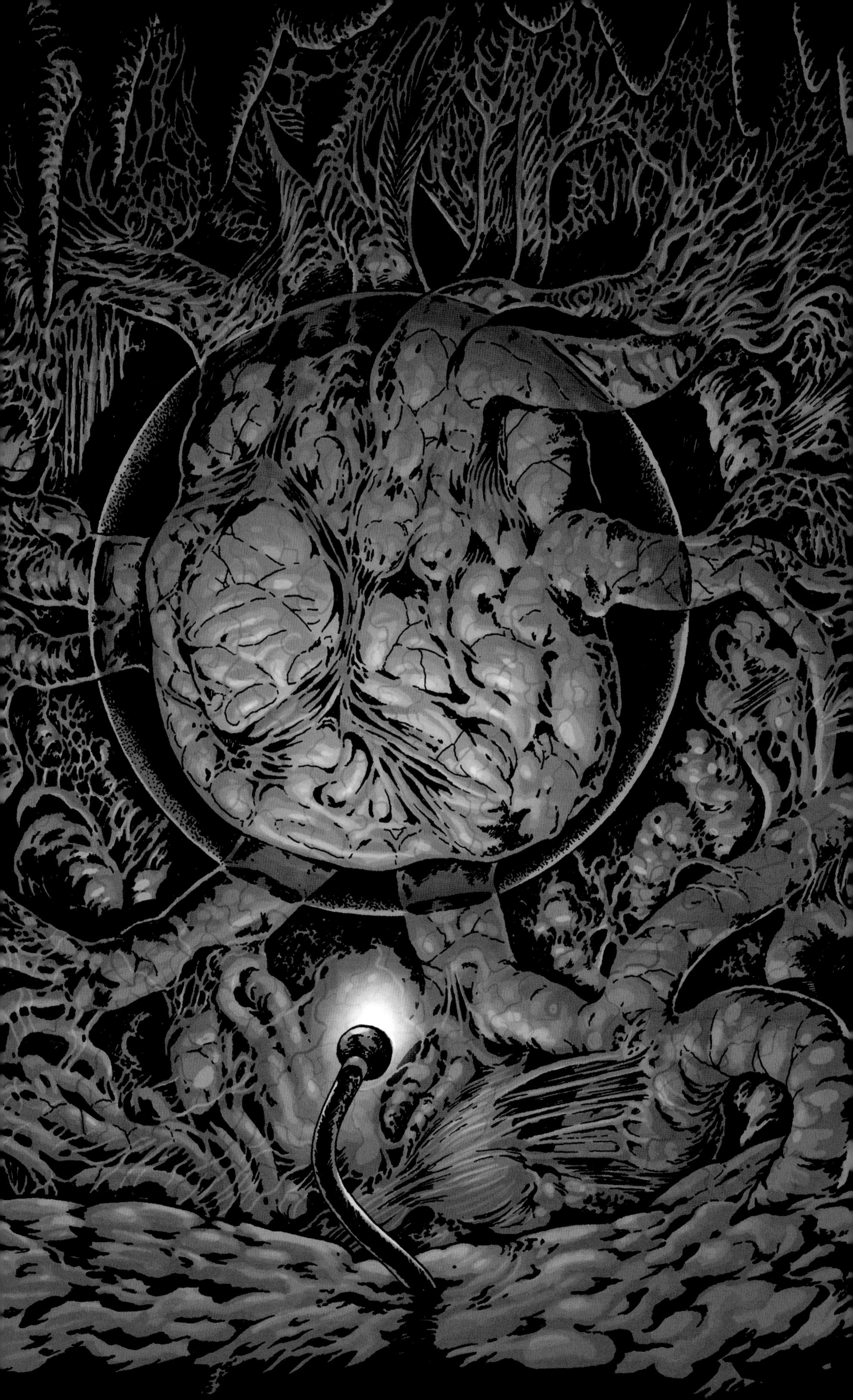

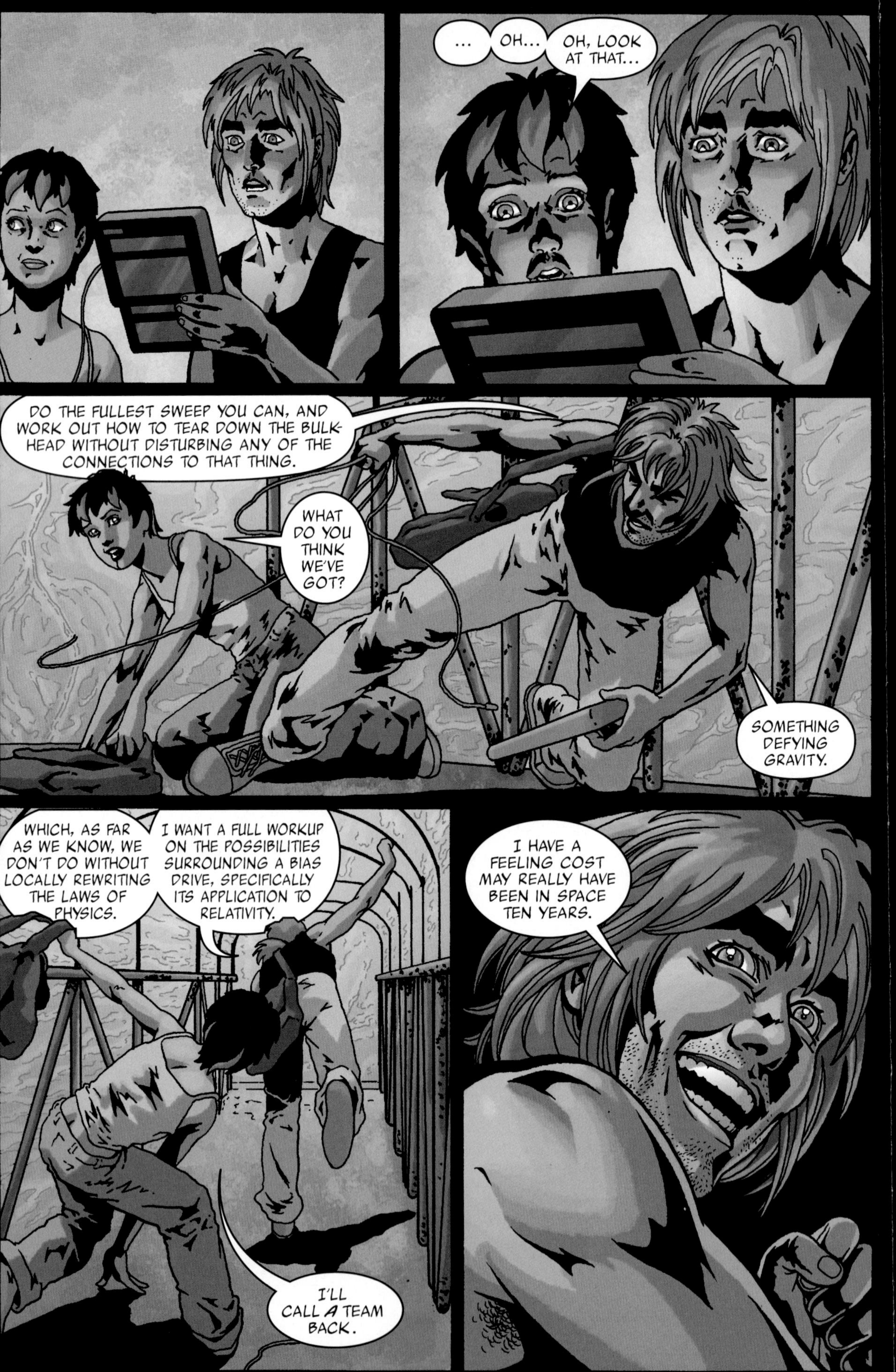
...
OH...
OH, LOOK AT THAT...
DO THE FULLEST SWEEP YOU CAN, AND WORK OUT HOW TO TEAR DOWN THE BULK-HEAD WITHOUT DISTURBING ANY OF THE CONNECTIONS TO THAT THING.
WHAT DO YOU THINK WE'VE GOT?
SOMETHING DEFYING GRAVITY.
WHICH, AS FAR AS WE KNOW, WE DON'T DO WITHOUT LOCALLY REWRITING THE LAWS OF PHYSICS.
I WANT A FULL WORKUP ON THE POSSIBILITIES SURROUNDING A BIAS DRIVE, SPECIFICALLY ITS APPLICATION TO RELATIVITY.
I'LL CALL A TEAM BACK.
I HAVE A FEELING COST MAY REALLY HAVE BEEN IN SPACE TEN YEARS.

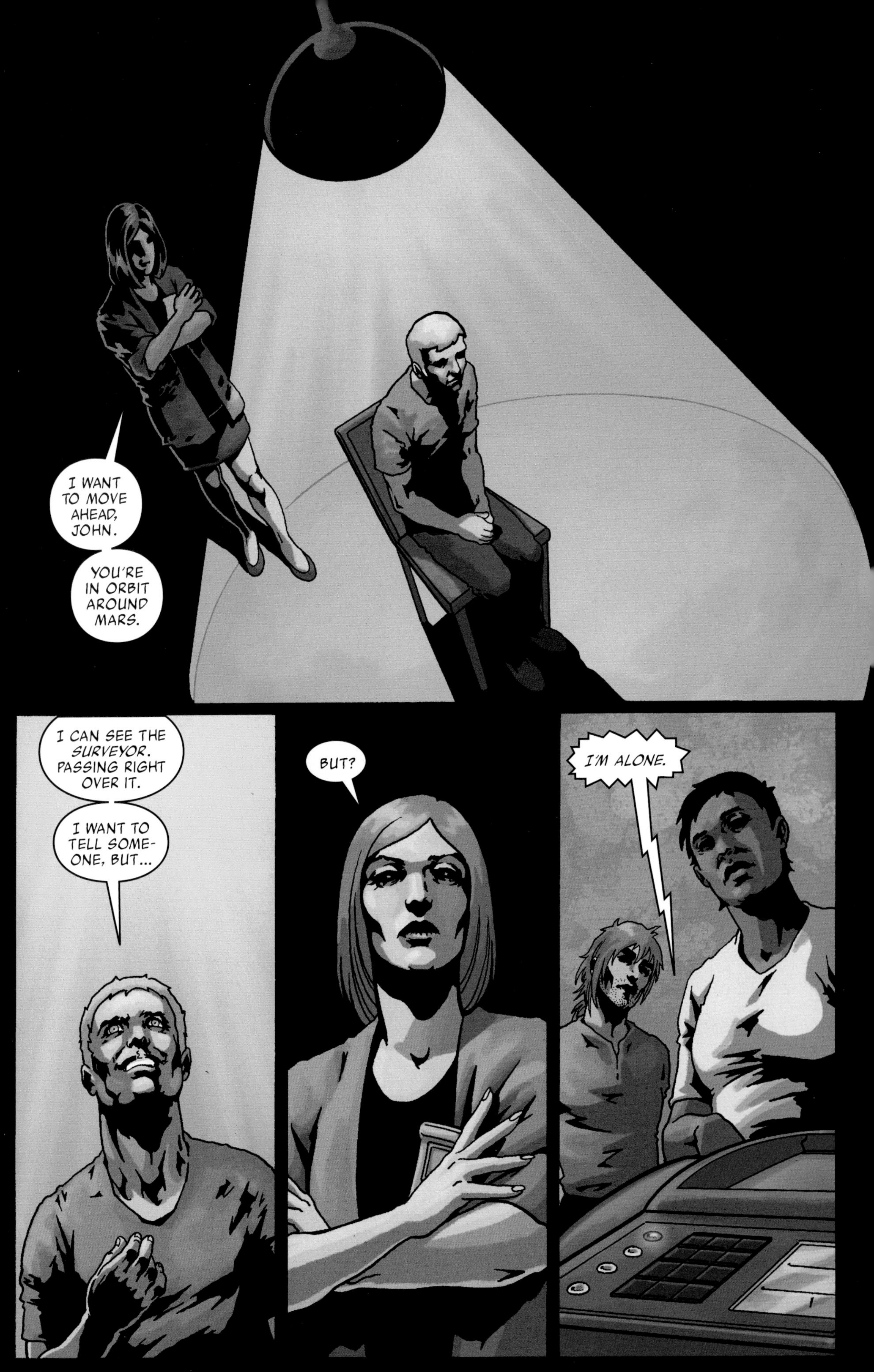
I WANT TO MOVE AHEAD, JOHN.
YOU'RE IN ORBIT AROUND MARS.
I CAN SEE THE *SURVEYOR*. PASSING RIGHT OVER IT.
I WANT TO TELL SOME-ONE, BUT...
BUT?
I'M ALONE.

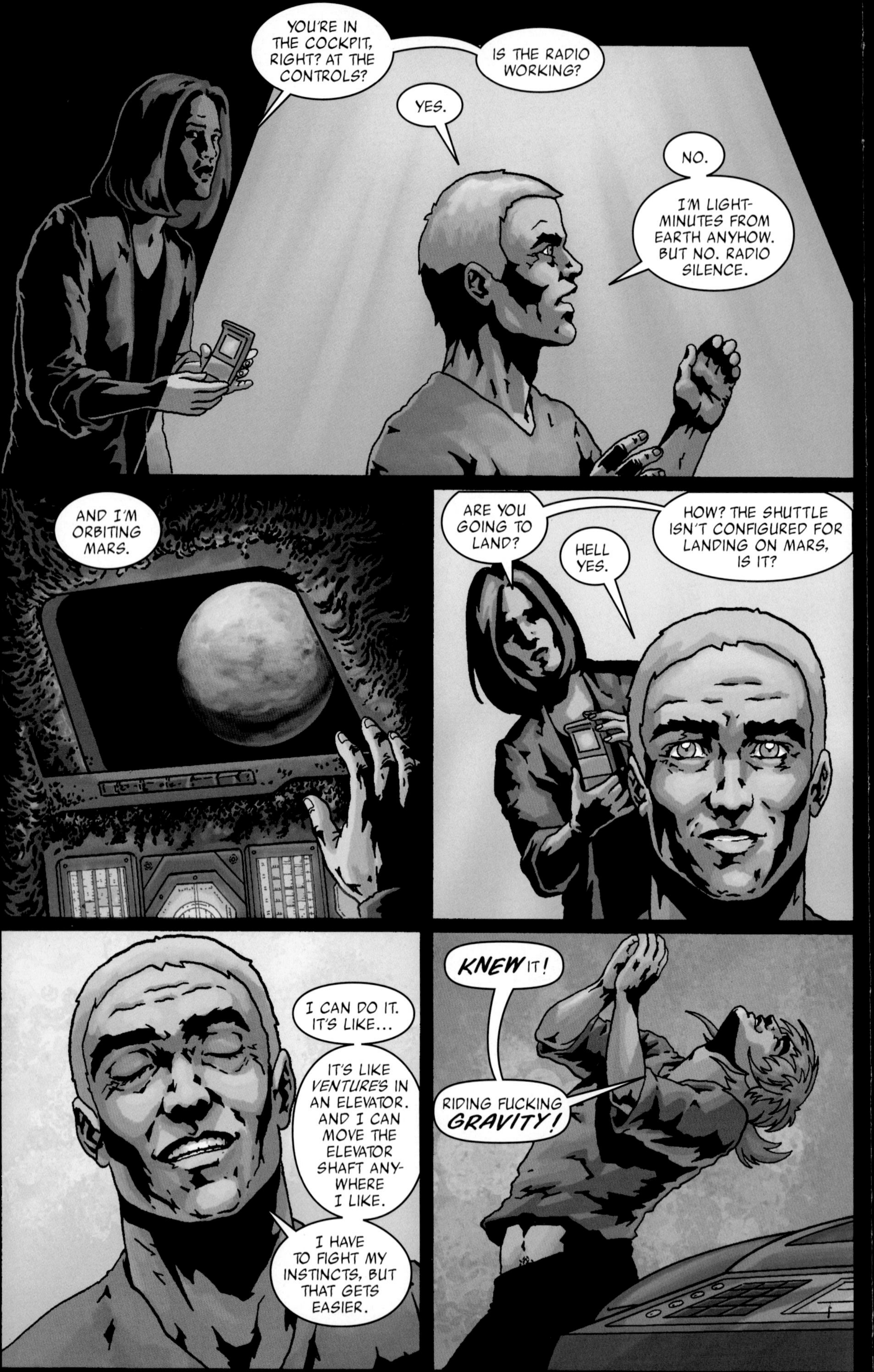
YOU'RE IN THE COCKPIT, RIGHT? AT THE CONTROLS?
YES.
IS THE RADIO WORKING?
NO.
I'M LIGHT-MINUTES FROM EARTH ANYHOW. BUT NO. RADIO SILENCE.
AND I'M ORBITING MARS.
ARE YOU GOING TO LAND?
HELL YES.
HOW? THE SHUTTLE ISN'T CONFIGURED FOR LANDING ON MARS, IS IT?
I CAN DO IT. IT'S LIKE...
IT'S LIKE *VENTURE'S* IN AN ELEVATOR. AND I CAN MOVE THE ELEVATOR SHAFT ANY-WHERE I LIKE.
I HAVE TO FIGHT MY INSTINCTS, BUT THAT GETS EASIER.
KNEW IT!
RIDING FUCKING **GRAVITY!**

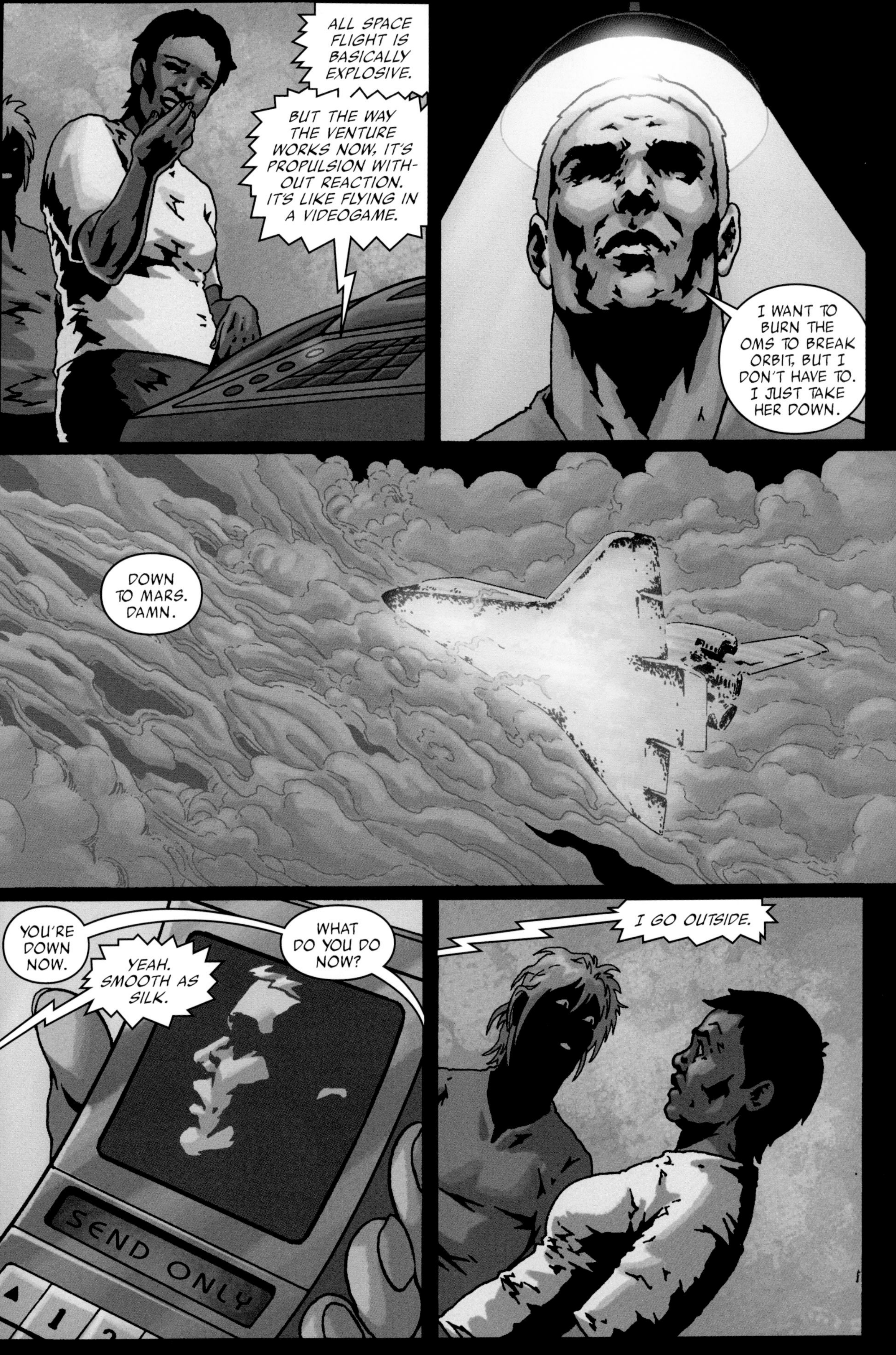
ALL SPACE FLIGHT IS BASICALLY EXPLOSIVE.
BUT THE WAY THE VENTURE WORKS NOW, IT'S PROPULSION WITH-OUT REACTION. IT'S LIKE FLYING IN A VIDEOGAME.
I WANT TO BURN THE OMS TO BREAK ORBIT, BUT I DON'T HAVE TO. I JUST TAKE HER DOWN.
DOWN TO MARS. DAMN.
YOU'RE DOWN NOW.
YEAH. SMOOTH AS SILK.
WHAT DO YOU DO NOW?
SEND ONLY
I GO OUTSIDE.

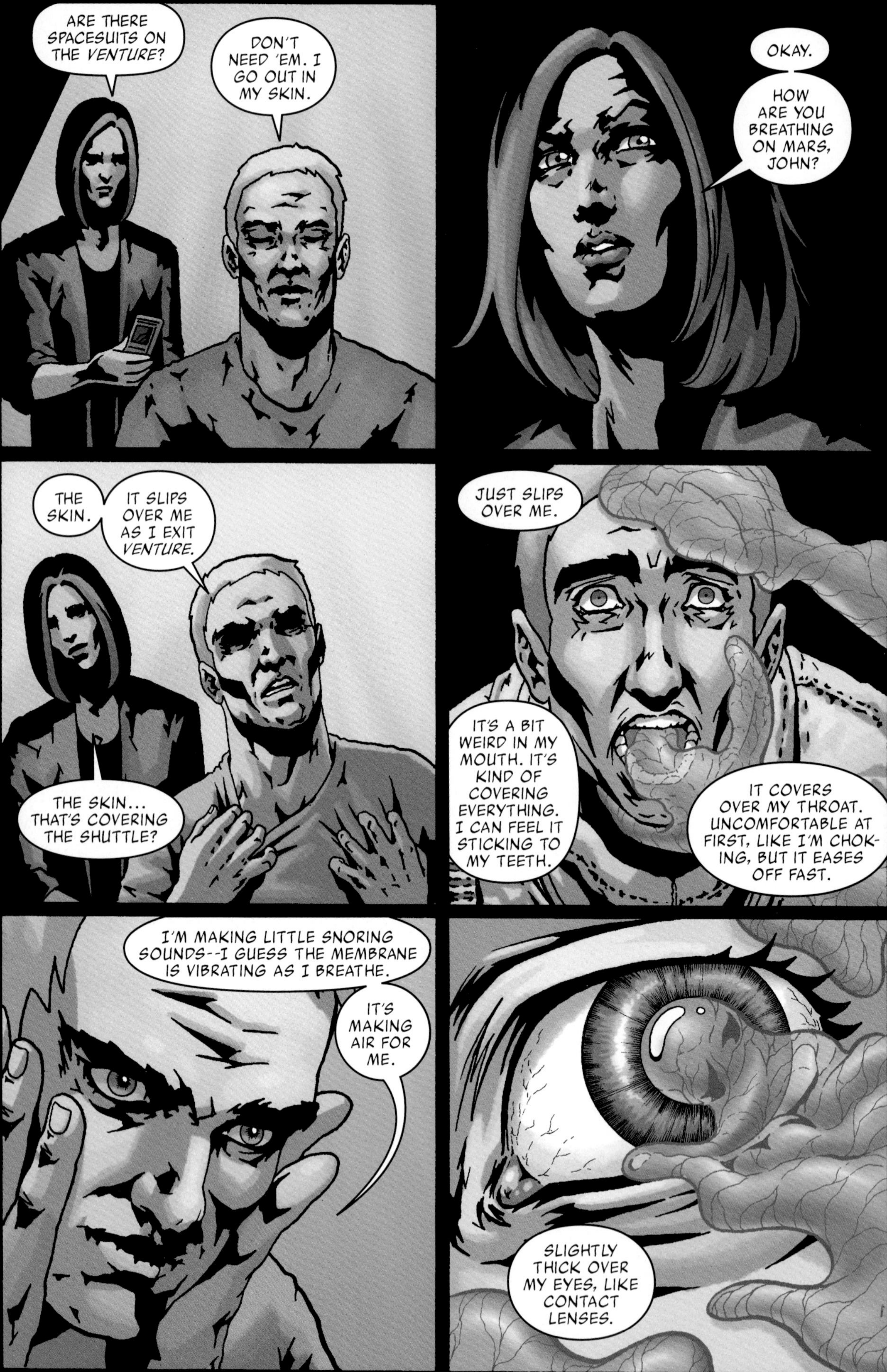
ARE THERE SPACESUITS ON THE *VENTURE*?
DON'T NEED 'EM. I GO OUT IN MY SKIN.
OKAY.
HOW ARE YOU BREATHING ON MARS, JOHN?
THE SKIN.
IT SLIPS OVER ME AS I EXIT *VENTURE*.
THE SKIN... THAT'S COVERING THE SHUTTLE?
JUST SLIPS OVER ME.
IT'S A BIT WEIRD IN MY MOUTH. IT'S KIND OF COVERING EVERYTHING. I CAN FEEL IT STICKING TO MY TEETH.
IT COVERS OVER MY THROAT. UNCOMFORTABLE AT FIRST, LIKE I'M CHOKING, BUT IT EASES OFF FAST.
I'M MAKING LITTLE SNORING SOUNDS--I GUESS THE MEMBRANE IS VIBRATING AS I BREATHE.
IT'S MAKING AIR FOR ME.
SLIGHTLY THICK OVER MY EYES, LIKE CONTACT LENSES.

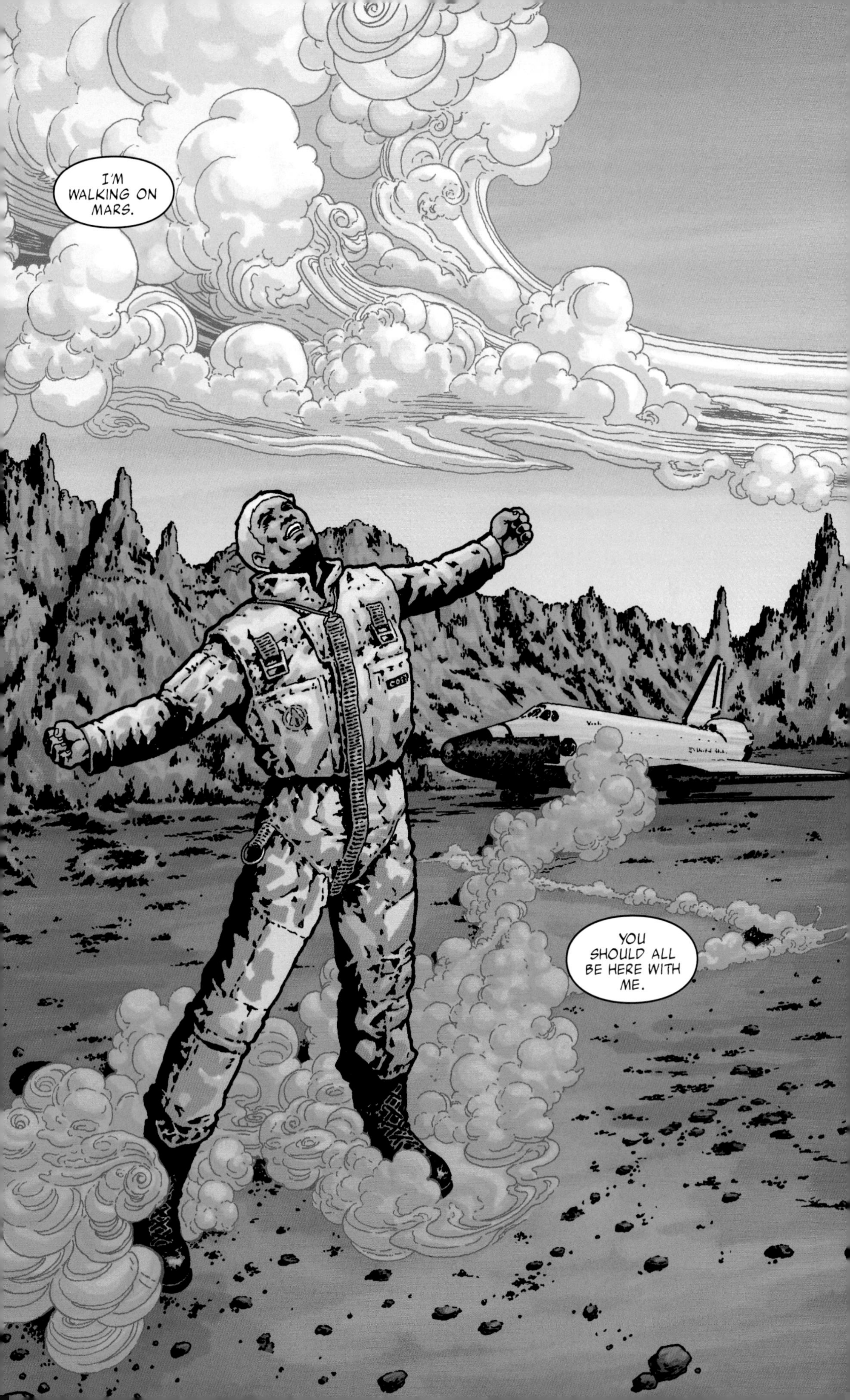
I'M WALKING ON MARS.
YOU SHOULD ALL BE HERE WITH ME.

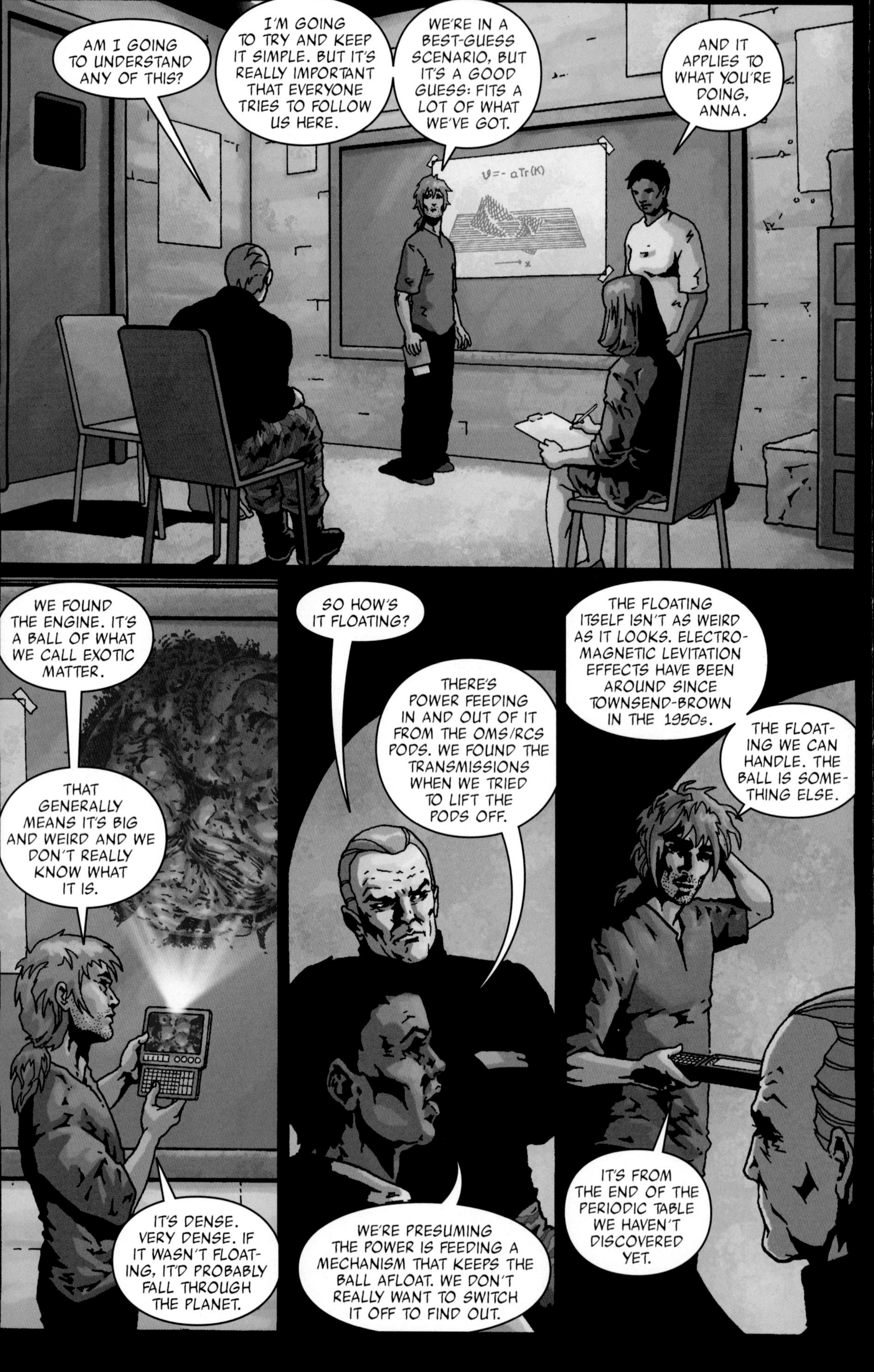

AM I GOING TO UNDERSTAND ANY OF THIS?
I'M GOING TO TRY AND KEEP IT SIMPLE. BUT IT'S REALLY IMPORTANT THAT EVERYONE TRIES TO FOLLOW US HERE.
WE'RE IN A BEST-GUESS SCENARIO, BUT IT'S A GOOD GUESS: FITS A LOT OF WHAT WE'VE GOT.
AND IT APPLIES TO WHAT YOU'RE DOING, ANNA.
WE FOUND THE ENGINE. IT'S A BALL OF WHAT WE CALL EXOTIC MATTER.
THAT GENERALLY MEANS IT'S BIG AND WEIRD AND WE DON'T REALLY KNOW WHAT IT IS.
IT'S DENSE. VERY DENSE. IF IT WASN'T FLOAT-ING, IT'D PROBABLY FALL THROUGH THE PLANET.
SO HOW'S IT FLOATING?
THERE'S POWER FEEDING IN AND OUT OF IT FROM THE OMS/RCS PODS. WE FOUND THE TRANSMISSIONS WHEN WE TRIED TO LIFT THE PODS OFF.
WE'RE PRESUMING THE POWER IS FEEDING A MECHANISM THAT KEEPS THE BALL AFLOAT. WE DON'T REALLY WANT TO SWITCH IT OFF TO FIND OUT.
THE FLOATING ITSELF ISN'T AS WEIRD AS IT LOOKS. ELECTRO-MAGNETIC LEVITATION EFFECTS HAVE BEEN AROUND SINCE TOWNSEND-BROWN IN THE 1950s.
THE FLOAT-ING WE CAN HANDLE. THE BALL IS SOME-THING ELSE.
IT'S FROM THE END OF THE PERIODIC TABLE WE HAVEN'T DISCOVERED YET.

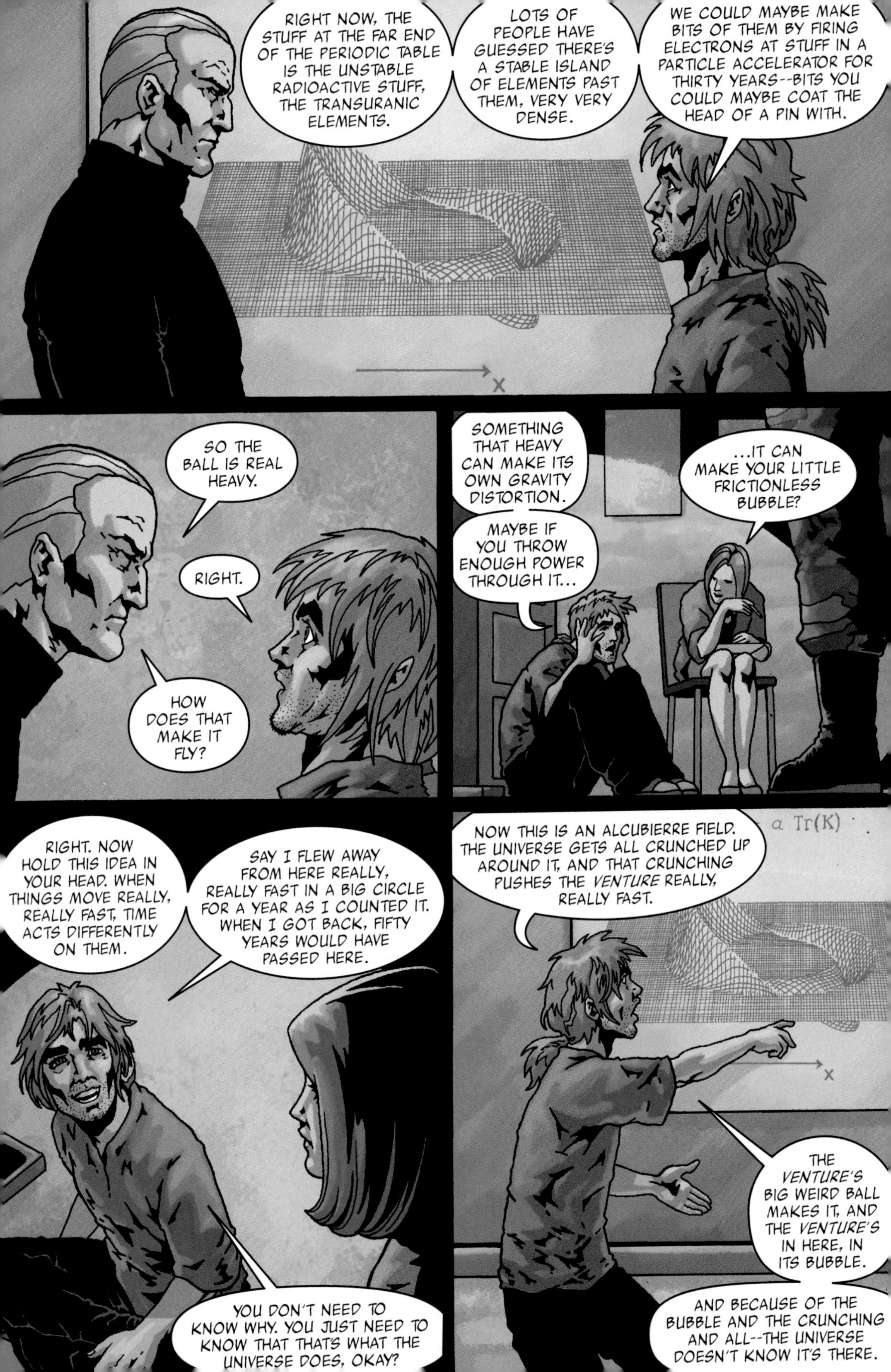
RIGHT NOW, THE STUFF AT THE FAR END OF THE PERIODIC TABLE IS THE UNSTABLE RADIOACTIVE STUFF, THE TRANSURANIC ELEMENTS.
LOTS OF PEOPLE HAVE GUESSED THERE'S A STABLE ISLAND OF ELEMENTS PAST THEM, VERY VERY DENSE.
WE COULD MAYBE MAKE BITS OF THEM BY FIRING ELECTRONS AT STUFF IN A PARTICLE ACCELERATOR FOR THIRTY YEARS--BITS YOU COULD MAYBE COAT THE HEAD OF A PIN WITH.
X
SO THE BALL IS REAL HEAVY.
RIGHT.
HOW DOES THAT MAKE IT FLY?
SOMETHING THAT HEAVY CAN MAKE ITS OWN GRAVITY DISTORTION.
MAYBE IF YOU THROW ENOUGH POWER THROUGH IT...
...IT CAN MAKE YOUR LITTLE FRICTIONLESS BUBBLE?
RIGHT. NOW HOLD THIS IDEA IN YOUR HEAD. WHEN THINGS MOVE REALLY, REALLY FAST, TIME ACTS DIFFERENTLY ON THEM.
SAY I FLEW AWAY FROM HERE REALLY, REALLY FAST IN A BIG CIRCLE FOR A YEAR AS I COUNTED IT. WHEN I GOT BACK, FIFTY YEARS WOULD HAVE PASSED HERE.
YOU DON'T NEED TO KNOW WHY. YOU JUST NEED TO KNOW THAT THAT'S WHAT THE UNIVERSE DOES, OKAY?
a Tr(K)
NOW THIS IS AN ALCUBIERRE FIELD. THE UNIVERSE GETS ALL CRUNCHED UP AROUND IT, AND THAT CRUNCHING PUSHES THE *VENTURE* REALLY, REALLY FAST.
X
THE *VENTURE'S* BIG WEIRD BALL MAKES IT, AND THE *VENTURE'S* IN HERE, IN ITS BUBBLE.
AND BECAUSE OF THE BUBBLE AND THE CRUNCHING AND ALL--THE UNIVERSE DOESN'T KNOW IT'S THERE.

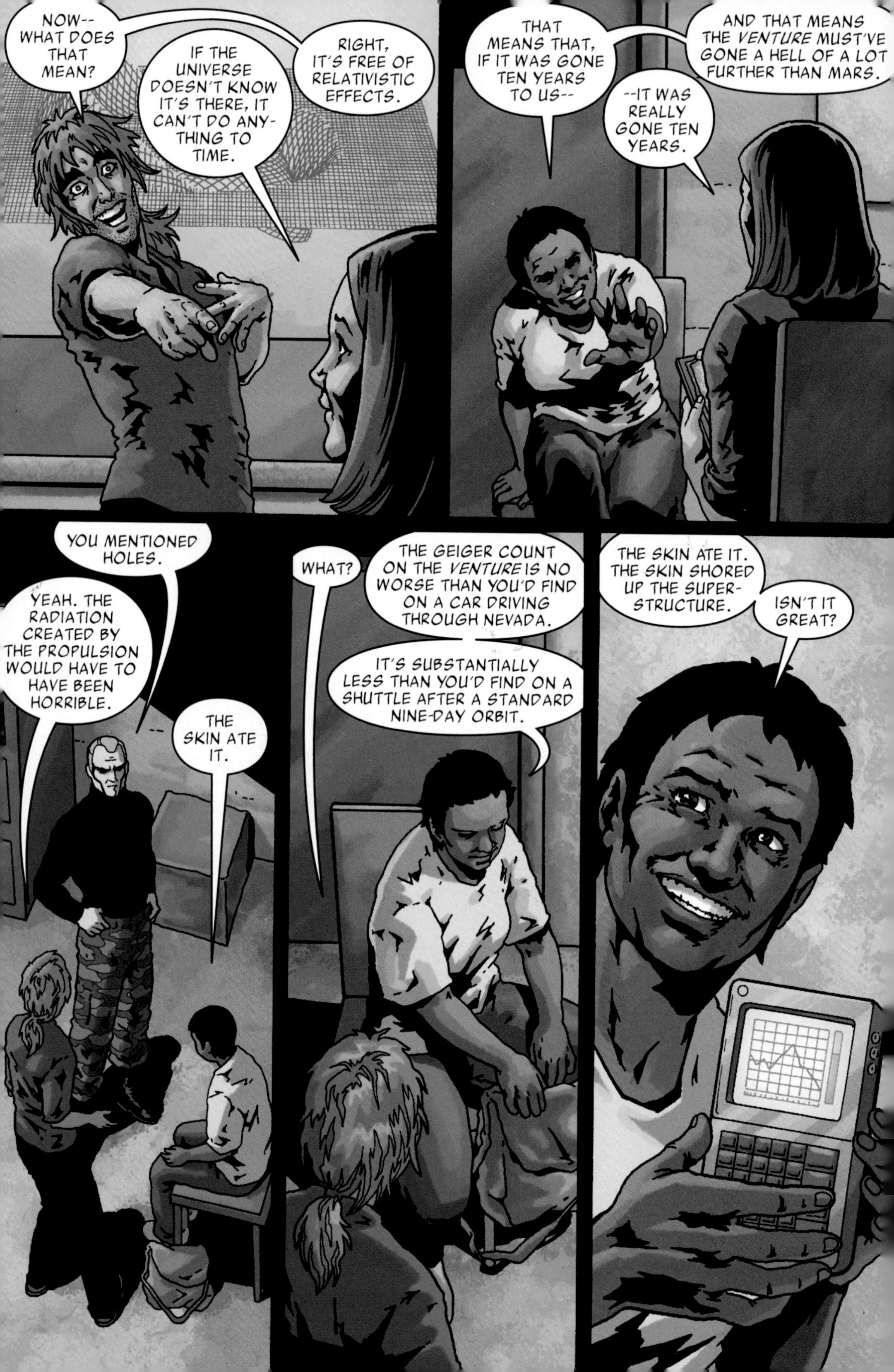
NOW-- WHAT DOES THAT MEAN?
IF THE UNIVERSE DOESN'T KNOW IT'S THERE, IT CAN'T DO ANY-THING TO TIME.
RIGHT, IT'S FREE OF RELATIVISTIC EFFECTS.
THAT MEANS THAT, IF IT WAS GONE TEN YEARS TO US--
--IT WAS REALLY GONE TEN YEARS.
AND THAT MEANS THE *VENTURE* MUST'VE GONE A HELL OF A LOT FURTHER THAN MARS.
YOU MENTIONED HOLES.
YEAH. THE RADIATION CREATED BY THE PROPULSION WOULD HAVE TO HAVE BEEN HORRIBLE.
THE SKIN ATE IT.
WHAT?
THE GEIGER COUNT ON THE *VENTURE* IS NO WORSE THAN YOU'D FIND ON A CAR DRIVING THROUGH NEVADA.
IT'S SUBSTANTIALLY LESS THAN YOU'D FIND ON A SHUTTLE AFTER A STANDARD NINE-DAY ORBIT.
THE SKIN ATE IT. THE SKIN SHORED UP THE SUPER-STRUCTURE.
ISN'T IT GREAT?

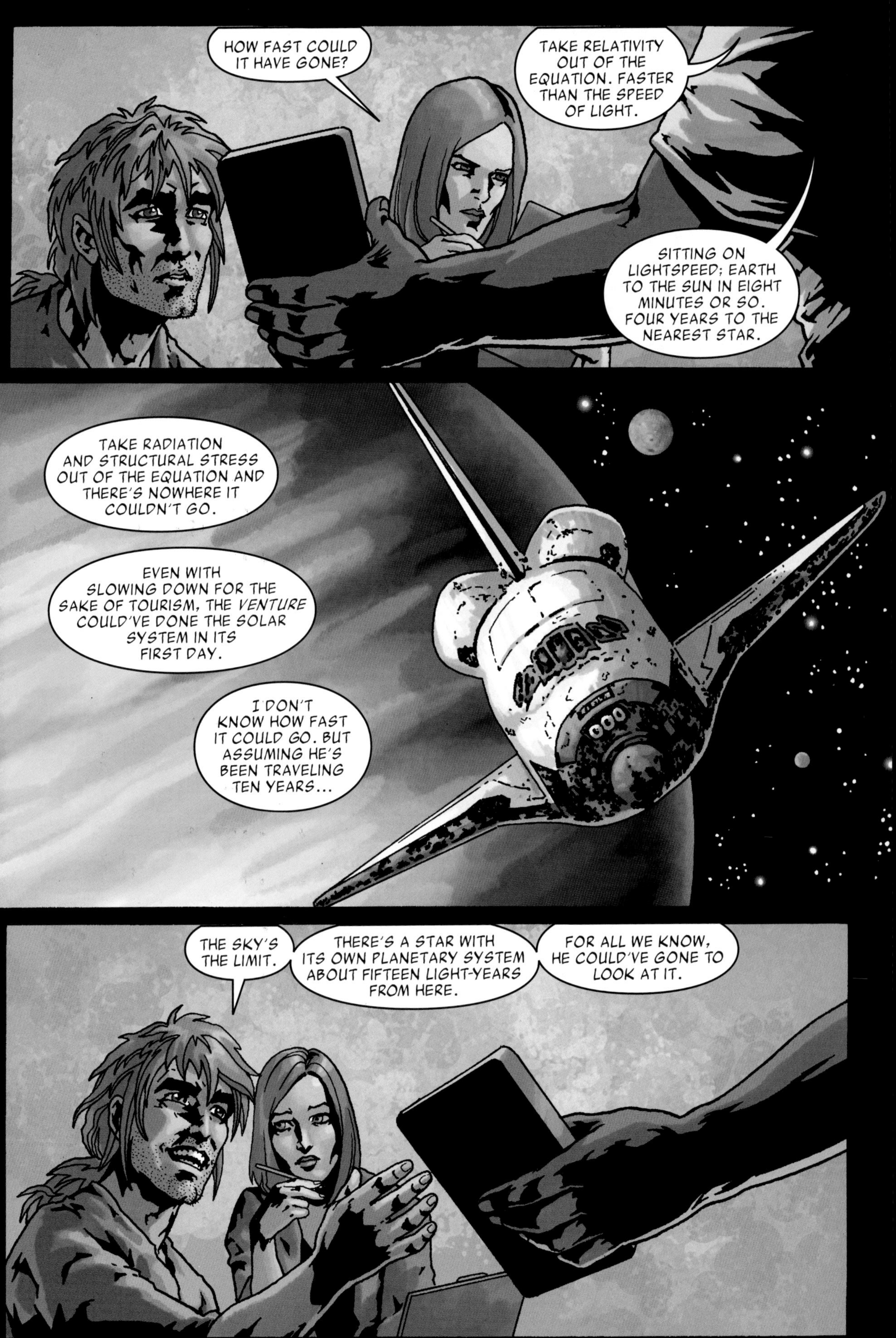
HOW FAST COULD IT HAVE GONE?
TAKE RELATIVITY OUT OF THE EQUATION. FASTER THAN THE SPEED OF LIGHT.
SITTING ON LIGHTSPEED; EARTH TO THE SUN IN EIGHT MINUTES OR SO. FOUR YEARS TO THE NEAREST STAR.
TAKE RADIATION AND STRUCTURAL STRESS OUT OF THE EQUATION AND THERE'S NOWHERE IT COULDN'T GO.
EVEN WITH SLOWING DOWN FOR THE SAKE OF TOURISM, THE *VENTURE* COULD'VE DONE THE SOLAR SYSTEM IN ITS FIRST DAY.
I DON'T KNOW HOW FAST IT COULD GO. BUT ASSUMING HE'S BEEN TRAVELING TEN YEARS...
THE SKY'S THE LIMIT.
THERE'S A STAR WITH ITS OWN PLANETARY SYSTEM ABOUT FIFTEEN LIGHT-YEARS FROM HERE.
FOR ALL WE KNOW, HE COULD'VE GONE TO LOOK AT IT.

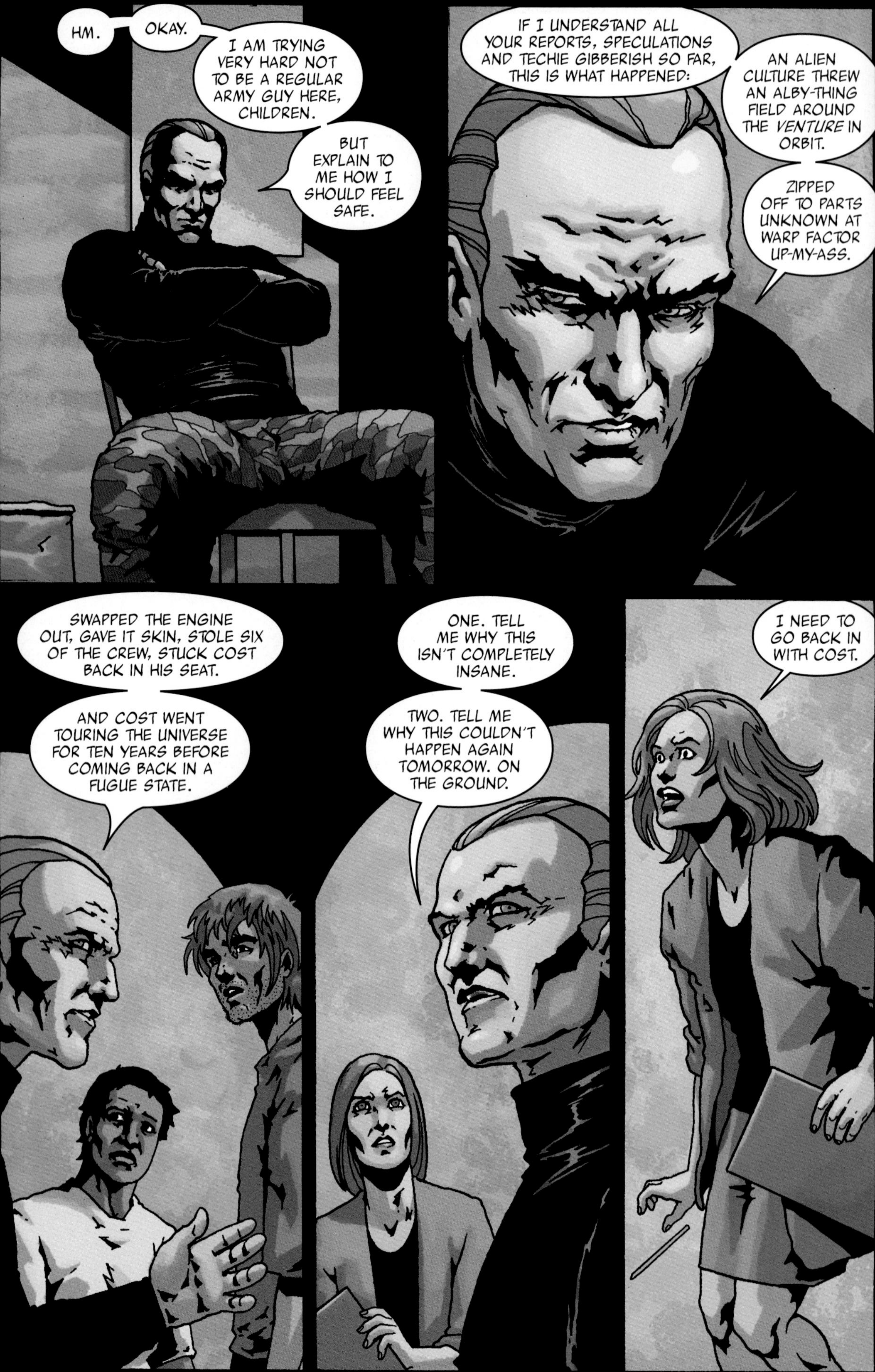
HM.
OKAY.
I AM TRYING VERY HARD NOT TO BE A REGULAR ARMY GUY HERE, CHILDREN.
BUT EXPLAIN TO ME HOW I SHOULD FEEL SAFE.
IF I UNDERSTAND ALL YOUR REPORTS, SPECULATIONS AND TECHIE GIBBERISH SO FAR, THIS IS WHAT HAPPENED:
AN ALIEN CULTURE THREW AN ALBY-THING FIELD AROUND THE *VENTURE* IN ORBIT.
ZIPPED OFF TO PARTS UNKNOWN AT WARP FACTOR UP-MY-ASS.
SWAPPED THE ENGINE OUT, GAVE IT SKIN, STOLE SIX OF THE CREW, STUCK COST BACK IN HIS SEAT.
AND COST WENT TOURING THE UNIVERSE FOR TEN YEARS BEFORE COMING BACK IN A FUGUE STATE.
ONE. TELL ME WHY THIS ISN'T COMPLETELY INSANE.
TWO. TELL ME WHY THIS COULDN'T HAPPEN AGAIN TOMORROW. ON THE GROUND.
I NEED TO GO BACK IN WITH COST.

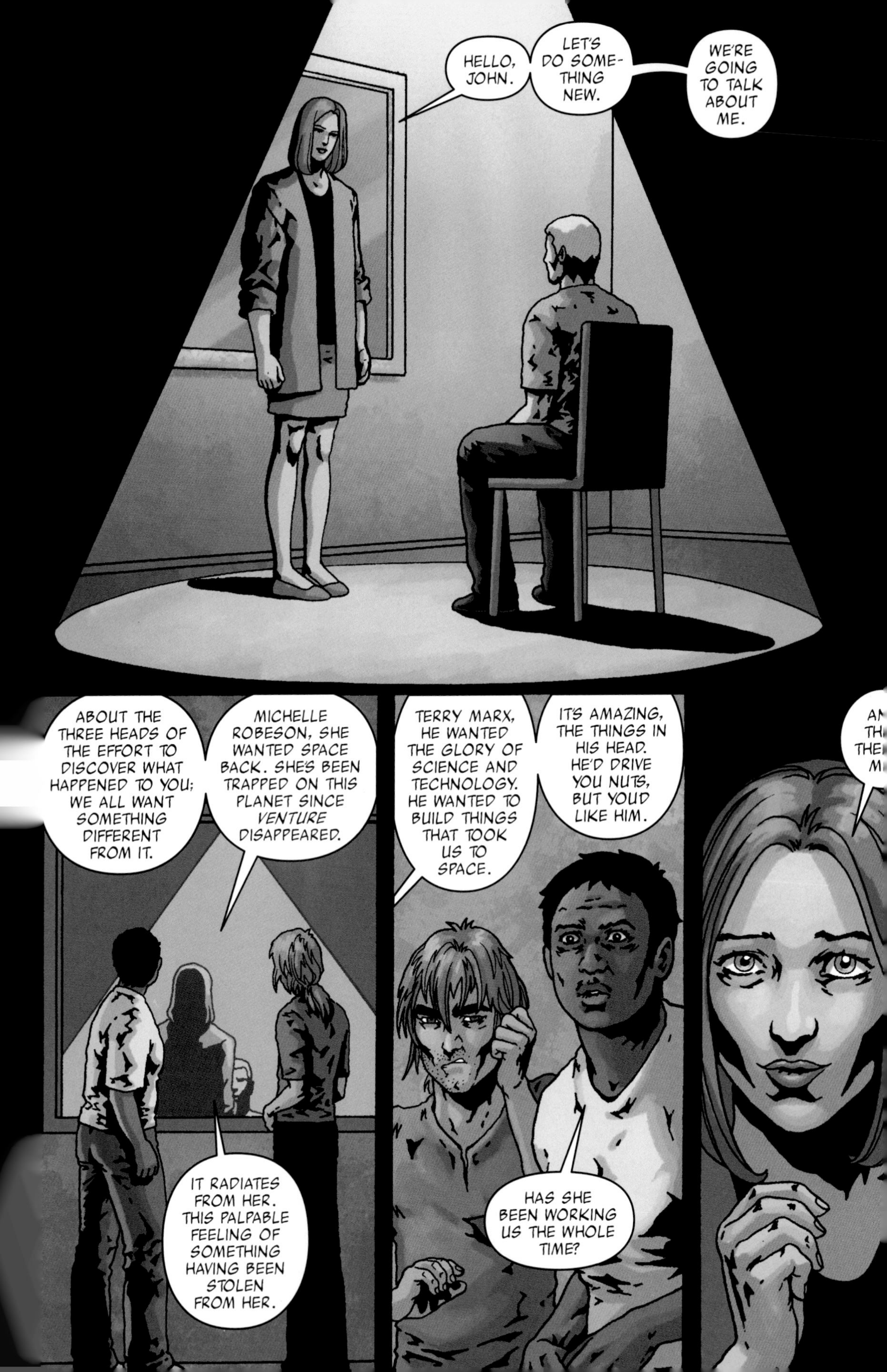
HELLO, JOHN.
LET'S DO SOME-THING NEW.
WE'RE GOING TO TALK ABOUT ME.
ABOUT THE THREE HEADS OF THE EFFORT TO DISCOVER WHAT HAPPENED TO YOU; WE ALL WANT SOMETHING DIFFERENT FROM IT.
MICHELLE ROBESON, SHE WANTED SPACE BACK. SHE'S BEEN TRAPPED ON THIS PLANET SINCE *VENTURE* DISAPPEARED.
IT RADIATES FROM HER. THIS PALPABLE FEELING OF SOMETHING HAVING BEEN STOLEN FROM HER.
TERRY MARX, HE WANTED THE GLORY OF SCIENCE AND TECHNOLOGY. HE WANTED TO BUILD THINGS THAT TOOK US TO SPACE.
IT'S AMAZING, THE THINGS IN HIS HEAD. HE'D DRIVE YOU NUTS, BUT YOUD LIKE HIM.
HAS SHE BEEN WORKING US THE WHOLE TIME?

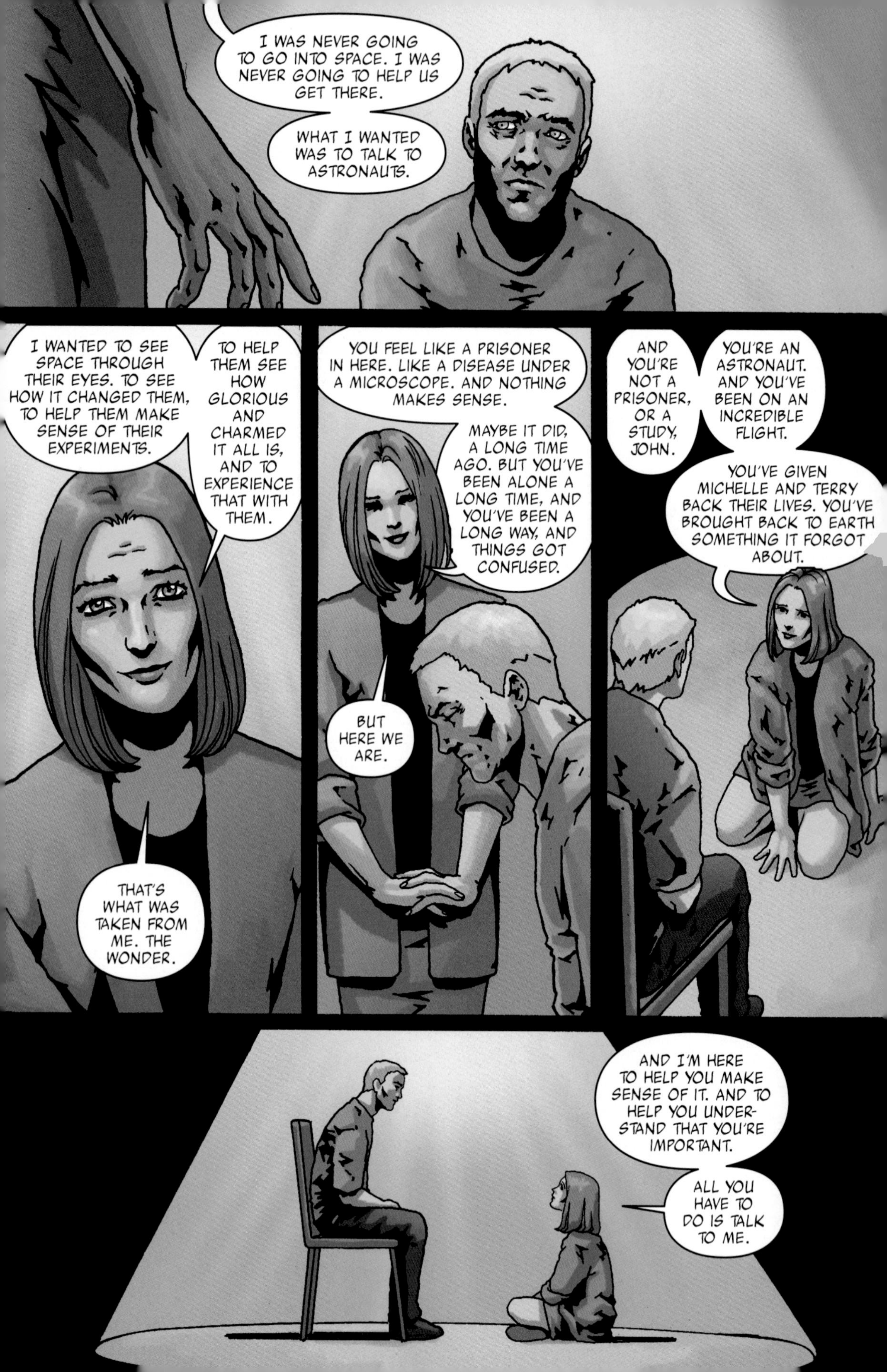
I WAS NEVER GOING TO GO INTO SPACE. I WAS NEVER GOING TO HELP US GET THERE.
WHAT I WANTED WAS TO TALK TO ASTRONAUTS.
I WANTED TO SEE SPACE THROUGH THEIR EYES. TO SEE HOW IT CHANGED THEM, TO HELP THEM MAKE SENSE OF THEIR EXPERIMENTS.
TO HELP THEM SEE HOW GLORIOUS AND CHARMED IT ALL IS, AND TO EXPERIENCE THAT WITH THEM.
THAT'S WHAT WAS TAKEN FROM ME. THE WONDER.
YOU FEEL LIKE A PRISONER IN HERE. LIKE A DISEASE UNDER A MICROSCOPE. AND NOTHING MAKES SENSE.
MAYBE IT DID, A LONG TIME AGO. BUT YOU'VE BEEN ALONE A LONG TIME, AND YOU'VE BEEN A LONG WAY, AND THINGS GOT CONFUSED.
BUT HERE WE ARE.
AND YOU'RE NOT A PRISONER, OR A STUDY, JOHN.
YOU'RE AN ASTRONAUT. AND YOU'VE BEEN ON AN INCREDIBLE FLIGHT.
YOU'VE GIVEN MICHELLE AND TERRY BACK THEIR LIVES. YOU'VE BROUGHT BACK TO EARTH SOMETHING IT FORGOT ABOUT.
AND I'M HERE TO HELP YOU MAKE SENSE OF IT. AND TO HELP YOU UNDER-STAND THAT YOU'RE IMPORTANT.
ALL YOU HAVE TO DO IS TALK TO ME.

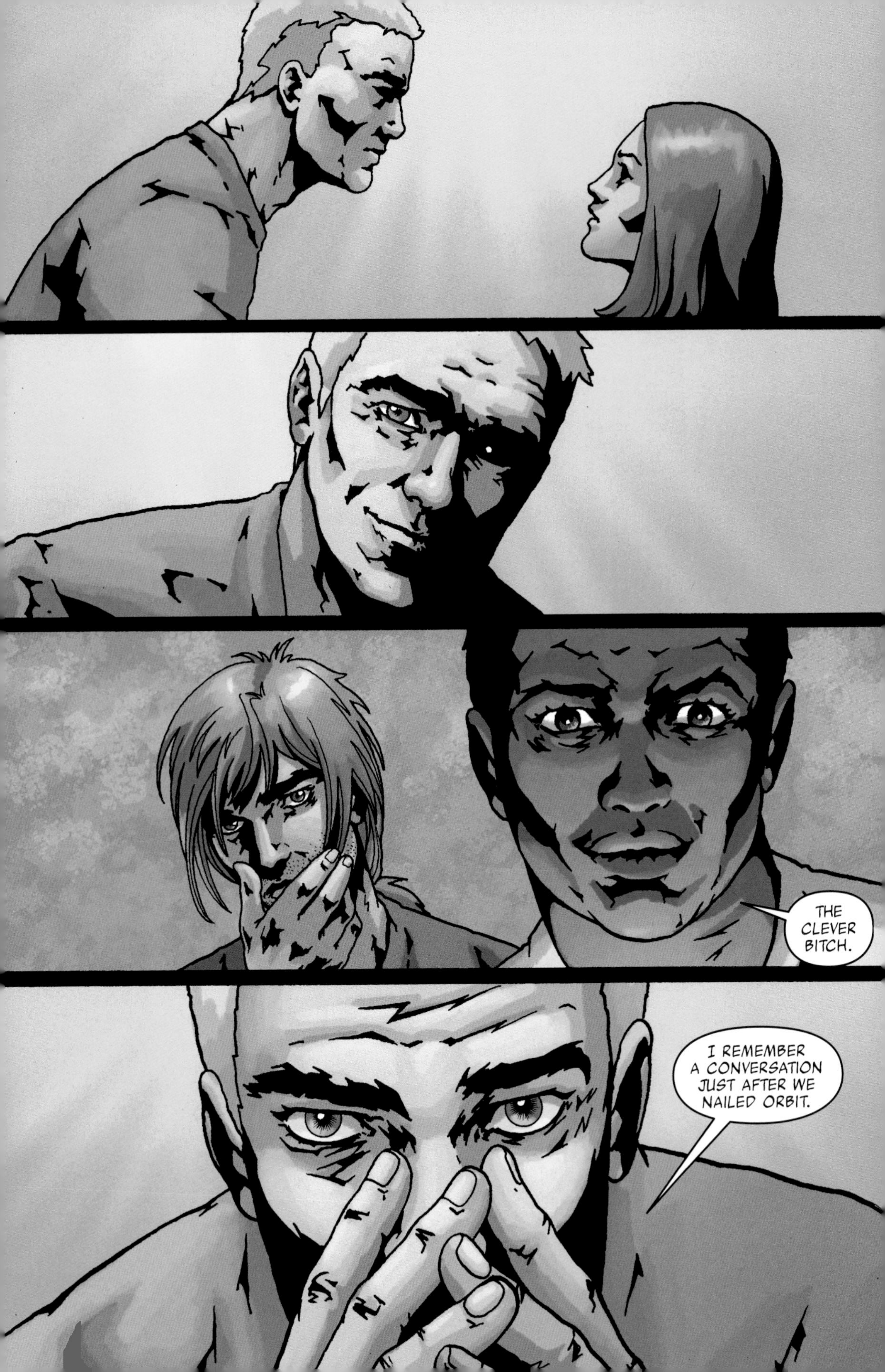
THE CLEVER BITCH.
I REMEMBER A CONVERSATION JUST AFTER WE NAILED ORBIT.

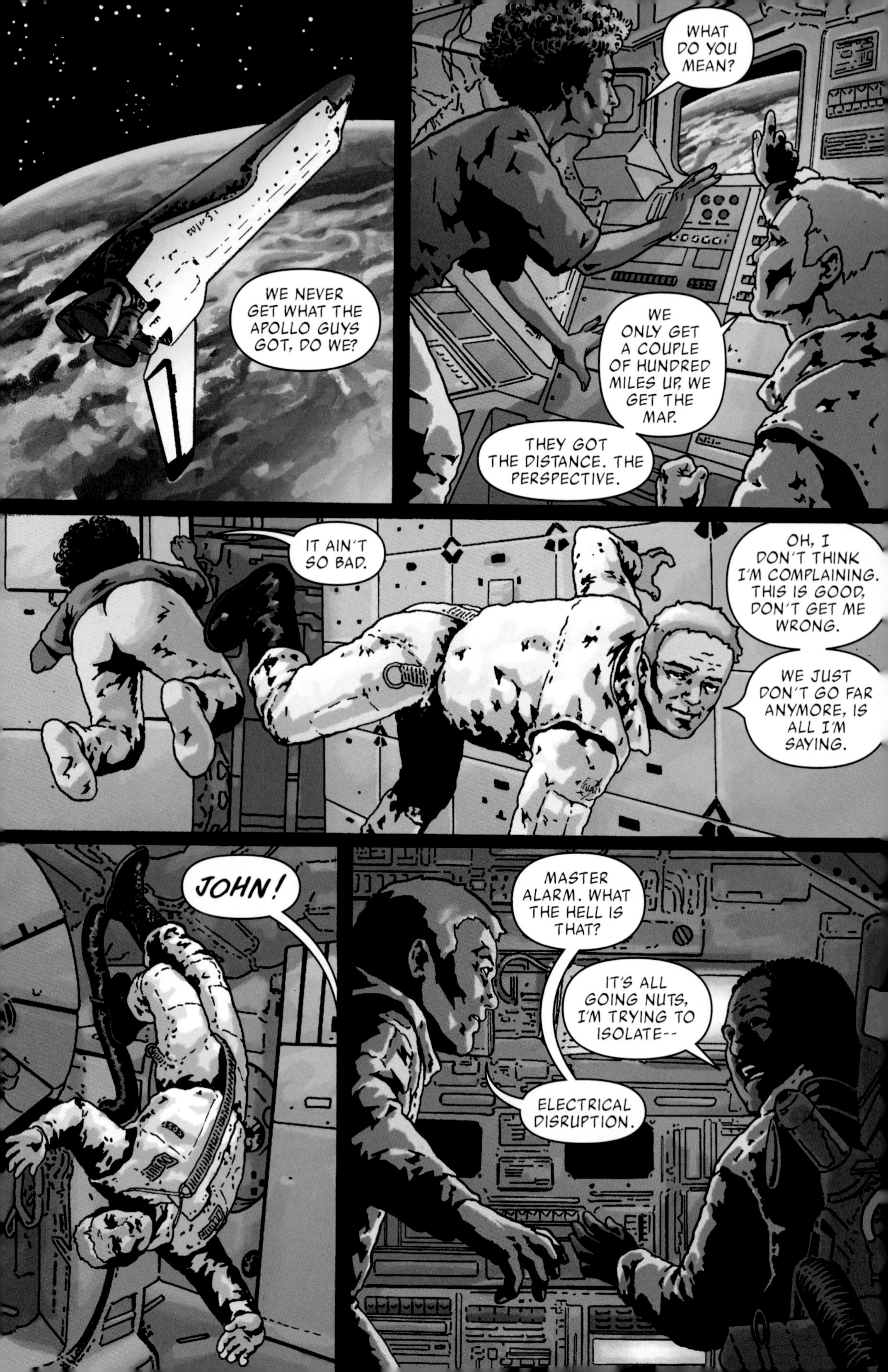
WE NEVER GET WHAT THE APOLLO GUYS GOT, DO WE?
WHAT DO YOU MEAN?
WE ONLY GET A COUPLE OF HUNDRED MILES UP, WE GET THE MAP.
THEY GOT THE DISTANCE. THE PERSPECTIVE.
IT AIN'T SO BAD.
OH, I DON'T THINK I'M COMPLAINING. THIS IS GOOD, DON'T GET ME WRONG.
WE JUST DON'T GO FAR ANYMORE, IS ALL I'M SAYING.
JOHN!
MASTER ALARM. WHAT THE HELL IS THAT?
IT'S ALL GOING NUTS, I'M TRYING TO ISOLATE--
ELECTRICAL DISRUPTION.

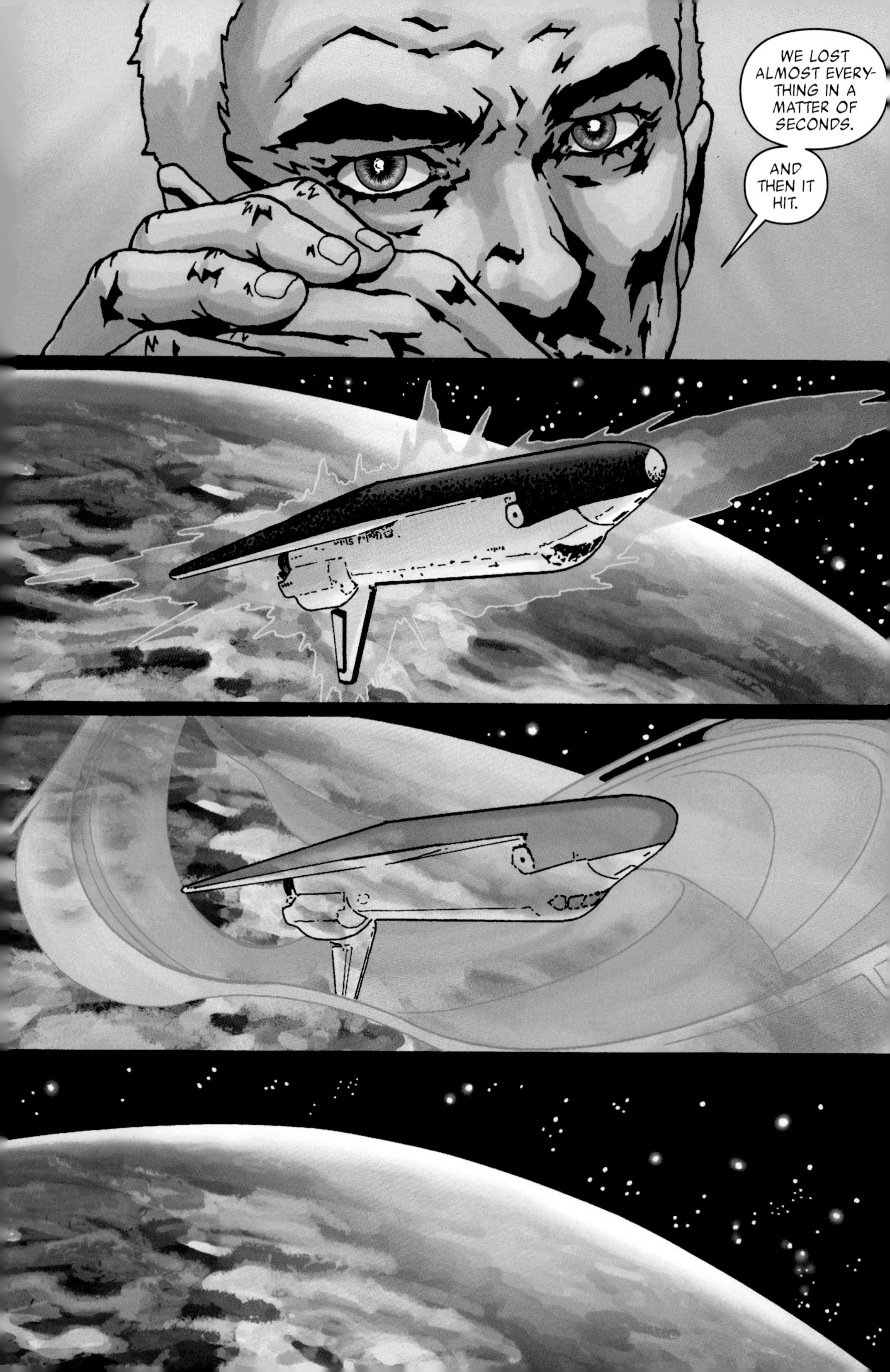
WE LOST ALMOST EVERYTHING IN A MATTER OF SECONDS.
AND THEN IT HIT.

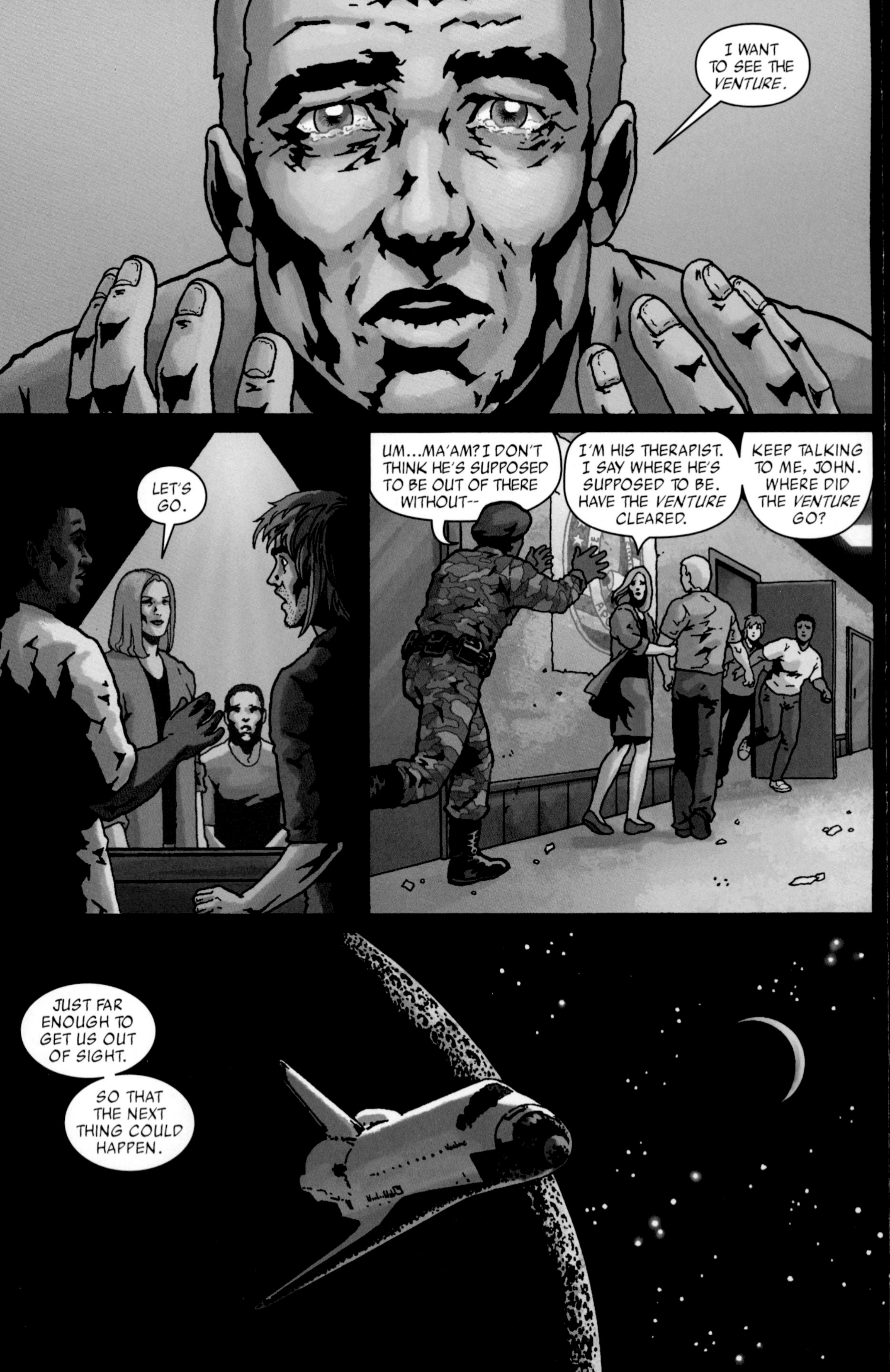
I WANT TO SEE THE *VENTURE*.
LET'S GO.
UM...MA'AM? I DON'T THINK HE'S SUPPOSED TO BE OUT OF THERE WITHOUT--
I'M HIS THERAPIST. I SAY WHERE HE'S SUPPOSED TO BE. HAVE THE *VENTURE* CLEARED.
KEEP TALKING TO ME, JOHN. WHERE DID THE *VENTURE* GO?
JUST FAR ENOUGH TO GET US OUT OF SIGHT.
SO THAT THE NEXT THING COULD HAPPEN.

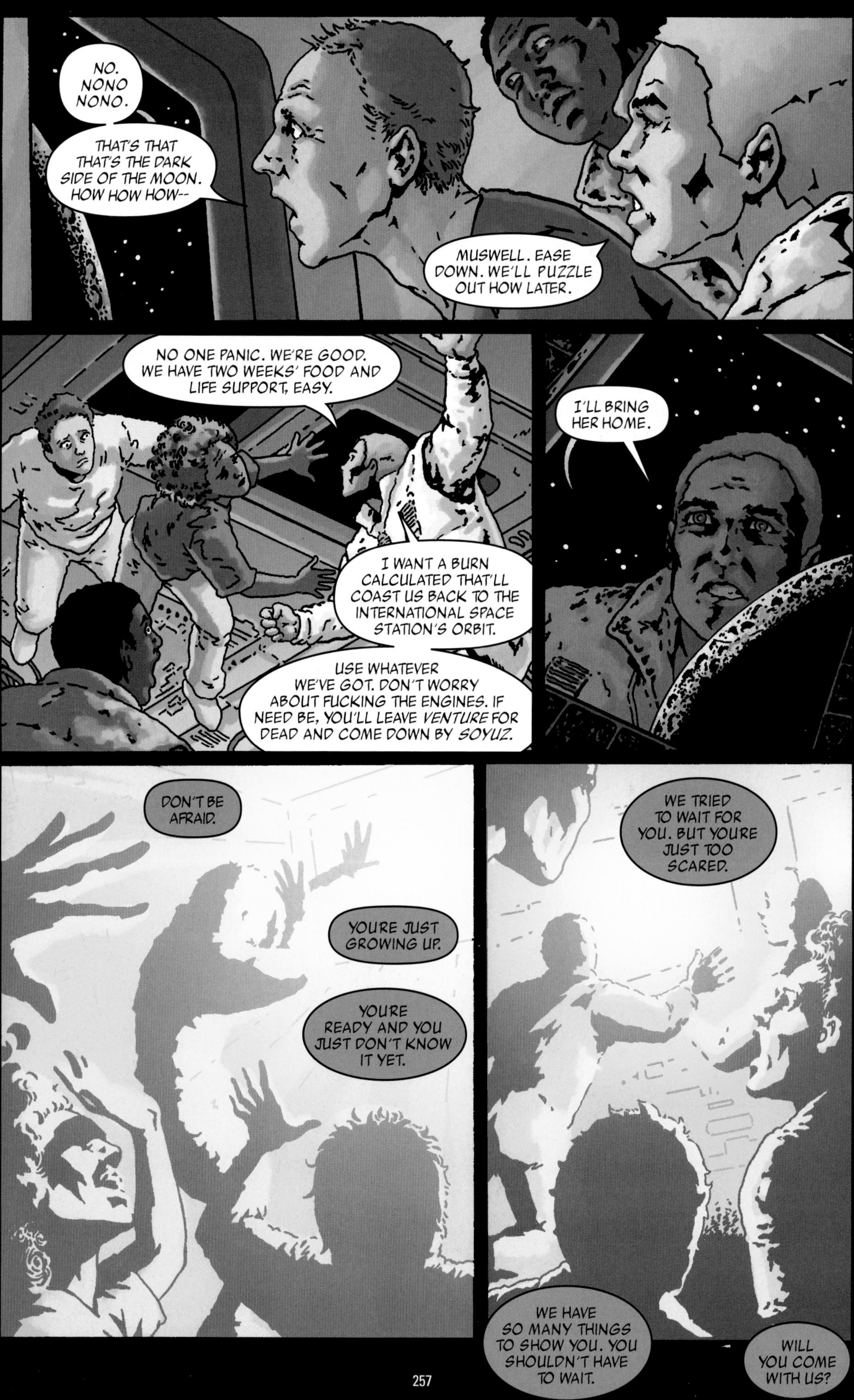
NO. NONO NONO.
THAT'S THAT THAT'S THE DARK SIDE OF THE MOON. HOW HOW HOW--
MUSWELL. EASE DOWN. WE'LL PUZZLE OUT HOW LATER.
NO ONE PANIC. WE'RE GOOD. WE HAVE TWO WEEKS' FOOD AND LIFE SUPPORT, EASY.
I WANT A BURN CALCULATED THAT'LL COAST US BACK TO THE INTERNATIONAL SPACE STATION'S ORBIT.
USE WHATEVER WE'VE GOT. DON'T WORRY ABOUT FUCKING THE ENGINES. IF NEED BE, YOU'LL LEAVE *VENTURE* FOR DEAD AND COME DOWN BY *SOYUZ*.
I'LL BRING HER HOME.
DON'T BE AFRAID.
YOU'RE JUST GROWING UP.
YOU'RE READY AND YOU JUST DON'T KNOW IT YET.
WE TRIED TO WAIT FOR YOU. BUT YOU'RE JUST TOO SCARED.
WE HAVE SO MANY THINGS TO SHOW YOU. YOU SHOULDN'T HAVE TO WAIT.
WILL YOU COME WITH US?

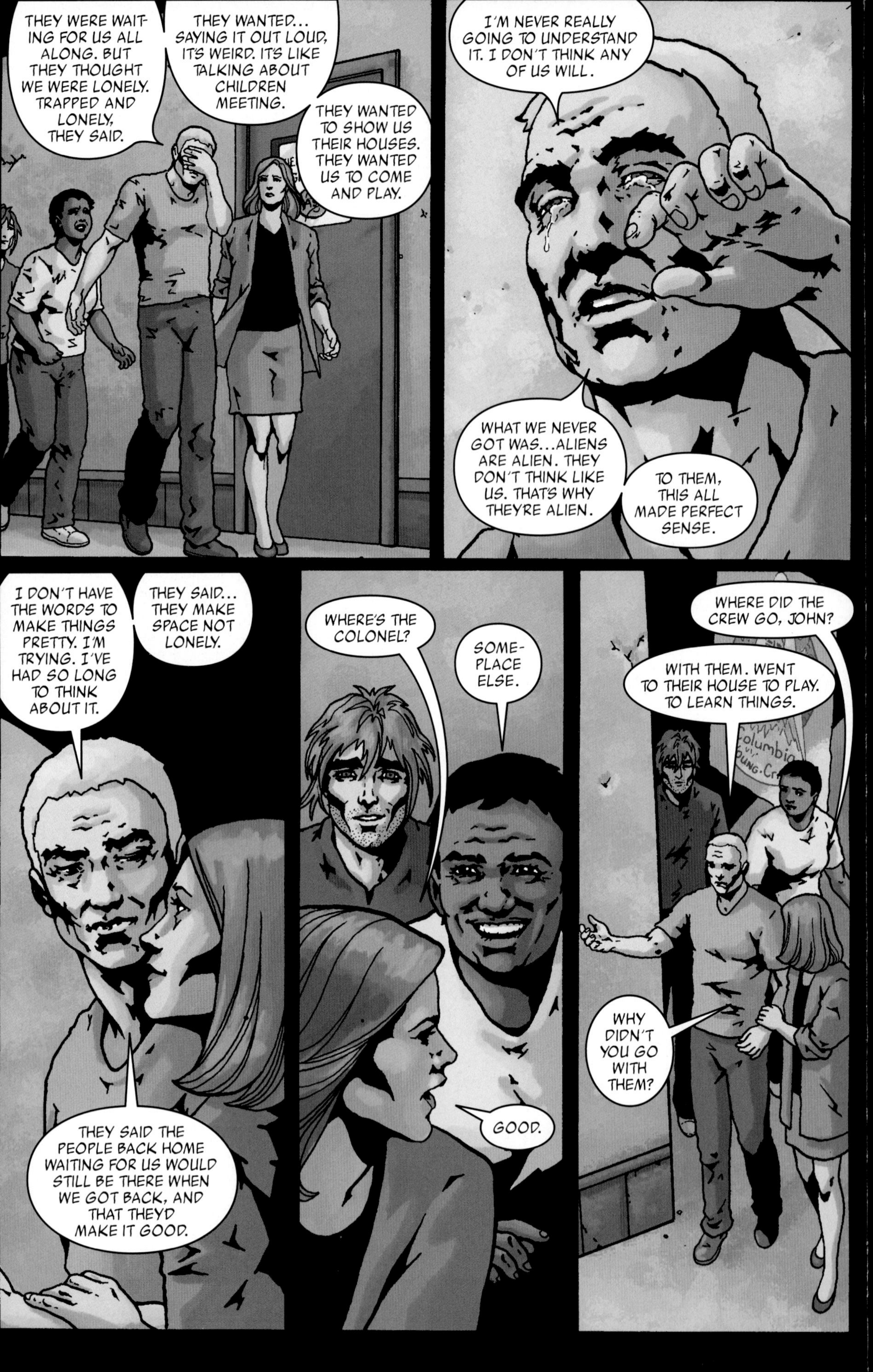
THEY WERE WAITING FOR US ALL ALONG. BUT THEY THOUGHT WE WERE LONELY. TRAPPED AND LONELY, THEY SAID.
THEY WANTED... SAYING IT OUT LOUD, IT'S WEIRD. IT'S LIKE TALKING ABOUT CHILDREN MEETING.
THEY WANTED TO SHOW US THEIR HOUSES. THEY WANTED US TO COME AND PLAY.
I'M NEVER REALLY GOING TO UNDERSTAND IT. I DON'T THINK ANY OF US WILL.
WHAT WE NEVER GOT WAS...ALIENS ARE ALIEN. THEY DON'T THINK LIKE US. THAT'S WHY THEY'RE ALIEN.
TO THEM, THIS ALL MADE PERFECT SENSE.
I DON'T HAVE THE WORDS TO MAKE THINGS PRETTY. I'M TRYING. I'VE HAD SO LONG TO THINK ABOUT IT.
THEY SAID... THEY MAKE SPACE NOT LONELY.
THEY SAID THE PEOPLE BACK HOME WAITING FOR US WOULD STILL BE THERE WHEN WE GOT BACK, AND THAT THEY'D MAKE IT GOOD.
WHERE'S THE COLONEL?
SOME-PLACE ELSE.
GOOD.
WHERE DID THE CREW GO, JOHN?
WITH THEM. WENT TO THEIR HOUSE TO PLAY. TO LEARN THINGS.
WHY DIDN'T YOU GO WITH THEM?

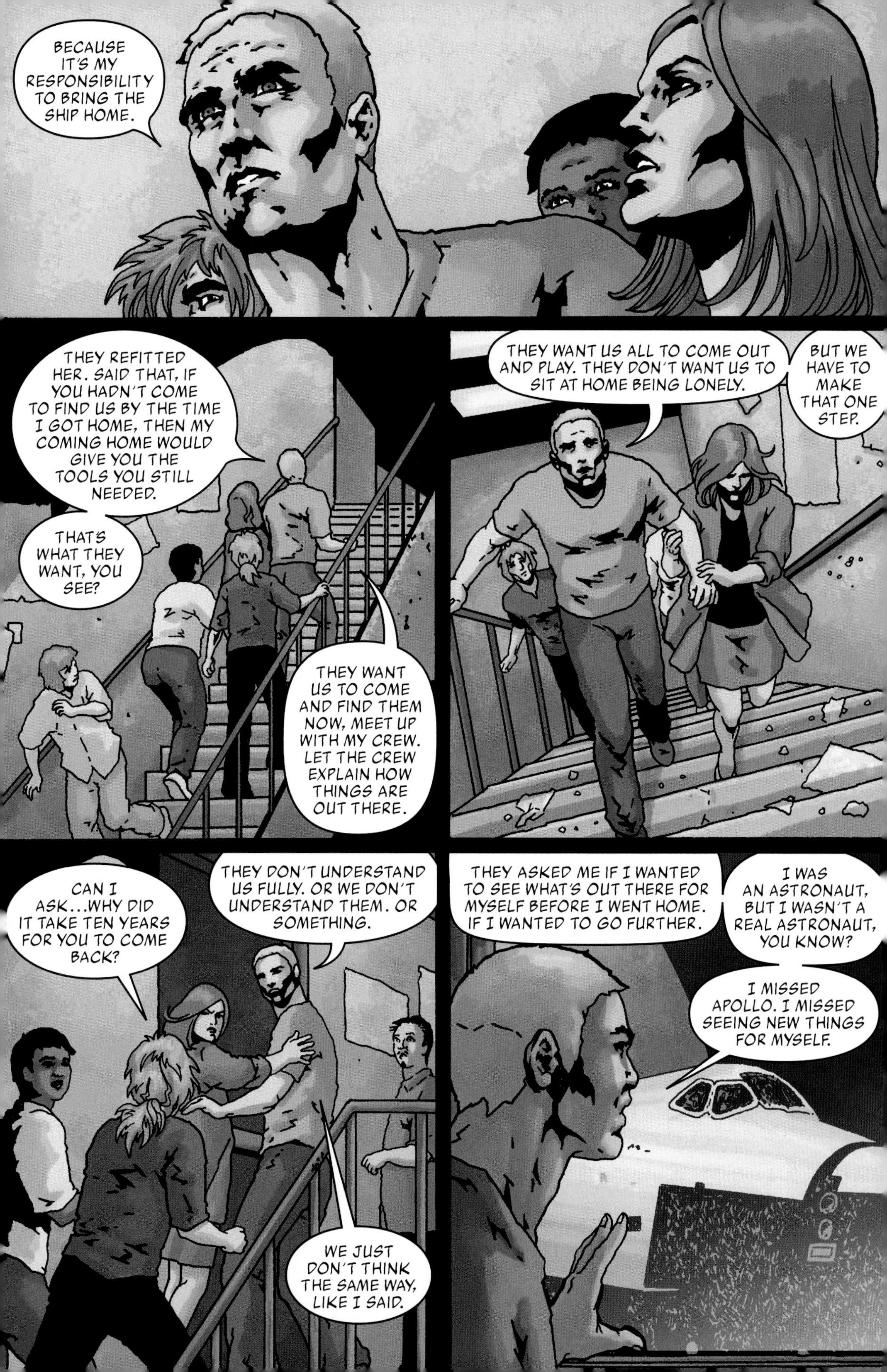
BECAUSE IT'S MY RESPONSIBILITY TO BRING THE SHIP HOME.
THEY REFITTED HER. SAID THAT, IF YOU HADN'T COME TO FIND US BY THE TIME I GOT HOME, THEN MY COMING HOME WOULD GIVE YOU THE TOOLS YOU STILL NEEDED.
THAT'S WHAT THEY WANT, YOU SEE?
THEY WANT US TO COME AND FIND THEM NOW, MEET UP WITH MY CREW. LET THE CREW EXPLAIN HOW THINGS ARE OUT THERE.
THEY WANT US ALL TO COME OUT AND PLAY. THEY DON'T WANT US TO SIT AT HOME BEING LONELY.
BUT WE HAVE TO MAKE THAT ONE STEP.
CAN I ASK...WHY DID IT TAKE TEN YEARS FOR YOU TO COME BACK?
THEY DON'T UNDERSTAND US FULLY. OR WE DON'T UNDERSTAND THEM. OR SOMETHING.
WE JUST DON'T THINK THE SAME WAY, LIKE I SAID.
THEY ASKED ME IF I WANTED TO SEE WHAT'S OUT THERE FOR MYSELF BEFORE I WENT HOME. IF I WANTED TO GO FURTHER.
I WAS AN ASTRONAUT, BUT I WASN'T A REAL ASTRONAUT, YOU KNOW?
I MISSED APOLLO. I MISSED SEEING NEW THINGS FOR MYSELF.

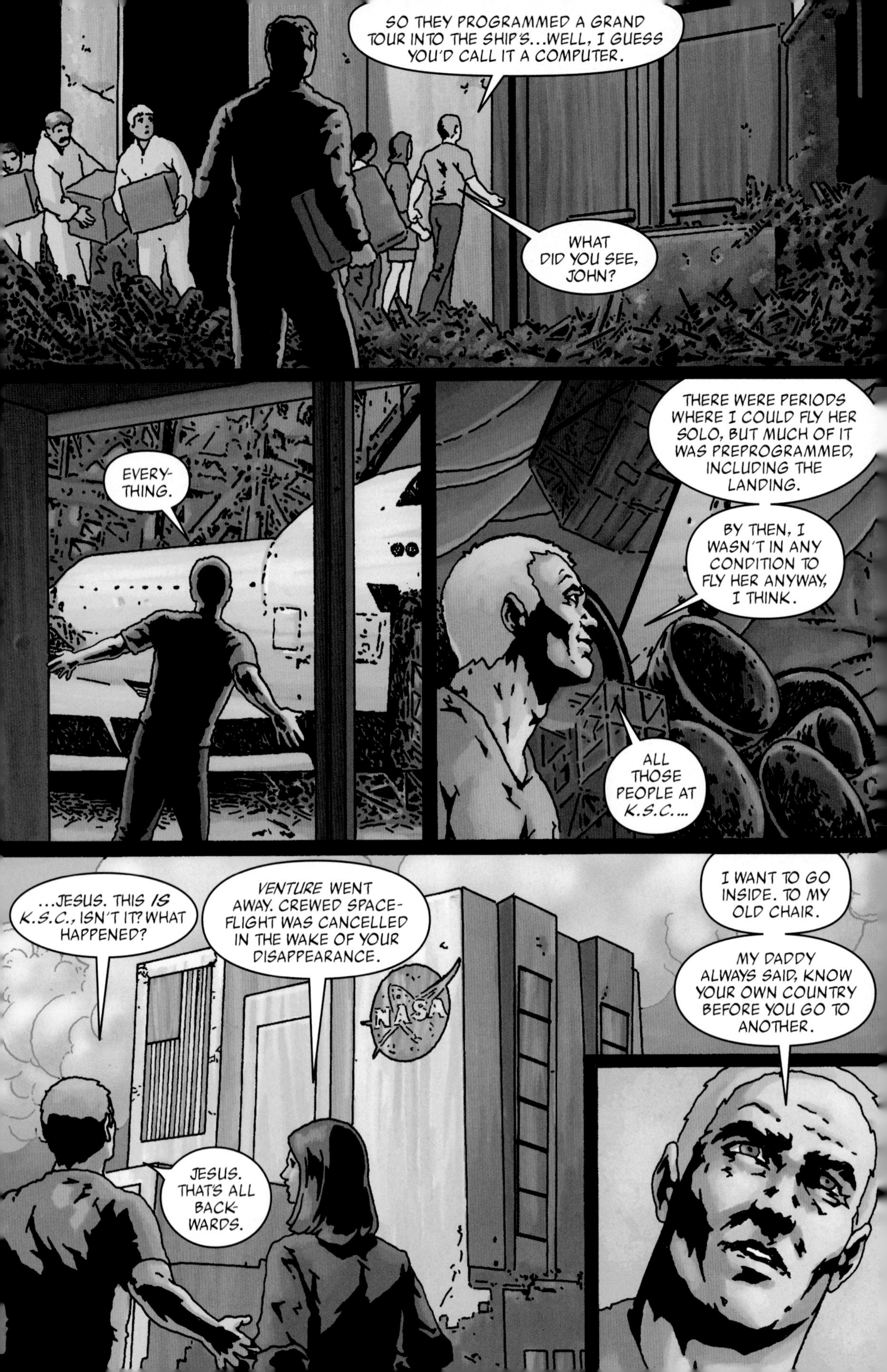
SO THEY PROGRAMMED A GRAND TOUR INTO THE SHIP'S...WELL, I GUESS YOU'D CALL IT A COMPUTER.
WHAT DID YOU SEE, JOHN?
EVERY-THING.
THERE WERE PERIODS WHERE I COULD FLY HER SOLO, BUT MUCH OF IT WAS PREPROGRAMMED, INCLUDING THE LANDING.
BY THEN, I WASN'T IN ANY CONDITION TO FLY HER ANYWAY, I THINK.
ALL THOSE PEOPLE AT K.S.C....
...JESUS. THIS *IS* K.S.C., ISN'T IT? WHAT HAPPENED?
VENTURE WENT AWAY. CREWED SPACE-FLIGHT WAS CANCELLED IN THE WAKE OF YOUR DISAPPEARANCE.
JESUS. THAT'S ALL BACK-WARDS.
I WANT TO GO INSIDE. TO MY OLD CHAIR.
MY DADDY ALWAYS SAID, KNOW YOUR OWN COUNTRY BEFORE YOU GO TO ANOTHER.
NASA

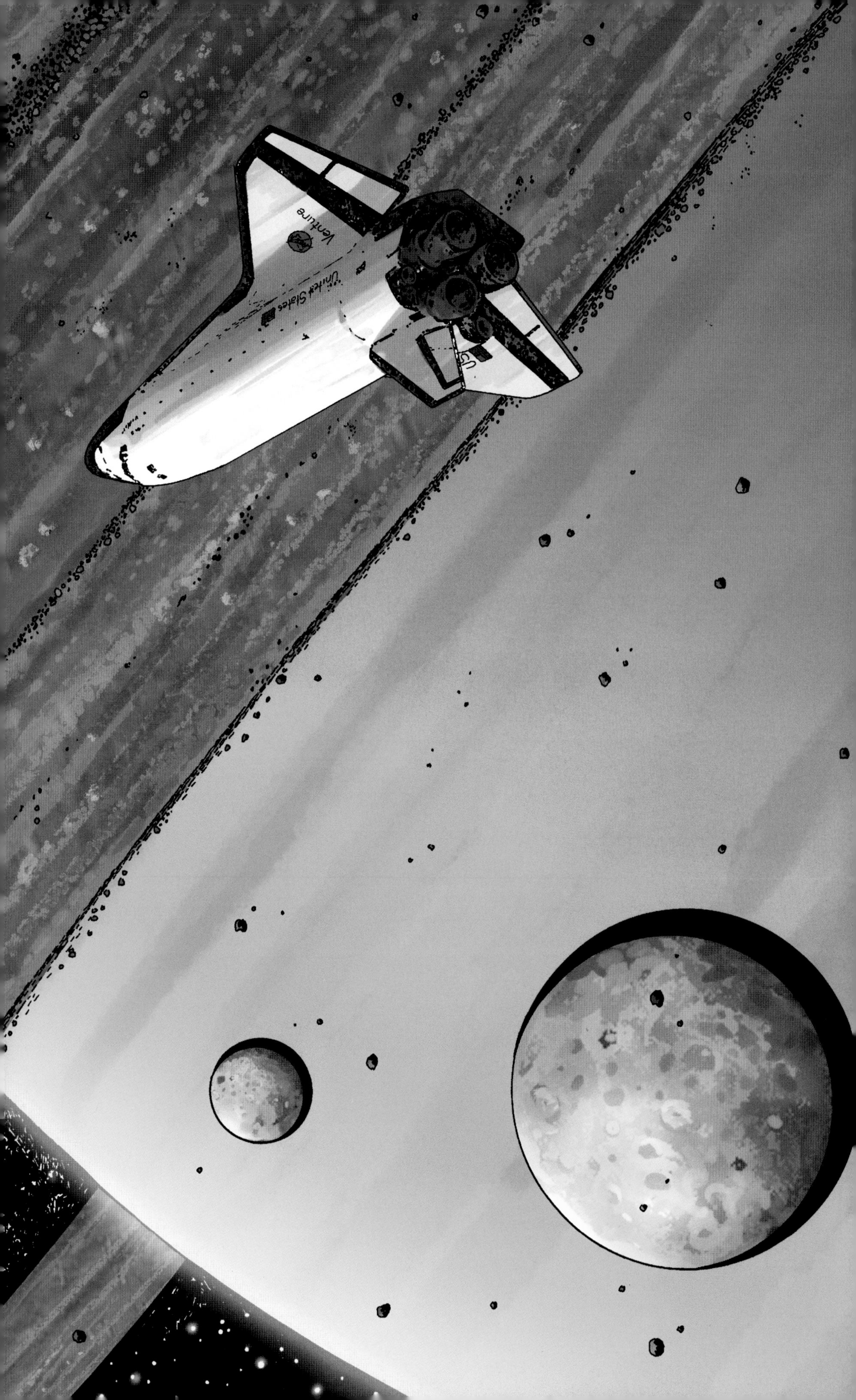
Venture
United States

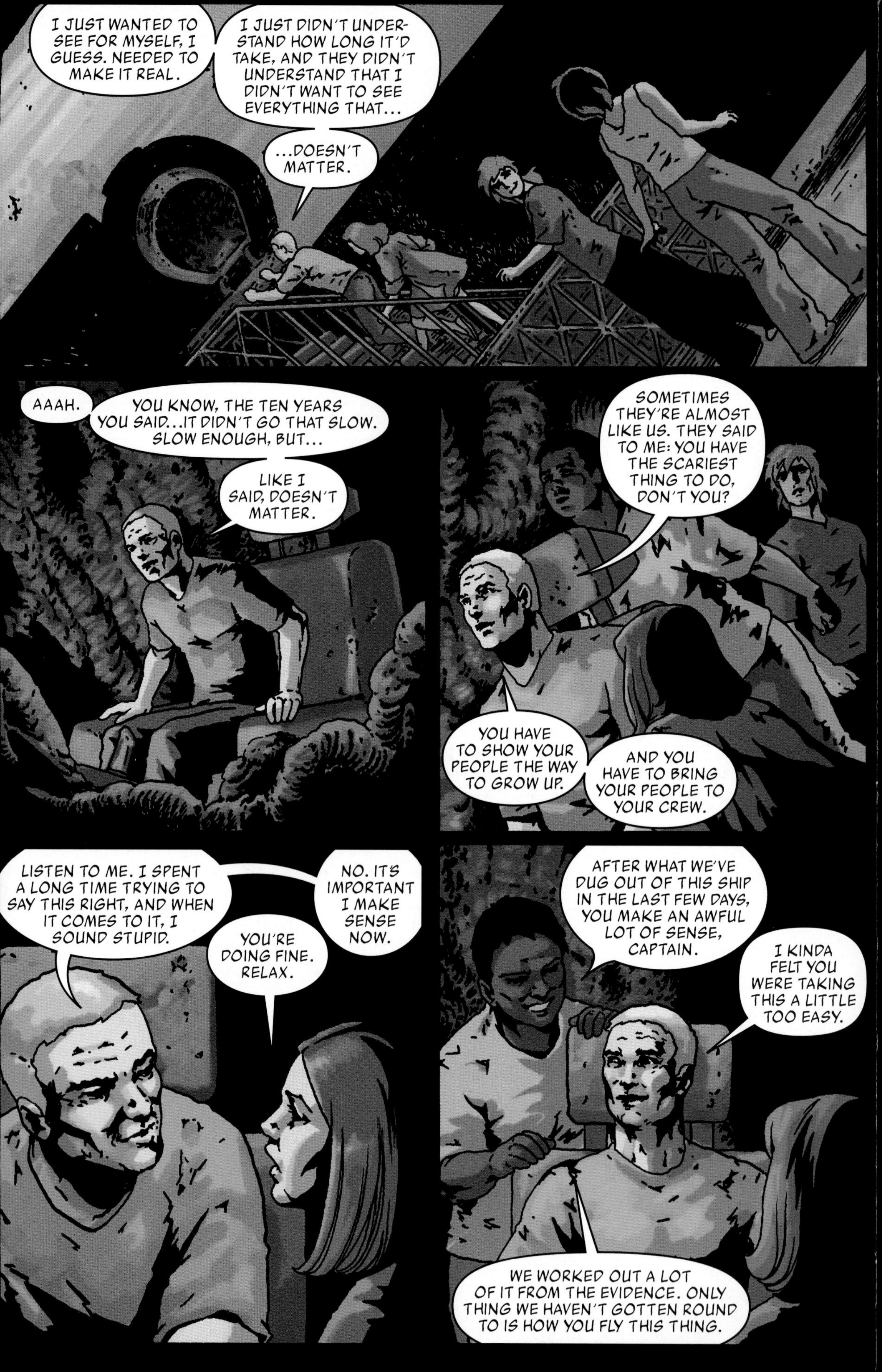
I JUST WANTED TO SEE FOR MYSELF, I GUESS. NEEDED TO MAKE IT REAL.
I JUST DIDN'T UNDERSTAND HOW LONG IT'D TAKE, AND THEY DIDN'T UNDERSTAND THAT I DIDN'T WANT TO SEE EVERYTHING THAT...
...DOESN'T MATTER.
AAAH.
YOU KNOW, THE TEN YEARS YOU SAID...IT DIDN'T GO THAT SLOW. SLOW ENOUGH, BUT...
LIKE I SAID, DOESN'T MATTER.
SOMETIMES THEY'RE ALMOST LIKE US. THEY SAID TO ME: YOU HAVE THE SCARIEST THING TO DO, DON'T YOU?
YOU HAVE TO SHOW YOUR PEOPLE THE WAY TO GROW UP.
AND YOU HAVE TO BRING YOUR PEOPLE TO YOUR CREW.
LISTEN TO ME. I SPENT A LONG TIME TRYING TO SAY THIS RIGHT, AND WHEN IT COMES TO IT, I SOUND STUPID.
YOU'RE DOING FINE. RELAX.
NO. IT'S IMPORTANT I MAKE SENSE NOW.
AFTER WHAT WE'VE DUG OUT OF THIS SHIP IN THE LAST FEW DAYS, YOU MAKE AN AWFUL LOT OF SENSE, CAPTAIN.
I KINDA FELT YOU WERE TAKING THIS A LITTLE TOO EASY.
WE WORKED OUT A LOT OF IT FROM THE EVIDENCE. ONLY THING WE HAVEN'T GOTTEN ROUND TO IS HOW YOU FLY THIS THING.

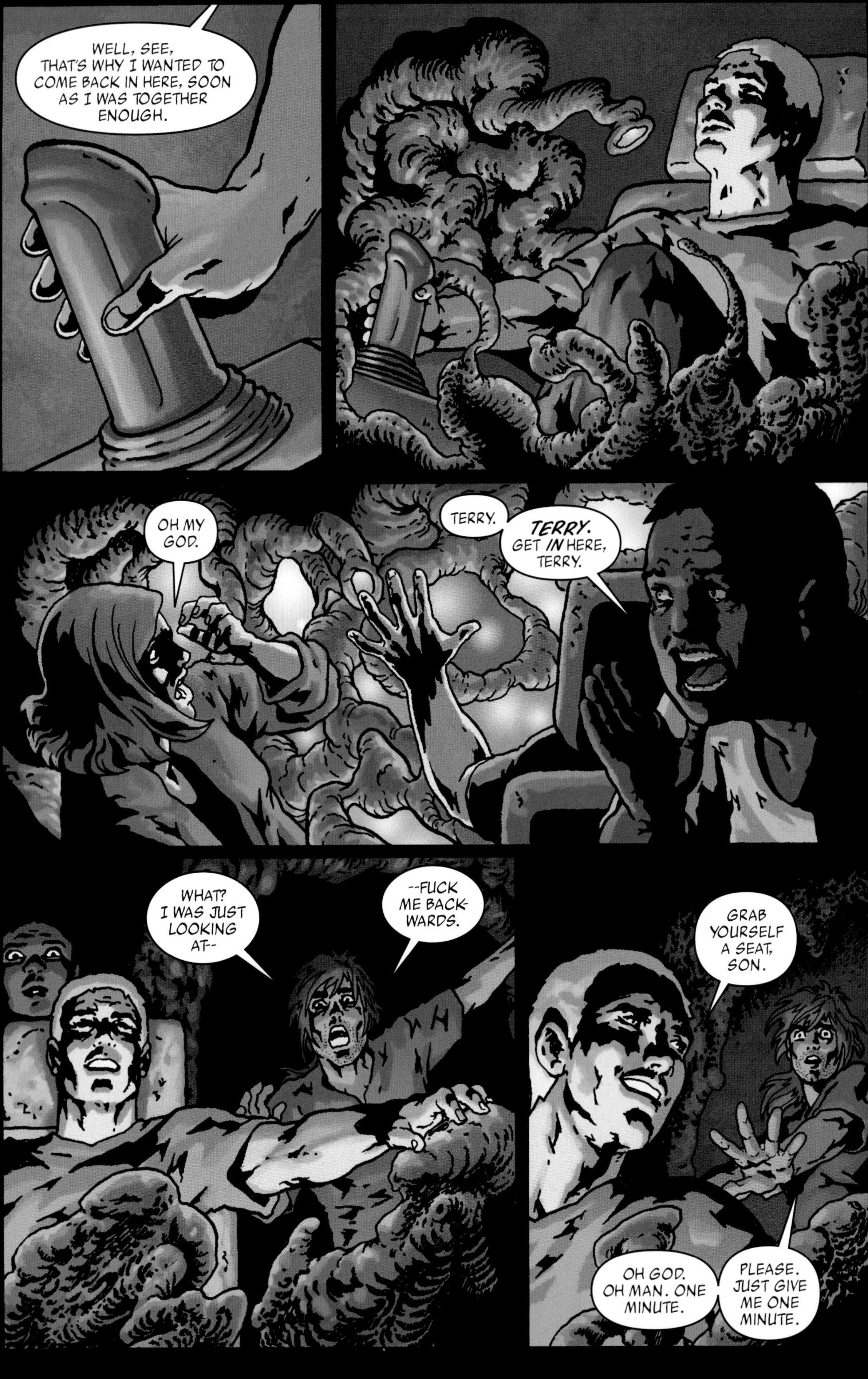
WELL, SEE, THAT'S WHY I WANTED TO COME BACK IN HERE, SOON AS I WAS TOGETHER ENOUGH.
OH MY GOD.
TERRY.
TERRY. GET IN HERE, TERRY.
WHAT? I WAS JUST LOOKING AT--
--FUCK ME BACK-WARDS.
GRAB YOURSELF A SEAT, SON.
OH GOD. OH MAN. ONE MINUTE.
PLEASE. JUST GIVE ME ONE MINUTE.

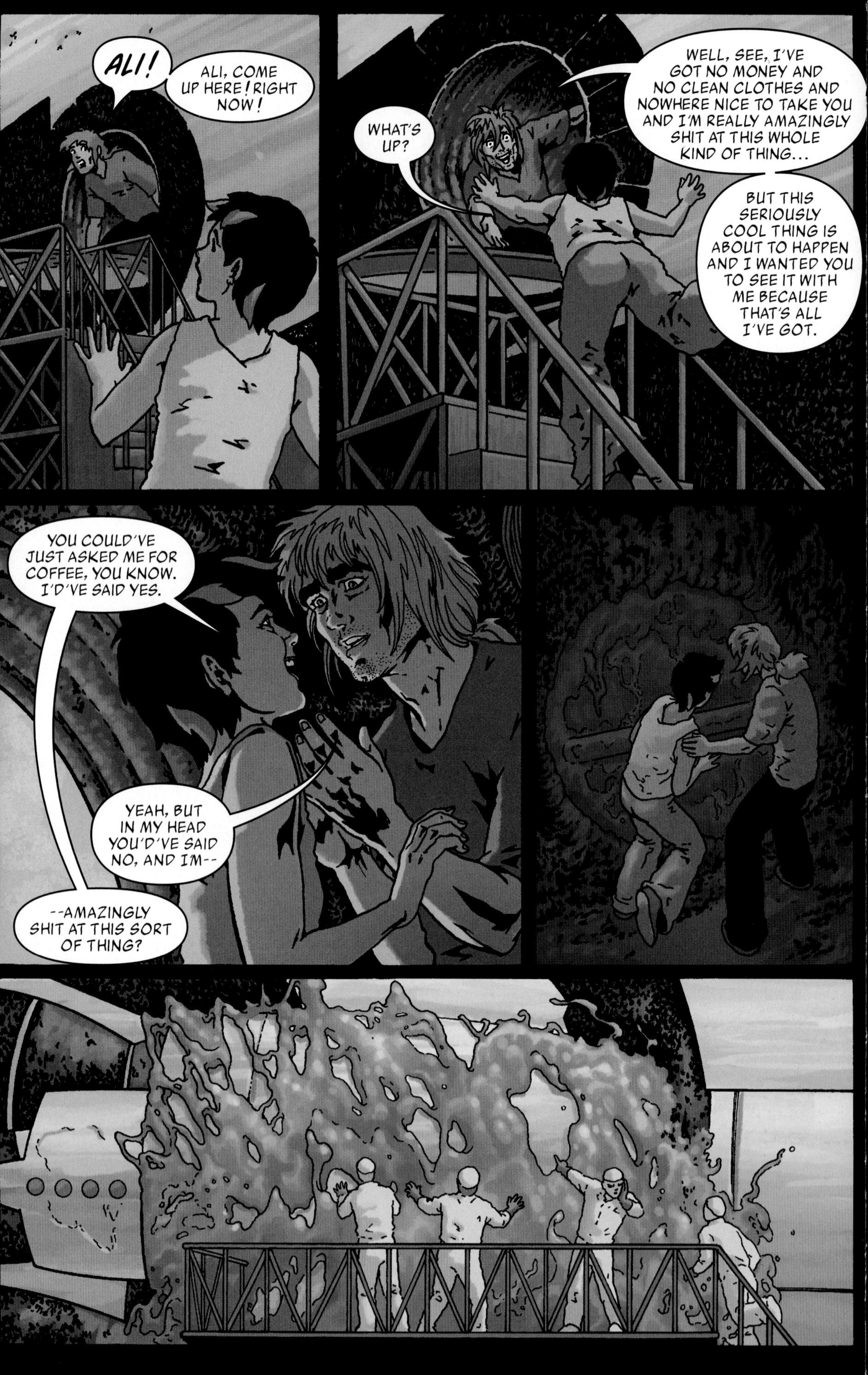
ALI!
ALI, COME UP HERE! RIGHT NOW!
WHAT'S UP?
WELL, SEE, I'VE GOT NO MONEY AND NO CLEAN CLOTHES AND NOWHERE NICE TO TAKE YOU AND I'M REALLY AMAZINGLY SHIT AT THIS WHOLE KIND OF THING...
BUT THIS SERIOUSLY COOL THING IS ABOUT TO HAPPEN AND I WANTED YOU TO SEE IT WITH ME BECAUSE THAT'S ALL I'VE GOT.
YOU COULD'VE JUST ASKED ME FOR COFFEE, YOU KNOW. I'D'VE SAID YES.
YEAH, BUT IN MY HEAD YOU'D'VE SAID NO, AND I'M--
--AMAZINGLY SHIT AT THIS SORT OF THING?

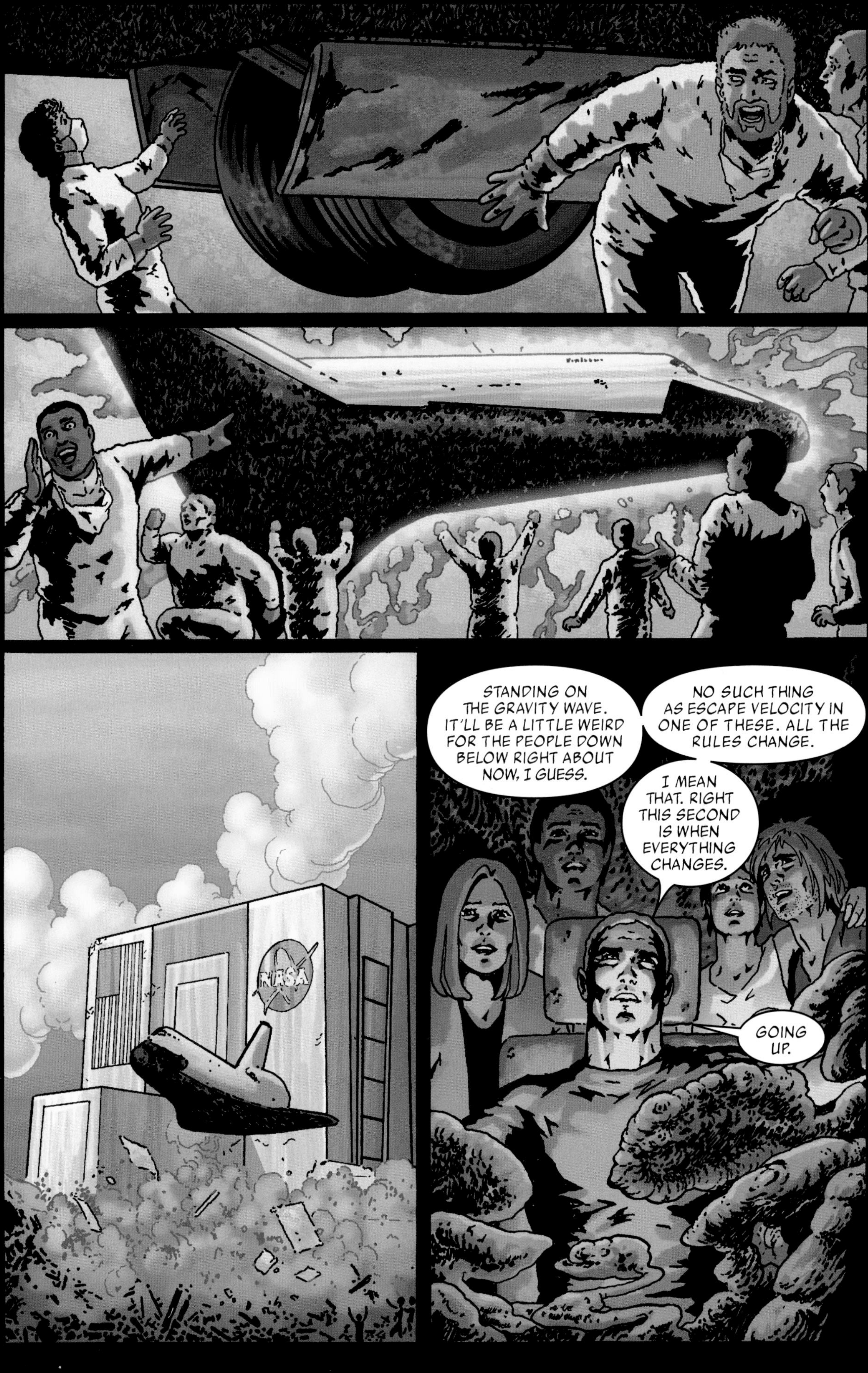
STANDING ON THE GRAVITY WAVE. IT'LL BE A LITTLE WEIRD FOR THE PEOPLE DOWN BELOW RIGHT ABOUT NOW, I GUESS.
NO SUCH THING AS ESCAPE VELOCITY IN ONE OF THESE. ALL THE RULES CHANGE.
I MEAN THAT. RIGHT THIS SECOND IS WHEN EVERYTHING CHANGES.
GOING UP.

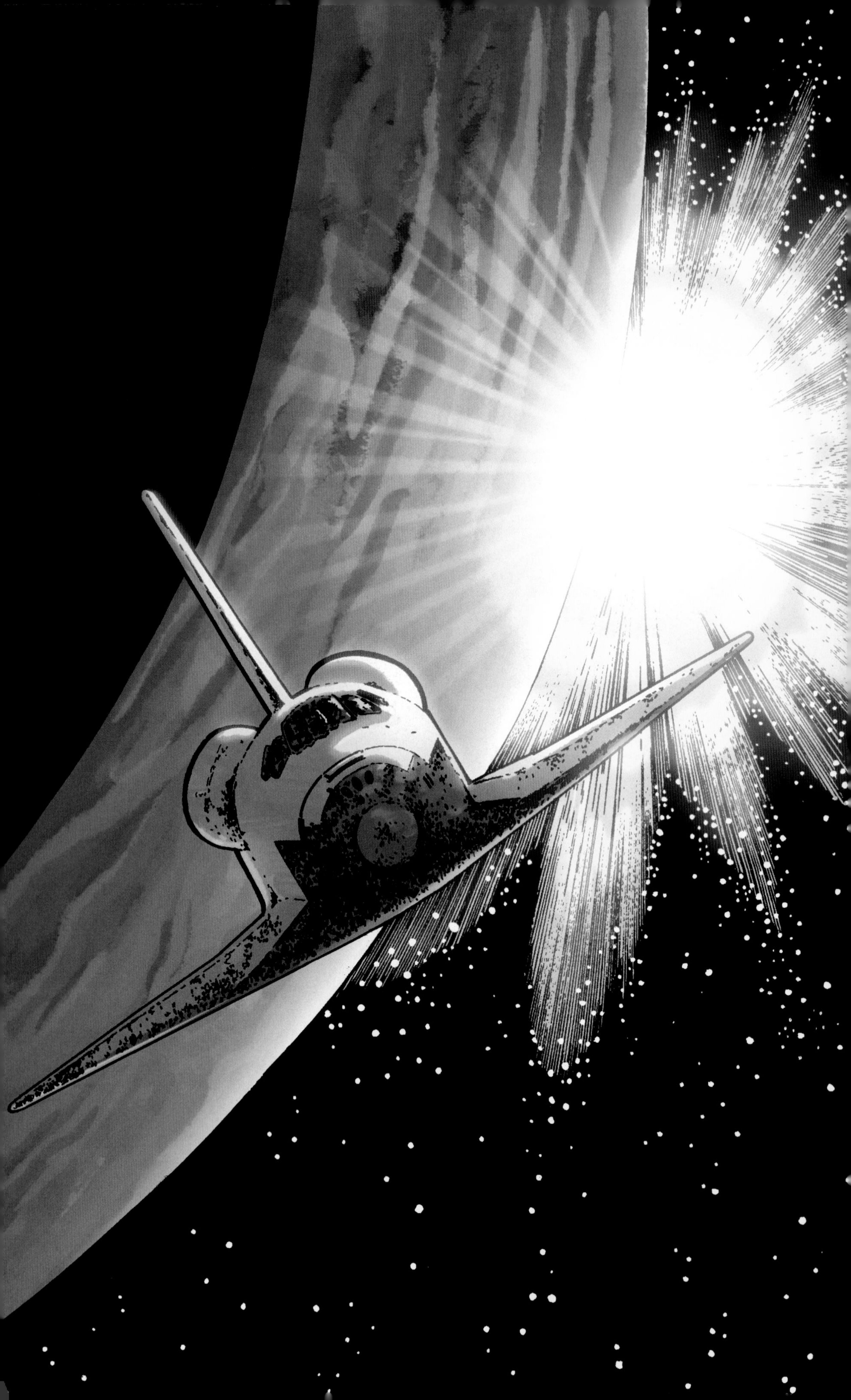

GETTING UP AGAIN

An **ORBITER** Afterword by **WARREN ELLIS**

My first memory is of being held up in front of a tiny black-and-white TV set by my mother and being told, "Remember this. This is history, this is." July 1969. I was seventeen months old. Neil Armstrong had gotten that sticky hatch open and was making that odd little jump from the end of the ladder to the soil of the Moon.

I didn't sleep much as a kid — probably exacerbated by an insane dog that used to attempt to sleep in the cot with me — and it was probably on those sleepless nights that my father built the Apollo 11 model I treasured for years afterwards. It was the complete stack — the stages unscrewed to reveal each section's engine bells — right down to the tiny Command Module and lander in the top under the escape rocket tower.

I had the bug. Just as my father infected me with science fiction and comics. The first comic I ever read was one he brought home for me. *Countdown*, featuring comics versions of popular science fiction TV shows of the time. I remember devouring a series of books that I found in the local library a few years after Viking, about children in an invented British space program. They used children because adults constituted a weight penalty, in the panicky mathematics of chemical thrust against payload mass. My dad's model Apollo stack was brought into focus; that huge bloody thing needed to throw that tiny little capsule to the Moon. And: there wasn't going to be a British space program. The Russians weren't going to put people on the Moon, and it was putting people out there that was important. We understand environments through experience, not robot telemetry. All my hopes for a science fiction future, for performing the exploration the human being is hardwired for, were pinned on the American space program.

School stopped for an hour, the day the first Shuttle launched. We watched it on a TV wheeled into the school assembly hall. We didn't do that the first time an Ariane — the European workhorse booster, nominally "closer" to us here in Britain — banged off. It wasn't crewed. It did not have the aura of the future that American spaceflight glowed with.

As I write this, I'm thirty-four years old.

I have another Apollo 11 model in my office. Colleen sends NASA astronaut ice-cream packages for my daughter Lilith, who's seven. I came up with the basic concept for ORBITER three years ago. I began writing it in 2001. My father died one year ago.

I wrote the final scene of ORBITER a couple of months ago.

Eight days ago, Kennedy Space Center lost the signal from Columbia as it passed thirty-nine miles above Texas on reentry trajectory, moving at twelve thousand five hundred miles an hour.

I was on the Internet at the time, reading the BBC news, when the ticker flashed up the alert; loss of signal fifteen minutes ago. A Space Shuttle has no abort contingency at that stage in the approach. It's too high and too fast. The control surfaces don't have enough atmosphere to usefully bite into, too deep for OMS/RCS to have any real effect, too fast for attitude jets to correct hard. At eighteen times the speed of sound, escaping into the air off the egress pole would've been like jumping in front of a speeding truck. The Shuttle is infamous for handling like a flying brick in its return mode, as an unpowered glider. Flying Shuttle is — as everyone has learned, once again — experimental flight. *Columbia* was flying mission STS-107. This means that none of the fleet has been up more than thirty times.

I brought up the webcast NASA TV and BBC News 24 streams on my screen. On the former, KSC Mission Control was appallingly silent. The BBC had footage from Texas, of the plasma-stream "contrail" from *Columbia* arcing over a perfect blue sky, with a hot flaring light at its apex. The flare was wrong.

Attitude jets were firing off the left wing. Temperature sensors were burning away. Despite a large amount of telemetry being routed away from the cockpit and down to KSC, the crew knew that the bird was sick. A minute is a very long time when you're thirty-nine miles high, the fastest thing in the air, and the laws of nature are scorching their way into the superstructure of your ship.

Florida was just waking up, waiting for the double-boom of supersonics that heralded the

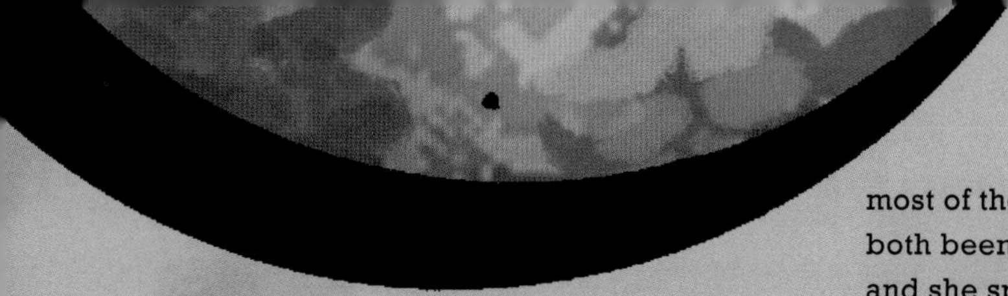

return of a Shuttle. And waited.

The flare became two flares. And three. And four.

I called Colleen, not knowing she was in California on business. Hooked up with my friend Matt in Kansas City, and we spent the day working the various news services, keeping each other informed, looking for a sign that, I don't know, someone had gotten out, that *Columbia* had pulled off an emergency landing, that this was impossible to avoid and there hadn't been *Challenger*-level incompetence, that crewed American spaceflight hadn't been shot in the heart.

Human remains were found in Texas a few hours later.

My family gave me a lot of space that day.

When *Challenger* cracked up on launch, the Shuttle fleet was grounded for two and a half years. As I write this, there's talk of the remaining Shuttles staying down for at least a year. And the very sense of human spaceflight is being questioned. As you read this book, you'll find why that gave me an especial chill. After that was said, a business associate in Los Angeles emailed to call me a prophet. I would rather not be. I hope I'm not.

The much-talked-about Prometheus initiative for nuclear thrust currently has application only to robot missions. Going flat-out, in an Apollo-scale manner, it'd take ten years to crew-rate a nuclear-electric mission, where a reactor powers an ion-drive system. A nuclear-thermal system, where a module rides a spike of superhot gas squirted out of the reactor, will, in my opinion, never be crew-rated.

Since I was seventeen months old, space has gotten progressively further away. Even Shuttle was designed only to perform shallow hundred-mile-high orbits.

The current American President is publicly recommitting to NASA. But his father's inauguration address told his nation that they were going to Mars. NASA has always been a political football, and it is entirely possible to re-fund NASA and treat it with respect and still suspend crewed spaceflight for a considerable period of time.

I caught up with Colleen on Monday. I don't think she'll mind my telling you that she cried most of the way home from California. We've both been space freaks from early childhood, and she spent a lot of time at NASA centers, talking with NASA people, in the production of ORBITER. And we both said the same thing.

This book needs to come out now.

It has something to say. Now is the time to get back up. I wrote it in the face of the disappointment of the International Space Station, the wounded Russian program, the crushed Japanese space initiative, the intellectual poverty of the European Space Agency, and of the site of the beautiful Shuttles never getting further than an eight-minute burn away. There has to be more, I wrote. We're losing space, I wrote, when there is so much out there for us. It meant something huge to Colleen and me; and it means more now.

This is a book about returning to space in the face of fear and adversity. It's a book about glory. About going back to space, because it's waiting for us, and it's where we're meant to be. We can't allow human space exploration to become our history.

Human spaceflight remains experimental. It is very dangerous. It demands great ingenuity. But we are old enough, now, to do these things. Growing up is hard. But we cannot remain children, standing on the shore or in front of the TV set.

Colleen and I have dedicated ORBITER in the names of the seven astronauts lost on Columbia. We also place it in the service of those who will go after, with equal courage and intelligence, to make us great.

And more will go on. Because it's too important a thing to allow it to die in the sky

— **WARREN ELLIS**
Southend, England
February 2003

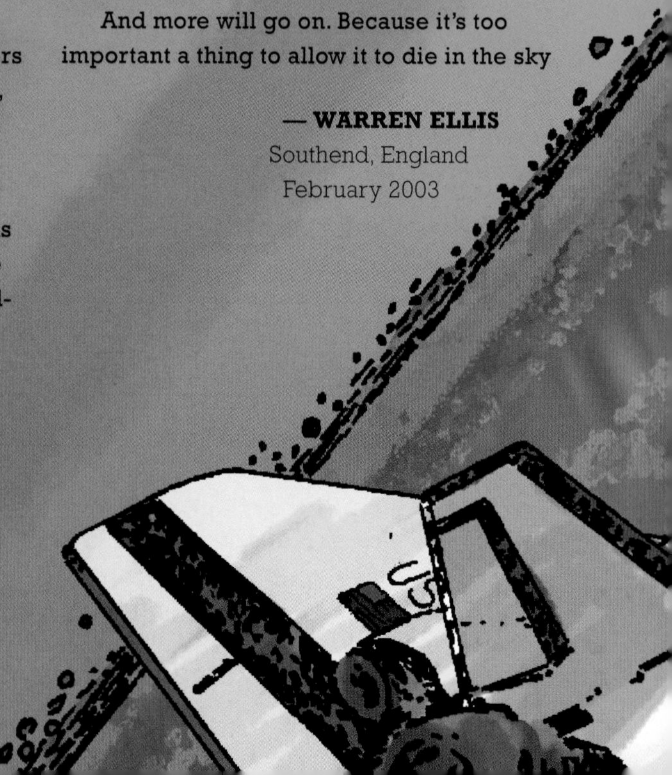

BACK FROM THE FUTURE

Sketches, designs and preliminary art by
CHRIS SPROUSE, MICHAEL GOLDEN AND COLLEEN DORAN

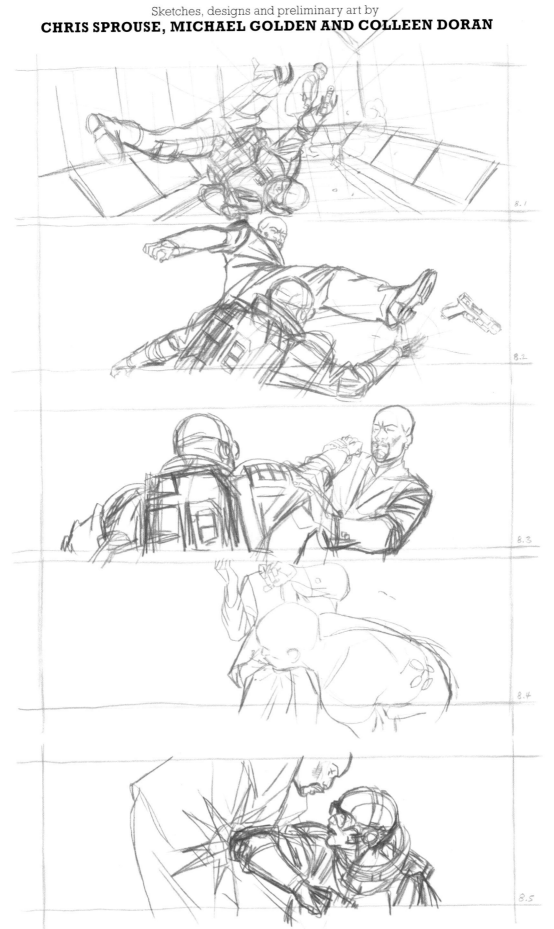

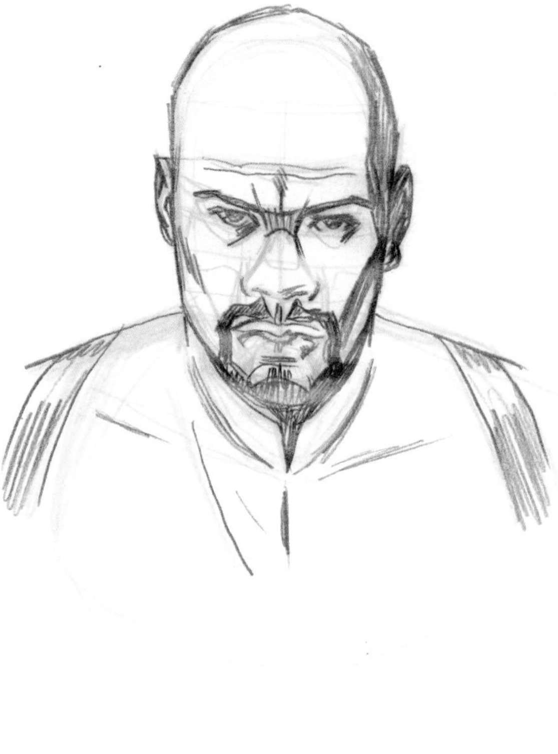

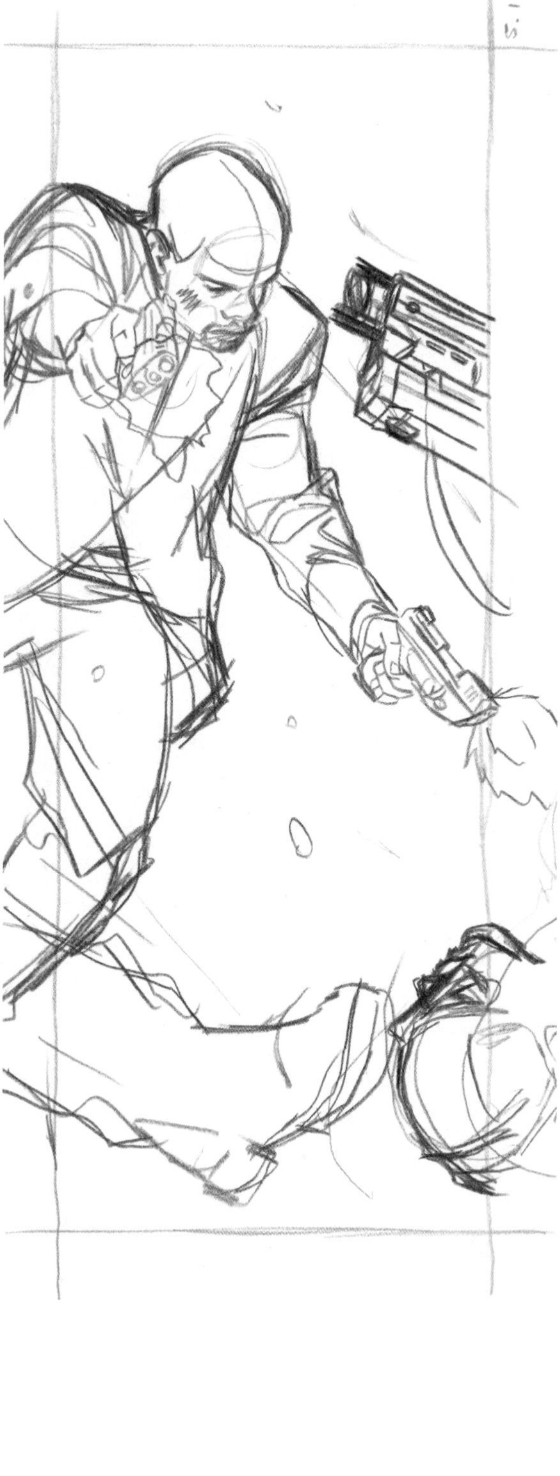

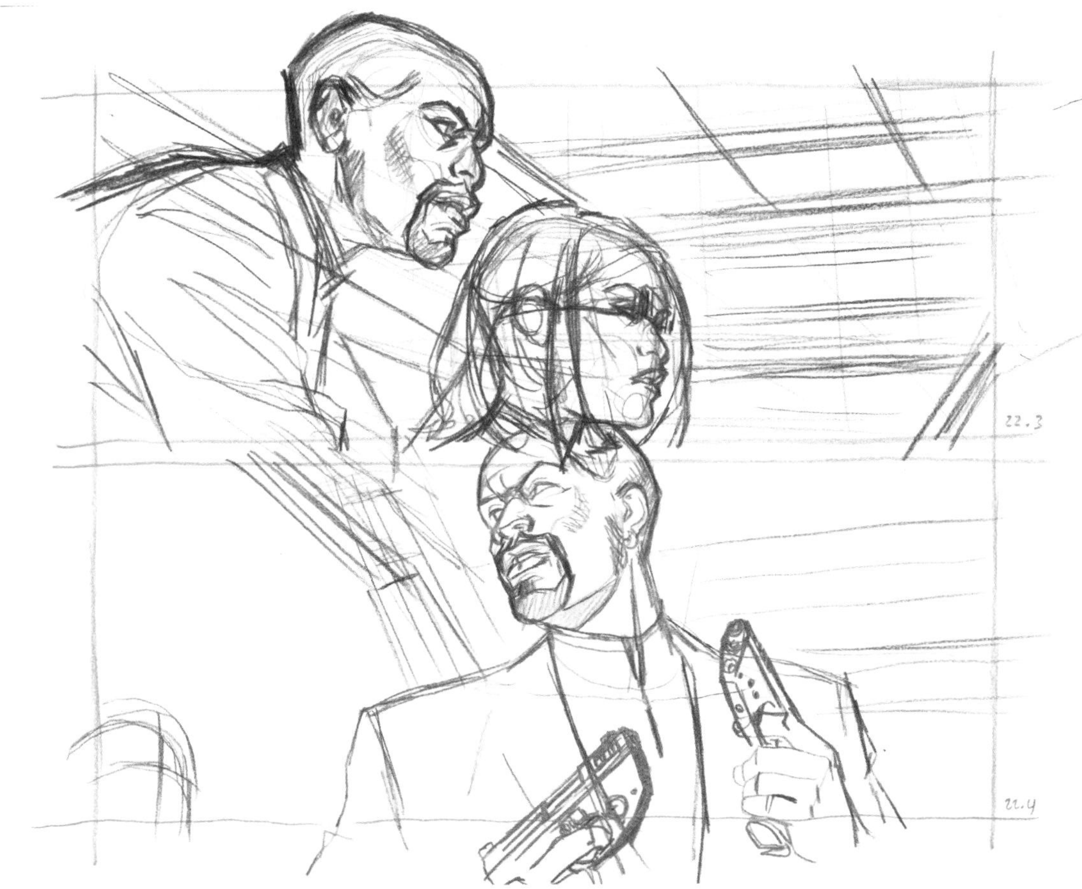
22.3
22.4

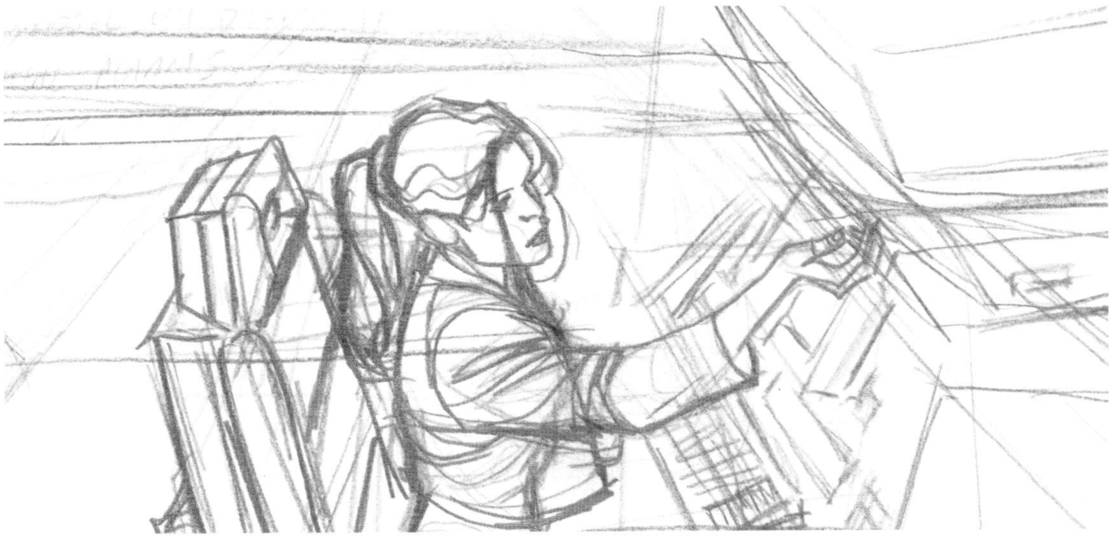

FOR PAGE ⑨
PANEL ②

FOR PAGE ⑨
PANEL ②

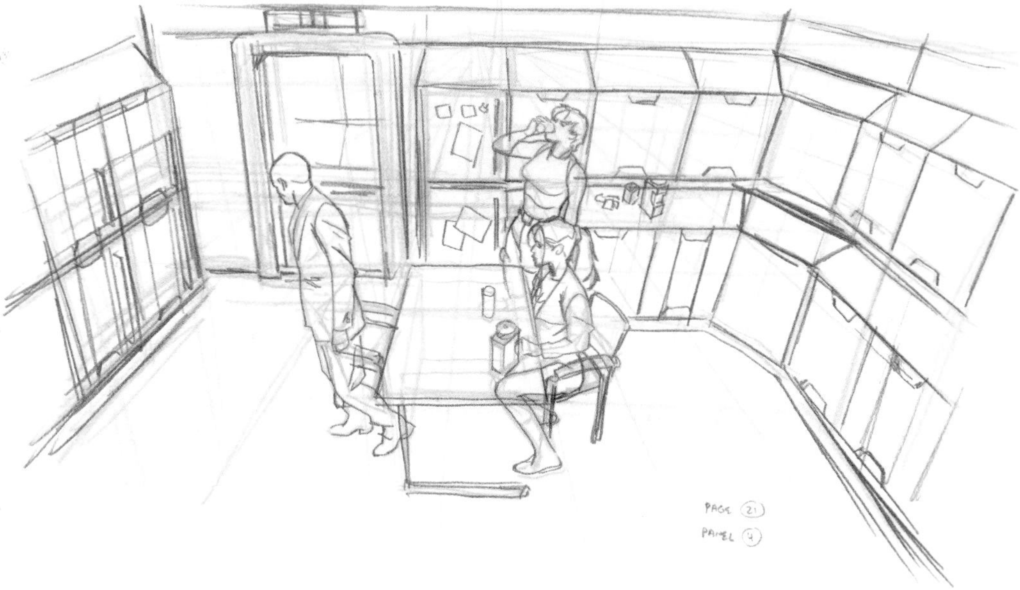
PAGE 21
PANEL 4

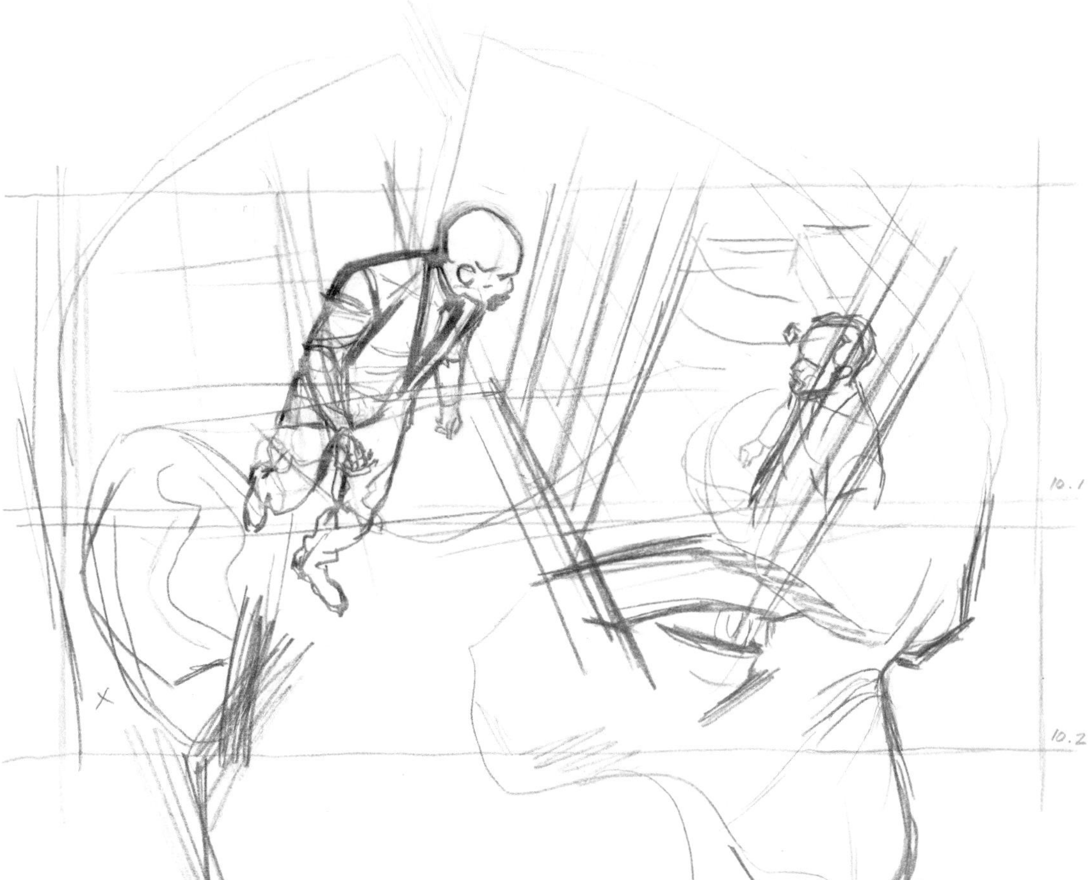
10.1
10.2

Fadia Aziz

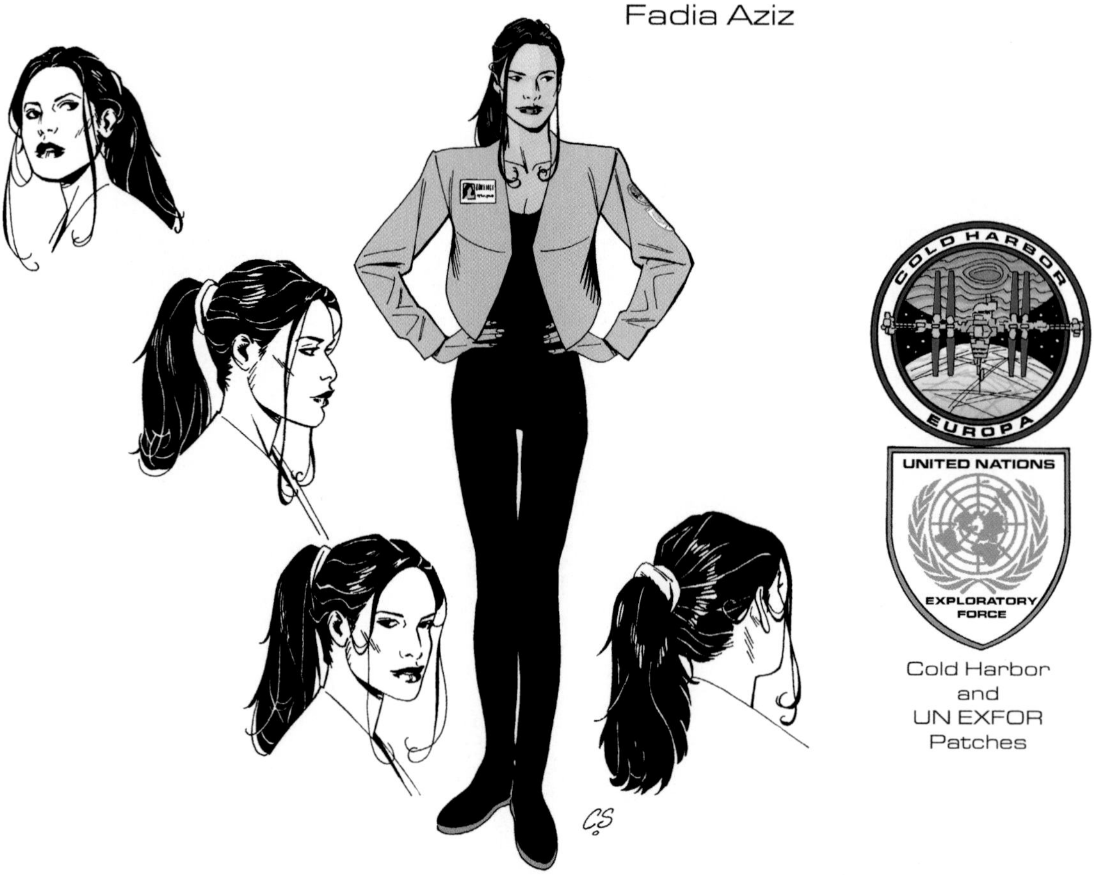
COLD HARBOR
EUROPA
UNITED NATIONS
EXPLORATORY FORCE
Cold Harbor and UN EXFOR Patches
CS

Nathan Kane

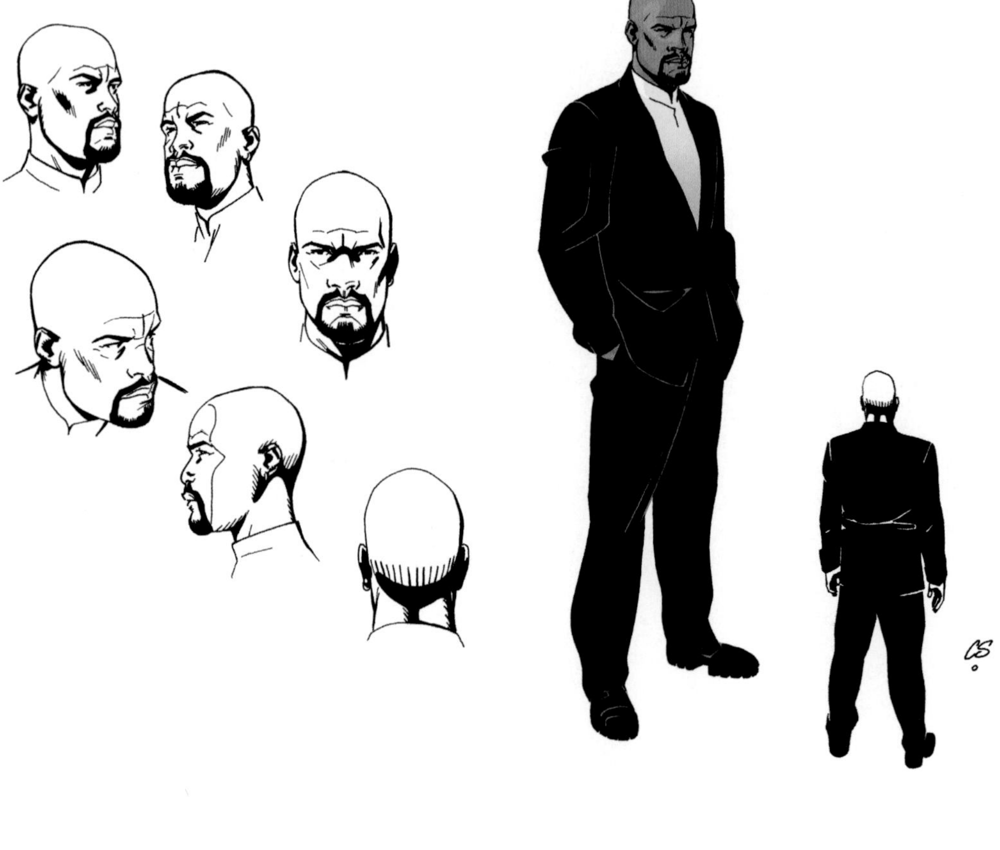
CS

Cold Harbor Staff

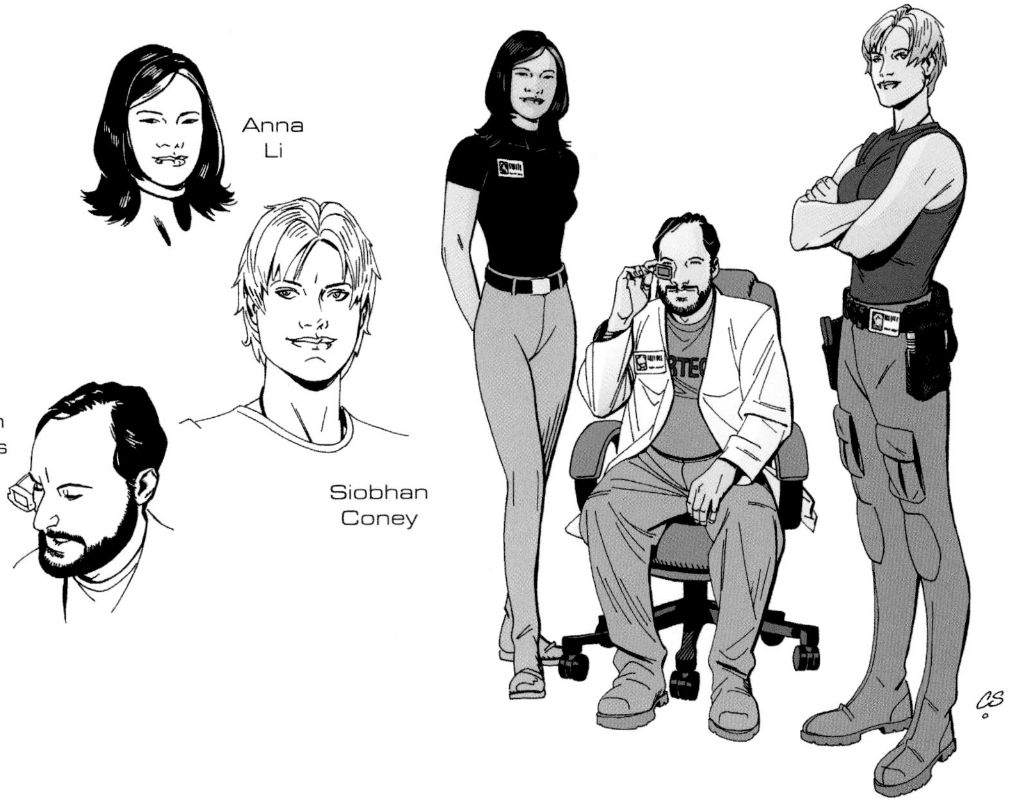
Anna
Li
John
Wells
Siobhan
Coney
CS

Doors Station Manager

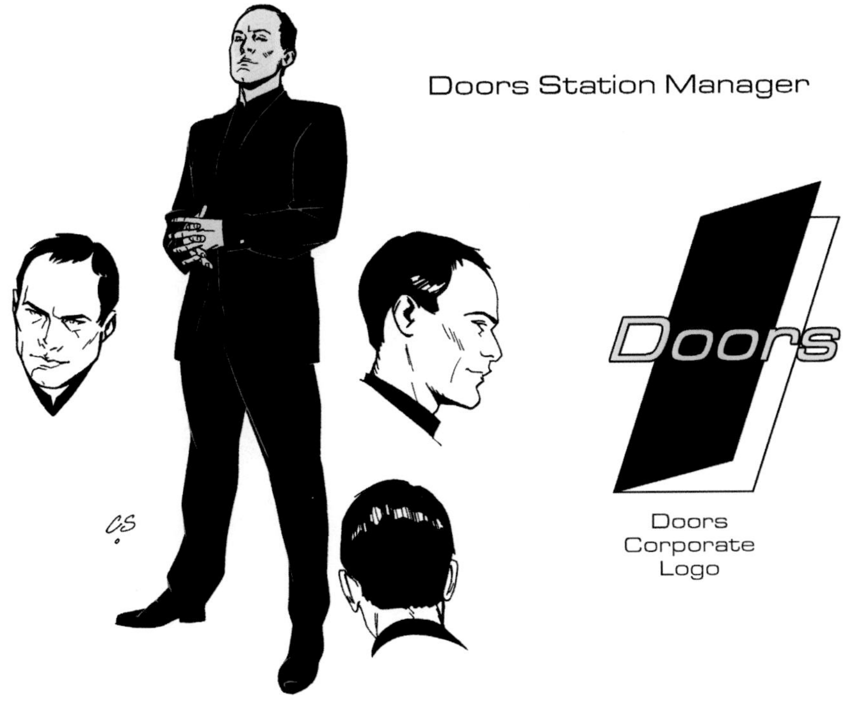
CS
Doors
Doors
Corporate
Logo

Acid Pistol

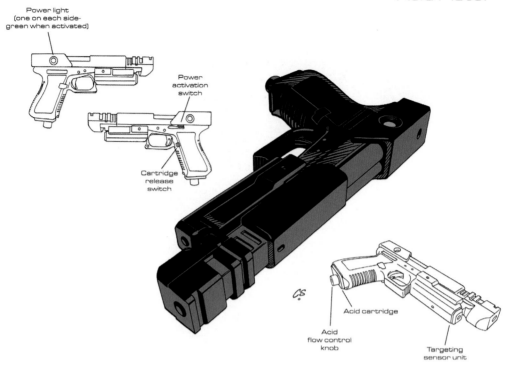

Power light
(one on each side-
green when activated)

Power
activation
switch

Cartridge
release
switch

Acid cartridge

Acid
flow control
knob

Targeting
sensor unit

Kane's Gun

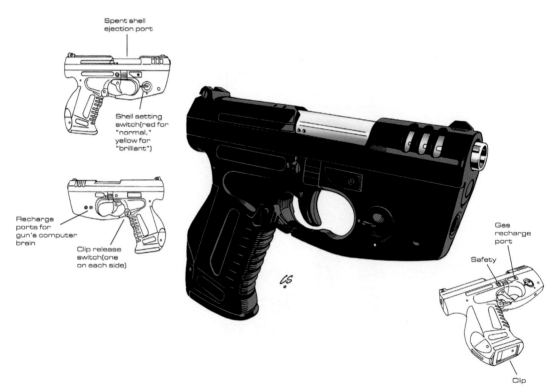

Spent shell
ejection port

Shell setting
switch(red for
"normal,"
yellow for
"brilliant")

Recharge
ports for
gun's computer
brain

Clip release
switch(one
on each side)

Gas
recharge
port

Safety

Clip

OCEAN
ISSUE # 6
5
INTERIORS
KANE FLIPS
M2
- PISTOL WHIP! -
LIGHTS ON!
DOUBLE PAGE SPREAD: CUT AS SHOWN, ABUT PAGE EDGES, TAPE ON BACK, DO NOT OVERLAP

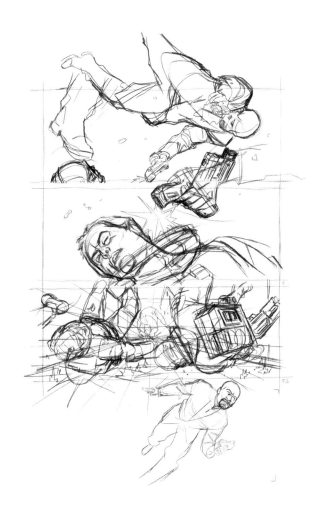

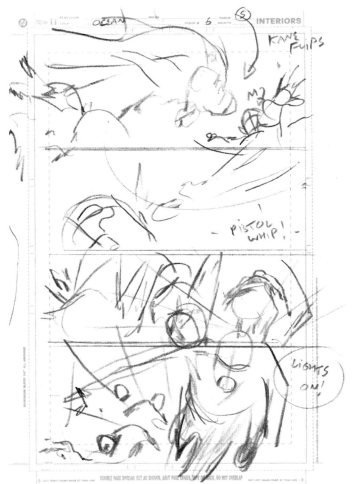

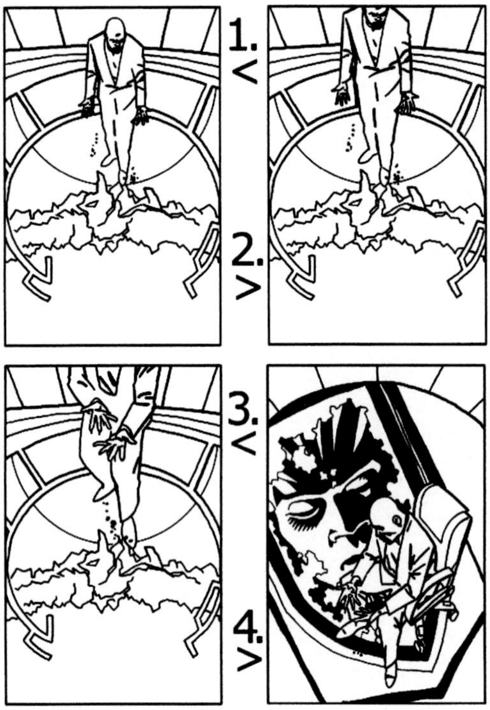
1. <
2. >
3. <
4. >

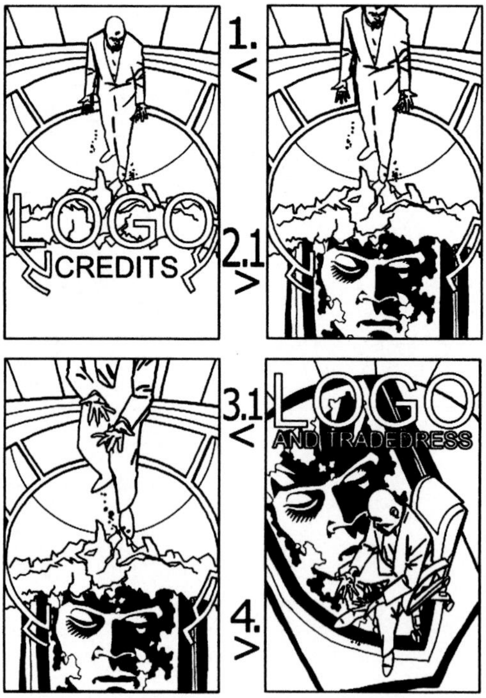
1. <
LOGO
CREDITS
2.1 >
3.1 <
LOGO
AND TRADEDRESS
4. >

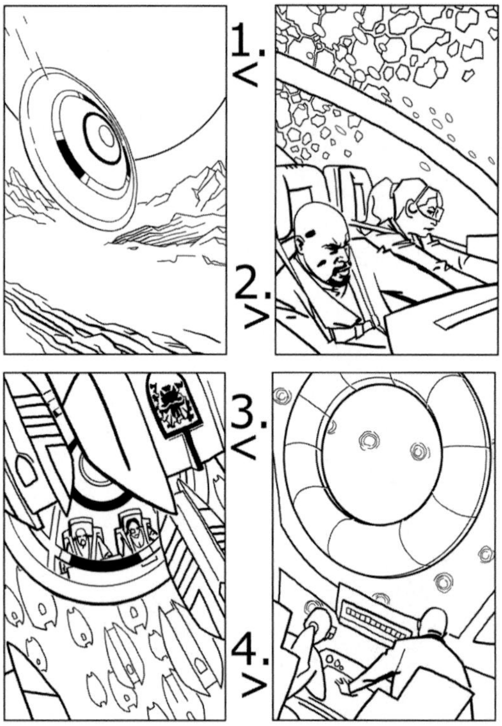
1. <
2. >
3. <
4. >

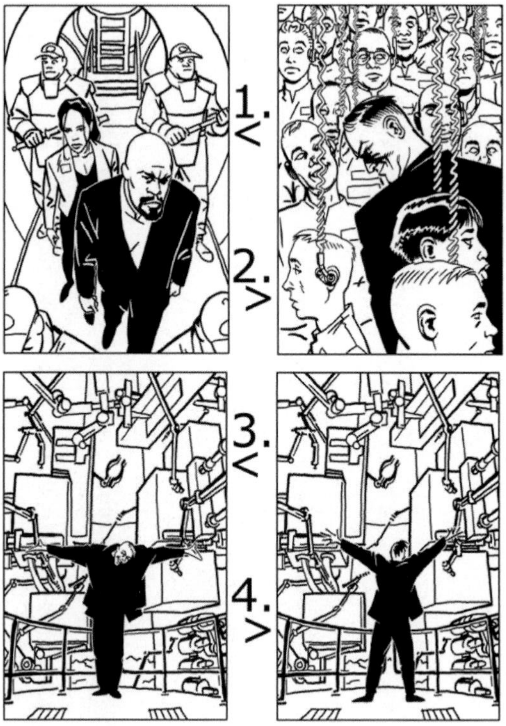
1. <
2. >
3. <
4. >

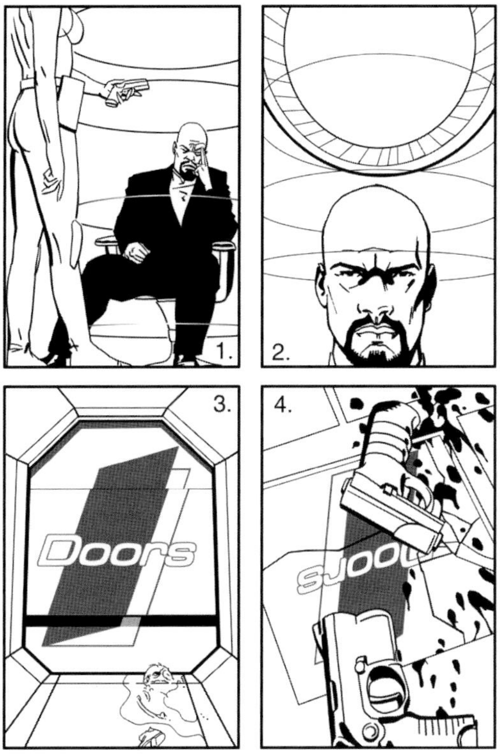
1.
2.
3.
Doors
4.

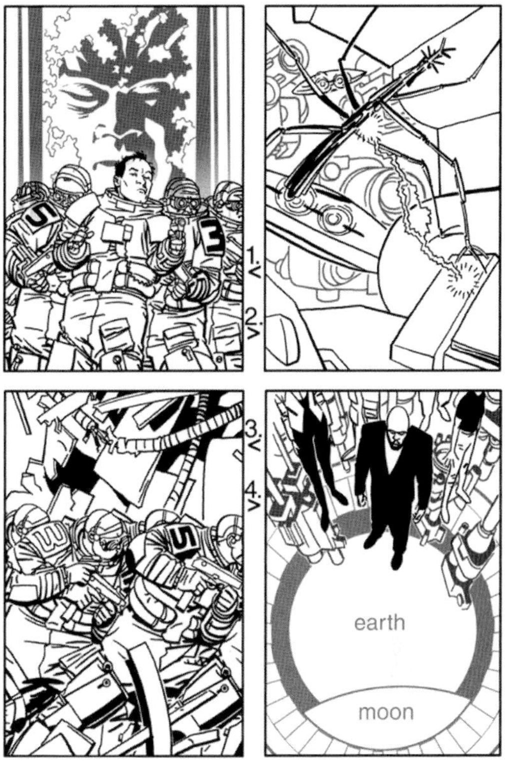
1.
<
2.
>
3.
<
4.
>
earth
moon

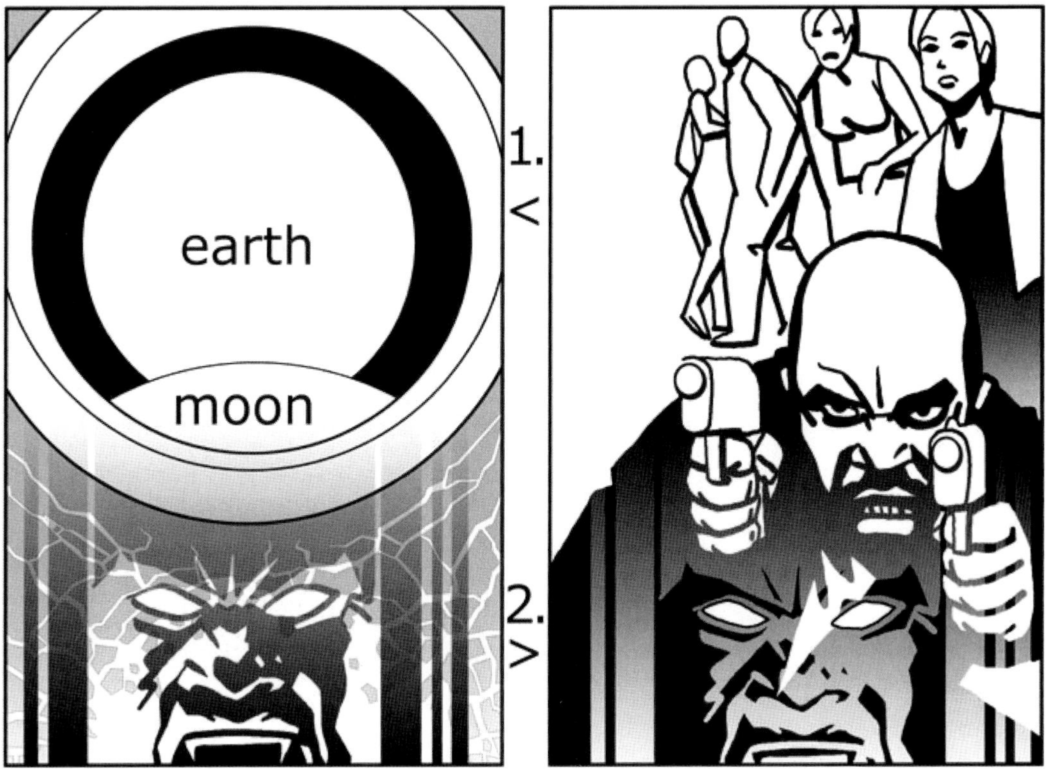
earth
moon
1.
<
2.
>

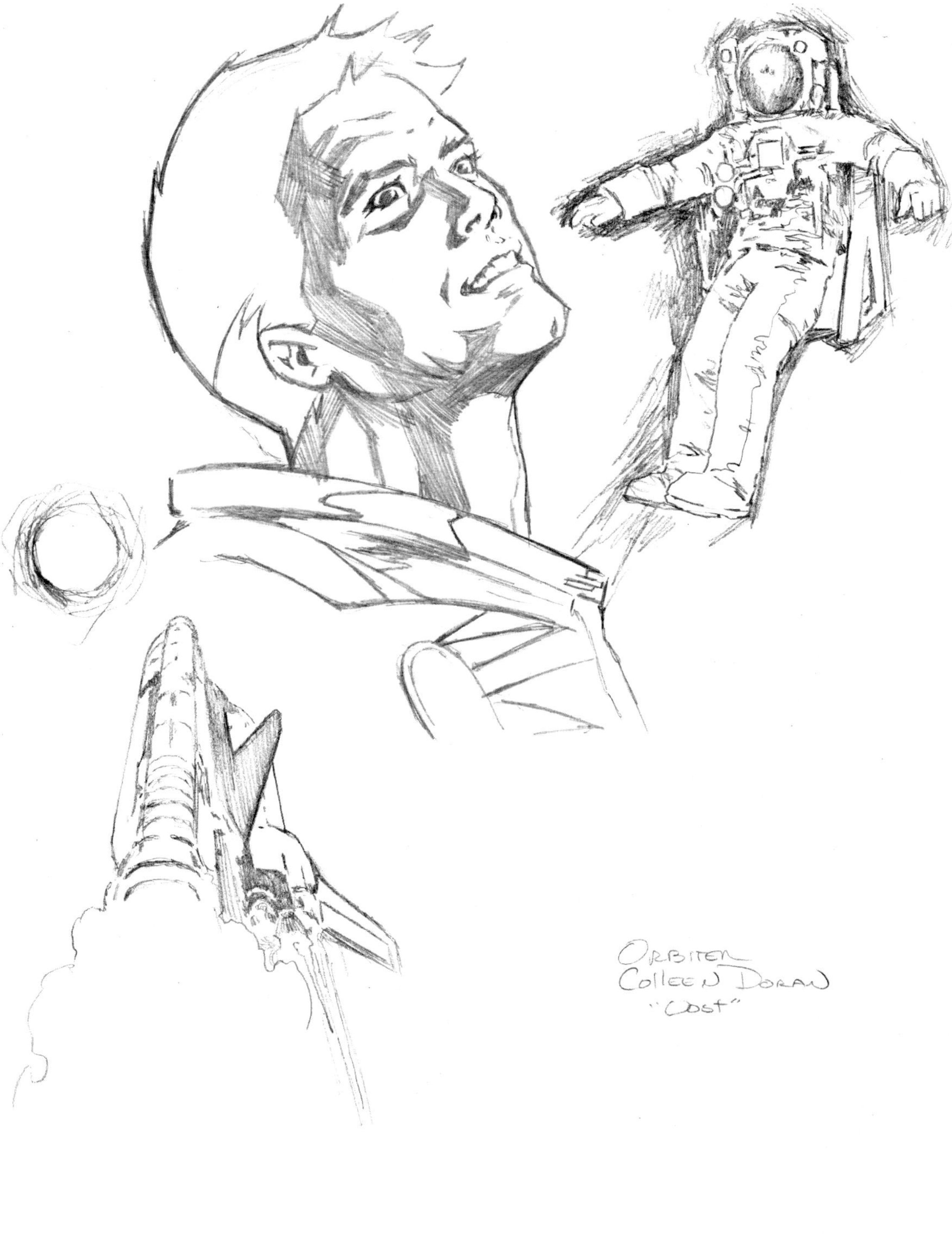
Orbiter
Colleen Doran
"Lost"

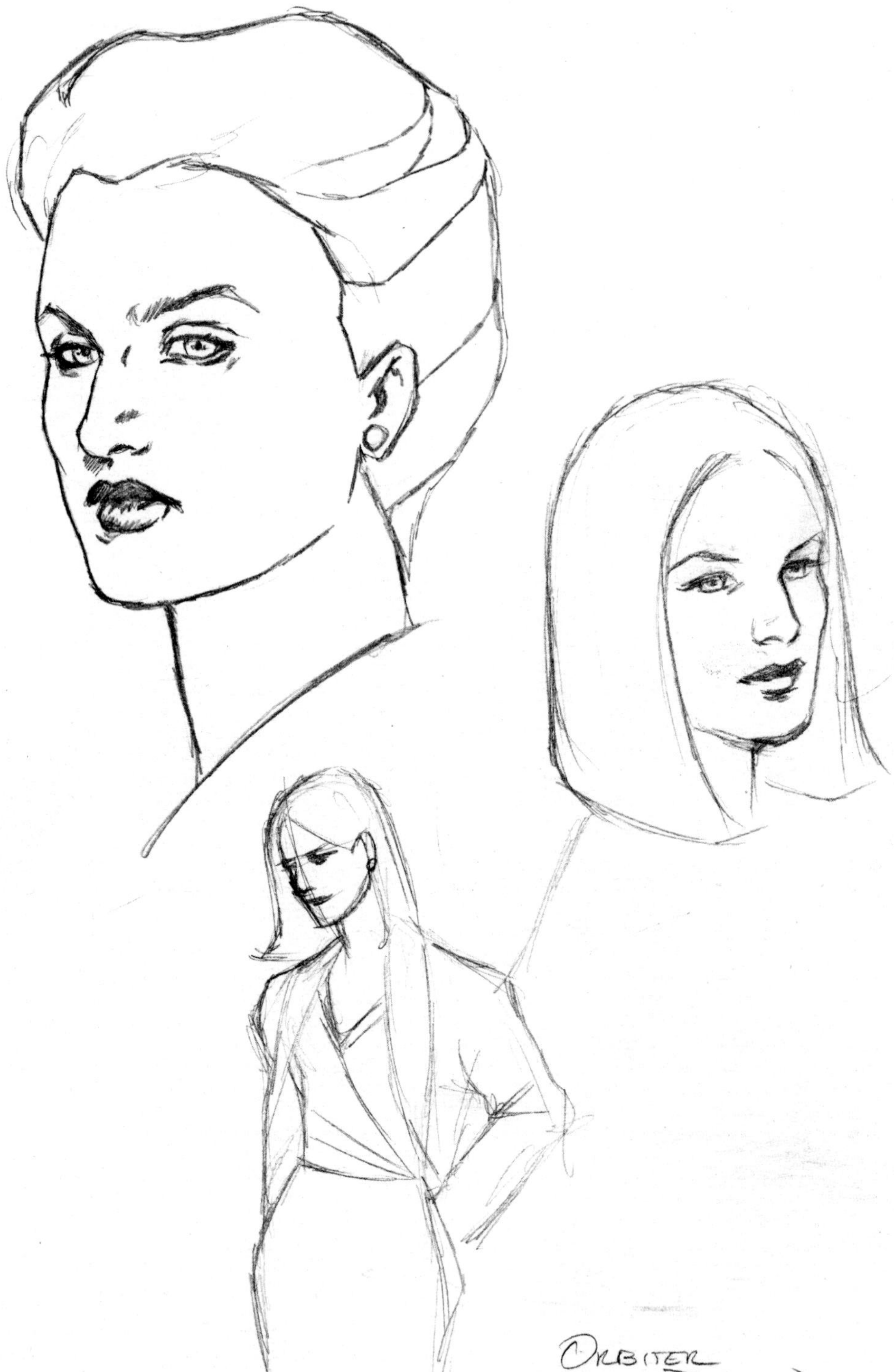
ORBITER
Colleen Doran
"ANNA"

ORBITER
Colleen Doran
"Bukovic"

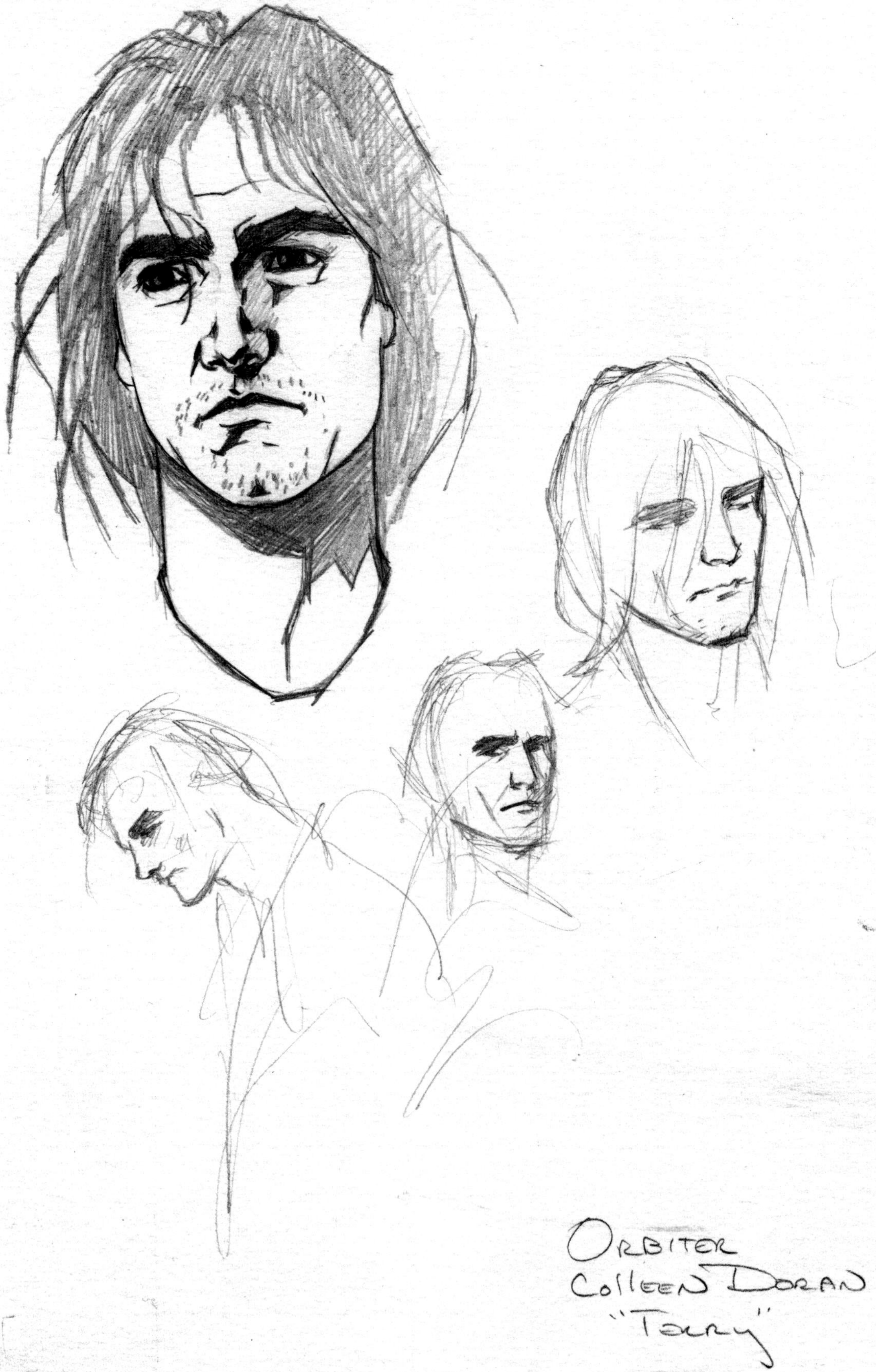
ORBITER
COLLEEN DORAN
"TERRY"

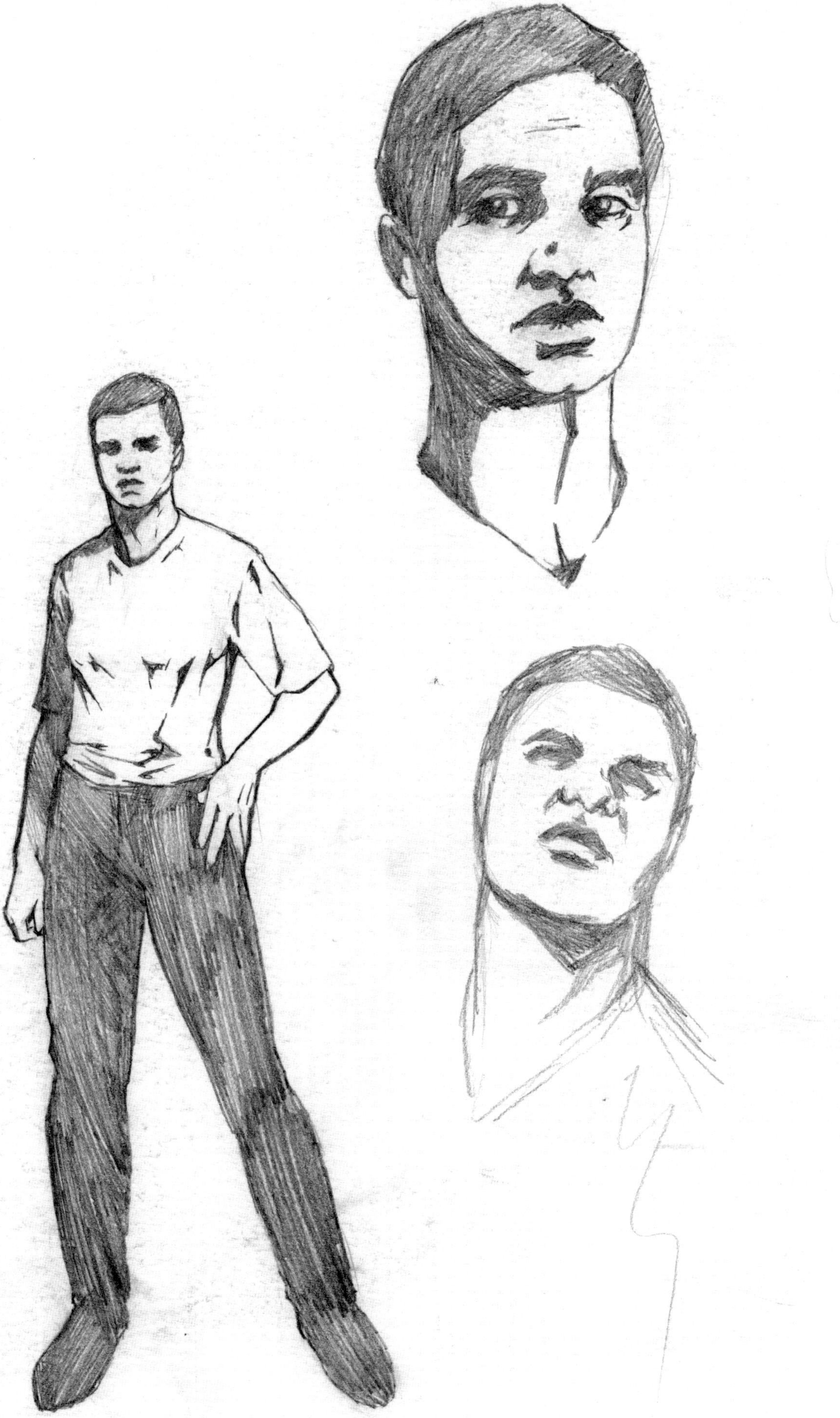

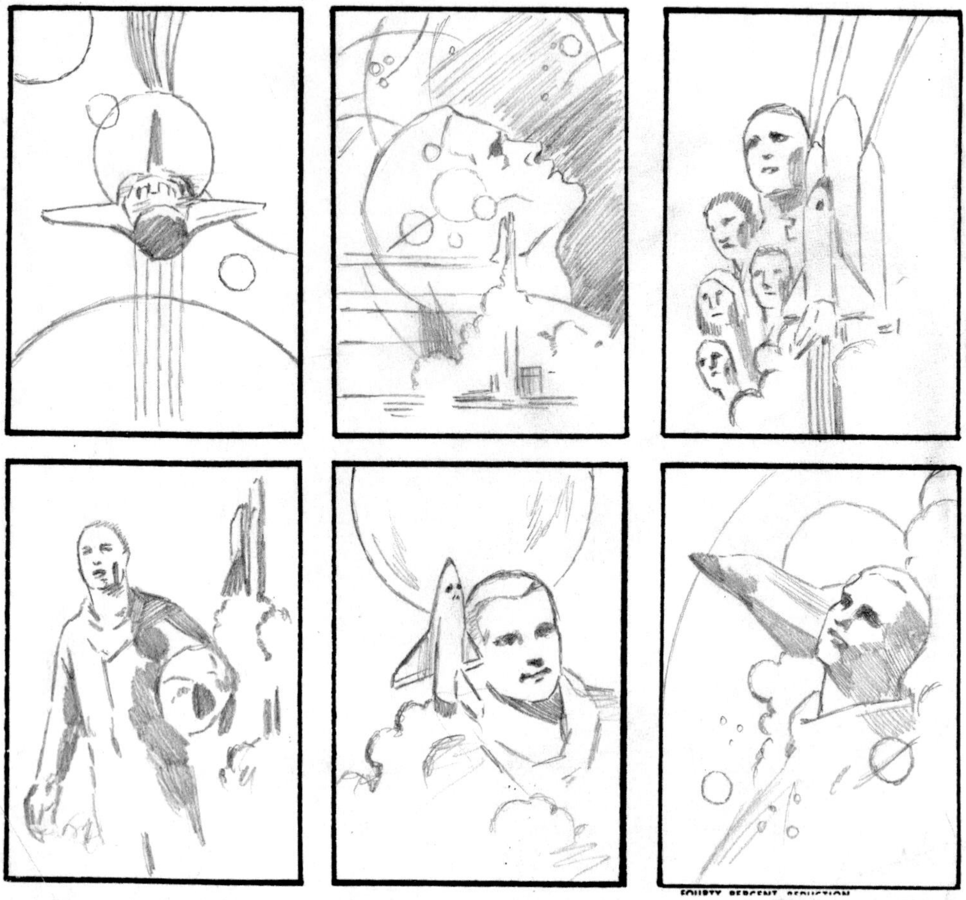

FOURTY PERCENT REDUCTION

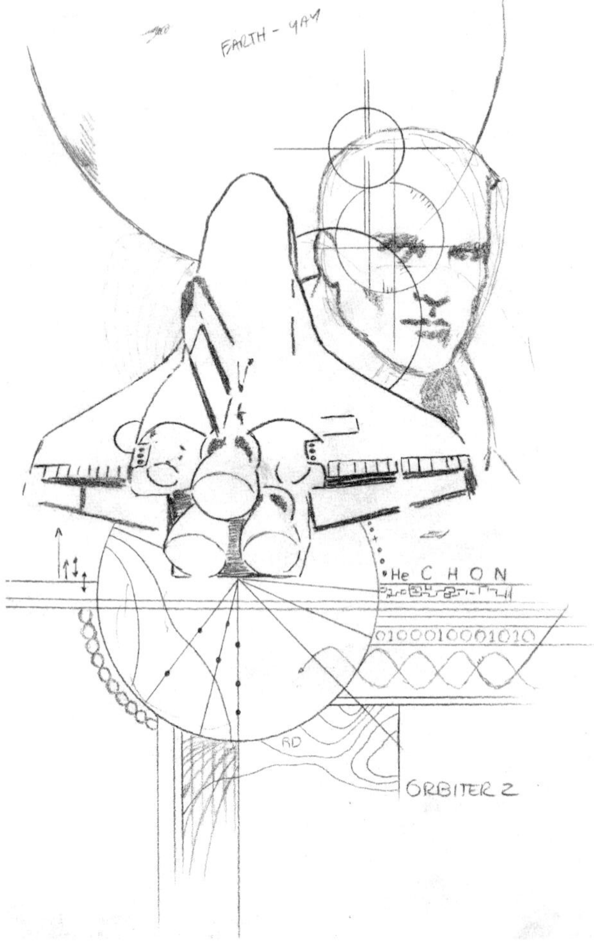
He C H O N
0100010001010
ORBITER 2

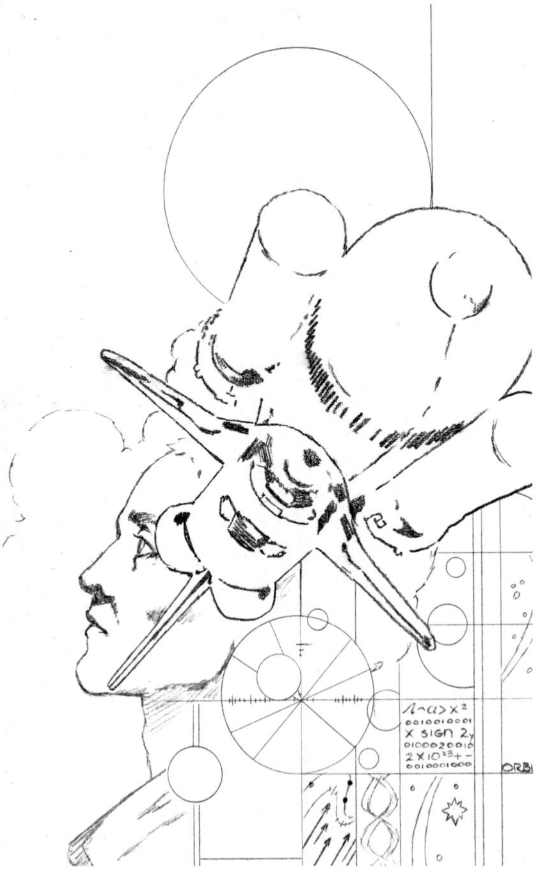
X SIGN 2y
ORBI

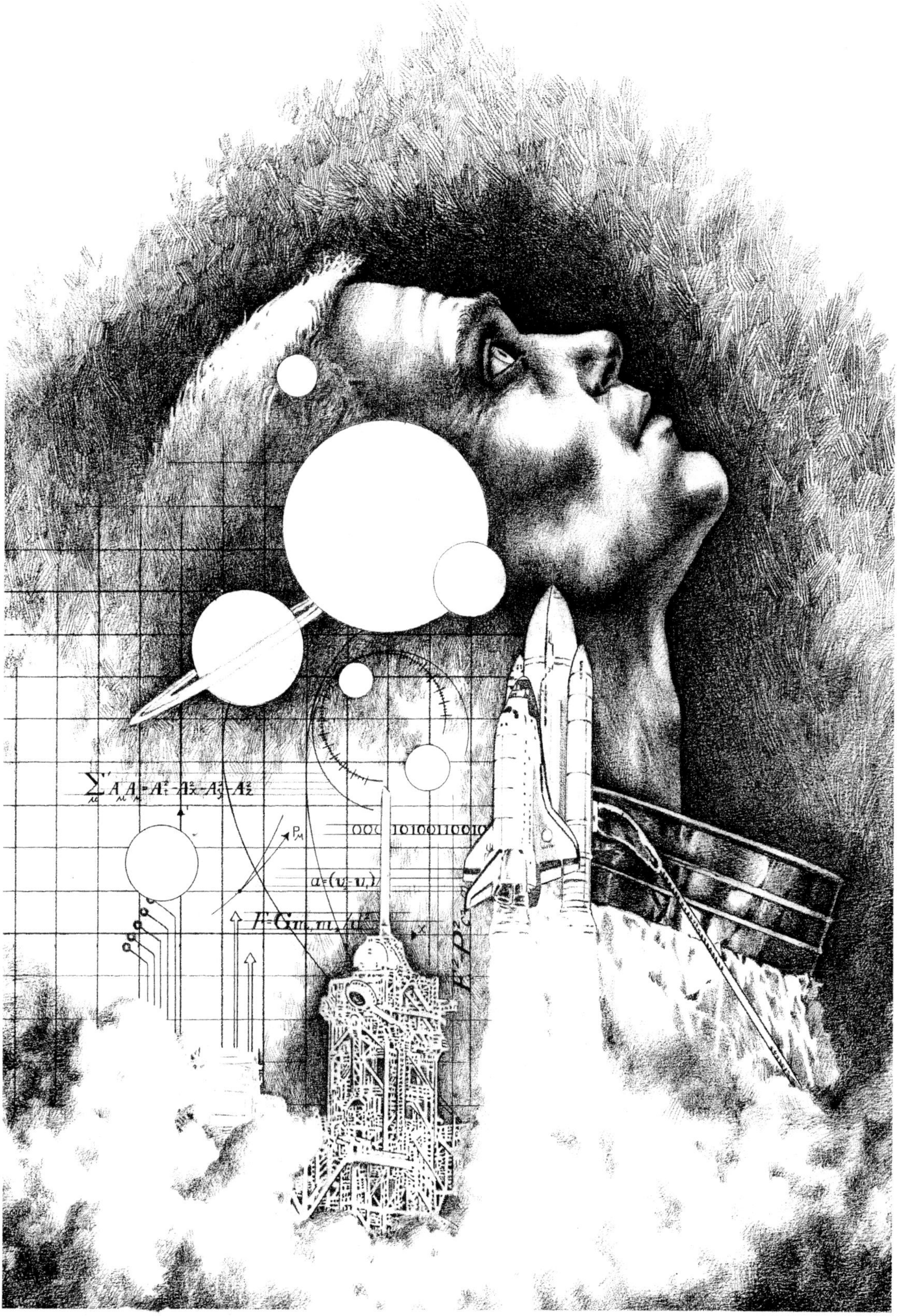

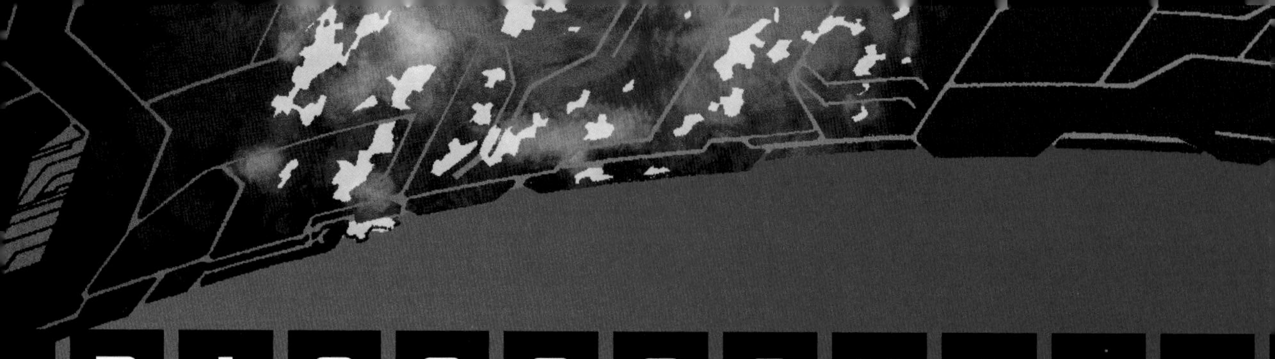

BIOGRAPHIES

WARREN ELLIS is the creator and writer of a host of critically acclaimed and award-winning graphic novels, including TRANSMETROPOLITAN, THE AUTHORITY, PLANETARY, RED, GLOBAL FREQUENCY, ORBITER, *Ultimate Fantastic Four*, *Ultimate Galactus*, *Ministry of Space*, *Gravel*, *FreakAngels*, and *Fell*. Outside of comics he has also written screenplays, video games, nonfiction books, short stories, and novels, and he maintains a nigh-ubiquitous online presence through every portal the Internet has to offer. His celebrated life and career are the subjects of several books as well as a documentary film entitled *Warren Ellis: Captured Ghosts*, released in 2012. He lives in southeast England with his girlfriend and daughter.

CHRIS SPROUSE began working in comics in 1989, cutting his teeth on such series as LEGION OF SUPER-HEROES, LEGIONNAIRES and HAMMERLOCKE. In 1999 he co-created the world of TOM STRONG with Alan Moore, and since then he has drawn countless adventures featuring Earth's Greatest Science Hero in the titles TOM STRONG, TOM STRONG AND THE PLANET OF PERIL, and TOM STRONG AND THE ROBOTS OF DOOM. In addition to his work on OCEAN, Sprouse has also contributed to THE AUTHORITY, BATMAN: THE RETURN OF BRUCE WAYNE, and THE MULTIVERSITY — THE SOCIETY OF SUPER-HEROES: CONQUERORS FROM THE COUNTER-WORLD. He currently lives in Ohio.

KARL STORY began his comics career in 1988 working on First Publishing's *The Badger*. In 1991 he co-founded Gaijin Studios in Atlanta, which became his base of operations for nearly two decades. Since then he has contributed to a multitude of books, including *Generation X*, *Savage Dragon*, LEGIONNAIRES, NIGHTWING, BATMAN, TOM STRONG, TERRA OBSCURA, THE AMERICAN WAY, OCEAN, MIDNIGHTER, and *Serenity: Leaves on the Wind*. He lives and works just outside Atlanta.

A professional illustrator since the age of fifteen, **COLLEEN DORAN** has contributed to such comic books as THE SANDMAN, LUCIFER, WONDER WOMAN, *The Amazing Spider-Man*, and *Captain America*, as well as *The Book of Lost Souls* by *Babylon 5* creator J. Michael Straczynski and the graphic novel adaptations of Anne Rice's *The Master of Rampling Gate* and Disney's *Beauty and the Beast*. She has illustrated two original graphic novels for Vertigo — ORBITER, written by Warren Ellis, and GONE TO AMERIKAY, written by Derek McCulloch — and she is currently working on upcoming projects with Neil Gaiman for Dark Horse, J. Michael Straczynski for Image, and Stan Lee for Simon & Schuster.